PRAETERIT

JOHN RUSKIN was born in London in 1819. His father was a wine merchant, born and brought up in Scotland; his mother, a devout Evangelical Christian, gave him the early religious training that influenced him throughout his life. He was largely taught at home as a boy, and later became an undergraduate at Christ Church, Oxford. In 1843 he began his career as a critic with the publication of the first volume of *Modern Painters*, a passionate celebration of the painting of J. M. W. Turner. Seventeen years, and four further volumes, were needed to bring that work to completion in 1860. Two further works on art and architecture belong to these years—*The Seven Lamps of Architecture* (1849) and *The Stones of Venice* (1851–3). He married Effie Gray in 1848. The marriage was unhappy, and was annulled in 1854. In 1858 he met Rose La Touche, and his frustrated love for her shadowed his later years. Throughout the late 1850s and 1860s he wrote a series of essays and lectures addressing political and economic issues, including *Unto This Last* (1860), *Sesame and Lilies* (1865), and *The Queen of the Air* (1869). His work as Oxford's first Slade Professor of Fine Art began in 1870. In the following year he started to publish *Fors Clavigera*, a series of letters to the 'Workmen and Labourers of Great Britain', associated with the foundation of the reforming Guild of St George. His mental health became increasingly fragile in the 1870s, and the first of a series of serious and damaging breakdowns came in 1878. He began to publish his autobiography, *Praeterita*, in 1885; it was still incomplete when a final breakdown, in 1889, brought his publishing career to an end. He died in 1900.

FRANCIS O'GORMAN is Professor of Victorian Literature at the University of Leeds.

OXFORD WORLD'S CLASSICS

*For over 100 years Oxford World's Classics have brought
readers closer to the world's great literature. Now with over 700
titles—from the 4,000-year-old myths of Mesopotamia to the
twentieth century's greatest novels—the series makes available
lesser-known as well as celebrated writing.*

*The pocket-sized hardbacks of the early years contained
introductions by Virginia Woolf, T. S. Eliot, Graham Greene,
and other literary figures which enriched the experience of reading.
Today the series is recognized for its fine scholarship and
reliability in texts that span world literature, drama and poetry,
religion, philosophy, and politics. Each edition includes perceptive
commentary and essential background information to meet the
changing needs of readers.*

OXFORD WORLD'S CLASSICS

JOHN RUSKIN

Praeterita

Edited with an Introduction and Notes by
FRANCIS O'GORMAN

OXFORD
UNIVERSITY PRESS

OXFORD
UNIVERSITY PRESS

Great Clarendon Street, Oxford, OX2 6DP,
United Kingdom

Oxford University Press is a department of the University of Oxford.
It furthers the University's objective of excellence in research, scholarship,
and education by publishing worldwide. Oxford is a registered trade mark of
Oxford University Press in the UK and in certain other countries

Editorial matter © Francis O'Gorman 2012
Chronology © Dinah Birch 2004

The moral rights of the authors have been asserted

First published as an Oxford World's Classics paperback 2012
Impression: 9

British Library Cataloguing in Publication Data
Data available

Library of Congress Cataloging in Publication Data
Library of Congress Control Number: 2012002668

ISBN 978-0-19-280241-5

Printed in Great Britain by
Clays Ltd, Elcograf S.p.A.

ACKNOWLEDGEMENTS

MANY people have assisted me with this edition. For particular matters of explanation, I am grateful to Stuart Eagles, Ray Haslam, Howard Hull, Rory McTurk, Jay Prosser, Mark Purcell, John Whale, and Stephen Wildman. A number of people have read the Introduction or Notes and offered valuable suggestions for improvement: I am especially grateful to Alan Davis, Rachel Dickinson, and Bernard Richards. Dr Richards has been particularly generous in adding information to the text. James S. Dearden has been invaluable in sharing unpublished knowledge of *Praeterita*, not least in relation to Ruskin and London, and about Charles Richardson. I am particularly grateful to him for revealing the location of Charles's grave, and for ideas about the nature of Billiter Street. I am grateful to Mrs K. Samuelson for further information about Billiter Street in the first part of the nineteenth century, and to the Matlock Local Studies Library for information about the man Ruskin misleadingly calls 'Caxton'. Thanks too to Joanie Roes in Australia, a direct descendant of Bridget Ruskin Richardson, Ruskin's cousin, for more information about this side of JR's family.

Many thanks to my mother, Joyce O'Gorman, for the long translations from the French: all other translations, unless indicated otherwise, are my own. Dinah Birch has provided me with more than two decades of friendship and Ruskin wisdom, and I am deeply grateful for this; my thanks, also, for much Ruskin discussion over many years to Van Akin Burd, Keith Hanley, Robert Hewison, Sarah Quill, Nicholas Shrimpton, and Michael Wheeler, as well as to current members of the Ruskin Centre at the University of Lancaster. Many thanks are due to Judith Luna of OUP for advice throughout the editing of this volume. My best thanks and love are to Katherine Mullin.

CONTENTS

INTRODUCTION

WHEN the art historian Kenneth Clark began his 'Introduction' in 1949 to the important Hart-Davis edition of *Praeterita*, he helped commence the slow recovery of John Ruskin among readers. Ruskin's visibility in the nineteenth century as a critic of art and society had been unequalled. He had hoped the best for England—its art, its trade, its buildings, its schools and universities, its treatment of the poor, its attitude to what we now call the environment. And he had been one of England's most devastating critics. But by the end of the Great War, John Ruskin was either forgotten or derided. He was as unpalatable as the Victorian age itself: moralistic, anti-modern, illiberal. The once-great critic of the nineteenth century had become an emblem for what had been wrong with the recent past. It took some time before the tide began, gradually, to turn. Derrick Leon's *Ruskin: The Great Victorian* (1949) was crucial in offering an early, newly thoughtful and sympathetic reassessment. John Rosenberg's *The Darkening Glass: A Portrait of Ruskin's Genius* (1961) introduced Ruskin to students, and put him back into circulation, as Clive Wilmer's edition of *Unto this Last and Other Writings* (Penguin, 1985) and Dinah Birch's *John Ruskin: Selected Writings* (Oxford World's Classics, 2004) keep him in circulation now. Some influential feminist critics in the 1970s and 1980s were impatient with the author of *Sesame and Lilies* (1865), though gendered readings have now been refined. Today, Ruskin's arguments are still a matter of contest. But his significance is settled. He is widely studied. Now, there are scholars and journalists, furniture makers and pension managers, gardeners and artists, organic farmers and poets, economists and politicians, preachers and teachers who remember his work and admire him.[1] The Hart-Davis edition, later reprinted by Oxford University Press and for several decades the only accessible (though unannotated) version of Ruskin's autobiography, did his state some service.

Lord Clark, who gave British television viewers the famous series his commissioner insisted on calling *Civilisation* (1969), literally began his 'Introduction' with a bracing line. '*Praeterita*', he said, 'is the only one of Ruskin's writings intended to give pleasure.'[2] It was a good opening,

---

[1] This is a selective list based in part on a few of the current Companions of the Guild of St George.

[2] John Ruskin, *Praeterita*, introd. Kenneth Clark (London: Hart-Davis, 1949), p. vii.

and it is tempting to believe it. Clark even had Ruskin for his authority. But, for all Lord Clark's sympathetic understanding of a writer whom few in the 1940s were ready to read, he was wrong about *Praeterita*. Ruskin had neither a single audience in mind, nor a single purpose. Sometimes, in the midst of ill health, he struggled to know why he was writing his autobiography at all. The autobiography is an extended praise of the Alps, of the discovery of the genius of Turner, of a life lived with an increasing sense of the ministry and meaning of art, of the life-enhancing wonders of the early Italian Renaissance. But it is not singly so. About pleasure, Ruskin could not quite decide. 'All great art is praise' (*LE* xv. 351), he had said in *The Laws of Fésole* (1877–8).[3] The critic's first responsibility was to celebrate what was itself celebratory. Ruskin had spent his life in celebration, however much he is popularly remembered for his denunciations more than his affirmations. Yet this long, late history of the making of a critic could not confine itself to sources of joy. In the 'Author's Preface' to *Praeterita*, Ruskin said he was keen to omit passages of his life that brought no happiness in remembering (p. 5). Readers will look in vain for his mysterious falling-out with the English landscape painter to whom he had dedicated much of his early career, J. M. W. Turner (1775–1851); for Ruskin's eventual vexation with the Pre-Raphaelite painters whom he had earlier supported; for much about his politics; for much about his complex relationship with his parents. They will look in vain for anything at all about his six-year marriage to Effie Gray (1828–97)—and Ruskin's decision to omit detail of his marriage is one of the reasons why we learn so little about Venice in this book, because his two major early visits to the city in preparation for *The Stones of Venice* (1851–3) were undertaken with his wife, whom he no longer wished to remember. But these omissions did not leave everything else an unalloyed delight. Loss, the failing of pleasure, and its unreachableness through the past, are *Praeterita*'s recurrent themes.

There may appear, for contemporary readers, something almost uncanny about Ruskin's ability to build his life story around that which can be known no more. This starts with ordinary things. The house

³ All references to Ruskin's work other than *Praeterita*, unless indicated otherwise, are to *The Library Edition of the Works of John Ruskin*, ed. E. T. Cook and Alexander Wedderburn, 39 vols. (London: Allen, 1903–12), and are given as volume and page number. This edition (*LE*) was made available as a hard copy digital reprint in Cambridge University Press's 'Cambridge Library Collection' from 2009, and is also available free online from the University of Lancaster's Ruskin Centre (www.lancs.ac.uk/users/ruskinlib/Pages/Works.html).

at Hunter Street, London, in which Ruskin was born; the house at
Herne Hill in which he wrote the 'Author's Preface'; the house at
Denmark Hill his parents bought when their prosperity made it possible and their social status required it—all are gone: only Brantwood,
on the eastern shore of Coniston Water in the English Lake District,
remains. It was Ruskin's home from 1872 to his death. *Praeterita* cares
a great deal about houses as it cares about places more generally. It is,
in part, a remembered history of visiting. And it recalls much that is
changed. The University of Oxford that Ruskin recollects in 'Quem
Tu, Melpomene' and 'Christ Church Choir' has long passed away,
changed, not least, by the mid-Victorian reformers. What Ruskin
boldly calls in 'The Col de la Faucille' the three 'centres of my life's
thought' (p. 103)—Rouen, Geneva, and Pisa—are now, as modern
commercial cities, dramatically altered from those Ruskin knew. When
Ruskin speaks of Chamonix and the Alps (part of what he meant by
'Geneva'), he did not know the ski destination the snows would become.
In Pisa, Ruskin was entranced by the Campo Santo, the now austere
cloister next to the cathedral church of Santa Maria Assunta. It was,
Ruskin said in *The Stones of Venice*, one of the 'three most precious
buildings in Italy' (*LE* xi. 403),[4] and its frescoes formed in *Praeterita*
the subject of 'Campo Santo'. A firestorm after Allied bombardment
on 27 July 1944 swept through the cloisters, destroying the painting.
And what of Florence? Ruskin saw that city disappearing during his
lifetime. 'When I first saw Florence, in 1840,' he says in 'Macugnaga',
the 'great street leading into the Baptistery square from the south had
not been rebuilt, but consisted of irregular ancient houses, with far
projecting bracketed roofs. I mourned over their loss bitterly in 1845;
but for the rest, Florence was still, then, what no one who sees her now
could conceive' (p. 228).

Ruskin describes a world the modern reader can see has gone, and he
was already a witness to its passing. Remembering with wonder, and
often with pain, shapes this personal history. By the last chapter, it is
hard to exaggerate the density of regret that Ruskin can imply in the
briefest line. 'I have been sorrowful enough for myself', he says in
'Joanna's Care', 'since ever I lost sight of that peach-blossom avenue'
(p. 362). They are innocent words, perhaps, and seem hardly capable
of possessing much consequence. But they refer to walks in the garden at his parents' house on Denmark Hill with the young Irish girl,

---

⁴ The other two were the Sistine Chapel in the Vatican and the Scuola di San Rocco,
Venice.

Rose La Touche, whom from the 1860s he had hoped to marry and who died in 1875 at the age of 27. Those lost peach-blossoms, with their faintest glimpse of fragile purity, are the smallest—and thus the most crushing—hints of private sorrow. Never to know a functioning marriage, Ruskin did not cease to feel that his life had been blighted by the absence of a woman's daily love, and, in particular, by Rose's death. What is saved, what is peculiarly *present*, is that which is secured through pen and paper. Writing, here, does more than merely dryly record what the past was like. In *Praeterita* (Ruskin thought the title meant 'past things'), words offer a self, a *life*, made through memory.

Readers expecting a chronological narration will find this only in the broadest sense. Each chapter of *Praeterita*, mostly associated with a particular location, moves the story just about forward through time (though once at breakneck speed). But Ruskin keeps returning to earlier points. Readers should not worry too much if they are confused. Sometimes, certainly, Ruskin's memories are simply at fault—he mistakes dates as much as he forgets or ignores other facts. *Praeterita* is full of errors. But he also declines to be constricted by a narrative pattern that runs smoothly in a straight line, or which deals only with things that can be neatly narrated. Ruskin, the lover of Gothic architecture's twists and turns, the childhood admirer of the curving road in Maria Edgeworth's 'Harry and Lucy' (1801) that he reproduces in 'The Banks of Tay' (p. 35), replicates nothing merely tidy, symmetrical, or mathematical in his own story. It is easy to think that it was the twentieth century that began to consider how best to represent 'real' lives in autobiography or in fiction, the individual 'behind' the facts. The inner lives to which James Joyce, Katherine Mansfield, Dorothy Richardson, and Virginia Woolf attended can inadvertently persuade us that the Victorians—especially Victorian *men*—kept their deeper, more 'real' selves locked away. But Ruskin's autobiography is no mere linear record of the plain facts of 'what happened'. *Praeterita* finds that in order to approach an authentic presentation of Ruskin's mind, events sometimes need to be told from different perspectives, several times, to catch more of what they meant or of what they might now imply. It finds that objects and places may better serve the revelation of its author than direct efforts of telling. *Praeterita* sometimes finds it is necessary to contradict to reach more complicated truths, and that myths may be better than empirical histories to suggest a life's deepest structures and meanings (the loss of Eden, of walled and secure spaces, of young women, shape Ruskin's narration in *Praeterita* as if they are archetypes or *ur*-narratives). Memoir writers tend to leave out 'the person to whom things happened'. They say ' "this is what happened"; but they do not say what the person was like to whom it happened'.[5] That is Virginia Woolf. But there is something of *Praeterita* in those words too.

The 'self' of *Praeterita* has limits, nevertheless. Ruskin wanted to show first of all how his *mind* had grown into what it was. John Henry Newman's *Apologia Pro Vita Sua* (1864) is a suggestive shadow here, another account of the formation of a man's ideas and beliefs rather than an autobiography in a more extensive sense. *Praeterita* is offered as an intellectual history primarily, though not a dry one, for Ruskin's affections matter profoundly to what he has become. 'How I learned the things I taught', he says in 'Macugnaga', 'is the major, and properly, only question regarded in this history' (p. 234). The American journalist and academic Henry Adams would take a similar theme in his more tightly structured *The Education of Henry Adams* (1907) to reveal the inadequacy of his formal education as preparation for the modern world. But Ruskin did not really mean formal teaching: he meant the teaching he had absorbed from all that was around him. That 'major, and properly, only question' is a capacious topic—and Ruskin is not entirely fair about *Praeterita*'s scope. But limits and privacy remain. As much as *Praeterita* is a fresh way of approaching a personal history, the story of the growth of a mind, it is partial too. 'Who could tell from my books,' Ruskin said in a section intended for *Proserpina* (1875–86), his study of botany,

except in the source and common event of the abandonment of a sectarian doctrine, what has been the course of religious effort and speculation in me? Who could learn anything of friendships or loves, and the help or harm they have done me? Who could find the roots of my personal angers? Or see the dark sprays of them in the sky? (*LE* xxxv. 628)

Praeterita offers the beginning of some answers to those questions, and Ruskin is often more visible than he says. But this personal history is still, primarily, the history of part of a life. Despite his admiration of the personal candour of Thomas Carlyle's *Reminiscences* (1881), Ruskin keeps his secrets.

His preferred image is of an opening flower. That suggests that Ruskin is speaking of the development of what is already there, of what exists in potential. The 'great error of thoughtless biographers', he declares in 'The Springs of Wandel', is to 'attribute to the accident which introduces some new phase of character, all the circumstance of

---

[5] Virginia Woolf, *Moments of Being* ('A Sketch of the Past' [1939–40]) (London: Grafton, 1978), 75.

character which gave the accident importance' (p. 17). Recognizing the self outside patterns of change, Ruskin attempts the history of what, in this respect, he does not think has a history. So 'stubborn and chemically unalterable', he remarks in 'Roslyn Chapel', are the 'laws of life' that now,

looking back to that brook shore of 1837, whence I could see the whole of my youth, I find myself in nothing whatsoever changed. Some of me is dead, more of me stronger. I have learned a few things, forgotten many; in the total of me, I am but the same youth, disappointed and rheumatic. (p. 144)

The gentle wit is part of Ruskin's characteristic voice. Comic retrospection was something he learned from Charles Dickens, particularly from *David Copperfield* (1849–50), a novel that, with *Great Expectations* (1860–1), helped shape Ruskin's conception of how to write autobiography. If there is regret in looking back to that brook shore, there is also distance—even a lightness of being, a lightness about being.

The stubborn self is drawn out by events, people, books. So who and what *did* make Ruskin who he was? His parents; the Bible; his faith in God; his youthful love for Adèle Domecq, the daughter of his father's business partner, who clouded his time at Oxford; William Wordsworth (1770–1850); the novels and poetry of Sir Walter Scott (1771–1832); the valuable gift of Samuel Rogers's collection of travel poems, *Italy* (1822–8); the Alps; the paintings and drawings of Turner; the revelation that accurately observed natural form should be the starting point of art; Gothic architecture; northern Italy; eastern France; Ruskin's many friends; his later love for Rose. *Praeterita* is a long rhapsody on what places, companionship, and the writing of others can do to and for a sensitive mind. If Ruskin's autobiography records only qualified domestic affections, it is also the remarkable history of a man's love. It is an account of one man's passions, a man who hopes those passions may be others' too—passions for the meaning of the natural world made by God; for the expressive creativity of human beings using God's gifts.

Yet the hope is unobtrusive. *Praeterita* may be a study of the foundations of Ruskin's teaching, but it does not often adopt the tone of the teacher. It is intimate: its voice is that of the study or sitting room, not the lecture hall. At the beginning of *The Renaissance* (1873), Walter Pater (1839–94)—in many ways Ruskin's antagonist as a writer about the meaning of art—had defined the critic's role against Ruskin and Matthew Arnold (1822–88). A critic's first question, Pater said, should not be about the general truths of art, but about personal response.

'What is this song or picture,' he wrote in the 'Preface' to *The Renaissance*, 'this engaging personality presented in life or in a book, to *me*? What effect does it really produce on me?'[6] Ruskin had never forgotten himself in writing of art across his career. Yet he had intended primarily to speak beyond personal response about verities that were permanent; about, precisely, those 'general truths of art'. But in *Praeterita*, modestly, he speaks mostly of himself, as if compiling more of a private history of taste than elsewhere. Ruskin's inwardness, as he composes a history of himself, can sometimes imply that he is writing *for* himself. 'Eloquence', said the Utilitarian philosopher John Stuart Mill (1806–73), 'is *heard*; poetry *over* heard.'[7] So, at times, is *Praeterita*. Ruskin forgets his reader, or simply imagines that he or she can follow him through all the details of his past, through named inns and streets of sixty years ago; past local chemists and visiting doctors; through all the aiguilles, slopes, and snows of the French and Swiss Alps; through the villages of the Jura and the novels of Scott; through illustrations to long-forgotten children's books; through monastic history and the popular educational textbooks of the early nineteenth century. In all the dazzle of Ruskin's recall, *Praeterita* sometimes creates an exceptional need for other words and images: for glosses, accompanying illustrations, maps, translations, biographies, explanations. In his absorption, Ruskin forgets the need to take his readers with him. Yet the intimacy of the text strangely deepens in these instants: if we are baffled, we are also, for a moment, closer.

Praeterita's experimentalism can be overstated. Some readers have been persuaded that the text's peculiarities, omissions, and overlaps are *only* the result of a newly creative mind, forging a fresh, subtle mode of self-writing. Indeed, readers have often, historically, fallen into two (sometimes hostile) camps. Literary-minded readers have emphasized the daring inventiveness of the text as an innovative, but more or less coherent, way of relating a view of self. Those more factually and bibliographically minded have, alternatively, emphasized the chanciness and brokenness of the text and the individual story it tries to tell as a product of textual history rather than authorial invention.[8] Both are worth keeping in mind. Neither is the complete explanation.

---

[6] Walter Pater, *Studies in the History of the Renaissance*, ed. Matthew Beaumont (Oxford: OUP, 2010), 3.

[7] *The Collected Works of John Stuart Mill*, ed. J. M. Robson, 33 vols. (Toronto: U. of Toronto P., 1963–91), i. 348.

[8] For one version of this argument see George Landow's review now reproduced on http://victorianweb.org/authors/ruskin/hilton.html.

Certainly, to dwell on literary inventiveness only does no proper justice to the facts of the autobiography's troubled composition, and those are more than usually important for a reader to know. For a start, *Praeterita* did not begin as it ended. Its earliest chapters had an earlier life. They came from passages in Ruskin's open letters to 'the workmen and labourers of Great Britain', given the quirky title of *Fors Clavigera* (1871–84).[9] These were letters where Ruskin, in personal and demanding prose, sketched out his ambitions for the Guild of St George, which he founded in the early 1870s. This was Ruskin's alternative community of shared ownership, religious tolerance, hierarchical governance, hand labour, and enabling education. The famous opening of *Praeterita*, in its original context, was a response to a political question: to which party did Ruskin belong? 'I am not a Liberal', Ruskin had said to his *Fors* readers in October 1871, '—quite the polar contrary of that' (*LE* xxvii. 166). Indeed, it would have been hard to accuse him of liberalism in the pugnacious prose of *Fors*. In July that year Ruskin had also told his readers that he was 'a Communist of the old school—reddest also of the red' (ibid. 116). He meant that he was a believer in communities, but he was playfully courting his readers' bewilderment. So what, really, *was* he in the 1870s? 'It is time you should know,' Ruskin said in October 1871, 'and I will tell you plainly. I am, and my father was before me, a violent Tory of the old school' (ibid. 167). The story of the formation of Ruskin's political beliefs began there, with that tribute to order, hierarchy, the values of the past, the values of his *own* past. Yet when Ruskin, thinking a separate volume of autobiography might serve some purpose, lifted the opening material from that October *Fors*, he started the book he named *Praeterita* at the second sentence. He gave no indication (except for the briefest apologetic note at the head of 'The Springs of Wandel') that he had once been answering a political question in what had originally been an obscure series of political letters on social reform.

Ruskin's imagined audiences change. The small original audience of *Fors* gives way to others. Ruskin in *Praeterita* seems to speak primarily to his Oxford friends in the Oxford chapters and to his artistic friends in the discussions of the state of British art in the first half of the nineteenth century. Sometimes, Ruskin writes for a moment directly to the

---

[9] Ruskin explains that his title means a number of things built around 'Force, Fortitude, and Fortune' and 'Club-bearer, Key-bearer, or Nail-bearer' (*LE* xxvii. 28): 'Nail bearing,' he says later, 'or, in the full idea, nail-and-hammer bearing; driving the iron home with hammer-stroke, so that nothing shall be moved; and fastening each of us at last to the Cross we have chosen to carry' (ibid. 231). Ruskin often thought of his own life, from the 1870s, as guided by a higher or fateful 'Fors' (e.g. pp. 264, 357).

individuals who corresponded with him during the course of *Praeterita*, sometimes with complaints—one, mentioned in 'The Banks of Tay', accuses him of scorning people of no ancestry. Another expects more on Oxford. Ruskin writes in memory of, but also, in a way, *to* his parents, the planets around which, as he put it, his life moved. He seems, more often, to envisage shadier figures: unnamed, idealized men and women who shared his parents' values, who cared for the old days before the railways, mass tourism, and the political movements that so offended Ruskin. Ruskin's watchful cousin, Joan Severn (1846–1924), was on his mind too, and she played an important role in the shape of *Praeterita*. Joan was a necessary figure in the domestic and emotional stability of Ruskin's life. His love for her was real. But there were difficulties—and she was perpetually on edge about *Praeterita*. What would Ruskin say that would embarrass those who knew him, and, in particular, those who lived with him now? Undeniably, there would be trouble about Rose La Touche. The difficulty was not, readers today will want to know, that the relationship had been between an older man and a young girl. The problems were other family discomforts that were better kept from public knowledge. Percy La Touche, Rose's brother, had hoped for permission to marry Joan. But the relationship had been broken off. What embarrassment might *Praeterita* reveal to the world about that? Ruskin had thought Rose's ghost had appeared to him. Joan must have doubted that revealing this would do him much credit. Rose's mother, Maria (Ruskin always called her 'Lacerta'), had had no easy relationship with her daughter's lover, and may have been a little in love with Ruskin herself. Joan could hardly have wanted to bring those memories back.

Was Joan displeased to discover that Ruskin's original plans had included introducing herself, in a midpoint chapter called 'Joanna's Care', as, in effect, a family servant? She had arrived from Scotland as a young woman to be his mother's companion on the death of John James, Ruskin's father, who had died in 1864. Certainly, by 1889, there were times when Ruskin doubted (correctly) he would ever finish the autobiography. He seems, loyally, to have hastened on with 'Joanna's Care'. It proved the final chapter he wrote. Perhaps he hoped to thank and reassure Joan who was, practically, and would be in time actually, Mistress of Brantwood. As it turned out, she was heavily involved with the chapter herself, even contributing portions of the writing.[10] But Ruskin was not fawning, and it is possible to discern the tensions at

[10] Tim Hilton asserts that Ruskin dictated the final paragraphs of the chapter to Joan (*John Ruskin: The Later Years* (New Haven: Yale UP, 2000), 573): but the last page exists in his handwriting, with his corrections. It is reproduced in *LE* xxxv, facing page 562.

Brantwood in the manoeuvring of his prose, here, as elsewhere. Some of Ruskin's remarks ('I had seen her three years before, but not long enough to remember her distinctly' (p. 346)) may have a touch of sharpness or distance in them (compare his account of meeting Lady Mount-Temple in 'Rome'). But, most significantly, much of the chapter is not about Joan at all. 'Joanna's Care' concerns primarily the country that she came from, and that allows Ruskin, in turn, to write about his own Scotland, particularly the Borders. This was the Scotland which, as his subtitle to *Proserpina* proudly declared, 'my father knew' (*LE* xxv. 189). 'Joanna's Care' is also the last and fullest of *Praeterita*'s celebrations of the truthfulness of Walter Scott, and of truthfulness itself as the foundation of art. That was nothing but faithful to Ruskin's mind and life's work—but it also conveniently hid difficulties at home.

Other matters shaped the course of *Praeterita*. Ruskin did not always have the material he wanted. Pages of his diaries, which provided the main substance for his memories, were sometimes missing (even more are missing now). Sometimes, he merely reproduced—or *nearly* reproduced—what the diaries said and added nothing further, leaving the reader with little sense of what significance the passages had to the older man. Other sources he simply could not reach. For part of the time, he was away from Brantwood, stranded from his books and papers. In the late summer of 1887, there had been a falling-out in his Lake District home. Tempers were high. Joan may well have been fearful that Ruskin, in periods of his increasingly upsetting, violent, and debilitating mental illness, might exclude her from her expected inheritance. Ruskin himself, aged 68, was gravely ill, though by no means all the time. A restorative trip to France in that summer had reached no further than the port town of Folkestone, on the south coast of Kent. There Ruskin, in effect, was abandoned by Joan and Baxter, his valet (it seems there had been a violent scene in a hotel). Ruskin was without free access to his own money and without medical help. Ending up in a boarding house in Sandgate, west along the coast, Ruskin maintained a fretful correspondence with Joan back at Brantwood, which he did not expect to see again. He was cared for by strangers: compassionate, but no doubt puzzled, townsfolk. A visit to the National Gallery in London led him to strike up a friendship with a young girl, Kathleen Olander. That gave him purpose and hope, but it resulted in a marriage proposal and more embarrassment.[11] His close friends seem not to have

---

[11] Much later in life, Kathleen Olander (then Prynne) wrote a commentary to her letters from JR in *The Gulf of Years: Letters from John Ruskin to Kathleen Olander* (London: Allen, 1953).

realized his condition. In Folkestone, Ruskin wrote 'Otterburn', fit-fully recording his continuing delight in the skies.[12] At Sandgate, he produced 'The Grande Chartreuse', which rushes awkwardly through the 1850s to reach his 'unconversion' in 1858. Ruskin's biographer, Tim Hilton, may be right to suggest that 'The Grande Chartreuse' proceeds at such a pace 'not only to travel past the period of his mar-riage but to clear the ground for the entrance of Rose'.[13] Certainly, the closer Ruskin got to Rose in *Praeterita* (she eventually appears properly in 'L'Esterelle', written at Sallenches in September 1888), the more Joan worried. Later, in 'Joanna's Care', there is one line peculiarly weighted with private meaning from this miserable episode. That was Ruskin's reference, with apparent warmth, to Joan's establishment in the Ruskin family while Margaret Ruskin was alive: 'nor virtually', Ruskin says, 'have [Joan] and I ever parted since' (p. 347). After Folkestone and Sandgate, it was a provocative line, written with thoroughly mixed motives.

Praeterita is a compound of fresh, personal ways of relating a man's conception of his 'real' self, and a text problematized by circumstance. At its highest power, the autobiography contains some of Ruskin's most arresting and humane writing. He disclaims any ability to create. 'I never saw any boy's work in my life showing so little original faculty', he remarks characteristically of his poetry and drawing as a youth in 'Under New Tutorships' (p. 49). Despite the foray into fiction that was involved in his fairy tale *The King of the Golden River* (1851),[14] Ruskin may have thought himself the last person able to write a novel. Yet his sense of place and, even more engagingly, his portraits of individuals that bring out personality with luminous clarity, mean that *Praeterita* reveals a novelist's imagination and sense of human otherness. When Ruskin describes a man or woman from the past, they seem for a moment to stand before us. Even the very last paragraph has still some-thing of the glow of Ruskin's greatest writing.

And yet, on the other side, Ruskin's sickness meant that, at its most troubled, *Praeterita* struggles. It can offer little help to the reader in stories that break off, incomplete and inconsequential; in memories that are too fragmentary to bear much meaning. And it loses its way more thoroughly on a few occasions. Perhaps Ruskin's collapsing mind

[12] Cf. Alan Davis, ' "Moonlight in a rage": Fragments of Autobiography in Two Late Ruskin Drawings', in *John Ruskin: The Brantwood Years* (Lancaster: The Ruskin Programme, 2000), 1–19.

[13] *John Ruskin: The Later Years*, 547.

[14] *The King of the Golden River* was written in 1841 but not published till 1851.

can actually be followed in the decline that takes place from the beginning of 'The State of Denmark' to the end. In 'Mont Velan', he can only repeat, in his own translation or paraphrase, a textbook history of Switzerland, Eusèbe-Henri-Alban Gaullieur's study, *La Suisse: historique et pittoresque* (1855). Ruskin is palely considering his old theme, the dignity of Europe before the Renaissance. But this time, the reader may well feel the desire to skip. 'Mont Velan' was followed by another period of Ruskin's illness, and 'L'Esterelle', the next chapter, did not appear until nine months later. Although often vigorous and clear-minded, Ruskin was writing *Praeterita* between periods of serious mental breakdown. The history of such breakdowns is not unknown in the autobiographies of Victorian authors (insofar that there *are* autobiographies). John Stuart Mill remembered in the early draft of his *Autobiography* (1873) the autumn of 1826 when he had felt that he had 'nothing left to live for'.[15] But *Praeterita* is a life history written on occasions from the edges of mental breakdown itself. Ruskin had once said, in *Modern Painters*, V (1860), of Turner's *Apollo and Python* (1811),[16] that it represented, in its deepest meaning, a great conflict: the 'strife of purity with pollution; of life with forgetfulness; of love, with the grave' (*LE* vii. 420). Those words, much later, echo in the last chapters of *Praeterita*.

Ruskin's complete works stretch well beyond the thirty-nine volumes of the enormous *Library Edition* published by Ruskin's old pupil, George Allen, between 1903 and 1912. One of the challenges of reading Ruskin, amid all of this, is to know where to start. *Praeterita* will—and will not—do. Of course, it is Ruskin's own account of himself, and as such uniquely revealing. Yet despite its range and substance, and despite the fact that it is personal testimony, *Praeterita* gives a very odd version of John Ruskin indeed. That is *because* it is Ruskin's own. *Praeterita* is, primarily, the history of the formation of ideas, of opinions, seen from the self. It is not, in this respect, a public story. Ruskin is in no expository frame of mind, and he sees little purpose in giving a summary of the facts about his life that had made him the public figure he was. The reader will find no convenient digest of his understanding of Gothic architecture from *The Seven Lamps of Architecture* (1849) to his analysis of Venetian history in terms of moral fall in *The Stones of Venice*. Indeed, in this autobiography of the most celebrated English Venetian historian of the nineteenth century, Venice is barely mentioned at all. Ruskin offers no précis of the massive project of

---

[15] *The Collected Works of John Stuart Mill*, ed. Robson, i. 138.
[16] Now in the Tate Collection, London.

Modern Painters (1843–60), nor analyses his controversial presentation of an alternative form of morally responsible capitalism in *Unto This Last* (1860) and *Munera Pulveris* (1862–3). He does not reaffirm his cautious but consequential celebration of the Pre-Raphaelites as potential inheritors of the wisdom of medieval artists, nor does he return to *The Ethics of the Dust* (1866) or *The Queen of the Air* (1869) and his understanding of the usefulness of ancient myth as a way of identifying enduring moral truths that human beings have long forgotten. Ruskin the teacher; Ruskin before his public; Ruskin the writer and thinker and visionary: where are they? Yet *Praeterita* asks the reader to distinguish between being and doing, between what a man has made and what has made him. It asks the reader, too, to recognize the deepest foundations of a life's work, on which all else was built. *Praeterita* tells the story of the mind that made those public statements possible. It describes the formation of a man who drew unending strength from the best meanings of the past, and from reverent attention to the natural world understood as revelatory of God's will. Those are *Praeterita*'s enduring subjects because they are Ruskin's most enduring convictions and experiences. They are who he is. Not knowing these, nothing else makes sense.

Ruskin read buildings as much as he read books; he read paintings and statues; he read the meanings of the natural world. He looked at what we would now call cultural forms, as well as natural forms, as the expression of intended, willed meaning, which was either man's (in culture) or God's (in nature). Art was at its greatest when it was man's best expression of God's meaning. Ruskin was a cultural critic before the term was invented, as he was a public intellectual before that was. Such meaning in visible form needed, he thought, not interpretation first but understanding: texts, in the fullest and most modern sense of that term, did not need commentary to start with, but exposition. *Praeterita* is a history of reading cultural forms (mostly Turner and Italian art) and of natural forms (mostly the Alps). But it is also, more plainly, about reading words. Whether Ruskin's subjects are the popular songs that Joan sang to him in evenings at Brantwood; or textbooks of chemistry and geography; whether Homer's *Iliad* or stories recorded from Tuscan peasants; whether reading the Psalmist or Carlyle, Ruskin listens for the teaching that words offer. Looking back over his own life, the stories of Maria Edgeworth are unforgotten; the language of Samuel Rogers's *Italy* shapes *Praeterita* more than half a century after Ruskin first read it; the lessons he learned from Agassiz's *Recherches sur les poissons fossiles* (1833–43) and from Pope's translations of

Homer remain. The Bible is the first sustaining literary presence of his life; Dante's *Divina Commedia* the second. 'I remorsefully bethink me no word has been said of the dawn and sunrise of Dickens on us', Ruskin says in 'Fontainebleau' (p. 192), well into the second volume of *Praeterita*. Reading aloud had united Ruskin and his parents as a family, as it had for the Brontë sisters, around the table at Haworth Parsonage. Listening as well as reading was part of who the Ruskins were. *Praeterita* figures a man's mind partly constituted by the writing of others. Words express the self, and others' words are part of it. They are breathed like air.

Even the associations of books mattered. Ruskin could be outraged about what a slight to a book could mean. He, and his father before him, had used Alexander Adam's *Principles of Latin and English Grammar* (1772). Adam had been headmaster of Edinburgh's Royal High School where John James Ruskin had studied. Using Adam's *Grammar* was, in part, a tribute to Ruskin's father, and to the Edinburgh they both knew. It was Scott's Edinburgh too, as it had been Scott's school. Adam's *Grammar* bound them together. But Ruskin's new teacher in London, the Reverend Thomas Dale, would have none of it. Seeing the young Ruskin with that volume, the clergyman 'threw it back to me', Ruskin declared in *Fiction, Fair and Foul* (1880–1),

with a fierce bang upon his desk, saying (with accent and look of seven-times-heated scorn): 'That's a *Scotch* thing' Now, my father being Scotch, and an Edinburgh High School boy, and my mother having laboured in that book with me since I could read, and all my happiest holiday time having been spent on the North Inch of Perth, these four words, with the action accompanying them, contained as much insult, pain, and loosening of my respect for my parents, love of my father's country, and honour for its worthies, as it was possible to compress into four syllables and an ill-mannered gesture. Which were therefore pure, double-edged and point-envenomed blasphemy. For to make a boy despise his mother's care, is the straightest way to make him also despise his Redeemer's voice; and to make him scorn his father and his father's house, the straightest way to make him deny his God, and his God's Heaven. (*LE* xxxiv. 365–6)

It is hard to think of a more sobering instance of the casual damage a teacher may do with a few words. Ruskin's analysis is far-reaching, pulling out layer of meaning after layer, and exposing terrible significance from casualness. He reads far into an act of prohibited reading. Perhaps it is too much, too unforgiving, too overheated. But Ruskin thought part of his family, and his faith, had been cast away. Books could carry great meanings, and they asked for responsible treatment.

Praeterita is contingent and purposeful, incomplete but held together; it is the history of a life lived in public that is peculiarly personal. It is modest, and brave. It sometimes forgets its readers, but it is also a history of care. Ruskin's autobiography comprises the story of a man who saw around him, wherever he was, willed meanings from which he could learn. A Gothic cathedral taught, and so did a snow-capped mountain; a Scottish drawing-room ballad offered human insight into how to live and so did advice from a friend. Ruskin cherished the visible teaching that made existence precious, which deepened it, and which, where possible, guided it. He had with him an enduring sense, wherever he was, of the testimonies of men and women through their creations, and of God through His. Art offered in quite literal terms a way of existing. Destruction of those creations—buildings, pictures, scenes—was a form of death, an irreplaceable loss of paths to wise and compassionate existence, and of the sources of joy. Charlotte Brontë, reading *Modern Painters*, I (1843) for the first time, thought that Ruskin had taught her how to see:

> I have lately been reading *Modern Painters* and I have derived from the work much genuine pleasure and, I hope, some edification; at any rate, it made me feel how ignorant I had previously been on the subject which it treats. Hitherto I have only had instinct to guide me in judging of art; I feel more as if I had been walking blindfold—this book seems to give me eyes[.][17]

Praeterita offers a life which, for all its grief, was rich in the knowledge of what had been seen. And seen not in any passive sense, but seen and *read*. It is a broken history of understanding brought through the eye. Ruskin's autobiography, for all its problems, tells of a life lived with exceptional attention to what noble men and women had meant through their creations, and what God intended men and women to understand of His love. *Praeterita* speaks of grandeur and the highest of human achievement, but its author is also the admirer of the best all human beings have achieved, however modest or forgotten. Ending with almost the last words Ruskin wrote for print, *Praeterita* is an account, a confession, of a man who took nothing easily, and who suffered bitterly. It is also, despite its confusions and sorrows, the compelling testimony of a writer who knew, looking back, that he had lived in the fullest sense amid revelation.

[17] *The Letters of Charlotte Brontë*, ed. Margaret Smith, 3 vols. (Oxford: Clarendon, 1995–2004), ii. 94 (letter to W. S. Williams, 31 July 1848).

NOTE ON THE TEXT

John Ruskin issued many of his publications in parts: *Praeterita* was no exception. It is something of a mistake to regard it as a 'book' at all, and a single volume edition such as this one gives a misleading impression of how it was first written and received. Initial portions, as discussed in the Introduction, p. xvi, appeared in *Fors Clavigera*, letters 10 (October 1871), 28, 33, 46, 51, 52, 53, 54, 56, 63, and 65 (March 1877). *Praeterita* itself began with the publication of Chapters I and II by George Allen in July 1885. Ruskin had made, and continued to make, plans for its final shape. Several versions of those plans exist, some reproduced, for instance, in the *Library Edition*, xxxv. 633–4, and another in the second volume of Tim Hilton's *John Ruskin: The Later Years*.[1] The numbering of Ruskin's paragraphs (or groups of paragraphs), largely introduced into his publications in the 1880s, is retained here in accordance with convention.

The topics of missing chapters, insofar as they can be reconstructed from the mere titles or brief notes that Ruskin left, include Chamonix; the writing of *Unto this Last* and Ruskin's stay at Mornex; Neuchâtel, the deaths of John James Ruskin and of Lady Trevelyan (who died in Ruskin's presence in 1866); Venice 'from the beginning' (*LE* xxxv. 635) till Venice in 1876; Broadlands and (presumably) Ruskin's spiritualist experience at the home of the Lord and Lady Mount-Temple; the 1882 journey to Italy, including a last visit to Ilaria del Caretto in Lucca, and a farewell to Italy. The pattern of association of place and a particular theme/event was evidently to be continued.

For the instalments of the completed chapters (some of which pay particular attention, as *Fors* did, to contemporary events as they were occurring), publication was as follows:

Volume I, Chapter I (July 1885); Chapter II (July 1885); Chapter III (30 July 1885); Chapter IV (29 September 1885); Chapter V (28 October 1885); Chapter VI (17 November 1885); Chapter VII (4 December 1885); Chapter VIII (21 January 1886); Chapter IX (9 February 1886);

---

[1] (New Haven: Yale UP, 2000), 506–7. There is discussion of textual history, and additional scholarly material about *Praeterita*, in Bernard Richards's *Praeterita Continued*, an exploration using many of Ruskin's words of what fifteen of the unwritten chapters might have looked like had they been completed (Oxford, privately printed, 2008–).

Chapter X (18 February 1886); Chapter XI (6 March 1886); Chapter XII (1 April 1886).

Volume II, Chapter I (14 May 1886); Chapter II (14 May 1886); Chapter III (24 May 1886); Chapter IV (10 June 1886); Chapter V (9 July 1886); Chapter VI (22 October 1886); Chapter VII (22 October 1886); Chapter VIII (27 November 1886); Chapter IX (1 January 1887); Chapter X (15 March 1887); Chapter XI (9 June 1887); Chapter XII (8 November 1887).

Volume III, Chapter I (19 May 1888); Chapter II (28 September 1888); Chapter III (3 June 1889); Chapter IV (6 July 1889).

These individual parts are now extremely rare. There were relatively few instalments sold, and *Praeterita* was originally, in essence, a private publication, bought by or given to friends and allies. Swiftly, nevertheless, it was issued in volume form. The first twelve chapters were produced (with some variants from the separate chapters) as Volume I in 1886 and the second twelve as Volume II in 1887. The four chapters of Volume III were issued posthumously. Ruskin had intended his autobiography to be accompanied by a collection of documents under the name *Dilecta: Correspondence, Diary Notes, and Extracts from Books, Illustrating 'Praeterita', arranged by John Ruskin*. Part 1 of this text was issued on 30 September 1886; Part 2 on 13 January 1887. Part 3 was issued posthumously, with the incomplete third volume of *Praeterita*. *Dilecta* was included in the Hart-Davis edition of *Praeterita* and provides in some ways a sketchy indication of how unwritten elements of the autobiography could have developed.

Ruskin described himself as possessing 'a peculiar fineness in the pleasures of sight' (*LE* xxxv. 628). *Praeterita* should include, like many of Ruskin's books, illustrations. In its range of visual reference, any edition would, certainly, profit now from substantial supporting visual material. The reader is, certainly, encouraged to consult a map of the French and Swiss Alps and images of the artefacts Ruskin discusses where their identity can be unequivocally established. A small number of Ruskin's corrected proofs are in the Ruskin Centre at the University of Lancaster (1996B2709), and indicate his habit both of shortening the text to fit the fixed number of pages, and introducing changes that did not affect the overall length. *Praeterita* itself was sometimes written in pieces, even on scraps of paper that the publisher was asked to incorporate. It was haphazard. Some fragments may have been lost in transit. Material is still occasionally discovered. When Ruskin spoke of how things 'bind and blend themselves together' (p. 362) in 'Joanna's

Care', he was glancing not merely at how his imagination worked but at how, literally, he was assembling his story.

Some errors have been silently corrected and some standardization of punctuation and spelling introduced for consistency and clarity. Editorial notes are signalled by an asterisk in the text; all footnotes are by Ruskin, who was frequently a glosser of his own writing.

SELECT BIBLIOGRAPHY

Other Editions

Library Edition (1908), vol. xxxv.

Praeterita, introd. Kenneth Clark (London: Rupert Hart-Davis, 1949; repr. by OUP, 1978 and 1989).

Praeterita, ed. A. O. J. Cockshut and James S. Dearden (Keele: Ryburn, 1994).

Praeterita and Dilecta, introd. Tim Hilton (London: Everyman, 2005).

John Ruskin: Selected Writings, ed. Dinah Birch (Oxford: OUP, 2004), includes the Preface, and portions of three chapters of *Praeterita*, pp. 279–97.

Correspondence (relevant to Praeterita)

Burd, Van Akin (ed.), *The Winnington Letters: John Ruskin's Correspondence with Margaret Alexis Bell and the Children at Winnington Hall* (London: Allen and Unwin, 1969).

—— (ed.), *The Ruskin Family Letters*, 2 vols. (Ithaca, NY: Cornell UP, 1973).

—— (ed.), *Christmas Story: John Ruskin's Venetian Letters of 1876–1877* (Newark, NJ: U of Delaware P, 1990).

Bradley, John Lewis (ed.), *Ruskin's Letters from Venice, 1851–1852* (New Haven: Yale UP, 1955).

—— (ed.), *The Letters of John Ruskin to Lord and Lady Mount-Temple* (Columbus, Ohio: Ohio State UP, 1964).

—— and Ousby, Ian (eds.), *The Correspondence of John Ruskin and Charles Eliot Norton* (Cambridge: CUP, 1987).

Cate, George Allen (ed.), *The Correspondence of Thomas Carlyle and John Ruskin* (Stanford, Calif.: Stanford UP, 1982).

Dickinson, Rachel (ed.), *John Ruskin's Correspondence with Joan Severn: Sense and Nonsense Letters* (Oxford: Legenda, 2009).

Hayman, John (ed.), *Letters from the Continent, 1858* (Toronto: U of Toronto P, 1982).

Lutyens, Mary (ed.), *Young Mrs Ruskin in Venice: Unpublished Letters of Mrs John Ruskin Written from Venice between 1849–1852* (New York: Vanguard, 1967).

Shapiro, Harold I. (ed.), *Ruskin in Italy: His Letters to His Parents, 1845* (Oxford: Clarendon, 1972).

Surtees, Virginia (ed.), *Sublime and Instructive: Letters from John Ruskin to Louisa, Marchioness of Waterford, Anna Blunden, and Ellen Heaton* (London: Joseph, 1972).

—— *Reflections on a Friendship: John Ruskin's Letters to Pauline Trevelyan 1848–1866* (London: Allen & Unwin, 1979).

Diaries

Many of JR's manuscript diaries are now preserved at the Ruskin Centre, University of Lancaster: this collection is available in microfilm form from Adam Matthew as *Ruskin and Victorian Intellectual Life: Manuscripts of John Ruskin (1819–1900) from the Ruskin Library, University of Lancaster*, Part 1: *Diaries, 1835–1888*; Part 2: *Correspondence with Joan Severn, 1864–1899*. The *Diaries of John Ruskin*, ed. Joan Evans and John Howard Whitehouse, 3 vols. (Oxford: Clarendon, 1956–9), reproduces only selections of that material. Helen Gill Viljoen's edition of *The Brantwood Diary of John Ruskin* (New Haven: Yale UP, 1971) and James S. Dearden's edition of *A Tour to the Lakes in Cumberland: John Ruskin's Diary for 1830* (Aldershot: Scolar, 1990) should also be consulted. The *Victorian Lives and Letters Consortium* (led by David Sorensen) is proposing to issue digital versions of the complete archived diary journals of John Ruskin from 2013 (led by Francis O'Gorman).

Biography

Bachelor, John, *John Ruskin: No Wealth but Life* (London: Chatto & Windus, 2000).

Hilton, Tim, *John Ruskin: The Early Years* (New Haven: Yale UP, 1985).

—— *John Ruskin: The Later Years* (New Haven: Yale UP, 2000).

Hunt, John Dixon, *The Wider Sea: A Life of John Ruskin* (London: Dent, 1982).

Kempster, P. A., and Alty, J. E., 'John Ruskin's Relapsing Encephalopathy', *Brain: A Journal of Neurology*, 131 (2008), 2520–5.

Severn, Arthur, *The Professor: Arthur Severn's Memoir of John Ruskin*, ed. James S. Dearden (London: Allen & Unwin, 1967).

Spates, James L., 'John Ruskin's Dark Star: New Lights on His Life Based on the Unpublished Biographical Materials and Reasearch of Helen Gill Viljoen', *Bulletin of the John Rylands University Library of Manchester*, 82 (2000), 135–91.

—— *The Imperfect Round: Helen Gill Viljoen's Life of Ruskin* (New York: Long View, 2005).

Viljoen, H. G., *Ruskin's Scottish Heritage* (Urbana, Ill.: University of Illinois Press, 1956).

Bibliography

The best is accessible from http://www.lancs.ac.uk/users/ruskinlib/Pages/bibliog.html.

Critical Works on, or Including Significant Discussion of, Praeterita

Arrowsmith, William, 'Ruskin's Fireflies', in John Dixon Hunt and Faith M. Holland (eds.), *The Ruskin Polygon: Essays on the Imagination of John Ruskin* (Manchester: Manchester UP, 1982), 198–235.

Birch, Dinah, 'A Life in Writing: Ruskin and the Uses of Suburbia', in J. B. Bullen (ed.), *Writing and Victorianism* (London: Longman, 1997), 234–49.

—— 'The Critic as Autobiographer: Ruskin and His Artists', in Robert Hewison (ed.), *Ruskin's Artists: Studies in the Victorian Visual Economy* (Aldershot: Ashgate, 2000), 221–33.

—— 'Ruskin's Revised Eighteenth Century', in Francis O'Gorman and Katherine Turner (eds.), *The Victorians and the Eighteenth Century: Reassessing the Tradition* (Aldershot: Ashgate, 2004), 163–81.

—— and O'Gorman, Francis (eds.), *Ruskin and Gender* (Basingstoke: Palgrave, 2002).

Columbus, Charlotte Kemper, 'Ruskin's *Praeterita* as Thanatography', in George P. Landow (ed.), *Approaches to Victorian Autobiography* (Athens, Ohio: Ohio UP, 1979), 109–27.

Emerson, Sheila, *Ruskin: The Genesis of Invention* (Cambridge: CUP, 1993).

Fellows, Jay, *Ruskin's Maze: Mastery and Madness in His Art* (Princeton: Princeton UP, 1981).

Fitch, Raymond E., *The Poison Sky: Myth and Apocalypse in Ruskin* (Athens, Ohio: Ohio UP, 1982).

Hanson, David C., 'Ruskin's *Praeterita* and Landscape in Evangelical Children's Education', *Nineteenth-Century Literature*, 44 (1989), 45–66.

—— 'Ruskin, Dante, and the Dark Waters of *Praeterita*', *Nineteenth-Century Prose*, 35 (2008), 58–93.

Helsinger, Elizabeth K., *Ruskin and the Art of the Beholder* (Cambridge, Mass.: Harvard UP, 1982).

Henderson, Heather, *The Victorian Self: Autobiography and Biblical Narrative* (Ithaca, NY: Cornell UP, 1989), esp. ch. 2, '"That there should be time no longer": Revelation and Recurrence in Ruskin's *Praeterita*'.

Milbank, Alison, 'Ruskin's Grotesque: *Praeterita* as Dantesque Journey to the Real', *Nineteenth-Century Prose*, 35 (2008), 37–57.

Miller, J. Hillis, 'Prosopopoeia and *Praeterita*', in Laurence S. Lockridge et al. (eds.), *Nineteenth-Century Lives: Essays Presented to Jerome Hamilton Buckley* (Cambridge: CUP, 1989), 125–39.

O'Gorman, Francis, '"The Clue of Shakespearian Power over Me": Ruskin, Shakespeare and Influence', in Gail Marshall and Adrian Poole (eds.), *Victorian Shakespeare*, ii (Basingstoke: Palgrave, 2003), 203–18.

—— 'Romance and Victorian Autobiography: Margaret Oliphant, Edmund Gosse and John Ruskin's "needle to the north"', in Corinne Saunders (ed.), *Blackwell Companion to Romance* (Oxford: Blackwell, 2004), 360–74.

Redford, Bruce B., 'Ruskin Unparadized: Emblems of Eden in *Praeterita*', *Studies in English Literature*, 22 (1982), 675–87.

Sawyer, Paul L., *Ruskin's Poetic Argument: The Design of the Major Works* (Ithaca, NY: Cornell UP, 1985), esp. ch. 13, 'Time Present and Time Past'.

Tambling, Jeremy, 'Late Style: Approaching Madness in *Praeterita*', *English*, 58 (2009), 116–36.

Photographic Response

Riddy, John, *Praeterita: A Series of Photographs Suggested by the Autobiography of John Ruskin* (University of Oxford: Ruskin School of Drawing and Fine Art, 2000).

Societies, Museums, and Websites

The Ruskin Society (http://www.midwarks.info/ruskinsoc/).

A digital version of Ruskin's Walkley Museum by Dr Marcus Waithe (http://www.ruskinatwalkley.org/).

The Ruskin Gallery at the Millennium Gallery, Sheffield (http://www.museums-sheffield.org.uk/coresite/html/ruskin.asp).

See also the many Ruskin-related events at Brantwood (http://www.brantwood.org.uk/index.htm).

More generally, the British Association of Victorian Studies (http://www.bavsuk.org/index.htm) and the North American Victorian Studies Association (http://www.cla.purdue.edu/english/navsa/) host Victorian-related scholarly activity across the year.

A CHRONOLOGY OF JOHN RUSKIN

	Life	Historical and Cultural Background
1819	John Ruskin born 8 February at 54 Hunter Street, London.	Mary Anne Evans (George Eliot) and Queen Victoria born; Peterloo massacre.
1823	Family moves to Herne Hill, Camberwell, south of London.	
1825	Tour of France and Belgium.	
1829	First poem printed.	Dante Gabriel Rossetti born; Euphemia 'Effie' Gray born.
1830	Tour of the Lake District.	Accession of William IV.
1832	Ruskin is probably given Samuel Rogers's *Italy*, with vignettes after Turner.	First Reform Act; Walter Scott dies.
1833	Tour of Germany, Italy, and Switzerland; meets Adèle Domecq.	Factory Act. Thomas Carlyle, *Sartor Resartus*
1834	Enrols at Dr Thomas Dale's school; two geological papers published in *Magazine of National History*.	William Morris born; Samuel Coleridge dies.
1835	Tour of France, Italy and Switzerland; first visits Venice.	
1836	Writes essay in defence of Turner, who discourages publication.	Charles Dickens, *Sketches by Boz*
1837	Becomes gentleman commoner at Christ Church, Oxford. Visits Lake District. *The Poetry of Architecture* (to 1838).	Accession of Queen Victoria; John Constable dies. Carlyle, *French Revolution* Dickens, *Oliver Twist*
1838	Visits Lake District and Scotland.	'People's Charter'; beginnings of Chartism.
1839	Wins Newdigate prize for poetry at Oxford. Meets Wordsworth. Begins to collect Turners. Adèle Domecq marries.	Carlyle, *Chartism*
1840	Travels in France and Italy (to 1841) with parents, suffering from poor health.	Queen Victoria marries Prince Albert.

	Life	Historical and Cultural Background
1841	Treatment at Leamington Spa. Meets 'Effie' Gray; writes *The King of the Golden River* for her.	Thomas Babington Macaulay, *Lays of Ancient Rome* Ralph Waldo Emerson, *Essays* Carlyle, *Heroes and Hero-Worship*
1842	Takes honorary double fourth at Oxford. Family moves to Denmark Hill.	Income tax introduced. William Wordsworth, *Poems* J. M. W. Turner, *Slavers*
1843	*Modern Painters* (vol. i).	Wordsworth Poet Laureate; Robert Southey dies.
1844	In Switzerland and France.	Irish potato famine (to 1845). Robert Chambers, *Vestiges of the Natural History of Creation* Benjamin Disraeli, *Coningsby*
1845	In France, Switzerland, Italy, without his parents.	John Henry Newman converts to Roman Catholicism.
1846	*Modern Painters* (vol. ii). Repeats 1845 tour with his parents.	Corn Laws repealed. Brontës, *Poems* David Friedrich Strauss, *Life of Jesus* (trans. George Eliot)
1847	Treatment at Leamington Spa and Scotland.	Charlotte Brontë, *Jane Eyre* Emily Brontë, *Wuthering Heights* William Thackeray, *Vanity Fair*
1848	10 April: marries Effie Gray. Travels in Normandy.	Communist Manifesto; revolutions in Europe; Chartist petition; Pre-Raphaelite Brotherhood formed.
1849	*The Seven Lamps of Architecture*. Travels in Italy and France; winters (to 1850) in Venice.	Charlotte Brontë, *Shirley* Macaulay, *History of England*
1850	*Poems, Essay on Baptism* (to 1851).	Wordsworth dies; Alfred Tennyson Poet Laureate; Roman Catholic hierarchy re-established in England. Wordsworth, *The Prelude* Tennyson, *In Memoriam* Dickens, *David Copperfield*
1851	*The Stones of Venice* (vol. i), *Pre-Raphaelitism, The King of the Golden River, Notes on the Construction of Sheepfolds*; winters (to 1852) in Venice.	Turner dies; Great Exhibition in Crystal Palace, London.
1852	Moves to 30 Herne Hill.	Augustus Welby Pugin dies. Dickens, *Bleak House* (to 1853)

	Life	*Historical and Cultural Background*
1853	*The Stones of Venice* (vols. ii and iii), *Giotto and his Works in Padua*. Holiday at Glenfinlas with Effie and Millais.	Crimean War (to 1856). William Holman Hunt, *The Light of the World* Matthew Arnold, *Poems* Charlotte Brontë, *Villette*
1854	*Lectures on Architecture and Painting, The Opening of the Crystal Palace*. Marriage annulled on grounds of non-consummation. Travels in France, Switzerland, Italy. Teaches at Working Men's College.	Battle of Balaclava. Dickens, *Hard Times* Elizabeth Gaskell, *North and South*
1855	*Notes on the Royal Academy* (to 1859, 1875). Meets Charles Eliot Norton.	Benjamin Woodward and Thomas Deane, Oxford Museum (to 1860). Robert Browning, *Men and Women*
1856	*Modern Painters* (vols. iii and iv), *The Harbours of England*. Travels in France, Switzerland.	Bessemer's Steel Process. James Anthony Froude, *History of England*
1857	*The Elements of Drawing, The Political Economy of Art*. Arranges Turner Bequest (to 1858).	Indian Mutiny (to 1859). Elizabeth Barrett Browning, *Aurora Leigh*
1858	*Inaugural Address at the Cambridge School of Art*. Travels in France, Switzerland, Italy; 'unconversion' from Evangelicalism. Meets Rose La Touche (aged 10).	George Eliot, *Scenes of Clerical Life* Carlyle, *Frederick the Great*
1859	*The Two Paths, The Elements of Perspective, The Oxford Museum, The Unity of Art*. Travels in Germany, Switzerland; visits Winnington School.	Charles Darwin, *On the Origin of Species* John Stuart Mill, *On Liberty* George Eliot, *Adam Bede*
1860	*Modern Painters* (vol. v). *Unto This Last* serialized in *Cornhill* (published in book form in 1862).	Italian unification. *Essays and Reviews*
1861	Several tours; suffers depression.	Elizabeth Barrett Browning dies; American Civil War (to 1865); Prince Albert dies.

Life	*Historical and Cultural Background*
1862	*Essays on Political Economy* serialized in *Fraser's* (published in book form as *Munera Pulveris* in 1872). Travels in France, Italy.	George Meredith, *Modern Love*
1863	Stays in Mornex, buys land in Chamonix.	Thackeray dies; Albert Memorial, London. John Stuart Mill, *Utilitarianism*
1864	*Cestus of Aglaia* (to 1865). John James Ruskin dies, leaving fortune to Ruskin; his cousin Joan Agnew comes to Denmark Hill to care for Margaret Ruskin.	Pasteurization invented. John Henry Newman, *Apologia Pro Vita Sua*
1865	*Sesame and Lilies*. Member of Governor Eyre defence committee.	Abraham Lincoln assassinated; American Civil War ends. Charles Dodgson (Lewis Carroll), *Alice's Adventures in Wonderland*
1866	*The Ethics of the Dust, The Crown of Wild Olive*. Proposes to Rose La Touche. Travels in France, Switzerland.	Nobel invents dynamite. Algernon Charles Swinburne, *Poems and Ballads*
1867	*Time and Tide*.	Second Reform Act. Karl Marx, *Das Kapital* Carlyle, *Shooting Niagara*
1868	Lectures in Dublin and northern France.	Robert Browning, *The Ring and the Book*
1869	*The Queen of the Air, The Flamboyant Architecture of the Somme*. Elected first Slade Professor of Fine Art at Oxford.	Suez Canal; Girton College, Cambridge, founded. Matthew Arnold, *Culture and Anarchy* John Stuart Mill, *The Subjection of Women*
1870	*Verona and its Rivers, Lectures on Art*. Founds school of drawing at Oxford.	Dickens dies; Franco-Prussian War; Forster's Education Act.
1871	*Fors Clavigera: Letters to the Workmen and Labourers of Great Britain* (monthly to 1878, and 1880–4). Donates sum to St George's Fund (origin of Guild of St George). Illness at Matlock. Buys Brantwood in the Lake District. Margaret Ruskin dies. Sells Denmark Hill. Endows Drawing Mastership at Oxford.	Abolition of religious tests at Oxford and Cambridge. Charles Darwin, *The Descent of Man*, George Eliot, *Middlemarch*

	Life	Historical and Cultural Background
1872	*Aratra Pentelici, The Eagle's Nest.* Rose La Touche ill; rejects Ruskin's marriage proposal.	Secret ballot.
1873	*Ariadne Fiorentina* (to 1876), *Love's Meinie* (to 1881). George Allen becomes his sole publisher.	John Stuart Mill dies. Walter Pater, *Studies in the History of the Renaissance*
1874	*Val d'Arno.* Hinksey Road diggings; travels in France, Italy.	Impressionist Exhibition, Paris. Thomas Hardy, *Far From the Madding Crowd*
1875	Death of Rose La Touche. *Mornings in Florence* (to 1877), *Deucalion* (to 1883), *Proserpina* (to 1886). Founds St George's Museum in Sheffield.	Russo–Turkish war. Anthony Trollope, *The Way We Live Now*
1876	*Bibliotheca Pastorum* (ed.; to 1877). Travels in Switzerland, delirium in Venice (to 1877).	Queen Victoria Empress of India. George Eliot, *Daniel Deronda*
1877	*Guide to the Academy at Venice, The Laws of Fesole* (to 1879), *St Mark's Rest* (to 1884).	Society for the Preservation of Ancient Buildings founded.
1878	First madness. Whistler *v.* Ruskin libel case. Arranges Turner Exhibition at the Fine Art Society, London.	Salvation Army founded. Thomas Hardy, *The Return of the Native*
1879	*Notes on Prout and Hunt.* Resigns Slade Professorship at Oxford.	Gladstone's Midlothian campaign; Afghan and Zulu wars. Henrik Ibsen, *A Doll's House*
1880	*Elements of English Prosody, Bible of Amiens* (to 1885), *Fiction, Fair and Foul* (to 1881), *Letters to the Clergy on the Lord's Prayer and the Church, Arrows of the Chace, A Joy for Ever.* Travels in northern France.	George Eliot dies.
1881	Second madness.	Disraeli dies; Carlyle dies. Henry James, *Portrait of a Lady*
1882	Third madness; travels in France, Italy.	Dante Gabriel Rossetti dies; Charles Darwin dies; Anthony Trollope dies. James Anthony Froude, *Carlyle: The First Forty Years*

	Life	*Historical and Cultural Background*
1883	*The Art of England* (to 1884). Resumes Slade Professorship.	Royal College of Music founded. Friedrich Nietzsche, *Thus Spake Zarathustra*
1884	*The Storm-Cloud of the Nineteenth Century*; *The Pleasures of England* (to 1885).	Third Reform Act. *Oxford English Dictionary* (to 1928)
1885	Resigns Slade Professorship; fourth madness; *Praeterita* (to 1889), *On the Old Road*.	Fall of Khartoum. *Dictionary of National Biography* (ed. Leslie Stephen) Pater, *Marius the Epicurean*
1886	Fifth madness; *Dilecta* (to 1900).	Repeal of Contagious Diseases Act. Nietzsche, *Beyond Good and Evil*
1887	*Hortus Inclusus*.	Queen's Golden Jubilee. Arthur Conan Doyle, *A Study in Scarlet*
1888	Last tour—France, Switzerland, Italy; proposes to Kathleen Olander.	Matthew Arnold dies. Mary Ward, *Robert Elsmere* William Morris, *A Dream of John Ball*
1889	Mental incapacity ends career; lives retired life in Brantwood, cared for by Joan Severn.	Robert Browning dies. Pater, *Appreciations*
1890		First underground railway. William Morris, *News from Nowhere* William Booth, *In Darkest England*
1891		Free elementary education. William Butler Yeats, *The Countess Cathleen*
1892		Tennyson dies. George Bernard Shaw, *Widowers' Houses*
1893		Independent Labour Party founded; Benjamin Jowett dies.
1894		Christina Rossetti dies. George Moore, *Esther Waters*
1895		Cinematography invented; Jameson Raid. Joseph Conrad, *Almayer's Folly*
1896		William Morris dies; John Everett Millais dies. Arthur Morrison, *A Child of the Jago*
1897		Queen's Diamond Jubilee; Tate Gallery, London, opens.
1898		Arnold Bennett, *A Man from the North*

	Life	Historical and Cultural Background
1899		Boer War (to 1900).
		Leo Tolstoy, *Resurrection*
		Edward Elgar, *Enigma Variations*
1900	Dies 20 January at Brantwood, buried in Coniston churchyard.	Relief of Ladysmith and Mafeking.
		Joseph Conrad, *Lord Jim*
		Sigmund Freud, *The Interpretation of Dreams*
1901		Queen Victoria dies.

PRAETERITA

OUTLINES OF SCENES AND THOUGHTS
PERHAPS WORTHY OF MEMORY
IN MY PAST LIFE

CONTENTS

Contents

VOLUME III

AUTHOR'S PREFACE

I HAVE written these sketches of effort and incident in former years for my friends; and for those of the public who have been pleased by my books.

I have written them therefore, frankly, garrulously, and at ease; speaking of what it gives me joy to remember at any length I like—sometimes very carefully of what I think it may be useful for others to know; and passing in total silence things which I have no pleasure in reviewing, and which the reader would find no help in the account of.* My described life has thus become more amusing than I expected to myself, as I summoned its long past scenes for present scrutiny:—its main methods of study, and principles of work, I feel justified in commending to other students; and very certainly any habitual readers of my books will understand them better, for having knowledge as complete as I can give them of the personal character which, without endeavour to conceal, I yet have never taken pains to display, and even, now and then, felt some freakish pleasure in exposing to the chance of misinterpretation.

I write these few prefatory words on my father's* birthday, in what was once my nursery in his old house,*—to which he brought my mother and me, sixty-two years since, I being then four years old. What would otherwise in the following pages have been little more than an old man's recreation in gathering visionary flowers* in fields of youth, has taken, as I wrote, the nobler aspect of a dutiful offering at the grave of parents who trained my childhood to all the good it could attain, and whose memory makes declining life cheerful in the hope of being soon again with them.*

HERNE HILL,
  10th May, 1885.

VOLUME I

CHAPTER I

THE SPRINGS OF WANDEL*

[*The reader must be advised that the first two chapters are reprinted, with slight revision, from Fors Clavigera, having been written there chiefly for the political lessons, which appear now introduced somewhat violently.*]

1. I AM, and my father was before me, a violent* Tory of the old school;—Walter Scott's school, that is to say, and Homer's. I name these two out of the numberless great Tory writers, because they were my own two masters. I had Walter Scott's novels and the Iliad, (Pope's translation,*) for constant reading when I was a child, on week-days: on Sunday their effect was tempered by Robinson Crusoe and the Pilgrim's Progress; my mother having it deeply in her heart to make an evangelical clergyman of me. Fortunately, I had an aunt more evangelical than my mother; and my aunt gave me cold mutton for Sunday's dinner, which—as I much preferred it hot—greatly diminished the influence of the Pilgrim's Progress, and the end of the matter was, that I got all the noble imaginative teaching of Defoe and Bunyan, and yet—am not an evangelical clergyman.

2. I had, however, still better teaching than theirs, and that compulsorily, and every day of the week.

Walter Scott and Pope's Homer were reading of my own election, and my mother forced me, by steady daily toil, to learn long chapters of the Bible by heart; as well as to read it every syllable through, aloud, hard names and all, from Genesis to the Apocalypse, about once a year: and to that discipline—patient, accurate, and resolute—I owe, not only a knowledge of the book, which I find occasionally serviceable, but much of my general power of taking pains, and the best part of my taste in literature. From Walter Scott's novels I might easily, as I grew older, have fallen to other people's novels; and Pope might, perhaps, have led me to take Johnson's English, or Gibbon's, as types of language; but, once knowing the 32nd of Deuteronomy, the 119th Psalm, the 15th of 1st Corinthians, the Sermon on the Mount, and most of the Apocalypse, every syllable by heart, and having always a way of thinking with myself what words meant, it was not possible for me, even in the foolishest times of youth, to write entirely superficial or formal English; and the affectation of trying to write like Hooker and George Herbert* was the most innocent I could have fallen into.

3. From my own chosen masters, then, Scott and Homer, I learned the Toryism which my best afterthought has only served to confirm.

That is to say, a most sincere love of kings,* and dislike of everybody who attempted to disobey them. Only, both by Homer and Scott, I was taught strange ideas about kings, which I find for the present much obsolete; for, I perceived that both the author of the Iliad and the author of Waverley made their kings, or king-loving persons, do harder work than anybody else. Tydides or Idomeneus* always killed twenty Trojans to other people's one, and Redgauntlet* speared more salmon than any of the Solway fishermen, and—which was particularly a subject of admiration to me—I observed that they not only did more, but in proportion to their doings, *got* less than other people—nay, that the best of them were even ready to govern for nothing! and let their followers divide any quantity of spoil or profit. Of late it has seemed to me that the idea of a king has become exactly the contrary of this, and that it has been supposed the duty of superior persons generally to govern less, and get more, than anybody else. So that it was, perhaps, quite as well that in those early days my contemplation of existent kingship was a very distant one.

4. The aunt who gave me cold mutton on Sundays was my father's sister.* She lived at Bridge-end, in the town of Perth, and had a garden full of gooseberry-bushes, sloping down to the Tay, with a door opening to the water, which ran past it, clear-brown over the pebbles three or four feet deep; swift-eddying,—an infinite thing for a child to look down into.

5. My father began business as a wine-merchant, with no capital, and a considerable amount of debts bequeathed him by my grandfather.* He accepted the bequest, and paid them all before he began to lay by anything for himself,—for which his best friends called him a fool, and I, without expressing any opinion as to his wisdom, which I knew in such matters to be at least equal to mine, have written on the granite slab over his grave* that he was 'an entirely honest merchant.' As days went on he was able to take a house in Hunter Street, Brunswick Square, No. 54,* (the windows of it, fortunately for me, commanded a view of a marvellous iron post, out of which the water-carts were filled through beautiful little trap-doors, by pipes like boa-constrictors; and I was never weary of contemplating that mystery, and the delicious dripping consequent); and as years went on, and I came to be four or

five years old, he could command a postchaise and pair for two months
in the summer, by help of which, with my mother and me, he went the
round of his country customers (who liked to see the principal of
the house his own traveller); so that, at a jog-trot pace, and through the
panoramic opening of the four windows of a postchaise, made more
panoramic still to me because my seat was a little bracket in front, (for
we used to hire the chaise regularly for the two months out of Long
Acre,* and so could have it bracketed and pocketed as we liked), I saw
all the high-roads, and most of the cross ones, of England and Wales,
and great part of lowland Scotland, as far as Perth, where every other
year we spent the whole summer; and I used to read the Abbot at
Kinross, and the Monastery in Glen Farg,* which I confused with
'Glendearg,' and thought that the White Lady had as certainly lived by
the streamlet in that glen of the Ochils, as the Queen of Scots in the
island of Loch Leven.*

6. To my farther great benefit, as I grew older, I thus saw nearly all
the noblemen's houses in England; in reverent and healthy delight of
uncovetous admiration,—perceiving, as soon as I could perceive any
political truth at all, that it was probably much happier to live in a small
house, and have Warwick Castle to be astonished at, than to live in
Warwick Castle and have nothing to be astonished at; but that, at all
events, it would not make Brunswick Square in the least more pleasantly habitable, to pull Warwick Castle down. And at this day, though I
have kind invitations enough to visit America, I could not, even for
a couple of months, live in a country so miserable as to possess no
castles.

7. Nevertheless, having formed my notion of kinghood chiefly from
the FitzJames of the Lady of the Lake,* and of noblesse from the
Douglas there, and the Douglas in Marmion,* a painful wonder soon
arose in my child-mind, why the castles should now be always empty.
Tantallon was there; but no Archibald of Angus:—Stirling, but no
Knight of Snowdoun.* The galleries and gardens of England were
beautiful to see—but his Lordship and her Ladyship were always in
town, said the housekeepers and gardeners. Deep yearning took hold
of me for a kind of 'Restoration,' which I began slowly to feel that
Charles the Second had not altogether effected, though I always wore a
gilded oak-apple very piously in my button-hole on the 29th of May.*
It seemed to me that Charles the Second's Restoration had been, as
compared with the Restoration I wanted, much as that gilded oak-apple
to a real apple. And as I grew wiser, the desire for sweet pippins instead
of bitter ones, and Living Kings instead of dead ones, appeared to me

rational as well as romantic; and gradually it has become the main purpose of my life to grow pippins, and its chief hope, to see Kings.[1]

8. I have never been able to trace these prejudices to any royalty of descent: of my father's ancestors I know nothing, nor of my mother's more than that my maternal grandmother* was the landlady of the Old King's Head in Market Street, Croydon; and I wish she were alive again, and I could paint her Simone Memmi's King's Head,* for a sign.

My maternal grandfather was, as I have said,* a sailor, who used to embark, like Robinson Crusoe, at Yarmouth, and come back at rare intervals, making himself very delightful at home. I have an idea he had something to do with the herring business, but am not clear on that point,* my mother never being much communicative concerning it. He spoiled her, and her (younger) sister, with all his heart, when he was at home; unless there appeared any tendency to equivocation, or imaginative statements, on the part of the children, which were always unforgiveable. My mother being once perceived by him to have distinctly told him a lie, he sent the servant out forthwith to buy an entire bundle of new broom twigs to whip her with. 'They did not hurt me so much as one' (twig) 'would have done,' said my mother, 'but I *thought* a good deal of it.'

9. My grandfather was killed at two-and-thirty, by trying to ride, instead of walk, into Croydon; he got his leg crushed by his horse against a wall; and died of the hurt's mortifying. My mother was then seven or eight years old, and, with her sister, was sent to quite a fashionable (for Croydon) day-school, Mrs Rice's, where my mother was taught evangelical principles, and became the pattern girl and best needlewoman in the school; and where my aunt absolutely refused evangelical principles, and became the plague and pet of it.

10. My mother, being a girl of great power, with not a little pride, grew more and more exemplary in her entirely conscientious career, much laughed at, though much beloved, by her sister; who had more wit, less pride, and no conscience. At last my mother, formed into a consummate housewife, was sent for to Scotland to take care of my paternal grandfather's house; who was gradually ruining himself; and who at last effectually ruined, and killed, himself. My father came up to London; was a clerk in a merchant's house for nine years, without a holiday; then began business on his own account; paid his father's debts; and married his exemplary Croydon cousin.

---

[1] The St George's Company* was founded for the promotion of agricultural instead of town life: and my only hope of prosperity for England, or any other country, in whatever life they lead, is in their discovering and obeying men capable of Kinghood.

11. Meantime my aunt* had remained in Croydon, and married a baker. By the time I was four years old, and beginning to recollect things,—my father rapidly taking higher commercial position in London,—there was traceable—though to me, as a child, wholly incomprehensible,—just the least possible shade of shyness on the part of Hunter Street, Brunswick Square, towards Market Street, Croydon. But whenever my father was ill,—and hard work and sorrow had already set their mark on him,—we all went down to Croydon to be petted by my homely aunt; and walk on Duppas Hill, and on the heather of Addington.

12. My aunt lived in the little house still standing—or which was so four months ago—the fashionablest in Market Street, having actually two windows over the shop, in the second storey; but I never troubled myself about that superior part of the mansion, unless my father happened to be making drawings in Indian ink, when I would sit reverently by and watch; my chosen domains being, at all other times, the shop, the bakehouse, and the stones round the spring of crystal water at the back door (long since let down into the modern sewer); and my chief companion, my aunt's dog, Towzer, whom she had taken pity on when he was a snappish, starved vagrant; and made a brave and affectionate dog of: which was the kind of thing she did for every living creature that came in her way, all her life long.

13. Contented, by help of these occasional glimpses of the rivers of Paradise, I lived until I was more than four years old in Hunter Street, Brunswick Square, the greater part of the year; for a few weeks in the summer breathing country air by taking lodgings in small cottages (real cottages, not villas, so-called) either about Hampstead, or at Dulwich, at 'Mrs Ridley's,' the last of a row in a lane which led out into the Dulwich fields on one side, and was itself full of buttercups in spring, and blackberries in autumn. But my chief remaining impressions of those days are attached to Hunter Street. My mother's general principles of first treatment were, to guard me with steady watchfulness from all avoidable pain or danger; and, for the rest, to let me amuse myself as I liked, provided I was neither fretful nor troublesome. But the law was, that I should find my own amusement. No toys of any kind were at first allowed;—and the pity of my Croydon aunt for my monastic poverty in this respect was boundless. On one of my birthdays, thinking to overcome my mother's resolution by splendour of temptation, she bought the most radiant Punch and Judy she could find in all the Soho bazaar—as big as a real Punch and Judy, all dressed in scarlet and gold, and that would dance, tied to the leg of a chair. I must have

been greatly impressed, for I remember well the look of the two figures, as my aunt herself exhibited their virtues. My mother was obliged to accept them; but afterwards quietly told me it was not right that I should have them; and I never saw them again.

14. Nor did I painfully wish, what I was never permitted for an instant to hope, or even imagine, the possession of such things as one saw in toy-shops. I had a bunch of keys to play with, as long as I was capable only of pleasure in what glittered and jingled; as I grew older, I had a cart, and a ball; and when I was five or six years old, two boxes of well-cut wooden bricks. With these modest, but, I still think, entirely sufficient possessions, and being always summarily whipped if I cried, did not do as I was bid, or tumbled on the stairs, I soon attained serene and secure methods of life and motion; and could pass my days contentedly in tracing the squares and comparing the colours of my carpet;—examining the knots in the wood of the floor, or counting the bricks in the opposite houses; with rapturous intervals of excitement during the filling of the water-cart, through its leathern pipe, from the dripping iron post at the pavement edge; or the still more admirable proceedings of the turncock, when he turned and turned till a fountain sprang up in the middle of the street. But the carpet, and what patterns I could find in bed covers, dresses, or wall-papers to be examined, were my chief resources, and my attention to the particulars in these was soon so accurate, that when at three and a half I was taken to have my portrait painted by Mr Northcote, I had not been ten minutes alone with him before I asked him why there were holes in his carpet. The portrait in question represents a very pretty child with yellow hair, dressed in a white frock like a girl, with a broad light-blue sash and blue shoes to match; the feet of the child wholesomely large in proportion to its body; and the shoes still more wholesomely large in proportion to the feet.

15. These articles of my daily dress were all sent to the old painter for perfect realization; but they appear in the picture more remarkable than they were in my nursery, because I am represented as running in a field at the edge of a wood with the trunks of its trees striped across in the manner of Sir Joshua Reynolds; while two rounded hills, as blue as my shoes, appear in the distance, which were put in by the painter at my own request; for I had already been once, if not twice, taken to Scotland; and my Scottish nurse having always sung to me as we approached the Tweed or Esk,—

'For Scotland, my darling, lies full in thy view,
With her barefooted lassies, and mountains so blue,'

the idea of distant hills was connected in my mind with approach to the extreme felicities of life, in my Scottish aunt's garden of gooseberry bushes, sloping to the Tay. But that, when old Mr Northcote asked me (little thinking, I fancy, to get any answer so explicit) what I would like to have in the distance of my picture, I should have said 'blue hills' instead of 'gooseberry bushes,' appears to me—and I think without any morbid tendency to think over-much of myself—a fact sufficiently curious, and not without promise, in a child of that age.

16. I think it should be related also that having, as aforesaid, been steadily whipped if I was troublesome, my formed habit of serenity was greatly pleasing to the old painter; for I sat contentedly motionless, counting the holes in his carpet, or watching him squeeze his paint out of its bladders,—a beautiful operation, indeed, to my thinking;—but I do not remember taking any interest in Mr Northcote's application of the pigments to the canvas; my ideas of delightful art, in that respect, involving indispensably the possession of a large pot, filled with paint of the brightest green, and of a brush which would come out of it soppy. But my quietude was so pleasing to the old man that he begged my father and mother to let me sit to him for the face of a child which he was painting in a classical subject;* where I was accordingly repre-sented as reclining on a leopard skin, and having a thorn taken out of my foot by a wild man of the woods.

17. In all these particulars, I think the treatment, or accidental con-ditions, of my childhood, entirely right, for a child of my temperament: but the mode of my introduction to literature appears to me question-able, and I am not prepared to carry it out in St George's schools,* without much modification. I absolutely declined to learn to read by syllables; but would get an entire sentence by heart with great facility, and point with accuracy to every word in the page as I repeated it. As, however, when the words were once displaced, I had no more to say, my mother gave up, for the time, the endeavour to teach me to read, hoping only that I might consent, in process of years, to adopt the popular system of syllabic study. But I went on to amuse myself, in my own way, learnt whole words at a time, as I did patterns; and at five years old was sending for my 'second volumes' to the circulating library.*

18. This effort to learn the words in their collective aspect, was assisted by my real admiration of the look of printed type, which I began to copy for my pleasure, as other children draw dogs and horses. The following inscription, facsimile'd from the fly-leaf of my Seven Champions of Christendom,* (judging from the independent views taken in it of the character of the letter L, and the relative elevation of G,)

I believe to be an extremely early art study of this class; and as by the will of Fors,* the first lines of the note, written after an interval of fifty years, underneath my copy of it, in direction to Mr Burgess, presented some notable points of correspondence with it, I thought it well he should engrave them together, as they stood.

The noble knight like a bowl and daring hero then entered the valey where the Dragon had his abode who no sooner had sight of him but his leathern throat sent forth a sound most

Bolton Abbey

Dear Burgess   24th Jan. 75*

Will you kindly facsimile with moderate care, the above piece of ancient manuscript for Fors.

19. My mother had, as she afterwards told me, solemnly 'devoted me to God' before I was born; in imitation of Hannah.*

Very good women are remarkably apt to make away with their children prematurely, in this manner: the real meaning of the pious act being, that, as the sons of Zebedee are not (or at least they hope not), to sit on the right and left of Christ, in His kingdom, their own sons may perhaps, they think, in time be advanced to that respectable position in eternal life; especially if they ask Christ very humbly for it every day; and they always forget in the most naïve way that the position is not His to give!*

20. 'Devoting me to God,' meant, as far as my mother knew herself what she meant, that she would try to send me to college, and make a clergyman of me: and I was accordingly bred for 'the Church.' My father, who—rest be to his soul—had the exceedingly bad habit of yielding to my mother in large things and taking his own way in little ones, allowed me, without saying a word, to be thus withdrawn from the sherry trade as an unclean thing; not without some pardonable participation in my mother's ultimate views for me. For, many and many a year afterwards, I remember, while he was speaking to one of our

artist friends, who admired Raphael,* and greatly regretted my endeavours to interfere with that popular taste,—while my father and he were condoling with each other on my having been impudent enough to think I could tell the public about Turner and Raphael,—instead of contenting myself, as I ought, with explaining the way of their souls' salvation to them—and what an amiable clergyman was lost in me,—'Yes,' said my father, with tears in his eyes—(true and tender tears, as ever father shed,) 'he would have been a Bishop.'*

21. Luckily for me, my mother, under these distinct impressions of her own duty, and with such latent hopes of my future eminence, took me very early to church;—where, in spite of my quiet habits, and my mother's golden vinaigrette, always indulged to me there, and there only, with its lid unclasped that I might see the wreathed open pattern above the sponge, I found the bottom of the pew so extremely dull a place to keep quiet in, (my best story-books being also taken away from me in the morning,) that, as I have somewhere said before,* the horror of Sunday used even to cast its prescient gloom as far back in the week as Friday—and all the glory of Monday, with church seven days removed again, was no equivalent for it.

22. Notwithstanding, I arrived at some abstract in my own mind of the Rev. Mr Howell's sermons; and occasionally, in imitation of him, preached a sermon at home over the red sofa cushions;—this performance being always called for by my mother's dearest friends, as the great accomplishment of my childhood. The sermon was, I believe, some eleven words long; very exemplary, it seems to me, in that respect—and I still think must have been the purest gospel, for I know it began with, 'People, be good.'

23. We seldom had company, even on week days; and I was never allowed to come down to dessert, until much later in life—when I was able to crack nuts neatly. I was then permitted to come down to crack other people's nuts for them—(I hope they liked the ministration)—but never to have any myself; nor anything else of dainty kind, either then or at other times. Once at Hunter Street, I recollect my mother giving me three raisins, in the forenoon, out of the store cabinet; and I remember perfectly the first time I tasted custard, in our lodgings in Norfolk Street—where we had gone while the house was being painted, or cleaned, or something. My father was dining in the front room, and did not finish his custard; and my mother brought me the bottom of it into the back room.

24. But for the reader's better understanding of such further progress of my poor little life as I may trespass on his patience in

describing, it is now needful that I give some account of my father's mercantile position in London.

The firm of which he was head partner may be yet remembered by some of the older city houses, as carrying on their business in a small counting-house on the first floor of narrow premises, in as narrow a thoroughfare of East London,—Billiter Street, the principal traverse from Leadenhall Street into Fenchurch Street.

The names of the three partners were given in full on their brass plate under the counting-house bell,—Ruskin, Telford, and Domecq.

25. Mr Domecq's name should have been the first, by rights, for my father and Mr Telford were only his agents. He was the sole proprietor of the estate which was the main capital of the firm,—the vineyard of Macharnudo, the most precious hillside, for growth of white wine, in the Spanish peninsula. The quality of the Macharnudo vintage essentially fixed the standard of Xeres 'sack,' or 'dry'—secco—sherris, or sherry, from the days of Henry the Fifth to our own;—the unalterable and unrivalled chalk-marl of it putting a strength into the grape which age can only enrich and darken,—never impair.*

26. Mr Peter Domecq was, I believe, Spanish born; and partly French, partly English bred; a man of strictest honour, and kindly disposition; how descended, I do not know; how he became possessor of his vineyard, I do not know; what position he held, when young, in the firm of Gordon, Murphy, and Company, I do not know; but in their house he watched their head clerk, my father, during his nine years of duty, and when the house broke up, asked him to be his own agent in England. My father saw that he could fully trust Mr Domecq's honour, and feeling;—but not so fully either his sense, or his industry; and insisted, though taking only his agent's commission, on being both nominally, and practically, the head-partner of the firm.

27. Mr Domecq lived chiefly in Paris; rarely visiting his Spanish estate, but having perfect knowledge of the proper processes of its cultivation, and authority over its labourers almost like a chief's over his clan. He kept the wines at the highest possible standard; and allowed my father to manage all matters concerning their sale, as he thought best. The second partner, Mr Henry Telford, brought into the business what capital was necessary for its London branch. The premises in Billiter Street belonged to him; and he had a pleasant country house at Widmore, near Bromley; a quite far-away Kentish village in those days.

He was a perfect type of an English country gentleman of moderate fortune; unmarried, living with three unmarried sisters,—who, in the refinement of their highly educated, unpretending, benevolent, and felicitous lives, remain in my memory more like the figures in a beautiful story than realities. Neither in story, nor in reality, have I ever again heard of, or seen, anything like Mr Henry Telford;—so gentle, so humble, so affectionate, so clear in common sense, so fond of horses,—and so entirely incapable of doing, thinking, or saying, anything that had the slightest taint in it of the racecourse or the stable.

28. Yet I believe he never missed any great race; passed the greater part of his life on horseback; and hunted during the whole Leicestershire season; but never made a bet, never had a serious fall, and never hurt a horse. Between him and my father there was absolute confidence, and the utmost friendship that could exist without community of pursuit. My father was greatly proud of Mr Telford's standing among the country gentlemen; and Mr Telford was affectionately respectful to my father's steady industry and infallible commercial instinct. Mr Telford's actual part in the conduct of the business was limited to attendance in the counting-house during two months at Midsummer, when my father took his holiday, and sometimes for a month at the beginning of the year, when he travelled for orders. At these times Mr Telford rode into London daily from Widmore, signed what letters and bills needed signature, read the papers, and rode home again; any matters needing deliberation were referred to my father, or awaited his return. All the family at Widmore would have been limitlessly kind to my mother and me, if they had been permitted any opportunity; but my mother always felt, in cultivated society,—and was too proud to feel with patience,—the defects of her own early education; and therefore (which was the true and fatal sign of such defect) never familiarly visited any one whom she did not feel to be, in some sort, her inferior.

Nevertheless, Mr Telford had a singularly important influence in my education. By, I believe, his sisters' advice, he gave me, as soon as it was published, the illustrated edition of Rogers' Italy. This book was the first means I had of looking carefully at Turner's work:* and I might, not without some appearance of reason, attribute to the gift the entire direction of my life's energies. But it is the great error of thoughtless biographers to attribute to the accident which introduces some new phase of character, all the circumstances of character which gave the accident importance. The essential point to be noted, and accounted for, was that I could understand Turner's work, when I saw it;—not by what chance, or in what year, it was first seen. Poor Mr Telford, nevertheless, was always held by papa and mamma primarily responsible for my Turner insanities.

29. In a more direct, though less intended way, his help to me was important. For, before my father thought it right to hire a carriage for the above mentioned Midsummer holiday, Mr Telford always lent us his own travelling chariot.

Now the old English chariot is the most luxurious of travelling carriages, for two persons, or even for two persons and so much of third personage as I possessed at three years old. The one in question was hung high, so that we could see well over stone dykes and average hedges out of it; such elevation being attained by the old-fashioned folding steps, with a lovely padded cushion fitting into the recess of the door,—steps which it was one of my chief travelling delights to see the hostlers fold up and down; though my delight was painfully alloyed by envious ambition to be allowed to do it myself:—but I never was,—lest I should pinch my fingers.

30. The 'dickey,'—(to think that I should never till this moment have asked myself the derivation* of that word, and now be unable to get at it!)—being, typically, that commanding seat in her Majesty's mail, occupied by the Guard; and classical, even in modern literature, as the scene of Mr Bob Sawyer's arrangements with Sam,*—was thrown far back in Mr Telford's chariot, so as to give perfectly comfortable room for the legs (if one chose to travel outside on fine days), and to afford beneath it spacious area to the boot, a storehouse of rearward miscellaneous luggage. Over which—with all the rest of forward and superficial luggage—my nurse Anne* presided, both as guard and packer; unrivalled, she, in the flatness and precision of her in-laying of dresses, as in turning of pancakes; the fine precision, observe, meaning also the easy wit and invention of her art; for, no more in packing a trunk than commanding a campaign, is precision possible without foresight.

31. Among the people whom one must miss out of one's life, dead, or worse than dead, by the time one is past fifty, I can only say for my own part, that the one I practically and truly miss most next to father and mother, (and putting losses of imaginary good out of the question,) is this Anne, my father's nurse, and mine. She was one of our 'many,'[1] (our many being always but few,) and from her girlhood to her old age, the entire ability of her life was given to serving us. She had a natural gift and speciality for doing disagreeable things; above all, the service of a sick room; so that she was never quite in her glory unless some of us were ill. She had also some parallel speciality for *saying* disagreeable

---

[1] Formerly 'Meinie,' 'attendant company.'

things; and might be relied upon to give the extremely darkest view of any subject, before proceeding to ameliorative action upon it. And she had a very creditable and republican aversion to doing immediately, or in set terms, as she was bid; so that when my mother and she got old together, and my mother became very imperative and particular about having her teacup set on one side of her little round table, Anne would observantly and punctiliously put it always on the other; which caused my mother to state to me, every morning after breakfast, gravely, that if ever a woman in this world was possessed by the Devil, Anne was that woman. But in spite of these momentary and petulant aspirations to liberality and independence of character, poor Anne remained very servile in soul all her days; and was altogether occupied, from the age of fifteen to seventy-two, in doing other people's wills instead of her own, and seeking other people's good instead of her own: nor did I ever hear on any occasion of her doing harm to a human being, except by saving two hundred and some odd pounds for her relations; in consequence of which some of them, after her funeral, did not speak to the rest for several months.

32. The dickey then aforesaid, being indispensable for our guard Anne, was made wide enough for two, that my father might go outside also when the scenery and day were fine. The entire equipage was not a light one of its kind; but, the luggage being carefully limited, went gaily behind good horses on the then perfectly smooth mail roads; and posting,* in those days, being universal, so that at the leading inns in every country town, the cry 'Horses out!' down the yard, as one drove up, was answered, often instantly, always within five minutes, by the merry trot through the archway of the booted and bright-jacketed rider, with his caparisoned* pair,—there was no driver's seat in front: and the four large, admirably fitting and sliding windows, admitting no drop of rain when they were up, and never sticking as they were let down, formed one large moving oriel,* out of which one saw the country round, to the full half of the horizon. My own prospect was more extended still, for my seat was the little box containing my clothes, strongly made, with a cushion on one end of it; set upright in front (and well forward), between my father and mother. I was thus not the least in their way, and my horizon of sight the widest possible. When no object of particular interest presented itself, I trotted, keeping time with the postboy on my trunk cushion for a saddle, and whipped my father's legs for horses; at first theoretically only, with dexterous motion of wrist; but ultimately in a quite practical and efficient manner, my father having presented me with a silver-mounted postillion's whip.

33. The Midsummer holiday,* for better enjoyment of which Mr Telford provided us with these luxuries, began usually on the fifteenth of May, or thereabouts;—my father's birthday was the tenth; on that day I was always allowed to gather the gooseberries for his first gooseberry pie of the year,* from the tree between the buttresses on the north wall of the Herne Hill garden; so that we could not leave before that *festa*. The holiday itself consisted in a tour for orders through half the English counties; and a visit (if the counties lay northward) to my aunt in Scotland.

34. The mode of journeying was as fixed as that of our home life. We went from forty to fifty miles a day, starting always early enough in the morning to arrive comfortably to four o'clock dinner. Generally, therefore, getting off at six o'clock, a stage or two were done before breakfast, with the dew on the grass, and first scent from the hawthorns; if in the course of the midday drive there were any gentleman's house to be seen,—or, better still, a lord's—or, best of all, a duke's,—my father baited the horses, and took my mother and me reverently through the state rooms; always speaking a little under our breath to the housekeeper, major domo, or other authority in charge; and gleaning worshipfully what fragmentary illustrations of the history and domestic ways of the family might fall from their lips.

35. In analyzing above, page 9, the effect on my mind of all this, I have perhaps a little antedated the supposed resultant impression that it was probably happier to live in a small house than a large one. But assuredly, while I never to this day pass a lattice-windowed cottage without wishing to be its cottager, I never yet saw the castle which I envied to its lord; and although in the course of these many worshipful pilgrimages I gathered curiously extensive knowledge, both of art and natural scenery, afterwards infinitely useful, it is evident to me in retrospect that my own character and affections were little altered by them; and that the personal feeling and native instinct of me had been fastened, irrevocably, long before, to things modest, humble, and pure in peace, under the low red roofs of Croydon, and by the cress-set rivulets in which the sand danced and minnows darted above the Springs of Wandel.

CHAPTER II

HERNE HILL ALMOND BLOSSOMS

36. WHEN I was about four years old my father found himself able to buy the lease of a house on Herne Hill, a rustic eminence four miles south of the 'Standard in Cornhill';* of which the leafy seclusion remains, in all essential points of character, unchanged to this day: certain Gothic splendours, lately indulged in by our wealthier neighbours, being the only serious innovations; and these are so graciously concealed by the fine trees of their grounds, that the passing viator* remains unappalled by them; and I can still walk up and down the piece of road between the Fox tavern and the Herne Hill station, imagining myself four years old.

37. Our house was the northernmost of a group which stand accurately on the top or dome of the hill, where the ground is for a small space level, as the snows are, (I understand,) on the dome of Mont Blanc; presently falling, however, in what may be, in the London clay formation, considered a precipitous slope, to our valley of Chamouni (or of Dulwich) on the east; and with a softer descent into Cold Harbour*-lane[1] on the west: on the south, no less beautifully declining to the dale of the Effra, (doubtless shortened from Effrena, signifying the 'Unbridled' river; recently, I regret to say, bricked over for the convenience of Mr Biffin,* chemist, and others); while on the north, prolonged indeed with slight depression some half mile or so, and receiving, in the parish of Lambeth, the chivalric title of 'Champion Hill,' it plunges down at last to efface itself in the plains of Peckham, and the rural barbarism of Goose Green.

38. The group, of which our house was the quarter, consisted of two precisely similar partner-couples of houses, gardens and all to match; still the two highest blocks of buildings seen from Norwood on the crest of the ridge; so that the house itself, three-storied, with garrets above, commanded, in those comparatively smokeless days, a very notable view from its garret windows, of the Norwood hills on one side, and the winter sunrise over them; and of the valley of the Thames on the other, with Windsor telescopically clear in the distance, and Harrow, conspicuous always in fine weather to open vision against the summer sunset. It had front and back garden in sufficient proportion to its size; the front, richly

---

[1] Said in the History of Croydon to be a name which has long puzzled antiquaries, and nearly always found near Roman military stations.

set with old evergreens, and well-grown lilac and laburnum; the back, seventy yards long by twenty wide, renowned over all the hill for its pears and apples, which had been chosen with extreme care by our predecessor, (shame on me to forget the name of a man to whom I owe so much!*)—and possessing also a strong old mulberry tree, a tall white-heart cherry tree, a black Kentish one, and an almost unbroken hedge, all round, of alternate gooseberry and currant bush; decked, in due season, (for the ground was wholly beneficent,) with magical splendour of abundant fruit: fresh green, soft amber, and rough-bristled crimson bending the spinous branches; clustered pearl and pendant ruby joyfully discoverable under the large leaves that looked like vine.

39. The differences of primal importance which I observed between the nature of this garden, and that of Eden, as I had imagined it, were, that, in this one, *all* the fruit was forbidden;* and there were no companionable beasts:* in other respects the little domain answered every purpose of Paradise to me; and the climate, in that cycle of our years, allowed me to pass most of my life in it. My mother never gave me more to learn than she knew I could easily get learnt, if I set myself honestly to work, by twelve o'clock. She never allowed anything to disturb me when my task was set; if it was not said rightly by twelve o'clock, I was kept in till I knew it, and in general, even when Latin Grammar came to supplement the Psalms, I was my own master for at least an hour before half-past one dinner, and for the rest of the afternoon.

40. My mother, herself finding her chief personal pleasure in her flowers, was often planting or pruning beside me, at least if I chose to stay beside *her*. I never thought of doing anything behind her back which I would not have done before her face; and her presence was therefore no restraint to me; but, also, no particular pleasure, for, from having always been left so much alone, I had generally my own little affairs to see after; and, on the whole, by the time I was seven years old, was already getting too independent, mentally, even of my father and mother; and, having nobody else to be dependent upon, began to lead a very small, perky, contented, conceited, Cock-Robinson-Crusoe* sort of life, in the central point which it appeared to me, (as it must naturally appear to geometrical animals,) that I occupied in the universe.

41. This was partly the fault of my father's modesty; and partly of his pride. He had so much more confidence in my mother's judgment as to such matters than in his own, that he never ventured even to help, much less to cross her, in the conduct of my education; on the other hand, in the fixed purpose of making an ecclesiastical gentleman of me, with the superfinest of manners, and access to the highest circles of

fleshly and spiritual society, the visits to Croydon, where I entirely loved my aunt, and young baker-cousins, became rarer and more rare: the society of our neighbours on the hill could not be had without breaking up our regular and sweetly selfish manner of living; and on the whole, I had nothing animate to care for, in a childish way, but myself, some nests of ants, which the gardener would never leave undisturbed for me, and a sociable bird or two; though I never had the sense or perseverance to make one really tame. But that was partly because, if ever I managed to bring one to be the least trustful of me, the cats got it.

Under these circumstances, what powers of imagination I possessed, either fastened themselves on inanimate things—the sky, the leaves, and pebbles, observable within the walls of Eden,—or caught at any opportunity of flight into regions of romance, compatible with the objective realities of existence in the nineteenth century, within a mile and a quarter of Camberwell Green.

42. Herein my father, happily, though with no definite intention other than of pleasing me, when he found he could do so without infringing any of my mother's rules, became my guide. I was particularly fond of watching him shave; and was always allowed to come into his room in the morning (under the one in which I am now writing), to be the motionless witness of that operation. Over his dressing-table hung one of his own water-colour drawings, made under the teaching of the elder Nasmyth; I believe, at the High School of Edinburgh.* It was done in the early manner of tinting, which, just about the time when my father was at the High School, Dr Monro was teaching Turner; namely, in grey under-tints of Prussian blue and British ink, washed with warm colour afterwards on the lights. It represented Conway Castle, with its Frith, and, in the foreground, a cottage, a fisherman, and a boat at the water's edge.[1]

43. When my father had finished shaving, he always told me a story about this picture. The custom began without any initial purpose of his, in consequence of my troublesome curiosity whether the fisherman lived in the cottage, and where he was going to in the boat. It being settled, for peace' sake, that he *did* live in the cottage, and was going in the boat to fish near the castle, the plot of the drama afterwards gradually thickened; and became, I believe, involved with that of the tragedy of Douglas,* and of the Castle Spectre,* in both of which pieces my father had performed in private theatricals, before my mother, and a select Edinburgh audience, when he was a boy of sixteen, and she, at grave twenty, a model

---

[1] This drawing is still over the chimney-piece of my bedroom at Brantwood.*

housekeeper, and very scornful and religiously suspicious of theatricals. But she was never weary of telling me, in later years, how beautiful my father looked in his Highland dress, with the high black feathers.

44. In the afternoons, when my father returned (always punctually) from his business, he dined, at half-past four, in the front parlour, my mother sitting beside him to hear the events of the day, and give counsel and encouragement with respect to the same;—chiefly the last, for my father was apt to be vexed if orders for sherry fell the least short of their due standard, even for a day or two. I was never present at this time, however, and only avouch what I relate by hearsay and probable conjecture; for between four and six it would have been a grave misdemeanour in me if I so much as approached the parlour door. After that, in summer time, we were all in the garden as long as the day lasted; tea under the white-heart cherry tree; or in winter and rough weather, at six o'clock in the drawing-room,—I having my cup of milk, and slice of bread-and-butter, in a little recess, with a table in front of it, wholly sacred to me; and in which I remained in the evenings as an Idol in a niche, while my mother knitted, and my father read to her,—and to me, so far as I chose to listen.

45. The series of the Waverley novels, then drawing towards its close, was still the chief source of delight in all households caring for literature; and I can no more recollect the time when I did not know them than when I did not know the Bible; but I have still a vivid remembrance of my father's intense expression of sorrow mixed with scorn, as he threw down *Count Robert of Paris*,* after reading three or four pages; and knew that the life of Scott was ended: the scorn being a very complex and bitter feeling in him,—partly, indeed, of the book itself, but chiefly of the wretches who were tormenting and selling the wrecked intellect,* and not a little, deep down, of the subtle dishonesty which had essentially caused the ruin. My father never could forgive Scott his concealment of the Ballantyne partnership.*

46. Such being the salutary pleasures of Herne Hill, I have next with deeper gratitude to chronicle what I owe to my mother for the resolutely consistent lessons which so exercised me in the Scriptures as to make every word of them familiar to my ear in habitual music,— yet in that familiarity reverenced, as transcending all thought, and ordaining all conduct.[1]

This she effected, not by her own sayings or personal authority; but simply by compelling me to read the book thoroughly, for myself.

---

[1] Compare the 52nd paragraph of chapter iii. of *The Bible of Amiens*.*

As soon as I was able to read with fluency, she began a course of Bible work with me, which never ceased till I went to Oxford. She read alternate verses with me, watching, at first, every intonation of my voice, and correcting the false ones, till she made me understand the verse, if within my reach, rightly, and energetically. It might be beyond me altogether; that she did not care about; but she made sure that as soon as I got hold of it at all, I should get hold of it by the right end.

In this way she began with the first verse of Genesis, and went straight through, to the last verse of the Apocalypse; hard names, numbers, Levitical law, and all; and began again at Genesis the next day. If a name was hard, the better the exercise in pronunciation,—if a chapter was tiresome, the better lesson in patience,—if loathsome, the better lesson in faith that there was some use in its being so outspoken. After our chapters, (from two to three a day, according to their length, the first thing after breakfast, and no interruption from servants allowed,—none from visitors, who either joined in the reading or had to stay upstairs,—and none from any visitings or excursions, except real travelling,) I had to learn a few verses by heart, or repeat, to make sure I had not lost, something of what was already known; and, with the chapters thus gradually possessed from the first word to the last, I had to learn the whole body of the fine old Scottish paraphrases,* which are good, melodious, and forceful verse; and to which, together with the Bible itself, I owe the first cultivation of my ear in sound.

It is strange that of all the pieces of the Bible which my mother thus taught me, that which cost me most to learn, and which was, to my child's mind, chiefly repulsive—the 119th Psalm—has now become of all the most precious to me, in its overflowing and glorious passion of love for the Law of God,* in opposition to the abuse of it by modern preachers of what they imagine to be His gospel.

47. But it is only by deliberate effort that I recall the long morning hours of toil, as regular as sunrise,—toil on both sides equal—by which, year after year, my mother forced me to learn these paraphrases, and chapters, (the eighth of 1st Kings being one*—try it, good reader, in a leisure hour!) allowing not so much as a syllable to be missed or misplaced; while every sentence was required to be said over and over again till she was satisfied with the accent of it. I recollect a struggle between us of about three weeks, concerning the accent of the 'of' in the lines

> 'Shall any following spring revive
> The ashes of the urn?'*

—I insisting, partly in childish obstinacy, and partly in true instinct for rhythm, (being wholly careless on the subject both of urns and their contents,) on reciting it with an accented *of*. It was not, I say, till after three weeks' labour, that my mother got the accent lightened on the 'of' and laid on the ashes, to her mind. But had it taken three years she would have done it, having once undertaken to do it. And, assuredly, had she not done it,—well, there's no knowing what would have happened; but I'm very thankful she *did*.

48. I have just opened my oldest (in use) Bible,—a small, closely, and very neatly printed volume it is, printed in Edinburgh by Sir D. Hunter Blair and J. Bruce, Printers to the King's Most Excellent Majesty, in 1816. Yellow, now, with age, and flexible, but not unclean, with much use, except that the lower corners of the pages at 8th of 1st Kings, and 32nd Deuteronomy, are worn somewhat thin and dark, the learning of these two chapters having cost me much pains. My mother's list of the chapters with which, thus learned, she established my soul in life,[1] has just fallen out of it. I will take what indulgence the incurious reader can give me, for printing the list thus accidentally occurrent:—

Exodus,	chapters	15th and 20th.
2 Samuel	"	1st, from 17th verse to the end.
1 Kings	"	8th.
Psalms	"	23rd, 32nd, 90th, 91st, 103rd, 112th, 119th, 139th.
Proverbs	"	2nd, 3rd, 8th, 12th.
Isaiah	"	58th.
Matthew	"	5th, 6th, 7th.
Acts	"	26th.
1 Corinthians	"	13th, 15th.
James	"	4th.
Revelation	"	5th, 6th.

And truly, though I have picked up the elements of a little further knowledge—in mathematics, meteorology, and the like, in after life,—and owe not a little to the teaching of many people, this maternal installation of my mind in that property of chapters, I count very confidently the most precious, and, on the whole, the one *essential* part of all my education.

---

[1] This expression in *Fors* has naturally been supposed by some readers to mean that my mother at this time made me vitally and evangelically religious. The fact was far otherwise. I meant only that she gave me secure *ground* for all future life, practical or spiritual. See the paragraph next following.

And it is perhaps already time to mark what advantage and mischief, by the chances of life up to seven years old, had been irrevocably determined for me.

I will first count my blessings (as a not unwise friend once recommended me to do, continually; whereas I have a bad trick of always numbering the thorns in my fingers and not the bones in them).

And for best and truest beginning of all blessings, I had been taught the perfect meaning of Peace, in thought, act, and word.

I never had heard my father's or mother's voice once raised in any question with each other; nor seen an angry, or even slightly hurt or offended, glance in the eyes of either. I had never heard a servant scolded; nor even suddenly, passionately, or in any severe manner, blamed. I had never seen a moment's trouble or disorder in any household matter; nor anything whatever either done in a hurry, or undone in due time. I had no conception of such a feeling as anxiety; my father's occasional vexation in the afternoons, when he had only got an order for twelve butts after expecting one for fifteen, as I have just stated, was never manifested to *me*; and itself related only to the question whether his name would be a step higher or lower in the year's list of sherry exporters; for he never spent more than half his income, and therefore found himself little incommoded by occasional variations in the total of it. I had never done any wrong that I knew of—beyond occasionally delaying the commitment to heart of some improving sentence, that I might watch a wasp on the window pane, or a bird in the cherry tree; and I had never seen any grief.

49. Next to this quite priceless gift of Peace, I had received the perfect understanding of the natures of Obedience and Faith. I obeyed word, or lifted finger, of father or mother, simply as a ship her helm; not only without idea of resistance, but receiving the direction as a part of my own life and force, and helpful law, as necessary to me in every moral action as the law of gravity in leaping. And my practice in Faith was soon complete: nothing was ever promised me that was not given; nothing ever threatened me that was not inflicted, and nothing ever told me that was not true.

Peace, obedience, faith; these three for chief good; next to these, the habit of fixed attention with both eyes and mind—on which I will not further enlarge at this moment, this being the main practical faculty of my life, causing Mazzini to say of me, in conversation authentically reported, a year or two before his death, that I had 'the most analytic mind in Europe.' An opinion in which, so far as I am acquainted with Europe, I am myself entirely disposed to concur.

Lastly, an extreme perfection in palate and all other bodily senses, given by the utter prohibition of cake, wine, comfits, or, except in carefullest restriction, fruit; and by fine preparation of what food was given me. Such I esteem the main blessings of my childhood;—next, let me count the equally dominant calamities.

50. First, that I had nothing to love.

My parents were—in a sort—visible powers of nature to me, no more loved than the sun and the moon: only I should have been annoyed and puzzled if either of them had gone out; (how much, now, when both are darkened!)—still less did I love God; not that I had any quarrel with Him, or fear of Him; but simply found what people told me was His service, disagreeable; and what people told me was His book, not entertaining. I had no companions to quarrel with, neither; nobody to assist, and nobody to thank. Not a servant was ever allowed to do anything for me, but what it was their duty to do; and why should I have been grateful to the cook for cooking, or the gardener for gardening,—when the one dared not give me a baked potato without asking leave, and the other would not let my ants' nests alone, because they made the walks untidy? The evil consequence of all this was not, however, what might perhaps have been expected, that I grew up selfish or unaffectionate; but that, when affection did come, it came with violence utterly rampant and unmanageable, at least by me, who never before had anything to manage.

51. For (second of chief calamities) I had nothing to endure. Danger or pain of any kind I knew not: my strength was never exercised, my patience never tried, and my courage never fortified. Not that I was ever afraid of anything,—either ghosts, thunder, or beasts; and one of the nearest approaches to insubordination which I was ever tempted into as a child, was in passionate effort to get leave to play with the lion's cubs in Wombwell's menagerie.*

52. Thirdly. I was taught no precision nor etiquette of manners; it was enough if, in the little society we saw, I remained unobtrusive, and replied to a question without shyness: but the shyness came later, and increased as I grew conscious of the rudeness arising from the want of social discipline, and found it impossible to acquire, in advanced life, dexterity in any bodily exercise, skill in any pleasing accomplishment, or ease and tact in ordinary behaviour.

53. Lastly, and chief of evils. My judgment of right and wrong, and powers of independent action,[1] were left entirely undeveloped; because

---

[1] *Action*, observe, I say here: in *thought* I was too independent, as I said above.

the bridle and blinkers were never taken off me. Children should have their times of being off duty, like soldiers; and when once the obedience, if required, is certain, the little creature should be very early put for periods of practice in complete command of itself; set on the bare-backed horse of its own will, and left to break it by its own strength. But the ceaseless authority exercised over my youth left me, when cast out at last into the world, unable for some time to do more than drift with its vortices.

54. My present verdict, therefore, on the general tenor of my education at that time, must be, that it was at once too formal and too luxurious; leaving my character, at the most important moment for its construction, cramped indeed, but not disciplined; and only by protection innocent instead of by practice virtuous. My mother saw this herself, and but too clearly, in later years; and whenever I did anything wrong, stupid, or hard-hearted,—(and I have done many things that were all three,)—always said, 'It is because you were too much indulged.'

55. Thus far, with some omissions, I have merely reprinted the account of these times given in *Fors*: and I fear the sequel may be more trivial, because much is concentrated in the foregoing broad statement, which I have now to continue by slower steps;—and yet less amusing, because I tried always in *Fors* to say things, if I could, a little piquantly; and the rest of the things related in this book will be told as plainly as I can. But whether I succeeded in writing piquantly in Fors or not, I certainly wrote often obscurely; and the description above given of Herne Hill seems to me to need at once some reduction to plainer terms.

56. The actual height of the long ridge of Herne Hill, above Thames,—at least above the nearly Thames-level of its base at Camberwell Green, is, I conceive, not more than one hundred and fifty feet: but it gives the whole of this fall on both sides of it in about a quarter of a mile; forming, east and west, a succession of quite beautiful pleasure-ground and gardens, instantly dry after rain, and in which, for children, running down is pleasant play, and rolling a roller up, vigorous work. The view from the ridge on both sides was, before railroads came, entirely lovely: westward at evening, almost sublime, over softly wreathing distances of domestic wood;—Thames herself not visible, nor any fields except immediately beneath; but the tops of twenty square miles of politely inhabited groves. On the other side, east and south, the Norwood hills, partly rough with furze, partly wooded with birch and oak, partly in pure green bramble copse, and rather steep

pasture, rose with the promise of all the rustic loveliness of Surrey and Kent in them, and with so much of space and height in their sweep, as gave them some fellowship with hills of true hill-districts. Fellowship now inconceivable, for the Crystal Palace,* without ever itself attaining any true aspect of size, and possessing no more sublimity than a cucumber frame between two chimneys, yet by its stupidity of hollow bulk, dwarfs the hills at once; so that now one thinks of them no more but as three long lumps of clay, on lease for building. But then, the Norwood, or North wood, so called as it was seen from Croydon, in opposition to the South wood of the Surrey downs, drew itself in sweeping crescent good five miles round Dulwich to the south, broken by lanes of ascent, Gipsy Hill, and others; and, from the top, commanding views towards Dartford, and over the plain of Croydon,—in contemplation of which I one day frightened my mother out of her wits by saying 'the eyes were coming out of my head!' She thought it was an attack of coup-de-soleil.*

57. Central in such amphitheatre, the crowning glory of Herne Hill was accordingly, that, after walking along its ridge southward from London through a mile of chestnut, lilac, and apple trees, hanging over the wooden palings on each side—suddenly the trees stopped on the left, and out one came on the top of a field sloping down to the south into Dulwich valley—open field animate with cow and buttercup, and below, the beautiful meadows and high avenues of Dulwich; and beyond, all that crescent of the Norwood hills; a footpath, entered by a turnstile, going down to the left, always so warm that invalids could be sheltered there in March, when to walk elsewhere would have been death to them; and so quiet, that whenever I had anything difficult to compose or think of, I used to do it rather there than in our own garden. The great field was separated from the path and road only by light wooden open palings, four feet high, needful to keep the cows in. Since I last composed, or meditated there, various improvements have taken place; first the neighbourhood wanted a new church, and built a meagre Gothic one with a useless spire, for the fashion of the thing, at the side of the field; then they built a parsonage behind it, the two stopping out half the view in that direction. Then the Crystal Palace came, for ever spoiling the view through all its compass, and bringing every show-day, from London, a flood of pedestrians down the footpath, who left it filthy with cigar ashes for the rest of the week: then the railroads came, and expatiating roughs by every excursion train, who knocked the palings about, roared at the cows, and tore down what branches of blossom they could reach over the palings on the

enclosed side. Then the residents, on the enclosed side, built a brick wall to defend themselves. Then the path got to be insufferably hot as well as dirty, and was gradually abandoned to the roughs, with a policeman on watch at the bottom. Finally, this year, a six foot high close paling has been put down the other side of it, and the processional excursionist has the liberty of obtaining what notion of the country air and prospect he may, between the wall and that, with one bad cigar before him, another behind him, and another in his mouth.

58. I do not mean this book to be in any avoidable way disagreeable or querulous; but expressive generally of my native disposition—which, though I say it, is extremely amiable, when I'm not bothered: I will grumble elsewhere when I must, and only notice this injury alike to the resident and excursionist at Herne Hill, because questions of right-of-way are now of constant occurrence; and in most cases, the mere *path* is the smallest part of the old Right, truly understood. The Right is of the cheerful view and sweet air which the path commanded.

Also, I may note in passing, that for all their talk about Magna Charta,* very few Englishmen are aware that one of the main provisions of it is that Law should not be sold;[1] and it seems to me that the law of England might preserve Banstead and other downs free to the poor of England, without charging me, as it has just done, a hundred pounds for its temporary performance of that otherwise unremunerative duty.*

59. I shall have to return over the ground of these early years, to fill gaps, after getting on a little first; but will yet venture here the tediousness of explaining that my saying 'in Herne Hill garden all fruit was forbidden,' only meant, of course, forbidden unless under defined restriction; which made the various gatherings of each kind in its season a sort of harvest festival; and which had this further good in its apparent severity, that, although in the at last indulgent areas, the peach which my mother gathered for me when she was sure it was ripe, and the cherry pie for which I had chosen the cherries red all round, were, I suppose, of more ethereal flavour to me than they could have been to children allowed to pluck and eat at their will; still the unalloyed and long continuing pleasure given me by our fruit-tree avenue was in its blossom, not in its bearing. For the general epicurean enjoyment of existence, potatoes well browned, green pease well boiled,—broad beans of the true bitter,—and the pots of damson and currant for whose annual filling we were dependent more on the

---

[1] 'To no one will We sell, to no one will We deny or defer, Right, or Justice.'

greengrocer than the garden, were a hundredfold more important to me than the dozen or two of nectarines of which perhaps I might get the halves of three,—(the other sides mouldy)—or the bushel or two of pears which went directly to the store-shelf. So that, very early indeed in my thoughts of trees, I had got at the principle given fifty years afterwards in 'Proserpina,' that the seeds and fruits of them were for the sake of the flowers, not the flowers for the fruit.* The first joy of the year being in its snowdrops, the second, and cardinal one, was in the almond blossom,—every other garden and woodland gladness following from that in an unbroken order of kindling flower and shadowy leaf; and for many and many a year to come,—until indeed, the whole of life became autumn to me,—my chief prayer for the kindness of heaven, in its flowerful seasons, was that the frost might not touch the almond blossom.

CHAPTER III

THE BANKS OF TAY

60. THE reader has, I hope, observed that in all I have hitherto said, emphasis has been laid only on the favourable conditions which surrounded the child whose history I am writing, and on the docile and impressionable quietness of its temper.

No claim has been made for it to any special power or capacity; for, indeed, none such existed, except that patience in looking, and precision in feeling, which afterwards, with due industry, formed my analytic power.

In all essential qualities of genius, except these, I was deficient; my memory only of average power. I have literally never known a child so incapable of acting a part, or telling a tale. On the other hand, I have never known one whose thirst for visible fact was at once so eager and so methodic.

61. I find also that in the foregoing accounts, modest as I meant them to be, higher literature is too boastfully spoken of as my first and exclusive study. My little Pope's *Iliad*, and, in any understanding of them, my Genesis and Exodus, were certainly of little account with me till after I was ten. My calf milk of books was, on the lighter side, composed of *Dame Wiggins of Lee*, the *Peacock at Home*, and the like nursery rhymes; and on the graver side, of Miss Edgeworth's *Frank*, and *Harry and Lucy*, combined with Joyce's *Scientific Dialogues*.*

The earliest dated efforts I can find, indicating incipient motion of brain-molecules, are six 'poems' on subjects selected from those works; between the fourth and fifth of which my mother has written: 'January, 1826. This book begun about September or October, 1826, finished about January, 1827.' The whole of it, therefore, was written and printed in imitation of book-print, in my seventh year.* The book is a little red one, ruled with blue, six inches high by four wide, containing forty-five leaves pencilled in imitation of print on both sides,—the title-page, written in the form here approximately imitated, on the inside of the cover.

HARRY AND LUCY

CONCLUDED

BEING THE LAST

PART OF

EARLY LESSONS

in four volumes

vol I

with copper

plates

PRINTED and composed by a little boy
and also drawn

62. Of the promised four volumes, it appears that (according to my practice to this day*) I accomplished but one and a quarter, the first volume consisting only of forty leaves, the rest of the book being occupied by the aforesaid six 'poems,' and the forty leaves losing ten of their pages in the 'copper plates,' of which the one, purporting to represent 'Harry's new road,' is, I believe, my first effort at mountain drawing. The passage closing the first volume of this work is, I think, for several reasons, worth preservation. I print it, therefore, with its own divisions of line, and three variations of size in imitated type. Punctuation must be left to the reader's kind conjecture. The hyphens, it is to be noticed, were put long or short, to make the print even, not that it ever succeeds in being so, but the variously spaced lines here imitate it pretty well.

Harry knew very well–
what it was and went
on with his drawing but
Lucy soon called him aw–
ay and bid him observe
a great black cloud from–
the north which seemed ra
ther electrical. Harry ran
for an electrical apparatus which
his father had given him and the–
cloud electrified his apparatus positively
after that another cloud came which
electrified his apparatus negatively
and then a long train of smaller
ones but before this cloud came
a great cloud of dust rose from

the ground and followed the pos
itive cloud and at length seemed
to come in contact with it and
when the other cloud came
a flash of lightning was seen
to dart through the cloud of
dust upon which the negative
cloud spread very much and
dissolved in rain which pres
ently cleared the sky
After this phenomenon was over
and also the surprise Harry began
to wonder how electricity
could get where there was
so much water but he soon-
observed a rainbow and a-
rising mist under it which
his fancy soon transform

ed into a female form. He
then remembered the witch of
the waters at the Alps who
was raised from them by-
takeing some water in the-
hand and throwing it into
the air pronouncing some
unintelligable words. And
though it was a tale it-
affected Harry now when
he saw in the clouds some-
    end of Harry   thing
     and Lucy   like it.

63. The several reasons aforesaid, which induce me to reprint this piece of, too literally, 'composition,' are—the first, that it is a tolerable specimen of my seven years old spelling;—tolerable only, not *fair*, since it was extremely unusual with me to make a mistake at all, whereas here there are two (takeing and unintelligable), which I can only account for by supposing I was in too great a hurry to finish my volume;—the second, that the adaptation of materials for my story out of Joyce's *Scientific Dialogues*[1] and *Manfred*,* is an extremely perfect type of the

[1] The original passage is as follows, vol. vi., edition of 1821, p. 138:—
'Dr Franklin mentions a remarkable appearance which occurred to Mr Wilke, a considerable electrician. On the 20th of July, 1758, at three o'clock in the afternoon, he observed a great quantity of dust rising from the ground, and covering a field, and part of the town in which he then was. There was no wind, and the dust moved gently towards the east, where there appeared a great black cloud, which electrified his apparatus positively to a very high degree. This cloud went towards the west, the dust followed it, and continued to rise higher and higher, till it composed a thick pillar, in the form of a sugar-loaf, and at length it seemed to be in contact with the cloud. At some distance from this, there came another great cloud, with a long stream of smaller ones, which electrified his apparatus negatively; and when they came near the positive cloud, a flash of lightning was seen to dart through the cloud of dust, upon which the negative clouds spread very much, and dissolved in rain, which presently cleared the atmosphere.'

interwoven temper of my mind, at the beginning of days just as much as at their end—which has always made foolish scientific readers doubt my books because there was love of beauty in them, and foolish aesthetic readers doubt my books because there was love of science in them;—the third, that the extremely reasonable method of final judgment, upon which I found my claim to the sensible reader's respect for these dipartite writings, cannot be better illustrated than by this proof, that, even at seven years old, no tale, however seductive, could 'affect' Harry, until he had seen—in the clouds, or elsewhere—'something like it.'

Of the six poems which follow, the first is on the Steam-engine, beginning,

> 'When furious up from mines the water pours,
> And clears from rusty moisture all the ores;'

and the last on the Rainbow, 'in blank verse,' as being of a didactic character, with observations on the ignorant and unreflective dispositions of certain people.

> 'But those that do not know about that light,
> Reflect not on it; and in all that light,
> Not one of all the colours do they know.'

64. It was only, I think, after my seventh year had been fulfilled in these meditations, that my mother added the Latin lesson to the Bible-reading, and accurately established the daily routine which was sketched in the foregoing chapter. But it extremely surprises me, in trying, at least for my own amusement, if not the reader's, to finish the sketch into its corners, that I can't recollect now what used to happen first in the morning, except breakfasting in the nursery, and if my Croydon cousin Bridget happened to be staying with us, quarrelling with her which should have the brownest bits of toast. That must have been later on, though, for I could not have been promoted to toast at the time I am thinking of. Nothing is well clear to me of the day's course, till, after my father had gone to the City by the coach, and my mother's household orders been quickly given, lessons began at half-past nine, with the Bible readings above described, and the two or three verses to be learned by heart, with a verse of paraphrase;—then a Latin declension or a bit of verb, and eight words of vocabulary from Adam's Latin Grammar,* (the best that ever was,) and the rest of the day was my own. Arithmetic was wholesomely remitted till much later; geography I taught myself fast enough in my own way; history was never

thought of, beyond what I chose to read of Scott's *Tales of a Grandfather*.*
Thus, as aforesaid, by noon I was in the garden on fine days, or left to
my own amusements on wet ones; of which I have farther at once to
note that nearly as soon as I could crawl, my toy-bricks of lignum vitae*
had been constant companions: and I am graceless in forgetting by
what extravagant friend, (I greatly suspect my Croydon aunt,) I was
afterwards gifted with a two-arched bridge, admirable in fittings of
voussoir* and keystone, and adjustment of the level courses of masonry
with bevelled edges, into which they dovetailed, in the style of Waterloo
Bridge.* Well-made centreings, and a course of inlaid steps down to
the water, made this model largely, as accurately, instructive: and I was
never weary of building, *un*building,—(it was too strong to be thrown
down, but had always to be *taken* down,)—and rebuilding it. This
inconceivable passive—or rather impassive—contentment in doing,
or reading, the same thing over and over again, I perceive to have been
a great condition in my future power of getting thoroughly to the bottom of matters.

65. Some people would say that in getting these toys lay the chance
that guided me to an early love of architecture; but I never saw or heard
of another child so fond of its toy bricks, except Miss Edgeworth's
Frank.* To be sure, in this present age,—age of universal brickfield
though it be,—people don't give their children toy bricks, but toy
puff-puffs; and the little things are always taking tickets and arriving at
stations, without ever fathoming—none of them will take pains enough
to do *that*,—the principle of a puff-puff! And what good could they get
of it if they did,—unless they could learn also, that no principle of
Puff-puff would ever supersede the principle of Breath?

But I not only mastered, with Harry and Lucy, the entire motive principle of puff-puff; but also, by help of my well-cut bricks, very utterly
the laws of practical stability in towers and arches, by the time I was
seven or eight years old: and these studies of structure were farther
animated by my invariable habit of watching, with the closest attention,
the proceedings of any bricklayers, stone-sawyers, or paviours,*—whose
work my nurse would allow me to stop to contemplate in our walks; or,
delight of delights, might be seen at ease from some fortunate window
of inn or lodging on our journeys. In those cases the day was not long
enough for my rapturous and riveted observation.

66. Constantly, as aforesaid, in the garden when the weather was
fine, my time there was passed chiefly in the same kind of close watching
of the ways of plants. I had not the smallest taste for growing them, or
taking care of them, any more than for taking care of the birds, or the

trees, or the sky, or the sea. My whole time passed in staring at them, or into them. In no morbid curiosity, but in admiring wonder, I pulled every flower to pieces till I knew all that could be seen of it with a child's eyes; and used to lay up little treasures of seeds, by way of pearls and beads,—never with any thought of sowing them. The old gardener only came once a week, for what sweeping and weeding needed doing; I was fain to learn to sweep the walks with him, but was discouraged and shamed by his always doing the bits I had done over again. I was extremely fond of digging holes, but that form of gardening was not allowed. Necessarily, I fell always back into my merely contemplative mind, and at nine years old began a poem, called Eudosia,—I forget wholly where I got hold of this name, or what I understood by it,—'On the Universe,'* though I could understand not a little by it, now. A couplet or two, as the real beginning at once of *Deucalion** and *Proserpina*, may be perhaps allowed, together with the preceding, a place in this grave memoir; the rather that I am again enabled to give accurate date—September 28th, 1828—for the beginning of its 'First book,' as follows:—

> 'When first the wrath of heaven o'erwhelmed the world,
> And o'er the rocks, and hills, and mountains, hurl'd
> The waters' gathering mass; and sea o'er shore,—
> Then mountains fell, and vales, unknown before,
> Lay where they were. Far different was the Earth
> When first the flood came down, than at its second birth.
> Now for its produce!—Queen of flowers, O rose,
> From whose fair coloured leaves such odour flows,
> Thou must now be before thy subjects named,
> Both for thy beauty and thy sweetness famed.
> Thou art the flower of England, and the flow'r
> Of Beauty too—of Venus' odrous bower.
> And thou wilt often shed sweet odours round,
> And often stooping, hide thy head on ground.[1]
> And then the lily, towering up so proud,
> And raising its gay head among the various crowd,
> There the black spots upon a scarlet ground,
> And there the taper-pointed leaves are found.'

67. In 220 lines, of such quality, the first book ascends from the rose to the oak. The second begins—to my surprise, and in extremely

---

[1] An awkward way—chiefly for the rhyme's sake—of saying that roses are often too heavy for their stalks.

exceptional violation of my above-boasted custom—with an ecstatic apostrophe to what I had never seen!

> 'I sing the Pine, which clothes high Switzer's[1] head,
> And high enthroned, grows on a rocky bed,
> On gulphs so deep, on cliffs that are so high,
> He that would dare to climb them dares to die.'

This enthusiasm, however, only lasts—mostly exhausting itself in a description, verified out of *Harry and Lucy*, of the slide of Alpnach,—through 76 lines, when the verses cease, and the book being turned upside down, begins at the other end with the information that 'Rock-crystal is accompanied by Actynolite, Axinite, and Epidote, at Bourg d'Oisans in Dauphiny.' But the garden-meditations never ceased, and it is impossible to say how much strength was gained, or how much time uselessly given, except in pleasure, to these quiet hours and foolish rhymes. Their happiness made all the duties of outer life irksome, and their unprogressive reveries might, the reader may think, if my mother had wished, have been changed into a beginning of sound botanical knowledge. But, while there were books on geology and mineralogy which I could understand, all on botany were then,—and they are little mended now,—harder than the Latin grammar. The mineralogy was enough for me seriously to work at, and I am inclined finally to aver that the garden-time could not have been more rightly passed, unless in weeding.

68. At six punctually I joined my father and mother at tea, being, in the drawing-room, restricted to the inhabitation of the sacred niche above referred to, a recess beside the fireplace, well lighted from the lateral window in the summer evenings, and by the chimney-piece lamp in winter, and out of all inconvenient heat, or hurtful draught. A good writing-table before it shut me well in, and carried my plate and cup, or books in service. After tea, my father read to my mother what pleased themselves, I picking up what I could, or reading what I liked better instead. Thus I heard all the Shakespeare comedies and historical plays again and again,—all Scott, and all Don Quixote, a favourite book of my father's, and at which I could then laugh to ecstasy; now, it is one of the saddest, and, in some things, the most offensive of books to me.*

My father was an absolutely beautiful reader of the *best* poetry and prose;—of Shakespeare, Pope, Spenser, Byron, and Scott; as of

---

[1] Switzer, clearly short for Switzerland.

Goldsmith, Addison, and Johnson. Lighter ballad poetry he had not fineness of ear to do justice to: his sense of the strength and wisdom of true meaning, and of the force of rightly ordered syllables, made his delivery of Hamlet, Lear, Caesar, or Marmion, melodiously grand and just; but he had no idea of modulating the refrain of a ballad, and had little patience with the tenor of its sentiment. He looked always, in the matter of what he read, for heroic will and consummate reason; never tolerated the morbid love of misery for its own sake, and never read, either for his own pleasure or my instruction, such ballads as Burd Helen, the Twa Corbies,* or any other rhyme or story which sought its interest in vain love or fruitless death.

But true, pure, and ennobling sadness began very early to mingle its undertone with the constant happiness of those days;—a ballad music, beautiful in sincerity, and hallowing them like cathedral chant. Concerning which,—I must go back now to the days I have only heard of with the hearing of the ear, and yet of which some are to me as if mine eyes had seen them.

69. It must have been a little after 1780 that my paternal grandmother, Catherine Tweddale, ran away with my paternal grandfather when she was not quite sixteen; and my aunt Jessie, my father's only sister, was born a year afterwards;* a few weeks after which event, my grandmother, not yet seventeen, was surprised, by a friend who came into her room unannounced, dancing a threesome reel, with two chairs for her partners; she having found at the moment no other way of adequately expressing the pleasure she took in this mortal life, and its gifts and promises.

The latter failed somewhat afterwards; and my aunt Jessie, a very precious and perfect creature, beautiful in her dark-eyed, Highland way,—utterly religious, in her quiet Puritan way,—and very submissive to Fates mostly unkind, was married to a somewhat rough tanner,* with a fairly good business in the good town of Perth: and, when I was old enough to be taken first to visit them, my aunt and my uncle the tanner lived in a square-built grey stone house in the suburb of Perth known as 'Bridge-End,' the house some fifty yards north of the bridge; its garden sloping steeply to the Tay, which eddied, three or four feet deep of sombre crystal, round the steps where the servants dipped their pails.

70. A mistaken correspondent in *Fors* once complained of my coarse habit of sneering at people of no ancestry. I have no such habit; though not always entirely at ease in writing of my uncles the baker and the tanner. And my readers may trust me when I tell them that, in now

remembering my dreams in the house of the entirely honest chief baker of Market Street, Croydon, and of Peter—not Simon—the tanner,* whose house was by the riverside of Perth, I would not change the dreams, far less the tender realities, of those early days, for anything I hear now remembered by lords or dames, of their days of childhood in castle halls, and by sweet lawns and lakes in park-walled forest.

Lawn and lake enough indeed I had, in the North Inch of Perth, and pools of pausing Tay, before Rose Terrace, (where I used to live after my uncle died, briefly apoplectic, at Bridge-End,) in the peace of the fair Scotch summer days, with my widowed aunt, and my little cousin Jessie,* then traversing a bright space between her sixth and ninth year; dark-eyed deeply,[1] like her mother, and similarly pious; so that she and I used to compete in the Sunday evening Scriptural examinations; and be as proud as two little peacocks because Jessie's elder brothers, and sister Mary, used to get 'put down,' and either Jessie or I was always 'Dux.'* We agreed upon this that we would be married when we were a little older; not considering it to be preparatorily necessary to be in any degree wiser.

71. Strangely, the kitchen servant-of-all-work in the house at Rose Terrace was a very old 'Mause,'—before, my grandfather's servant in Edinburgh,—who might well have been the prototype of the Mause of 'Old Mortality,'[2]* but had even a more solemn, fearless, and patient faith, fastened in her by extreme suffering; for she had been nearly starved to death when she was a girl, and had literally picked the bones out of cast-out dust-heaps to gnaw; and ever afterwards, to see the waste of an atom of food was as shocking to her as blasphemy. 'Oh, Miss Margaret!' she said once to my mother, who had shaken some crumbs off a dirty plate out of the window, 'I had rather you had knocked me down.' She would make her dinner upon anything in the house that the other servants wouldn't eat;—often upon potato skins, giving her own dinner away to any poor person she saw; and would

---

[1] As opposed to the darkness of mere iris, making the eyes like black cherries.

[2] Vulgar modern Puritanism has shown its degeneracy in nothing more than in its incapability of understanding Scott's exquisitely finished portraits of the Covenanter. In 'Old Mortality' alone, there are four which cannot be surpassed; the typical one, Elizabeth, faultlessly sublime and pure; the second, Ephraim Macbriar, giving the too common phase of the character, which is touched with ascetic insanity; the third, Mause, coloured and made sometimes ludicrous by Scottish conceit, but utterly strong and pure at heart; the last, Balfour, a study of supreme interest, showing the effect of the Puritan faith, sincerely held, on a naturally and incurably cruel and base spirit. Add to these four studies, from this single novel, those in the 'Heart of Midlothian,' and Nicol Jarvie and Andrew Fairservice from 'Rob Roy,' and you have a series of theological analyses far beyond those of any other philosophical work that I know, of any period.

always stand during the whole church service, (though at least seventy years old when I knew her, and very feeble,) if she could persuade any wild Amorite* out of the streets to take her seat. Her wrinkled and worn face, moveless in resolution and patience, incapable of smile, and knit sometimes perhaps too severely against Jessie and me, if we wanted more creamy milk to our porridge, or jumped off our favourite box on Sunday,—('Never mind, John,' said Jessie to me, once seeing me in an unchristian state of provocation on this subject, 'when we're married, we'll jump off boxes all day long, if we like!')—may have been partly instrumental in giving me that slight bias against Evangelical religion, which I confess to be sometimes traceable in my later works;* but I never can be thankful enough for having seen, in our own 'Old Mause,' the Scottish Puritan spirit in its perfect faith and force; and been enabled therefore afterwards to trace its agency in the reforming policy of Scotland, with the reverence and honour it deserves.

72. My aunt, a pure dove-priestess, if ever there was one, of Highland Dodona,* was of a far gentler temper; but still, to me, remained at a wistful distance. She had been much saddened by the loss of three of her children before her husband's death. Little Peter,* especially, had been the corner-stone of her love's building; and it was thrown down swiftly:—white swelling came in the knee; he suffered much, and grew weaker gradually, dutiful always, and loving, and wholly patient. She wanted him one day to take half a glass of port wine, and took him on her knee, and put it to his lips. 'Not now, mamma; in a minute,' said he; and put his head on her shoulder, and gave one long, low sigh, and died. Then there was Catherine; and—I forget the other little daughter's name, I did not see them; my mother told me of them;—eagerly always about Catherine, who had been her own favourite. My aunt had been talking earnestly one day with her husband about these two children; planning this and that for their schooling and what not: at night, for a little while she could not sleep; and as she lay thinking, she saw the door of the room open, and two spades come into it, and stand at the foot of her bed. Both the children were dead within brief time afterwards. I was about to write 'within a fortnight'—but I cannot be sure of remembering my mother's words accurately.*

73. But when I was in Perth, there were still—Mary, her eldest daughter, who looked after us children when Mause was too busy; James and John, William and Andrew; (I can't think whom the un-apostolic William was named after). But the boys were then all at school or college,—the scholars, William and Andrew, only came home to tease Jessie and me, and eat the biggest jargonel pears;* the collegians

were wholly abstract; and the two girls and I played in our quiet ways
on the North Inch, and by the 'Lead,' a stream 'led' from the Tay
past Rose Terrace into the town for molinary purposes;* and long ago,
I suppose, bricked over or choked with rubbish; but then lovely, and a
perpetual treasure of flowing diamond to us children. Mary, by the
way, was ascending towards twelve—fair, blue-eyed, and moderately
pretty; and as pious as Jessie, without being quite so zealous.

74. My father rarely stayed with us in Perth, but went on business
travel through Scotland, and even my mother became a curiously unim-
portant figure at Rose Terrace. I can't understand how she so rarely
walked with us children; she and my aunt seemed always to have their
own secluded ways. Mary, Jessie, and I were allowed to do what we
liked on the Inch: and I don't remember doing any lessons in these Perth
times, except the above-described competitive divinity on Sunday.

Had there been anybody then to teach me anything about plants or
pebbles, it had been good for me; as it was, I passed my days much as
the thistles and tansy* did, only with perpetual watching of all the ways
of running water,—a singular awe developing itself in me, both of the
pools of Tay, where the water changed from brown to blue-black, and
of the precipices of Kinnoull; partly out of my own mind, and partly
because the servants always became serious when we went up Kinnoull
way, especially if I wanted to stay and look at the little crystal spring of
Bower's Well.

75. 'But you say you were not afraid of anything?' writes a friend,
anxious for the unassailable veracity of these memoirs. Well, I said, not
of ghosts, thunder, or beasts,—meaning to specify the commonest
terrors of mere childhood. Every day, as I grew wiser, taught me a
reasonable fear; else I had not above described myself as the most reasonable person of my acquaintance. And by the swirls of smooth blackness, broken by no fleck of foam, where Tay gathered herself like
Medusa.[1]* I never passed without awe, even in those thoughtless days;
neither do I in the least mean that I could walk among tombstones
in the night (neither, for that matter, in the day), as if they were only
paving stones set upright. Far the contrary; but it is important to the
reader's confidence in writings which have seemed inordinately impres-
sional and emotional, that he should know I was never subject to—
I should perhaps rather say, sorrowfully, never capable of—any manner of illusion or false imagination, nor in the least liable to have my
nerves shaken by surprise. When I was about five years old, having

[1] I always think of Tay as a goddess river, as Greta a nymph one.

been on amicable terms for a while with a black Newfoundland, then on probation for watch dog at Herne Hill; after one of our long summer journeys my first thought on getting home was to go to see Lion. My mother trusted me to go to the stable with our one serving-man, Thomas, giving him strict orders that I was not to be allowed within stretch of the dog's chain. Thomas, for better security, carried me in his arms. Lion was at his dinner, and took no notice of either of us; on which I besought leave to pat him. Foolish Thomas stooped towards him that I might, when the dog instantly flew at me, and bit a piece clean out of the corner of my lip on the left side. I was brought up the back stairs, bleeding fast, but not a whit frightened, except lest Lion should be sent away. Lion indeed had to go; but not Thomas: my mother was sure he was sorry, and I think blamed herself the most. The bitten side of the (then really pretty) mouth, was spoiled for evermore, but the wound, drawn close, healed quickly; the last use I made of my moveable lips before Dr Aveline drew them into ordered silence for a while, was to observe, 'Mama, though I can't speak, I can play upon the fiddle.' But the house was of another opinion, and I never attained any proficiency upon that instrument worthy of my genius. Not the slightest diminution of my love of dogs, nor the slightest nervousness in managing them, was induced by the accident.

I scarcely know whether I was in any real danger or not when, another day, in the same stable, quite by myself, I went head foremost into the large water-tub kept for the garden. I think I might have got awkwardly wedged if I had tried to draw my feet in after me: instead, I used the small watering-pot I had in my hand to give myself a good thrust up from the bottom, and caught the opposite edge of the tub with my left hand, getting not a little credit afterwards for my decision of method. Looking back to the few chances that have in any such manner tried my head, I believe it has never failed me when I wanted it, and that I am much more likely to be confused by sudden admiration than by sudden danger.

76. The dark pools of Tay, which have led me into this boasting, were under the high bank at the head of the North Inch,—the path above them being seldom traversed by us children unless at harvest time, when we used to go gleaning* in the fields beyond; Jessie and I afterward grinding our corn in the kitchen pepper-mill, and kneading and toasting for ourselves cakes of pepper bread, of quite unpurchaseable quality.

In the general course of this my careful narration, I rebut with as much indignation as may be permitted without ill manners, the charge of partiality to anything merely because it was seen when I was young. I hesitate, however, in recording as a constant truth for the world, the impression left on me when I went gleaning with Jessie, that Scottish sheaves are more golden than are bound in other lands, and that no harvests elsewhere visible to human eyes are so like the 'corn of heaven'[1] as those of Strath-Tay and Strath-Earn.

CHAPTER IV

UNDER NEW TUTORSHIPS

77. WHEN I was about eight or nine I had a bad feverish illness at Dunkeld, during which I believe I was in some danger, and am sure I was very uncomfortable. It came on after a long walk in which I had been gathering quantities of foxgloves and pulling them to pieces to examine their seeds, and there were hints about their having poisoned me; very absurd, but which extended the gathering awe from river eddies to foxglove dells. Not long after that, when we were back at home, my cousin Jessie fell ill, and died very slowly, of water on the brain.* I was very sorry, not so much in any strength of early affection, as in the feeling that the happy, happy* days at Perth were for ever ended, since there was no more Jessie.

Before her illness took its fatal form,—before, indeed, I believe it had at all declared itself—my aunt dreamed one of her foresight dreams, simple and plain enough for any one's interpretation;—that she was approaching the ford of a dark river, alone, when little Jessie came running up behind her, and passed her, and went through first. Then she passed through herself, and looking back from the other side, saw her old Mause approaching from the distance to the bank of the stream. And so it was, that Jessie, immediately afterwards, sickened rapidly and died; and a few months, or it might be nearly a year afterwards, my aunt died of decline; and Mause, some two or three years later, having had no care after her mistress and Jessie were gone, but when she might go to them.

78. I was at Plymouth with my father and mother when my Scottish aunt died, and had been very happy with my nurse on the hill east of the town, looking out on the bay and breakwater; and came in to find my father, for the first time I had ever seen him, in deep distress of sobbing tears.

---

[1] Psalm lxxviii. 24.

I was very sorry that my aunt was dead, but, at that time, (and a good deal since, also,) I lived mostly in the present, like an animal, and my principal sensation was,—What a pity it was to pass such an uncomfortable evening—and we at Plymouth!

The deaths of Jessie and her mother of course ended our Scottish days. The only surviving daughter, Mary, was thenceforward adopted by my father and mother, and brought up with me. She was fourteen when she came to us, and I four years younger;—so with the Perth days, closed the first decade of my life. Mary was a rather pretty, blue-eyed, clumsily-made girl, very amiable and affectionate in a quiet way, with no parts, but good sense and good principle, honestly and inoffensively pious, and equal tempered, but with no pretty girlish ways or fancies. She became a serene additional neutral tint in the household harmony; read alternate verses of the Bible with my mother and me in the mornings, and went to a day school in the forenoon. When we travelled she took somewhat of a governess position towards me, we being allowed to explore places together without my nurse;—but we generally took old Anne too for better company.

79. It began now to be of some importance what church I went to on Sunday morning. My father, who was still much broken in health, could not go to the long Church of England service, and, my mother being evangelical, he went contentedly, or at least submissively, with her and me to Beresford Chapel, Walworth,*where the Rev. E. Andrews preached, regularly, a somewhat eloquent, forcible, and ingenious sermon, not tiresome to him:—the prayers were abridged from the Church Service, and we, being the grandest people in the congregation, were allowed—though, as I now remember, not without offended and reproachful glances from the more conscientious worshippers—to come in when even those short prayers were half over. Mary and I used each to write an abstract of the sermon in the afternoon, to please ourselves,—Mary dutifully, and I to show how well I could do it. We never went to church in afternoon or evening. I remember yet the amazed and appalling sensation, as of a vision preliminary to the Day of Judgment, of going, a year or two later, first into a church by candlelight.

80. We had no family worship, but our servants were better cared for than is often the case in ostentatiously religious houses. My mother used to take them when girls, from families known to her, sister after sister, and we never had a bad one.

On the Sunday evening my father would sometimes read us a sermon of Blair's, or it might be, a clerk or a customer would dine with us, when the conversation, in mere necessary courtesy, would take generally the direction of sherry. Mary and I got through the evening how we could, over the *Pilgrim's Progress*, Bunyan's *Holy War*, Quarles's *Emblems*, Foxe's *Book of Martyrs*, Mrs Sherwood's *Lady of the Manor*,—a very awful book to me, because of the stories in it of wicked girls who had gone to balls, dying immediately after of fever,—and Mrs Sherwood's *Henry Milner*,—of which more presently,—the *Youth's Magazine*, *Alfred Campbell the Young Pilgrim*, and, though rather as a profane indulgence, permitted because of the hardness of our hearts, Bingley's *Natural History*.* We none of us cared for singing hymns or psalms as such, and were too honest to amuse ourselves with them as sacred music, besides that we did not find their music amusing.

81. My father and mother, though due cheques for charities were of course sent to Dr Andrews, and various civilities at Christmas, in the way of turkeys or boxes of raisins, intimated their satisfaction with the style of his sermons and purity of his doctrine,—had yet, with their usual shyness, never asked for his acquaintance, or even permitted the state of their souls to be inquired after in pastoral visits. Mary and I, however, were charmed merely by the distant effect of him, and used to walk with Anne up and down in Walworth, merely in the hope of seeing him pass on the other side of the way. At last, one day, when, by extreme favour of Fortune, he met us in a great hurry on our own side of it, and nearly tumbled over me, Anne, as he recovered himself, dropped him a low curtsey; whereupon he stopped, inquired who we were, and was extremely gracious to us; and we, coming home in a fever of delight, announced, not much to my mother's satisfaction, that the Doctor had said he would call some day! And so, little by little, the blissful acquaintance was made. I might be eleven or going on twelve by that time. Miss Andrews, the eldest sister of the 'Angel in the House,'* was an extremely beautiful girl of seventeen; she sang 'Tambourgi, Tambourgi'[1]* with great spirit and a rich voice, went at blackberry time on rambles with us at the Norwood Spa, and made me feel generally that there was something in girls that I did not understand, and that was curiously agreeable. And at last, because I was so fond of the Doctor, and he had the reputation (in Walworth) of being a good scholar, my father thought he might pleasantly initiate me in Greek, such initiation having been already too long deferred. The Doctor, it afterwards turned out, knew little more of Greek than the letters, and declensions of nouns; but he wrote the letters prettily, and had an

---

[1] Hebrew melodies.

accurate and sensitive ear for rhythm. He began me with the odes of Anacreon, and made me scan both them and my Virgil thoroughly, sometimes, by way of interlude, reciting bits of Shakespeare to me with force and propriety. The Anacreontic metre* entirely pleased me, nor less the Anacreontic sentiment. I learned half the odes by heart merely to please myself, and learned with certainty, what in later study of Greek art it has proved extremely advantageous to me to know, that the Greeks liked doves, swallows, and roses just as well as I did.

82. In the intervals of these unlaborious Greek lessons, I went on amusing myself—partly in writing English doggerel, partly in map drawing, or copying Cruikshank's illustrations to Grimm,* which I did with great, and to most people now incredible, exactness, a sheet of them being, by good hap, well preserved, done when I was between ten and eleven. But I never saw any boy's work in my life showing so little original faculty, or grasp by memory. I could literally draw nothing, not a cat, not a mouse, not a boat, not a bush, 'out of my head,' and there was, luckily, at present no idea on the part either of parents or preceptor, of teaching me to draw out of other people's heads.

Nevertheless, Mary, at her day school, was getting drawing lessons with the other girls. Her report of the pleasantness and zeal of the master, and the frank and somewhat unusual execution of the drawings he gave her to copy, interested my father, and he was still more pleased by Mary's copying, for a proof of industry while he was away on his winter's journey—copying, in pencil so as to produce the effect of a vigorous engraving, the little water-colour by Prout of a wayside cottage, which was the foundation of our future water-colour collection, being then our only possession in that kind—of other kind, two miniatures on ivory completed our gallery.

83. I perceive, in thinking over the good work of that patient black and white study, that Mary could have drawn, if she had been well taught and kindly encouraged. But her power of patient copying did not serve her in drawing from nature, and when, that same summer, I between ten and eleven (1829), we went to stay at Matlock in Derbyshire, all that she proved able to accomplish was an outline of Caxton's New Bath Hotel,* in which our efforts in the direction of art, for that year, ended.

But, in the glittering white broken spar, specked with galena,* by which the walks of the hotel garden were made bright, and in the shops of the pretty village, and in many a happy walk among its cliffs, I pursued my mineralogical studies on fluor, calcite, and the ores of lead, with indescribable rapture when I was allowed to go into a cave.

My father and mother showed far more kindness than I knew, in yielding to my subterranean passion; for my mother could not bear dirty places, and my father had a nervous feeling that the ladders would break, or the roof fall, before we got out again. They went with me, nevertheless, wherever I wanted to go,—my father even into the terrible Speedwell mine at Castleton, where, for once, I was a little frightened myself.

From Matlock we must have gone on to Cumberland, for I find in my father's writing the legend, 'Begun 28th November, 1830, finished 11th January, 1832,' on the fly-leaf of the 'Iteriad,'* a poem in four books, which I indited, between those dates, on the subject of our journey among the Lakes, and of which some little notice may be taken farther on.

84. It must have been in the spring of 1831 that the important step was taken of giving me a drawing master. Mary showed no gift of representing any of the scenes of our travels, and I began to express some wish that I could draw myself. Whereupon, Mary's pleasant drawing master, to whom my father and mother were equitable enough not to impute Mary's want of genius, was invited to give *me* also an hour in the week.

I suppose a drawing master's business can only become established by his assertion of himself to the public as the possessor of a style; and teaching in that only. Nevertheless, Mr Runciman's memory sustains disgrace in my mind in that he gave no impulse nor even indulgence to the extraordinary gift I had for drawing delicately with the pen point. Any work of that kind was done thenceforward only to please myself. Mr Runciman gave me nothing but his own mannered and inefficient drawings to copy, and greatly broke the force both of my mind and hand.

Yet he taught me much, and suggested more. He taught me perspective, at once accurately and simply—an invaluable bit of teaching. He compelled me into a swiftness and facility of hand which I found afterwards extremely useful, though what I have just called the 'force,' the strong accuracy of my line, was lost. He cultivated in me,—indeed founded,—the habit of looking for the essential points in the things drawn, so as to abstract them decisively, and he explained to me the meaning and importance of composition, though he himself could not compose.

85. A very happy time followed, for about two years. I was, of course, far behind Mary in touch-skill of pencil drawing, and it was good for her that this superiority was acknowledged, and due honour

done her for the steady pains of her unimpulsive practice and unwearied attention. For, as she did not write poems like me, nor collect spars
like me, nor exhibit any prevailing vivacity of mind in any direction,
she was gradually sinking into far too subordinate a position to my
high-mightiness. But I could make no pretence for some time to rival
her in free-hand copying, and my first attempts from nature were not
felt by my father to be the least flattering to his vanity.

These were made under the stimulus of a journey to Dover with the
forethought of which my mother comforted me through an illness of
1829. I find my quite first sketchbook, an extremely inconvenient
upright small octavo in mottled and flexible cover, the paper pure
white, and ribbedly gritty, filled with outlines, irregularly defaced by
impulsive efforts at finish, in arbitrary places and corners, of Dover and
Tunbridge Castles and the main tower of Canterbury Cathedral.
These, with a really good study, supplemented by detached detail, of
Battle Abbey, I have set aside for preservation; the really first sketch
I ever made from nature being No. 1, of a street in Sevenoaks. I got
little satisfaction and less praise by these works; but the native architectural instinct is instantly developed in these,—highly notable for any
one who cares to note such nativities. Two little pencillings from
Canterbury south porch and central tower, I have given to Miss Gale,
of Burgate House, Canterbury; the remnants of the book itself to
Mrs Talbot, of Tyn-y-Ffynon, Barmouth, both very dear friends.

86. But before everything, at this time, came my pleasure in merely
watching the sea. I was not allowed to row, far less to sail, nor to walk
near the harbour alone; so that I learned nothing of shipping or anything else worth learning, but spent four or five hours every day in
simply staring and wondering at the sea,—an occupation which never
failed me till I was forty. Whenever I could get to a beach it was enough
for me to have the waves to look at, and hear, and pursue and fly from.
I never took to natural history of shells, or shrimps, or weeds, or jelly-
fish. Pebbles?—yes if there were any; otherwise, merely stared all day
long at the tumbling and creaming strength of the sea. Idiotically, it
now appears to me, wasting all that priceless youth in mere dream and
trance of admiration; it had a certain strain of Byronesque passion in it,
which meant something: but it was a fearful loss of time.

87. The summer of 1832 must, I think, have been passed at home,
for my next sketch-book contains only some efforts at tree-drawing in
Dulwich, and a view of the bridge over the now bricked-up 'Effra,' by
which the Norwood road then crossed it at the bottom of Herne Hill:
the road itself, just at the place where, from the top of the bridge, one

looked up and down the streamlet, bridged now into putridly damp shade by the railway, close to Herne Hill Station.* This sketch was the first in which I was ever supposed to show any talent for drawing. But on my thirteenth (?) birthday, 8th February, 1832, my father's partner, Mr Henry Telford, gave me Rogers' *Italy*, and determined the main tenor of my life.

At that time I had never heard of Turner, except in the well remembered saying of Mr Runciman's, that 'the world had lately been much dazzled and led away by some splendid ideas thrown out by Turner.' But I had no sooner cast eyes on the Rogers vignettes than I took them for my only masters, and set myself to imitate them as far as I possibly could by fine pen shading.

88. I have told this story so often that I begin to doubt its time. It is curiously tiresome that Mr Telford did not himself write my name in the book, and my father who writes in it, 'The gift of Henry Telford, Esq.,' still more curiously, for him, puts no date: if it was a year later, no matter; there is no doubt however that early in the spring of 1833 Prout published his *Sketches in Flanders and Germany*. I well remember going with my father into the shop where subscribers entered their names, and being referred to the specimen print, the turreted window over the Moselle, at Coblentz. We got the book home to Herne Hill before the time of our usual annual tour; and as my mother watched my father's pleasure and mine in looking at the wonderful places, she said, why should not we go and see some of them in reality? My father hesitated a little, then with glittering eyes said—why not? And there were two or three weeks of entirely rapturous and amazed preparation. I recollect that very evening bringing down my big geography book,* still most precious to me; (I take it down now, and for the first time put my own initials under my father's name in it)—and looking with Mary at the outline of Mont Blanc, copied from Saussure, at p. 201, and reading some of the very singular information about the Alps which it illustrates. So that Switzerland must have been at once included in the plans,—soon prosperously, and with result of all manner of good, by God's help fulfilled.

89. We went by Calais and Brussels to Cologne; up the Rhine to Strasburg, across the Black Forest to Schaffhausen, then made a sweep through North Switzerland by Basle, Berne, Interlachen, Lucerne, Zurich, to Constance,—following up the Rhine still to Coire, then over Splugen to Como, Milan, and Genoa; meaning, as I now remember, for Rome. But, it being June already, the heat of Genoa warned us of imprudence: we turned, and came back over the Simplon to Geneva, saw Chamouni, and so home by Lyons and Dijon.

To do all this in the then only possible way, with post-horses, and, on the lakes, with oared boats, needed careful calculation of time each day. My father liked to get to our sleeping place as early as he could, and never would stop the horses for me to draw anything (the extra pence to postillion for waiting being also an item of weight in his mind);—thus I got into the bad habit, yet not without its discipline, of making scrawls as the carriage went along, and working them up 'out of my head' in the evening. I produced in this manner, throughout the journey, some thirty sheets or so of small pen and Indian ink drawings, four or five in a sheet; some not inelegant, all laborious, but for the most part one just like another, and without exception stupid and characterless to the last degree.

90. With these flying scrawls on the road, I made, when staying in towns, some elaborate pencil and pen outlines, of which perhaps half-a-dozen are worth register and preservation. My father's pride in a study of the doubly-towered Renaissance church of Dijon was great. A still more laborious Hôtel de Ville of Brussels remains with it at Brantwood. The drawing of that Hôtel de Ville by me now at Oxford is a copy of Prout's, which I made in illustration of the volume in which I wrote the beginning of a rhymed history of the tour.

For it had excited all the poor little faculties that were in me to their utmost strain, and I had certainly more passionate happiness, of a quality utterly indescribable to people who never felt the like, and more, in solid quantity, in those three months, than most people have in all their lives. The impression of the Alps first seen from Schaffhausen, of Milan and of Geneva, I will try to give some account of afterwards,—my first business now is to get on.

91. The winter of '33, and what time I could steal to amuse myself in, out of '34, were spent in composing, writing fair, and drawing vignettes for the decoration of the aforesaid poetical account of our tour, in imitation of Rogers' *Italy*. The drawings were made on separate pieces of paper and pasted into the books; many have since been taken out, others are there for which the verses were never written, for I had spent my fervour before I got up the Rhine. I leave the unfinished folly in Joanie's* care, that none but friends may see it.*

Meantime, it having been perceived by my father and mother that Dr Andrews could neither prepare me for the University, nor for the duties of a bishopric, I was sent as a day scholar to the private school kept by the Rev. Thomas Dale, in Grove Lane, within walking distance of Herne Hill. Walking down with my father after breakfast, carrying my blue bag of books, I came home to half-past one dinner, and prepared my lessons in the evening for next day. Under these conditions I saw little of my fellow-scholars, the two sons of Mr Dale, Tom and James; and three boarders, the sons of Colonel Matson, of Woolwich; of Alderman Key, of Denmark Hill; and a fine lively boy, Willoughby Jones, afterwards Sir W., and only lately, to my sorrow, dead.

92. Finding me in all respects what boys could only look upon as an innocent, they treated me as I suppose they would have treated a girl; they neither thrashed nor chaffed me,—finding, indeed, from the first that chaff had no effect on me. Generally I did not understand it, nor in the least mind it if I did, the fountain of pure conceit in my own heart sustaining me serenely against all deprecation, whether by master or companion. I was fairly intelligent of books, had a good quick and holding memory, learned whatever I was bid as fast as I could, and as well; and since all the other boys learned always as little as they could, though I was far in retard of them in real knowledge, I almost always knew the day's lesson best. I have already described, in the first chapter of *Fiction, Fair and Foul,* Mr Dale's rejection of my clearly known old grammar as a 'Scotch thing.'* In that one action he rejected himself from being my master; and I thenceforward learned all he told me only because I had to do it.

93. While these steps were taken for my classical advancement, a master was found for me, still in that unlucky Walworth, to teach me mathematics. Mr Rowbotham was an extremely industrious, deserving, and fairly well-informed person in his own branches, who, with his wife, and various impediments and inconveniences in the way of children, kept a 'young gentleman's Academy' near the Elephant and Castle, in one of the first houses which have black plots of grass in front, fenced by iron railings from the Walworth Road.

He knew Latin, German, and French grammar; was able to teach the 'use of the globes' as far as needed in a preparatory school, and was, up to far beyond the point needed for me, a really sound mathematician. For the rest, utterly unacquainted with men or their history, with nature and its meanings; stupid and disconsolate, incapable of any manner of mirth or fancy, thinking mathematics the only proper occupation of human intellect, asthmatic to a degree causing often helpless suffering, and hopelessly poor, spending his evenings, after his school-drudgery was over, in writing manuals of arithmetic and algebra, and compiling French and German grammars, which he allowed the booksellers to cheat him out of,—adding perhaps, with all his year's lamp-labour, fifteen or twenty pounds to his income;—a more wretched, innocent, patient, insensible, unadmirable, uncomfortable, intolerable being never was produced in this aera of England by the culture characteristic of her metropolis.

94. Under the tuition, twice a week in the evening, of Mr Rowbotham, (invited always to substantial tea with us before the lesson as a really efficient help to his hungry science, after the walk up Herne Hill, painful to asthma,) I prospered fairly in 1834, picking up some bits of French grammar, of which I had really felt the want,—I had before got hold, somehow, of words enough to make my way about with,—and I don't know how, but I recollect, at Paris, going to the Louvre under charge of Salvador,* (I wanted to make a sketch from Rembrandt's *Supper at Emmaus*,*) and on Salvador's application to the custode for permission, it appeared I was not old enough to have a ticket,—fifteen was then the earliest admission-age; but seeing me look woebegone, the good-natured custode said he thought if I went in to the 'Board,' or whatever it was, of authorities, and asked for permission myself, they would give it me. Whereupon I instantly begged to be introduced to the Board, and the custode taking me in under his coat lappets, I did verily, in what broken French was feasible to me, represent my case to several gentlemen of an official and impressive aspect, and got my permission, and outlined the *Supper at Emmaus* with some real success in expression, and was extremely proud of myself. But my narrow knowledge of the language, though thus available for business, left me sorrowful and ashamed after the fatal dinner at Mr Domecq's,* when the little Elise, then just nine, seeing that her elder sisters did not choose to trouble themselves with me, and being herself of an entirely benevolent and pitiful temper, came across the drawing-room to me in my desolation, and leaning an elbow on my knee, set herself deliberately to chatter to me mellifluously for an hour and a half by the timepiece,—requiring no answer, of which she saw I was incapable, but satisfied with my grateful and respectful attention, and admiring interest, if not exactly always in what she said, at least in the way she said it. She gave me the entire history of her school, and of the objectionable characters of her teachers, and of the delightful characters of her companions, and of the mischief she got into, and the surreptitious enjoyments they devised, and the joys of coming back to the Champs Elysées, and the general likeness of Paris to the Garden of Eden. And the hour and a half seemed but too short, and left me resolved, anyhow, to do my best to learn French.

95. So, as I said, I progressed in this study to the contentment of Mr Rowbotham, went easily through the three first books of Euclid, and got as far as quadratics in Algebra. But there I stopped, virtually,

for ever. The moment I got into sums of series, or symbols expressing the relations instead of the real magnitudes of things,—partly in want of faculty, partly in an already well-developed and healthy hatred of things vainly bothering and intangible,—I jibbed—or stood stunned. Afterwards at Oxford they dragged me through some conic sections, of which the facts representable by drawing became afterwards of extreme value to me; and taught me as much trigonometry as made my mountain work, in plan and elevation, unaccusable. In elementary geometry I was always happy, and, for a boy, strong; and my conceit, developing now every hour more venomously as I began to perceive the weaknesses of my masters, led me to spend nearly every moment I could command for study in my own way, through the year 1835, in trying to trisect an angle.* For some time afterwards I had the sense to reproach myself for the waste of thoughtful hours in that year, little knowing or dreaming how many a year to come, from that time forth, was to be worse wasted.

While the course of my education was thus daily gathering the growth of me into a stubborn little standard bush, various frost-stroke was stripping away from me the poor little flowers—or herbs—of the forest, that had once grown, happily for me, at my side.

CHAPTER V

PARNASSUS AND PLYNLIMMON*

96. I HAVE allowed, in the last chapter, my record of boyish achievements and experiments in art to run on to a date much in advance of the early years which were most seriously eventful for me in good and evil. I resume the general story of them with the less hesitation, because, such as it is, nobody else can tell it; while, in later years, my friends in some respects know me better than I know myself.

The second decade of my life was cut away still more sharply from the perfectly happy time of childhood, by the death of my Croydon aunt; death of 'cold' literally, caught in some homely washing operations in an east wind. Her brown and white spaniel, Dash, lay beside her body and on her coffin, till they were taken away from him; then he was brought to Herne Hill, and I think had been my companion some time before Mary came to us.

With the death of my Croydon aunt ended for me all the days by Wandel streams, as at Perth by Tay; and thus when I was ten years old, an exclusively Herne Hill-top life set in (when we were not travelling), of no very beneficial character.

97. My Croydon aunt left four sons—John, William, George, and Charles; and two daughters—Margaret and Bridget.* All hand-some lads and pretty lasses; but Margaret, in early youth, met with some mischance that twisted her spine, and hopelessly deformed her. She was clever, and witty, like her mother; but never of any interest to me, though I gave a kind of brotherly, rather than cousinly, affection to all my Croydon cousins. But I never liked invalids,* and don't to this day; and Margaret used to wear her hair in ringlets, which I couldn't bear the sight of.

Bridget was a very different creature; a black-eyed, or, with preci-sion, dark hazel-eyed, slim-made, lively girl; a little too sharp in the features to be quite pretty, a little too wiry-jointed to be quite graceful; capricious, and more or less selfish in temper, yet nice enough to be once or twice asked to Perth with us, or to stay for a month or two at Herne Hill; but never attaching herself much to us, neither us to her. I felt her an inconvenience in my nursery arrangements, the nursery having become my child's study as I grew studious; and she had no mind, or, it might be, no leave, to work with me in the garden.

98. The four boys were all of them good, and steadily active. The eldest, John, with wider business habits than the rest, went soon to push his fortune in Australia, and did so; the second, William, pros-pered also in London.

The third brother, George, was the best of boys and men, but of small wit. He extremely resembled a rural George the Fourth, with an expansive, healthy, benevolent eagerness of simplicity in his face, greatly bettering him as a type of British character. He went into the business in Market Street, with his father, and both were a great joy to all of us in their affectionateness and truth: neither of them in all their lives ever did a dishonest, unkind, or otherwise faultful thing—but still less a clever one! For the present, I leave them happily filling and driving their cart of quartern loaves in morning round from Market Street.

99. The fourth, and youngest, Charles, was like the last-born in a fairy tale, ruddy as the boy David,* bright of heart, not wanting in common sense, or even in *good* sense; and affectionate, like all the rest. He took to his schooling kindly, and became grammatical, polite, and presentable in our high Herne Hill circle. His elder brother, John, had taken care of his education in more important matters: very early in the child's life he put him on a barebacked pony, with the simple elementary

instruction that he should be thrashed if he came off. And he stayed on. Similarly, for first lesson in swimming, he pitched the boy like a pebble into the middle of the Croydon Canal, jumping in, of course, after him; but I believe the lad squattered to the bank without help, and became when he was only 'that high' a fearless master of horse and wave.

100. My mother used to tell these two stories with the greater satisfaction, because, in her own son's education, she had sacrificed her pride in his heroism to her anxiety for his safety; and never allowed me to go to the edge of a pond, or be in the same field with a pony. As ill-luck also would have it, there was no manner of farm or marsh near us, which might of necessity modify these restrictions; but I have already noted with thankfulness the good I got out of the tadpole-haunted ditch in Croxted Lane;* while also, even between us and tutorial Walworth, there was one Elysian field for me in the neglected grass of Camberwell Green. There *was* a pond in the corner of it, of considerable size, and unknown depth,—probably, even in summer, full three feet in the middle; the sable opacity of its waters adding to the mystery of danger. Large, as I said, for a pond, perhaps sixty or seventy yards the long way of the Green, fifty the short; while on its western edge grew a stately elm, from whose boughs, it was currently reported, and conscientiously believed, a wicked boy had fallen into the pond on Sunday, and forthwith the soul of him into a deeper and darker pool.

It was one of the most valued privileges of my early life to be permitted by my nurse to contemplate this judicial pond with awe, from the other side of the way. The loss of it, by the sanitary conversion of Camberwell Green into a bouquet for Camberwell's button-hole, is to this day matter of perennial lament to me.

101. In the carrying out of the precautionary laws above described I was, of course, never allowed, on my visits to Croydon, to go out with my cousins, lest they should lead me into mischief; and no more adventurous joys were ever possible to me there, than my walks with Anne or my mother where the stream from Scarborough pond ran across the road; or on the crisp turf of Duppas Hill; my watchings of the process of my father's drawings in Indian ink, and my own untired contemplations of the pump and gutter on the other side of the so-called street, but really lane,—not more than twelve feet from wall to wall. So that, when at last it was thought that Charles, with all his good natural gifts and graces, should be brought from Croydon town to London city, and initiated into the lofty life and work of its burgess orders; and when, accordingly, he was, after various taking of counsel and making of enquiry, apprenticed to Messrs Smith, Elder, & Co.,* of 65 Cornhill,

with the high privilege of coming out to dine at Herne Hill every Sunday, the new and beaming presence of cousin Charles became a vivid excitement, and admirable revelation of the activities of youth to me, and I began to get really attached to him.

I was not myself the sort of creature that a boy could care much for,—or indeed any human being, except papa and mama, and Mrs Richard Gray (of whom more presently); being indeed nothing more than a conceited and unentertainingly troublesome little monkey. But Charles was always kind to me, and naturally answered with some cousinly or even brotherly tenderness my admiration of him, and delight in him.

102. At Messrs Smith & Elder's he was an admittedly exemplary apprentice, rapidly becoming a serviceable shop-man, taking orders intelligently, and knowing well both his books and his customers. As all right-minded apprentices and good shopmen do, he took personal pride in everything produced by the firm; and on Sundays always brought a volume or two in his pocket to show us the character of its most ambitious publications; especially choosing, on my behalf, any which chanced to contain good engravings. In this way I became familiar with Stanfield and Harding long before I possessed a single engraving myself from either of them; but the really most precious, and continuous in deep effect upon me, of all gifts to my childhood, was from my Croydon aunt, of the *Forget-me-not** of 1827, with a beautiful engraving in it of Prout's 'Sepulchral monument at Verona.'

Strange, that the true first impulse to the most refined instincts of my mind should have been given by my totally uneducated, but entirely good and right-minded, mother's sister.

103. But more magnificent results came of Charles's literary connection, through the interest we all took in the embossed and gilded small octavo which Smith & Elder published annually, by title 'Friendship's Offering.' This was edited by a pious Scotch missionary, and minor—very much minor—key, poet, Thomas Pringle; mentioned once or twice with a sprinkling of honour in Lockhart's *Life of Scott*.* A strictly conscientious and earnest, accurately trained, though narrowly learned, man, with all the Scottish conceit, restlessness for travel, and petulant courage of the Parks and Livingstones;* with also some pretty tinges of romance and inklings of philosophy to mellow him, he was an admitted, though little regarded, member of the best literary circles, and acquainted, in the course of catering for his little embossed octavo, with everybody in the outer circles, and lower, down to little me. He had been patronised by Scott; was on terms of polite

correspondence with Wordsworth and Rogers; of familiar intercourse with the Ettrick Shepherd;* and had himself written a book of poems on the subject of Africa, in which antelopes were called springboks, and other African manners and customs carefully observed.

104. Partly to oblige the good-natured and lively shop-boy, who told wonderful things of his little student cousin;—partly in the look-out for thin compositions of tractable stucco, wherewith to fill interstices in the masonry of 'Friendship's Offering,' Mr Pringle visited us at Herne Hill, heard the traditions of my literary life, expressed some interest in its farther progress,—and sometimes took a copy of verses away in his pocket. He was the first person who intimated to my father and mother, with some decision, that there were as yet no wholly trustworthy indications of my one day occupying a higher place in English literature than either Milton or Byron; and accordingly I think none of us attached much importance to his opinions. But he had the sense to recognise, through the parental vanity, my father's high natural powers, and exquisitely romantic sensibility; nor less my mother's tried sincerity in the evangelical faith, which he had set himself apart to preach: and he thus became an honoured, though never quite cordially welcomed, guest on occasions of state Sunday dinner; and more or less an adviser thenceforward of the mode of my education. He himself found interest enough in my real love of nature and ready faculty of rhyme, to induce him to read and criticize for me some of my verses with attention; and at last, as a sacred Elusinian initiation and Delphic pilgrimage,* to take me in his hand one day when he had a visit to pay to the poet Rogers.

105. The old man, previously warned of my admissible claims, in Mr Pringle's sight, to the beatitude of such introduction, was sufficiently gracious to me, though the cultivation of germinating genius was never held by Mr Rogers to be an industry altogether delectable to genius in its zenith. Moreover, I was unfortunate in the line of observations by which, in return for his notice, I endeavoured to show myself worthy of it. I congratulated him with enthusiasm on the beauty of the engravings by which his poems were illustrated,—but betrayed, I fear me, at the same time some lack of an equally vivid interest in the composition of the poems themselves. At all events, Mr Pringle—I thought at the time, somewhat abruptly—diverted the conversation to subjects connected with Africa. These were doubtless more calculated to interest the polished minstrel of St James's Place;* but again I fell into misdemeanours by allowing my own attention, as my wandering eyes too frankly confessed, to determine itself on the pictures glowing from

the crimson-silken walls; and accordingly, after we had taken leave, Mr Pringle took occasion to advise me that, in future, when I was in the company of distinguished men, I should listen more attentively to their conversation.*

106. These, and such other—(I have elsewhere related* the Ettrick Shepherd's favouring visit to us, also obtained by Mr Pringle)— glorifications and advancements being the reward of my literary efforts, I was nevertheless not beguiled by them into any abandonment of the scientific studies which were indeed natural and delightful to me. I have above registered their beginnings in the sparry walks at Matlock: but my father's business also took him often to Bristol, where he placed my mother, with Mary and me, at Clifton. Miss Edgeworth's story of Lazy Lawrence, and the visit to Matlock by Harry and Lucy,* gave an almost romantic and visionary charm to mineralogy in those dells; and the piece of iron oxide with bright Bristol diamonds,—No. 51 of the Brantwood collection,—was I think the first stone on which I began my studies of silica. The diamonds of it were bright with many an association besides, since from Clifton we nearly always crossed to Chepstow,—the rapture of being afloat, for half-an-hour even, on that muddy sea, concentrating into these impressive minutes the pleasures of a year of other boys' boating,—and so round by Tintern and Malvern, where the hills, extremely delightful in themselves to me because I was allowed to run free on them, there being no precipices to fall over nor streams to fall into, were also classical to me through Mrs Sherwood's 'Henry Milner,' a book which I loved long, and respect still. So that there was this of curious and precious in the means of my education in these years, that my romance was always ratified to me by the seal of locality—and every charm of locality spiritualized by the glow and the passion of romance.

107. There was one district, however, that of the Cumberland lakes, which needed no charm of association to deepen the appeal of its realities. I have said somewhere that my first memory in life was of Friar's Crag on Derwentwater;*—meaning, I suppose, my first memory of things afterwards chiefly precious to me; at all events, I knew Keswick before I knew Perth, and after the Perth days were ended, my mother and I stayed either there, at the Royal Oak, or at Lowwood Inn, or at Coniston Waterhead, while my father went on his business journeys to Whitehaven, Lancaster, Newcastle, and other northern towns. The inn at Coniston was then actually at the upper end of the lake, the road from Ambleside to the village passing just between it and the water; and the view of the long reach of lake, with its softly wooded lateral

hills, had for my father a tender charm which excited the same feeling as that with which he afterwards regarded the lakes of Italy. Lowwood Inn also was then little more than a country cottage,—and Ambleside a rural village; and the absolute peace and bliss which any one who cared for grassy hills and for sweet waters might find at every footstep, and at every turn of crag or bend of bay, was totally unlike anything I ever saw, or read of, elsewhere.

108. My first sight of bolder scenery was in Wales; and I have written,—more than it would be wise to print,*—about the drive from Hereford, to Rhaiadyr, and under Plynlimmon to Pont-y-Monach: the joy of a walk with my father in the Sunday afternoon towards Hafod, dashed only with some alarmed sense of the sin of being so happy among the hills, instead of writing out a sermon at home;—my father's presence and countenance not wholly comforting me, for we both of us had alike a subdued consciousness of being profane and rebellious characters, compared to my mother.

From Pont-y-Monach we went north, gathering pebbles on the beach at Aberystwith, and getting up Cader Idris with help of ponies:— it remained, and rightly, for many a year after, a king of mountains to me. Followed Harlech and its sands, Festiniog, the pass of Aberglaslyn, and marvel of Menai Straits and Bridge, which I looked at, then, as Miss Edgeworth had taught me, with reverence for the mechanical skill of man,—little thinking, poor innocent, what use I should see the creature putting his skill to, in the half century to come.

The Menai *Bridge* it was, remember, good reader, not *tube*;—but the trim plank roadway swinging smooth between its iron cobwebs from tower to tower.*

109. And so on to Llanberis and up Snowdon, of which ascent I remember, as the most exciting event, the finding for the first time in my life a real 'mineral' for myself, a piece of copper pyrites! But the general impression of Welsh mountain form was so true and clear that subsequent journeys little changed or deepened it.

And if only then my father and mother had seen the real strengths and weaknesses of their little John;—if they had given me but a shaggy scrap of a Welsh pony, and left me in charge of a good Welsh guide, and of his wife, if I needed any coddling, they would have made a man of me there and then, and afterwards the comfort of their own hearts, and probably the first geologist of my time in Europe.

If only! But they could no more have done it than thrown me like my cousin Charles into Croydon Canal, trusting me to find my way out by the laws of nature.

110. Instead, they took me back to London, and my father spared time from his business hours, once or twice a week, to take me to a four-square, sky-lighted, sawdust-floored prison of a riding-school in Moorfields, the smell of which, as we turned in at the gate of it, was a terror and horror and abomination to me: and there I was put on big horses that jumped, and reared, and circled, and sidled; and fell off them regularly whenever they did any of those things; and was a disgrace to my family, and a burning shame and misery to myself, till at last the riding-school was given up on my spraining my right-hand forefinger (it has never come straight again since),—and a well-broken Shetland pony bought for me, and the two of us led about the Norwood roads by a riding master with a leading string. I used to do pretty well as long as we went straight, and then get thinking of something and fall off when we turned a corner. I might have got some inkling of a seat in Heaven's good time, if no fuss had been made about me, nor inquiries instituted whether I had been off or on; but as my mother, the moment I got home, made searching scrutiny into the day's disgraces, I merely got more and more nervous and helpless after every tumble; and this branch of my education was at last abandoned, my parents consoling themselves, as best they might, in the conclusion that my not being able to learn to ride was the sign of my being a singular genius.

111. The rest of the year was passed in such home employment as I have above described;—but, either in that or the preceding year, my mineralogical taste received a new and very important impulse from a friend who entered afterwards intimately into our family life, but of whom I have not yet spoken.

My illness at Dunkeld, above noticed, was attended by two physicians,—my mother,—and Dr Grant. The Doctor must then have been a youth who had just obtained his diploma. I do not know the origin of his acquaintance with my parents; but I know that my father had almost paternal influence over him; and was of service to him, to what extent I know not, but certainly continued and effective, in beginning the world. And as I grew older I used often to hear expressions of much affection and respect for Dr Grant from my father and mother, coupled with others of regret or blame that he did not enough bring out his powers, or use his advantages.

Ever after the Dunkeld illness, Dr Grant's name was associated in my mind with a brown powder—rhubarb, or the like—of a gritty and acrid nature, which, by his orders, I had then to take. The name thenceforward always sounded to me gr-r-ish and granular; and a certain dread, not amounting to dislike—but, on the contrary, affectionate, (for *me*)—made the Doctor's presence somewhat solemnizing to me; the rather as he never jested, and had a brownish, partly austere, and sere, wrinkled, and—rhubarby, in fact, sort of a face. For the rest, a man entirely kind and conscientious, much affectionate to my father, and acknowledging a sort of ward-to-guardian's duty to him, together with the responsibility of a medical adviser, acquainted both with his imagination and his constitution.

112. I conjecture that it must have been owing to Dr Grant's being of fairly good family, and in every sense and every reality of the word a gentleman, that, soon after coming up to London, he got a surgeon's appointment in one of His Majesty's frigates commissioned for a cruise on the west coast of South America. Fortunately the health of her company gave the Doctor little to do professionally; and he was able to give most of his time to the study of the natural history of the coast of Chili and Peru. One of the results of these shore expeditions was the finding such a stag-beetle as had never before been seen. It had peculiar or colossal nippers, and—I forget what 'chiasos' means in Greek, but its jaws were chiasoi.* It was brought home beautifully packed in a box of cotton; and, when the box was opened, excited the admiration of all beholders, and was called the 'Chiasognathos Grantii.'* A second result was his collection of a very perfect series of Valparaiso humming birds, out of which he spared, for a present to my mother, as many as filled with purple and golden flutter two glass cases as large as Mr Gould's at the British Museum, which became resplendent decorations of the drawing-room at Herne Hill,—were to me, as I grew older, conclusive standards of plume texture and colour,—and are now placed in the best lighted recess of the parish school at Coniston.

113. The third result was more important still. Dr Grant had been presented by the Spanish masters of mines with characteristic and rich specimens of the most beautiful vein-stones of Copiapo. It was a mighty fact for me, at the height of my child's interest in minerals, to see our own parlour table loaded with foliated silver and arborescent gold. Not only the man of science, but the latent miser in me, was developed largely in an hour or two! In the pieces which Dr Grant gave me, I counted my treasure grain by grain; and recall to-day, in acute sympathy with it, the indignation I felt at seeing no instantly reverential change in cousin Charles's countenance, when I informed him that the film on the surface of an unpresuming specimen, amounting in quantity to about the sixteenth part of a sixpence, was 'native silver'!

Soon after his return from this prosperous voyage, Dr Grant settled himself in a respectable house half-way down Richmond Hill, where gradually he obtained practice and accepted position among the gentry of that town and its parkly neighbourhood. And every now and then, in the summer mornings, or the gaily frost-white winter ones, we used, papa and mamma, and Mary and I, to drive over Clapham and Wandsworth Commons to a breakfast picnic with Dr Grant at the 'Star and Garter.'* Breakfasts much impressed on my mind, partly by the pretty view from the windows; but more, because while my orthodox breakfast, even in travelling, was of stale baker's bread, at these starry picnics I was allowed new French roll.

114. Leaving Dr Grant, for the nonce, under these pleasant and dignifiedly crescent circumstances, I must turn to the friends who of all others, not relatives, were most powerfully influential on my child life,—Mr and Mrs Richard Gray.

Some considerable time during my father's clerkdom had been passed by him in Spain, in learning to know sherry, and seeing the ways of making and storing it at Xerez, Cadiz, and Lisbon. At Lisbon he became intimate with another young Scotsman of about his own age, also employed, I conceive, as a clerk, in some Spanish house, but himself of no narrow clerkly mind. On the contrary, Richard Gray went far beyond my father in the romantic sentiment, and scholarly love of good literature, which so strangely mingled with my father's steady business habits. Equally energetic, industrious, and high-principled, Mr Gray's enthusiasm was nevertheless irregularly, and too often uselessly, coruscant;* being to my father's, as Carlyle says of French against English fire at Dettingen, 'faggot against anthracite.'* Yet, I will not venture absolutely to maintain that, under Richard's erratic and effervescent influence, an expedition to Cintra, or an assistance at a village festa, or even at a bull-fight, might not sometimes, to that extent, invalidate my former general assertion that, during nine years, my father never had a holiday. At all events, the young men became close and affectionate friends; and the connection had a softening, cheering, and altogether beneficent effect on my father's character. Nor was their brotherly friendship any whit flawed or dimmed, when, a little while before leaving Spain,* Mr Gray married an extremely good and beautiful Scotch girl, Mary Monro.

115. Extremely good, and, in the gentlest way;—entirely simple, meek, loving, and serious; not clever enough to be any way naughty, but saved from being stupid by a vivid nature, full of enthusiasm like her husband's. Both of them evangelically pious, in a vivid, not virulent, way; and each of them sacredly, no less than passionately, in love with the other, they were the entirely best-matched pair I have yet seen

in this match-making world and dispensation. Yet, as fate would have it, they had the one grief of having no children, which caused it, in years to come, to be Mrs Gray's principal occupation in life to spoil *me*. By the time I was old enough to be spoiled, Mr Gray, having fairly prospered in business, and come to London, was established, with his wife, her mother, and her mother's white French poodle, Petite, in a dignified house in Camberwell Grove. An entirely happy family; old Mrs Monro as sweet as her daughter, perhaps slightly wiser; Richard rejoicing in them both with all his heart; and Petite, having, perhaps, as much sense as any two of them, delighted in, and beloved by all three.

116. Their house was near the top of the Grove,—which was a real grove in those days, and a grand one, some three-quarters of a mile long, steepishly down hill,—beautiful in perspective as an unprecedently 'long-drawn aisle;'* trees, elm, wych elm, sycamore and aspen, the branches meeting at top; the houses on each side with trim stone pathways up to them, through small plots of well-mown grass; three or four storied, mostly in grouped terraces,—well-built, of sober-coloured brick, with high and steep slated roof—not gabled, but polygonal; all well to do, well kept, well broomed, dignifiedly and pleasantly vulgar, and their own Grove-world all in all to them. It was a pleasant mile and a furlong or two's walk from Herne Hill to the Grove; and whenever Mrs Gray and my mother had anything to say to each other, they walked—up the hill or down—to say it; and Mr Gray's house was always the same to us as our own at any time of day or night. But our house not at all so to the Grays, having its formalities inviolable; so that during the whole of childhood I had the sense that we were, in some way or other, always above our friends and relations,—more or less patronizing everybody, favouring them by our advice, instructing them by our example, and called upon, by what was due both to ourselves, and the constitution of society, to keep them at a certain distance.

117. With one exception; which I have deep pleasure in remembering. In the first chapter of the Antiquary, the landlord at Queen's Ferry sets down to his esteemed guest a bottle of Robert Cockburn's best port; with which Robert Cockburn duly supplied Sir Walter himself, being at that time, if not the largest, the leading importer of the finest Portugal wine, as my father of Spanish.* But Mr Cockburn was primarily an old Edinburgh gentleman, and only by condescension a wine-merchant; a man of great power and pleasant sarcastic wit, moving in the first circles of Edinburgh; attached to my father by many links of

association with the 'auld toun,' and sincerely respecting him. He was much the stateliest and truest piece of character who ever sate at our merchant feasts.

Mrs Cockburn was even a little higher,—as representative of the Scottish lady of the old school,—indulgent yet to the new. She had been Lord Byron's first of first loves; she was the Mary Duff of Lachin-y-Gair. When I first remember her, still extremely beautiful in middle age, full of sense; and, though with some mixture of proud severity, extremely kind.

118. They had two sons, Alexander and Archibald, both in business with their father, both clever and energetic, but both distinctly resolute—as indeed their parents desired—that they would be gentlemen first, salesmen second: a character much to be honoured and retained among us; nor in their case the least ambitious or affected: gentlemen they were,—born so, and more at home on the hills than in the counting-house, and withal attentive enough to their business. The house, nevertheless, did not become all that it might have been in less well-bred hands.

The two sons, one or other, often dined with us, and were more distinctly friends than most of our guests. Alexander had much of his father's humour; Archibald, a fine, young, dark Highlander, was extremely delightful to me, and took some pains with me, for the sake of my love of Scott, telling me anything about fishing or deer-stalking that I cared to listen to. For, even from earliest days, I cared to listen to the adventures of other people, though I never coveted any for myself. I read all Captain Marryat's novels, without ever wishing to go to sea; traversed the field of Waterloo without the slightest inclination to be a soldier; went on ideal fishing with Izaak Walton without ever casting a fly; and knew Cooper's 'Deerslayer' and 'Pathfinder' almost by heart,* without handling anything but a pop-gun, or having any paths to find beyond the solitudes of Gipsy-Hill. I used sometimes to tell myself stories of campaigns in which I was an ingenious general, or caverns in which I discovered veins of gold; but these were merely to fill vacancies of fancy, and had no reference whatever to things actual or feasible. I already disliked growing older,—never expected to be wiser, and formed no more plans for the future than a little black silkworm does in the middle of its first mulberry leaf.*

CHAPTER VI

SCHAFFHAUSEN AND MILAN

119. THE visit to the field of Waterloo, spoken of by chance in last chapter, must have been when I was five years old,—on the occasion of papa and mamma's taking a fancy to see Paris in its festivities following the coronation of Charles X. We stayed several weeks in Paris, in a quiet family inn, and then some days at Brussels,—but I have no memory whatever of intermediate stages. It seems to me, on revision of those matin times, that I was very slow in receiving impressions, and needed to stop two or three days at least in a place, before I began to get a notion of it; but the notion, once got, was, as far as it went, always right; and since I had no occasion afterwards to modify it, other impressions fell away from that principal one, and disappeared altogether. Hence what people call my prejudiced views of things,—which are, in fact, the exact contrary, namely, post-judiced. (I do not mean to introduce this word for general service, but it saves time and print just now.)

120. Another character of my perceptions I find curiously steady— that I was only interested by things near me, or at least clearly visible and present. I suppose this is so with children generally; but it remained—and remains—a part of my grown-up temper. In this visit to Paris, I was extremely taken up with the soft red cushions of the arm-chairs, which it took one half an hour to subside into after sitting down,—with the exquisitely polished floor of the salon, and the good-natured French 'Boots' (more properly 'Brushes'), who skated over it in the morning till it became as reflective as a mahogany table,—with the pretty court full of flowers and shrubs in beds and tubs, between our rez-de-chaussée* windows and the outer gate,—with a nice black servant belonging to another family, who used to catch the house-cat for me; and with an equally good-natured fille de chambre, who used to catch it back again, for fear I should teaze it, (her experience of English boy-children having made her dubious of my intentions);—all these things and people I remember,—and the Tuileries garden, and the 'Tivoli' gardens, where my father took me up and down a 'Russian mountain,' and I saw fireworks of the finest. But I remember nothing of the Seine, nor of Notre Dame, nor of anything in or even out of the town, except the windmills on Mont Martre.*

121. Similarly at Brussels. I recollect no Hôtel de Ville, no stately streets, no surprises, or interests, except only the drive to Waterloo and slow walk over the field. The defacing mound was not then built—it

was only nine years since the fight; and each bank and hollow of the ground was still a true exponent of the courses of charge or recoil. Fastened in my mind by later reading, that sight of the slope of battle remains to me entirely distinct, while the results of a later examination of it after the building of the mound, have faded mostly away.

I must also note that the rapture of getting on board a steamer, spoken of in last letter, was of later date; as a child I cared more for a beach on which the waves broke, or sands in which I could dig, than for wide sea. There was no 'first sight' of the sea for me. I had gone to Scotland in Captain Spinks' cutter, then a regular passage boat, when I was only three years old; but the weather was fine, and except for the pleasure of tattooing myself with tar among the ropes, I might as well have been ashore; but I grew into the sense of ocean, as the Earth shaker,* by the rattling beach, and lisping sand.

122. I had meant, also in this place, to give a word or two to another poor relative, Nanny Clowsley, an entirely cheerful old woman, who lived, with a Dutch clock and some old teacups, in a single room (with small bed in alcove) on the third storey of a gabled house, part of the group of old ones lately pulled down on Chelsea side of Battersea bridge. But I had better keep what I have to say of Chelsea well together, early and late,* only, in speaking of shingle, I must note the use to me of the view out of Nanny Clowsley's window right down upon the Thames tide, with its tossing wherries at the flow, and stranded barges at ebb.

And now, I must get on, and come to the real first sights of several things.

123. I said that, for our English tours, Mr Telford usually lent us his chariot. But for Switzerland, now taking Mary, we needed stronger wheels and more room; and for this, and all following tours abroad, the first preparation and the beginning of delight was the choosing a carriage to our fancy, from the hireable reserves at Mr Hopkinson's, of Long Acre.

The poor modern slaves and simpletons who let themselves be dragged like cattle, or felled timber, through the countries they imagine themselves visiting, can have no conception whatever of the complex joys, and ingenious hopes, connected with the choice and arrangement of the travelling carriage in old times. The mechanical questions first, of strength—easy rolling—steady and safe poise of persons and luggage; the general stateliness of effect to be obtained for the abashing of plebeian beholders; the cunning design and distribution of store-cellars under the seats, secret drawers under front windows, invisible pockets under padded lining, safe from dust, and accessible only by insidious slits, or necromantic valves like Aladdin's trap-door;* the fitting of cushions where they would not slip, the rounding of corners for more delicate repose; the prudent attachments and springs of blinds; the perfect fitting of windows, on which one-half the comfort of a travelling carriage really depends; and the adaptation of all these concentrated luxuries to the probabilities of who would sit where, in the little apartment which was to be virtually one's home for five or six months;— all this was an imaginary journey in itself, with every pleasure, and none of the discomfort, of practical travelling.

124. On the grand occasion of our first continental journey—which was meant to be half a year long—the carriage was chosen with, or in addition fitted with, a front seat outside for my father and Mary, a dickey, unusually large, for Anne and the courier, and four inside seats, though those in front very small, that papa and Mary might be received inside in stress of weather. I recollect, when we had finally settled which carriage we would have, the polite Mr Hopkinson, advised of my dawning literary reputation, asking me (to the joy of my father) if I could translate the motto of the former possessor, under his painted arms,—'*Vix ea nostra voco*,'*—which I accomplishing successfully, farther wittily observed that however by right belonging to the former possessor, the motto was with greater propriety applicable to *us*.

125. For a family carriage of this solid construction, with its luggage, and load of six or more persons, four horses were of course necessary to get any sufficient way on it; and half-a-dozen such teams were kept at every post-house. The modern reader may perhaps have as much difficulty in realizing these savagely and clumsily locomotive periods, though so recent, as any aspects of migratory Saxon or Goth; and may not think me vainly garrulous in their description.

The French horses, and more or less those on all the great lines of European travelling, were properly stout trotting cart-horses, well up to their work and over it; untrimmed, long-tailed, good-humouredly licentious, whinnying and frolicking with each other when they had a chance; sagaciously steady to their work; obedient to the voice mostly, to the rein only for more explicitness; never touched by the whip, which was used merely to express the driver's exultation in himself and them,—signal obstructive vehicles in front out of the way, and advise all the inhabitants of the villages and towns traversed on the day's journey, that persons of distinction were honouring them by their transitory presence. If everything was right, the four horses were driven by one postillion riding the shaft horse; but if the horses were young, or the riders unpractised, there was a postillion for the leaders also. As a rule, there were four steady horses and a good driver, rarely drunk, often very young, the men of stronger build being more useful for other work, and any clever young rider able to manage the well-trained and merry-minded beasts, besides being lighter on their backs. Half the weight of the cavalier, in such cases, was in his boots, which were often brought out slung from the saddle like two buckets, the postillion, after the horses were harnessed, walking along the pole and getting into them.

126. Scarcely less official, for a travelling carriage of good class than its postillions, was the courier, or properly, avant-courier, whose primary office it was to ride in advance at a steady gallop, and order the horses at each post-house to be harnessed and ready waiting, so that no time might be lost between stages. His higher function was to make all bargains and pay all bills, so as to save the family unbecoming cares and mean anxieties, besides the trouble and disgrace of trying to speak French or any other foreign language. He, farther, knew the good inns in each town, and all the good rooms in each inn, so that he could write beforehand to secure those suited to his family. He was also, if an intelligent man and high-class courier, well acquainted with the proper sights to be seen in each town, and with all the occult means to be used for getting sight of those that weren't to be seen by the vulgar. Murray,* the reader will remember, did not exist in those days; the courier was a private Murray, who knew, if he had any wit, not the things to be seen only, but those you would yourself best like to see, and gave instructions to your valet-de-place* accordingly, interfering only as a higher power in cases of difficulty needing to be overcome by money or tact. He invariably attended the ladies in their shopping expeditions, took them to the fashionable shops, and arranged as he thought proper the prices of articles. Lastly, he knew, of course, all the other high-class couriers on the road, and told you, if you wished to know, all the people of consideration who chanced to be with you in the inn.

127. My father would have considered it an insolent and revolutionary trespass on the privileges of the nobility to have mounted his courier to ride in advance of us; besides that, wisely liberal of his money for comfort and pleasure, he never would have paid the cost of an extra horse for show. The horses were, therefore, ordered in advance, when possible, by the postillions of any preceding carriage (or, otherwise, we did not mind waiting till they were harnessed), and we carried our courier behind us in the dickey with Anne, being in all his other functions and accomplishments an indispensable luxury to us. Indispensable, first,

because none of us could speak anything but French, and that only enough to ask our way in; for all specialties of bargaining, or details of information, we were helpless, even in France,—and might as well have been migratory sheep, or geese, in Switzerland or Italy. Indispensable, secondly, to my father's peace of mind, because, with perfect liberality of temper, he had a great dislike to being over-reached. He perfectly well knew that his courier would have his commission, and allowed it without question; but he knew also that his courier would not be cheated by other people, and was content in his representative. Not for ostentation, but for real enjoyment and change of sensation from his suburban life, my father liked large rooms; and my mother, in mere continuance of her ordinary and essential habits, liked clean ones; clean, and large, means, a good inn and a first floor. Also my father liked a view from his windows, and reasonably said, 'Why should we travel to see less than we may?'—so that meant first floor *front*. Also my father liked delicate cookery, just because he was one of the smallest and rarest eaters; and my mother liked good meat. That meant, dinner without limiting price, in reason. Also, though my father never went into society, he all the more enjoyed getting a glimpse, reverentially, of fashionable people—I mean, people of rank,—he scorned fashion, and it was a great thing to him to feel that Lord and Lady —— were on the opposite landing, and that, at any moment, he might conceivably meet and pass them on the stairs. Salvador, duly advised, or penetratively perceptive of these dispositions of my father, entirely pleasing and admirable to the courier mind, had carte-blanche in all administrative functions and bargains. We found our pleasant rooms always ready, our good horses always waiting, everybody took their hats off when we arrived and departed. Salvador presented his accounts weekly, and they were settled without a word of demur.

128. To all these conditions of luxury and felicity, can the modern steam-puffed tourist conceive the added ruling and culminating one—that we were never in a hurry? coupled with the correlative power of always starting at the hour we chose, and that if we weren't ready, the horses would wait? As a rule, we breakfasted at our own home time—eight; the horses were pawing and neighing at the door (under the archway, I should have said) by nine. Between nine and three,—reckoning seven miles an hour, including stoppages, for minimum pace,— we had done our forty to fifty miles of journey, sate down to dinner at four,—and I had two hours of delicious exploring by myself in the evening; ordered in punctually at seven to tea, and finishing my sketches till half-past nine,—bed-time.

On longer days of journey we started at six, and did twenty miles before breakfast, coming in for four o'clock dinner as usual. In a quite long day we made a second stop, dining at any nice village hostelry, and coming in for late tea, after doing our eighty or ninety miles. But these pushes were seldom made unless to get to some pleasant cathedral town for Sunday, or pleasant Alpine village. We never travelled on Sunday; my father and I nearly always went—as philosophers—to mass, in the morning, and my mother, in pure good-nature to us, (I scarcely ever saw in her a trace of feminine curiosity,) would join with us in some such profanity as a drive on the Corso, or the like, in the afternoon. But we all, even my father, liked a walk in the fields better, round an Alpine châlet village.

129. At page 53 I threatened more accurate note of my first impressions of Switzerland and Italy in 1833. Of customary Calais I have something to say later on,—here I note only our going up Rhine to Strasburg, where, with all its miracles of building, I was already wise enough to feel the cathedral stiff and iron-worky; but was greatly excited and impressed by the high roofs and rich fronts of the wooden houses, in their sudden indication of nearness to Switzerland; and especially by finding the scene, so admirably expressed by Prout in the 36th plate of his Flanders and Germany, still uninjured. And then, with Salvador was held council in the inn-parlour of Strasburg, whether—it was then the Friday afternoon—we should push on to-morrow for our Sunday's rest to Basle, or to Schaffhausen.

130. How much depended—if ever anything 'depends' on anything else,—on the issue of that debate! Salvador inclined to the straight and level Rhine-side road, with the luxury of the Three Kings* attainable by sunset. But at Basle, it had to be admitted, there were no Alps in sight, no cataract within hearing, and Salvador honourably laid before us the splendid alternative possibility of reaching, by traverse of the hilly road of the Black Forest, the gates of Schaffhausen itself, before they closed for the night.

The Black Forest! The fall of Schaffhausen! The chain of the Alps! within one's grasp for Sunday! What a Sunday, instead of customary Walworth and the Dulwich fields! My impassioned petition at last carried it, and the earliest morning saw us trotting over the bridge of boats to Kehl, and in the eastern light I well remember watching the line of the Black Forest hills enlarge and rise, as we crossed the plain of the Rhine. 'Gates of the hills'; opening for me to a new life—to cease no more, except at the Gates of the Hills whence one returns not.

131. And so, we reached the base of the Schwartzwald, and entered

an ascending dingle; and scarcely, I think, a quarter of an hour after entering, saw our first 'Swiss cottage.'[1] How much it meant to all of us,—how much prophesied to me, no modern traveller could the least conceive, if I spent days in trying to tell him. A sort of triumphant shriek—like all the railway whistles going off at once at Clapham Junction*—has gone up from the Fooldom of Europe at the destruction of the myth of William Tell.* To us, every word of it was true—but mythically luminous with more than mortal truth; and here, under the black woods, glowed the visible, beautiful, tangible testimony to it in the purple larch timber, carved to exquisiteness by the joy of peasant life, continuous, motionless there in the pine shadow on its ancestral turf,—unassailed and unassailing, in the blessedness of righteous poverty, of religious peace.

The myth of William Tell is destroyed forsooth? and you have tunnelled Gothard,* and filled, it may be, the Bay of Uri;—and it was all for you and your sake that the grapes dropped blood from the press of St Jacob, and the pine club struck down horse and helm in Morgarten Glen?*

132. Difficult enough for you to imagine, that old travellers' time when Switzerland was yet the land of the Swiss, and the Alps had never been trod by foot of man. Steam, never heard of yet, but for short fair weather crossing at sea (were there paddle-packets across Atlantic?* I forget). Any way, the roads by land were safe; and entered once into this mountain Paradise, we wound on through its balmy glens, past cottage after cottage on their lawns, still glistering in the dew.

The road got into more barren heights by the mid-day, the hills arduous; once or twice we had to wait for horses, and we were still twenty miles from Schaffhausen at sunset; it was past midnight when we reached her closed gates. The disturbed porter had the grace to open them—not quite wide enough; we carried away one of our lamps in collision with the slanting bar as we drove through the arch. How much happier the privilege of dreamily entering a mediaeval city, though with the loss of a lamp, than the free ingress of being jammed between a dray and a tramcar at a railroad station!

133. It is strange that I but dimly recollect the following morning; I fancy we must have gone to some sort of church or other; and certainly, part of the day went in admiring the bow-windows projecting into the clean streets. None of us seem to have thought the Alps would be visible without profane exertion in climbing hills. We dined at four,

---

[1] Swiss, in character and real habit—the political boundaries are of no moment.

as usual, and the evening being entirely fine, went out to walk, all of us,—my father and mother and Mary and I.

We must have still spent some time in town-seeing, for it was drawing towards sunset when we got up to some sort of garden promenade—west of the town, I believe; and high above the Rhine, so as to command the open country across it to the south and west. At which open country of low undulation, far into blue,—gazing as at one of our own distances from Malvern of Worcestershire, or Dorking of Kent,—suddenly—behold—beyond!

134. There was no thought in any of us for a moment of their being clouds. They were clear as crystal, sharp on the pure horizon sky, and already tinged with rose by the sinking sun. Infinitely beyond all that we had ever thought or dreamed,—the seen walls of lost Eden could not have been more beautiful to us; not more awful, round heaven, the walls of sacred Death.

It is not possible to imagine, in any time of the world, a more blessed entrance into life, for a child of such a temperament as mine. True, the temperament belonged to the age: a very few years,—within the hundred,—before that, no child could have been born to care for mountains, or for the men that lived among them, in that way. Till Rousseau's time, there had been no 'sentimental' love of nature; and till Scott's, no such apprehensive love of 'all sorts and conditions of men,'* not in the soul merely, but in the flesh. St Bernard of La Fontaine, looking out to Mont Blanc with his child's eyes, sees above Mont Blanc the Madonna; St Bernard of Talloires, not the Lake of Annecy, but the dead between Martigny and Aosta.* But for me, the Alps and their people were alike beautiful in their snow, and their humanity; and I wanted, neither for them nor myself, sight of any thrones in heaven but the rocks, or of any spirits in heaven but the clouds.

135. Thus, in perfect health of life and fire of heart, not wanting to be anything but the boy I was, not wanting to have anything more than I had; knowing of sorrow only just so much as to make life serious to me, not enough to slacken in the least its sinews; and with so much of science mixed with feeling as to make the sight of the Alps not only the revelation of the beauty of the earth, but the opening of the first page of its volume,—I went down that evening from the garden-terrace of Schaffhausen with my destiny fixed in all of it that was to be sacred and useful. To that terrace, and the shore of the Lake of Geneva, my heart and faith return to this day, in every impulse that is yet nobly alive in them, and every thought that has in it help or peace.

136. The morning after that Sunday's eve at Schaffhausen was also

cloudless, and we drove early to the falls, seeing again the chain of the Alps by morning light, and learning, at Lauffen, what an Alpine river was. Coming out of the gorge of Balstall, I got another ever memorable sight of the chain of the Alps, and these distant views, never seen by the modern traveller, taught me, and made me feel, more than the close marvels of Thun and Interlachen. It was again fortunate that we took the grandest pass into Italy,—that the first ravine of the main Alps I saw was the Via Mala, and the first lake of Italy, Como.

We took boat on the little recessed lake of Chiavenna, and rowed down the whole way of waters, passing another Sunday at Cadenabbia, and then, from villa to villa, across the lake, and across, to Como, and so to Milan by Monza.

It was then full, though early, summer time; and the first impression of Italy always ought to be in her summer. It was also well that, though my heart was with the Swiss cottager, the artificial taste in me had been mainly formed by Turner's rendering of those very scenes, in Rogers' *Italy*. The 'Lake of Como,' the two moonlight villas, and the 'Farewell,' had prepared me for all that was beautiful and right in the terraced gardens, proportioned arcades, and white spaces of sunny wall, which have in general no honest charm for the English mind. But to me, they were almost native through Turner,—familiar at once, and revered. I had no idea then of the Renaissance evil* in them; they were associated only with what I had been told of the 'divine art' of Raphael and Leonardo, and, by my ignorance of dates, associated with the stories of Shakespeare. Portia's villa,—Juliet's palace,*—I thought to have been like these.

Also, as noticed in the preface to reprint of vol. ii. of *Modern Painters*, I had always a quite true perception of size, whether in mountains or buildings, and with the perception, joy in it; so that the vastness of scale in the Milanese palaces, and the 'mount of marble, a hundred spires,'* of the duomo, impressed me to the full at once: and not having yet the taste to discern good Gothic from bad, the mere richness and fineness of lace-like tracery against the sky was a consummate rapture to me—how much more getting up to it and climbing among it, with the Monte Rosa seen between its pinnacles across the plain!

137. I had been partly prepared for this view by the admirable presentment of it in London, a year or two before, in an exhibition, of which the vanishing has been in later life a greatly felt loss to me,— Burford's panorama in Leicester Square,* which was an educational institution of the highest and purest value, and ought to have been supported by the Government as one of the most beneficial school

instruments in London. There I had seen, exquisitely painted, the view from the roof of Milan Cathedral, when I had no hope of ever seeing the reality, but with a joy and wonder of the deepest;—and now to be there indeed, made deep wonder become fathomless.

Again, most fortunately, the weather was clear and cloudless all day long, and as the sun drew westward, we were able to drive to the Corso, where, at that time, the higher Milanese were happy and proud as ours in their park, and whence, no railway station intervening, the whole chain of the Alps was visible on one side, and the beautiful city with its dominant frost-crystalline Duomo on the other. Then the drive home in the open carriage through the quiet twilight, up the long streets, and round the base of the Duomo, the smooth pavement under the wheels adding with its silentness to the sense of dream wonder in it all,—the perfect air in absolute calm, the just seen majesty of encompassing Alps, the perfectness—so it seemed to me—and purity, of the sweet, stately, stainless marble against the sky. What more, what else, could be asked of seemingly immutable good, in this mutable world?

138. I wish in general to avoid interference with the reader's judgment on the matters which I endeavour serenely to narrate; but may, I think, here be pardoned for observing to him the advantage, in a certain way, of the contemplative abstraction from the world which, during this early continental travelling, was partly enforced by our ignorance, and partly secured by our love of comfort. There is something peculiarly delightful—nay, delightful inconceivably by the modern German-plated and French-polished tourist, in passing through the streets of a foreign city without understanding a word that anybody says! One's ear for all sound of voices then becomes entirely impartial; one is not diverted by the meaning of syllables from recognizing the absolute guttural, liquid, or honeyed quality of them: while the gesture of the body and the expression of the face have the same value for you that they have in a pantomime; every scene becomes a melodious opera to you, or a picturesquely inarticulate *Punch*. Consider, also, the gain in so consistent tranquillity. Most young people nowadays, or even lively old ones, travel more in search of adventures than of information. One of my most valued records of recent wandering is a series of sketches by an amiable and extremely clever girl, of the things that happened to her people and herself every day that they were abroad. Here it is brother Harry, and there it is mamma, and now paterfamilias, and now her little graceful self, and anon her merry or remonstrant sisterhood, who meet with enchanting hardships, and enviable misadventures; bind themselves with fetters of friendship, and glance into

sparklings of amourette,* with any sort of people in conical hats and
fringy caps: and it is all very delightful and condescending; and, of
course, things are learnt about the country that way which can be
learned in no other way, but only about that part of it which interests
itself in you, or which you have pleasure in being acquainted with.
Virtually, you are thinking of yourself all the time; you necessarily talk
to the cheerful people, not to the sad ones; and your head is for the
most part vividly taken up with very little things. I don't say that our
isolation was meritorious, or that people in general should know no
language but their own. Yet the meek ignorance has these advantages.
We did not travel for adventures, nor for company, but to see with our
eyes, and to measure with our hearts. If you have sympathy, the aspect
of humanity is more true to the depths of it than its words; and even in
my own land, the things in which I have been least deceived are those
which I have learned as their Spectator.

CHAPTER VII

PAPA AND MAMMA

139. THE work to which, as partly above described, I set myself during
the year 1834 under the excitement remaining from my foreign travels,
was in four distinct directions, in any one of which my strength might
at that time have been fixed by definite encouragement. There was first
the effort to express sentiment in rhyme; the sentiment being really
genuine, under all the superficial vanities of its display; and the rhymes
rhythmic, only without any ideas in them. It was impossible to explain,
either to myself or other people, why I liked staring at the sea, or scam-
pering on a moor; but, one had pleasure in making some sort of melodious noise about it, like the waves themselves, or the peewits. Then,
secondly, there was the real love of engraving, and of such characters of
surface and shade as it could give. I have never seen drawing, by a
youth, so entirely industrious in delicate line; and there was really the
making of a fine landscape, or figure outline, engraver in me. But fate
having ordered otherwise, I mourn the loss to engraving less than that
before calculated, or rather incalculable, one, to geology! Then there
was, thirdly, the violent instinct for architecture; but I never could have
built or carved anything, because I was without power of design; and
have perhaps done as much in that direction as it was worth doing with
so limited faculty. And then, fourthly, there was the unabated, never to

be abated, geological instinct, now fastened on the Alps. My fifteenth birthday gift being left to my choice, I asked for Saussure's 'Voyages dans les Alpes,'* and thenceforward began progressive work, carrying on my mineralogical dictionary by the help of Jameson's three-volume *Mineralogy,** (an entirely clear and serviceable book;) comparing his descriptions with the minerals in the British Museum, and writing my own more eloquent and exhaustive accounts in a shorthand of many ingeniously symbolic characters, which it took me much longer to write my descriptions in, than in common text, and which neither I nor anybody else could read a word of, afterwards.

140. Such being the quadrilateral plan of my fortifiable dispositions, it is time now to explain, with such clue as I have found to them, the somewhat peculiar character and genius of both my parents; the influence of which was more important upon me, then, and far on into life, than any external conditions, either of friendship or tutorship, whether at the University, or in the world.

It was, in the first place, a matter of essential weight in the determination of subsequent lines, not only of labour but of thought, that while my father, as before told, gave me the best example of emotional reading,—*reading*, observe, proper, not recitation, which he disdained and I disliked,—my mother was both able to teach me, and resolved that I should learn, absolute accuracy of diction and precision of accent in prose; and made me know, as soon as I could speak plain, what I have in all later years tried to enforce on my readers, that accuracy of diction means accuracy of sensation, and precision of accent, precision of feeling. Trained, herself in girlhood, only at Mrs Rice's country school, my mother had there learned severely right principles of truth, charity, and housewifery, with punctilious respect for the purity of that English which in her home surroundings she perceived to be by no means as undefiled as the ripples of Wandel. She was the daughter, as aforesaid, of the early widowed landlady of the King's Head Inn and Tavern, which still exists, or existed a year or two since, presenting its side to Croydon market-place, its front and entrance door to the narrow alley which descends, steep for pedestrians, impassable to carriages, from the High Street to the lower town.

141. Thus native to the customs and dialect of Croydon Agora,* my mother, as I now read her, must have been an extremely intelligent, admirably practical, and naïvely ambitious girl; keeping, without contention, the headship of her class, and availing herself with steady discretion of every advantage the country school and its modest mistress could offer her. I never in her after-life heard her speak with regret,

and seldom without respectful praise, of any part of the discipline of Mrs Rice.

I do not know for what reason, or under what conditions, my mother went to live with my Scottish grandfather and grandmother, first at Edinburgh, and then at the house of Bower's Well, on the slope of the Hill of Kinnoul, above Perth. I was stupidly and heartlessly careless of the past history of my family as long as I could have learnt it; not till after my mother's death did I begin to desire to know what I could never more be told.

But certainly the change, for her, was into a higher sphere of society,—that of real, though sometimes eccentric, and frequently poor, gentlemen and gentlewomen. She must then have been rapidly growing into a tall, handsome, and very finely made girl, with a beautiful mild firmness of expression; a faultless and accomplished housekeeper, and a natural, essential, unassailable, yet inoffensive, prude. I never heard a single word of any sentiment, accident, admiration, or affection disturbing the serene tenor of her Scottish stewardship; yet I noticed that she never spoke without some slight shyness before my father, nor without some pleasure, to other people, of Dr Thomas Brown.

142. That the Professor of Moral Philosophy was a frequent guest at my grandmother's tea-table, and fond of benignantly arguing with Miss Margaret, is evidence enough of the position she held in Edinburgh circles; her household skills and duties never therefore neglected— rather, if anything, still too scrupulously practised. Once, when she had put her white frock on for dinner, and hurried to the kitchen to give final glance at the state and order of things there, old Mause, having run against the white frock with a black saucepan, and been, it seems, rebuked by her young mistress with too little resignation to the will of Providence in that matter, shook her head sorrowfully, saying, 'Ah, Miss Margaret, ye are just like Martha,* careful and troubled about mony things.'

143. When my mother was thus, at twenty, in a Desdemona-like prime of womanhood, intent on highest moral philosophy,—'though still the house affairs would draw her thence'*—my father was a dark-eyed, brilliantly active, and sensitive youth of sixteen. Margaret became to him an absolutely respected and admired—mildly liked—governess and confidante. Her sympathy was necessary to him in all his flashingly transient amours; her advice in all domestic business or sorrow, and her encouragement in all his plans of life.

These were already determined for commerce;—yet not to the abandonment of liberal study. He had learned Latin thoroughly, though with no large range of reading, under the noble traditions of Adam at the High School of Edinburgh: while, by the then living and universal influence of Sir Walter, every scene of his native city was exalted in his imagination by the purest poetry, and the proudest history, that ever hallowed or haunted the streets and rocks of a brightly inhabited capital. I have neither space, nor wish, to extend my proposed account of things that have been, by records of correspondence;—it is too much the habit of modern biographers to confuse epistolary talk with vital fact. But the following letter from Dr Thomas Brown to my father, at this critical juncture of his life, must be read, in part as a testimony to the position he already held among the youths of Edinburgh, and yet more as explaining some points of his blended character, of the deepest significance afterwards, both to himself and to me.

144.   "8, N. St. David's Street,
                              "Edinburgh, *February 18th*, 1807.

'My dear Sir,—When I look at the date of the letter which you did me the honour to send me as your adviser in literary matters—an office which a *proficient* like you scarcely requires—I am quite ashamed of the interval which I have suffered to elapse. I can truly assure you, however, that it has been unavoidable, and has not arisen from any want of interest in your intellectual progress. Even when you were a mere boy I was much delighted with your early zeal and attainments; and for your own sake, as well as for your excellent mother's, I have always looked to you with great regard, and with the belief that you would distinguish yourself in whatever profession you might adopt.

'You seem, I think, to repent too much the time you have devoted to the Belles Lettres. I confess I do not regret this for you. You must, I am sure, have felt the effect which such studies have in giving a general refinement to the manners and to the heart, which, to anyone who is not to be strictly a *man of science*, is the most valuable effect of literature. You must remember that there is a great difference between studying *professionally*, and studying for relaxation and ornament. In the society in which you are to mix, the writers in Belles Lettres will be mentioned fifty times, when more abstract science will not be mentioned once; and there is this great advantage in that sort of knowledge, that the display of it, unless very immoderate indeed, is not counted pedantry, when the display of other intellectual attainments might run some risk of the imputation. There is indeed one evil in the reading of poetry and other light productions, that it is apt to be indulged in to downright *gluttony*, and to occupy time which should be given to business; but I am sure I can rely on *you* that you will not so misapply your time. There is, however, *one science*, the first and greatest of sciences to all men, and to merchants particularly—the science of Political Economy.* To this I think your chief attention should be directed. It is in truth the science of your own profession, which counteracts the—(word lost with seal)—and narrow habits which that profession is sometimes apt to produce; and which is of perpetual appeal in every discussion on mercantile and financial affairs. A merchant well instructed in Political Economy must always be fit to lead the views of his brother merchants—without it, he is a mere trader. Do not lose a day, therefore, without providing yourself with a copy of Adam Smith's "Wealth of Nations,"* and read and re-read it with attention—as I am sure you must read it with delight. In giving you this advice I consider you as a *merchant*, for as that is to be your profession in life, your test of the importance of any acquirement should be how far it will tend to render you an *honourable and distinguished merchant*;*—a character of no small estimation in this commercial country. I therefore consider the physical sciences as greatly subordinate in relation to your prospects in life, and the society in which you will be called to mingle. All but chemistry require a greater preparation in mathematics than you probably have, and chemistry it is quite impossible to understand without some opportunity of seeing experiments systematically carried on. If, however, you have the opportunity to attend any of the lecturers on that science in London, it will be well worth your while, and in that case I think you should purchase either Dr Thompson's or Mr Murray's new system of chemistry,* so as to keep up constantly with your lecturer. Even of physics in general it is pleasant to have some view, however superficial, and therefore though you cannot expect without mathematics to have anything but a superficial view, you had better try to attain it. With this view you may read Gregory's "Economy of Nature,"* which though not a good book, and not always accurate, is, I believe, the best popular book we have, and sufficiently accurate for your purposes. Remember, however, that though you may be permitted to be a superficial natural philosopher, no such indulgence is to be given you in Political Economy.

'The only other circumstance remaining for me to request of you is that you will not suffer yourself to lose any of the languages you have acquired. Of the modern languages there is less fear, as your mercantile communications will in some measure keep them alive; but merchants do not correspond in Latin, and you may perhaps lose it unconsciously.

Independently, however, of the admirable writers of whom you would thus deprive yourself, and considering the language merely as the accomplishment of a gentleman, it is of too great value to be carelessly resigned.

'Farewell, my dear sir. Accept the regard of all this family, and believe me, with every wish to be of service to you,

> "Your sincere friend,
> "T. Brown."

145. It may easily be conceived that a youth to whom such a letter as this was addressed by one of the chiefs of the purely intellectual circles of Edinburgh, would be regarded with more respect by his Croydon cousin than is usually rendered by grown young women to their schoolboy friends.

Their frank, cousinly relation went on, however, without a thought on either side of any closer ties, until my father, at two or three and twenty, after various apprenticeship in London, was going finally to London to begin his career in his own business. By that time he had made up his mind that Margaret, though not the least an ideal heroine to him, was quite the best sort of person he could have for a wife, the rather as they were already so well used to each other; and in a quiet, but enough resolute way, asked her if she were of the same mind, and would wait until he had an independence to offer her. His early tutress consented with frankly confessed joy, not indeed in the Agnes Wickfield way, 'I have loved you all my life,'* but feeling and admitting that it was great delight to be allowed to love him now. The relations between Grace Nugent and Lord Colambre* in Miss Edgeworth's 'Absentee' extremely resemble those between my father and mother, except that Lord Colambre is a more eager lover. My father chose his wife much with the same kind of serenity and decision with which afterwards he chose his clerks.

146. A time of active and hopeful contentment for both the young people followed, my mother being perhaps the more deeply in love, while John depended more absolutely on her sympathy and wise friendship than is at all usual with young men of the present day in their relations with admired young ladies. But neither of them ever permitted their feelings to degenerate into fretful or impatient passion. My mother showed her affection chiefly in steady endeavour to culti- vate her powers of mind, and form her manners, so as to fit herself to be the undespised companion of a man whom she considered much her superior: my father in unremitting attention to the business on the

success of which his marriage depended: and in a methodical regularity of conduct and correspondence which never left his mistress a moment of avoidable anxiety, or gave her motive for any serious displeasure.

On these terms the engagement lasted nine years; at the end of which time, my grandfather's debts having been all paid, and my father established in a business gradually increasing, and liable to no grave contingency, the now not very young people were married* in Perth one evening after supper, the servants of the house having no suspicion of the event until John and Margaret drove away together next morning to Edinburgh.

147. In looking back to my past thoughts and ways, nothing astonishes me more than my want of curiosity about all these matters; and that, often and often as my mother used to tell with complacency the story of this carefully secret marriage, I never asked, 'But, mother, why so secret, when it was just what all the friends of both of you so long expected, and what all your best friends so heartily wished?'

But, until lately, I never thought of writing any more about myself than was set down in diaries, nor of my family at all: and thus too carelessly, and, as I now think, profanely, neglected the traditions of my people. 'What does it all matter, now?' I said; 'we are what we are, and shall be what we make ourselves.'

Also, until very lately, I had accustomed myself to consider all that my parents had done, so far as their own happiness was concerned, entirely wise and exemplary. Yet the reader must not suppose that what I have said in my deliberate writings on the propriety of long engagements had any reference to this singular one in my own family. Of the heroism and patience with which the sacrifice was made, on both sides, I cannot judge:—but that it was greater than I should myself have been capable of, I know, and I believe that it was unwise. For during these years of waiting, my father fell gradually into a state of ill-health, from which he never entirely recovered; and in close of life, they both had to leave their child, just when he was beginning to satisfy the hopes they had formed for him.

148. I have allowed this tale of the little I knew of their early trials and virtues to be thus chance told, because I think my history will, in the end, be completest if I write as its connected subjects occur to me, and not with formal chronology of plan. My reason for telling it in this place was chiefly to explain how my mother obtained her perfect skill in English reading, through the hard effort which, through the years of waiting, she made to efface the faults, and supply the defects, of her early education; effort which was aided and directed unerringly by her

natural—for its intensity I might justly call it supernatural—purity of heart and conduct, leading her always to take most delight in the right and clear language which only can relate lovely things. Her unquestioning evangelical faith in the literal truth of the Bible placed me, as soon as I could conceive or think, in the presence of an unseen world; and set my active analytic power early to work on the questions of conscience, free will, and responsibility, which are easily determined in days of innocence; but are approached too often with prejudice, and always with disadvantage, after men become stupified by the opinions, or tainted by the sins, of the outer world: while the gloom, and even terror, with which the restrictions of the Sunday, and the doctrines of the *Pilgrim's Progress*, the *Holy War*, and Quarles' *Emblems*, oppressed the seventh part of my time, was useful to me as the only form of vexation which I was called on to endure; and redeemed by the otherwise uninterrupted cheerfulness and tranquillity of a household wherein the common ways were all of pleasantness, and its single and strait path, of perfect peace.*

149. My father's failure of health, following necessarily on the long years of responsibility and exertion, needed only this repose to effect its cure. Shy to an extreme degree in general company, all the more because he had natural powers which he was unable to his own satisfaction to express,—his business faculty was entirely superb and easy. he gave his full energy to counting-house work in the morning, and his afternoons to domestic rest. With instant perception and decision in all business questions; with principles of dealing which admitted of no infraction, and involved neither anxiety nor concealment, the counting-house work was more of an interest, or even an amusement, to him, than a care. His capital was either in the Bank, or in St Catherine's Docks,* in the form of insured butts of the finest sherry in the world; his partner, Mr Domecq, a Spaniard as proud as himself, as honourable, and having perfect trust in him,—not only in his probity, but his judgment,—accurately complying with all his directions in the preparation of wine for the English market, and no less anxious than he to make every variety of it, in its several rank, incomparably good. The letters to Spain therefore needed only brief statement that the public of that year wanted their wine young or old, pale or brown, and the like; and the letters to customers were as brief in their assurances that if they found fault with their wine, they did not understand it, and if they wanted an extension of credit, they could not have it. These Spartan brevities of epistle were, however, always supported by the utmost care in executing his correspondents' orders; and by the unusual attention

shown them in travelling for those orders himself, instead of sending an agent or a clerk. His domiciliary visits of this kind were always conducted by him with great *savoir faire** and pleasant courtesy, no less than the most attentive patience: and they were productive of the more confidence between him and the country merchant, that he was perfectly just and candid in appraisement of the wine of rival houses, while his fine palate enabled him always to sustain triumphantly any and every ordeal of blindfold question which the suspicious customer might put him to. Also, when correspondents of importance came up to town, my father would put himself so far out of his way as to ask them to dine at Herne Hill, and try the contents of his own cellar. These London visits fell into groups, on any occasions in the metropolis of interest more than usual to the provincial mind. Our business dinners were then arranged so as to collect two or three country visitors together, and the table made symmetrical by selections from the house's customers in London, whose conversation might be most instructive to its rural friends.

Very early in my boy's life I began much to dislike these commercial feasts, and to form, by carefully attending to their dialogue, when it chanced to turn on any other subject than wine, an extremely low estimate of the commercial mind as such;—estimate which I have never had the slightest reason to alter.

Of our neighbours on Herne Hill we saw nothing, with one exception only, afterwards to be noticed. They were for the most part well-to-do London tradesmen of the better class, who had little sympathy with my mother's old-fashioned ways, and none with my father's romantic sentiment.

150. There was probably the farther reason for our declining the intimacy of our immediate neighbours, that most of them were far more wealthy than we, and inclined to demonstrate their wealth by the magnificence of their establishments. My parents lived with strict economy, kept only female servants,[1] used only tallow candles in plated candlesticks, were content with the leasehold territory of their front and back gardens,—scarce an acre altogether,—and kept neither horse nor carriage. Our shop-keeping neighbours, on the contrary, had usually great cortège of footmen and glitter of plate, extensive pleasure grounds, costly hot-houses, and carriages driven by coachmen in wigs. It may be perhaps doubted by some of my readers whether the coldness

---

[1] Thomas left us, I think partly in shame for my permanently injured lip;* and we never had another indoor manservant.

of acquaintanceship was altogether on our side; but assuredly my father was too proud to join entertainments for which he could give no like return, and my mother did not care to leave her card on foot at the doors of ladies who dashed up to hers in their barouche.*

151. Protected by these monastic severities and aristocratic dignities, from the snares and disturbances of the outer world, the routine of my childish days became fixed, as of the sunrise and sunset to a nestling. It may seem singular to many of my readers that I remember with most pleasure the time when it was most regular and most solitary. The entrance of my cousin Mary into our household was coincident with the introduction of masters above described, and with other changes in the aims and employments of the day, which, while they often increased its interest, disturbed its tranquillity. The ideas of success at school or college, put before me by my masters, were ignoble and comfortless, in comparison with my mother's regretful blame, or simple praise: and Mary, though of a mildly cheerful and entirely amiable disposition, necessarily touched the household heart with the sadness of her orphanage, and something interrupted its harmony by the difference, which my mother could not help showing, between the feelings with which she regarded her niece and her child.

152. And although I have dwelt with thankfulness on the many joys and advantages of these secluded years, the vigilant reader will not, I hope, have interpreted the accounts rendered of them into general praise of a like home education in the environs of London. But one farther good there was in it, hitherto unspoken; that great part of my acute perception and deep feeling of the beauty of architecture and scenery abroad, was owing to the well-formed habit of narrowing myself to happiness within the four brick walls of our fifty by one hundred yards of garden; and accepting with resignation the aesthetic external surroundings of a London suburb, and, yet more of a London chapel. For Dr Andrews' was the Londonian chapel in its perfect type, definable as accurately as a Roman basilica,*—an oblong, flat-ceiled barn, lighted by windows with semi-circular heads, brick-arched, filled by small-paned glass held by iron bars, like fine threaded halves of cobwebs; galleries propped on iron pipes, up both sides; pews, well shut in, each of them, by partitions of plain deal, and neatly brass-latched deal doors, filling the barn floor, all but its two lateral straw-matted passages; pulpit, sublimely isolated, central from sides and clear of altar rails at end; a stout, four-legged box of well-grained wainscot, high as the level of front galleries, and decorated with a cushion of crimson velvet, padded six inches thick, with gold tassels at the

corners; which was a great resource to me when I was tired of the sermon, because I liked watching the rich colour of the folds and creases that came in it when the clergyman thumped it.

153. Imagine the change between one Sunday and the next,—from the morning service in this building, attended by the families of the small shopkeepers of the Walworth Road, in their Sunday trimmings; (our plumber's wife, fat, good, sensible Mrs Goad, sat in the next pew in front of us, sternly sensitive to the interruption of her devotion by our late arrivals); fancy the change from this, to high mass in Rouen Cathedral, its nave filled by the white-capped peasantry of half Normandy!

Nor was the contrast less enchanting or marvellous between the street architecture familiar to my eyes, and that of Flanders and Italy, as an exposition of mercantile taste and power. My father's counting-house was in the centre of Billiter Street, some years since effaced from sight and memory of men,* but a type, then, of English city state in perfection. We now build house fronts as advertisements, spending a hundred thousand pounds in the lying mask of our bankruptcies. But in my father's time both trade and building were still honest. His counting-house was a room about fifteen feet by twenty, including desks for two clerks, and a small cupboard for sherry samples, on the first floor, with a larger room opposite for private polite receptions of elegant visitors, or the serving of a chop for himself if he had to stay late in town. The ground floor was occupied by friendly Messrs Wardell and Co., a bottling retail firm, I believe.* The only advertisement of the place of business was the brass plate under the bell-handle, inscribed 'Ruskin, Telford, and Domecq,' brightly scrubbed by the single female servant in charge of the establishment, old Maisie,—abbreviated or tenderly diminished into the 'sie,' from I know not what Christian name—Marion, I believe, as Mary into Mause. The whole house, three-storied, with garrets, was under her authority, with, doubtless, assistant morning charwoman,—cooking, waiting, and answering the door to distinguished visitors, all done by Maisie, the visitors being expected of course to announce themselves by the knocker with a flourish in proportion to their eminence in society. The businessmen rang the counting-house bell aforesaid, (round which the many coats of annual paint were cut into a beautiful slant section by daily scrubbing, like the coats of an agate;) and were admitted by lifting of latch, manipulated by the head clerk's hand in the counting-house, without stirring from his seat.

154. This unpretending establishment, as I said, formed part of the

western side of Billiter Street, a narrow trench—it may have been thirty feet wide—admitting, with careful and precise driving, the passing each other of two brewers' drays. I am not sure that this was possible at the ends of the street, but only at a slight enlargement opposite the brewery in the middle. Effectively a mere trench between three-storied houses of prodigious brickwork, thoroughly well laid, and presenting no farther entertainment whatever to the aesthetic beholder than the alternation of the ends and sides of their beautifully level close courses of bricks, and the practised and skilful radiation of those which formed the window' lintels.

Typical, I repeat, of the group of London edifices, east of the Mansion House, and extending to the Tower; the under-hill picturesquenesses of which, however, were in early days an entirely forbidden district to me, lest I should tumble into the docks; but Fenchurch and Leadenhall Streets, familiar to me as the perfection of British mercantile state and grandeur,—the reader may by effort, though still dimly, conceive the effect on my imagination of the fantastic gables of Ghent, and orange-scented cortiles of Genoa.

155. I can scarcely account to myself, on any of the ordinary principles of resignation, for the undimmed tranquillity of pleasure with which, after these infinite excitements in foreign lands, my father would return to his desk opposite the brick wall of the brewery,* and I to my niche behind the drawing-room chimney piece. But to both of us, the steady occupations, the beloved samenesses, and the sacred customs of home were more precious than all the fervours of wonder in things new to us, or delight in scenes of incomparable beauty. Very early, indeed, I had found that novelty was soon exhausted, and beauty, though inexhaustible, beyond a certain point or time of enthusiasm, no more to be enjoyed; but it is not so often observed by philosophers that home, healthily organized, is always enjoyable; nay, the sick thrill of pleasure through all the brain and heart with which, after even so much as a month or two of absence, I used to catch the first sight of the ridge of Herne Hill, and watch for every turn of the well-known road and every branch of the familiar trees, was—though not so deep or overwhelming—more intimately and vitally powerful than the brightest passions of joy in strange lands, or even in the unaccustomed scenery of my own. To my mother, her ordinary household cares, her reading with Mary and me, her chance of a chat with Mrs Gray, and the unperturbed preparation for my father's return, and for the quiet evening, were more than all the splendours or wonders of the globe between poles and equator.

156. Thus we returned—full of new thoughts, and faithful to the old, to this exulting rest of home in the close of 1833. An unforeseen shadow was in the heaven of its charmed horizon.

Every day at Cornhill, Charles became more delightful and satisfactory to everybody who knew him. How a boy living all day in London could keep so bright a complexion, and so crisply Achillean curls of hair—and all the gay spirit of his Croydon mother—was not easily conceivable; but he became a perfect combination of the sparkle of Jin Vin with the steadiness of Tunstall,* and was untroubled by the charms of any unattainable Margaret,* for his master had no daughter; but, as worse chance would have it, a son: so that looking forward to possibilities as a rising apprentice ought, Charles saw that there were none in the house for him beyond the place of cashier, or perhaps only head-clerk. His elder brother, who had taught him to swim by throwing him into Croydon canal, was getting on fast as a general trader in Australia, and naturally longed to have his best-loved brother there for a partner. Bref, it was resolved that Charles should go to Australia. The Christmas time of 1833 passed heavily, for I was very sorry; Mary, a good deal more so: and my father and mother, though in their hearts caring for nobody in the world but me, were grave at the thought of Charles's going so far away; but, honestly and justifiably, thought it for the lad's good. I think the whole affair was decided, and Charles's outfit furnished, and ship's berth settled, and ship's captain interested in his favour, in something less than a fortnight, and down he went to Portsmouth to join his ship joyfully, with the world to win. By due post came the news that he was at anchor off Cowes, but that the ship could not sail because of the west wind. And post succeeded post, and still the west wind blew. We liked the west wind for its own sake, but it was a prolonging of farewell which teazed us, though Charles wrote that he was enjoying himself immensely, and the captain, that he had made friends with every sailor on board, besides the passengers.

157. And still the west wind blew. I do not remember how long—some ten days or fortnight, I believe. At last, one day my mother and Mary went with my father into town on some shopping or sight-seeing business of a cheerful character; and I was left at home, busy also about something that cheered me greatly, I know not what; but when I heard the others come in, and upstairs into the drawing-room, I ran eagerly down and into the room, beginning to tell them about this felicity that had befallen me, whatever it was. They all stood like statues, my father and mother very grave. Mary was looking out of the

window—the farthest of the front three from the door. As I went on, boasting of myself, she turned round suddenly, her face all streaming with tears, and caught hold of me, and put her face close to mine, that I might hear the sobbing whisper, 'Charles is gone.'

158. The west wind had still blown, clearly and strong, and the day before there had been a fresh breeze of it round the isle, at Spithead, exactly the kind of breeze that drifts the clouds, and ridges the waves, in Turner's Gosport.

The ship was sending her boat on shore for some water, or the like—her little cutter, or somehow sailing, boat. There was a heavy sea running, and the sailors, and, I believe, also a passenger or two, had some difficulty in getting on board. 'May I go, too?' said Charles to the captain, as he stood seeing them down the side. 'Are you not afraid?' said the captain. 'I never was afraid of anything in my life,' said Charles, and went down the side and leaped in.

The boat had not got fifty yards from the ship before she went over, but there were other boats sailing all about them, like gnats in midsummer. Two or three scudded to the spot in a minute, and every soul was saved, except Charles, who went down like a stone.

22nd January, 1834.

All this we knew by little and little. For the first day or two we would not believe it, but thought he must have been taken up by some other boat and carried to sea. At last came word that his body had been thrown ashore at Cowes: and his father went down to see him buried. That done, and all the story heard, for still the ship stayed, he came to Herne Hill, to tell Charles's 'auntie' all about it. (The old man never called my mother anything else than auntie.) It was in the morning, in the front parlour—my mother knitting in her usual place at the fireside, I at my drawing, or the like, in my own place also. My uncle told all the story, in the quiet, steady sort of way that the common English do, till just at the end he broke down into sobbing, saying (I can hear the words now), 'They caught the cap off of his head, and yet they couldn't save him.'*

CHAPTER VIII

VESTER, CAMENAE*

159. THE death of Charles closed the doors of my heart again for that time; and the self-engrossed quiet of the Herne Hill life continued for another year, leaving little to be remembered, and less to be told. My parents made one effort, however, to obtain some healthy companionship for me, to which I probably owe more than I knew at the moment.

Some six or seven gates down the hill towards the field, (which I have to return most true thanks to its present owner, Mr Sopper, for having again opened to the public sight in consequence of the passage above describing the greatness of its loss both to the neighbour and the stranger), some six or seven gates down that way, a pretty lawn, shaded by a low spreading cedar, opened before an extremely neat and carefully kept house, where lived two people, modest in their ways as my father and mother, themselves,—Mr and Mrs Fall, happier, however, in having son and daughter instead of an only child. Their son, Richard, was a year younger than I, but already at school at Shrewsbury, and somewhat in advance of me therefore in regular discipline; extremely gentle and good-natured,—his sister, still younger, a clever little girl, her mother's constant companion: and both of them unpretending, but rigid, examples of all Herne Hill proprieties, true religions, and useful learnings. I shudder still at the recollection of Mrs Fall's raised eyebrows one day at my pronunciation of 'naiveté' as 'naivette.'

160. I think it must have been as early as 1832* that my father, noticing with great respect the conduct of all matters in this family, wrote to Mr Fall in courteous request that 'the two boys' might be permitted, when Richard was at home, to pursue their holiday tasks, or recreations, so far as it pleased them, together. The proposal was kindly taken: the two boys took stock of each other,—agreed to the arrangement,—and, as I had been promoted by that time to the possession of a study, all to myself, while Richard had only his own room, (and *that* liable to sisterly advice or intrusion,) the course which things fell into was that usually, when Richard was at home, he came up past the seven gates about ten in the morning; did what lessons he had to do at the same table with me, occasionally helping me a little with mine; and then we went together for afternoon walk with Dash, Gipsy, or whatever dog chanced to be dominant.

161. I do not venture to affirm that the snow of those Christmas holidays was whiter than it is now, though I might give some reasons

for supposing that it remained longer white. But I affirm decisively that it used to fall deeper in the neighbourhood of London than has been seen for the last twenty or twenty-five years. It was quite usual to find in the hollows of the Norwood Hills the field fences buried under crested waves of snow, while, from the higher ridges, half the counties of Kent and Surrey shone to the horizon like a cloudless and terrorless Arctic sea.

Richard Fall was entirely good-humoured, sensible, and practical; but had no particular tastes; a distaste, if anything, for *my* styles both of art and poetry. He stiffly declined arbitration on the merits of my compositions; and though with pleasant cordiality in daily companionship, took rather the position of putting up with me, than of pride in his privilege of acquaintance with a rising author. He was never unkind or sarcastic; but laughed me inexorably out of writing bad English for rhyme's sake, or demonstrable nonsense either in prose or rhyme. We got gradually accustomed to be together, and far on into life were glad when any chance brought us together again.

162. The year 1834 passed innocuously enough, but with little profit, in the quadripartite industries before described, followed for my own pleasure;—with minglings of sapless effort in the classics, in which I neither felt, nor foresaw, the least good.

Innocuously *enough*, I say,—meaning, with as little mischief as a well-intentioned boy, virtually masterless, could suffer from having all his own way, and daily confirming himself in the serious impression that his own way was always the best.

I cannot analyse, at least without taking more trouble than I suppose any reader would care to take with me, the mixed good and evil in the third rate literature which I preferred to the Latin classics. My volume of the Forget-me-not, which gave me that precious engraving of Verona (curiously also another by Prout of St Mark's at Venice), was somewhat above the general caste of annuals in its quality of letter-press; and contained three stories, 'The Red-nosed Lieutenant,' by the Rev. George Croly; 'Hans in Kelder,' by the author of 'Chronicles of London Bridge;' and 'The Comet,' by Henry Neele, Esq.,* which were in their several ways extremely impressive to me. The partly childish, partly dull, or even, as aforesaid, idiotic, way I had of staring at the same things all day long, carried itself out in reading, so that I could read the same things all the year round. As there was neither advantage nor credit to be got by remembering fictitious circumstances, I was, if anything, rather proud of my skill in forgetting, so as the sooner to recover the zest of the tales; and I suppose these favourites, and a good many less important ones of the sort, were read some twenty times a year, during the earlier epoch of teens.

163. I wonder a little at my having been allowed so long to sit in that drawing-room corner with only my Rogers' *Italy*, my *Forget-me-not*, the *Continental Annual* and *Friendship's Offering*,* for my working library; and I wonder a little more that my father, in his passionate hope that I might one day write like Byron, never noticed that Byron's early power was founded on a course of general reading of the masters in every walk of literature, such as is, I think, utterly unparalleled in any other young life, whether of student or author. But I was entirely incapable of such brain-work, and the real gift I had in drawing involved the use in its practice of the best energy of the day. *Hans in Kelder*, and *The Comet*, were my manner of rest.

I do not know when my father first began to read Byron to me, with any expectation of my liking him; all primary training, after the Iliad, having been in Scott; but it must have been about the beginning of the teen period, else I should recollect the first effect of it. *Manfred* evidently, I had got at, like *Macbeth*, for the sake of the witches. Various questionable changes were made, however, at that 1831 turning of twelve, in the Hermitage discipline of Herne Hill. I was allowed to taste wine; taken to the theatre; and, on festive days, even dined with my father and mother at four: and it was then generally at dessert that my father would read any otherwise suspected delight: the *Noctes Ambrosianae** regularly when they came out—without the least missing of the naughty words; and at last, the shipwreck in *Don Juan*,*—of which, finding me rightly appreciative, my father went on with nearly all the rest. I recollect that he and my mother looked across the table at each other with something of alarm, when, on asking me a few festas afterwards what we should have for after dinner reading, I instantly answered 'Juan and Haidée.'* My selection was not adopted, and, feeling there was something wrong somewhere, I did not press it, attempting even some stutter of apology which made matters worse. Perhaps I was given a bit of *Childe Harold* instead, which I liked at that time nearly as well; and, indeed, the story of Haidée soon became too sad for me. But very certainly, by the end of this year 1834, I knew my Byron pretty well all through, all but *Cain*, *Werner*, the *Deformed Transformed*, and *Vision of Judgment*,* none of which I could understand, nor did papa and mamma think it would be well I should try to.

164. The ingenuous reader may perhaps be so much surprised that mamma fell in with all this, that it becomes here needful to mark for him some peculiarities in my mother's prudery which he could not

discover for himself, from anything hitherto told of her. He might indeed guess that, after taking me at least six times straight through the Bible, she was not afraid of plain words to, or for, me; but might not feel that in the energy and affectionateness of her character, she had as much sympathy with all that is noble and beautiful in Byron as my father himself; nor that her Puritanism was clear enough in common sense to see that, while Shakespeare and Burns lay open on the table all day, there was no reason for much mystery with Byron (though until later I was not allowed to read him for myself). She had trust in my disposition and education, and was no more afraid of my turning out a Corsair or a Giaour than a Richard III, or a——Solomon.* And she was perfectly right, so far. I never got the slightest harm from Byron: what harm came to me was from the facts of life, and from books of a baser kind, including a wide range of the works of authors popularly considered extremely instructive—from Victor Hugo down to Doctor Watts.*

165. Farther, I will take leave to explain in this place what I meant by saying that my mother was an 'inoffensive' prude. She was herself as strict as Alice Bridgenorth;* but she understood the doctrine of the religion she had learnt, and, without ostentatiously calling herself a miserable sinner, knew that according that doctrine, and probably in fact, Madge Wildfire* was no worse a sinner than she. She was like her sister in universal charity—had sympathy with every passion, as well as every virtue, of true womanhood; and, in her heart of hearts, perhaps liked the real Margherita Cogni quite as well as the ideal wife of Faliero.*

166. And there was one more feature in my mother's character which must be here asserted at once, to put an end to the notion of which I see traces in some newspaper comments on my past descriptions of her, that she was in any wise like Esther's religious aunt in *Bleak House*.* Far on the contrary, there was a hearty, frank, and sometimes even irrepressible, laugh in my mother! Never sardonic, yet with a very definitely Smollettesque turn in it! so that, between themselves, she and my father enjoyed their *Humphrey Clinker* extremely, long before *I* was able to understand either the jest or gist of it. Much more, she could exult in a harmless bit of Smollettesque reality. Years and years after this time, in one of our crossings of the Simplon, just at the top, where we had stopped to look about us, Nurse Anne sat down to rest herself on the railings at the roadside, just in front of the monastery;—the off roadside, from which the bank slopes steeply down outside the fence. Turning to observe the panoramic picturesque, Anne lost her balance, and went backwards over the railings

down the bank. My father could not help suggesting that she had done it expressly for the entertainment of the Holy Fathers; and neither he nor my mother could ever speak of the 'performance' (as they called it) afterwards, without laughing for a quarter of an hour.

167. If, however, there was the least bitterness or irony in a jest, my mother did not like it; but my father and I liked it all the more, if it were just; and, so far as I could understand it, I rejoiced in all the sarcasm of *Don Juan*. But my firm decision, as soon as I got well into the later cantos of it, that Byron was to be my master in verse, as Turner in colour, was made of course in that gosling (or say cygnet) epoch of existence, without consciousness of the deeper instincts that prompted it: only two things I consciously recognized, that his truth of observation was the most exact, and his chosen expression the most concentrated, that I had yet found in literature. By that time my father had himself put me through the two first books of Livy, and I knew, therefore, what close-set language was; but I saw then that Livy, as afterwards that Horace and Tacitus, were studiously, often laboriously and sometimes obscurely, concentrated: while Byron wrote, as easily as a hawk flies, and as clearly as a lake reflects, the exact truth in the precisely narrowest terms; nor only the exact truth, but the most central and useful one.

168. Of course I could no more measure Byron's greater powers at that time than I could Turner's; but I saw that both were right in all things that *I* knew right from wrong in; and that they must thenceforth be my masters, each in his own domain. The modern reader, not to say also, modern scholar, is usually so ignorant of the essential qualities of Byron, that I cannot go farther in the story of my own novitiate under him without illustrating, by rapid example, the things which I saw to be unrivalled in his work.

For this purpose I take his common prose, rather than his verse, since his modes of rhythm involve other questions than those with which I am now concerned. Read, for chance-first, the sentence on Sheridan, in his letter to Thomas Moore, from Venice, June 1st (or dawn of June 2nd!), 1818. 'The Whigs abuse him; however, he never left them, and such blunderers deserve neither credit nor compassion. As for his creditors—remember Sheridan never had a shilling, and was thrown, with great powers and passions, into the thick of the world, and placed upon the pinnacle of success, with no other external means to support him in his elevation. Did Fox pay *his* debts? or did Sheridan take a subscription? Was ——'s drunkenness more excusable than his? Were his intrigues more notorious than those of all his contemporaries?

and is his memory to be blasted and theirs respected? Don't let yourself be led away by clamour, but compare him with the coalitioner Fox, and the pensioner Burke, as a man of principle; and with ten hundred thousand in personal views; and with none in talent, for he beat them all out and out. Without means, without connection, without character (which might be false at first, and drive him mad afterwards from desperation), he beat them all, in all he ever attempted. But, alas poor human nature! Good-night, or rather morning. It is four, and the dawn gleams over the Grand Canal, and unshadows the Rialto.'*

169. Now, observe, that passage is noble, primarily because it contains the utmost number that will come together into the space, of absolutely just, wise, and kind thoughts. But it is more than noble, it is *perfect*, because the quantity it holds is not artificially or intricately concentrated, but with the serene swiftness of a smith's hammer-strokes on hot iron; and with choice of terms which, each in its place, will convey far more than they mean in the dictionary. Thus, 'however' is used instead of 'yet,' because it stands for 'howsoever,' or, in full, for 'yet whatever they did.' 'Thick' of society, because it means, not merely the crowd, but the *fog* of it; 'ten hundred thousand' instead of 'a million,' or 'a thousand thousand,' to take the sublimity out of the number, and make us feel that it is a number of nobodies. Then the sentence in parenthesis, 'which might be false,' etc., is indeed obscure, because it was impossible to clarify it without a regular pause, and much loss of time; and the reader's sense is therefore left to expand it for himself into 'it was, perhaps, falsely said of him at first, that he had no character,' etc. Finally, the dawn 'unshadows'—lessens the shadow on—the Rialto, but does not *gleam* on that, as on the broad water.

170. Next, take the two sentences on poetry, in his letters to Murray* of September 15th, 1817, and April 12th, 1818; (for the collected force of these compare the deliberate published statement in the answer to Blackwood in 1820.)

1817. 'With regard to poetry in general, I am convinced, the more I think of it, that he (Moore), and *all* of us—Scott, Southey, Wordsworth, Moore, Campbell, I,—are all in the wrong, one as much as another; that we are upon a wrong revolutionary poetical system, or systems, not worth a damn in itself, and from which none but Rogers and Crabbe are free: and that the present and next generations will finally be of this opinion. I am the more confirmed in this by having lately gone over some of our classics, particularly Pope, whom I tried in this way: I took Moore's poems, and my own, and some others, and went over them side by side with Pope's, and I was really astonished (I ought not to have been so) and mortified, at the ineffable distance in point of sense, learning, effect, and even *imagination*, passion, and *invention*, between the little Queen Anne's man, and us of the Lower Empire. Depend upon it, it is all Horace then, and Claudian now, among us; and if I had to begin again, I would mould myself accordingly. Crabbe's the man; but he has got a coarse and impracticable subject, and . . . is retired upon half-pay, and has done enough, unless he were to do as he did formerly.'

1818. 'I thought of a preface, defending Lord Hervey against Pope's attack, but Pope—quoad Pope, the poet,—against all the world, in the unjustifiable attempts begun by Warton, and carried on at this day by the new school of critics and scribblers, who think themselves poets because they do *not* write like Pope. I have no patience with such cursed humbug and bad taste; your whole generation are not worth a canto of the Rape of the Lock, or the Essay on Man, or the Dunciad,*or "anything that is his."'

171. There is nothing which needs explanation in the brevities and amenities of these two fragments, except, in the first of them, the distinctive and exhaustive enumeration of the qualities of great poetry,—and note especially the order in which he puts these.

A. Sense. That is to say, the first thing you have to think of is whether the would-be poet is a wise man—so also in the answer to Blackwood, 'They call him (Pope) the poet of reason!—is that any reason why he should not be a poet?'

B. Learning. The Ayrshire ploughman* may have good gifts, but he is out of court with relation to Homer, or Dante, or Milton.

C. Effect. Has he *efficiency* in his verse?—does it tell on the ear and the spirit in an instant? See the 'effect' on her audience of Beatrice's 'ottave,' in the story at p. 286 of Miss Alexander's *Songs of Tuscany*.*

D. Imagination. Put thus low because many novelists and artists have this faculty, yet are not poets, or even good novelists or painters; because they have not sense to manage it, nor the art to give it effect.

E. Passion. Lower yet, because all good men and women have as much as either they or the poet ought to have.

F. Invention. And this lowest, because one may be a good poet without having this at all. Byron had scarcely any himself, while Scott had any quantity—yet never could write a play.

172. But neither the force and precision, nor the rhythm, of Byron's language, were at all the central reasons for my taking him for master. Knowing the Song of Moses and the Sermon on the Mount by heart, and half the Apocalypse besides, I was in no need of tutorship either in

the majesty or simplicity of English words; and for their logical arrangement, I had had Byron's own master, Pope, since I could lisp. But the
thing wholly new and precious to me in Byron was his measured and
living *truth*—measured, as compared with Homer; and living, as compared with everybody else. My own inexorable measuring wand,—not
enchanter's, but cloth-worker's and builder's,—reduced to mere
incredibility all the statements of the poets usually called sublime. It
was of no use for Homer to tell me that Pelion was put on the top of
Ossa.* I knew perfectly well it wouldn't go on the top of Ossa. Of no
use for Pope to tell me that trees where his mistress looked would
crowd into a shade, because I was satisfied that they would do nothing
of the sort.* Nay, the whole world, as it was described to me either by
poetry or theology, was every hour becoming more and more shadowy
and impossible. I rejoiced in all stories of Pallas and Venus, of Achilles
and Eneas, of Elijah and St John:* but, without doubting in my heart
that there were real spirits of wisdom and beauty, nor that there had
been invincible heroes and inspired prophets, I felt already, with fatal
and increasing sadness, that there was no clear utterance about any of
them—that there were for *me* neither Goddess guides nor prophetic
teachers; and that the poetical histories, whether of this world or the
next, were to me as the words of Peter to the shut up disciples—'as idle
tales; and they believed them not.'*

173. But here at last I had found a man who spoke only of what he
had seen, and known; and spoke without exaggeration, without mystery, without enmity, and without mercy. 'That *is* so;—make what you
will of it!' Shakespeare said the Alps voided their rheum on the valleys,*
which indeed is precisely true, with the final truth, in that matter, of
James Forbes,—but it was told in a mythic manner, and with an
unpleasant British bias to the nasty. But Byron, saying that 'the glacier's
cold and restless mass moved onward day by day,'* said plainly what he
saw and knew,—no more. So also, the Arabian Nights had told me of
thieves who lived in enchanted caves, and beauties who fought with
genii in the air; but Byron told me of thieves with whom he had ridden
on their own hills, and of the fair Persians or Greeks who lived and died
under the very sun that rose over my visible Norwood hills.

And in this narrow, but sure, truth, to Byron, as already to me, it
appeared that Love was a transient thing, and Death a dreadful one. He
did not attempt to console me for Jessie's death, by saying she was
happier in Heaven; or for Charles's, by saying it was a Providential
dispensation to me on Earth. He did not tell me that war was a just
price for the glory of captains, or that the National command of murder

diminished its guilt. Of all things within range of human thought he felt the facts, and discerned the natures with accurate justice.

But even all this he might have done, and yet been no master of mine, had not he sympathized with me in reverent love of beauty, and indignant recoil from ugliness. The witch of the Staubbach in her rainbow was a greatly more pleasant vision than Shakespeare's, like a rat without a tail, or Burns's, in her cutty sark.* The sea-king Conrad* had an immediate advantage with me over Coleridge's long, lank, brown, and ancient, mariner,* and whatever Pope might have gracefully said, or honestly felt of Windsor woods* and streams, was mere tinkling cymbal* to me, compared with Byron's love of Lachin-y-Gair.*

174. I must pause here, in tracing the sources of his influence over me, lest the reader should mistake the analysis which I am now able to give them, for a description of the feelings possible to me at fifteen. Most of these, however, were assuredly within the knot of my unfolding mind—as the saffron of the crocus yet beneath the earth; and Byron—though he could not teach me to love mountains or sea more than I did in childhood, first animated them for me with the sense of real human nobleness and grief. He taught me the meaning of Chillon and of Meillerie,* and bade me seek first in Venice—the ruined homes of Foscari and Falier.*

And observe, the force with which he struck depended again on there being unquestionable reality of person in his stories, as of principle in his thoughts. Romance, enough and to spare, I had learnt from Scott—but his Lady of the Lake was as openly fictitious as his White Maid of Avenel:* while Rogers was a mere dilettante, who felt no difference between landing where Tell leaped ashore, or standing where 'St Preux has stood.'* Even Shakespeare's Venice was visionary; and Portia as impossible as Miranda.* But Byron told me of, and reanimated for me, the real people whose feet had worn the marble I trod on.

175. One word only, though it trenches* on a future subject, I must permit myself about his rhythm. Its natural flow in almost prosaic simplicity and tranquillity interested me extremely, in opposition alike to the symmetrical clauses of Pope's logical metre, and to the balanced strophes of classic and Hebrew verse. But though I followed his manner instantly in what verses I wrote for my own amusement, my respect for the structural, as opposed to fluent, force of the classic measures, supported as it was partly by Byron's contempt for his own work, and partly by my own architect's instinct for 'the principle of the pyramid,' made me long endeavour, in forming my prose style, to keep the cadences of Pope and Johnson for all serious statement. Of Johnson's

influence on me I have to give account in the last chapter of this volume; meantime, I must get back to the days of mere rivulet-singing, in my poor little watercress life.

176. I had a sharp attack of pleurisy in the spring of '35, which gave me much gasping pain, and put me in some danger for three or four days, during which our old family physician, Dr Walshman, and my mother, defended me against the wish of all other scientific people to have me bled. 'He wants all the blood he has in him to fight the illness,' said the old doctor, and brought me well through, weak enough, however, to claim a fortnight's nursing and petting afterwards, during which I read the 'Fair Maid of Perth,' learned the song of 'Poor Louise,'* and feasted on Stanfield's drawing of St Michael's Mount, engraved in the 'Coast Scenery,'* and Turner's Santa Saba, Pool of Bethesda, and Corinth, engraved in the Bible series,* lent me by Richard Fall's little sister. I got an immense quantity of useful learning out of those four plates, and am very thankful to possess now the originals of the Bethesda and Corinth.

Moreover, I planned all my proceedings on the journey to Switzerland, which was to begin the moment I was strong enough. I shaded in cobalt a 'cyanometer'* to measure the blue of the sky with; bought a ruled notebook for geological observations, and a large quarto for architectural sketches, with square rule and foot-rule ingeniously fastened outside. And I determined that the events and sentiments of this journey should be described in a poetic diary in the style of *Don Juan*, artfully combined with that of *Childe Harold*. Two cantos of this work were indeed finished—carrying me across France to Chamouni— where I broke down, finding that I had exhausted on the Jura all the descriptive terms at my disposal, and that none were left for the Alps. I must try to give, in the next chapter, some useful account of the same part of the journey in less exalted language.

CHAPTER IX

THE COL DE LA FAUCILLE

177. ABOUT the moment in the forenoon when the modern fashionable traveller, intent on Paris, Nice, and Monaco, and started by the morning mail from Charing Cross, has a little recovered himself from the qualms of his crossing, and the irritation of fighting for seats at Boulogne, and begins to look at his watch to see how near he is to the

buffet of Amiens, he is apt to be baulked and worried by the train's useless stop at one inconsiderable station, lettered ABBEVILLE. As the carriage gets in motion again, he may see, if he cares to lift his eyes for an instant from his newspaper, two square towers, with a curiously attached bit of traceried arch, dominant over the poplars and osiers of the marshy level he is traversing. Such glimpse is probably all he will ever wish to get of them; and I scarcely know how far I can make even the most sympathetic reader understand their power over my own life.

The country town in which they are central,—once, like Croyland,* a mere monk's and peasant's refuge (so for some time called 'Refuge'),—among the swamps of Somme, received about the year 650 the name of 'Abbatis Villa,'—'Abbot's-ford,' I had like to have written: house and village, I suppose we may rightly say,—as the chief dependence of the great monastery founded by St Riquier at his native place, on the hillside five miles east of the present town. Concerning which saint I translate from the Dict^re des Sciences Eccles^ques,* what it may perhaps be well for the reader, in present political junctures,* to remember for more weighty reasons than any arising out of such interest as he may take in my poor little nascent personality.

178. 'St Riquier, in Latin "Sanctus Richarius," born in the village of Centula, at two leagues from Abbeville, was so touched by the piety of two holy priests of Ireland, whom he had hospitably received, that he also embraced "la pénitence." Being ordained priest, he devoted himself to preaching, and so passed into England. Then, returning into Ponthieu, he became, by God's help, powerful in work and word in leading the people to repentance. He preached at the court of Dagobert, and, a little while after that prince's death, founded the monastery which bore his name, and another, called Forest-Moutier, in the wood of Crécy, where he ended his life and penitence.'

I find further in the Ecclesiastical History of Abbeville, published in 1646 at Paris by François Pelican, 'Rue St Jacques, à l'enseigne du Pelican,'* that St Riquier was himself of royal blood, that St Angilbert, the seventh abbot, had married Charlemagne's second daughter Bertha—'qui se rendit aussi Religieuse de l'ordre de Saint Benoist.'* Louis, the eleventh abbot, was cousin-german to Charles the Bald; the twelfth was St Angilbert's son, Charlemagne's grandson. Raoul, the thirteenth abbot, was the brother of the Empress Judith; and Carloman, the sixteenth, was the son of Charles the Bald.

179. Lifting again your eyes, good reader, as the train gets to its speed, you may see gleaming opposite on the hillside the white village and its abbey,—not, indeed, the walls of the home of these princes and

princesses, (afterwards again and again ruined,) but the still beautiful
abbey built on their foundations by the monks of St Maur.

In the year when the above quoted history of Abbeville was written
(say 1600 for surety), the town, then familiarly called 'Faithful
Abbeville,' contained 40,000 souls, 'living in great unity among themselves, of a marvellous frankness, fearing to do wrong to their neighbour, the women modest, honest, full of faith and charity, and adorned
with a goodness and beauty toute innocente: the noblesse numerous,
hardy, and adroit in arms, the masterships (maistrises) of arts and
trades, with excellent workers in every profession, under sixty-four
Mayor-Bannerets, who are the chiefs of the trades, and elect the mayor
of the city, who is an independent Home Ruler, de grande probité,
d'authorité, et sans reproche,* aided by four eschevins* of the present,
and four of the past year; having authority of justice, police, and war,
and right to keep the weights and measures true and unchanged, and to
punish those who abuse them, or sell by false weight or measure, or sell
anything without the town's mark on it.' Moreover, the town contained, besides the great church of St Wulfran, thirteen parish churches,
six monasteries, eight nunneries, and five hospitals, among which
churches I am especially bound to name that of St George, begun by
our own Edward in 1368, on the 10th of January; transferred and
reconsecrated in 1469 by the Bishop of Bethlehem, and enlarged by the
Marguilliers* in 1536, 'because the congregation had so increased that
numbers had to remain outside on days of solemnity.'

These reconstructions took place with so great ease and rapidity at
Abbeville, owing partly to the number of its unanimous workmen,
partly to the easily workable quality of the stone they used, and partly
to the uncertainty of a foundation always on piles, that there is now
scarce vestige left of any building prior to the fifteenth century.
St Wulfran itself, with St Riquier, and all that remain of the parish
churches (four only, now, I believe, besides St Wulfran), are of the
same flamboyant Gothic,—walls and towers alike coeval with the
gabled timber houses of which the busier streets chiefly consisted when
first I saw them.

180. I must here, in advance, tell the general reader that there have
been, in sum, three centres of my life's thought: Rouen, Geneva, and
Pisa. All that I did at Venice was bye-work, because her history had
been falsely written before, and not even by any of her own people
understood; and because, in the world of painting, Tintoret was virtually unseen, Veronese unfelt, Carpaccio not so much as named, when
I began to study them; something also was due to my love of gliding

about in gondolas. But Rouen, Geneva, and Pisa have been tutresses of all I know, and were mistresses of all I did, from the first moments I entered their gates.

In this journey of 1835 I first saw Rouen and Venice—Pisa not till 1840; nor could I understand the full power of any of those great scenes till much later. But for Abbeville, which is the preface and interpretation of Rouen, I was ready on that 5th of June, and felt that here was entrance for me into immediately healthy labour and joy.

181. For here I saw that art (of its local kind), religion, and present human life, were yet in perfect harmony. There were no dead six days and dismal seventh in those sculptured churches; there was no beadle to lock me out of them, or pew-shutter to shut me in. I might haunt them, fancying myself a ghost; peep round their pillars, like Rob Roy;* kneel in them, and scandalize nobody; draw in them, and disturb none. Outside, the faithful old town gathered itself, and nestled under their buttresses like a brood beneath the mother's wings; the quiet, uninjurious aristocracy of the newer town opened into silent streets, between self-possessed and hidden dignities of dwelling, each with its courtyard and richly trellised garden. The commercial square, with the main street of traverse, consisted of uncompetitive shops, such as were needful, of the native wares: cloth and hosiery spun, woven, and knitted within the walls; cheese of neighbouring Neuchatel; fruit of their own gardens, bread from the fields above the green coteaux;* meat of their herds, untainted by American tin;* smith's work of sufficient scythe and ploughshare, hammered on the open anvil; groceries dainty, the coffee generally roasting odoriferously in the street, before the door; for the modistes,*—well, perhaps a bonnet or two from Paris, the rest, wholesome dress for peasant and dame of Ponthieu. Above the prosperous, serenely busy and beneficent shop, the old dwelling-house of its ancestral masters; pleasantly carved, proudly roofed, keeping its place, and order, and recognised function, unfailing, unenlarging, for centuries. Round all, the breezy ramparts, with their long waving avenues; through all, in variously circuiting cleanness and sweetness of navigable river and active millstream, the green chalk-water of the Somme.

My most intense happinesses have of course been among mountains. But for cheerful, unalloyed, unwearying pleasure, the getting in sight of Abbeville on a fine summer afternoon, jumping out in the courtyard of the Hotel de l'Europe, and rushing down the street to see St Wulfran again before the sun was off the towers, are things to cherish the past for,—to the end.

182. Of Rouen, and its Cathedral, my saying remains yet to be said, if days be given me, in 'Our Fathers have told us.'* The sight of them, and following journey up the Seine to Paris, then to Soissons and Rheims, determined as aforesaid, the first centre and circle of future life-work. Beyond Rheims, at Bar-le-Duc, I was brought again within the greater radius of the Alps, and my father was kind enough to go down by Plombiéres to Dijon, that I might approach them by the straightest pass of Jura.

The reader must pardon my relating so much as I think he may care to hear of this journey of 1835, rather as what *used* to happen, than as limitable to that date; for it is extremely difficult for me now to separate the circumstances of any one journey from those of subsequent days, in which we stayed at the same inns, with variation only from the blue room to the green, saw the same sights, and rejoiced the more in every pleasure—that it was not new.

And this latter part of the road from Paris to Geneva, beautiful without being the least terrific or pathetic, but in the most lovable and cheerful way, became afterwards so dear and so domestic to me, that I will not attempt here to check my gossip of it.

183. We used always to drive out of the yard of La Cloche at Dijon in early morning—seven, after joyful breakfast at half-past six. The small saloon on the first floor to the front had a bedroom across the passage at the west end of it, whose windows commanded the cathedral towers over a low roof on the opposite side of the street. This was always mine, and its bed was in an alcove at the back, separated only by a lath partition from an extremely narrow passage leading from the outer gallery to Anne's room. It was a delight for Anne to which I think she looked forward all across France, to open a little hidden door from this passage, at the back of the alcove exactly above my pillow, and surprise, or wake, me in the morning.

I think I only remember once starting in rain. Usually the morning sun shone through the misty spray and far thrown diamonds of the fountain in the south-eastern suburb, and threw long poplar shadows across the road to Genlis.

Genlis, Auxonne, Dole, Mont-sous-Vaudrey—three stages of 12 or 14 kilometres each, two of 18; in all about 70 kilometres = 42 miles, from Dijon gate to Jura foot—we went straight for the hills always, lunching on French plums and bread.

Level plain of little interest to Auxonne. I used to wonder how any mortal creature could be content to live within actual sight of Jura, and never go to see them, all their lives! At Auxonne, cross the Saone, wide and beautiful in clear shallows of green stream—little more, yet, than a noble mountain torrent; one saw in an instant it came from Jura. Another hour of patience, and from the broken yellow limestone slopes of Dole—there, at last, they were—the long blue surges of them fading as far as eye could see to the south, more abruptly near to the north-east, where the bold outlier, almost island, of them, rises like a precipitous Wrekin, above Salins. Beyond Dole, a new wildness comes into the more undulating country, notable chiefly for its clay-built cottages with enormously high thatched gables of roof. Strange, that I never inquired into the special reason of that form, nor looked into a single cottage to see the mode of its inhabitation!

184. The village, or rural town, of Poligny, clustered out of well-built old stone houses, with gardens and orchards; and gathering at the midst of it into some pretence or manner of a street, straggles along the roots of Jura at the opening of a little valley, which in Yorkshire or Derbyshire limestone would have been a gorge between nodding cliffs, with a pretty pattering stream at the bottom: but, in Jura is a far retiring theatre of rising terraces, with bits of field and garden getting foot on them at various heights; a spiry convent in its hollow, and well-built little nests of husbandry-building set in corners of meadow, and on juts of rock;—no stream, to speak of, nor springs in it, nor the smallest conceivable reason for its being there, but that God made it.

'Far' retiring, I said,—perhaps a mile into the hills from the outer plain, by half a mile across, permitting the main road from Paris to Geneva to serpentine and zigzag capriciously up the cliff terraces with innocent engineering, finding itself every now and then where it had no notion of getting to, and looking, in a circumflex of puzzled level, where it was to go next;—retrospect of the plain of Burgundy enlarging under its backward sweeps, till at last, under a broken bit of steep final crag, it got quite up the side, and out over the edge of the ravine, where said ravine closes as unreasonably as it had opened, and the surprised traveller finds himself, magically as if he were Jack of the Beanstalk, in a new plain of an upper world. A world of level rock, breaking at the surface into yellow soil, capable of scanty, but healthy, turf, and sprinkled copse and thicket; with here and there, beyond, a blue surge of pines, and over those, if the evening or morning were clear, always one small bright silvery likeness of a cloud.

185. These first tracts of Jura differ in many pleasant ways from the limestone levels round Ingleborough, which are their English types. The Yorkshire moors are mostly by a hundred or two feet higher, and exposed to drift of rain under violent, nearly constant, wind. They break

into wide fields of loose blocks, and rugged slopes of shale; and are mixed with sands and clay from the millstone grit, which nourish rank grass, and lodge in occasional morass: the wild winds also forbidding any vestige or comfort of tree, except here and there in a sheltered nook of new plantation. But the Jura sky is as calm and clear as that of the rest of France; if the day is bright on the plain, the bounding hills are bright also; the Jura rock, balanced in the make of it between chalk and marble, weathers indeed into curious rifts and furrows, but rarely breaks loose, and has long ago clothed itself either with forest flowers, or with sweet short grass, and all blossoms that love sunshine. The pure air, even on this lower ledge of a thousand feet above sea, cherishes their sweetest scents and liveliest colours, and the winter gives them rest under thawless serenity of snow.

186. A still greater and stranger difference exists in the system of streams. For all their losing themselves and hiding, and intermitting, their presence is distinctly felt on a Yorkshire moor; one sees the places they have been in yesterday, the wells where they will flow after the next shower, and a tricklet here at the bottom of a crag, or a tinkle there from the top of it, is always making one think whether this is one of the sources of Aire, or rootlets of Ribble, or beginnings of Bolton Strid, or threads of silver which are to be spun into Tees.

But no whisper, nor murmur, nor patter, nor song, of streamlet disturbs the enchanted silence of open Jura. The rain-cloud clasps her cliffs, and floats along her fields; it passes, and in an hour the rocks are dry, and only beads of dew left in the Alchemilla leaves,—but of rivulet, or brook,—no vestige yesterday, or to-day, or to-morrow. Through unseen fissures and filmy crannies the waters of cliff and plain have alike vanished, only far down in the depths of the main valley glides the strong river, unconscious of change.

187. One is taught thus much for one's earliest lesson, in the two stages from Poligny to Champagnole, level over the absolutely crisp turf and sun-bright rock, without so much water anywhere as a cress could grow in, or a tadpole wag his tail in,—and then, by a zigzag of shady road, forming the Park and Boulevard of the wistful little village, down to the single arched bridge that leaps the Ain, which pauses underneath in magnificent pools of clear pale green: the green of spring leaves; then clashes into foam, half weir, half natural cascade, and into a confused race of currents beneath hollow overhanging of crag festooned with leafage. The only marvel is, to anyone knowing Jura structure, that rivers should be visible anywhere at all, and that the rocks should be consistent enough to carry them in open air through the

great valleys, without perpetual 'pertes'* like that of the Rhone. Below the Lac de Joux the Orbe thus loses itself indeed, reappearing seven hundred feet[1] beneath in a scene of which I permit myself to quote my Papa Saussure's description.

188. 'A semicircular rock at least two hundred feet high, composed of great horizontal rocks hewn vertical, and divided[2] by ranks of pine which grow on their projecting ledges, closes to the west the valley of Valorbe. Mountains yet more elevated and covered with forests, form a circuit round this rock, which opens only to give passage to the Orbe, whose source is at its foot. Its waters, of a perfect limpidity, flow at first with a majestic tranquillity upon a bed tapestried with beautiful green moss (Fontinalis antipyretica), but soon, drawn into a steep slope, the thread of the current breaks itself in foam against the rocks which occupy the middle of its bed, while the borders, less agitated, flowing always on their green ground, set off the whiteness of the midst of the river; and thus it withdraws itself from sight, in following the course of a deep valley covered with pines, whose blackness is rendered more striking by the vivid green of the beeches which are scattered among them.

'Ah, if Petrarch had seen this spring and had found there his Laura, how much would not he have preferred it to that of Vaucluse, more abundant, perhaps, and more rapid, but of which the sterile rocks have neither the greatness of ours, nor the rich parure, which embellishes them.'

I have never seen the source of the Orbe, but would commend to the reader's notice the frequent beauty of these great springs in literally *rising* at the base of cliffs, instead of falling, as one would have imagined likely, out of clefts in the front of them. In our own English anti-type of the source of Orbe, Malham Cove, the flow of water is, in like manner, wholly at the base of the rock, and seems to rise to the ledge of its outlet from a deeper interior pool.

189. The old Hotel de la Poste at Champagnole stood just above the bridge of Ain, opposite the town, where the road got level again as it darted away towards Geneva. I think the year 1842 was the first in which we lengthened the day from Dijon by the two stages beyond Poligny; but afterwards, the Hotel de la Poste at Champagnole became a kind of home to us: going out, we had so much delight there, and coming home, so many thoughts, that a great space of life seemed to be

---

[1] Six hundred and eighty French feet. Saussure, §§ 385.
[2] 'Taillés à pic, et entrecoupées.'*

passed in its peace. No one was ever in the house but ourselves; if a family stopped every third day or so, it was enough to maintain the inn, which, besides, had its own farm; and those who did stop, rushed away for Geneva early in the morning. We, who were to sleep again at Morez, were in no hurry; and in returning always left Geneva on Friday, to get the Sunday at Champagnole.

190. But my own great joy was in the early June evening, when we had arrived from Dijon, and I got out after the quickly dressed trout and cutlet for the first walk on rock and under pine.

With all my Tory prejudice (I mean, principle), I have to confess that one great joy of Swiss—above all, Jurassic Swiss—ground to me, is in its effectual, not merely theoretic, *liberty*. Among the greater hills, one can't always go just where one chooses,—all around is the too far, or too steep,—one wants to get to this, and climb that, and can't do either;—but in Jura one can go every way, and be happy everywhere. Generally, if there was time, I used to climb the islet of crag to the north of the village, on which there are a few grey walls of ruined castle, and the yet traceable paths of its 'pleasance,' whence to look if the likeness of white cloud were still on the horizon. Still there, in the clear evening, and again and again, each year more marvellous to me; the derniers rochers, and calotte* of Mont Blanc. Only those; that is to say just as much as may be seen over the Dome du Gouté from St Martin's. But it looks as large from Champagnole as it does there—glowing in the last light like a harvest moon.

If there were not time to reach the castle rock, at least I could get into the woods above the Ain, and gather my first Alpine flowers. Again and again, I feel the duty of gratitude to the formalities and even vulgarities of Herne Hill, for making me to feel by contrast the divine wildness of Jura forest.

Then came the morning drive into the higher glen of the Ain, where the road began first to wind beside the falling stream. One never understands how those winding roads steal with their tranquil slope from height to height; it was but an hour's walking beside the carriage,—an hour passed like a minute; and one emerged on the high plain of St Laurent, and the gentians began to gleam among the roadside grass, and the pines swept round the horizon with the dark infinitude of ocean.

191. All Switzerland was there in hope and sensation, and what was less than Switzerland was in some sort better, in its meek simplicity and healthy purity. The Jura cottage is not carved with the stately richness of the Bernese, nor set together with the antique strength of Uri.

It is covered with thin slit fine shingles, side-roofed as it were to the ground for mere dryness' sake, a little crossing of laths here and there underneath the window its only ornament. It has no daintiness of garden nor wealth of farm about it,—is indeed little more than a delicately-built chalet, yet trim and domestic, mildly intelligent of things other than pastoral, watch-making and the like, though set in the midst of the meadows, the gentian at its door, the lily of the valley wild in the copses hard by.

My delight in these cottages, and in the sense of human industry and enjoyment through the whole scene, was at the root of all pleasure in its beauty; see the passage afterwards written in the 'Seven Lamps' insisting on this as if it were general to human nature thus to admire through sympathy.* I have noticed since, with sorrowful accuracy, how many people there are who, wherever they find themselves, think only 'of their position.' But the feeling which gave me so much happiness, both then and through life, differed also curiously, in its impersonal character, from that of many even of the best and kindest persons.

192. In the beginning of the Carlyle-Emerson correspondence, edited with too little comment by my dear friend Charles Norton, I find at page 18 this—to me entirely disputable, and to my thought, so far as undisputed, much blameable and pitiable—exclamation of my master's: 'Not till we can think that here and there one is thinking of us, one is loving us, does this waste earth become a peopled garden.'* My training, as the reader has perhaps enough perceived, produced in me the precisely opposite sentiment. *My* times of happiness had always been when *nobody* was thinking of me; and the main discomfort and drawback to all proceedings and designs, the attention and interference of the public—represented by my mother and the gardener. The garden was no waste place to me, because I did not suppose myself an object of interest either to the ants or the butterflies; and the only qualification of the entire delight of my evening walk at Champagnole or St Laurent was the sense that my father and mother *were* thinking of me, and would be frightened if I was five minutes late for tea.

I don't mean in the least that I could have done without them. They were, to me, much more than Carlyle's wife to him;* and if Carlyle had written, instead of, that he wanted Emerson to think of him in America, that he wanted his father and mother to be thinking of him at Ecclefechan, it had been well. But that the rest of the world was waste to him unless he had admirers in it, is a sorry state of sentiment enough; and I am somewhat tempted, for once, to admire the exactly opposite temper of my own solitude. My entire delight was in observing without being myself noticed,—if I could have been invisible, all the better. I was absolutely interested in men and their ways, as I was interested in marmots and chamois, in tomtits and trout. If only they would stay still and let me look at them, and not get into their holes and up their heights! The living inhabitation of the world—the grazing and nesting in it,—the spiritual power of the air, the rocks, the waters, to be in the midst of it, and rejoice and wonder at it, and help it if I could,— happier if it needed no help of mine,—this was the essential love *of Nature* in me, this the root of all that I have usefully become, and the light of all that I have rightly learned.

193. Whether we slept at St Laurent or Morez, the morning of the next day was an eventful one. In ordinarily fine weather, the ascent from Morez to Les Rousses, walked most of the way, was mere enchantment; so also breakfast, and fringed-gentian gathering, at Les Rousses. Then came usually an hour of tortured watching the increase of the noon clouds; for, however early we had risen, it was impossible to reach the Col de la Faucille before, two o'clock, or later if we had bad horses, and at two o'clock, if there are clouds above Jura, there will be assuredly clouds on the Alps.

It is worth notice, Saussure himself not having noticed it, that this main pass of Jura, unlike the great passes of the Alps, reaches its traverse-point very nearly under the highest summit of that part of the chain. The col, separating the source of the Bienne, which runs down to Morez and St Claude, from that of the Valserine, which winds through the midst of Jura to the Rhone at Bellegarde, is a spur of the Dole itself, under whose prolonged masses the road is then carried six miles farther, ascending very slightly to the Col de la Faucille, where the chain opens suddenly, and a sweep of the road, traversed in five minutes at a trot, opens the whole Lake of Geneva, and the chain of the Alps along a hundred miles of horizon.

194. I have never seen that view perfectly but once—in this year 1835; when I drew it carefully in my then fashion, and have been content to look back to it as the confirming sequel of the first view of the Alps from Schaffhausen. Very few travellers, even in old times, saw it at all; tired of the long posting journey from Paris, by the time they got to the col they were mostly thinking only of their dinners and rest at Geneva; the guide books said nothing about it; and though, for everybody, it was an inevitable task to ascend the Righi, nobody ever thought there was anything to be seen from the Dole.

Both mountains have had enormous influence on my whole life;—the Dole continually and calmly; the Righi at sorrowful intervals, as will be seen.* But the Col de la Faucille, on that day of 1835, opened to me in distinct vision the Holy Land of my future work and true home in this world. My eyes had been opened, and my heart with them, to see and to possess royally such a kingdom! Far as the eye could reach—that land and its moving or pausing waters; Arve, and his gates of Cluse, and his glacier fountains; Rhone, and the infinitude of his sapphire lake,—his peace beneath the narcissus meads of Vevay—his cruelty beneath the promontories of Sierre. And all that rose against and melted into the sky, of mountain and mountain snow; and all that living plain, burning with human gladness—studded with white homes,—a milky way of star-dwellings cast across its sunlit blue.

CHAPTER X

QUEM TU, MELPOMENE*

195. WHETHER in the biography of a nation, or of a single person, it is alike impossible to trace it steadily through successive years. Some forces are failing while others strengthen, and most act irregularly, or else at uncorresponding periods of renewed enthusiasm after intervals of lassitude. For all clearness of exposition, it is necessary to follow first one, then another, without confusing notices of what is happening in other directions.

I must accordingly cease talk of pictorial and rhythmic efforts of the year 1835, at this point; and go back to give account of another segment of my learning, which might have had better consequence than ever came of it, had the stars so pleased.

196. I cannot, and perhaps the reader will be thankful, remember anything of the Apolline instincts under which I averred to incredulous papa and mamma that, 'though I could not speak, I could play upon the fiddle.' But even to this day, I look back with starts of sorrow to a lost opportunity of showing what was in me, of that manner of genius, on the occasion of a grand military dinner in the state room of the Sussex, at Tunbridge Wells; where, when I was something about eight or nine years old, we were staying in an unadventurous manner, enjoying the pantiles,* the common, the sight, if not the taste, of the lovely fountain, and drives to the High Rocks. After the military dinner there was military music, and by connivance of waiters, Anne and I got in, some-how, mixed up with the dessert. I believe I was rather a pretty boy then, and dressed in a not wholly civilian manner, in a sort of laced and

buttoned surtout.* My mind was extremely set on watching the instrumental manœuvres of the band,—with admiration of all, but burning envy of the drummer.

The colonel took notice of my rapt attention, and sent an ensign to bring me round to him; and after getting, I know not how, at my mind in the matter, told me I might go and ask the drummer to give me his lovely round-headed sticks, and he would. I was in two minds to do it, having good confidence in my powers of keeping time. But the dismal shyness conquered:—I shook my head woefully, and my musical career was blighted. No one will ever know what I could then have brought out of that drum, or (if my father had perchance taken me to Spain) out of a tambourine.

197. My mother, busy in graver matters, had never cultivated the little she had been taught of music, though her natural sensibility to it was great. Mrs Richard Gray used sometimes to play gracefully to me, but if ever she struck a false note, her husband used to put his fingers in his ears, and dance about the room, exclaiming, 'O Mary, Mary dear!' and so extinguish her. Our own Perth Mary played dutifully her scales, and little more; but I got useful help, almost unconsciously, from a family of young people who ought, if my chronology had been systematic, to have been affectionately spoken of long ago.

In above describing my father's counting-house, I said the door was opened by a latch pulled by the head clerk. This head clerk, or, putting it more modestly, topmost of two clerks, Henry Watson, was a person of much import in my father's life and mine; import which, I perceive, looking back, to have been as in many respects tender and fortunate, yet in others extremely doleful, both to us and himself.

The chief fault in my father's mind, (I say so reverently, for its faults, were few, but necessarily, for they were very fatal,) was his dislike of being excelled. He knew his own power—felt that he had not nerve to use or display it, in full measure; but all the more, could not bear, in his own sphere, any approach to equality. He chose his clerks first for trustworthiness, secondly for—*in*capacity. I am not sure that he would have sent away a clever one, if he had chanced on such a person; but he assuredly did not look for mercantile genius in them, but rather for subordinates who would be subordinate for ever. Frederick the Great chose his clerks in the same way; but then, his clerks never supposed themselves likely to be king, while a merchant's clerks are apt to hope they may at least become partners, if not successors. Also, Friedrich's clerks were absolutely fit for *their* business; but my father's clerks were, in many ways, utterly unfit for theirs. Of which unfitness my father greatly complaining, nevertheless by no means bestirred himself to find fitter ones. He used to send Henry Watson on business tours, and assure him afterwards that he had done more harm than good: he would now and then leave Henry Ritchie to write a business letter; and, I think, find with some satisfaction that it was needful afterwards to write two, himself, in correction of it. There was scarcely a day when he did not come home in some irritation at something that one or other of them had done, or not done. But they stayed with him till his death.

198. Of the second in command, Mr Ritchie, I will say what is needful in another place,* but the clerk of confidence, Henry Watson, has already been left unnoticed too long. He was, I believe, the principal support of a widowed mother and three grown-up sisters, amiable, well educated, and fairly sensible women, all of them; refined beyond the average tone of their position,—and desirous, not vulgarly, of keeping themselves in the upper-edge circle of the middle class. Not vulgarly, I say, as caring merely to have carriages stopping at their door, but with real sense of the good that *is* in good London society, in London society's way. They liked, as they did not drop their own h's,* to talk with people who did not drop theirs; to hear what was going on in polite circles; and to have *entrée* to a pleasant dance, or rightly given concert. Being themselves both good and pleasing musicians, (the qualities are not united in all musicians,) this was not difficult for them;—nevertheless it meant necessarily having a house in a street of tone, near the Park, and being nicely dressed, and giving now and then a little reception themselves. On the whole, it meant the total absorption of Henry's salary, and of the earnings, in some official, or otherwise plumaged occupations, of two brothers besides, David and William. The latter, now I think of it, was a West-End wine merchant,* supplying the nobility with Clos-Vougeot, Hochheimer, dignifiedly still Champagne,* and other nectareous drinks, of which the bottom fills up half the bottle, and which are only to be had out of the cellars of Grand Dukes and Counts of the Empire. The family lived, to the edge of their means,—not too narrowly: the young ladies enjoyed themselves, studied German—and at that time it was thought very fine and poetical to study German;—sang extremely well, gracefully and easily; had good taste in dress, the better for being a little matronly and old-fashioned: and the whole family thought themselves extremely *élite*, in a substantial and virtuous manner.

199. When Henry Watson was first taken, (then, I believe, a boy of sixteen,) I know not by what chance, or on what commendation, into my father's counting-house, the opening was thought by his family

a magnificent one; they were very thankful and happy, and, of course, in their brother's interest, eager to do all they could to please my father and mother. They found, however, my mother not very easily pleased; and presently began themselves to be not a little surprised and *dis*pleased by the way things went on, both in the counting-house and at Herne Hill. At the one, there was steady work; at the other, little show: the clerks could by no means venture to leave their desks for a garden-party, and after dark were allowed only tallow candles. That the head of the Firm should live in the half of a party-walled house, beyond the suburb of Camberwell, was a degradation and disgrace to everybody connected with the business! and that Henry should be obliged every morning to take omnibus into the eastern City, and work within scent of Billingsgate, instead of walking elegantly across Piccadilly to an office in St James's Street, was alike injurious to him, and disparaging to my father's taste and knowledge of the world. Also, to the feminine circle, my mother was a singular, and sorrowfully intractable, phenomenon. Taking herself no interest in German studies, and being little curious as to the events, and little respectful to the opinions, of Mayfair, she was apt to look with some severity, perhaps a tinge of jealousy, on what she thought pretentious in the accomplishments, or affected in the manners, of the young people: while they, on the other hand, though quite sensible of my mother's worth, grateful for her good will, and in time really attached to her, were not disposed to pay much attention to the opinions of a woman who knew only her own language;—and were more restive than responsive under kindnesses which frequently took the form of advice.

200. These differences in feeling, irreconcilable though they were, did not hinder the growth of consistently pleasant and sincerely affectionate relations between my mother and the young housewives. With what best of girl nature was in them, Fanny, Helen, and foolishest, cleverest little Juliet, enjoyed, in spring time, exchanging for a day or two the dusty dignity of their street of tone in Mayfair for the lilacs and laburnums of Herne-hill: and held themselves, with their brother Henry, always ready at call to come out on any occasion of the hill's hospitality to some respected correspondent of the House, and sing to us the prettiest airs from the new opera, with a due foundation and tonic intermixture of classical German.

Henry had a singularly beautiful tenor voice; and the three sisters, though not, any one of them, of special power, sang their parts with sufficient precision, with intelligent taste, and with the pretty unison of sisterly voices. In this way, from early childhood, I was accustomed to hear a great range of good music completely and rightly rendered, without breakings down, missings out, affectations of manner, or vulgar prominence of execution. Had the quartette sung me English glees, or Scotch ballads, or British salt water ones, or had any one of the girls had gift enough to render higher music with its proper splendour, I might easily have been led to spare some time from my maps and mineralogy for attentive listening. As it was, the scientific German compositions were simply tiresome to me, and the pretty modulations of Italian, which I understood no syllable of, pleasant only as the trills of the blackbirds, who often listened, and expressed their satisfaction by joining in the part-songs through the window that opened to the back garden in the spring evenings. Yet the education of my ear and taste went on without trouble of mine. I do not think I ever heard any masterly professional music, until, as good hap was, I heard the best, only to *be* heard during a narrow space of those young days.

201. I too carelessly left without explanation the casual sentence about 'fatal dinner at Mr Domecq's' when I was fourteen, above, Chap. IV., p. 55. My father's Spanish partner was at that time living in the Champs Elysées, with his English wife and his five daughters; the eldest, Diana, on the eve of her marriage with one of Napoleon's officers, Count Maison; the four others, much younger, chanced to be at home on vacation from their convent school: and we had happy family dinner with them, and mamma and the girls and a delightful old French gentleman, Mr Badell, played afterwards at 'la toilette de Madame'* with me; only I couldn't remember whether I was the necklace or the garters; and then Clotilde and Cécile played 'les Echos' and other fascinations of dance-melody,—only I couldn't dance; and at last Elise had to take pity on me as above described. But the best, if not the largest, part of the conversation among the elders was of the recent death of Bellini, the sorrow of all Paris for him, and the power with which his 'I Puritani' was being rendered by the reigning four great singers for whom it was written.*

202. It puzzles me that I have no recollection of any first sight and hearing of an opera. Not even, for that matter, of my first going to a theatre, though I was full twelve, before being taken; and afterwards, it was a matter of intense rapture, of a common sort, to be taken to a pantomime. And I greatly enjoy theatre to this day—it is one of the pleasures that have least worn out; yet, while I remember Friar's Crag at Derwentwater when I was four years old, and the courtyard of our Paris inn at five, I have no memory whatever, and am a little proud to have none, of my first theatre. To be taken now at Paris to the feebly

dramatic 'Puritani' was no great joy to me; but I then heard, and it will always be a rare, and only once or twice in a century possible, thing to hear, four great musicians, all rightly to be called of genius, singing together, with sincere desire to assist each other, not eclipse; and to exhibit, not only their own power of singing, but the beauty of the music they sang.

203. Still more fortunately it happened that a woman of *faultless* genius led the following dances,—Taglioni;* a person of the highest natural faculties, and stainlessly simple character, gathered with sincerest ardour and reverence into her art. My mother, though she allowed me without serious remonstrance to be taken to the theatre by my father, had the strictest Puritan prejudice against the stage; yet enjoyed it so much that I think she felt the sacrifice she made in not going with us to be a sort of price accepted by the laws of virtue for what was sinful in her concession to my father and me. She went, however, to hear and see this group of players, renowned, without any rivals, through all the cities of Europe;—and, strange and pretty to say, her instinct of the innocence, beauty, and wonder, in every motion of the Grace of her century, was so strong, that from that time forth my mother would always, at a word, go with us to see Taglioni.

Afterwards, a season did not pass without my hearing twice or thrice, at least, those four singers; and I learned the better because my ear was never jaded the intention of the music written for them, or studied by them; and am extremely glad now that I heard *their* renderings of Mozart and Rossini, neither of whom can be now said ever to be heard at all, owing to the detestable quickening of the time. Grisi and Malibran sang at least one third slower than any modern cantatrice;[1] and Patti, the last time I heard her, massacred Zerlina's part in 'La ci darem,' as if the audience and she had but the one object of getting Mozart's air done with, as soon as possible.*

204. Afterwards, (the confession may as well be got over at once,) when I had got settled in my furrow at Christ Church, it chanced that the better men of the college had founded a musical society, under instruction of the cathedral organist, Mr Marshall, an extremely simple, good-natured, and good-humoured person, by whose encouragement I was brought to the point of trying to learn to sing, 'Come mai posso vivere se Rosina non m'ascolta,' and to play the two lines of prelude to the 'A te o cara,'* and what notes I could manage to read of

---

[1] It is a pretty conceit of musical people to call themselves scientific, when they have not yet fixed their unit of time!

accompaniments to other songs of similarly tender purport. In which, though never even getting so far as to read with ease, I nevertheless, between my fine rhythmic ear, and true lover's sentiment, got to understand some principles of musical art, which I shall perhaps be able to enforce with benefit on the musical public mind, even to-day, if only I can get first done with this autobiography.*

What the furrow at Christ Church was to be like, or where to lead, none of my people seem at this time to have been thinking. My mother, watching the naturalistic and methodic bent of me, was, I suppose, tranquil in the thought of my becoming another White of Selborne, or Vicar of Wakefield, victorious in Whistonian,* and every other controversy. My father perhaps conceived more cometic* or meteoric career for me, but neither of them put the matter seriously in hand, however deeply laid up in heart: and I was allowed without remonstrance to go on measuring the blue of the sky, and watching the flight of the clouds, till I had forgotten most of the Latin I ever knew, and all the Greek, except Anacreon's ode to the rose.

205. Some little effort was made to pull me together in 1836 by sending me to hear Mr Dale's lectures at King's College, where I explained to Mr Dale, on meeting him one day in the court of entrance, that porticoes should not be carried on the top of arches; and considered myself exalted because I went in at the same door with boys who had square caps on.* The lectures were on early English literature, of which, though I had never read a word of any before Pope, I thought myself already a much better judge than Mr Dale. His quotation of 'Knut the king came sailing by'* stayed with me; and I think that was about all I learnt during the summer. For, as my adverse stars would have it, that year, my father's partner, Mr Domecq, thought it might for once be expedient that he should himself pay a complimentary round of visits to his British customers, and asked if meanwhile he might leave his daughters at Herne Hill to see the lions at the Tower, and so on. How we got them all into Herne Hill corners and cupboards would be inexplicable but with a plan of the three stories! The arrangements were half Noah's ark, half Doll's house, but we got them all in: Clotilde, a graceful oval-faced blonde of fifteen; Cécile, a dark, finely-browed, beautifully-featured girl of thirteen; Elise, again fair, round-faced like an English girl, a treasure of good nature and good sense; Caroline, a delicately quaint little thing of eleven. They had all been born abroad, Clotilde at Cadiz, and of course convent-bred; but lately accustomed to be much in society during vacation at Paris. Deeper than any one dreamed, the sight of them in the Champs Elysées had

sealed itself in me, for they were the first well-bred and well-dressed girls I had ever seen—or at least spoken to. I mean of course, by well-dressed, perfectly simply dressed, with Parisian cutting and fitting. They were all 'bigoted'—as Protestants would say; quietly firm, as they ought to say—Roman Catholics; spoke Spanish and French with perfect grace, and English with broken precision: were all fairly sensible, Clotilde sternly and accurately so, Elise gaily and kindly, Cécile serenely, Caroline keenly. A most curious galaxy, or southern cross,* of unconceived stars, floating on a sudden into my obscure firmament of London suburb.

206. How my parents could allow their young novice to be cast into the fiery furnace of the outer world in this helpless manner the reader may wonder, and only the Fates know; but there was this excuse for them, that they had never seen me the least interested or anxious about girls—never caring to stay in the promenades at Cheltenham or Bath, or on the parade at Dover; on the contrary, growling and mewing if I was ever kept there, and off to the sea or the fields the moment I got leave; and they had educated me in such extremely orthodox English Toryism and Evangelicalism that they could not conceive their scientific, religious, and George the Third revering youth, wavering in his constitutional balance towards French Catholics.* And I had never *said* anything about the Champs Elysées! Virtually convent-bred more closely than the maids themselves, without a single sisterly or cousinly affection for refuge or lightning rod, and having no athletic skill or pleasure to check my dreaming, I was thrown, bound hand and foot, in my unaccomplished simplicity, into the fiery furnace, or fiery cross, of these four girls,—who of course reduced me to a mere heap of white ashes in four days. Four days, at the most, it took to reduce me to ashes, but the Mercredi des cendres* lasted four years.

Anything more comic in the externals of it, anything more tragic in the essence, could not have been invented by the skilfullest designer in either kind. In my social behaviour and mind I was a curious combination of Mr Traddles, Mr Toots, and Mr Winkle.* I had the real fidelity and single-mindedness of Mr Traddles, with the conversational abilities of Mr Toots, and the heroic ambition of Mr Winkle;—all these illuminated by imagination like Mr Copperfield's, at his first Norwood dinner.*

207. Clotilde (Adèle Clotilde in full, but her sisters called her Clotilde, after the queen-saint, and I Adèle, because it rhymed to shell, spell, and knell) was only made more resplendent by the circlet of her sisters' beauty; while my own shyness and unpresentableness were

farther stiffened, or rather sanded, by a patriotic and Protestant conceit, which was tempered neither by politeness nor sympathy; that,
while in company I sate jealously miserable like a stock fish (in truth,
I imagine, looking like nothing so much as a skate in an aquarium trying to get up the glass), on any blessed occasion of tête-à-tête I endeavoured to entertain my Spanish-born, Paris-bred, and Catholic-hearted
mistress with my own views upon the subjects of the Spanish Armada,
the Battle of Waterloo, and the doctrine of Transubstantiation.*

To these modes of recommending myself, however, I did not fail to
add what display I could make of the talents I supposed myself to possess. I wrote with great pains, and straining of my invention, a story
about Naples (which I had never seen), and 'the Bandit Leoni,' whom
I represented as typical of what my own sanguinary and adventurous
disposition would have been had I been brought up a bandit; and 'the
Maiden Giuletta,' in whom I portrayed all the perfections of my mistress. Our connection with Messrs Smith & Elder enabled me to get
this story printed in 'Friendship's Offering;'* and Adèle laughed over
it in rippling ecstasies of derision, of which I bore the pain bravely, for
the sake of seeing her thoroughly amused.

I dared not address any sonnets straight to herself; but when she
went back to Paris, wrote her a French letter seven quarto pages long,
descriptive of the desolations and solitudes of Herne Hill since her
departure. This letter, either Elise or Caroline wrote to tell me she had
really read, and 'laughed immensely at the French of.' Both Caroline
and Elise pitied me a little, and did not like to say she had also laughed
at the contents.

208. The old people, meanwhile, saw little harm in all this.
Mr Domecq, who was extremely good-natured, and a good judge of
character, rather liked me, because he saw that I was good-natured
also, and had some seedling brains, which would come up in time: in
the interests of the business he was perfectly ready to give me any of his
daughters I liked, who could also be got to like me, but considered that
the time was not come to talk of such things. My father was entirely of
the same mind, besides being pleased at my getting a story printed in
'Friendship's Offering,' glad that I saw something of girls with good
manners, and in hopes that if I wrote poetry about them, it might be as
good as the *Hours of Idleness*.* My mother, who looked upon the idea of
my marrying a Roman Catholic as too monstrous to be possible in the
decrees of Heaven, and too preposterous to be even guarded against on
earth, was rather annoyed at the whole business, as she would have
been if one of her chimneys had begun smoking,—but had not the

slightest notion her house was on fire. She saw more, however, than my father, into the depth of the feeling, but did not, in her motherly tenderness, like to grieve me by any serious check to it. She hoped, when the Domecqs went back to Paris, we might see no more of them, and that Adèle's influence and memory would pass away—with next winter's snow.

209. Under these indulgent circumstances,—bitterly ashamed of the figure I had made, but yet not a whit dashed back out of my daily swelling foam of furious conceit, supported as it was by real depth of feeling, and (note it well, good reader) by a true and glorious sense of the newly revealed miracle of human love, in its exaltation of the physical beauty of the world I had till then sought by its own light alone,—I set myself in that my seventeenth year, in a state of majestic imbecility, to write a tragedy on a Venetian subject, in which the sorrows of my soul were to be enshrined in immortal verse,—the fair heroine, Bianca, was to be endowed with the perfections of Desdemona and the brightness of Juliet,—and Venice and Love were to be described, as never had been thought of before. I may note in passing, that on my first sight of the Ducal Palace, the year before, I had deliberately announced to my father and mother, and—it seemed to me stupidly incredulous—Mary, that I meant to make such a drawing of the Ducal Palace as never had been made before. This I proceeded to perform by collecting some hasty memoranda on the spot, and finishing my design elaborately out of my head at Treviso. The drawing still exists,—for a wonder, out of perspective, which I had now got too conceited to follow the rules of,—and with the diaper pattern of the red and white marbles represented as a bold panelling in relief. No figure disturbs the solemn tranquillity of the Riva, and the gondolas—each in the shape of a Turkish crescent standing on its back on the water—float about without the aid of gondoliers.

I remember nothing more of that year, 1836,* than sitting under the mulberry tree in the back garden, writing my tragedy. I forget whether we went travelling or not, or what I did in the rest of the day. It is all now blank to me, except Venice, Bianca, and looking out over Shooter's Hill, where I could see the last turn of the road to Paris.

Some Greek, though I don't know what, must have been read, and some mathematics, for I certainly knew the difference between a square and cube root when I went to Oxford, and was put by my tutor into Herodotus,* out of whom I immediately gathered materials enough to write my Scythian drinking song, in imitation of the *Giaour*.

210. The reflective reader can scarcely but have begun to doubt, by

this time, the accuracy of my statement that I took no harm from Byron. But he need not. The particular form of expression which my folly took was indeed directed by him; but this form was the best it could have taken. I got better practice in English by imitating the *Giaour* and *Bride of Abydos** than I could have had under any other master, (the tragedy was of course Shakespearian!) and the state of my mind was—my mind's own fault, and that of surrounding mischance or mismanagement—not Byron's. In that same year, 1836, I took to reading Shelley also, and wasted much time over the Sensitive Plant and Epipsychidion;* and I took a good deal of harm from *him*, in trying to write lines like 'prickly and pulpous and blistered and blue;'* or 'it was a little lawny islet by anemone and vi'let,—like mosaic paven,'* etc.; but in the state of frothy fever I was in, there was little good for me to be got out of anything. The perseverance with which I tried to wade through the Revolt of Islam,* and find out (I never did, and don't know to this day) who revolted against whom, or what, was creditable to me; and the Prometheus really made me understand something of Aeschylus*. I am not sure that, for what I was to turn out, my days of ferment could have been got over much easier: at any rate, it was better than if I had been learning to shoot, or hunt, or smoke, or gamble. The entirely inscrutable thing to me, looking back on myself, is my total want of all reason, will, or design in the business: I had neither the resolution to win Adèle, the courage to do without her, the sense to consider what was at last to come of it all, or the grace to think how disagreeable I was making myself at the time to everybody about me. There was really no more capacity nor intelligence in me than in a just fledged owlet, or just open-eyed puppy, disconsolate at the existence of the moon.

211. Out of my feebly melodious complaints to that luminary, however, I was startled by a letter to my father from Christ Church, advising him that there was room for my residence in the January term of 1837, and that I must come up to matriculate* in October of the instant year, 1836.

Strangely enough, my father had never enquired into the nature and manner of matriculation, till he took me up to display in Oxford;—he, very nearly as much a boy as I, for anything we knew of what we were about. He never had any doubt about putting me at the most fashionable college, and of course my name had been down at Christ Church* years before I was called up; but it had never dawned on my father's mind that there were two, fashionable and unfashionable, orders, or castes, of undergraduate at Christ Church, one of these being called

Gentlemen-Commoners, the other Commoners; and that these last seemed to occupy an almost bisectional point between the Gentlemen-Commoners and the Servitors. All these 'invidious' distinctions are now done away with in our Reformed University.* Nobody sets up for the special rank of a gentleman, but nobody will be set down as a commoner; and though, of the old people, anybody will beg or canvass for a place for their children in a charity school, everybody would be furious at the thought of his son's wearing, at college, the gown of a Servitor.

212. How far I agree with the modern British citizen in these lofty sentiments, my general writings have enough shown, but I leave the reader to form his own opinions without any contrary comment of mine, on the results of the exploded system of things in my own college life.

My father did not like the word 'commoner,'—all the less, because our relationships in general were not uncommon. Also, though himself satisfying his pride enough in being the head of the sherry trade, he felt and saw in his son powers which had not their full scope in the sherry trade. His ideal of my future,—now entirely formed in conviction of my genius,—was that I should enter at college into the best society, take all the prizes every year, and a double first to finish with; marry Lady Clara Vere de Vere; write poetry as good as Byron's, only pious; preach sermons as good as Bossuet's, only Protestant; be made, at forty, Bishop of Winchester, and at fifty, Primate of England.*

213. With all these hopes, and under all these temptations, my father was yet restrained and embarrassed in no small degree by his old and steady sense of what was becoming to his station in life: and he consulted anxiously, but honestly, the Dean of Christ Church, (Gaisford,) and my college tutor that was to be, Mr Walter Brown, whether a person in his position might without impropriety enter his son as a gentleman-commoner. I did not hear the dialogues, but the old Dean must have answered with a grunt, that my father had every right to make me a gentleman-commoner if he liked, and could pay the fees; the tutor, more attentively laying before him the conditions of the question, may perhaps have said, with courtesy, that it would be good for the college to have a reading man among the gentlemen-commoners, who, as a rule, were not studiously inclined; but he was compelled also to give my father a hint, that as far as my reading had already gone, it was not altogether certain I could pass the entrance examination which had to be sustained by commoners. This last suggestion was conclusive. It was not to be endured that the boy who had been expected to carry all before him, should get himself jammed in the first turnstile.

I was entered as a Gentleman-Commoner without farther debate, and remember still, as if it were yesterday, the pride of first walking out of the Angel Hotel, and past University College, holding my father's arm, in my velvet cap and silk gown.

214. Yes, good reader, the velvet and silk made a difference, not to my mother only, but to me! Quite one of the telling and weighty points in the home debates concerning this choice of Hercules,* had been that the commoner's gown was not only of ugly stuff, but had no flowing lines in it, and was virtually only a black rag tied to one's shoulders. One was thrice a gownsman in a flowing gown.

So little, indeed, am I disposed now in maturer years to deride these unphilosophical feelings, that instead of effacing distinction of dress at the University (except for the boating clubs), I would fain have seen them extended into the entire social order of the country. I think that nobody but duchesses should be allowed to wear diamonds; that lords should be known from common people by their stars, a quarter of a mile off; that every peasant girl should boast her county by some dainty ratification of cap or bodice; and that in the towns a vintner should be known from a fishmonger by the cut of his jerkin.

That walk to the Schools, and the waiting, outside the Divinity School, in comforting admiration of its door, my turn for matriculation, continue still for me, a pleasure. But I remember nothing more that year; nor anything of the first days of the next, until early in January we drove down to Oxford, only my mother and I, by the beautiful Henley road, weary a little as we changed horses for the last stage from Dorchester; solemnized, in spite of velvet and silk, as we entered among the towers in the twilight; and after one more rest under the domestic roof of the Angel, I found myself the next day at evening, alone, by the fireside, entered into command of my own life, in my own college room in Peckwater.

CHAPTER XI

CHRIST CHURCH CHOIR

215. ALONE, by the fireside of the little back room, which looked into the narrow lane, chiefly then of stabling, I sate collecting my resolution for college life.

I had not much to collect; nor, so far as I knew, much to collect it against. I had about as clear understanding of my whereabouts, or foresight of my fortune, as Davie Gellatly* might have had in my place; with these farther inferiorities to Davie, that I could neither dance, sing, nor roast eggs. There was not the slightest fear of my gambling, for I had never touched a card, and looked upon dice as people now do on dynamite. No fear of my being tempted by the strange woman, for was not I in love? and besides, never allowed to be out after half-past nine. No fear of my running in debt, for there were no Turners to be had in Oxford, and I cared for nothing else in the world of material possession. No fear of my breaking my neck out hunting, for I couldn't have ridden a hack down the High Street; and no fear of my ruining myself at a race, for I never had been but at one race in my life, and had not the least wish to win anybody else's money.

I expected some ridicule, indeed, for these my simple ways, but was safe against ridicule in my conceit: the only thing I doubted myself in, and very rightly, was the power of applying for three years to work in which I took not the slightest interest. I resolved, however, to do my parents and myself as much credit as I could, said my prayers very seriously, and went to bed in good hope.

216. And here I must stay, for a minute or two, to give some account of the state of mind I had got into during the above-described progress of my education, touching religious matters.

As far as I recollect, the steady Bible reading with my mother ended with our first continental journey, when I was fourteen; one could not read three chapters after breakfast while the horses were at the door. For this lesson was substituted my own private reading of a chapter, morning and evening, and, of course, saying the Lord's Prayer after it, and asking for everything that was nice for myself and my family; after which I waked or slept, without much thought of anything but my earthly affairs, whether by night or day.

It had never entered into my head to doubt a word of the Bible, though I saw well enough already that its words were to be understood otherwise than I had been taught; but the more I believed it, the less it did me any good. It was all very well for Abraham to do what angels bid him,*—so would I, if any angels bid me; but none had ever appeared to me that I knew of, not even Adèle, who couldn't be an angel because she was a Roman Catholic.

217. Also, if I had lived in Christ's time, of course I would have gone with Him up to the mountain, or sailed with Him on the Lake of Galilee;* but that was quite another thing from going to Beresford chapel, Walworth, or St Bride's, Fleet Street. Also, though I felt myself somehow called to imitate Christian in the *Pilgrim's Progress*,

I couldn't see that either Billiter Street and the Tower Wharf, where my father had his cellars, or the cherry-blossomed garden at Herne Hill, where my mother potted her flowers, could be places I was bound to fly from as in the City of Destruction.* Without much reasoning on the matter, I had virtually concluded from my general Bible reading that, never having meant or done any harm that I knew of, I could not be in danger of hell: while I saw also that even the crême de la crême of religious people seemed to be in no hurry to go to heaven. On the whole, it seemed to me, all that was required of *me* was to say my prayers, go to church, learn my lessons, obey my parents, and enjoy my dinner.

218. Thus minded, in the slowly granted light of the winter morning I looked out upon the view from my college windows, of Christ Church library and the smooth gravelled square of Peckwater, vexed a little because I was not in an oriel window looking out on a Gothic chapel:* but quite unconscious of the real condemnation I had fallen under, or of the loss that was involved to me in having nothing but Christ Church library, and a gravelled square, to see out of window during the spring-times of two years of youth.

At the moment I felt that, though dull, it was all very grand; and that the architecture, though Renaissance, was bold, learned, well-proportioned, and variously didactic. In reality, I might just as well have been sent to the dungeon of Chillon, except for the damp; better indeed, if I could have seen the three small trees from the window slit, and good groining and pavement, instead of the modern vulgar upholstery of my room furniture.

Even the first sight of college chapel* disappointed me, after the large churches abroad; but its narrow vaults had very different offices.

On the whole, of important places and services for the Christian souls of England, the choir* of Christ Church was at that epoch of English history virtually the navel, and seat of life. There remained in it the traditions of Saxon, Norman, Elizabethan, religion unbroken, —the memory of loyalty, the reality of learning, and, in nominal obedience at least, and in the heart of them with true docility, stood every morning, to be animated for the highest duties owed to their country, the noblest of English youth. The greater number of the peers of England, and as a rule, the best of her squirealty, passed necessarily through Christ Church.

The cathedral itself was an epitome of English history. Every stone, every pane of glass, every panel of woodwork, was true, and of its time,—not an accursed sham of architect's job. The first shrine of

St Frideswide* had indeed been destroyed, and her body rent and scattered on the dust by the Puritan; but her second shrine was still beautiful in its kind,—most lovely English work both of heart and hand. The Norman vaults above were true English Norman; bad and rude enough, but the best we could do with our own wits, and no French help. The roof was true Tudor,—grotesque, inventively constructive, delicately carved; it, with the roof of the hall staircase, summing the builder's skill of the fifteenth century.* The west window, with its clumsy painting of the Adoration of the Shepherds,* a monument of the transition from window to picture which ended in Dutch pictures of the cattle without either shepherds or Christ,—but still, the best men could do of the day; and the plain final woodwork of the stalls represented still the last art of living England in the form of honest and comfortable carpentry.

219. In this choir, written so closely and consecutively with indisputable British history, met every morning a congregation representing the best of what Britain had become,—orderly, as the crew of a man-of-war, in the goodly ship of their temple. Every man in his place, according to his rank, age, and learning; every man of sense or heart there recognizing that he was either fulfilling, or being prepared to fulfil, the gravest duties required of Englishmen. A well-educated foreigner, admitted to that morning service, might have learned and judged more quickly and justly what the country had been and still had power to be, than by months of stay in court or city. There, in his stall, sat the greatest divine of England,—under his commandant niche, her greatest scholar,*—among the tutors the present Dean Liddell; and a man of curious intellectual power and simple virtue, Osborne Gordon. The group of noblemen gave, in the Marquis of Kildare, Earl of Desart, Earl of Emlyn, and Francis Charteris, now Lord Wemyss,—the brightest types of high race and active power. Henry Acland and Charles Newton among the senior undergraduates, and I among the freshmen, showed, if one had known it, elements of curious possibilities in coming days. None of us then conscious of any need or chance of change, least of all the stern captain, who with rounded brow and glittering dark eye, led in his old thunderous Latin the responses of the morning prayer.

For all that I saw, and was made to think, in that cathedral choir, I am most thankful to this day.

220. The influence on me of the next goodliest part of the college buildings,—the hall,—was of a different and curiously mixed character. Had it only been used, as it only ought to have been, for festivity and

magnificence,—for the refectory daily, the reception of guests, the delivery of speeches on state occasions, and the like,—the hall, like the cathedral, would have had an entirely salutary and beneficently solemnizing effect on me, hallowing to me my daily bread, or, if our Dean Abbot* had condescended sometimes to dine with us, our incidental venison. But with the extremely bad taste (which, to my mind, is our cardinal modern sin, the staple to the hinge of our taste for money, and distaste for money's worth, and every other worthiness)—in that bad taste, I say, the Abbot allowed our Hall to be used for 'collections.' The word is wholly abominable to my mind, whether as expressing extorted charities in church, or extracted knowledge in examination. 'Collections,' in scholastic sense, meant the college examination at the end of every term, at which the Abbot had always the worse than bad taste to be present as our inquisitor, though he had never once presided at our table as our host. Of course the collective quantity of Greek possessed by all the undergraduate heads in hall, was to *him*, infinitesimal. Scornful at once, and vindictive, thunderous always, more sullen and threatening as the day went on, he stalked with baleful emanation of Gorgonian cold* from dais to door, and door to dais, of the majestic torture chamber,—vast as the great council hall of Venice,* but degraded now by the mean terrors, swallow-like under its eaves, of doleful creatures who had no counsel in them, except how to hide their crib in time, at each fateful Abbot's transit. Of course *I* never used a crib, but I believe the Dean would rather I had used fifty, than borne the puzzled and hopeless aspect which I presented towards the afternoon, over whatever I had to do. And as my Latin writing was, I suppose, the worst in the university,—as I never by any chance knew a first from a second future,* or, even to the end of my Oxford career, could get into my head where the Pelasgi lived, or where the Heraclidae returned from,*—it may be imagined with what sort of countenance the Dean gave me his first and second fingers to shake at our parting, or with what comfort I met the inquiries of my father and mother as to the extent to which I was, in college opinion, carrying all before me.

221. As time went on, the aspect of my college hall to me meant little more than the fear and shame of those examination days; but even in the first surprise and sublimity of finding myself dining there, were many reasons for the qualification of my pleasure. The change from our front parlour at Herne Hill, some fifteen feet by eighteen, and meat and pudding with my mother and Mary, to a hall about as big as the nave of Canterbury Cathedral, with its extremity lost in mist, its roof in darkness, and its company, an innumerable, immeasurable vision in

vanishing perspective, was in itself more appalling to me than appetizing; but also, from first to last, I had the clownish feeling of having no business there.

In the cathedral, however born or bred, I felt myself present by as good a right as its bishop,—nay, that in some of its lessons and uses, the building was less his than mine. But at table, with this learned and lordly perspective of guests, and state of worldly service, I had nothing to do; my own proper style of dining was for ever, I felt, divided from this—impassably. With baked potatoes under the mutton, just out of the oven, into the little parlour off the shop in Market Street, or beside a gipsy's kettle on Addington Hill (not that I had ever been beside a gipsy's kettle, but often wanted to be); or with an oat-cake and butter—for I was always a gourmand—in a Scotch shepherd's cottage, to be divided with his collie, I was myself, and in my place: but at the gentlemen-commoners' table, in Cardinal Wolsey's dining-room, I was, in all sorts of ways at once, less than myself, and in all sorts of wrong places at once, out of my place.

222. I may as well here record a somewhat comic incident, extremely trivial, which took place a little while afterwards; and which, in spite of its triviality, farther contributed to diminish in my own mind the charm of Christ Church hall. I had been received as a good-humoured and inoffensive little cur, contemptuously, yet kindly, among the dogs of race at the gentlemen-commoners' table; and my tutor, and the men who read in class with me, were beginning to recognize that I had some little gift in reading with good accent, thinking of what I read, and even asking troublesome questions about it, to the extent of being one day eagerly and admiringly congratulated by the whole class the moment we got out into quad, on the consummate manner in which I had floored our tutor. I having had no more intention to floor, or consciousness of flooring, the tutor, than a babe unborn, but had only happened, to the exquisite joy of my companions, to ask him something which he didn't happen to know. But, a good while before attaining this degree of public approval, I had made a direct attempt to bring myself into favourable notice, which had been far less successful.

It was an institution of the college that every week the undergraduates should write an essay on a philosophical subject, explicatory of some brief Latin text of Horace, Juvenal, or other accredited and pithy writer; and, I suppose, as a sort of guarantee to the men that what they wrote was really looked at, the essay pronounced the best was read aloud in hall on Saturday afternoon, with enforced attendance of the other undergraduates. Here, at least, was something in which I felt that my little faculties had some scope, and both conscientiously, and with real interest in the task, I wrote my weekly essay with all the sagacity and eloquence I possessed. And therefore, though much flattered, I was not surprised, when, a few weeks after coming up, my tutor announced to me, with a look of approval, that I was to read my essay in hall next Saturday.

223. Serenely, and on good grounds, confident in my powers of reading rightly, and with a decent gravity which I felt to be becoming on this my first occasion of public distinction, I read my essay, I have reason to believe, not ungracefully; and descended from the rostrum to receive—as I doubted not—the thanks of the gentlemen-commoners for this creditable presentment of the wisdom of that body. But poor Clara, after her first ball, receiving her cousin's compliments in the cloak-room, was less surprised than I by my welcome from my cousins of the long-table. Not in envy, truly, but in fiery disdain, varied in expression through every form and manner of English language, from the Olympian sarcasm of Charteris to the level-delivered volley of Grimston, they explained to me that I had committed grossest *lèse-majesté** against the order of gentlemen-commoners; that no gentleman-commoner's essay ought ever to contain more than twelve lines, with four words in each; and that even indulging to my folly, and conceit, and want of *savoir faire*, the impropriety of writing an essay with any meaning in it, like vulgar students,—the thoughtlessness and audacity of writing one that would take at least a quarter of an hour to read, and then reading it all, might for this once be forgiven to such a greenhorn, but that Coventry wasn't the word for the place I should be sent to if ever I did such a thing again. I am happy at least in remembering that I bore my fall from the clouds without much hurt, or even too ridiculous astonishment. I at once admitted the justice of these representations, yet do not remember that I modified the style of my future essays materially in consequence, neither do I remember what line of conduct I had proposed to myself in the event of again obtaining the privilege of edifying the Saturday's congregation. Perhaps my essays really diminished in value, or perhaps even the tutors had enough of them. All I know is, I was never asked to.

224. I ought to have noticed that the first introductions to the men at my table were made easier by the chance of my having been shut up for two days of storm at the Hospice of the Grimsel,* in 1835, with some thirty travellers from various countries, among whom a Christ Church gentleman-commoner, Mr Strangways, had played chess with me, and been a little interested in the way I drew granite among

the snow. He at once acknowledged me in Hall for a fellow-creature; and the rest of his set, finding they could get a good deal out of me in amusement without my knowing it, and that I did not take upon myself to reform their manners from any Evangelical, or otherwise impertinent, point of view, took me up kindly; so that, in a fortnight or so, I had fair choice of what companions I liked, out of the whole college.

Fortunately for me—beyond all words, fortunately—Henry Acland, by about a year and a half my senior, chose *me*; saw what helpless possibilities were in me, and took me affectionately in hand. His rooms, next the gate on the north side of Canterbury,* were within fifty yards of mine, and became to me the only place where I was happy. He quietly showed me the manner of life of English youth of good sense, good family, and enlarged education; we both of us already lived in elements far external to the college quadrangle. He told me of the plains of Troy;* a year or two afterwards I showed him, on his marriage journey, the path up the Montanvert; and the friendship between us has never changed, but by deepening, to this day.

225. Of other friends, I had some sensible and many kind ones; an excellent college tutor;* and later on, for a private one, the entirely right-minded and accomplished scholar already named, Osborne Gordon. At the corner of the great quadrangle lived Dr Buckland, always ready to help me,—or, a greater favour still, to be helped by me, in diagram drawing for his lectures. My picture of the granite veins in Trewavas Head, with a cutter weathering the point in a squall, in the style of Copley Fielding, still, I believe, forms part of the resources of the geological department. Mr Parker, then first founding the Architectural Society, and Charles Newton, already notable in his intense and curious way of looking into things, were there to sympathize with me, and to teach me more accurately the study of architecture. Within eight miles were the pictures of Blenheim. In all ways, opportunities, and privileges, it was not conceivable that a youth of my age could have been placed more favourably—if only he had had the wit to know them, and the will to use them. Alas! there I stood—or tottered—partly irresolute, partly idiotic, in the midst of them: nothing that I can think of among men, or birds, or beasts, quite the image of me, except poor little Shepherdess Agnes's picture of the 'Duckling Astray.'*

226. I count it is just a little to my credit that I was not ashamed, but pleased, that my mother came to Oxford with me to take such care of me as she could. Through all three years of residence, during term time, she had lodging in the High Street (first in Mr Adams's pretty

house of sixteenth century wood-work), and my father lived alone all through the week at Herne Hill, parting with wife and son at once for the son's sake. On the Saturday, he came down to us, and I went with him and my mother, in the old domestic way, to St Peter's, for the Sunday morning service: otherwise, they never appeared with me in public, lest my companions should laugh at me, or any one else ask malicious questions concerning vintner papa and his old-fashioned wife.

None of the men, through my whole college career, ever said one word in depreciation of either of them, or in sarcasm at my habitually spending my evenings with my mother. But once, when Adèle's elder sister came with her husband to see Oxford, and I mentioned, somewhat unnecessarily, at dinner, that she was the Countess Diane de Maison, they had no mercy on me for a month afterwards.

The reader will please also note that my mother did not come to Oxford because she could not part with me,—still less, because she distrusted me. She came simply that she might be at hand in case of accident or sudden illness. She had always been my physician as well as my nurse; on several occasions her timely watchfulness had saved me from the most serious danger; nor was her caution now, as will be seen, unjustified by the event. But for the first two years of my college life I caused her no anxiety; and my day was always happier because I could tell her at tea whatever had pleased or profited me in it.

227. The routine of day is perhaps worth telling. I never missed chapel; and in winter got an hour's reading before it. Breakfast at nine,—half-an-hour allowed for it to a second, for Captain Marryat with my roll and butter. College lectures till one. Lunch, with a little talk to anybody who cared to come in, or share their own commons with me. At two, Buckland or other professor's lecture. Walk till five, hall dinner, wine either given or accepted, and quiet chat over it with the reading men, or a frolic with those of my own table; but I always got round to the High Street to my mother's tea at seven, and amused myself till Tom[1] rang in, and I got with a run to Canterbury gate, and settled to a steady bit of final reading till ten. I can't make out more than six hours' real work in the day, but that was constantly and unflinchingly given.*

228. My Herodotean history, at any rate, got well settled down into me, and remains a greatly precious possession to this day. Also my college tutor, Mr Walter Brown, became somewhat loved by me, and

---

[1] I try to do without notes, but for the sake of any not English reader must explain that 'Tom' is the name of the great bell of Oxford, in Christ Church western tower.

with gentleness encouraged me into some small acquaintance with Greek verbs. My mathematics progressed well under another tutor whom I liked, Mr Hill; the natural instinct in me for pure geometry being keen, and my grasp of it, as far as I had gone, thorough. At my 'little go'* in the spring of '38, the diagrams of Euclid being given me, as was customary with the Euclid examination paper, I handed the book back to the examiner, saying scornfully, 'I don't want any figures, Sir.' 'You had better take them,' replied he, mildly; which I did, as he bid me; but I could then, and can still, dictate blindfold the demonstration of any problem, with any letters, at any of its points. I just scraped through, and no more, with my Latin writing, came creditably off with what else had to be done, and my tutor was satisfied with me,—not enough recognizing that the 'little go' had asked, and got out of me, pretty nearly all I had in me, or was ever likely to have in that kind.

229. It was extremely unfortunate for me that the two higher lecturers of the college, Kynaston (afterwards Master of St Paul's) in Greek, and Hussey, the censor, in I don't recollect what of disagreeable, were both to my own feeling repellent. They both despised me, as a homeboy, to begin with; Kynaston with justice, for I had not Greek enough to understand anything he said; and when good-naturedly one day, in order to bring out as best he might my supposed peculiar genius and acquirements, he put me on at the ορα δέ γ'εῖσω τριγ λύφωυ, ὅποι κευὸυ δέμας καθεῖυαι, of the Iphigenia in Tauris,* and found, to his own and all the class's astonishment and disgust, that I did not know what a triglyph* was,—never spoke to me with any patience again, until long afterwards at St Paul's, where he received me, on an occasion of school ceremony, with affection and respect.

Hussey was, by all except the best men of the college, felt to be a censorious censor; and the manners of the college were unhappily such as to make any wise censor censorious. He had, by the judgment of heaven, a grim countenance; and was to me accordingly, from first to last, as a Christ Church Gorgon or Erinnys;* whose passing cast a shadow on the air as well as on the gravel.

I am amused, as I look back, in now perceiving what an aesthetic view I had of all my tutors and companions,—how consistently they took to me the aspect of pictures, and how I from the first declined giving any attention to those which were not well painted enough. My ideal of a tutor was founded on what Holbein or Durer had represented in Erasmus or Melanchthon, or, even more solemnly, on Titian's Magnificoes or Bonifazio's Bishops.* No presences of that kind appeared either in Tom* or Peckwater; and even Doctor Pusey (who also never spoke to me) was not in the least a picturesque or tremendous figure, but only a sickly and rather ill put together English clerical gentleman, who never looked one in the face, or appeared aware of the state of the weather.

230. My own tutor was a dark-eyed, animated, pleasant, but not in the least impressive person, who walked with an unconscious air of assumption, noticeable by us juniors not to his advantage. Kynaston was ludicrously like a fat schoolboy. Hussey, grim and brown as I said, somewhat lank, incapable of jest, equally incapable of enthusiasm; for the rest, doing his duty thoroughly, and a most estimable member of the college and university,—but to me, a resident calamity far greater than I knew, whose malefic influence I recognize in memory only.

Finally, the Dean himself, though venerable to me, from the first, in his evident honesty, self-respect, and real power of a rough kind, was yet in his general aspect too much like the sign of the Red Pig which I afterwards saw set up in pudding raisins, with black currants for eyes, by an imaginative grocer in Chartres fair; and in the total bodily and ghostly* presence of him was to me only a rotundly progressive terror, or sternly enthroned and niched Anathema.*

There was one tutor, however, out of my sphere, who reached my ideal, but disappointed my hope, then,—as perhaps his own, since;— a man sorrowfully under the dominion of the Greek ἀνάγκη—the present Dean.* He was, and is, one of the rarest types of nobly-presenced Englishmen, but I fancy it was his adverse star that made him an Englishman at all—the prosaic and practical element in him having prevailed over the sensitive one. He was the only man in Oxford among the masters of my day who knew anything of art; and his keen saying of Turner, that he 'had got hold of a false ideal,' would have been infinitely helpful to me at that time, had he explained and enforced it. But I suppose he did not see enough in me to make him take trouble with me,—and, what was much more serious, he saw not enough in himself to take trouble, in that field, with himself.

231. There was a more humane and more living spirit, however, inhabitant of the north-west angle of the Cardinal's Square:* and a great many of the mischances which were only harmful to me through my own folly may be justly held, and to the full, counterbalanced by that one piece of good fortune, of which I had the wit to take advantage. Dr Buckland was a Canon of the Cathedral, and he, with his wife and family, were all sensible and good-natured, with originality enough in the sense of them to give sap and savour to the whole college.

Originality—passing slightly into grotesqueness, and a little diminishing their effective power. The Doctor had too much humour ever to follow far enough the dull side of a subject. Frank* was too fond of his bear cub to give attention enough to the training of the cubbish element in himself; and a day scarcely passed without Mit's committing herself in some manner disapproved by the statelier college demoiselles. But all were frank, kind, and clever, vital in the highest degree; to me, medicinal and saving.

Dr Buckland was extremely like Sydney Smith in his staple of character; no rival with him in wit, but like him in humour, common sense, and benevolently cheerful doctrine of Divinity. At his breakfast-table I met the leading scientific men of the day, from Herschel* downwards, and often intelligent and courteous foreigners,—with whom my stutter of French, refined by Adèle into some precision of accent, was sometimes useful. Every one was at ease and amused at that breakfast-table,—the menû and service of it usually in themselves interesting. I have always regretted a day of unlucky engagement on which I missed a delicate toast of mice; and remembered, with delight, being waited upon one hot summer morning by two graceful and polite little Carolina lizards,* who kept off the flies.

232. I have above noticed the farther and incalculable good it was to me that Acland took me up in my first and foolishest days, and with pretty irony and loving insight,—or, rather, sympathy with what was best, and blindness to what was worst in me,—gave me the good of seeing a noble young English life in its purity, sagacity, honour, reckless daring, and happy piety; its English pride shining prettily through all, like a girl's in her beauty. It is extremely interesting to me to contrast the Englishman's silently conscious pride in what he *is*, with the vexed restlessness and wretchedness of the Frenchman, in his thirst for 'gloire,' to be gained by agonized effort to become something he is *not*.

One day when the Cherwell was running deep over one of its most slippery weirs, question arising between Acland and me whether it were traversable, and I declaring it too positively to be impassable, Acland instantly took off boot and sock, and walked over and back. He ran no risk but of a sound ducking, being, of course, a strong swimmer: and I suppose him wise enough not to have done it had there been real danger. But he would certainly have run the margin fine, and possessed in its quite highest, and in a certain sense, most laughable degree, the constitutional English serenity in danger, which, with the foolish of us, degenerates into delight in it, but with the wise, whether soldier or physician, is the basis of the most fortunate action and swiftest decision of deliberate skill. When, thirty years afterwards,* Dr Acland was wrecked in the steamer *Tyne*, off the coast of Dorset, the steamer having lain wedged on the rocks all night,—no one knew what rocks,—and the dawn breaking on half-a-mile of dangerous surf between the ship and shore,—the officers, in anxious debate, the crew, in confusion, the passengers, in hysterics or at prayers, were all astonished, and many scandalized, at the appearance of Dr Acland from the saloon in punctilious morning dress, with the announcement that 'breakfast was ready.' To the impatient clamour of indignation with which his unsympathetic conduct was greeted, he replied by pointing out that not a boat could go on shore, far less come out from it, in that state of the tide, and that in the meantime, as most of them were wet, all cold, and at the best must be dragged ashore through the surf, if not swim for their lives in it, they would be extremely prudent to begin the day, as usual, with breakfast. The hysterics ceased, the confusion calmed, what wits anybody had became available to them again, and not a life was ultimately lost.

233. In all this playful and proud heroism of his youth, Henry Acland delighted me as a leopard or a falcon would, without in the least affecting my own character by his example. I had been too often adjured and commanded to take care of myself, ever to think of following him over slippery weirs, or accompanying him in pilot boats through white-topped shoal water; but both in art and science he could pull me on, being years ahead of me, yet glad of my sympathy, for, till I came, he was literally alone in the university in caring for either. To Dr Buckland, geology was only the pleasant occupation of his own merry life. To Henry Acland physiology was an entrusted gospel of which he was the solitary and first preacher to the heathen; and already in his undergraduate's room in Canterbury he was designing—a few years later in his professional room in Tom quad, he was realizing,—the introduction of physiological study which has made the university what she has now become.

Indeed, the curious point in Acland's character was its early completeness. Already in these yet boyish days, his judgment was unerring, his aims determined, his powers developed; and had he not, as time went on, been bound to the routine of professional work, and satisfied in the serenity, not to say arrested by the interests, of a beautiful home life,——it is no use thinking or saying what he might have been; those who know him best are the most thankful that he is what he is.

234. Next to Acland, but with a many-feet-thick wall between, in my aesthetic choice of idols, which required primarily of man or woman

that they should be comely, before I regarded any of their farther qualities, came Francis Charteris. I have always held Charteris the most
ideal Scotsman, and on the whole the grandest type of European
Circassian* race hitherto visible to me; and his subtle, effortless, inevitable, unmalicious sarcasm, and generally sufficient and available sense,
gave a constantly natural, and therefore inoffensive, hauteur to his delicate beauty. He could do what he liked with anyone,—at least with anyone of good humour and sympathy; and when one day, the old sub-dean
coming out of Canterbury gate at the instant Charteris was dismounting
at it in forbidden pink, and Charteris turned serenely to him as he took
his foot out of the stirrup, to inform him that 'he had been out with the
Dean's hounds,' the old man and the boy were both alike pleased.

Charteris never failed in anything, but never troubled himself about
anything. Naturally of high ability and activity, he did all he chose with
ease,—neither had falls in hunting, nor toil in reading, nor ambition
nor anxiety in examination,—nor disgrace in recklessness of life. He
was partly checked, it may be in some measure weakened, by hectic
danger in his constitution, possibly the real cause of his never having
made his mark in after life.

235. The Earl of Desart, next to Charteris, interested me most of
the men at my table. A youth of the same bright promise, and of kind
disposition, he had less natural activity, and less—being Irish,—
common sense, than the Scot; and the University made no attempt to
give him more. It has been the pride of recent days to equalize the position, and disguise the distinction of noble and servitor. Perhaps it
might have been wiser, instead of effacing the distinction, to reverse
the manner of it. In those days the happy servitor's tenure of his college-
room and revenue depended on his industry, while it was the privilege
of the noble to support with lavish gifts the college, from which he
expected no return, and to buy with sums equivalent to his dignity
the privileges of rejecting alike its instruction and its control. It seems
to me singular, and little suggestive of sagacity in the common English
character, that it had never occurred to either an old dean, or a young
duke, that possibly the Church of England and the House of Peers
might hold a different position in the country in years to come if the
entrance examination had been made severer for the rich than the poor;
and the nobility and good breeding of a student expected to be bla-
zoned consistently by the shield on his seal, the tassel on his cap, the
grace of his conduct, and the accuracy of his learning.

In the last respect, indeed, Eton and Harrow boys are for ever distinguished,—whether idle or industrious in after life,—from youth of

general England; but how much of the best capacity of her noblesse is
lost by her carelessness of their university training, she may soon have
more serious cause to calculate than I am willing to foretell.

I have little to record of my admired Irish fellow-student than that
he gave the supper at which my freshman's initiation into the body of
gentlemen-commoners was to be duly and formally ratified. Curious
glances were directed to me under the ordeal of the necessary
toasts,—but it had not occurred to the hospitality of my entertainers
that I probably knew as much about wine as they did. When we broke
up at the small hours, I helped to carry the son of the head of my
college* downstairs, and walked across Peckwater to my own rooms,
deliberating, as I went, whether there was any immediately practicable
trigonometric method of determining whether I was walking straight
towards the lamp over the door.

236. From this time—that is to say, from about the third week after
I came into residence—it began to be recognized that, muff or milksop
though I might be, I could hold my own on occasion; and in next term,
when I had to return civilities, that I gave good wine, and that of curious quality, without any bush;* and saw with good-humour the fruit
I had sent for from London thrown out of the window to the porter's
children: farther, that I could take any quantity of jests, though I could
not make one, and could be extremely interested in hearing conversation on topics I knew nothing about,—to that degree that Bob Grimston
condescended to take me with him one day to a tavern across Magdalen
Bridge, to hear him elucidate from the landlord some points of the
horses entered for the Derby, an object only to be properly accomplished
by sitting with indifference on a corner of the kitchen table, and carrying
on the dialogue with careful pauses, and more by winks than words.

The quieter men of the set were also some of them interested in
my drawing; and one or two—Scott Murray, for instance, and
Lord Kildare—were as punctual as I in chapel, and had some thoughts
concerning college life and its issues, which they were glad to share
with me. In this second year of residence, my position in college was
thus alike pleasant, and satisfactorily to my parents, eminent: and I was
received without demur into the Christ Church society, which had
its quiet club-room at the corner of Oriel Lane, looking across to the
'beautiful gate' of St Mary's; and on whose books were entered the
names of most of the good men belonging to the upper table and its set,
who had passed through Christ Church for the last ten or twelve years.

237. Under these luxurious, and—in the world's sight—honourable, conditions, my mind gradually recovering its tranquillity and

spring, and making some daily, though infinitesimal, progress towards the attainment of common sense, I believe that I did harder and better work in my college reading than I can at all remember. It seems to me now as if I had known Thucydides, as I knew Homer (Pope's!), since I could spell; but the fact was, that for a youth who had so little Greek to bless himself with at seventeen, to know every syllable of his Thucydides at half past eighteen meant some steady sitting at it. The perfect honesty of the Greek soldier, his high breeding, his political insight, and the scorn of construction with which he knotted his meaning into a rhythmic strength that writhed and wrought every way at once, all interested me intensely in him as a writer; while his subject, the central tragedy of all the world, the suicide of Greece, was felt by me with a sympathy in which the best powers of my heart and brain were brought up to their fullest, for my years.

I open, and lay beside me as I write, the perfectly clean and well-preserved third volume of Arnold, over which I spent so much toil, and burnt with such sorrow; my close-written abstracts still dovetailed into its pages, and read with surprised gratitude the editor's final sentence in the preface dated 'Fox How, Ambleside, January, 1835.'

'Not the wildest extravagance of atheistic wickedness in modern times can go further than the sophists of Greece went before them. Whatever audacity can dare and subtlety contrive, to make the words "good" and "evil" change their meaning, has been already tried in the days of Plato, and by his eloquence, and wisdom, and faith unshaken, put to shame.'

CHAPTER XII

ROSLYN CHAPEL

238. I MUST yet return, before closing the broken record of these first twenty years, to one or two scattered days in 1836, when things happened which led forward into phases of work to be given account of in next volume.

I cannot find the date of my father's buying his first Copley Fielding,—'Between King's House and Inveroran, Argyllshire.' It cost a tremendous sum, for *us*—forty-seven guineas; and the day it came home was a festa, and many a day after, in looking at it, and fancying the hills and the rain were real.

My father and I were in absolute sympathy about Copley Fielding, and I could find it in my heart now to wish I had lived at the Land's End, and never seen any art but Prout's and his. We were very much set up at making his acquaintance, and then very happy in it: the modestest of presidents* he was; the simplest of painters, without a vestige of romance, but the purest love of daily sunshine and the constant hills. Fancy him, while Stanfield and Harding and Roberts were grand-touring in Italy, and Sicily, and Stiria, and Bohemia, and Illyria, and the Alps, and the Pyrenees, and the Sierra Morena,—Fielding never crossing to Calais, but year after year returning to Saddleback and Ben Venue, or, less ambitious yet, to Sandgate and the Sussex Downs.

239. The drawings I made in 1835 were really interesting even to artists, and appeared promising enough to my father to justify him in promoting me from Mr Runciman's tutelage to the higher privileges of art-instruction. Lessons from any of the members of the Water-Colour Society cost a guinea, and six were supposed to have efficiency for the production of an adequately skilled water-colour amateur. There was, of course, no question by what master they should be given; and I know not whether papa or I most enjoyed the six hours in Newman Street:* my father's intense delight in Fielding's work making it a real pleasure to the painter that he should stay chatting while I had my lesson. Nor was my father's talk (if he could be got to talk) unworthy any painter's attention, though he never put out his strength but in writing. I chance in good time on a letter from Northcote in 1830, showing how much value the old painter put on my father's judgment of a piece of literary work which remains classical to this day, and is indeed the best piece of existing criticism founded on the principles of Sir Joshua's school:

240. 'DEAR SIR,—I received your most kind and consoling letter, yet I was very sorry to find you had been so ill, but hope you have now recovered your health. The praise you are so good as to bestow on me and the Volume of Conversations* gives me more pleasure than perhaps you apprehend, as the book was published against my consent, and, in its first appearance in the magazines, totally without my knowledge. I have done all in my power to prevent its coming before the public, because there are several hard and cruel opinions of persons that I would not have them see in a printed book; besides that, Hazlitt, although a man of real abilities, yet had a desire to give pain to others, and has also frequently exaggerated that which I had said in confidence to him. However, I thank God that this book, which made me tremble at its coming before the world, is received with unexpected favour on

to my part, and the approbation of a mind like yours give (*sic*—short for "cannot but give") me the greatest consolation I can receive, and sets my mind more at ease.

'Please to present my respectful compliments to Mrs Ruskin, who I hope is well, and kind remembrances to your son.

'I remain always, dear Sir,

'Your most obliged friend[1]

'And very humble servant,

'JAMES NORTHCOTE.

'ARGYLL HOUSE,
  '*October* 13th, 1830.
'To John J. Ruskin, Esq.'

241. And thus the proposed six lessons in Newman Street ran on into perhaps eight or nine, during which Copley Fielding taught me to wash colour smoothly in successive tints, to shade cobalt through pink madder into yellow ochre for skies, to use a broken scraggy touch for the tops of mountains, to represent calm lakes by broad strips of shade with lines of light between them (usually at about the distance of the lines of this print), to produce dark clouds and rain with twelve or twenty successive washes, and to crumble burnt umber with a dry brush for foliage and foreground. With these instructions, I succeeded in copying a drawing which Fielding made before me, some twelve inches by nine, of Ben Venue and the Trosachs, with brown cows standing in Loch Achray, so much to my own satisfaction that I put my work up over my bedroom chimney-piece the last thing at night, and woke to its contemplation in the morning with a rapture, mixed of self-complacency and the sense of new faculty, in which I floated all that day, as in a newly-discovered and strongly buoyant species of air.

In a very little while, however, I found that this great first step did not mean consistent progress at the same pace. I saw that my washes, however careful or multitudinous, did not in the end look as smooth as Fielding's, and that my crumblings of burnt umber became uninteresting after a certain number of repetitions.

With still greater discouragement, I perceived the Fielding processes to be inapplicable to the Alps. My scraggy touches did not to my satisfaction represent aiguilles, nor my ruled lines of shade, the

---

[1] In memory of the quiet old man who thus honoured us with his friendship, and in most true sense of their value, I hope to reprint the parts of the *Conversations* which I think he would have wished to be preserved.*

Lake of Geneva. The water-colour drawing was abandoned, with a dim under-current of feeling that I had no gift for it,—and in truth I had none for colour arrangement,—and the pencil outline returned to with resolute energy.

242. I had never, up to this time, seen a Turner drawing, and scarcely know whether to lay to the score of dulness, or prudence, the tranquillity in which I copied the engravings of the Rogers vignettes, without so much as once asking where the originals were. The facts being that they lay at the bottom of an old drawer in Queen Anne Street,* inaccessible to me as the bottom of the sea,—and that, if I had seen them, they would only have destroyed my pleasure in the engravings,—my rest in these was at least fortunate: and the more I consider of this and other such forms of failure in what most people would call laudable curiosity, the more I am disposed to regard with thankfulness, and even respect, the habits which have remained with me during life, of always working resignedly at the thing under my hand till I could do it, and looking exclusively at the thing before my eyes till I could see it.

On the other hand, the Academy Turners were too far beyond all hope of imitation to disturb me, and the impressions they produced before 1836 were confused; many of them, like the Quilleboeuf, or the 'Keelmen heaving in coals,'* being of little charm in colour; and the Fountain of Indolence, or Golden Bough,* perhaps seeming to me already fantastic, beside the naturalism of Landseer; and the human interest and intelligible finish of Wilkie.

243. But in 1836 Turner exhibited three pictures, in which the characteristics of his later manner were developed with his best skill and enthusiasm: Juliet and her Nurse, Rome from Mount Aventine, and Mercury and Argus.* His freak in placing Juliet at Venice instead of Verona, and the mysteries of lamplight and rockets with which he had disguised Venice herself, gave occasion to an article in *Blackwood's Magazine** of sufficiently telling ribaldry, expressing, with some force, and extreme discourtesy, the feelings of the pupils of Sir George Beaumont at the appearance of these unaccredited views of Nature.

The review raised me to the height of 'black anger' in which I have remained pretty nearly ever since; and having by that time some confidence in my power of words, and—not merely judgment, but sincere *experience*—of the charm of Turner's work, I wrote an answer to Blackwood, of which I wish I could now find any fragment.* But my father thought it right to ask Turner's leave for its publication; it was copied in my best hand, and sent to Queen Anne Street, and the old man returned kindly answer, as follows:—

'47, QUEEN ANN (*sic*) STREET WEST,
'*October 6th*, 1836.

'MY DEAR SIR,—I beg to thank you for your zeal, kindness, and the trouble you have taken in my behalf, in regard of the criticism of Blackwood's Magazine for October, respecting my works; but I never move in these matters, they are of no import save mischief and the meal tub, which Maga fears for by my having invaded the flour tub.

'*P.S.*—If you wish to have the manuscript back, have the goodness to let me know. If not, with your sanction, I will send it on to the possessor of the picture of Juliet.'

I cannot give the signature of this letter, which has been cut off for some friend! In later years it used to be, to my father, 'Yours most truly,' and to me, 'Yours truly.'

The 'possessor of the picture' was Mr Munro of Novar, who never spoke to me of the first chapter of 'Modern Painters' thus coming into his hands. Nor did I ever care to ask him about it; and still, for a year or two longer, I persevered in the study of Turner engravings only, and the use of Copley Fielding's method for such efforts at colour as I made on the vacation journeys during Oxford days.

244. We made three tours in those summers, without crossing Channel. In 1837, to Yorkshire and the Lakes; in 1838, to Scotland; in 1839, to Cornwall.

On the journey of 1837, when I was eighteen, I felt, for the last time, the pure childish love of nature which Wordsworth so idly takes for an intimation of immortality.* We went down by the North Road, as usual; and on the fourth day arrived at Catterick Bridge, where there is a clear pebble-bedded stream, and both west and east some rising of hills, foretelling the moorlands and dells of upland Yorkshire; and there the feeling came back to me—as it could never return more.

It is a feeling only possible to youth, for all care, regret, or knowledge of evil destroys it; and it requires also the full sensibility of nerve and blood, the conscious strength of heart, and hope; not but that I suppose the purity of youth may feel what is best of it even through sickness and the waiting for death; but only in thinking death itself God's sending.

245. In myself, it has always been quite exclusively confined to *wild*, that is to say, wholly natural places, and especially to scenery animated

by streams, or by the sea. The sense of the freedom, spontaneous, unpolluted power of nature was essential in it. I enjoyed a lawn, a garden, a daisied field, a quiet pond, as other children do; but by the side of Wandel, or on the downs of Sandgate, or by a Yorkshire stream under a cliff, I was different from other children, that ever I have noticed: but the feeling cannot be described by any of us that have it. Wordsworth's 'haunted me like a passion'* is no description of it, for it is not *like*, but *is*, a passion; the point is to define how it *differs* from other passions,—what sort of human, pre-eminently human, feeling it is that loves a stone for a stone's sake, and a cloud for a cloud's. A monkey loves a monkey for a monkey's sake, and a nut for the kernel's, but not a stone for a stone's. I took stones for bread, but not certainly at the Devil's bidding.*

I was different, be it once more said, from other children even of my own type, not so much in the actual nature of the feeling, but in the mixture of it. I had, in my little clay pitcher, vialfuls, as it were, of Wordsworth's reverence, Shelley's sensitiveness, Turner's accuracy, all in one. A snowdrop was to me, as to Wordsworth, part of the Sermon on the mount;* but I never should have written sonnets to the celandine, because it is of a coarse, yellow and imperfect form. With Shelley, I loved blue sky and blue eyes, but never in the least confused the heavens with my own poor little Psychidion.* And the reverence and passion were alike kept in their places by the constructive Turnerian element; and I did not weary myself in wishing that a daisy could see the beauty of its shadow, but in trying to draw the shadow rightly, myself.

246. But so stubborn and chemically inalterable the laws of the prescription were, that now, looking back from 1886 to that brook shore of 1837, whence I could see the whole of my youth, I find myself in nothing whatsoever *changed*. Some of me is dead, more of me stronger. I have learned a few things, forgotten many; in the total of me, I am but the same youth, disappointed and rheumatic.

And in illustration of this stubbornness, not by stiffening of the wood with age, but in the structure of the pith, let me insist a minute or two more on the curious joy I felt in 1837 in returning to the haunts of boyhood. No boy could possibly have been more excited than I was by seeing Italy and the Alps; neither boy nor man ever knew better the difference between a Cumberland cottage and Venetian palace, or a Cumberland stream and the Rhone:—my very knowledge of this difference will be found next year expressing itself in the first bit of promising literary work* I ever did; but, after all the furious excitement and wild joy of the Continent, the coming back to a Yorkshire stream-side felt like returning to heaven. We went on into well known Cumberland; my father took me up Scawfell and Helvellyn, with a clever Keswick guide, who knew mineralogy, Mr Wright; and the summer passed beneficently and peacefully.

247. A little incident which happened, I fancy in the beginning of '38, shows that I had thus recovered some tranquillity and sense, and might at that time have been settled down to simple and healthy life, easily enough, had my parents seen the chance.

I forgot to say, when speaking of Mr and Mrs Richard Gray, that, when I was a child, my mother had another religious friend, who lived just at the top of Camberwell Grove, or between it and the White Gate,—Mrs Withers; an extremely amiable and charitable person, with whom my mother organized, I imagine, such schemes of alms-giving as her own housekeeping prevented her seeing to herself. Mr Withers was a coal-merchant, ultimately not a successful one. Of him I remember only a reddish and rather vacant face; of Mrs Withers, no material aspect, only the above vague but certain facts; and that she was a familiar element in my mother's life, dying out of it however without much notice or miss, before I was old enough to get any clear notion of her.

In this spring of '38, however, the widowed Mr Withers, having by that time retired to the rural districts in reduced circumstances, came up to town on some small vestige of carboniferous business, bringing his only daughter with him to show my mother;—who, for a wonder, asked her to stay with us, while her father visited his umquwhile* clientage at the coal-wharves. Charlotte Withers was a fragile, fair, freckled, sensitive slip of a girl about sixteen; graceful in an unfinished and small wild-flower sort of a way, extremely intelligent, affectionate, wholly right-minded and mild in piety. An altogether sweet and deli-cate creature of ordinary sort, not pretty, but quite pleasant to see, especially if her eyes were looking your way, and her mind with them.

248. We got to like each other in a mildly confidential way in the course of a week. We disputed on the relative dignities of music and painting; and I wrote an essay nine foolscap pages long,* proposing the entire establishment of my own opinions, and the total discomfiture and overthrow of hers, according to my usual manner of paying court to my mistresses. Charlotte Withers, however, thought I did her great honour, and carried away the essay as if it had been a school prize.

And, as I said, if my father and mother had chosen to keep her a month longer, we should have fallen quite melodiously and quietly in love; and they might have given me an excellently pleasant little wife, and set me up, geology and all, in the coal business, without any resistance or farther trouble on my part. I don't suppose the idea ever occurred to them; Charlotte was not the kind of person they proposed for me. So Charlotte went away at the week's end, when her father was ready for her. I walked with her to Camberwell Green, and we said good-bye, rather sorrowfully, at the corner of the New Road; and that possibility of meek happiness vanished for ever. A little while afterwards, her father 'negotiated' a marriage for her with a well-to-do Newcastle trader, whom she took because she was bid. He treated her pretty much as one of his coal sacks, and in a year or two she died.

249. Very dimly, and rather against my own will, the incident showed me what my mother had once or twice observed to me, to my immense indignation, that Adèle was not the only girl in the world; and my enjoyment of our tour in the Trosachs was not described in any more Byronian heroics; the tragedy also having been given up, because, when I had described a gondola, a bravo, the heroine Bianca, and moonlight on the Grand Canal, I found I had not much more to say.

Scott's country took me at last well out of it all. It is of little use to the reader now to tell him that still at that date the shore of Loch Katrine, at the east extremity of the lake, was exactly as Scott had seen it, and described,

> 'Onward, amid the copse 'gan peep,
> A narrow inlet, still and deep.'*

In literal and lovely truth, that was so:—by the side of the footpath (it was no more) which wound through the Trosachs, deep and calm under the blaeberry bushes, a dark winding clear-brown pool, not five feet wide at first, reflected the entangled moss of its margin, and arch of branches above, with scarcely a gleam of sky.

That inlet of Loch Katrine was in itself an extremely rare thing; I have never myself seen the like of it in lake shores. A winding recess of deep water, without any entering stream to account for it—possible only, I imagine, among rocks of the quite abnormal confusion of the Trosachs; and besides the natural sweetness and wonder of it made sacred by the most beautiful poem that Scotland ever sang by her stream sides. And all that the nineteenth century conceived of wise and right to do with this piece of mountain inheritance, was to thrust the nose of a steamer* into it, plank its blaeberries over with a platform, and drive the populace headlong past it as fast as they can scuffle.

It had been well for me if I had climbed Ben Venue and Ben Ledi, hammer in hand, as Scawfell and Helvellyn. But I had given myself some literary work instead, to which I was farther urged by the sight of Roslyn and Melrose.

250. The idea had come into my head in the summer of '37, and, I imagine, rose immediately out of my sense of the contrast between the cottages of Westmoreland and those of Italy. Anyhow, the November number of Loudon's *Architectural Magazine* for 1837 opens with 'Introduction to the Poetry of Architecture; or, The Architecture of the Nations of Europe considered in its Association with Natural Scenery and National Character,' by Kataphusin.* I could not have put in fewer, or more inclusive words, the definition of what half my future life was to be spent in discoursing of; while the nom-de-plume I chose, 'According to Nature,' was equally expressive of the temper in which I was to discourse alike on that and every other subject. The adoption of a nom-de-plume at all, implied (as also the concealment of name* on the first publication of 'Modern Painters') a sense of a power of judgment in myself, which it would not have been becoming in a youth of eighteen to claim. Had either my father or tutor then said to me, 'Write as it is becoming in a youth to write,—let the reader discover what you know, and be persuaded to what you judge,' I perhaps might not now have been ashamed of my youth's essays. Had they said to me more sternly, 'Hold your tongue till you need not ask the reader's condescension in listening to you,' I might perhaps have been satisfied with my work when it was mature.

As it is, these youthful essays, though deformed by assumption, and shallow in contents, are curiously right up to the points they reach; and already distinguished above most of the literature of the time, for the skill of language which the public at once felt for a pleasant gift in me.

251. I have above said that had it not been for constant reading of the Bible, I might probably have taken Johnson for my model of English. To a useful extent I have always done so; in these first essays, partly because I could not help it, partly of set, and well set, purpose.

On our foreign journeys, it being of course desirable to keep the luggage as light as possible, my father had judged that four little volumes of Johnson—the *Idler* and the *Rambler**—did, under names wholly appropriate to the circumstances, contain more substantial literary nourishment than could be, from any other author, packed into so portable compass. And accordingly, in spare hours, and on wet days, the turns and returns of reiterated *Rambler* and iterated *Idler* fastened themselves in my ears and mind; nor was it possible for me, till long afterwards, to quit myself of Johnsonian symmetry and balance in sentences intended, either with swordsman's or paviour's blow, to cleave an enemy's crest, or drive down the oaken pile of a principle. I never for an instant compared Johnson to Scott, Pope, Byron, or any of the really great writers whom I loved. But I at once and for ever recognized in him a man entirely sincere, and infallibly wise in the view and estimate he gave of the common questions, business, and ways of the world. I valued his sentences not primarily because they were symmetrical, but because they were just, and clear; it is a method of judgment rarely used by the average public, who ask from an author always, in the first place, arguments in favour of their own opinions, in elegant terms; and are just as ready with their applause for a sentence of Macaulay's, which may have no more sense in it than a blot pinched between doubled paper, as to reject one of Johnson's, telling against their own prejudice,—though its symmetry be as of thunder answering from two horizons.

252. I hold it more than happy that, during those continental journeys, in which the vivid excitement of the greater part of the day left me glad to give spare half-hours to the study of a thoughtful book, Johnson was the one author accessible to me. No other writer could have secured me, as he did, against all chance of being misled by my own sanguine and metaphysical temperament. He taught me carefully to measure life, and distrust fortune; and he secured me, by his adamantine common-sense, for ever, from being caught in the cobwebs of German metaphysics,* or sloughed in the English drainage of them.

I open, at this moment, the larger of the volumes of the Idler to which I owe so much. After turning over a few leaves, I chance on the closing sentence of No. 65, which transcribing, I may show the reader in sum what it taught me,—in words which, writing this account of myself, I conclusively obey.

'Of these learned men, let those who aspire to the same praise imitate the diligence, and avoid the scrupulosity. Let it be always remembered that life is short, that knowledge is endless, and that many doubts deserve not to be cleared. Let those whom nature and study have qualified to teach mankind, tell us what they have learned while they are yet able to tell it, and trust their reputation only to themselves.'

It is impossible for me now to know how far my own honest desire for truth, and compassionate sense of what is instantly helpful to creatures who are every instant perishing, might have brought me, in their own time, to think and judge as Johnson thought and measured,— even had I never learned of him. He at least set me in the straight path from the beginning, and, whatever time I might waste in vain pleasure, or weak effort, he saved me for ever from false thoughts and futile speculations.

253. Why, I know not, for Mr Loudon was certainly not tired of me, the Kataphusin papers close abruptly,* as if their business was at its natural end, without a word of allusion in any part of them, or apology for the want of allusion, to the higher forms of civil and religious architecture. I find, indeed, a casual indication of some ulterior purpose in a ponderous sentence of the paper on the Westmoreland cottage, announcing that 'it will be seen hereafter, when we leave the lowly valley for the torn ravine, and the grassy knoll for the ribbed precipice, that if the continental architects cannot adorn the pasture with the humble roof, they can crest the crag with eternal battlements.'* But this magnificent promise ends in nothing more tremendous than a 'chapter on chimneys,' illustrated as I find this morning to my extreme surprise, by a fairly good drawing of the building which is now the principal feature in the view from my study window,—Coniston Hall.

On the whole, however, these papers, written at intervals during 1838, indicate a fairly progressive and rightly consolidated range of thought on these subjects, within the chrysalid torpor of me.

254. From the Trosachs we drove to Edinburgh: and, somewhere on the road near Linlithgow, my father, reading some letters got by that day's post, coolly announced to my mother and me that Mr Domecq was going to bring his four daughters to England again, to finish their schooling at New Hall, near Chelmsford.

And I am unconscious of anything more in that journey, or of anything after it, until I found myself driving down to Chelmsford. My mother had no business of course to take *me* with her to pay a visit in a convent; but I suppose felt it would be too cruel to leave me behind. The young ladies were allowed a chat with us in the parlour, and invited (with acceptance) to spend their vacations always at Herne Hill. And so began a second aera of that part of my life which is *not* 'worthy of memory,' but only of the 'Guarda e Passa.'*

There was some solace during my autumnal studies in thinking that she was really in England, really over *there*,—I could see the sky over Chelmsford from my study window,—and that she was shut up in a convent and couldn't be seen by anybody, or spoken to, but by nuns; and that perhaps she wouldn't quite like it, and would like to come to Herne Hill again, and bear with me a little.

255. I wonder mightily now what sort of a creature I should have turned out, if at this time Love had been with me instead of against me; and instead of the distracting and useless pain, I had had the joy of

approved love, and the untellable, incalculable motive of its sympathy and praise.

It seems to me such things are not allowed in this world. The men capable of the highest imaginative passion are always tossed on fiery waves by it: the men who find it smooth water, and not scalding, are of another sort. My father's second clerk, Mr Ritchie, wrote unfeelingly to his colleague, bachelor Henry, who would not marry for his mother's and sisters' sakes, 'If you want to know what happiness is, get a wife, and half a dozen children, and come to Margate.' But Mr Ritchie remained all his life nothing more than a portly gentleman with gooseberry eyes, of the Irvingite persuasion.*

There must be great happiness in the love-matches of the typical English squire. Yet English squires make their happy lives only a portion for foxes.*

256. Of course, when Adèle and her sisters came back at Christmas, and stayed with us four or five weeks, every feeling and folly that had been subdued or forgotten, returned in redoubled force. I don't know what would have happened if Adèle had been a perfectly beautiful and amiable girl, and had herself in the least liked me. I suppose then my mother would have been overcome. But though extremely lovely at fifteen, Adèle was not prettier than French girls in general at eighteen; she was firm, and fiery, and high principled; but, as the light traits already noticed of her enough show, not in the least amiable; and although she would have married me, had her father wished it, was always glad to have me out of her way. My love was much too high and fantastic to be diminished by her loss of beauty; but I perfectly well saw and admitted it, having never at any time been in the slightest degree blinded by love, as I perceive other men are, out of my critic nature. And day followed on day, and month to month, of complex absurdity, pain, error, wasted affection, and rewardless semi-virtue, which I am content to sweep out of the way of what better things I can recollect at this time, into the smallest possible size of dust heap, and wish the Dustman Oblivion good clearance of them.

With this one general note, concerning children's conduct to their parents, that a great quantity of external and irksome obedience may be shown them, which virtually is no obedience, because it is not cheerful and total. The *wish* to disobey is already disobedience; and although at this time I was really doing a great many things I did not like, to please my parents, I have not now *one* self-approving thought or consolation in having done so, so much did its sullenness and maimedness pollute the meagre sacrifice.

257. But, before I quit, for this time, the field of romance, let me write the epitaph of one of its sweet shadows, which some who knew the shadow may be glad I should write. The ground floor, under my father's counting-house at Billiter Street, I have already said was occupied by Messrs Wardell & Co. The head of this firm was an extremely intelligent and refined elderly gentleman, darkish, with spiritedly curling and projecting dark hair, and bright eyes; good-natured and amiable in a high degree, well educated, not over wise, always well pleased with himself, happy in a sensible wife, and a very beautiful, and entirely gentle and good, only daughter. Not over wise, I repeat, but an excellent man of business; older, and, I suppose, already considerably richer, than my father. He had a handsome house at Hampstead, and spared no pains on his daughter's education.

It must have been some time about this year 1839, or the previous one, that my father having been deploring to Mr Wardell the discomfortable state of mind I had got into about Adèle, Mr Wardell proposed to him to try whether some slight diversion of my thoughts might not be effected by a visit to Hampstead. My father's fancy was still set on Lady Clara Vere de Vere; but Miss Wardell was everything that a girl should be, and an heiress,—of perhaps something more than my own fortune was likely to come to. And the two fathers agreed that nothing could be more fit, rational, and desirable, than such an arrangement. So I was sent to pass a summer afternoon, and dine at Hampstead.

258. It would have been an extremely delightful afternoon for any youth not a simpleton. Miss Wardell had often enough heard me spoken of by her father as a well-conducted youth, already of some literary reputation—author of the 'Poetry of Architecture'—winner of the Newdigate,*—First class man in expectation. She herself had been brought up in a way closely resembling my own, in severe seclusion by devoted parents, at a suburban villa with a pretty garden, to skip, and gather flowers, in. The chief difference was that, from the first, Miss Wardell had had excellent masters, and was now an extremely accomplished, intelligent, and faultless maid of seventeen; fragile and delicate to a degree enhancing her beauty with some solemnity of fear, yet in perfect health, as far as a fast-growing girl could be; a softly moulded slender brunette, with her father's dark curling hair transfigured into playful grace round the pretty, modest, not unthoughtful, gray-eyed face. Of the afternoon at Hampstead, I remember only that it was a fine day, and that we walked in the garden; mamma, as her mere duty to me in politeness at a first visit, superintending,—it would have been wiser to have left us to get on how we could. I very heartily

and reverently admired the pretty creature, and would fain have done, or said, anything I could to please her. Literally to *please* her, for that is, indeed, my hope with all girls, in spite of what I have above related of my mistaken ways of recommending myself. My primary thought is how to serve *them*, and make them happy, and if they could use me for a plank bridge over a stream, or set me up for a post to tie a swing to, or anything of the sort not requiring me to talk, I should be always quite happy in such promotion. This sincere devotion to them, with intense delight in whatever beauty or grace they chance to have, and in most cases, perceptive sympathy, heightened by faith in their right feelings, for the most part gives me considerable power with girls: but all this prevents me from ever being in the least at ease with them,—and I have no doubt that during the whole afternoon at Hampstead, I gave little pleasure to my companion. For the rest, though I extremely admired Miss Wardell, she was not my sort of beauty. I like oval faces, crystalline blonde, with straightish, at the utmost wavy, (or, in length, wreathed) hair, and the form elastic, and foot firm. Miss Wardell's dark and tender grace had no power over me, except to make me extremely afraid of being tiresome to her. On the whole, I suppose I came off pretty well, for she afterwards allowed herself to be brought out to Herne Hill to see the pictures, and so on; and I recollect her looking a little frightenedly pleased at my kneeling down to hold a book for her, or some such matter.

259. After this second interview, however, my father and mother asking me seriously what I thought of her, and I explaining to them that though I saw all her beauty, and merit, and niceness, she yet was not my sort of girl,—the negotiations went no farther at that time, and a little while after, were ended for all time; for at Hampstead they went on teaching the tender creature High German, and French of Paris, and Kant's *Metaphysics*, and Newton's *Principia*;* and then they took her to Paris, and tired her out with seeing everything every day, all day long, besides the dazzle and excitement of such a first outing from Hampstead; and she at last getting too pale and weak, they brought her back to some English seaside place, I forget where: and there she fell into nervous fever and faded away, with the light of death flickering clearer and clearer in her soft eyes, and never skipped in Hampstead garden more.

How the parents, especially the father, lived on, I never could understand; but I suppose they were honestly religious without talking of it, and they had nothing to blame themselves in, except not having known better. The father, though with grave lines altering his face for ever, went steadily on with his business, and lived to be old.

260. I cannot be sure of the date of either Miss Withers' or Miss Wardell's death; that of Sybilla Dowie (told in Fors*), more sad than either, was much later; but the loss of her sweet spirit, following her lover's, had been felt by us before the time of which I am now writing. I had never myself seen Death, nor had any part in the grief or anxiety of a sick chamber; nor had I ever seen, far less conceived, the misery of unaided poverty. But I had been made to think of it; and in the deaths of the creatures whom I had seen joyful, the sense of deep pity, not sorrow for myself, but for them, began to mingle with all the thoughts, which, founded on the Homeric, Aeschylean, and Shakespearian tragedy, had now begun to modify the untried faith of childhood. The blue of the mountains became deep to me with the purple of mourning,—the clouds that gather round the setting sun,* not subdued, but raised in awe as the harmonies of a Miserere,*—and all the strength and framework of my mind, lurid, like the vaults of Roslyn, when weird fire gleamed on its pillars, foliage-bound, and far in the depth of twilight, 'blazed every rose-carved buttress fair.'*

END OF VOL. I

VOLUME II

CHAPTER I
OF AGE

1. THIS second volume must, I fear, be less pleasing to the general reader, with whom the first has found more favour than I had hoped,—not because I tire of talking, but that the talk must be less of other persons, and more of myself. For as I look deeper into the mirror, I find myself a more curious person than I had thought. I used to fancy that everybody would like clouds and rocks as well as I did, if once told to look at them; whereas, after fifty years of trial, I find that is not so, even in modern days; having long ago known that, in ancient ones, the clouds and mountains which have been life to me, were mere inconvenience and horror to most of mankind.

2. I related, in the first volume, page 61, some small part of my pleasures under St Vincent's rock at Clifton and the beginning of quartz-study there with the now No. 51 of the Brantwood series. Compare with these childish sentiments, those of the maturely judging John Evelyn, at the same place, 30th June, 1654:—

'The city' (Bristol) 'wholly mercantile, as standing neere the famous Severne, commodiously for Ireland and the Western world. Here I first saw the manner of refining suggar, and casting it into loaves, where we had a collation of eggs fried in the suggar furnace,[1] together with excellent Spanish wine: but what appeared most stupendious to me, was the rock of St Vincent, a little distance from yᵉ towne, the precipice whereoff is equal to anything of that nature I have seen in yᵉ most confragose* cataracts of the Alpes, the river gliding between them at an extraordinary depth. Here we went searching for diamonds, and to the Hot Wells at its foote. There is also on the side of this horrid Alp a very romantic seate: and so we returned to Bathe in the evening.'

3. Of course Evelyn uses the word 'horrid'* only in its Latin sense; but his mind is evidently relieved by returning to Bath; and although, farther on, he describes without alarm the towne and county of Nottingham as 'seeming to be but one entire rock, as it were,' he

---

[1] Note (by Evelyn's editor in 1827): 'A kind of entertainment like that we now have of eating beefsteaks drest on the stoker's shovel, and drinking porter at the famous brewhouses in London.'

explains his toleration of that structure in the close of his sentence—
'an exceeding pleasant shire, full of gentry.' Of his impressions of the
'stupendious' rocks of Fontainebleau, and ungentle people of the
Simplon, I have to speak in another place.*

In these and many other such particulars I find the typical English
mind, both then and now, so adverse to my own, as also to those of my
fellow companions through the sorrows of this world, that it becomes
for me a matter of acute Darwinian interest to trace my species from
origin to extinction: and I have, therefore, to warn the reader, and ask
his pardon, that while a modest person writes his autobiography chiefly
by giving accounts of the people he has met, I find it only possible,
within my planned limits, to take note of those who have had distinct
power in the training or the pruning of little me to any good.

4. I return first to my true master in mathematics, poor
Mr Rowbotham. Of course he missed his Herne Hill evenings sadly
when I went to Oxford. But always, when we came home, it was understood that once in the fortnight, or so, as he felt himself able, he
should still toil up the hill to tea. We were always sorry to see him at
the gate; but felt that it was our clear small duty to put up with his sigh-
ing for an hour or two in such rest as his woful life could find. Nor
were we without some real affection for him. His face had a certain
grandeur, from its constancy of patience, bewildered innocence, and
firm lines of faculty in geometric sort. Also he brought us news from
the mathematical and grammatical world, and told us some interesting details of manufacture, if he had been on a visit to his friend
Mr Crawshay. His own home became yearly more wretched, till one
day its little ten-years-old Peepy choked himself with his teetotum.*
The father told us, with real sorrow, the stages of the child's protracted
suffering before he died; but observed, finally, that it was better he
should have been taken away,—both for him and his parents. Evidently
the poor mathematical mind was relieved from one of its least soluble
burdens, and the sad face, that evening, had an expression of more than
usual repose.

I never forgot the lesson it taught me of what human life meant in
the suburbs of London.

5. The rigidly moral muse of Mr Pringle had by this time gone to
Africa, or, let us hope, Arabia Felix,* in the other world; and the
reins of my poetical genius had been given into the hand of kindly
Mr W. H. Harrison in the Vauxhall Road, of whom account has already
been given in the first chapter of 'On the Old Road'* enough to carry
us on for the present.

I must next bring up to time the history of my father's affectionate physician, Dr Grant. Increasing steadily in reputation, he married a widowed lady, Mrs Sidney, of good position in Richmond; and became the guardian of her two extremely nice and clever daughters, Augusta and Emma, who both felt great respect, and soon great regard, for their stepfather, and were every day more dutiful and pleasing children to him. Estimating my mother's character also as they ought, later on, they were familiar visitors to us; the younger, Emma, having good taste for drawing, and other quiet accomplishments and pursuits. At the time I am now looking back to, however, the Star and Garter breakfasts had become rarer, and were connected mostly with visits to Hampton Court, where the great vine, and the maze, were of thrilling attraction to me; and the Cartoons* began to take the aspect of mild nightmare and nuisance which they have ever since retained.

My runs with cousin Mary in the maze,* (once, as in Dantesque alleys of lucent verdure in the Moon, with Adèle and Elise,) always had something of an enchanted and Faery-Queen glamour in them: and I went on designing more and more complicated mazes in the blank leaves of my lesson books—wasting, I suppose, nearly as much time that way as in the trisection of the angle. Howbeit, afterwards, the coins of Cnossus, and characters of Daedalus, Theseus, and the Minotaur,* became intelligible to me as to few: and I have much unprinted MSS about them, intended for expansion in 'Ariadne Florentina,' and other labyrinthine volumes, but which the world must get on now without the benefit of, as it can.*

6. Meantime, from the Grove, whitehaired mamma Monro,* and silvery-fringed Petite, had gone to their rest. Mrs Gray cared no longer for the pride of her house, or shade of her avenue; while more and more, Mr Gray's devotion to Don Quixote, and to my poetry in 'Friendship's Offering,' interfered with his business habits. At last it was thought that, being true Scots both of them, they might better prosper over the Border. They went to Glasgow, where Mr Gray took up some sort of a wine business, and read Rob Roy instead of Don Quixote. We went to Glasgow to see them, on our Scottish tour, and sorrowfully perceived them to be going downwards, even in their Scottish world. For a little change, they were asked to Oxford that autumn, to see their spoiled Johnnie carrying all before him: and the good couple being seated in Christ Church Cathedral under the organ, and seeing me walk in with my companions in our silken sleeves, and with accompanying flourishes by Mr Marshall on the trumpet stop,* and Rembrandtesque effects of candlelight upon the Norman columns,

were both of them melted into tears; and remained speechless with reverent delight all the evening afterwards.

7. I have left too long without word the continual benevolence towards us of the family at Widmore, Mr Telford and his three sisters; the latter absolutely well-educated women—wise, without either severity or ostentation, using all they knew for the good of their neighbours, and exhibiting in their own lives every joy of sisterly love and active homeliness. Mr Henry Telford's perfectly quiet, slightly melancholy, exquisitely sensitive face, browned by continual riding from Bromley to Billiter Street, remains with me, among the most precious of the pictures which, unseen of any guest, hang on the walls of my refectory.

Mr and Mrs Robert Cockburn, as the years drew on, became more and more kindly, but less and less approvingly, interested in our monastic ways at Herne Hill; and in my partly thwarted and uncomfortable, partly singular, development of literary character. Mrs Cockburn took earnest pains with my mother to get her to send me more into society, that I might be licked a little into shape. But my mother was satisfied with me as I was: and besides, Mrs Cockburn and she never got quite well on together. My mother, according to her established manner, would no more dine with her than with any one else, and was even careless in returning calls; and Mrs Cockburn—which was wonderful in a woman of so much sense—instead of being merely sorry for my mother's shyness, and trying to efface her sense of inferiority in education and position, took this somewhat in pique. But among the fateful chances of my own life in her endeavours to do something for me, and somehow break the shell of me, she one day asked me to dine with Lockhart, and see his little harebell-like daintiness of a daughter.* I suppose Mrs Cockburn must have told him of my love of Scott, yet I do not remember manifesting that sentiment in any wise during dinner: I recollect only, over the wine, making some small effort to display my Oxonian orthodoxy and sound learning, with respect to the principles of Church Establishment; and being surprised, and somewhat discomfited, by finding that Mr Lockhart knew the Greek for 'bishop' and 'elder' as well as I did. On going into the drawing-room, however, I made every effort to ingratiate myself with the little dark-eyed, high-foreheaded Charlotte, and was very sorry,—but I don't think the child was,—when she was sent to bed.

8. But the most happy turn of Fortune's wheel for me, in this year '39, was the coming of Osborne Gordon to Herne Hill to be my private tutor, and read with me in our little nursery. Taking up the ravelled ends of yet workable and spinnable flax in me, he began to twist them,

at first through much wholesome pain, into such tenor as they were really capable of.

The first thing he did was to stop all pressure in reading. His inaugural sentence was, 'When you have got too much to do, don't do it,'— a golden saying which I have often repeated since, but not enough obeyed.

To Gordon himself, his own proverb was less serviceable. He was a man of quite exceptional power, and there is no saying what he might have done, with any strong motive. Very early, a keen, though entirely benevolent, sense of the absurdity of the world took away his heart in working for it:—perhaps I should rather have said, the density and unmalleability of the world, than absurdity. He thought there was nothing to be done with it, and that after all it would get on by itself. Chiefly, that autumn, in our walks over the Norwood hills, he, being then an ordained, or on the point of being ordained, priest, surprised me greatly by avoiding, evidently with the sense of its being useless bother, my favourite topic of conversation, namely, the torpor of the Protestant churches, and their duty, as it to me appeared, before any thought of missionary work, out of Europe, or comfortable settling to pastoral work at home, to trample finally out the smouldering 'diabolic fire' of the Papacy, in all Papal-Catholic lands. For I was then by training, thinking, and the teaching of such small experience as I had, as zealous, pugnacious, and self-sure a Protestant as you please. The first condition of my being so was, of course, total ignorance of Christian history; the second,—one for which the Roman Church is indeed guiltily responsible,—that all the Catholic Cantons of Switzerland, counting Savoy also as a main point of Alpine territory, are idle and dirty, and all Protestant ones busy and clean—a most impressive fact to my evangelical mother, whose first duty and first luxury of life consisted in purity of person and surroundings; while she and my father alike looked on idleness as indisputably Satanic. They failed not, therefore, to look carefully on the map for the bridge, or gate, or vale, or ridge, which marked the separation of Protestant from the benighted Catholic cantons; and it was rare if the first or second field and cottage, beyond the border, did not too clearly justify their exulting,—though also indignant and partly sorrowful,—enforcement upon me of the natural consequences of Popery.

9. The third reason for my strength of feeling at this time was a curious one. In proportion to the delight I felt in the ceremonial of foreign churches, was my conviction of the falseness of religious sentiment founded on these enjoyments. I had no foolish scorn of them, as

the proper expressions of the Catholic Faith; but infinite scorn of the lascivious sensibility which could change its beliefs because it delighted in these, and be 'piped into a new creed by the whine of an organ pipe.'*
So that alike my reason, and romantic pleasure, on the Continent, combined to make a bitter Protestant of me;—yet not a malicious nor ungenerous one. I never suspected Catholic priests of dishonesty, nor doubted the purity of the former Catholic Church. I was a Protestant Cavalier, not Protestant Roundhead,*—entirely desirous of keeping all that was noble and traditional in religious ritual, and reverent to the existing piety of the Catholic peasantry. So that the 'diabolic fire' which I wanted trampled out, was only the corrupt Catholicism which rendered the vice of Paris and the dirt of Savoy possible; and which I was quite right in thinking it the duty of every Christian priest to attack, and end the schism and scandal of it.

10. Osborne, on the contrary, was a practical Englishman, of the shrewdest, yet gentlest type; keenly perceptive of folly, but disposed to pardon most human failings as little more. His ambition was restricted to the walls of Christ Church; he was already the chiefly trusted aid of the old Dean; probably, next to him, the best Greek scholar in Oxford, and perfectly practised in all the college routine of business. He thought that the Church of England had—even in Oxford—enough to do in looking after her own faults; and addressed himself, in our conversations on Forest Hill, mainly to mollify my Protestant animosities, enlarge my small acquaintance with ecclesiastical history, and recall my attention to the immediate business in hand, of enjoying our walk, and recollecting what we had read in the morning.

In his proper work with me, no tutor could have been more diligent or patient. His own scholarly power was of the highest order; his memory (the necessary instrument of great scholarship) errorless and effortless; his judgment and feeling in literature sound; his interpretation of political events always rational, and founded on wide detail of well-balanced knowledge; and all this without in the least priding himself on his classic power, or wishing to check any of my impulses in other directions. He had taken his double first with the half of his strength, and would have taken a triple one without priding himself on it: he was amused by my facility in rhyming, recognized my true instinct in painting, and sympathised with me in love of country life and picturesque towns, but always in a quieting and reposeful manner. Once in after life, provoked at finding myself still unable to read Greek easily, I intimated to him a half-formed purpose to throw everything else aside, for a time, and make myself a sound Greek scholar. 'I think it would give you more trouble than it is worth,' said he. Another time, as I was making the drawing of 'Chamouni in afternoon sunshine' for him, (now at his sister's,) I spoke of the constant vexation I suffered because I could not draw better. 'And I,' he said, simply, 'should be very content if I could draw at all.'

11. During Gordon's stay with us, this 1839 autumn, we got our second Turner drawing. Certainly the most curious failure of memory—among the many I find—is that I don't know when I *saw* my first! I feel as if Mr Windus's parlour at Tottenham had been familiar to me since the dawn of existence in Brunswick Square.

Mr Godfrey Windus was a retired coachmaker, living in a cheerful little villa, with low rooms on the ground floor opening pleasantly into each other, like a sort of grouped conservatory, between his front and back gardens: their walls beset, but not crowded, with Turner drawings of the England series; while in his portfolio-stands, coming there straight from the publishers of the books they illustrated, were the entire series of the illustrations to Scott, to Byron, to the South Coast, and to Finden's Bible.*

Nobody, in all England, at that time,—and Turner was already sixty,—*cared*, in the true sense of the word, for Turner, but the retired coachmaker of Tottenham, and I.

Nor, indeed, could the public ever see the drawings, so as to begin to care for them. Mr Fawkes's were shut up at Farnley, Sir Peregrine Acland's, perishing of damp in his passages, and Mr Windus bought all that were made for engravers as soon as the engraver had done with them. The advantage, however, of seeing them all collected at his house,—he gave an open day each week, and to me the run of his rooms at any time,—was, to the general student, inestimable, and, for me, the means of writing 'Modern Painters.'

12. It is, I think, noteworthy that, although first attracted to Turner by the mountain truth in Rogers' Italy,—when I saw the drawings, it was almost wholly the pure artistic quality that fascinated me, whatever the subject; so that I was not in the least hindered by the beauty of Mr Windus's Llanberis or Melrose* from being quite happy when my father at last gave me, not for a beginning of Turner collection, but for a specimen of Turner's work, which was all—as it was supposed—I should ever need or aspire to possess, the 'Richmond Bridge, Surrey.'*

The triumphant talk between us over it, when we brought it home, consisted, as I remember, greatly in commendation of the quantity of Turnerian subject and character which this single specimen united:—'it had trees, architecture, water, a lovely sky, and a clustered bouquet of brilliant figures.'

And verily the Surrey Richmond remained for at least two years our only Turner possession, and the second we bought, the Gosport,* which came home when Gordon was staying with us, had still none of the delicate beauty of Turner except in its sky; nor were either my father or I the least offended by the ill-made bonnets of the lady-passengers in the cutter, nor by the helmsman's head being put on the wrong way.

The reader is not to think, because I speak thus frankly of Turner's faults, that I judge them greater, or know them better, now, than I did then. I knew them at this time of getting Richmond and Gosport just as well as other people; but knew also the power shown through these faults, to a degree quite wonderful for a boy;—it being my chief recreation, after Greek or trigonometry in the nursery-study, to go down and feast on my Gosport.

13. And so, after Christmas, I went back to Oxford for the last push, in January 1840, and did very steady work with Gordon, in St Aldate's;[1] the sense that I was coming of age somewhat increasing the feeling of responsibility for one's time. On my twenty-first birthday my father brought me for a present the drawing of Winchelsea,*—a curious choice, and an unlucky one. The thundrous sky and broken white light of storm round the distant gate and scarcely visible church, were but too true symbols of the time that was coming upon us; but neither he nor I were given to reading omens, or dreading them. I suppose he had been struck by the power of the drawing, and he always liked soldiers. I was disappointed, and saw for the first time clearly that my father's joy in Rubens and Sir Joshua could never become sentient of Turner's microscopic touch. But I was entirely grateful for his purpose, and very thankful to have any new Turner drawing whatsoever; and as at home the Gosport, so in St Aldate's the Winchelsea, was the chief recreation of my fatigued hours.

14. This Turner gift, however, was only complimentary. The same day my father transferred into my name in the stocks as much as would bring in at least £200 a year, and watched with some anxiety the use I should make of this first command of money. Not that I had ever been

---

[1] The street, named from its parish church, going down past Christ Church to the river. It was the regular course of a gentleman-commoner's residence to be promoted from Peckwater to Tom Quad, and turned out into the street for his last term. I have no notion at this minute who St Aldate was;*—American visitors may be advised that in Oxford it will be expected of them to call him St Old.

under definite restriction about it: at Oxford I ran what accounts with
the tradesmen I liked, and the bills were sent in to my mother weekly;
there was never any difficulty or demur on either side, and there was
nothing out of the common way in Oxford I wanted to buy, except the
engraving of Turner's Grand Canal, for my room wall,—and Monsieur
Jabot, the first I ever saw of Topffer's rivalless caricatures,* one day
when I had a headache. For anything on which my state or comfort in
the least depended, my father was more disposed to be extravagant
than I; but he had always the most curious suspicion of my taste for
minerals, and only the year before, in the summer term, was entirely
vexed and discomfited at my giving eleven shillings for a piece of
Cornish chalcedony. That I never thought of buying a mineral without
telling him what I had paid for it, besides advising him duly of the fact,
curiously marks the intimate confidence between us: but alas, my
respect for his judgment was at this time by these littlenesses gradually
diminished; and my confidence in my own painfully manifested to him
a very little while after he had permitted me the above stated measure
of independence. The Turner drawings hitherto bought,—Richmond,
Gosport, Winchelsea,—were all supplied by Mr Griffith, an agent in
whom Turner had perfect confidence, and my father none. Both were
fatally wrong. Had Turner dealt straight with my father, there is no
saying how much happiness might have come of it for all three of us;
had my father not been always afraid of being taken in by Mr Griffith,
he might at that time have bought some of the loveliest drawings
that Turner ever made, at entirely fair prices. But Mr Griffith's art-
salesmanship entirely offended my father from the first, and the best
drawings were always let pass, because Mr Griffith recommended
them, while Winchelsea and Gosport were both bought—among other
reasons—because Mr Griffith said they were not drawings which we
ought to have!

15. Among those of purest quality in his folios at this time was one
I especially coveted, the Harlech.* There had been a good deal of dealers' yea and nay about it, whether it was for sale or not; it was a smaller
drawing than most of the England and Wales series, and there were
many hints in the market about its being iniquitous in price. The
private view day of the Old Water Colour came; and, arm in arm
with my father, I met Mr Griffith in the crowd. After the proper five
minutes of how we liked the exhibition, he turned specially to me.
'I have some good news for you, the Harlech is ready for sale.' 'I'll take
it then,' I replied, without so much as a glance at my father, and without asking the price. Smiling a little ironically, Mr Griffith went on,

'And—seventy,'—implying that seventy was a low price, at once told me in answer to my confidence. But it was thirty above the Winchelsea, twenty-four above Gosport, and my father was of course sure that Mr Griffith had put twenty pounds on at the instant.

The mingled grief and scorn on his face told me what I had done; but I was too happy on pouncing on my Harlech to feel for him. All sorts of blindness and error on both sides, but, on his side, inevitable,— on mine, more foolish than culpable; fatal every way, beyond words.

16. I can scarcely understand my eagerness and delight in getting the Harlech at this time, because, during the winter, negotiations had been carried on in Paris for Adèle's marriage; and, it does not seem as if I had been really so much crushed by that event as I expected to be. There are expressions, however, in the foolish diaries I began to write, soon after, of general disdain of life, and all that it could in future bestow on me, which seem inconsistent with extreme satisfaction in getting a water-colour drawing, sixteen inches by nine. But whatever germs of better things remained in me, were then all centred in this love of Turner. It was not a piece of painted paper, but a Welsh castle and village, and Snowdon in blue cloud, that I bought for my seventy pounds. This must have been in the Easter holidays;—Harlech was brought home and safely installed in the drawing-room on the other side of the fireplace from my idol-niche: and I went triumphantly back to St Aldate's and Winchelsea.

In spite of Gordon's wholesome moderatorship, the work had come by that time to high pressure, until twelve at night from six in the morning, with little exercise, no cheerfulness, and no sense of any use in what I read, to myself or anybody else: things progressing also smoothly in Paris, to the abyss. One evening, after Gordon had left me, about ten o'clock, a short tickling cough surprised me, because pre-ceded by a curious sensation in the throat, and followed by a curious taste in the mouth, which I presently perceived to be that of blood. It must have been on a Saturday or Sunday evening, for my father, as well as my mother, was in the High Street lodgings. I walked round to them and told them what had happened.

17. My mother, an entirely skilled physician in all forms of con-sumptive disease, was not frightened, but sent round to the Deanery to ask leave for me to sleep out of my lodgings. Morning consultations ended in our going up to town, and town consultations in my being forbid any farther reading under pressure, and in the Dean's giving me, with many growls, permission to put off taking my degree for a year. During the month or two following, passed at Herne Hill, my

father's disappointment at the end of his hopes of my obtaining distinction in Oxford was sorrowfully silenced by his anxiety for my life. Once or twice the short cough, and mouth-taste—it was no more—of blood, returned; but my mother steadily maintained there was nothing serious the matter, and that I only wanted rest and fresh air. The doctors, almost unanimously,—Sir James Clark excepted,—gave gloomier views. Sir James cheerfully, but decidedly, ordered me abroad before autumn, to be as much in open carriages as possible, and to winter in Italy.

And Mr Telford consented to sit in the counting-house, and the clerks promised to be diligent; and my father, to whom the business was nothing, but for me, left his desk, and all other cares of life, but that of nursing me.

18. Of his own feelings, he said little; mine, in the sickly fermentation of temper I was in, were little deserving of utterance, describable indeed less as feelings than as the want of them, in all wholesome directions but one;—magnetic pointing to all presence of natural beauty, and to the poles of such art and science as interpreted it. My preparations for the journey were made with some renewal of spirit; my mother was steadily, bravely, habitually cheerful; while my father, capable to the utmost of every wise enjoyment in travelling, and most of all, of that in lovely landscape, had some personal joy in the thought of seeing South Italy. The attacks of the throat cough seemed to have ceased, and the line of our journey began to be planned with some of the old exultation.

That we might not go through Paris, the route was arranged by Rouen and the Loire to Tours, then across France by Auvergne, and down the Rhone to Avignon; thence, by the Riviera and Florence, to the South.

19. 'And is there to be no more Oxford?' asks Froude, a little reproachfully, in a recent letter concerning these memoranda; for he was at Oriel while I was at Christ Church, and does not think I have given an exhaustive view either of the studies or manners of the University in our day.

No, dear friend. I have no space in this story to describe the advantages I never used; nor does my own failure give me right to blame, even were there any use in blaming, a system now passed away. Oxford taught me as much Greek and Latin as she could; and though I think she might also have told me that fritillaries grew in Iffley meadow, it was better that she left me to find them for myself, than that she should have told me, as nowadays she would, that the painting on them was only to amuse the midges.* For the rest, the whole time I was there, my mind was simply in the state of a squash before 'tis a peascod,*—and remained so yet a year or two afterwards, I grieve to say;—so that for any account of my real life, the gossip hitherto given to its codling or cocoon condition has brought us but a little way. I must get on to the days of opening sight, and effective labour; and to the scenes of nobler education which all men who keep their hearts open, receive in the End of Days.

CHAPTER II

ROME

20. HOWEVER dearly bought, the permission to cease reading, and put what strength was left into my sketching again, gave healthy stimulus to all faculties which had been latently progressive in me; and the sketch-books and rulers were prepared for this journey on hitherto unexampled stateliness of system.

It had chanced, in the spring of the year, that David Roberts had brought home and exhibited his sketches in Egypt and the Holy Land.* They were the first studies ever made conscientiously by an English painter, not to exhibit his own skill, or make capital out of his subjects, but to give true portraiture of scenes of historical and religious interest. They were faithful and laborious beyond any outlines from nature I had ever seen, and I felt also that their severely restricted method was within reach of my own skill, and applicable to all my own purposes.

With Roberts' deficiencies or mannerism I have here no concern. He taught me, of absolute good, the use of the fine point instead of the blunt one; attention and indefatigable correctness in detail; and the simplest means of expressing ordinary light and shade on grey ground, flat wash for the full shadows, and heightening of the gradated lights by warm white.

21. I tried these adopted principles first in the courtyard of the Chateau de Blois: and came in to papa and mamma declaring that 'Prout would give his ears to make such a drawing as that.'

With some truth and modesty, I might have said he 'would have changed eyes with me;' for Prout's manner was gravely restricted by his nearness of sight. But also this Blois sketch showed some dawning notions of grace in proportion, and largeness of effect, which enabled me for the first time that year, to render continental subjects with just expression of their character and scale, and well-rounded solidification of pillars and sculpture.

22. The last days of the summer were well spent at Amboise, Tours, Aubusson, Pont Gibaud, and Le Puy; but as we emerged into the Rhone valley, autumn broke angrily on us; and the journey by Valence to Avignon was all made gloomy by the ravage of a just past inundation, of which the main mass at Montelimar had risen from six to eight feet in the streets, and the slime remained, instead of fields, over—I forget in fact, and can scarcely venture to conceive,—what extent of plain. The Rhone, through these vast gravelly levels a mere driving weight of discoloured water;—the Alps, on the other side, now in late autumn snowless up to their lower peaks, and showing few eminent ones;—the bise,* now first letting one feel what malignant wind could be,—might, perhaps, all be more depressing to me in my then state of temper; but I have never cared to see the lower Rhone any more; and to my love of cottage rather than castle, added at this time another strong moral principle, that if ever one was metamorphosed into a river, and could choose one's own size, it would be out of all doubt more prudent and delightful to be Tees or Wharfe than Rhone.

And then, for the first time, at Frejus, and on the Esterelle and the Western Riviera, I saw some initial letters of Italy, as distinct from Lombardy,—Italy of the stone pine and orange and palm, white villa and blue sea; and saw it with right judgment, as a wreck, and a viciously neglected one.

23. I don't think the reader has yet been informed that I inherited to the full my mother's love of tidiness and cleanliness; so that quite one of the most poetical charms of Switzerland to me, next to her white snows, was her white sleeves. Also I had my father's love of solidity and soundness,—of unveneered, unrouged, and well finished things; and here on the Riviera there were lemons and palms, yes,—but the lemons pale, and mostly skin; the palms not much larger than parasols; the sea—blue, yes, but its beach nasty; the buildings, pompous, luxurious, painted like Grimaldi,*—usually broken down at the ends, and in the middle, having sham architraves daubed over windows with no glass in them; the rocks shaly and ragged, the people filthy: and over everything, a coat of plaster dust.

I was in a bad humour? Yes, but everything I have described is as I say, for all that; and though the last time I was at Sestri* *I* wanted to stay there, the ladies with me wouldn't and couldn't, because of the filth of the inn; and the last time I was at Genoa, 1882, my walk round the ramparts was only to study what uglinesses of plants liked to grow in dust, and crawl, like the lizards, into clefts of ruin.

24. At Genoa I saw then for the first time the circular Pieta by Michael Angelo,* which was my initiation in all Italian art. For at this time I understood no jot of Italian painting, but only Rubens, Vandyke, and Velasquez. At Genoa, I did not even hunt down the Vandykes,* but went into the confused frontage of the city at its port, (no traversing blank quay blocking out the sea, then,) and drew the crescent of houses round the harbour, borne on their ancient arches;—a noble subject, and one of the best sketches I ever made.

From Genoa, more happy journey by the Eastern Riviera began to restore my spring of heart. I am just in time, in writing these memories, to catch the vision of the crossing Magra, in old time, and some of the other mountain streams of the two Rivieras.

It seems unbelievable to myself, as I set it down, but there were then only narrow mule bridges over the greater streams on either side of which were grouped the villages, where the river slackened behind its sea bar. Of course, in the large towns, Albenga, Savona, Ventimiglia, and so on, there were proper bridges; but at the intermediate hamlets (and the torrents round whose embouchures they grew were often formidable), the country people trusted to the slack of the water at the bar, and its frequent failure altogether in summer, for traverse of their own carrioles.* and had neither mind nor means to build Waterloo bridges for the convenience of English carriages and four. The English carriage got across the shingle how it could; the boys of the village, if the horses could not pull it through, harnessed themselves in front; and in windy weather, with deep water on the inside of the bar, and blue breakers on the other, one really began sometimes to think of the slackening wheels of Pharaoh.*

25. It chanced that there were two days of rain as we passed the Western Riviera; there was a hot night at Albenga before they came on, and my father wrote—which was extremely wrong of him—a parody of 'Woe is me, Alhama,'* the refrain being instead, 'Woe is me, Albenga'; the Moorish minarets of the old town and its Saracen legends, I suppose, having brought 'the Moorish King rode up and down'* into his head. Then the rain, with wild sirocco,* came on; and somewhere near Savona there was a pause at the brink of one of the streams, in rather angry flood, and some question if the carriage could get through. Loaded, it could not, and everybody was ordered to get out and be carried across, the carriage to follow, in such shifts as it might. Everybody obeyed these orders, and submitted to the national customs

with great hilarity, except my mother, who absolutely refused to be carried in the arms of an Italian ragged opera hero, more or less resembling the figures whom she had seen carrying off into the mountains the terrified Taglioni, or Cerito.* Out of the carriage she would not move, on any solicitation;—if they could pull the carriage through, they could pull her too, she said. My father was alike alarmed and angry, but as the surrounding opera corps de ballet seemed to look on the whole thing rather as a jest and an occasion for bajocco* gathering, than any crisis of fate, my mother had her way; a good team of bare-legged youngsters was put to, and she and the carriage entered the stream with shouting. Two-thirds through, the sand was soft, and horses and boys stopped to breathe. There was another, and really now serious, remonstrance with my mother, we being all nervous about quicksands, as if it had been the middle of Lancaster Bay. But stir she would not; the horses got their wind again, and the boys their way, and with much whip cracking and splashing, carriage and dama Inglese were victoriously dragged to dry land, with general promotion of good will between the two nations.

26. Of the passage of Magra, a day or two afterwards, my memory is vague as its own waves. There were all sorts of paths across the tract of troubled shingle, and I was thinking of the Carrara mountains beyond, all the while. Most of the streams fordable easily enough; a plank or two, loosely propped with a heap of stones, for pier and buttress, replaced after every storm, served the foot passenger. The main stream could neither be bridged nor forded, but was clumsily ferried, and at one place my mother had no choice really but between wading or being carried. She suffered the indignity, I think with some feeling of its being a consequence of the French Revolution, and remained cross all the way to Carrara.

We were going on to Massa to sleep, but had time to stop and walk up the dazzling white road to the lower quarry, and even to look into one or two 'studios,'—beginnings of my fixed contempt for rooms so called, ever since. Nevertheless, partly in my father's sense of what was kind and proper to be done,—partly by way of buying 'a trifle from Matlock,'*—and partly because he and I both liked the fancy of the group, we bought a two feet high 'Bacchus and Ariadne,' copied from I know not what (we supposed classic) original,* and with as much art in it as usually goes to a French timepiece. It remained long on a pedestal in the library at Denmark Hill, till it got smoked,* and was put out of the way.

With the passage of the Magra, and the purchase of the Bacchus and

Ariadne, to remain for a sort of monument of the two-feet high knowledge of classic art then possessed by me, ended the state of mind in
which my notions of sculpture lay between Chantrey and Roubilliac.
Across Magra I felt that I was in Italy proper; the next day we drove
over the bridge of Serchio into Lucca.

27. I am wrong in saying I 'felt,' *then*, I was in Italy proper. It is only
in looking back that I can mark the exact point where the tide began to
turn for me; and total ignorance of what early Christian art meant, and
of what living sculpture meant, were first pierced by vague wonder and
embarrassed awe, at the new mystery round me. The effect of Lucca on
me at this time is now quite confused with the far greater one in 1845.*
Not so that of the first sight of Pisa, where the solemnity and purity of
its architecture impressed me deeply;—yet chiefly in connection with
Byron and Shelley.* A masked brother of the Misericordia* first met us
in the cathedral of Lucca; but the possible occurrence of the dark figures in the open sunlight of the streets added greatly to the imaginative
effect of Pisa on my then nervous and depressed fancy. I drew the
Spina Chapel* with the Ponte-a-Mare beyond, very usefully and well;
but the languor of the muddy Arno as against Reuss, or Genevoise
Rhone, made me suspect all past or future descriptions of Italian rivers.
Singularly, I never saw Arno in full flood till 1882, nor understood till
then that all the rivers of Italy are mountain torrents. I am ashamed,
myself, to read, but feel it an inevitable duty to print, the piece of diary
which records my first impression of Florence.

28. 'November 13th, 1840. I have just been walking, or sauntering,
in the square of the statues, the air perfectly balmy; and I shall not soon
forget, I hope, the impression left by this square as it opened from the
river, with the enormous mass of tower above,—or of the Duomo
itself. I had not expected any mass of a church, rather something graceful, like La Salute at Venice; and, luckily, coming on it at the south-east
angle, where the gallery round the dome is complete, got nearly run
over before I recovered from the stun of the effect. Not that it is good
as architecture even in its own barbarous style. I cannot tell what to
think of it; but the wealth of exterior marble is quite overwhelming,
and the motion of magnificent figures in marble and bronze about the
great square, thrilling.

'Nov. 15th. I still cannot make up my mind about this place, though
my present feelings are of grievous disappointment. The galleries,
which I walked through yesterday, are impressive enough; but I had as
soon be in the British Museum, as far as enjoyment goes, except for the
Raphaels. I can understand nothing else, and not much of *them*.'

29. At Florence then, this time, the Newgate-like palaces* were rightly hateful to me; the old shop and market-streets rightly pleasant; the inside of the Duomo a horror, the outside a Chinese puzzle. All sacred art,—frescoes, tempera, what not, mere zero, as they were to the Italians themselves; the country round, dead wall and dusty olive;—the whole, a provocation and weariness, except for one master, M. Angelo.

I saw at once in him that there was emotion and human life, more than in the Greeks; and a severity and meaning which were not in Rubens. Everybody about me swearing that Michael Angelo was the finest thing in the world, I was extremely proud of being pleased with him; confirmed greatly in my notion of my own infallibility, and with help of Rogers in the Lorenzo Chapel,* and long sittings and standings about the Bacchus in the Uffizii, progressed greatly and vitally in Michael-Angelesque directions. But I at once pronounced the knife grinder in the Tribune a vulgar nuisance, as I do still; the Venus de Medicis, an uninteresting little person; Raphael's St John,* a piece of black bombast; and the Uffizii collection in general, an unbecoming medley, got together by people who knew nothing, and cared less than nothing,[1] about the arts. On the whole, when I last walked through the Uffizii in 1882 I was precisely of the same opinion, and proud of having arrived at it so quickly. It was not to be expected of me at that time to like either Angelico or Botticelli; and if I had, the upper corridor of the Uffizii was an entirely vile and contemptible place wherein to see the great Madonna of the one, or the Venus Marina* of the other. Both were then in the outer passage from the entrance to the Tribune.

These conclusions being comfortably arrived at, I sate myself down in the middle of the Ponte Vecchio, and made a very true and valuable sketch of the general perspective of its shops and the buildings beyond, looking towards the Duomo. I seem to have had time or will for no more in Florence; the Mercato Vecchio was too crowded to work in, and the carving of the Duomo could not be disengaged from its colour. Hopeful, but now somewhat doubtful, of finding things more to our mind in the south, we drove through the Porta Romana.

30. Siena, Radicofani, Viterbo, and the fourth day, Rome;—a gloomy journey, with gloomier rests. I had a bad weary headache at Siena; and the cathedral seemed to me every way absurd—over-cut, over-striped, over-crocketed, over-gabled, a piece of costly confection-ery, and faithless vanity. In the main it is so; the power of Siena was in

---

[1] That is, cared the wrong way,—liked them for their meanest skills, and worst uses.

her old cathedral, *her* Edward the Confessor's Westminster. Is the ruin of it yet spared?*

The volcanic desert of Radicofani, with gathering storm, and an ominously Aeolian* keyhole in a vile inn, remained long to all of us a terrific memory. At Viterbo I was better, and made a sketch of the convent on one side of the square, rightly felt and done. On the fourth day papa and mamma observed with triumph, though much worried by the jolting, that every mile nearer Rome the road got worse!

31. My stock of Latin learning, with which to begin my studies of the city, consisted of the two first books of Livy, never well known, and the names of places remembered without ever looking where they were on a map; Juvenal, a page or two of Tacitus, and in Virgil the burning of Troy, the story of Dido, the episode of Euryalus and the last battle. Of course, I had nominally read the whole Aeneid, but thought most of it nonsense. Of later Roman history, I had read English abstracts of the imperial vices, and supposed the malaria in the Campagna to be the consequence of the Papacy. I had never heard of a good Roman emperor, or a good pope; was not quite sure whether Trajan* lived before Christ or after, and would have thanked, with a sense of relieved satisfaction, anybody who might have told me that Marcus Antoninus was a Roman philosopher contemporary with Socrates.*

32. The first sight of St Peter's dome, twenty miles away, was little more to any of us than the apparition of a grey milestone, announcing twenty miles yet of stony road before rest. The first sluggish reach of Tiber, with its mud shore and ochreous water, was a quite vile and saddening sight to me,—as compared with breezy tide of Thames, seen from Nanny Clowsley's.* The Piazza del Popolo was as familiar to me, from paintings, as Cheapside, and much less interesting. We went, of course, to some hotel in the Piazza di Spagna, and I went to bed tired and sulky at finding myself in a big street of a big modern town, with nothing to draw, and no end of things to be bothered with. Next day, waking refreshed, of course I said, 'I am in Rome,' after Mr Rogers;* and accompanied papa and mamma, with a tinge of curiosity, to St Peter's.

Most people and books had told me I should be disappointed in its appearance of size. But I have not vainly boasted my habit and faculty of measuring magnitudes, and there was no question to me how big it was. The characters I was not prepared for were the clumsy dulness of the façade, and the entirely vile taste and vapid design of the interior. We walked round it, saw the mosaic copies of pictures we did not care for, the pompous tombs of people whose names we did not know, got out to the fresh air and fountains again with infinite sense of relief, and never again went near the place, any of us, except to hear music, or see processions and paraphernalia.

33. So we went home to lunch, and of course drove about the town in the afternoon, and saw the Forum, Coliseum, and so on. I had no distinct idea what the Forum was* or ever had been, or how the three pillars, or the seven, were connected with it, or the Arch of Severus,* standing without any road underneath, or the ragged block of buildings above, with their tower of the commonest possible eighteenth century type. There was, however, one extreme good in all this, that I saw things, with whatever faculty was in me, exactly for what they were; and though my religious instruction, as aforesaid, led me to suppose the malaria in the Campagna was the consequence of the Papacy, that did not in the least affect my clear and invincible perception that the outline of Soracte was good, and the outlines of tufo and pozzolana* foregrounds bad, whether it was Papal or Protestant pozzolana. What the Forum or Capitol had been, I did not in the least care; the pillars of the Forum I saw were on a small scale, and their capitals rudely carved, and the houses above them nothing like so interesting as the side of any close in the 'Auld toun' of Edinburgh.

34. Having ascertained these general facts about the city and its ruins, I had to begin my gallery work. Of course all the great religious paintings, Perugino's ante-chamber, Angelico's chapel, and the whole lower story of the Sistine,* were entirely useless to me. No soul ever bade me look at them, and I had no sense yet to find them out for myself. Everybody told me to look at the roof of the Sistine chapel, and I liked it; but everybody also told me to look at Raphael's Transfiguration, and Domenichino's St Jerome;* which also I did attentively, as I was bid, and pronounced—without the smallest hesitation—Domenichino's a bad picture, and Raphael's an ugly one; and thenceforward paid no more attention to what anybody said, (unless I happened to agree with it) on the subject of painting.

Sir Joshua's verdict on the Stanze* was a different matter, and I studied them long and carefully, admitting at once that there was more in them than I was the least able to see or understand, but decisively ascertaining that they could not give me the least pleasure,* and contained a mixture of Paganism and Papacy wholly inconsistent with the religious instruction I had received in Walworth.

Having laid these foundations of future study, I never afterwards had occasion seriously to interfere with them. Domenichino is always spoken of—as long as, in deference to Sir Joshua,* I name him at all—as an entirely bad painter; the Stanze, as never giving, or likely to give, anybody in a healthy state of mind,—that is to say, desirous of knowing what sibyls were really like, or how a Greek conceived the Muses,—the slightest pleasure; and the opposition of the Parnassus to the Disputa,* shown, in the 'Stones of Venice,'[1]* to foretell the fall of Catholic Theology.

35. The main wonders of Rome thus taken stock of, and the course of minor sight-seeing begun, we thought it time to present a letter of introduction which Henry Acland had given me to Mr Joseph Severn.

Although in the large octavo volume containing the works of Coleridge, Shelley, and Keats, which so often lay on my niche-table at Herne Hill, the Keats part had never attracted me, and always puzzled, I had got quite enough perception of his natural power, and felt enough regret for his death, to make me wait with reverence on his guardian friend. I forget exactly where Mr Severn lived at that time,* but his door was at the right of the landing at the top of a long flight of squarely reverting stair,—broad, to about the span of an English lane that would allow two carts to pass; and broad-stepped also, its gentle incline attained by some three inches of fall to a foot of flat. Up this I was advancing slowly,—it being forbidden me ever to strain breath,—and was within eighteen or twenty steps of Mr Severn's door, when it opened, and two gentlemen came out, closed it behind them with an expression of excluding the world for evermore from that side of the house, and began to descend the stairs to meet me, holding to my left. One was a rather short, rubicund, serenely beaming person; the other, not much taller, but paler, with a beautifully modelled forehead, and extremely vivid, though kind, dark eyes.

36. They looked hard at me as they passed, but in my usual shyness, and also because I have held it a first principle of manners not to waylay people;—above all, not to stop them when they are going out, I made no sign, and leaving them to descend the reverting stair in peace, climbed, at still slackening pace, the remaining steps to Mr Severn's door, and left my card and letter of introduction with the servant, who told me he had just gone out. His dark-eyed companion was George Richmond, to whom, also, Acland had given me a letter. Both Mr Severn and he came immediately to see us. My father and mother's quiet out-of-the-wayness at first interested, soon pleased, and at last won them, so completely, that before Christmas came, out of all people

---

[1] I have authorized the republication of this book in its original text and form, chiefly for the sake of its clear, and the reader will find, wholly incontrovertible, statement of the deadly influence of Renaissance Theology on the Arts in Italy, and on the religion of the World.

in Rome they chose us to eat their Christmas dinner with. Much more for my father's sake and mother's, than mine; not that they were uninterested in me also, but as *my* ways of out-of-the-wayness were by no means quiet, but perpetually firing up under their feet in little splutters and spitfires of the most appalling heresy; and those not only troublesome in immediate crackle, but carried out into steady, and not always refutable, objection to nearly everything sacred in their sight, of the autocratic masters and authentic splendours of Rome, their dialogues with me were apt to resolve themselves into delicate disguises of necessary reproof; and even with my father and mother, into consultation as to what was best to be done to bring me to anything like a right mind. The old people's confidence in *them* had been unbounded from the first, in consequence of Mr Severn's having said to Mr Richmond when they met me on the stairs, 'What a poetical countenance!'—and my recently fanatical misbehaviour in the affair of the Harlech, coupled with my now irrepressible impertinences to Raphael and Domenichino, began to give me in my parents' eyes something of the distant aspect of the Prodigal Son.*

37. The weight of adverse authority which I had thus to support was soon increased by the zeal of Mr Richmond's younger brother, Tom, whom I found, on the first occasion of my visiting them in their common studio, eagerly painting a torso with shadows of smalt blue, which, it was explained to me, were afterwards to be glazed so as to change into the flesh colour of Titian. As I did not at that time see anything particular in the flesh colour of Titian, and did not see the slightest probability—if there were—of its being imitable by that process, here was at once another chasm of separation opened between my friends and me, virtually never closed to the end of time; and in its immediately volcanic effect, decisive of the manner in which I spent the rest of my time in Rome and Italy. For, making up my mind thenceforward that the sentiment, of Raphael and tints of Titian were alike beyond me, if not wholly out of my way; and that the sculpture galleries of the Vatican were mere bewilderment and worry, I took the bit in my teeth, and proceeded to sketch what I could find in Rome to represent in my own way, bringing in primarily,—by way of defiance to Raphael, Titian, and the Apollo Belvidere* all in one,—a careful study of old clothes hanging out of old windows in the Jews' quarter.

38. The gauntlet being thus thrown, the two Mr Richmonds and my father had nothing for it but to amuse themselves as best they could with my unclassical efforts, not, taken on my own terms, without interest. I did the best I could for the Forum, in a careful general view; a study of

the aqueducts of the Campagna from St John Lateran, and of the Aventine from the Ponte Rotto, were extremely pleasant to most beholders; and at last even Mr Richmond was so far mollified as to ask me to draw the street of the Trinita di Monte for him, with which he had many happy associations. There was another practical chance for me in life at this crisis,—I might have made the most precious records of all the cities in Italy. But all my chances of being anything but what I am were thrown away, or broken short, one after another. An entirely, mocking and mirage-coloured one, as it seemed then, yet became, many a year later, a great and beautiful influence on my life.

39. Between my Protestantism and, as Tom Richmond rightly called it, Proutism, I had now abjured Roman shows altogether, and was equally rude and restive, whether I was asked to go to a church, a palace, or a gallery,—when papa and mamma began to perceive some dawn of docility in me about going to hear musical church services. This they naturally attributed to my native taste for Gregorian chants, and my increasing aptitude for musical composition. But the fact was, that at services of this kind there was always a chance of seeing, at intervals, above the bowed heads of the Italian crowd, for an instant or two before she also stooped—or sometimes, eminent in her grace above a stunted group of them,—a fair English girl,* who was not only the admitted Queen of beauty in the English circle of that winter in Rome, but was so, in the kind of beauty which I had only hitherto dreamed of as possible, but never yet seen living: statuesque severity with womanly sweetness joined. I don't think I ever succeeded in getting nearer than within fifty yards of her; but she was the light and solace of all the Roman winter to me, in the mere chance glimpses of her far away, and the hope of them.

40. Meantime, my father, to whom our Roman physician had given an encouraging report of me, recovered some of his natural cheerfulness, and enjoyed, with his niece, who if not an enthusiastic, was an indefatigable and attentive sight-seeker and seer, everything that Rome had to show; the musical festas especially, whenever his cross-grained boy consented, for Miss Tollemache's secret sake, to go with him; while Mr Severn and George Richmond became every day more kindly—nor, we felt, without real pleasure to themselves—helpful to us all. No *habitué* of the brightest circles of present London Society will doubt the privilege we had in better and better knowing George Richmond. But there is nothing in any circle that ever I saw or heard of, like what Mr Joseph Severn then was in Rome. He understood everybody, native and foreign, civil and ecclesiastic, in what was nicest

in them, and never saw anything else than the nicest; or saw what other people got angry about as only a humorous part of the nature of things. It was the nature of things that the Pope* should be at St Peter's, and the beggars on the Pincian steps. He forgave the Pope his papacy, reverenced the beggar's beard, and felt that alike the steps of the Pincian, and the Araceli, and the Lateran, and the Capitol, led to heaven, and everybody was going up, somehow; but might be happy where they were in the meantime. Lightly sagacious, lovingly humorous, daintily sentimental, he was in council with the cardinals to-day, and at picnic in Campagna with the brightest English belles to-morrow; and caught the hearts of all in the golden net of his good will and good understanding, as if life were but for him the rippling chant of his favourite song,—

'Gente, e qui l'uccellatore.'*

CHAPTER III

CUMAE*

41. IN my needful and fixed resolve to set the facts down continuously, leaving the reader to his reflections on them, I am slipping a little too fast over the surfaces of things; and it becomes at this point desirable that I should know, or at least try to guess, something of what the reader's reflections *are!* and whether in the main he is getting at the sense of the facts I tell him.

Does he think me a lucky or unlucky youth, I wonder? Commendable, on the whole, and exemplary—or the reverse? Of promising gifts—or merely glitter of morning, to pass at noon? I ask him at this point, because several letters from pleased acquaintances have announced to me, of late, that they have obtained quite new lights upon my character from these jottings, and like me much better than they ever did before. Which was not the least the effect I intended to produce on them; and which moreover is the exact opposite of the effect on my own mind of meeting myself, by turning back, face to face.

42. On the contrary, I suffer great pain, and shame, in perceiving with better knowledge the little that I was, and the much that I lost— of time, chance, and—duty, (a duty missed is the worst of loss); and I cannot in the least understand what my acquaintances have found, in anything hitherto told them of my childhood, more amiable than they might have guessed of the author of 'Time and Tide,'* or

'Unto This Last.'* The real fact being, whatever they make of it, that hitherto, and for a year or two on, yet, I was simply a little floppy and soppy tadpole,—little more than a stomach with a tail to it, flattening and wriggling itself up the crystal ripples and in the pure sands of the springhead of youth.

But there were always good eyes in me, and a good habit of keeping head up stream; and now the time was coming when I began to think about helping princesses by fetching up their balls from the bottom;* when I got a sudden glimpse of myself, in the true shape of me, extremely startling and discouraging:—here, in Rome it was, towards the Christmas time.

43. Among the living Roman arts of which polite travellers were expected to carry specimens home with them, one of the prettiest used to be the cutting cameos out of pink shells. We bought, according to custom, some coquillage of Gods and Graces; but the cameo cutters were also skilful in mortal portraiture, and papa and mamma, still expectant of my future greatness, resolved to have me carved in cameo.

I had always been content enough with my front face in the glass, and had never thought of contriving vision of the profile. The cameo finished, I saw at a glance to be well cut; but the image it gave of me was not to my mind. I did not analyse its elements at the time, but should now describe it as a George the Third's penny, with a halfpenny worth of George the Fourth, the pride of Amurath the Fifth,* and the temper of eight little Lucifers in a swept lodging.

Now I knew myself proud; yes, and of late, sullen; but did not in the least recognise pride or sulkiness for leading faults of my nature. On the contrary, I knew myself wholly reverent to all real greatness, and wholly good-humoured—when I got my own way. What more can you expect of average boy, or beast?

And it seemed hard to me that only the excrescent faults, and by no means the constant capacities, should be set forth, carved by the petty justice of the practical cameo. Concerning which, as also other later portraits of me, I will be thus far proud as to tell the disappointed spectator, once for all, that the main good of my face, as of my life, is in the eyes,—and only in those, seen near; that a very dear and wise French friend also told me, a long while after this, that the lips, though not Apolline, were kind: the George the Third and Fourth character I recognise very definitely among my people, as already noticed in my cousin George of Croydon; and of the shape of head, fore and aft, I have my own opinions, but do not think it time, yet, to tell them.

44. I think it, however, quite time to say a little more fully, not only what happened to me, now of age, but what was *in* me: to which end I permit a passage or two out of my diary, written for the first time this year wholly for my own use, and note of things I saw and thought; and neither to please papa, nor to be printed,—with corrections,—by Mr Harrison.

I see, indeed, in turning the old leaves, that I have been a little too morose in my record of impressions on the Riviera. Here is a page more pleasant, giving first sight of a place afterwards much important in my life—the promontory of Sestri di Levante.

'Sestri, Nov. 4th (1840). Very wet all morning; merely able to get the four miles to this most lovely village, the clouds drifting like smoke from the hills, and hanging in wreaths about the white churches on their woody slopes. Kept in here till three, then the clouds broke, and we got up the woody promontory that overhangs the village. The clouds were rising gradually from the Apennines, fragments entangled here and there in the ravines catching the level sunlight like so many tongues of fire; the dark blue outline of the hills clear as crystal against a pale distant purity of green sky, the sun touching here and there upon their turfy precipices, and the white, square villages along the gulph gleaming like silver to the north-west;—a mass of higher mountain, plunging down into broad valleys dark with olive, their summits at first grey with rain, then deep blue with flying showers—the sun suddenly catching the near woods at their base, already coloured exquisitely by the autumn, with such a burst of robing,—penetrating, glow as Turner only could even imagine, set off by the grey storm behind. To the south, an expanse of sea, varied by reflection of white Alpine cloud, and delicate lines of most pure blue, the low sun sending its line of light—forty miles long—from the horizon; the surges dashing far below against rocks of black marble, and lines of foam drifting back with the current into the open sea. Overhead, a group of dark Italian pine and evergreen oak, with such lovely ground about their roots as we have in the best bits of the islands of Derwentwater. This continued till near sunset, when a tall double rainbow rose to the east over the fiery woods, and as the sun sank, the storm of falling rain on the mountains became suddenly purple—nearly crimson; the rainbow, its hues scarcely traceable, one broad belt of crimson, the clouds above all fire. The whole scene such as can only come once or twice in a lifetime.'

45. I see that we got to Rome on a Saturday, November 28th. The actual first entry next morning is, perhaps, worth keeping:—

'Nov. 29th, Sunday. A great fuss about Pope officiating in the

Sistine Chapel—Advent Sunday.* Got into a crowd, and made myself very uncomfortable for nothing: no music worth hearing, a little mummery with Pope and dirty cardinals. Outside and west façade of St Peter's certainly very fine: the inside would make a nice ball-room, but is good for nothing else.'

'Nov. 30th. Drove up to the Capitol—a filthy, melancholy-looking, rubbishy place; and down to the Forum, which is certainly a very good subject; and then a little further on, amongst quantities of bricks and rubbish, till I was quite sick.'

With disgust, I meant; but from December 20th to 25th I had a qualm of real fever, which it was a wonder came to no worse. On the 30th I am afoot again; thus:—

'I have been walking backwards and forwards on the Pincian, being unable to do anything else since this confounded illness, and trying to find out why every imaginable delight palls so very rapidly on even the keenest feelings. I had all Rome before me; towers, cupolas, cypresses, and palaces mingled in every possible grouping; a light Decemberish mist, mixed with the slightest vestige of wood smoke, hovering between the distances, and giving beautiful grey outlines of every form between the eye and the sun; and over the rich evergreen oaks of the Borghese gardens,* a range of Apennine, with one principal pyramid of pure snow, like a piece of sudden comet-light fallen on the earth. It was not like moonlight, nor like sunlight, but as soft as the one, and as powerful as the other. And yet, with all this around me, I could not feel it. I was as tired of my walk, and as glad when I thought I had done duty, as ever on the Norwood road.'

46. There was a girl walking up and down with some children, her light cap prettily set on very well dressed hair: of whose country I had no doubt; long before I heard her complain to one of her charges, who was jabbering English as fast as the fountain tinkled on the other side of the road, 'Qu'elle n'en comprenait pas un mot.'* This girl after two or three turns sat down beside another *bonne*. There they sate laughing and chattering, with the expression of perfect happiness on their faces, thinking no more of the Alpine heights behind them, or the city beneath them, than of Constantinople; while I, with every feeling raised, I should think to a great degree above theirs, was in a state of actually severe mental pain, because I could perceive materials of the highest pleasure around me, and felt the time hang heavy on my hands. Here is the pride, you perceive, good reader, and the sullens—dum pituita molestat*—both plain enough. But it is no lofty pride in which I say my '*feelings*' were raised above the French *bonne's*. Very solemnly, I did not

think myself a better creature than she, nor so good; but only I knew there was a link between far Soracte and me,—nay, even between unseen Voltur and me,—which was not between her and them; and meant a wider, earthly, if not heavenly, horizon, under the birth-star.

47. Meantime, beneath the hill, my mother knitted, as quietly as if she had been at home, in the corner of the great Roman room in which she cared for nothing but the cleanliness, as distinguishing it from the accommodation of provincial inns; and the days turned, and it was time to think of the journey to Naples, before any of us were tired of Rome. And simple cousin Mary, whom I never condescended to ask for either sympathy or opinion, was really making better use of her Roman days than any of us. She was a sound, plain, musician; (having been finished by Moscheles*); attended to the church orchestras carefully, read her guide-books accurately, knew always where she was, and in her sincere religion, conquered her early Puritanism to the point of reverently visiting St Paul's grave and St Cecilia's house, and at last going up the Scala Santa on her knees, like any good girl of Rome.

48. So passed the days, till there was spring sunshine in the air as we climbed the Alban mount, and went down into the ravine under La Riccia, afterwards described in perhaps the oftenest quoted passage of 'Modern Painters.' The diary says: 'A hollow with another village on the hill opposite, a most elegant and finished group of church tower and roof, descending by delicate upright sprigs[1] of tree into a dark rich-toned depth of ravine, out of which rose nearer, and clear against its shade, a grey wall of rock, an absolute miracle for blending of bright lichenous colour.'

With a few sentences more, to similar effect, and then a bit of Pontine marsh description, dwelling much on the moving points of the 'black cattle, white gulls, black, bristly high-bred swine, and birds of all sorts, waders and dippers innumerable.' It is very interesting, at least to myself, to find how, so early as this, while I never drew anything but in pencil outline, I *saw* everything first in colour, as it ought to be seen.

49. I must give room to the detail of the day from Mola to Naples, because it shows, to proof enough, the constant watchfulness upon which the statements in 'Modern Painters' were afterwards founded, though neither that nor any other book had yet been dreamed of; and I wrote only to keep memory of things seen, for what good might come of the memory anyhow.

---

[1] I have substituted this word for a sketch like the end of a broom, which would convey no idea to anybody but myself.

'Naples, January 9th (1841). Dressed yesterday at Mola by a window commanding a misty sunrise over the sea—a grove of oranges sloping down to the beach, flushed with its light; Gaeta opposite, glittering along its promontory. Ran out to terrace at side of the house, a leaden bit of roof, with pots of orange and Indian fig. There was a range of Skiddaw-like mountains rising from the shore, the ravines just like those of Saddleback, or the west side of Skiddaw; the higher parts bright with fresh-fallen snow; the highest, misty with a touch of soft white, swift[1] cloud. Nearer, they softened into green, bare masses of hill, like Malvern, but with their tops covered with olives and lines of vine,—the village of Mola showing its white walls and level roofs above the olives, with a breath of blue smoke floating above them, and a long range of distant hills running out into the sea beyond. The air was fresh, and yet so pure and soft, and so full of perfume from the orange trees below the terrace, that it seemed more like an early summer morning than January. It got soon threatening, however, though the sun kept with us as we drove through the village;—confined streets, but bright and varied, down to the shore, and then under the slopes of the snowy precipice, now thoroughly dazzling with the risen sun, and between hedges of tall myrtle, into the plain of Garigliano. A heavy rain-cloud raced[2] us the ten miles, and stooped over us, stealing the blue sky inch by inch, till it had left only a strip of amber-blue[3] behind the Apennines, the near hills thrown into deep dark purple shade, the snow behind them, first blazing—the only strong light in the picture—then in shade, dark against the pure sky; the grey above, warm and lurid—a little washed with rain in parts; below, a copse of willow coming against the dark purples, nearly pure Indian yellow, a little touched with red. Then came a lovely bit of aqueduct, with coats of shattered mosaic, the hills seen through its arches, and pieces of bright green meadow mixing with the yellow of the willows. At Capua, detained by a rascally Dogana,*—we had one at Garigliano as well, howling beggars all about (Caffè del Giglio d'Oro), one ape of a creature clinging with its legs about another's neck, and chopping its jaws with its fists. Hence a dead flat of vines hanging from elms, and road perfectly straight, and cut utterly up by a deluge of rain. I was quite tired as it grew dark, fragments of blue and amber sky showing through

---

[1] Note the instant marking the *pace* of the cloud,—the work of 'Coeli Enarrant'* having been begun practically years before this. See below also of the rain-cloud.

[2] This distinct approach, or chase, by rain-cloud is opposed, in my last lectures on sky, to the *gathering* of rain-cloud all through the air, under the influence of plague wind.

[3] Palest transparent blue passing into gold.

colossal thunder clouds, and two or three pure stars labouring among the dark masses. It lightened fast as we got into Naples, and we were stopped again, first by Dogana, and then at passport office, till I lost temper and patience, and could have cried like a girl, for I was quite wearied with the bad roads, and disappointed with the approach to Naples, and cold. I could not help wondering at this. How little could I have imagined, sitting in my home corner, yearning for a glance of the hill snow, or the orange leaf, that I should, at entering Naples, be as thoroughly out of humour as ever after a monotonous day in London. More so!'

50. For full ten years, since earliest geologic reading, I had thoroughly known the structure and present look of Vesuvius and Monte Somma; nor had 'Friendship's Offering' and 'Forget-me-not,' in the days of the Bandit Leoni,* left me without useful notions of the Bay of Naples. But the beautiful forms of Monte St Angelo and Capri were new to me, and the first feeling of being in the presence of the power and mystery of the under earth, unspeakably solemn; though Vesuvius was virtually in repose, and the slow changes in the heaped white cloud above the crater were only like those of a thunder cloud.

The first sight of the Alps had been to me as a direct revelation of the benevolent will in creation. Long since, in the volcanic powers of destruction, I had been taught by Homer, and further forced by my own reason, to see, if not the personality of an Evil Spirit, at all events the permitted symbol of evil; unredeemed; wholly distinct from the conditions of storm, or heat, or frost, on which the healthy courses of organic life depended. In the same literal way in which the snows and Alpine roses of Lauterbrunnen were visible Paradise, here, in the valley of ashes and throat of lava, were visible Hell. If thus in the natural, how else should it be in the spiritual world?

I had never yet read a line of Dante. From the moment when I knew the words,—

> 'It now is evening there, where buried lies
> The body in which I cast a shade, removed
> To Naples from Brundusium's wall,'*

not Naples only, but Italy, became for ever flushed with the sacred twilight of them. But even now, what pieces I knew of Virgil, in that kind, became all at once true, when I saw the birdless lake;* for me also, the voice of it had teaching which was to be practically a warning law of future life:—

> 'Nec te
> Nequidquam lucis Hecate præfecit Avernis.'*

The legends became true,—*began* to come true, I should have said,—trains of thought now first rising which did not take clear current till forty years afterwards;* and in this first trickling, sorrowful in disappointment. 'There *were* such places then, and Sibyls *did* live in them!—but is this all?'

Frightful enough, yes, the spasmodic ground—the boiling sulphur lake—the Dog's grotto with its floor a foot deep in poisoned air that could be stirred with the hand. Awful, but also for the Delphi of Italy, ignoble. And all that was fairest in the whole sweep of isle and sea, I saw, as was already my wont, with precise note of its faults.

51. The common English traveller, if he can gather a black bunch of grapes with his own fingers, and have his bottle of Falernian* brought him by a girl with black eyes, asks no more of this world, nor the next; and declares Naples a Paradise. But I knew, from the first moment when my foot furrowed volcanic ashes, that no mountain form or colour could exist in perfection when everything was made of scoria,* and that blue sea was to be little boasted if it broke on black sand. And I saw also, with really wise anger, the horror of neglect in the governing power, which Mr Gladstone found, forsooth, in the Neapolitan prisons!* but which neither he nor any other Englishman, so far as I know, except Byron* and I, saw to have made the Apennines one prison wall, and all the modern life of Italy one captivity of shame and crime; alike against the honour of her ancestors, and the kindness of her God.

With these strong insights into the faults of others, there came also at Naples, I am thankful to say, some stroke of volcanic lightning on my own. The sense of the uselessness of all Naples and its gulph to me, in my then state of illness and gloom, was borne in upon me with reproach: the chrysalid envelope began to tear itself open here and there to some purpose, and I bade farewell to the last outlines of Monte St Angelo as they faded in the south, with dim notions of bettering my ways in future.

52. At Mola di Gaeta we stopped a whole day that I might go back to draw the castle of Itri. It was hinted darkly to us that Itri was of no good repute; we disdained all imputations on such a lovely place, and drove back there for a day's rambling. While I drew, my mother and Mary went at their own sweet wills up and down; Mary had by this time, at school and on the road, made herself mistress of syllables enough to express some sympathy with any contadina* who wore a pretty cap, or carried a pretty baby; and, the appearance of English women being rare at Itri, the contadine were pleased, and everything that was amiable to mamma and Mary. I made an excellent sketch, and

we returned in exultation to the orange-groves of Mola. We afterwards heard that the entire population of Itri consisted of banditti, and never troubled ourselves about banditti any more.

We stopped at Albano for the Sunday, and I went out in the morning for a walk through its ilex groves with my father and mother and Mary. For some time back, the little cough bringing blood had not troubled me, and I had been taking longer walks and otherwise counting on comparative safety, when here suddenly, in the gentle morning saunter through the shade, the cough came back—with a little darker stain on the handkerchief than usual. I sat down on a bank by the roadside, and my father's face was very grave.*

We got quietly back to the inn, where he found some sort of light carriole disposable, and set out, himself, to fetch the doctor from Rome.

It has always been one of the great shadows of thought to me, to fancy my father's feelings as he was driven that day those eighteen miles across the Campagna.

Good Di Gloag comforted him, and returned with him. But there was nothing new to be done, nor said.* Such chance attack was natural in the spring, he said, only I must be cautious for a while. My mother never lost her courage for an instant. Next day we went on to Rome, and it was the last time the cough ever troubled me.

53. The weather was fine at Easter, and I saw the Benediction,* and sate in the open air of twilight opposite the castle of St Angelo, and saw the dome-lines kindle on St Peter's, and the castle veil the sky with flying fire. Bearing with me from that last sight in Rome many thoughts that ripened slowly afterwards, chiefly convincing me how guiltily and meanly dead the Protestant mind was to the whole meaning and end of mediaeval Church splendour; and how meanly and guiltily dead the existing Catholic mind was, to the course by which to reach the Italian soul, instead of its eyes.

Re-opening, but a few days since, the book which my Christ Church official tutor, Walter Brown, recommended to me as the most useful code of English religious wisdom, the 'Natural History of Enthusiasm,'* I chanced on this following passage, which I think must have been one of the first to startle the complacency of my Puritan creed. My since experience in theological writing furnishes me with no more terrific example of the absence alike of charity and understanding in the leading masters of that sect, beyond all others into which the Church has ever been divided:—

'If it be for a moment forgotten that in every bell, and bowl, and vest of the Romish service there is hid a device against the liberty and welfare of mankind, and that its gold, and pearls, and fine linen are the deckings of eternal ruin; and if this apparatus of worship be compared with the impurities and the cruelties of the old Polytheistic rites, great praise may seem due to its contrivers. All the materials of poetic and scenic effect have been elaborated by the genius and taste of the Italian artists until a spectacle has been got up which leaves the most splendid shows of the ancient idol worship of Greece and Rome at a vast distance of inferiority.'

Yet I cannot distinctly remember being shocked, even at this passage, and I know there was much in the rest of the book that pleased me; but I had already the advantage over its author, and over all such authors, of knowing, when I saw them, sincere art from lying art, and happy faith from insolent dogmatism. I knew that the voices in the Trinita di Monte did not sing to deceive me; and that the kneeling multitude before the Pontiff were indeed bettered and strengthened by his benediction.

Although I had been able, weather favouring, to see the Easter ceremonies without danger, there was no sign, take all in all, of gain to my health from Roman winter. My own discouragement was great; and the first cautious journeyings back by Terni and Fuligno were sad enough; the night at Terni very deeply so. For in the evening, when we came back from seeing the falls, the servant of a young Englishman asked to speak with us, saying that he was alone in charge of his master, who had been stopped there by sudden, he feared mortal, illness. Would my father come and see him? My father went, and found a beautifully featured Scottish youth of three or four and twenty, indeed in the last day of decline. He died during the night, and we were of some use to the despairing servant afterwards. I forget now whether we ever knew who the youth was. I find his name in my diary, 'Farquharson,'* but no more.

As we drew northward, however, out of the volcanic country, I recovered heart; the enchanted world of Venice enlarging in front of me. I had only yet once seen her, and that six years ago, when still a child. That the fairy tale should come true now seemed wholly incredible, and the start from the gate of Padua in the morning,—Venice, asserted by people whom we could not but believe, to be really over there, on the horizon, in the sea! How to tell the feeling of it!

54. I have not yet fancied the reader's answer to the first question proposed in outset of this chapter,—does he think me a fortunate or unfortunate youth?

As to preparation for the future world, terrestrial or celestial, or future self in either, there may be two opinions—two or three perhaps—on the matter. But, there is no question that, of absolute happiness, I had the share of about a quarter of a million of average people, all to myself. I say 'people,' not 'boys.' I don't know what delight boys take in cricket, or boating, or throwing stones at birds, or learning to shoot them. But of average people in continuity of occupation, shopmen, clerks, Stock Exchange people, club and Pall Mall people, certainly there was no reckoning the quantity of happiness I had in comparison, followed indeed by times of reaction, or of puzzled satiety; and partly avenged by extremes of vexation at what vexed nobody else; but indisputably and infinitely precious in itself, every day complete at the end, as with Sydney Smith's salad: 'Fate cannot harm me; I have dined, to-day.'*

55. The two chapters closing the first, and beginning the second volume of the 'Stones of Venice' were written, I see on re-reading, in the melancholy experience of 1852, with honest effort to tell every traveller what was really to be seen. They do not attempt to recall my own joys of 1835 and 1841, when there was not even beginning of railway bridge;* when everything, muddy Brenta, vulgar villa, dusty causeway, sandy beach, was equally rich in rapture, on the morning that brought us in sight of Venice: and the black knot of gondolas in the canal of Mestre, more beautiful to me than a sunrise full of clouds all scarlet and gold.

But again, how to tell of it? or even explain it to myself,—the English mind, high or common, being utterly without trace of the feeling. Sir Philip Sidney goes to Venice, and seems unconscious that it is in the sea at all.* Elizabeth Lady Craven, in 1789, 'expected to see a gay clean-looking town, with quays on each side of the canals, but was extremely disappointed; the houses are in the water, and look dirty and uncomfortable on the outside; the innumerable quantity of gondolas too, that look like swimming coffins, added to the dismal scene, and, I confess, Venice on my arrival struck me with horror rather than pleasure.'*

After this, she goes to the Casini, and is happy. It does not appear she had ever read the Merchant, or Othello; still less has Evelyn* read them, though for him, as for Sidney, Othello's and Antonio's Venice was still all but living. My Venice, like Turner's, had been chiefly created for us by Byron; but for me, there was also still the pure childish passion of pleasure in seeing boats float in clear water. The beginning of everything was in seeing the gondola-beak come actually inside the door at Danieli's, when the tide was up, and the water two feet deep at the foot of the stairs; and then, all along the canal sides, actual marble walls rising out of the salt sea, with hosts of little brown crabs on them, and Titians inside.

56. Between May 6th and 16th I made notes on effects of light, afterwards greatly useful in 'modern Painters;' and two pencil drawings, Ca' Contarini Fasan, and the Giant's Staircase, of which, with two more made at Bologna in passing, and some half-dozen at Naples and Amalfi, I can say, now forty years later, with certitude, that they could not have been much better done. I knew absolutely nothing of architecture proper, had never drawn a, section nor a leaf moulding; but liked, as Turner did to the end of his days, anything that was graceful and rich, whether Gothic or Renaissance; was entirely certain and delicate in pencil-touch; and drew with an acuteness of delight in the thing as it actually stood, which makes the sketch living and like, from corner to corner. Thus much I could do, and *did* do, for the last time. Next year I began trying to do what I could not, and have gone on ever since, spending half of my days in that manner.

57. I find a sentence in diary on 6th May, which seems inconsistent with what I have said of the centres of my life work.*

'Thank God I am here; it is the Paradise of cities.'

*			*			*			*			*

'This, and Chamouni, are my two bournes* of Earth.'

But then, I *knew* neither Rouen nor Pisa, though I had seen both. (Geneva, when I spoke of it with them, is meant to include Chamouni.) Venice I regard more and more as a temptation. The diary says (where the stars are): 'There is moon enough to make half the sanities of the earth lunatic, striking its pure flashes of light on the grey water.'*

From Venice, by Padua, where St Antonio,—by Milan, where the Duomo,—were still faultless to me, and each a perfect bliss; to Turin— to Susa; my health still bettering in the sight of Alps, and what breeze came down from them—and over Cenis for the first time. I woke from a sound tired sleep in a little one-windowed room at Lans-le-bourg, at six of the summer morning, June 2nd, 1841; the red aiguilles on the north relieved against pure blue—the great pyramid of snow down the valley in one sheet of eastern light. I dressed in three minutes, ran down the village street, across the stream, and climbed the grassy slope on the south side of the valley, up to the first pines.

I had found my life again;—all the best of it. What good of religion, love, admiration or hope,* had ever been taught me, or felt by my best nature, rekindled at once; and my line of work, both by my own will and the aid granted to it by fate in the future, determined for me. I went down thankfully to my father and mother, and told them I was sure I should get well.

As to my mere physical state, the doctors had been entirely mistaken about me. I wanted bracing air, exercise, and rest from all artificial excitement. The air of the Campagna was the worst they could have sent me into—the life of Rome the worst they could have chosen.

58. The three following diary entries, which meant much afterwards, may summarily end what I fear has been a tiresome chapter.

I. 'Geneva, June 5th. Yesterday from Chambery,—a fresh north wind blowing away the dust. Much pleased with the respectable young wife of a confectioner, at one of the mid-towns where I went to get some Savoy biscuits—and asked for "a pound." "Mais, Monsieur, une livre sera un peu—volumineuse! je vous en donnerai la moitié; vous verrez si cela vous suffira;"*—"Ah, Louise" (to a little bright-eyed lady in the inner room, who was expressing her disapprobation of some of the affairs of life too loudly), "si tu n'es pas sage, tu vas savoir"*—but so playfully and kindly! Got here on a lovely afternoon near sunset, and the green bastions and bright Salève and rushing Rhone and far Jura, all so lovely that I was nearly vowing never to go into Italy again.'

II. 'June 6th. Pouring rain all day, and slow extempore sermon from a weak-voiced young man in a white arched small chapel, with a braying organ and doggerel hymns. Several times, about the same hour on Sunday mornings, a fit of self-reproach has come upon me for my idling at present, and I have formed resolutions to be always trying to get knowledge of some kind or other, or bodily strength, or some real available, continuing good, rather than the mere amusement of the time. It came on me to-day very strongly, and I would give anything and everything to keep myself in the temper, for I always slip out of it next day.'

III. 'Dec. 11th, 1842. Very odd! Exactly the same fit came on me in the same church, next year, and was the origin of Turner's work.'*

CHAPTER IV

FONTAINEBLEAU

59. WE reached Rochester on the 29th of June, and a month was spent at home, considering what was to be done next. My own feeling, ever since the morning at Lans-le-bourg, was that, if only left free in mountain air, I should get well, fast enough. After debate with London

doctors, it was thought best to give me my way; and, stipulating only that Richard Fall should go with me, papa and mamma sent me, early in August, on my first independent journey, into Wales.

But they desired me, on my way there, to stop at Leamington, and show myself to its dominant physician, Dr Jephson—called a quack by all the Faculty, yet of whom they had heard favourably from wise friends.

Jephson was no quack; but a man of the highest general power, and keenest medical instincts. He had risen, by stubborn industry and acute observation, from an apothecary's boy to be the first physician in Leamington; and was the first true physician I ever knew—nor since, till I knew Sir William Gull, have I met the match of him.

He examined me for ten minutes; then said, 'Stay here, and I'll put you to rights in six weeks.' I said I was not the least disposed to stay there, and was going into Wales, but would obey any directions and follow any prescriptions he chose to give me. No, he said, I must stay, or he could do nothing for me. I thought this did look a little like quackery, and accordingly made my bow, and proceeded on my journey into Wales, after writing a full account of the interview to my father.

60. At Pont-y-Monach lay for me a letter from him, bidding me go back to Leamington at once, and place myself under Jephson's care. Richard therefore went on to Snowdon by himself; and I, returning with what speed the mail could make, presented myself to the doctor penitently. He sent me into tiny lodgings near the Wells, where I spent six weeks of life extremely new to me; much grumbled at in my diary,—not unpleasant, now remembered.

Salt water from the Wells in the morning, and iron, visibly glittering in deposit at bottom of glass, twice a day. Breakfast at eight, with herb tea—dandelion, I think; dinner at one, supper at six, both of meat, bread, and water, only;—fish, meat, or fowl, as I chose, but only one dish of the meat chosen, and no vegetables nor fruit. Walk, forenoon and afternoon, and early to bed. Such the regimen suddenly enforced on my luxurious life.

To which discipline I submitted accurately: and found life still worth having on these terms, and the renewed hope of its continuance, extremely interesting.

61. Nor wanting in interest, the grotesquely prosaic position itself. Here I was, in a small square brick lodging-house, number what you like of its row, looking out on a bit of suburban paddock, and a broken paling; mean litter everywhere about; the muddy lingering of Leam,

about three yards broad, at the other side of the paddock; a ragged brambly bank at the other side of *it*. Down the row, beginnings of poor people's shops, then an aristocratic grocer and mercer or two, the circulating library, and the Pump Room.

After the Bay of Naples, Mount Aventine, and St Mark's Place, it felt like the first practical scene of a pantomime, after the transformation, and before the business begins. But I had been extremely dull under Mount Aventine; and did not, to my surprise, feel at all disposed to be dull here,—but somewhat amused, and with a pleasant feeling of things being really at last all right, for *me* at least; though it wasn't as grand as Peckwater, nor as pretty as St Mark's Place. Any how, I was down to Croydon level again in the world; and might do what I liked in my own lodgings, and hadn't any Collections to get ready for.

62. The first thing I did was to go to the library and choose a book to work at. After due examination, I bought Agassiz' 'Poissons Fossiles'!* and set myself to counting of scales and learning of hard names,— thinking as some people do still, that in that manner I might best advance in geology. Also I supplied myself with some Captain Marryat; and some beautiful new cakes of colour wherewith to finish a drawing, in Turner's grandest manner, of the Chateau of Amboise at sunset, with the moon rising in the distance, and shining through a bridge.

The 'Poissons Fossiles' turned out a most useful purchase, enabling me finally to perceive, after steady work on them, that Agassiz was a mere blockhead to have paid for all that good drawing of the nasty ugly things, and that it didn't matter a stale herring to any mortal whether they had any names or not.

For any positive or useful purpose, I could not more utterly have wasted my time; but it was no small gain to know that time spent in that sort of work *was* wasted; and that to have caught a chub in the Avon, and learned how to cook it spicily and herbaceously, so as to have pleased Izaak Walton, if the odour of it could reach him in the Anglers' Paradise, would have been a better result of six weeks' study than to be able to count and call by their right names every scale stuck in the mud of the universe.

Also I got a wholesome perception, from that book, of the true relation between artists and scientific gentlemen. For I saw that the real genius concerned in the 'Poissons Fossiles' was the lithographer's,* and not at all the scientific gentleman's; and that the book ought to have been called after the lithographer, *his* fishes, only with their scales counted and called bad names by subservient Mons. Agassiz.

63. The second thing of specific meaning that went on in Leamington

lodgings was the aforesaid highly laboured drawing of the Chateau of Amboise, 'out of my head;' representing the castle as about seven hundred feet above the river, (it is perhaps eighty or ninety,) with sunset light on it, in imitation of Turner; and the moon rising behind it, in imitation of Turner; and some steps and balustrades (which are not there) going down to the river, in imitation of Turner; with the fretwork of St Hubert's Chapel done very carefully in my own way,— I thought perhaps a little better than Turner.

This drawing, and the poem of the 'Broken Chain,'* which it was to illustrate, after being beautifully engraved by Goodall, turned out afterwards equally salutary exercises; proving to me that in those directions of imagination I was even a worse blockhead than Agassiz himself. Meantime, the autumn weather was fine, the corn was ripe, and once out of sight of the paddock, the pump room, and the Parade, the space of surrounding Warwickshire within afternoon walk was extremely impressive to me, in its English way. Warwick towers in sight over the near tree tops; Kenilworth, within an afternoon's walk; Stratford, to be reached by an hour's drive with a trotting pony; and, round them, as far as eye could reach, a space of perfect England, not hill and *dale*,—that might be anywhere,—but hill and *flat*, through which the streams linger, and where the canals wind without lock.

64. Under these peaceful conditions I began to look carefully at cornflowers, thistles, and hollyhocks; and find, by entry on Sept. 15th, that I was writing a bit of the 'King of the Golden River,'* and reading Alison's 'Europe' and Turner's 'Chemistry.'*

Anent the 'King of the River,' I remorsefully bethink me no word has been said of the dawn and sunrise of Dickens on us; from the first syllable of him in the 'Sketches,' altogether precious and admirable to my father and me; and the new number of Pickwick and following Nickleby* looked to, through whatever laborious or tragic realities might be upon us, as unmixed bliss, for the next day. But Dickens taught us nothing with which we were not familiar,—only painted it perfectly for us. We knew quite as much about coachmen and hostlers as he did; and rather more about Yorkshire. As a caricaturist, both in the studied development of his own manner, and that of the illustrative etchings, he put himself out of the pale of great authors; so that he never became an educational element of my life, but only one of its chief comforts and restoratives.

The 'King of the Golden River' was written to amuse a little girl,* and being a fairly good imitation of Grimm and Dickens, mixed with a little true Alpine feeling of my own, has been rightly pleasing to nice children, and good for them. But it is totally valueless, for all that. I can no more write a story than compose a picture.

65. Jephson kept his word, and let me go in six weeks, with my health, he told me,—I doubt not, truly,—in my own hands. And indeed, if I had continued to live on mutton and iron, learned to swim in the sea which I loved, and set myself wholly upon my geology and poissons—vivants instead of fossiles,*——Well, I suppose I should have been drowned like Charles, or lain, within a year or two,

> 'on a glacier, halfway up to heaven,
> Taking my final rest.'*

What might have been, the mute Fates know. I myself know only, with certainty, what ought *not* to have been,—that, getting released from Leamington, I took again to brown potatoes and cherry-pie; instead of learning to swim and climb, continued writing pathetic verses, and at this particularly foolish crisis of life, as aforesaid, trying to paint *twilight* like Turner. I was not simpleton enough to think I could follow him in daylight, but I thought I could do something like his Kenilworth Castle* at sunset, with the milkmaid and the moon.

66. I have passed without notice what the reader might suppose a principal event of my life,—the being introduced to him by Mr Griffith, at Norwood dinner, June 22nd, 1840.

The diary says, 'Introduced to-day to the man who beyond all doubt is the greatest of the age; greatest in every faculty of the imagination, in every branch of scenic[1] knowledge; at once the painter and poet of the day, J. M. W. Turner. Everybody had described him to me as coarse, boorish, unintellectual, vulgar. This I knew to be impossible. I found in him a somewhat eccentric, keen-mannered, matter-of-fact, English-minded—gentleman; good-natured evidently, bad-tempered evidently, hating humbug of all sorts, shrewd, perhaps a little selfish, highly intel-lectual, the powers of the mind not brought out with any delight in their manifestation, or intention of display, but flashing out occasion-ally in a word or a look.'*

Pretty close, that, and full, to be seen at a first glimpse, and set down the same evening.

67. Curiously, the drawing of Kenilworth was one of those that came out of Mr Griffith's folio after dinner; and I believe I must have talked some folly about it, as being 'a leading one of the England series'; which would displease Turner greatly. There were few things he hated

---

[1] Meaning, I suppose, knowledge of what could rightly be represented or composed as a scene.

more than hearing people gush about particular drawings. He knew it merely meant they could not see the others.

Anyhow, he stood silent; the general talk went on as if he had not been there. He wished me good-night kindly, and I did not see him again till I came back from Rome.

If he had but asked me to come and see him the next day! shown me a pencil sketch, and let me see him lay a wash! He would have saved me ten years of life, and would not have been less happy in the close of his own. One can only say, Such things are never to be; every soul of us has to do its fight with the Untoward, and for itself discover the Unseen.

68. So here I was at Leamington, trying to paint twilight at Amboise, and meditating over the Poissons Fossiles, and Michael Angelo. Set free of the Parade, I went to stay a few days with my college tutor, Walter Brown, Rector now of 'Wendlebury,' a village in the flats, eleven miles north of Oxford. Flats, not marshes: wholesome pastoral fields, separated by hedges; here and there a haystack, a gate, or a stile. The village consisted of twelve or fifteen thatched cottages, and the Rectory. The Rectory was a square house, with a garden fifty yards square. The church, close by, about four yards high by twenty yards long, had a square tower at the end, and a weather-cock.

Good Mr Walter Brown had married an entirely worthy, very plain, somewhat middle-aged wife, and settled himself down, with all his scholarship and good gifts, to promote the spiritual welfare of Wendlebury. He interested himself entirely in that object; dug his garden himself; took a scholar or two to prepare for Oxford examinations, with whom in the mornings he read in the old way; studied the 'Natural History of Enthusiasm,' and was perfectly happy and contented, to the end of his time.

69. Finding him proud of his little church and its weather-cock, I made a drawing of it for him, in my best manner, at sunset, with a moonrise behind. He objected a little to having the sky upside down, with the darkest blue at the bottom, to bring out the church; but somehow, everybody at this time had begun to believe in me, and think I knew more about drawing than other people: and the meekness with which Mr Brown would listen to me lecturing on Michael Angelo, from a series of outlines of the Last Judgment* which I had brought from Rome, with the muscles engraved all over the bodies like branch railroads, remains wholly phenomenal and mystic in my memory. Nobody is ever the least meek to me now, when I *do* know something about it.

But Mr Brown and his wife were in all ways extremely kind to me, and seemed to like having me with them. It was perhaps only their politeness: I can neither fancy nor find anything in myself at this time which could have been pleasant to anybody, unless the mere wish to be pleasant, which I had always; seeking to say, so far as I could honestly, what would be agreeable to whomsoever I spoke to.

70. From Wendlebury I went home, and made final preparation, with Gordon's help, for taking my degree in the spring. I find entry on Nov. 16th, 1841, at Herne Hill, 'I have got my rooms in order at last; I shall set to work on my reading to-morrow, methodically, but not hard.' Setting my rooms in order has, throughout life, been an occasionally complacent recreation to me; but I have never succeeded in keeping them in order three days after they were in it.

On the day following comes this: 'Mem., why is hoar-frost formed in larger crystals on the ribs and edges of leaves than in other places?' (on other parts of the leaf, I meant)—question which I had thought asked for the first time in my ice-study of '79,* and which is not answered yet.

The entry next day is also worth copying: 'Read the Clementina part of "Sir Charles Grandison."* I never met with anything which affected me so powerfully; at present I feel disposed to place this work above all other works of fiction I know. It is very, very grand; and has, I think, a greater practical effect on me for good than anything I ever read in my life.'

I find my first lessons from Harding were also at this time;* very delightful for what they were worth, though I saw well enough his shortcomings. But it was lovely to see him draw, in his own way, and up to a certain point. His knowledge of tree form was true, and entirely won for himself, with an honest original perception. Also, he was a violent hater of the old Dutch school, and I imagine the first who told me that they were 'sots, gamblers, and debauchees, delighting in the reality of the alehouse more than in its pictures.' All which was awakening and beneficial to no small extent.

71. And so the year 1842 dawned for me, with many things in its morning cloud. In the early spring of it, a change came over Turner's mind. He wanted to make some drawings to please himself; but also to be paid for making them. He gave Mr Griffith fifteen sketches for choice of subject by any one who would give him a commission. He got commissions for nine, of which my father let me choose at first one, then was coaxed and tricked into letting me have two. Turner got orders, out of all the round world besides, for seven more. With the sketches, four finished drawings were shown for samples of the sort of

thing Turner meant to make of them, and for immediate purchase by anybody.

Among them was the Splugen, which I had some hope of obtaining by supplication, when my father, who was travelling, came home. I waited dutifully till he should come. In the meantime it was bought, with the loveliest Lake Lucerne, by Mr Munro of Novar.*

72. The thing became to me grave matter for meditation. In a story by Miss Edgeworth, the father would have come home in the nick of time, effaced Mr Munro as he hesitated with the Splugen in his hand, and given the dutiful son that, and another. I found, after meditation, that Miss Edgeworth's way was not the world's, nor Providence's. I perceived then, and conclusively, that if you do a foolish thing, you suffer for it exactly the same, whether you do it piously or not. I knew perfectly well that this drawing was the best Swiss landscape yet painted by man; and that it was entirely proper for *me* to have it, and inexpedient that anybody else should. I ought to have secured it instantly, and begged my father's pardon, tenderly. He would have been angry, and surprised, and grieved; but loved me none the less, found in the end I was right, and been entirely pleased. I should have been very uncomfortable and penitent for a while, but loved my father all the more for having hurt him, and, in the good of the thing itself, finally satisfied and triumphant. As it was, the Splugen was a thorn in both our sides, all our lives. My father was always trying to get it; Mr Munro, aided by dealers, always raising the price on him, till it got up from 80 to 400 guineas. Then we gave it up,—with unspeakable wear and tear of best feelings on both sides.

73. And how about 'Thou shalt not covet,' etc.? Good reader, if you ask this, please consult my philosophical works. Here, I can only tell you facts, whether of circumstance or law. It is a law that if you do a foolish thing you suffer for it, whatever your motive. I do not say the motive itself may not be rewarded or punished on its own merits. In this case, nothing but mischief, as far as I know, came of the whole matter.

In the meantime, bearing the disappointment as best I could, I rejoiced in the sight of the sketches, and the hope of the drawings that were to be. And they gave me much more to think of than my mischance. I saw that these sketches were straight impressions from nature,—not artificial designs, like the Carthages and Romes.* And it began to occur to me that perhaps even in the artifice of Turner there might be more truth than I had understood. I was by this time very learned in *his* principles of composition; but it seemed to me that in these later subjects Nature herself was composing with him.

Considering of these matters, one day on the road to Norwood,* I noticed a bit of ivy round a thorn stem, which seemed, even to my critical judgment, not ill 'composed'; and proceeded to make a light and shade pencil study of it in my grey paper pocket-book, carefully, as if it had been a bit of sculpture, liking it more and more as I drew. When it was done, I saw that I had virtually lost all my time since I was twelve years old, because no one had ever told me to draw what was really there! All my time, I mean, given to drawing as an art; of course I had the records of places, but had never seen the beauty of anything, not even of a stone—how much less of a leaf!

I was neither so crushed nor so elated by the discovery as I ought to have been, but it ended the chrysalid days. Thenceforward my advance was steady, however slow.

74. This must have been in May, and a week or two afterwards I went up for my degree, but find no entry of it.* I only went up for a pass, and still wrote Latin so badly that there was a chance of my *not* passing! but the examiners forgave it because the divinity, philosophy, and mathematics were all above the average; and they gave me a complimentary double-fourth.*

When I was sure I had got through, I went out for a walk in the fields north of New College, (since turned into the Parks,) happy in the sense of recovered freedom, but extremely doubtful to what use I should put it. There I was, at two and twenty, with such and such powers, all second-rate except the analytic ones, which were as much in embryo as the rest, and which I had no means of measuring; such and such likings, hitherto indulged rather against conscience; and a dim sense of duty to myself, my parents, and a daily more vague shadow of Eternal Law.

What should I be, or do? my utterly indulgent father ready to let me do anything; with my room always luxuriously furnished in his house,—my expenses paid if I chose to travel. I was not heartless enough, yet, to choose to do that, alone. Perhaps it may deserve some dim praise that I never seriously thought of leaving my father and mother to explore foreign countries; and certainly the fear of grieving them was intermingled more or less with all my thoughts; but then, I did not much *want* to explore foreign countries. I had not the least love of adventure, but liked to have comfortable rooms always ordered, and a three-course dinner ready by four o'clock. Although no coward under circumstances of accidental danger, I extremely objected to any vestige of danger as a continuous element in one's life. I would not go to India for fear of tigers, nor to Russia for fear of bears, nor to Peru for fear of earthquakes;* and finally, though I had no rightly glowing or grateful affection for either father or mother, yet as they could not well do without me, so also I found I was not altogether comfortable without *them*.

75. So for the present, we planned a summer-time in Switzerland, not of travelling, but chiefly stay in Chamouni, to give me mountain air, and the long coveted power of examining the Mont Blanc rocks accurately. My mother loved Chamouni nearly as much as I; but this plan was of severe self-denial to my father, who did not like snow, nor wooden-walled rooms.

But he gave up all his own likings for me, and let me plan the stages through France as I chose, by Rouen, Chartres, Fontainebleau, and Auxerre. A pencil-sketch or two at first show only want of faith in my old manner, and more endeavour for light and shade, futile enough. The flat cross-country between Chartres and Fontainebleau, with an oppressive sense of Paris to the north, fretted me wickedly; when we got to the Fountain of Fair Water I lay feverishly wakeful through the night, and was so heavy and ill in the morning that I could not safely travel, and fancied some bad sickness was coming on. However, towards twelve o'clock the inn people brought me a little basket of wild strawberries; and they refreshed me, and I put my sketch-book in pocket and tottered out, though still in an extremely languid and woe-begone condition; and getting into a cart-road among some young trees, where there was nothing to see but the blue sky through thin branches, lay down on the bank by the roadside to see if I could sleep. But I couldn't, and the branches against the blue sky began to interest me, motionless as the branches of a tree of Jesse on a painted window.*

Feeling gradually somewhat livelier, and that I wasn't going to die this time, and be buried in the sand, though I couldn't for the present walk any farther, I took out my book, and began to draw a little aspen tree, on the other side of the cart-road, carefully.

76. How I had managed to get into that utterly dull cart-road, when there were sandstone rocks to be sought for, the Fates, as I have so often to observe, only know; but I was never fortunate enough to find at Fontainebleau any of the sublimities which I hear vaunted by French artists, and which disturbed poor Evelyn's mind nearly as much as the 'horrid Alp' of Clifton:—

'7th March (1644). I set forwards with some company towards Fontaine Bleau, a sumptuous palace of the King's like ours at Hampton Court. By the way we passe through a forest so prodigiously encompass'd with hideous rocks of whitish hard stone, heaped one on another in mountainous heights, that I think the like is nowhere to be found more horrid and solitary. On the summit of one of these gloomy precipices, intermingled with trees and shrubs, the stones hanging over and menacing ruin, is built an hermitage.'

I believe this passage to be accurately characteristic of the pure English mind about rocks. If they are only big enough to look as if they would break your head if they fell on it, it is all an Englishman asks, or can understand, of them. The modern thirst for self-glorification in getting to the top of them* is indeed often accompanied with good interest in geographical and other science; and nice boys and girls *do* enjoy their climbing, and lunching in fields of primula. But I never trace a word in one of their journals of sorrow for the destruction of any Swiss scene or Swiss character, so only that they have their own champagne at lunch.

77. The 'hideous rocks' of Fontainebleau were, I grieve to say, never hideous enough to please me. They always seemed to me no bigger than I could pack and send home for specimens, had they been worth carriage; and in my savage dislike of palaces and straight gravel walks, I never found out the spring which was the soul of the place. And to-day, I missed rocks, palace, and fountain all alike, and found myself lying on the bank of a cart-road in the sand, with no prospect whatever but that small aspen tree against the blue sky.

Languidly, but not idly, I began to draw it; and as I drew, the languor passed away: the beautiful lines insisted on being traced,—without weariness. More and more beautiful they became, as each rose out of the rest, and took its place in the air. With wonder increasing every instant, I saw that they 'composed' themselves, by finer laws than any known of men. At last, the tree was there, and everything that I had thought before about trees, nowhere.*

The Norwood ivy had not abased me in that final manner, because one had always felt that ivy was an ornamental creature, and expected it to behave prettily, on occasion. But that all the trees of the wood (for I saw surely that my little aspen was only one of their millions) should be beautiful—more than Gothic tracery, more than Greek vase-imagery, more than the daintiest embroiderers of the East could embroider, or the artfullest painters of the West could limn,—this was indeed an end to all former thoughts with me, an insight into a new silvan world.

Not silvan only. The woods, which I had only looked on as wilderness, fulfilled I then saw, in their beauty, the same laws which guided the clouds, divided the light, and balanced the wave. 'He hath made everything beautiful, in his time,'* became for me thenceforward the interpretation of the bond between the human mind and all visible things; and I returned along the wood-road feeling that it had led me far;—Farther than ever fancy had reached, or theodolite measured.

78. To my sorrow, and extreme surprise, I find no diary whatever of the feelings or discoveries of this year. They were too many, and bewildering, to be written. I did not even draw much,—the things I now saw were beyond drawings—but took to careful botany, while the month's time set apart for the rocks of Chamouni was spent in merely finding out what was to be done, and where. By the chance of guide dispensation, I had only one of the average standard, Michel Devouassoud, who knew his way to the show places, and little more; but I got the fresh air and the climbing; and thought over my Fontainebleau thoughts, by sweeter springs. The entry above quoted (p. 189), of Dec. 11th, the only one I can find of all the year's journeying, is very notable to me, in showing that the impulse which threw the new thoughts into the form of 'Modern Painters,' came to me in the fulfilment of the one disagreeable duty I persisted in,—going to church! But it came to me, two years following, in my true mother-town of Geneva.

We went home in 1842 by the Rhine and Flanders: and at Cologne and St Quentin I made the last drawings ever executed in my old manner. That of the great square at Cologne was given to Osborne Gordon, and remains I believe with his sister, Mrs Pritchard. The St Quentin has vanished into space.

79. We returned once more to the house at Herne Hill, and the lovely drawings Turner had made for me, Ehrenbreitstein and Lucerne, were first hung in its little front dining-room. But the Herne Hill days, and many joys with them, were now ended.

Perhaps my mother had sometimes—at Hampton Court, or Chatsworth, or Isola-Bella—admitted into her quiet soul the idea that it might be nice to have a larger garden. Sometimes a gold-tasseled Oxford friend would come out from Cavendish or Grosvenor Square to see me; and there was only the little back room opposite the nursery for him to wash his hands in. As his bank-balance enlarged, even my father thought it possible that his country customers might be more impressed by enjoying their after-dinner sherry with more room for their legs. And, now that I was of age and B.A. and so on—did not *I* also want a larger house?

No, good reader; but ever since first I could drive a spade, I had wanted to dig a canal, and make locks on it, like Harry in 'Harry and Lucy.'* And in the field at the back of the Denmark Hill house, now, in this hour of all our weaknesses, offered in temptation, I saw my way to a canal with any number of locks down towards Dulwich.

It is very wonderful to me, looking back, to remember this, and how entirely boyish—and very young-boyish, too—I was still, in all instincts of personal delight: while yet, looking out of myself, I saw farther than Kings of Naples or Cardinals of Rome.

80. Yet there was much, and very closely balanced, debate, before the house was taken. My mother wisely, though sadly, said it was too late for her;* she could not now manage a large garden: and my father, feeling his vanity had more than a word in the matter, besides all that might rightly be alleged of what was now convenient and becoming, hesitated painfully, as he had done about his first Copley Fielding.

But at last the lease of the larger house was bought: and everybody said how wise and proper; and my mother *did* like arranging the rows of pots in the big greenhouse; and the view from the breakfast-room into the field was really very lovely. And we bought three cows, and skimmed our own cream, and churned our own butter. And there was a stable, and a farmyard, and a haystack, and a pigstye, and a porter's lodge, where undesirable visitors could be stopped before startling us with a knock. But, for all these things, we never were so happy again. Never any more 'at home.'

81. At Champagnole, yes; and in Chamouni,—in La Cloche, at Dijon,—in La Cygne, at Lucerne.* All these places were of the old time. But though we had many happy days in the Denmark Hill house, none of our new ways ever were the same to us as the old: the basketfuls of peaches had not the flavour of the numbered dozen or score; nor were all the apples of the great orchard worth a single dishful of the Siberian crabs* of Herne Hill.

And I never got my canal dug, after all! Harry's making the lock-gates himself had indeed always seemed to me too magnificent! inimitable if not incredible: but also, I had never, till now that the need came, entered into the statistics of water supply. The gardeners wanted all that was in the butts for the greenhouse. Nothing but a dry ditch, incommodious to the cows, I saw to be possible, and resigned myself to destiny: yet the bewitching idea never went out of my head, and some water-works, on the model of Fontainebleau, were verily set aflowing—twenty years afterwards, as will be told.[1]

82. The next year, there was travelling enough for us up and down the new garden walks. Also, the first volume of 'Modern Painters' took

[1] See 'Joanna's Care.'

the best of the winter's leisure: the summer was broken by some formal term-keeping at Oxford.* There is nothing in diary worth noting, except a word about Camberwell church window;* to which I must return in connection with things yet far ahead.

The said first volume must have been out by my father's birthday; its success was assured by the end of the year, and on January 1st, 1844, 'my father brought me in the "Slaver"* for a New Year's gift,'—knowing well, this time, how to please me. I had it at the foot of my bed next morning like my own 'Loch Achray' of old. But the pleasure of one's own first painting everybody can understand. The pleasure of a new Turner to me, nobody ever will, and it's no use talking of it.

For the second volume,* (not meant to be the least like what it is,) I wanted more Chamouni. The journey of 1844 was planned entirely for central Alps, and on June 1st, 1844, we were happy by Lake Leman shore, again.

CHAPTER V

THE SIMPLON

83. MORE and more deeply every hour, in retracing Alpine paths,—by my fireside,—the wonder grows on me, what Heaven made the Alps for, and gave the chamois its foot, and the gentian its blue,—yet gave no one the heart to love them. And in the Alps, why especially that mighty central pass was so divinely planned, yet no one to pass it but against their wills, till Napoleon came, and made a road over it.*

Nor often, since, with any joy; though in truth there is no other such piece of beauty and power, full of human interest of the most strangely varied kind, in all the mountain scenery of the globe, as that traverse, with its two terminal cities, Geneva and Milan; its two lovely lakes of approach, Leman and Maggiore; its two tremendous valleys of vestibule, the Valais and Val d'Ossola; and its own, not desolate nor terrible, but wholly beautiful, upper region of rose and snow.

Of my early joy in Milan, I have already told; of Geneva, there is no telling, though I must now give what poor picture I may of the days we spent there, happy to young and old alike, again and again, in '33, '35, '42, and now, with full deliberation, in '44, knowing, and, in their repetitions twice, and thrice, and four times, magnifying, the well-remembered joys. And still I am more thankful, through every year of added life, that I was born in London, near enough to Geneva for me to reach it easily;*—and yet a city so contrary to everything Genevoise as best to teach me what the wonders of the little canton were.

84. A little canton, four miles square, and which did not wish to be six miles square! A little town, composed of a cluster of watermills, a street of penthouses, two wooden bridges, two dozen of stone houses on a little hill, and three or four perpendicular lanes up and down the hill. The four miles of acreage round, in grass, with modest gardens, and farm-dwelling houses; the people, pious, learned, and busy, to a man, to a woman—to a boy, to a girl, of them; progressing to and fro mostly on their feet, and only where they had business. And this bird's-nest of a place, to be the centre of religious and social thought, and of physical beauty, to all living Europe! That is to say, thinking and designing Europe,—France, Germany, and Italy. They, and their pieties, and their prides, their arts and their insanities, their wraths and slaughters, springing and flowering, building and fortifying, foaming and thundering round this inconceivable point of patience: the most lovely spot, and the most notable, without any possible dispute, of the European universe; yet the nations do not covet it, do not gravitate to it,—what is more wonderful, do not make a wilderness of it. They fight their battles at Chalons and Leipsic;* they build their cotton mills on the Aire,* and leave the Rhone running with a million of Aire power,—all pure. They build their pleasure houses on Thames shingle, and Seine mud, to look across to Lambeth, and—whatever *is* on the other side of the Seine. They found their military powers in the sand of Berlin,* and leave this precipice-guarded plain in peace. And yet it rules them,—is the focus of thought to them, and of passion, of science, and of *contrat sociale*,* of rational conduct, and of decent—and other—manners. Saussure's school and Calvin's,—Rousseau's and Byron's,—Turner's,—

And of course, I was going to say mine; but I didn't write all that last page to end so. Yet Geneva had better have ended with educating me and the likes of me, instead of the people who have hold of it now, with their polypous knots of houses, communal with 'London, Paris, and New York.'

Beneath which, and on the esplanades of the modern casino, New York and London now live—no more the Genevese. What their home once was, I must try to tell, as I saw it.

85. First, it was a notable town for keeping all its poor,—inside of it. In the very centre, where an English town has its biggest square, and its Exchange on the model of the Parthenon, built for the sake of the builder's commission on the cost,* there, on their little pile-propped

island, and by the steep lane-sides, lived the Genevoise poor; in their garrets,—their laborious upper spinning or watch-wheel cutting rooms,—their dark niches and angles of lane: mostly busy; the infirm and old all seen to and cared for, their porringers filled and their pallet-beds made, by household care.

But, outside the ramparts, no more poor. A sputter, perhaps, southward, along the Savoy road; but in all the champaign round, no mean rows of cubic lodgings with Doric porches; no squalid fields of mud and thistles; no deserts of abandoned brickfield and insolvent kitchen garden. On the instant, outside Geneva gates, perfectly smooth, clean, trim-hedged or prim-walled country roads; the main broad one intent on far-away things, its signal-posts inscribed 'Route de Paris;' branching from it, right and left, a labyrinth of equally well-kept ways for fine carriage wheels, between the gentlemen's houses with their farms; each having its own fifteen to twenty to fifty acres of mostly meadow, rich-waving always (in my time for being there) with grass and flowers, like a kaleidoscope. Stately plane trees, aspen and walnut,—sometimes in avenue,—casting breezy, never gloomy, shade round the dwelling-house. A dwelling-house indeed, all the year round; no travelling from it to fairer lands possible; no shutting up for seasons in town; hay-time and fruit-time, school-time and play, for generation after generation, within the cheerful white domicile with its green shutters and shingle roof,—pinnacled perhaps, humorously, at the corners, glittering on the edges with silvery tin. 'Kept up' the whole place, and all the neighbours' places, not ostentatiously, but perfectly: enough gardeners to mow, enough vintagers to press, enough nurses to nurse; no foxes to hunt, no birds to shoot;* but every household felicity possible to prudence and honour, felt and fulfilled from infancy to age.

86. Where the grounds came down to the waterside, they were mostly built out into it, till the water was four or five feet deep, lapping up, or lashing, under breeze, against the terrace wall. Not much boating; fancy wherries, unmanageable, or too adventurous, upon the wild blue; and Swiss boating a serious market and trade business, unfashionable in the high rural empyrean of Geneva. But between the Hotel des Etrangers, (one of these country-houses open to the polite stranger, some half-mile out of the gates, where Salvador took us in '33 and '35) and the town, there were one or two landing-places for the raft-like flat feluccas,* and glimpses of the open lake and things beyond,—glimpses only, shut off quickly by garden walls, until one came to the inlet of lake-water moat which bent itself under the ramparts back to the city gate. This was crossed, for people afoot who did not like going round

to that main gate, by the delicatest of filiform suspension bridges; strong enough it looked to carry a couple of lovers over in safety, or a nursemaid and children, but nothing heavier. One was allowed to cross it for a centime, which seemed to me always a most profitable transaction, the portress receiving placidly a sort of dirty flattened sixpence, (I forget its name) and returning me a waistcoat-pocketful of the loveliest little clean-struck centimes; and then one might stand on the bridge any time, in perfect quiet. (The Genevese didn't like paying the centime, and went round by the gate.) Two swans, drifting about underneath, over a couple of fathoms of purest green water, and the lake really opening from the moat, exactly where the Chamouni range of aiguilles rose beyond it far away. In our town walks we used always to time getting back to the little bridge at sunset, there to wait and watch.

87. That was the way of things on the north side; on the south, the town is still, in the main buildings of it, as then; the group of officially aristocratic houses round the cathedral and college presenting the same inaccessible sort of family dignity that they do to-day; only, since then, the Geneva Liberals——Well, I will not say what they have done; the main town stands still on its height of pebble-gravel, knit almost into rock; and still the upper terraces look across the variously mischievous Liberal works to the open southern country, rising in steady slope of garden, orchard, and vineyard—sprinkled with pretty farm-houses and bits of chateau, like a sea-shore with shells; rising always steeper and steeper, till the air gets rosy in the distance, then blue, and the great walnut-trees have become dots, and the farmsteads, minikin as if they were the fairy-finest of models made to be packed in a box; and then, instant—above vineyard, above farmstead, above field and wood, leaps up the Salève cliff, two thousand feet into the air.

88. I don't think anybody who goes to Geneva ever sees the Salève. For the most part, no English creature ever *does* see farther than over the way; and the Salève, unless you carefully peer into it, and make out what it is, pretends to be nothing,—a long, low swell like the South Downs, I fancy most people take it for, and look no more. Yet there are few rocks in the high Alps more awful than the 'Angle' of the Salève, at its foot—seven Shakespeare's Cliffs* set one on the top of another, and all of marble.[1]

On the other side of the high town the houses stand closer, leaving yet space for a little sycamore-shaded walk, whence one looks down on

---

[1] Not Parian, indeed, nor Carrara, but an extremely compact limestone, in which the compressed faulted veins are of marble indeed, and polish beautifully.

the whole southern reach of lake, opening wide to the horizon, and edged there like the sea, but in the summer sunshine looking as if it was the one well of blue which the sunbeams drank to make the sky of. Beyond it, ghostly ranges of incredible mountains—the Dent d'Oche, and first cliffs towards Fribourg; to the west, the long wave of Jura, fading into the air above Neuchatel.

That was the view for full noon, when the lake was brightest and bluest. Then you fell down a perpendicular lane into the lower town again, and you went to Mr Bautte's.*

89. Virtually there was no other jeweller in Geneva, in the great times. There were some respectable, uncompetitive shops, not dazzling, in the main street; and smaller ones, with an average supply of miniature watches, that would go well for ten years; and uncostly, but honest, trinketry. But one went to Mr Bautte's with awe, and of necessity, as one did to one's bankers. There was scarcely any external sign of Bautte whatever—a small brass plate at the side of a narrow arched door, into an alley—into a secluded alley—leading into a monastic courtyard, out of which—or rather out of the alley, where it opened to the court, you ascended a winding stair, wide enough for two only, and came to a green door, swinging, at the top of it; and there you paused to summon courage to enter.

A not large room, with a single counter at the further side. Nothing shown on the counter. Two confidential attendants behind it, and—it might possibly be Mr Bautte!—or his son—or his partner—or anyhow the Ruling power—at his desk beside the back window. You told what you wanted: it was necessary to know your mind, and to be sure you *did* want it; there was no showing of things for temptation at Bautte's. You wanted a bracelet, a brooch, a watch—plain or enamelled. Choice of what was wanted was quietly given. There were no big stones, nor blinding galaxies of wealth. Entirely sound workmanship in the purest gold that could be worked; fine enamel for the most part, for colour, rather than jewels; and a certain Bauttesque subtlety of linked and wreathed design, which the experienced eye recognized when worn in Paris or London. Absolutely just and moderate price; wear,—to the end of your days. You came away with a sense of duty fulfilled, of treasure possessed, and of a new foundation to the respectability of your family.

You returned into the light of the open street with a blissful sense of a parcel being made up to be sent after you, and in the consequently calm expatiation of mind, went usually to watch the Rhone.

Bautte's was in the main street, out of which one caught glimpses, down the short cross ones, of the passing water, as at Sandgate, or the like fishing towns, one got peeps of the sea. With twenty steps you were beside it.

90. For all other rivers there is a surface, and an underneath, and a vaguely displeasing idea of the bottom. But the Rhone flows like one lambent jewel; its surface is nowhere, its ethereal self is everywhere, the iridescent rush and translucent strength of it blue to the shore, and radiant to the depth.

Fifteen feet thick, of not flowing, but flying water; not water, neither,—melted glacier, rather, one should call it; the force of the ice is with it, and the wreathing of the clouds, the gladness of the sky, and the continuance of Time.

Waves of clear sea are, indeed, lovely to watch, but they are always coming or gone, never in any taken shape to be seen for a second. But here was one mighty wave that was always itself, and every fluted swirl of it, constant as the wreathing of a shell. No wasting away of the fallen foam, no pause for gathering of power, no helpless ebb of discouraged recoil; but alike through bright day and lulling night, the never-pausing plunge, and never-fading flash, and never-hushing whisper, and, while the sun was up, the ever-answering glow of unearthly aquamarine, ultramarine, violet-blue, gentian-blue, peacock-blue, river-of-paradise blue, glass of a painted window melted in the sun and the witch of the Alps flinging the spun tresses of it for ever from her snow.

91. The innocent way, too, in which the river used to stop to look into every little corner. Great torrents always seem angry, and great rivers too often sullen; but there is no anger, no disdain, in the Rhone. It seemed as if the mountain stream was in mere bliss at recovering itself again out of the lake-sleep, and raced because it rejoiced in racing, fain yet to return and stay. There were pieces of wave that danced all day as if Perdita were looking on to learn;* there were little streams that skipped like lambs and leaped like chamois;* there were pools that shook the sunshine all through them, and were rippled in layers of overlaid ripples, like crystal sand; there were currents that twisted the light into golden braids, and inlaid the threads with turquoise enamel; there were strips of stream that had certainly above the lake been millstreams, and were looking busily for mills to turn again; there were shoots of stream that had once shot fearfully into the air, and now sprang up again laughing that they had only fallen a foot or two;—and in the midst of all the gay glittering and eddied lingering, the noble bearing by of the midmost depth, so mighty, yet so terrorless

and harmless, with its swallows skimming instead of petrels, and the dear old decrepit town as safe in the embracing sweep of it as if it were set in a brooch of sapphire.

92. And the day went on, as the river; but I never felt that I wasted time in watching the Rhone. One used to get giddy sometimes, or discontentedly envious of the fish. Then one went back for a walk in the pent-house street, long ago gone. There was no such other street anywhere. Penthouses five stories high, not so much for the protection of the people in the street as to keep the plash of heavy rain from the house windows, so that these might be the more safely open. Beam-pillars of squared pine, with one cross-tie beam, the undecorative structural arrangement, Swiss to the very heart and pitch of it, picturesque in comfort, stately and ancient without decay, and rough, here in mid Geneva, more than in the hill solitudes.

93. We arrived at Geneva on 1st June, 1844,* with plan of another month at Chamouni; and fine things afterwards, which also came prosperously to pass. I had learned to draw now with great botanical precision; and could colour delicately, to a point of high finish. I was interested in everything, from clouds to lichens. Geneva was more wonderful to me, the Alps more living and mighty, than ever; Chamouni more peaceful.

We reached the Prieure on the 6th June, and found poor Michel Devouassoud's climbing days ended. He had got a chill, and a cough; medicined himself with absinthe, and was now fast dying. The body of guides had just sustained a graver loss, by the superannuation, according to law, in his sixtieth year, of Joseph Couttet, the Captain of Mont Blanc, and bravest at once and most sagacious of the old school of guides. Partly in regard for the old man, partly in respect for us, now favourably known in Chamouni, the law was relaxed by the Chef des Guides in our favour, and Couttet came to us on the morning of the 7th of June. My father explained to him that he wanted me taken charge of on the hills, and not permitted in any ambitious attempts, or taken into any dangerous places; and that, from what he had heard of Couttet's trustworthiness, and knowledge of his mountains, he had no doubt that I should be safe with him, and might learn more under his tutelage, in safety, than by the most daring expeditions under inferior masters. Couttet said little, but accepted the charge with a kindly glitter in his eyes, and a cheerful word or two, signifying that my father need not fear for me; and we set out together for the base of the Buet,—I on muleback, he walking.

For thirty years he remained my tutor and companion. Had he been my drawing-master also, it would have been better for me: if my work pleased Couttet, I found afterwards it was always good; and he knew perfectly when I was trying vainly to do what I could not, or foolishly what no one else would care for.

The month at Chamouni, however, passed with his approval, and to my perfect benefit. I made two foreground studies in colour, of considerable beauty; and, under his teaching, began to use my alpenstock easily, and to walk with firmness.

94. Of our habitual Chamouni life—papa's, mamma's, and mine— I shall give account further on.* I take from this year's diary only the note on first reaching the bases of the aiguilles.

'At last, on steep inclined planes of snow, reached the base of the little Charmoz; but was amazed to find that the size of the aiguilles seemed to diminish with every step of approach, after a certain point, and that, thus seen (the aiguille) Blaitière, though still 3,000 feet above us, looked a mere rock, ascendable in a quarter of an hour. Of course, after being used to the higher rocks, one begins to measure them in their own way; but where there is nothing to test scale—where the air is perfectly mistless, and the mountain masses are divided into sheets whose *edges* are the height of Dover cliffs, it is impossible effectually to estimate their magnitude but by trying them.'

This bit of moonlight is perhaps worth keeping: '28th June, half-past ten.—I never was dazzled by moonlight until now; but as it rose from behind the Mont Blanc du Tacul, the full moon almost blinded me: it burst forth into the sky like a vast star. For an hour before, the aiguilles had appeared as dark masses against a sky looking as transparent as clear sea, edged at their summits with fleeces of cloud breaking into glorious spray and foam of white fire. A meteor fell over the Dôme as the moon rose: now it is so intensely bright that I cannot see the Mont Blanc underneath it; the form is lost in its light.'

Many and many an hour of precious time and perfect sight was spent, during these years, in thus watching skies; much was written which would be useful—if I took a year to put it together,—to myself; but, in the present smoky world, to no other creature: and much was learned, which is of no use now to anybody; for to me it is only sorrowful memory, and to others, an old man's fantasy.

95. We left Chamouni on 4th July; on the 8th I find this entry at St Gingoulph: 'We dined late, which kept me later from my walk than I like, and it was wet with recent rain; but the glades of greensward under groves of Spanish chestnut all the greener for it. Such richness I never saw in Italy; the hay just cut, leaving the grass crisp and

short; the grey trunks and rich leaves mixed with mossy rock, and the cliffs above, nobler than Amalfi: the sunset sent down rays of opaque gold between me and the Jura, bringing out the successive rises of the Pays de Vaud; the Jura a golden shadow, sharp-edged and baseless in the sky.'

Hence, we crossed the Simplon to Baveno and back,—for the Simplon's and Lago Maggiore's sake only.

'Baveno, July 12th.—I have more feeling for Italy than ever, but it makes me deeply sad. The vines and pasture about this place make it a Paradise; the people are fine-featured, and singularly graceful in motion; but there is every appearance of hopeless vice. Four men have been playing cards and drinking, without stirring, in the inn-yard since twelve o'clock (noon). I had come in from an evening walk, and the gardens and enclosed spots of ground are foul as dunghills. The Isola Bella is fast going to decay—all the stucco of it green, damp, shattered, covered with weeds and dead leaves; yet the flowers and foliage of surpassing beauty.'

And to this day, the uselessness of San Carlo's memory* is to me one of the entirely wonderfullest things in Catholic history;—that Rome should go on sending missionaries to China, and, within a thousand yards across the water from St Carlo's isle, leave the people of her own Italy's Garden of Eden in guilt and misery. I call the Lago Maggiore district the Eden of Italy; for there are no solfataras* there, no earthquakes, no pestiferous marsh, no fever-striking sunshine. Purest air, richest earth, loveliest wave; and the same noble race that founded the architecture of Italy at Como.

Left to die, like the green lizards, in the blind clefts of their rocks, whence they see no God.

96. 'Village of Simplon, 15th June.*—At eight this evening I was sitting on the highest col of the Simplon, watching the light die on the Breithorn; nothing round me but rock and lichen, except one purple flower,' (coloured and very accurate drawing, at the side, of Linaria Alpina,*) 'and the forget-me-not, which grows everywhere. My walk home was very lovely, star after star coming out above my head, the white hills gleaming among them; the gulph of pines, with the torrent, black and awful below; lights breaking softly through cottage windows.

'Cassiopeia* is rising above a piny mountain, exactly opposite my window.'

The linaria must have been brought 'home' (the Simplon village inn was already more that to me than ever Denmark Hill), and painted next morning—it could not have been so rightly coloured at night; also the day had been a heavy one. At six, morning, I had visited Signor Zanetti, and reviewed his collection of pictures on Isola Pescatore; walked up most of the defile of Gondo; and the moment we got to the Simplon village, dashed off to catch the sunset from the col; five miles up hill against time, (and walk against time up a regular slope of eight feet in the hundred is the most trying foot-work I know,) five miles back under the stars, with the hills not *under* but *among* them, and careful entry, of which I have only given a sentence, make up a day which shows there was now no farther need to be alarmed about my health. My good father, who was never well in the high air, and hated the chills from patches of melting snow, stayed nevertheless all next day at the village, to let me climb the long-coveted peak west of the Simplon col. which forms the great precipice on the Brieg side. 'It commanded the Valais far down, the Bernese Alps in their whole extent, and two great mountains beyond the valley of Saas.' These were the Weisshorn, and lower peak nearer Zermatt.

97. That evening James Forbes and his wife were with us* in the otherwise untenanted salle-à-manger (see 'Deucalion,' Chap. X.), and next morning, the 17th, 'I set off at six to visit the Père Barras,' (formerly Clavendiér of the great St Bernard, now at the monastery of the Simplon,) 'On the Sempione,' (I meant the Fletsch-horn,) 'a field of cirri, bounded by a contour like that of common cirrostrati, convex and fishy, but composed of the most exquisite sandy and silky forms, all in most rapid motion, but forming and vanishing, as usual, exactly at the same point, so that the mass was stationary. Reached the col in two hours of very slow walking, and breakfasted with the Father. He showed me the spot where the green actynolite* is found, directly behind the convent. One of his dogs saw him with his hat on, and waited in the passage, barking furiously with delight. He parted from me half a mile down on this side (Brieg side), and I waited at the second gallery for the carriage.'

'19th July, Zermatt.—Clouds on the Matterhorn all day till sunset, when there were playing lights over the sky, and the Matterhorn appeared in full ruby, with a wreath of crimson cloud drifting from its top.'

That day Gordon was to come up from Chamouni to meet us; he had slept at Visp, and was first at Zermatt. Just as we came in sight of the Matterhorn he met us, with his most settledly practical and constitutional face—

'Yes, the Matterhorn is all very fine; but do you know there's nothing to eat?'

'Nonsense; we can eat anything here.'

'Well, the black bread's two months old, and there's nothing else but potatoes.'

'There must be milk, anyhow.'

Yes, there was milk, he supposed.

'You can sop your bread in it then; what could be nicer?'

But Gordon's downcast mien did not change; and I had to admit myself, when supper-time came, that one might almost as hopelessly have sopped the Matterhorn as the loaf.

98. Thus the Christian peasant had lived in the Alps, unthought of, for two thousand years—since Christ broke bread for His multitude;* and lived thus under the direct care of the Catholic Church—for Sion, the capital of the Valais, is one of the grandest of old bishoprics; and just below this valley of black bread, the little mountain towns of Visp and Brieg are more groups of tinkling towers and convent cloisters than civic dwelling-places. As for the Catholic State, for a thousand years, while at every sunset Monte Rosa glowed across the whole Lombard plain, not a Lombard noble knew where the mountain was.

Yet, it may be, I err in my pity. I have many things yet to say of the Valais; meantime this passage from Saussure records a social state in 1796, which, as compared with that of the poor in our great capitals, is one neither of discomfort nor disgrace:—

'La sobriété, compagne ordinaire de l'amour du travail, est encore une qualité remarquable des habitants de ces vallées. Ce pain de seigle, dont j'ai parlé qu'on ne mange que six mois après qu'il est cuit, on le ramollit dans du petit lait ou dans du lait de beurre, et cette espèce de soupe fait leur principale nourriture; le fromage et un peu de vieille vache ou de chèvre salées, se réservent pour les jours de fête ou pour le temps de grands travaux; car pour la viande fraîche, ils n'en mangent jamais, c'est un mets trop dispendieux. Les gens riches du pays vivent avec la même économie; je voyois notre hôte de Macugnaga, qui n'étoit rien moins que pauvre, aller tous les soirs prendre, dans un endroit fermé à clef, une pincée d'aulx dont il distribuoit gravement une gousse à sa femme, et autant à chacun de ses enfants, et cette gousse d'ail étoit l'assaisonnement unique d'un morceau de pain sec qu'ils brisoient entre deux pierres, & qu'ils mangeoient pour leur souper. Ceux d'entr'eux qui négocient au dehors, viennent au moins une fois tous les deux ans passer quelques mois dans leur village; et quoique hors de chez eux ils prennent l'habitude d'une meilleure nourriture, ils se remettent sans peine à celle de leur pays, et ne le quittent qu'avec un extrême regret; j'ai été témoin d'un ou deux de ces départs, qui m'ont attendri jusqu'aux larmes.'*

99. By the morning, however, our hosts had found some meat for the over-greedy foreigners, and the wine was good enough; but it was no place for papa and mamma to stay in; and, bravado apart, I liked black bread no better than they. So we went up to the Riffelberg, where I saw that on the north Monte Rosa was only a vast source of glacier, and, as a mountain, existed only for the Italian side: the Matterhorn was too much of an Egyptian obelisk to please me (I trace continually the tacit reference in my Cumberland-built soul to moorish Skiddaw and far-sweeping Saddleback as the proper types of majestic form); and I went down to Visp again next day without lamentation: my mother, sixty-three on next 2nd September, walking with me the ten miles from St Nicholas to Visp as lightly as a girl. And the old people went back to Brieg with me, that I might climb the Bell Alp (then unknown), whence I drew the panorama of the Simplon and Bernese range, now in Walkley Museum.* But the more I got, the more I asked. After drawing the Weisshorn and Aletsch-horn, I wanted to see the Aiguille Verte again, and was given another fortnight for Chamouni; the old people staying at the Trois Couronnes of Vevay. I spent the days usefully, going first up to the base of the Aiguille d'Argentière, which commands the glorious white ocean of the Tours glacier below, and, opposite, the four precipices of the Aiguille Verte on its north-east flank; and that day, 27th July, we saw a herd of more than thirty chamois* on the Argentière. 'Pour les voir, faut aller où ils sont,'* said Couttet; and he might have added, where other living things are not; for, whether by shepherd or traveller, the snows round the Aiguilles of Chardonnet and Argentière are the least trodden of all the Mont Blanc fields. The herd was in three groups, twelve in one of them only; and did not put itself to speed, but retired slowly when we got within a quarter of a mile of them, each stopping to look back from the ridge behind which they disappeared.

100. 'Iceland moss' (says the diary*), 'in enormous quantities amongst the Alpine roses, above the Argentière glacier—not growing at all, so far as I recollect, but on the hills on the north-east of the valley. Where we took the snow, the top of the glacier' (Tours) 'was wreathed in vast surges which took us from twenty minutes to half an hour (each) to climb,—green lovely lakes in their hollows, no crevices.' On the 29th July I went up the Buet, and down to Sixt, where I found myself very stiff and tired, and determined that the Alps were, on the whole, best seen from below. And after a walk to the Fer-à-cheval,

considering the wild strawberries there to taste of slate, I went rather penitently down to Geneva again.

Feeling also a little ashamed of myself before papa—in the consciousness that all his pining in cold air, and dining on black bread, and waiting, day after day, not without anxiety, while I rambled he knew not whither, had not in the least advanced the object nearest his heart,—the second volume of 'Modern Painters.' I had, on the contrary, been acutely and minutely at work in quite other directions—felt tempted now to write on Alpine botany, or devote myself to painting myrtilles and mica-slate* for the rest of my days. The Turner charm was indeed as potent as ever; but I felt that other powers were now telling on me besides his,—even beyond his; not in delight, but in vital strength; and that no word more could be written of him, till I had tried the range of these.

101. It surprises me to find, by entries at Paris (which I was reasonable enough now to bear the sight of again), in August of this year, how far I had advanced in picture knowledge since the Roman days; progress which I see no ground for, and remember no steps of,—except only a lesson given me by George Richmond at one of Mr Rogers' breakfasts (the old man used to ask me, finding me always reverent to him, joyful in his pictures, and sometimes amusing, as an object of curiosity to his guests),—date uncertain, but probably in 1842. Until that year, Rubens had remained the type of colour power to me, and (p. 175 above) Titian's flesh tints of little worth! But that morning, as I was getting talkative over the wild Rubens sketch, (War or Discord, or Victory or the Furies, I forget what,) Richmond said, pointing to the Veronese beneath it,* 'Why are you not looking at this,—so much greater in manner?' 'Greater,—how?' I asked, in surprise; 'it seems to me quite tame beside the Rubens.' 'That may be,' said Richmond, 'but the Veronese is true, the other violently conventional.' 'In what way true?' I asked, still not understanding. 'Well,' said Richmond, 'compare the pure shadows on the flesh, in Veronese, and its clear edge, with Rubens's ochre and vermilion, and outline of asphalt.'

102. No more was needed. From that moment, I saw what was meant by Venetian colour; yet during 1843, and early 1844, was so occupied with 'Modern Painters,' degree-getting, and studies of foliage and foreground, that I cannot understand how I had reached, in picture knowledge, the point shown by these following entries, of which indeed the first shows that the gain surprised me at the time, but foolishly regards it only as a change coming to pass in the Louvre on the instant, and does not recognize it as the result of growth: the fact

being, I suppose, that the habit of looking for true colour in nature had made me sensitive to the modesty and dignity of hues in painting also, before possessing no charm for me.

'Aug. 17th. I have had a change wrought in me, and a strong one, by this visit to the Louvre, and know not how far it may go, chiefly in my full understanding of Titian, John Bellini, and Perugino, and being able to abandon everything for them; or rather, being *un*able to look at anything else.'

103. I allow the following technical note only for proof of the length I had got to. There shall be no more of the kind let into PRAETERITA.

'1252 ("The Entombment"*) is the finest Titian in the gallery,—glowing, simple, broad, and grand. It is to be opposed to 1251 ("The Flagellation"), in which the shades are brown instead of grey, the outlines strong brown lines, the draperies broken up by folds, the lights very round and vivid, and foiled by deep shades, the flesh forms, the brightest lights, and the draperies subdued.

'In 1252 every one of these conditions is reversed. Even the palest flesh is solemn and dark, in juxtaposition with golden-white drapery; all the masses broad and flat, the shades grey, the outlines chaste and severe. It may be taken as an example of the highest dignity of expression wrought out by mere grandeur of colour and composition.

'I found myself finally in the Louvre, fixed by this Titian, and turning to it, and to the one (picture), exactly opposite, John and Gentile Bellini, by John Bellini.* I was a long time hesitating between this and Raphael's dark portrait; but decided for the John Bellini.

'Aug. 18th. To-morrow we leave. I have been watching the twilight on the Tuileries, which was very grand and clear; and planning works. I shall try to paint a Madonna some day, I believe.'

CHAPTER VI

THE CAMPO SANTO*

104. THE summer's work of 1844, so far from advancing the design of 'Modern Painters,' had thrown me off it—first into fine botany, then into difficult geology, and lastly, as that entry about the Madonna shows, into a fit of figure study which meant much. It meant, especially, at last some looking into ecclesiastical history,—some notion of the merit of fourteenth century painting, and the total abandonment of Rubens and Rembrandt for the Venetian school. Which, the reader will please

observe, signified not merely the advance in sense of colour, but in perception of truth and modesty in light and shade. And on getting home, I felt that in the cyclone of confused new knowledge, this was the thing first to be got firm.

Scarcely any book writing was done that winter,—and there are no diaries;* but, for the first time, I took up Turner's 'Liber Studiorum'* instead of engravings; mastered its principles, practised its method, and by spring-time in 1845 was able to study from nature accurately in full chiaroscuro, with a good frank power over the sepia tinting.

I must have read also, that winter, Rio's 'Poésie Chrétienne,' and Lord Lindsay's introduction to his 'Christian Art.'* And perceiving thus, in some degree, what a blind bat and puppy I had been, all through Italy, determined that at least I must see Pisa and Florence again before writing another word of 'Modern Painters.'

105. How papa and mamma took this new vagary, I have no recollection; resignedly, at least: perhaps they also had some notion that I might think differently, and it was to be hoped in a more orthodox and becoming manner, after another sight of the Tribune.* At all events, they concluded to give me my own way entirely this time; and what time I chose. My health caused them no farther anxiety; they could trust my word to take care of myself every day, just the same as if I were coming home to tea: my mother was satisfied of Couttet's skill as a physician, and care, if needed, as a nurse;—he was engaged for the summer in those capacities,—and, about the first week in April, I found myself dining on a trout of the Ain, at Champagnole; with Switzerland and Italy at my feet—for tomorrow.

106. Curiously, the principal opposition to this unprincipled escapade had been made by Turner. He knew that one of my chief objects was to see the motives of his last sketches on the St Gothard; and he feared my getting into some scrape in the then disturbed state of the cantons. He had probably himself seen some of their doings in 1843, when 'la vieille Suisse prit les armes, prévint les Bas Valaisans, qui furent vaincus et massacrés au Pont du Trient, près de Martigny;'[1]* and again an expedition of the Corps Francs of the liberal cantons 'pour expulser les Jesuits, et renverser le gouvernement,'* at Lucerne, had been summarily 'renversée'* itself by the Lucernois, 8th December, 1844, only three months before my intended start for the Alps. Every time Turner saw me during the winter, he said something to dissuade me from going abroad; when at last I went to say good-bye, he came

---

[1] 'La Suisse Historique,' par E. H. Gaullieur. Genève, 1855, p. 428.

down with me into the hall in Queen Anne Street, and opening the door just enough for me to pass, laid hold of my arm, gripping it strongly. 'Why *will* you go to Switzerland,—there'll be such a fidge about you, when you're gone.'

I am never able to collect myself in a moment, and am simply helpless on any sudden need for decision like this; the result being, usually, that I go on doing what I meant to do. If I say anything, it is sure to be wrong. I made no answer, but grasped his hand closely, and went. I believe he made up his mind that I was heartless and selfish; anyhow he took no more pains with me.*

107. As it chanced, even while I sat over my trout at Champagnole, there was another expedition of the Francs Corps—M. Gaullieur does not say against whom, but only that it had 'une issue encore plus tragique que la première.'* But there had been no instance of annoyance to English or any other travellers, in all the course of these Swiss squabbles since 1833, in which year—by the way, the first of our journeys—we drove under some posted field-batteries into Basle, just after the fight at Liesthal between the liberal townspeople and Catholic peasants. The landlord of the 'Three Kings' had been out; and run—or at least made the best speed he could—three leagues to the town gates.

It was no part of my plan, however, as my parents knew, to enter Switzerland in this spring-time: but to do what I could in Italy first. Geneva itself was quiet enough: Couttet met me there, and next day we drove over the ledges of the Salève, all aglow with primrose and soldanelle,* down upon Annecy.

108. I had with me, besides Couttet, a young servant who became of great use to me in succeeding years; with respect to whom I must glance back at some of the past revolutions in our domestic dynasties. The cook and housemaid at Herne Hill, in its mainly characteristic time—1827–1834—were sisters, Mary and Elizabeth Stone. I have never seen a fillet of veal rightly roasted, nor a Yorkshire pudding rightly basted, since Mary Stone left us to be married in 1836. Elizabeth, also not to be excelled in her line, was yet replaceable, when her career ended in the same catastrophe, by a third younger sister, Hannah; but I can't in the least remember who waited on us, till our perennial parlour-maid, Lucy Tovey, came to us in 1829—remaining with us till 1875. Her sister Harriet replaced Hannah Stone, who must needs be married, like Mary and Elizabeth, in 1834; nor did she leave us till the Denmark Hill household was broken up. But in 1842 another young housemaid came, Anne Hobbs, whose brother John Hobbs, called always at Denmark Hill, George, to distinguish him, in vocal summons,

from my father and me, became my body servant in the same year, and only left me to push his higher fortune in 1854. I could not say before, without interrupting graver matters, that the idea of my not being able to dress myself began at Oxford, where it was thought becoming in a gentleman-commoner to have a squire to manage his scout.* My good, honest, uninteresting Thomas Hughes, being vigilant that I put my waistcoat on right side outwards, went abroad with us, instead of Salvador; my father, after the first two journeys, being quite able to do his courier's work himself. When we came home in '42, Hughes wanted to promote himself to some honour or other in the public-house line, and George Hobbs, a sensible and merry-minded youth of eighteen, came in his stead. Couttet and he sat in the back seat of the light-hooded barouche which I took for this Italian journey; the hood seldom raised, as I never travelled in bad weather unless surprised by it; and the three of us walked that April morning up the Salève slope, and trotted down to Annecy, in great peace of mind.

109. At Annecy I made the first careful trial of my new way of work. I herewith reproduce the study; it is very pleasant to me still; and certainly any artist who once accustoms himself to the method cannot afterwards fall into any mean trickery or dull conventionalism. The outline must be made clearly and quietly, conveying as much accurate information as possible respecting the form and structure of the object; then, in washing, the chiaroscuro is lowered from the high lights with extreme care down to the middle tones, and the main masses left in full shade.

A rhyme written to Mont Blanc at Geneva, and another in vituperation of the idle people at Conflans, were, I think, the last serious exertions of my poetical powers.* I perceived finally that I could express nothing I had to say, rightly, in that manner; and the 'peace of mind' above referred to, which returns to me as the principal character of this opening journey, was perhaps, in part, the result of this extremely wholesome conclusion.

110. But also, the two full years, since the flash of volcanic lightning at Naples, had brought me into a deeper and more rational state of religious temper. I can scarcely yet call it religious thought; but the steadily read chapters, morning and evening, with the continual comparison between the Protestant and Papal services every Sunday abroad, made me feel that all dogmatic teaching was a matter of chance and habit; and that the life of religion depended on the force of faith, not the terms of it. In the sincerity and brightness of his imagination, I saw that George Herbert represented the theology of the Protestant

Church in a perfectly central and deeply spiritual manner: his 'Church Porch' I recognised to be blamelessly wise as a lesson to youth; and the exquisitely faithful fancy of the other poems (in the 'Temple') drew me into learning most of them by heart,—the 'Church Porch,' the 'Dialogue,' 'Employment,' 'Submission,' 'Gratefulness,' and, chief favourite, 'The Bag,'—deliberately and carefully. The code of feeling and law written in these verses may be always assigned as a standard of the purest unsectarian Christianity; and whatever has been wisest in thought or happiest in the course of my following life was founded at this time on the teaching of Herbert. The reader will perhaps be glad to see the poem that has been most useful to me, 'Submission,' in simpler spelling than in the grand editions:

> But that Thou art my wisdom, Lord,
> And both mine eyes are Thine,
> My mind would be extremely stirred
> For missing my design.

> Were it not better to bestow
> Some place and power on me?
> Then should Thy praises with me grow,
> And share in my degree.

> But when I thus dispute and grieve
> I do resume my sight,
> And pilfering what I once did give,
> Disseize Thee of Thy right.

> How know I, if Thou shouldst me raise,
> That I should then raise Thee?
> Perhaps great places and Thy praise
> Do not so well agree!

> Wherefore, unto my gift I stand,
> I will no more advise;
> Only do Thou lend me Thine hand,
> Since Thou hast both mine eyes.

111. In these, and other such favourite verses, George Herbert, as aforesaid, was to me at this time, and has been since, useful beyond every other teacher; not that I ever attained to any likeness of feeling, but at least knew where I was myself wrong, or cold, in comparison. A little more force was also put on Bible study at this time, because I held myself responsible for George's tenets as well as my own, and wished to set him a discreet example; he being well-disposed, and given to my guidance, with no harm as yet in any of his ways. So I read my

chapter with him morning and evening; and if there were no English church on Sundays, the Morning Service, Litany and all,* very reverently; after which we enjoyed ourselves, each in our own way, in the afternoons, George being always free, and Couttet, if he chose; but he had little taste for the Sunday promenades in a town, and was glad if I would take him with me to gather flowers, or carry stones. I never, until this time, had thought of travelling, climbing, or sketching on the Sunday: the first infringement of this rule by climbing the isolated peak above Gap, with both Couttet and George, after our morning service, remains a weight on my conscience to this day. But it was thirteen years later before I made a sketch on Sunday.*

112. By Gap and Sisteron to Frejus, along the Riviera to Sestri, where I gave a day to draw the stone-pines now at Oxford; and so straight to my first fixed aim, Lucca, where I settled myself for ten days,—as I supposed. It turned out forty years.

The town is some thousand paces square; the unbroken rampart walk round may be a short three miles. There are upwards of twenty churches in that space, dating between the sixth and twelfth centuries; a ruined feudal palace and tower, unmatched except at Verona: the streets clean—cheerfully inhabited, yet quiet; nor desolate, even now. Two of the churches representing the perfectest phase of round-arched building in Europe, and one of them containing the loveliest Christian tomb in Italy.*

The rampart walk, unbroken except by descents and ascents at the gates, commands every way the loveliest ranges of all the Tuscan Apennine: when I was there in 1845, besides the ruined feudal palace, there was a maintained Ducal Palace, with a living Duke in it, whose military band played every evening on the most floral and peaceful space of rampart. After a well-spent day, and a three-course dinner,—military band,—chains, double braided, of amethyst Apennine linked by golden clouds,—then the mountain air of April still soft as the marble towers grew unsubstantial in the starlight,—such the monastic discipline of Lucca to my novitiate mind.

113. I must stop to think a little how it was that so early as this I could fasten on the tomb of Ilaria di Caretto with certainty of its being a supreme guide to me ever after. If I get tiresome, the reader must skip; I write, for the moment, to amuse myself, and not him. The said reader, duly sagacious, must have felt, long since, that, though very respectable people in our way, we were all of us definitely vulgar people; just as my aunt's dog Towzer was a vulgar dog, though a very good and dear dog. Said reader should have seen also that we had not

set ourselves up to have a taste in anything. There was never any question about matching colours in furniture, or having the correct pattern in china. Everything for service in the house was bought plain, and of the best; our toys were what we happened to take a fancy to in pleasant places—a cow in stalactite from Matlock, a fisher-wife doll from Calais, a Swiss farm from Berne, Bacchus and Ariadne from Carrara. But, among these toys, principal on the drawing-room chimney-piece, always put away by my mother at night, and 'put out' in the afternoon, were some pieces of Spanish clay, to which, without knowing it, I owed a quantity of strenuous teaching. Native baked clay figures, painted and gilded by untaught persons who had the gift; manufacture mainly practised along the Xeres coast, I believe, and of late much decayed, but then flourishing, and its work as good as the worker could make it. There was a Don Whiskerandos* contrabandista, splendidly handsome and good-natured, on a magnificent horse at the trot, brightly caparisoned: everything finely finished, his gun loose in his hand. There was a lemonade seller, a pomegranate seller, a matador with his bull—animate all, and graceful, the colouring chiefly ruddy brown. Things of constant interest to me, and altogether wholesome; vestiges of living sculpture come down into the Herne Hill times, from the days of Tanagra.*

For loftier admiration, as before told, Chantrey in Lichfield, Roubilliac in Westminster,* were set forth to me, and honestly felt; a scratched white outline or two from Greek vases on the black Derbyshire marble did not interfere with my first general feeling about sculpture, that it should be living, and emotional; that the flesh should be like flesh, and the drapery like clothes; and that, whether trotting contrabandista, dancing girl, or dying gladiator,* the subject should have an interest of its own, and not consist merely of figures with torches or garlands standing alternately on their right and left legs. Of 'ideal' form and the like, I fortunately heard and thought nothing.

114. The point of connoisseurship I had reached, at sixteen, with these advantages and instincts, is curiously measured by the criticism of the Cathedral of Rheims in my Don Juan journal of 1835:

> The carving is not rich,—the Gothic heavy,
> The statues miserable; not a fold
> Of drapery well-disposed in all the bevy
> Of Saints and Bishops and Archbishops old
> That line the porches grey. But in the nave I
> Stared at the windows purple, blue, and gold:
> And the perspective's wonderfully fine
> When you look down the long columnar line.

By the 'carving' I meant the niche work, which is indeed curiously rude at Rheims; by the 'Gothic' the structure and mouldings of arch, which I rightly call 'heavy' as compared with later French types; while the condemnation of the draperies meant that they were not the least like those either of Rubens or Roubilliac. And ten years had to pass over me before I knew better; but every day between the standing in Rheims porch and by Ilaria's tomb had done on me some chiselling to the good; and the discipline from the Fontainebleau time till now had been severe. The accurate study of tree branches, growing leaves, and foreground herbage, had more and more taught me the difference between violent and graceful lines; the beauty of Clotilde and Cécile,* essentially French-Gothic, and the living Egeria of Araceli,* had fixed in my mind and heart, not as an art-ideal, but as a sacred reality, the purest standards of breathing womanhood; and here suddenly, in the sleeping Ilaria, was the perfectness of these, expressed with harmonies of line which I saw in an instant were under the same laws as the river wave, and the aspen branch, and the stars' rising and setting; but treated with a modesty and severity which read the laws of nature by the light of virtue.

115. Another influence, no less forcible, and more instantly effective, was brought to bear on me by my first quiet walk through Lucca.

Hitherto, all architecture, except fairy-finished Milan, had depended with me for its delight on being partly in decay. I revered the sentiment of its age, and I was accustomed to look for the signs of age in the mouldering of its traceries, and in the interstices deepening between the stones of its masonry. This looking for cranny and joint was mixed with the love of rough stones themselves, and of country churches built like Westmoreland cottages.

Here in Lucca I found myself suddenly in the presence of twelfth century buildings, originally set in such balance of masonry that they could all stand without mortar; and in material so incorruptible, that after six hundred years of sunshine and rain, a lancet could not now be put between their joints.

Absolutely for the first time I now saw what mediaeval builders were, and what they meant. I took the simplest of all façades for analysis, that of Santa Maria Foris-Portam, and thereon literally *began* the study of architecture.

In the third—and, for the reader's relief, last—place in these technical records, Fra Bartolomeo's picture of the Magdalene, with St Catherine of Siena,* gave me a faultless example of the treatment of pure Catholic tradition by the perfect schools of painting.

116. And I never needed lessoning more in the principles of the three great arts. After those summer days of 1845, I advanced only in knowledge of individual character, provincial feeling, and details of construction or execution. Of what was primarily right and ultimately best, there was never more doubt to me, and my art-teaching, necessarily, in its many local or personal interests, partial, has been from that time throughout consistent, and progressing every year to more evident completion.

The full happiness of that time to me cannot be explained except to consistently hard workers; and of those, to the few who can keep their peace and health. For the world appeared to me now exactly right. Hills as high as they should be, rivers as wide, pictures as pretty, and masters and men as wise—as pretty and wise could be. And I expected to bring everybody to be of my opinion, as soon as I could get out my second volume; and drove down to Pisa in much hope and pride, though grave in both.

For now I had read enough of Cary's Dante, and Sismondi's 'Italian Republics,' and Lord Lindsay,* to feel what I had to look for in the Campo Santo. Yet at this moment I pause to think what it was that I found.

Briefly, the entire doctrine of Christianity, painted so that a child could understand it. And what a child cannot understand of Christianity, no one need try to.

117. In these days of the religion of this and that,—briefly let us say, the religion of Stocks and Posts—in order to say a clear word of the Campo Santo, one must first say a firm word concerning Christianity itself. I find numbers, even of the most intelligent and amiable people, not knowing what the word means; because they are always asking how much is true, and how much they like, and never ask, first, what *was* the total meaning of it, whether they like it or not.

The total meaning was, and is, that the God who made earth and its creatures, took at a certain time upon the earth, the flesh and form of man; in that flesh sustained the pain and died the death of the creature He had made; rose again after death into glorious human life, and when the date of the human race is ended, will return in visible human form, and render to every man according to his work.* Christianity is the belief in, and love of, God thus manifested. Anything less than this, the mere acceptance of the sayings of Christ, or assertion of any less than divine power in His Being, may be, for aught I know, enough for virtue, peace, and safety; but they do not make people Christians, or enable them to understand the heart of the simplest believer in the old doctrine. One verse more of George Herbert will put the height of that doctrine into less debateable, though figurative, picture than any longer talk of mine:—

> Hast thou not heard that my Lord Jesus died?
>   Then let me tell thee a strange story.
> The God of power, as he did ride
>   In his majestic robes of glory,
>   Resolved to light; and so, one day
>   He did descend, undressing all the way.
>
> The stars his tire of light, and rings, obtained,
>   The cloud his bow, the fire his spear,
> The heavens his azure mantle gained,
>   And when they asked what he would wear,
>   He smiled, and said as he did go,
>   'He had new clothes a-making, here, below.'*

I write from memory;* the lines have been my lesson, ever since 1845, of the noblesse of thought which makes the simplest word best.

118. And the Campo Santo of Pisa is absolutely the same in painting as these lines in word. Straight to its purpose, in the clearest and most eager way; the purpose, highest that can be; the expression, the best possible to the workman according to his knowledge. The several parts of the gospel of the Campo Santo are written by different persons; but all the original frescoes are by men of honest genius. No matter for their names;* the contents of this wall-scripture are these.

First, the Triumph of Death, as Homer, Virgil, and Horace thought of death. Having been within sight of it myself, since Oxford days; and looking back already over a little Campo Santo of my own people, I was ready for that part of the lesson.

Secondly, the story of the Patriarchs, and of their guidance by the ministries of visible angels; that is to say, the ideal of the life of man in its blessedness, *before* the coming of Christ.

Thirdly, the story of Job, in direct converse with God himself, the God of nature, and without any reference to the work of Christ except in its final surety, 'Yet in my flesh I shall see God.'*

Fourthly, the life of St Ranier of Pisa, and of the desert saints, showing the ideal of human life in its blessedness *after* the coming of Christ.

Lastly, the return of Christ in glory, and the Last Judgment.

119. Now this code of teaching is absolutely general for the whole Christian world. There is no papal doctrine, nor antipapal; nor any question of sect or schism whatsoever. Kings, bishops, knights, hermits, are there, because the painters saw them, and painted them, naturally,

as we paint the nineteenth century product of common councilmen and engineers. But they did not conceive that a man must be entirely happy in this world and the next because he wore a mitre or helmet, as we do because he has made a fortune or a tunnel.

Not only was I prepared at this time for the teaching of the Campo Santo, but it was precisely what at that time I needed.

It realized for me the patriarchal life,* showed me what the earlier Bible meant to say; and put into direct and inevitable light the questions I had to deal with, alike in my thoughts and ways, under existing Christian tradition.

Questions clearly not to be all settled in that fortnight. Some, respecting the Last Judgment, such as would have occurred to Professor Huxley,—as for instance, that if Christ came to judgment in St James's Street, the people couldn't see him from Piccadilly,—had been dealt with by me before now; but there is one fact, and no question at all, concerning the Judgment, which was only at this time beginning to dawn on me, that men had been curiously judging *themselves* by always calling the day they expected, 'Dies Irae,' instead of 'Dies Amoris.'*

120. Meantime, my own first business was evidently to read what these Pisans had said of it, and take some record of the sayings; for at that time the old-fashioned ravages were going on, honestly and innocently. Nobody cared for the old plaster, and nobody pretended to. When any dignitary of Pisa was to be buried, they peeled off some Benozzo Gozzoli, or whatever else was in the way, and put up a nice new tablet to the new defunct; but what was left was still all Benozzo, (or repainting of old time, not last year's restoration). I cajoled the Abbé Rosini into letting me put up a scaffold level with the frescoes; set steadily to work with what faculty in outline I had; and being by this time practised in delicate curves, by having drawn trees and grass rightly, got far better results than I had hoped, and had an extremely happy fortnight of it! For as the triumph of Death was no new thought to me, the life of hermits was no temptation; but the stories of Abraham, Job, and St Ranier, well told, were like three new—Scott's novels, I was going to say, and will say, for I don't see my way to anything nearer the fact, and the work on them was pure delight. I got an outline of Abraham's parting with the last of the three angels; of the sacrifice of Job; of the three beggars, and a fiend or two, out of the Triumph of Death; and of the conversion of St Ranier, for which I greatly pitied him.

For he is playing, evidently with happiest skill, on a kind of zithern-harp, held upright as he stands, to the dance of four sweet Pisan maids, in a round, holding each other only by the bent little fingers of each hand. And one with graver face, and wearing a purple robe, approaches him, saying—I knew once what she said, but forget now; only it meant that his joyful life in that kind was to be ended. And he obeys her, and follows, into a nobler life.

I do not know if ever there was a real St Ranier; but the story of him remained for truth in the heart of Pisa as long as Pisa herself lived.

121. I got more than outline of this scene: a coloured sketch of the whole group, which I destroyed afterwards, in shame of its faults, all but the purple-robed warning figure; and that is lost, and the fresco itself now lost also, all mouldering and ruined by what must indeed be a cyclical-change in the Italian climate; the frescoes exposed to it of which I made note before 1850, seem to me to have suffered more in the twenty years since, than they had since they were painted: those at Verona alone excepted, where the art of fresco seems to have been practised in the fifteenth century in absolute perfection, and the colour to have been injured only by violence, not by time.

There was another lovely cloister in Pisa, without fresco, but exquisite in its arched perspective and central garden, and noble in its unbuttressed height of belfry tower;—the cloister of San Francesco: in these, and in the meadow round the baptistery, the routine of my Italian university life was now fixed for a good many years in main material points.

122. In summer I have been always at work, or out walking, by six o'clock, usually awake by half-past four; but I keep to Pisa for the present, where my monkish discipline arranged itself thus. Out, anyhow, by six, quick walk to the field, and as much done as I could, and back to breakfast at half-past eight. Steady bit of Sismondi over bread and butter, then back to Campo Santo, draw till twelve; quick walk to look about me and stretch my legs, in shade if it might be, before lunch, on anything I chanced to see nice in a fruit shop, and a bit of bread. Back to lighter work, or merely looking and thinking, for another hour and a half, and to hotel for dinner at four. Three courses and a flask of Aleatico* (a sweet yet rather astringent, red, rich for Italian, wine—provincial, and with lovely basket-work round the bottle). Then out for saunter with Couttet; he having leave to say anything he had a mind to, but not generally communicative of his feelings; he carried my sketch-book, but in the evening there was too much always to be hunted out, of city; or watched, of hills, or sunset; and I rarely drew,—to my sorrow, now. I wish I knew less, and had drawn more.

Homewards, from wherever we had got to, the moment the sun was down, and the last clouds had lost their colour. I avoided marshy places, if I could, at all times of the day, because I didn't like them; but I feared neither sun nor moon, dawn nor twilight, malaria nor anything else malefic, in the course of work, except only draughts and ugly people. I never would sit in a draught for half a minute, and fled from some sorts of beggars; but a crowd of the common people round me only made me proud, and try to draw as well as I could; mere rags or dirt I did not care an atom for.

123. As early as 1835, and as late as 1841, I had been accustomed, both in France and Italy, to feel that the crowd behind me was interested in my choice of subjects, and pleasantly applausive of the swift progress under my hand of street perspectives, and richness of surface decoration, such as might be symbolized by dextrous zigzags, emphatic dots, or graceful flourishes. I had the better pleasure, now, of feeling that my really watchful delineation, while still rapid enough to interest any stray student of drawing who might stop by me on his way to the Academy, had a quite unusual power of directing the attention of the general crowd to points of beauty, or subjects of sculpture, in the buildings I was at work on, to which they had never before lifted eyes, and which I had the double pride of first discovering for them, and then imitating—not to their dissatisfaction.

And well might I be proud; but how much more ought I to have been pitiful, in feeling the swift and perfect sympathy which the 'common people'—companion-people I should have said, for in Italy there is no common-ness—gave me, in Lucca, or Florence, or Venice, for every touch of true work that I laid in their sight.[1] How much more, I say, should it have been pitiful to me, to recognize their eager intellect, and delicate senses, open to every lesson and every joy of their ancestral art, far more deeply and vividly than in the days when every spring kindled them into battle, and every autumn was red with their blood: yet left now, alike by the laws and lords set over them, less happy in aimless life than of old in sudden death; never one effort made to teach them, to comfort them, to economize their industries, animate their pleasures, or guard their simplest rights from the continually more fatal oppression of unprincipled avarice, and unmerciful wealth.

---

[1] A letter, received from Miss Alexander as I correct this proof, gives a singular instance of this power in the Italian peasant. She says:—'I have just been drawing a magnificent Lombard shepherd, who sits to me in a waistcoat made from the skin of a yellow cow with the hairy side out, a shirt of homespun linen as coarse as sailcloth, a scarlet sash, and trousers woven (I should think) from the wool of the black sheep. He astonishes me all the time by the great amount of good advice which he gives me about my work; and always right! Whenever he looks at my unfinished picture, he can always tell me exactly what it wants.'

124. But all this I have felt and learned, like so much else, too late. The extreme seclusion of my early training left me long careless of sympathy for myself; and that which I gave to others never led me into any hope of being useful to them, till my strength of active life was past. Also, my mind was not yet catholic enough to feel that the Campo Santo belonged to its own people more than to me; and indeed, I had to read its lessons before I could interpret them. The world has for the most part been of opinion that I entered on the task of philanthropy too soon rather than too late: at all events, my conscience remained at rest during all those first times at Pisa, in mere delight in the glory of the past, and in hope for the future of Italy, without need of my becoming one of her demagogues. And the days that began in the cloister of the Campo Santo usually ended by my getting upon the roof of Santa Maria della Spina, and sitting in the sunlight that transfused the warm marble of its pinnacles, till the unabated brightness went down beyond the arches of the Ponte-a-Mare,—the few footsteps and voices of the twilight fell silent in the streets, and the city and her mountains stood mute as a dream, beyond the soft eddying of Arno.

CHAPTER VII

MACUGNAGA

125. WHEN first I saw Florence, in 1840, the great street leading into the Baptistery square from the south had not been rebuilt, but consisted of irregular ancient houses, with far projecting bracketed roofs. I mourned over their loss bitterly in 1845; but for the rest, Florence was still, then, what no one who sees her now could conceive.*

For one great feature, an avenue of magnificent cypress and laurel ascended, unbroken, from the Porta Romana to Bellosguardo, from whose height one could then wander round through lanes of olive, or through small rural vineyards, to San Miniato, which stood deserted, but not ruinous, with a narrow lawn of scented herbage before it, and sweet wild weeds about its steps, all shut in by a hedge of roses. The long ascending causeway between smaller cypresses than those of the Porta Romana, gave every conceivably loveliest view of the Duomo, and Cascine forest, and passing away of Arno towards the sunset.

126. In the city herself, the monasteries were still inhabited, religiously and usefully; and in most of them, as well as among the Franciscans at Fésole, I was soon permitted to go wherever I liked, and

draw whatever I chose. But my time was passed chiefly in the sacristy and choir of Santa Maria Novella, the sacristy of Santa Croce, and the upper passage of San Marco. In the Academia I studied the Angelicos only, Lippi and Botticelli being still far beyond me; but the Ghirlandajos in the choir of Santa Maria Novella, in their broad masses of colour, complied with the laws I had learned in Venice, while yet they swiftly and strictly taught me the fine personalities of the Florentine race and art. At Venice, one only knows a fisherman by his net, and a saint by his nimbus. But at Florence, angel or prophet, knight or hermit, girl or goddess, prince or peasant, cannot but be what they are, masque them how you will.

Nobody ever disturbed me in the Ghirlandajo apse. There were no services behind the high altar; tourists, even the most learned, had never in those days heard Ghirlandajo's name; the sacristan was paid his daily fee regularly whether he looked after me or not. The lovely chapel, with its painted windows and companies of old Florentines, was left for me to do what I liked in, all the forenoon; and I wrote a complete critical and historical account* of the frescoes from top to bottom of it, seated mostly astride on the desks, till I tumbled off backwards one day at the gap where the steps went down, but came to no harm, though the fall was really a more dangerous one than any I ever had in the Alps. The inkbottle was upset over the historical account however, and the closing passages a little shortened,—which saved some useful time.

127. When the chief bustle in the small sacristy, (a mere cupboard or ecclesiastical pantry, two steps up out of the transept) was over, with the chapel masses of the morning, I used to be let in there to draw the Angelico Annunciation,—about eleven inches by fourteen as far as I recollect, then one of the chief gems of Florence, seen in the little shrine it was painted for, now carried away by republican pillage, and lost in the general lumber of the great pillage-reservoir galleries. The monks let me sit close to it and work, as long as I liked, and went on with their cup-rinsings and cope-foldings without minding me. If any priest of the higher dignities came in, I was careful always to rise reverently, and get his kind look, or bow, or perhaps a stray crumb of benediction. When I was tired of drawing, I went into the Spezieria, and learned what ineffable sweetnesses and incenses were in the herbs and leaves that had gathered the sunbeams of Florence into their life; and bought little bundles of bottles, an inch long, and as thick as a moderately sized quill, with Araby the blest* and a spice island or two inside each. Then in the afternoon a bit of street or gallery work, and

after dinner, always up either to Fésole or San Miniato. In those days, I think it never rained but when one wanted it to, (and not always then); wherever you chanced to be, if you got tired, and had no friends to be bothered with, you lay down on the next bank and went to sleep, to the song of the cicadas, which, with a great deal of making believe, might at last, somehow, be thought nice.

128. I did make one friend in Florence, however, for love of Switzerland, Rudolph Durheim, a Bernese student, of solid bearish gifts and kindly strength. I took to him at first because of a clearly true drawing he had made of his little blue-eyed twelve-years-old simplicity of a goat-herd sister; but found him afterwards a most helpful and didactic friend. He objected especially to my losing time in sentiment or over-hot vaporization, and would have had me draw something every afternoon, whether it suited my fancy or not. 'Ça vaut déjà la peine,'* said he, stopping on the way to the Certosa, under a group of hill-side cottages; it was my first serious lesson in Italian backgrounds; and if we had worked on together, so and so might have happened, as so often afore-said. But we separated, to our sorrow then, and harm, afterwards. I went off into higher and vainer vaporization at Venice; he went back to Berne, and under the patronage of its aristocracy, made his black bread by dull portrait-painting to the end of a lost life. I saw the arid remnant of him in his Bernese painting, or daubing, room, many a year afterwards, and reproached the heartless Alps, for his sake.

129. Of other companionship in Florence, except Couttet's, I had none. I had good letters to Mr Millingen, and of course a formal one to the British Embassy. I called on Mr Millingen dutifully, but found he knew nothing after the fourth century B.C., and had as little taste for the Liber Studiorum as the Abbé Rosini. I waited on the Ambassador,* and got him to use British influence enough to let me into the convent of the Magdalen, wherein I have always since greatly praised Perugino's fresco, with a pleasant feeling that nobody else could see it. I never went near the Embassy afterwards, nor the Embassy near me, till I sent my P. P. C. card* by George, when I was going away, before ten in the morning, which caused Lord ——s porter to swear fearfully at George and his master both. And it was the last time I ever had anything to do with Embassies, except through the mediation of pitying friends.

There was yet another young draughtsman in Florence, who lessoned me to purpose—a French youth;—his family name Dieudonné; I knew him by no other. He had trained himself to copy Angelico, in pencil tint, wrought with the point, as pure as the down on a butterfly's wing, and with perfect expression: typical engraving in grey, of inconceivable delicacy. I have never seen anything the least approaching it since, but did not then enough know its value. Dieudonné's prices were necessarily beyond those of the water-colour copyists, and he would not always work, even when the price was ready for him. He went back to France, and was effaced in the politeness of Paris, as Rudolph in the rudeness of Berne. Hard homes alike, their native cities, to them both.

130. My own work in Florence, this time, was chiefly thinking and writing—progressive, but much puzzled, and its Epicurean pieties a little too dependent on enamel and gilding. A study in the rose-garden of San Miniato, and in the cypress avenue of the Porta Romana, remain to me, for memorials of perhaps the best days of early life.

Couttet, however, was ill at ease and out of temper in Florence, little tolerant of Italian manners and customs; and not satisfied that my studies in sacristies and cloisters were wise, or vials of myrrh and myrtle essence as good for me as the breeze over Alpine rose. He solaced himself by making a careful collection of all the Florentine wild-flowers for me exquisitely pressed and dried,—now, to my sorrow, lost or burned with all other herbaria; they fretted me by bulging always in the middle, and crumbling like parcels of tea, over my sketches.

At last the Arno dried up; or, at least, was reduced to the size of the Effra at Dulwich, with muddy shingle to the shore; and the grey 'pietra serena'* of Fésole was like hot iron in the sun, sprinkled with sand. Also, I had pretty well tired myself out, and, for the present, spent all my pictorial language;—so that we all of us were pleased to trot over the Apennines, and see the gleam of Monte Rosa again from Piacenza and Pavia. Once it was in sight, I went straight for it, and remember nothing more till we were well afoot in the Val Anzasca.

131. The afternoon rambles to Fésole and Bellosguardo, besides having often to stand for hours together writing notes in church or gallery, had kept me in fair training; and I did the twenty miles up hill from Vogogna to Macugnaga without much trouble, but in ever hotter indignation all the way at the extreme dulness of the Val Anzasca, 'the most beautiful valley in the Alps'*—according to modern guide books. But tourists who pass their time mostly in looking at black rocks through blue spectacles, cannot be expected to know much about a valley:— on the other hand, ever since the days of Glenfarg and Matlock, I have been a stream-tracker and cliff-hunter, and rank mountains more by the beauty of their glens than the height of their summits: also, it chanced that our three first journeys abroad had shown me the unquestionably grandest defiles of the Alps in succession—first the Via Mala,

then the St Gothard, then the tremendous granites of the Grimsel; then Rosenlaui and Lauterbrunnen, Val d'Aosta and Cormayeur; then the valley of the Inn and precipices of Innsbruck—and at last the Ortlerspitze and descent from the Stelvio to Como; with the Simplon and defile of Cluse now as well known as Gipsy Hill at Norwood: and the Val Anzasca has no feature whatever in any kind to be matched with any one of these. It is merely a deep furrow through continuous masses of shaly rock, blistered by the sun and rough with juniper, with scattered chestnut-trees and pastures below. There are no precipices, no defiles, no distinct summits on either flank; while the Monte Rosa, occasionally seen at the extremity of the valley, is a mere white heap, with no more form in it than a haycock after a thunder-shower.

132. Nor was my mind relieved by arrival at Macugnaga itself; I did not then, nor do I yet, understand why the village should have a name at all, more than any other group of half-a-dozen chalets in a sheltered dip of moorlands. There was a little inn, of which the upper floor was just enough for the landlord, Couttet, George and me;—once, during a month's stay, I remember seeing two British persons with knapsacks at the bottom of the stairs, who must also have slept in the house, I suppose. My own room was about seven feet wide by ten long; one window, two-feet-six square, at the side, looked straight into the green bank at the bottom of the Monte Moro, and another at the end, looked into vacant sky down the valley. A clear dashing stream, not ice fed, but mere fountain and rainfall, from the Moro, ran past the house just under the side window, and was the chief cause of my stay, and consolation of it. The group of chalets round had no inhabitants, that ever I saw:—the little chapel had a belfry, but I never remember hearing its bell, or seeing anybody go in or come out of it. I don't think even the goats had bells, so quiet the place was. The Monte Rosa glacier, a mile higher up, merely choked the valley; it seemed to come from nowhere and to be going nowhere; it had no pinnacles, no waves, no crevasses with action or method of fracture in them; no icefalls at the top, nor arched source of stream at the bottom; the sweep of rock above showed neither bedding nor buttressing of the least interest, and gave no impression of having any particular top, while yet the whole circuit of it was, to such poor climbing powers as mine, totally inaccessible, and even unapproachable, but with more trouble than it was worth.

133. Thus much I made out the first day after arriving, but thought there must be something to see somewhere, if I looked properly about; also, I had made solemn vows and complex postal arrangements for

a month under Monte Rosa, and I stayed my month accordingly, with variously humiliating and disagreeably surprising results.

The first, namely, that mountain air at this height, 4,000 ft. for sleeping level, varying to 6,000 or 7,000 ft. in the day's walks, was really not good for me, but quickened pulse and sickened stomach, and saddened one's notions alike of clouds, stones, and pastoral life.

The second, that my Florentine studies had not taught me how to draw clouds or stones any better; that the stream under my window was no more imitable than the Rhone itself, and that any single boulder in it would take all the month, or it might be six weeks, to paint the least to my mind.

The third, that Alpine geology was in these high centres of it as yet wholly inscrutable to me.

The fourth, that I was not, as I used to suppose, born for solitude, like Dr Zimmermann,* and that the whole south side of Monte Rosa did not contain as much real and comfortable entertainment for me as the Market Street of Croydon. Nor do I believe I could have stayed out my month at Macugnaga with any consistency, but that I had brought with me a pocket volume of Shakespeare, and set myself for the first time to read, seriously, Coriolanus, and Julius Caesar.

134. I see that in the earlier passages of this too dimly explicit narrative, no notice is taken of the uses of Shakespeare at Herne Hill, other than that he used to lie upon the table; nor can I the least trace his influence on my own mind or work, except as a part of the great reality and infinity of the world itself, and its gradually unfolding history and law. To my father, and to Richard Gray, the characters of Shakespearian comedy were all familiar personal friends; my mother's refusal to expose herself to theatric temptation began in her having fallen in love, for some weeks, when she was a girl, with Henry the Fifth at the Battle of Agincourt; nor can I remember in my own childhood any time when the plots of the great plays were unknown to me, or—I write the word now with more than surprise—misunderstood! I thought and felt about all of them then, just as I think and feel now; no character, small or great, has taken a new aspect to me; and the attentive reading which began first at Macugnaga meant only the discovery of a more perfect truth, or a deeper passion, in the words that had before rung in my ears with too little questioned melody. As for the full contents of any passage, or any scene, I never expected, nor expect, to know them, any more than every rock of Skiddaw, or flower of Jura.

135. But by the light of the little window at Macugnaga, and by the murmur of the stream beneath it, began the course of study which led

me into fruitful thought, out of the till then passive sensation of merely
artistic or naturalist life; and which have made of me—or at least I fain
would believe the friends who tell me so—a useful teacher, instead of
a vain labourer.

From that time forward, nearly all serious reading was done while
I was abroad; the heaviest box in the boot being always full of dictionar-
ies; and my Denmark Hill life resolved itself into the drudgery of
authorship and press correction, with infinite waste of time in saying the
same things over and over to the people who came to see our Turners.

In calling my authorship, drudgery, I do not mean that writing ever
gave me the kind of pain of which Carlyle so wildly complains,*—to
my total amazement and boundless puzzlement, be it in passing said;
for he talked just as vigorously as he wrote, and the book he makes bit-
terest moan over, Friedrich, bears the outer aspect of richly enjoyed
gossip, and lovingly involuntary eloquence of description or praise. My
own literary work, on the contrary, was always done as quietly and
methodically as a piece of tapestry. I knew exactly what I had got to say,
put the words firmly in their places like so many stitches, hemmed the
edges of chapters round with what seemed to me graceful flourishes,
touched them finally with my cunningest points of colour, and read
the work to papa and mamma at breakfast next morning, as a girl shows
her sampler.

136. 'Drudgery' may be a hard word for this often complacent, and
entirely painless occupation; still, the best that could be said for it, was
that it gave me no serious trouble; and I should think the pleasure of
driving, to a good coachman, of ploughing, to a good farmer, much
more of dressmaking, to an inventive and benevolent modiste, must
be greatly more piquant than the most proudly ardent hours of book-
writing have ever been to me, or as far as my memory ranges, to any
conscientious author of merely average power. How great work is done,
under what burden of sorrow, or with what expense of life, has not
been told hitherto, nor is likely to be; the best of late time has been
done recklessly or contemptuously. Byron would burn a canto if a
friend disliked it, and Scott spoil a story to please a bookseller.

As I have come on the extremely minor question of my own work,[1]
I may once for all complete all necessary account of it by confession
of my evermore childish delight in beginning a drawing; and usually
acute misery in trying to finish one. People sometimes praise me as

---

[1] *Manner* of work, I mean. How I learned the things I taught is the major, and properly, only question regarded in this history.

industrious, when they count the number of printed volumes which Mr Allen can now advertise. But the biography of the waste pencilling and passionately forsaken colouring, heaped in the dusty corners of Brantwood, if I could write it, would be far more pathetically exemplary or admonitory.

137. And as I transpose myself back through the forty years of desultory, yet careful, reading, which began in my mossy cell* of Macugnaga, it becomes a yet more pertinent question to me how much life has been also wasted in that manner, and what was not wasted, extremely weakened and saddened. Very certainly, Coriolanus and Julius Caesar did not in the least cheer or strengthen my heart in its Monte-Rosean solitude; and as I try to follow the clue of Shakespearian power over me since, I cannot feel that it has been anywise wholesome for me to have the world represented as a place where, for that best sort of people, everything always goes wrong; or to have my conceptions of that best sort of people so much confused by images of the worst. To have kinghood represented, in the Shakespearian cycle, by Richards II and III instead of I, by Henrys IV and VIII instead of II; by King John, finished into all truths of baseness and grief, while Henry V is only a king of fairy tale; or in the realm of imagination, by the folly of Lear, the cruelty of Leontes, the furious and foul guilt of Macbeth and the Dane. Why must the persons of Iago and Iachimo, of Tybalt and Edmund, of Isabel's brother and Helena's lord,* pollute, or wither with their shadows, every happy scene in the loveliest plays; and they, the loveliest, be all mixed and encumbered with languid and common work,—to one's best hope spurious, certainly, so far as original, idle and disgraceful?—and all so inextricably and mysteriously that the writer himself is not only unknowable, but inconceivable; and his wisdom so useless, that at this time of being and speaking, among active and purposeful Englishmen, I know not one who shows a trace of ever having felt a passion of Shakespeare's, or learnt a lesson from him.

Any way, for good or sorrow, my student's life, instead of mere instinct of rhythmic mimicry, began thus, not till I was six-and-twenty. It is so inconvenient to be always a year behind the Christian date, (and I am really so young of my age!) that I am going to suppose the reader's permission to be only a quarter of a century old at Macugnaga, and to count my years henceforward by the stars instead of the clock.

138. The month of Rome and Monte Rosa was at least, compared with the days at Florence, a time of rest; and when I got down to Domo d'Ossola again, I was fresh for the expedition in search of Turner's subject at Dazio Grande.

With Couttet and George, and a baggage mule, I walked up the Val Formazza, and across to Airolo; Couttet on this walk first formulating the general principle, 'Pour que George aille bien, il faut lui donner à manger souvent; et beaucoup à la fois.'* I had no objection whatever to this arrangement, and was only sorry my Chamouni tutor could not give the same good report of *me*. But on anything like a hard day's walk, the miles after lunch always seemed to me to become German instead of geographical. And although I much enjoyed the Val Formazza all the way up, Airolo next day was found to be farther off than it appeared on the map, and on the third morning I ordered a post-chaise, and gave up my long-cherished idea of making the pedestrian tour of Europe.

139. The work done at Faido and Dazio Grande is told and illustrated in the fourth volume of 'Modern Painters;' it was a little shortened by a letter from J. D. Harding, asking if I would like him to join me at any place I might have chosen for autumn sketching. Very gratefully, I sent word that I would wait for him at Baveno; where, accordingly, towards the close of August, we made fraternal arrangements for an Elysian fortnight's floating round Isola Bella. There was a spacious half of seat vacant in my little hooded carriage, and good room for Harding's folios with mine: so we trotted from Baveno to Arona, and from Arona to Como, and from Como to Bergamo, and Bergamo to Brescia, and Brescia to Verona, and took up our abode in the 'Two Towers' for as long as we chose.

I do not remember finding in any artistic biography the history of a happier epoch than it was to us both. I am bold to speak for Harding as for myself. Generally, the restlessness of ambition, or the strain of effort, or anxiety about money matters, taint or disturb the peace of a painter's travels: but Harding did not wish, or perhaps think it possible, to do better than, to his own mind, he always did; while I had no hope of becoming a second Turner, and no thoughts of becoming a thirtieth Academician. Harding was sure of regular sale for his summer's work, and under no difficulty in dividing the hotel bills with me: we both enjoyed the same scenes, though in different ways, which gave us subjects of surprising but not antagonistic talk: the weather was perfect, the roads smooth, and the inns luxurious.

140. I must not yet say more of Verona, than that, though truly Rouen, Geneva, and Pisa have been the centres of thought and teaching to me, Verona has given the colouring to all they taught. She has virtually represented the fate and the beauty of Italy to me; and whatever concerning Italy I have felt, or been able with any charm or force to

say, has been dealt with more deeply, and said more earnestly, for her sake.

It was only for Harding's sake that I went on to Venice that year; and, for the first week there, neither of us thought of anything but the market and fishing boats, and effects of light on the city and the sea; till, in the spare hour of one sunny but luckless day, the fancy took us to look into the Scuola di San Rocco. Hitherto, in hesitating conjectures of what might have been, I have scarcely ventured to wish, gravely, that it *had* been. But, very earnestly, I should have bid myself that day keep *out* of the School of St Roch, had I known what was to come of my knocking at its door. But for that porter's opening, I should (so far as one can ever know what they should) have written, The Stones of Chamouni, instead of The Stones of Venice; and the Laws of Fésole,* in the full code of them, before beginning to teach in Oxford: and I should have brought out in full distinctness and use what faculty I had of drawing the human face and form with true expression of their higher beauty.

But Tintoret swept me away at once into the 'mare maggiore'* of the schools of painting which crowned the power and perished in the fall of Venice; so forcing me into the study of the history of Venice herself; and through that into what else I have traced or told of the laws of national strength and virtue. I am happy in having done this so that the truth of it must stand; but it was not my own proper work; and even the sea-born strength of Venetian painting was beyond my granted fields of fruitful exertion. Its continuity and felicity became thenceforward impossible, and the measure of my immediate success irrevocably shortened.

141. Strangely, at the same moment, another adversity first made itself felt to me,—of which the fatality has been great to many and many besides myself.

It must have been during my last days at Oxford that Mr Liddell, the present Dean of Christ Church, told me of the original experiments of Daguerre.* My Parisian friends obtained for me the best examples of his results; and the plates sent to me in Oxford were certainly the first examples of the sun's drawing that were ever seen in Oxford, and, I believe, the first sent to England.

Wholly careless at that time of finished detail, I saw nothing in the Daguerreotype to help, or alarm me; and inquired no more concerning it, until now at Venice I found a French artist producing exquisitely bright small plates, (about four inches square,) which contained, under a lens, the Grand Canal or St Mark's Place as if a magician had reduced the reality to be carried away into an enchanted land. The little gems of picture cost a napoleon each; but with two hundred francs I bought the Grand Canal from the Salute to the Rialto; and packed it away in thoughtless triumph.

142. I had no time then to think of the new power, or its meanings; my days were over-weighted already. Every morning, at six by the Piazza clock, we were moored, Harding and I, among the boats in the fruit-market; then, after eight o'clock breakfast, he went on his own quest of full subjects, and I to the Scuola di San Rocco, or wherever else in Venice there were Tintorets. In the afternoon, we lashed our gondola to the stern of a fishing-boat, sailing, as the wind served, within or outside the Lido, and sketching the boat and her sails in their varied action,—or Venice, as she shone far away beyond her islands. Back to Danieli's for six o'clock table d'hote; where, after we had got a bit of fish and fillet of anything, the September days were yet long enough for a sunset walk.

143. A much regarded friend, Mr Boxall, RA, came on to Venice at this time, after finishing at Milan the beautiful drawing from Leonardo's Christ, which was afterwards tenderly, though inadequately, engraved.* Mrs Jameson was staying also at Danieli's to complete her notes on Venetian legends: and in the evening walk we were usually together, the four of us; Boxall, Harding, and I extremely embarrassing Mrs Jameson by looking at everything from our pertinaciously separate corners of an equilateral triangle. Mrs Jameson was absolutely without knowledge or instinct of painting; and had no sharpness of insight for anything else; but she was candid and industrious, with a pleasant disposition to make the best of all she saw, and to say, compliantly, that a picture was good, if anybody had ever said so before. Her peace of mind was restored in a little while, by observing that the three of us, however separate in our reasons for liking a picture, always fastened on the same pictures to like; and that she was safe, therefore, in saying that, for whatever other reason might be assigned, other people should like them also.

I got some most refined and right teaching from Mr Boxall; of which I remember as chiefly vital, his swift correction of my misgiven Wordsworth's line—

'So be it when I shall grow old,'*

as—

'So shall it be when I grow old.'

I read Wordsworth with better care and profit ever afterwards; but there was this much of reason for that particular mistake, that I was perfectly confident in my own heart's love of rainbows to the end, and felt no occasion to wish for what I was so sure would be.

144. But Mr Boxall's time, and Harding's, were at end before I had counted and described all the Tintorets in Venice, and they left me at that task, besides trying to copy the Adoration of the Magi* on four sheets of brown paper. Things had gone fairly well as long as Harding took me out to sea every afternoon; but now, left to myself, trying to paint the Madonna and Magi in the morning, and peering all the rest of the day into the shadowy corners of chapel and sacristy and palace-corridor, beside every narrow street that was paved with waves, my strength began to fail fast. Couttet got anxious, and looked more gravely every morning into my eyes. 'Ç'a ne va pas bien,' said he. 'Vous ne le sentirez pas à présent, mais vous le sentirez après.'* I finished my list, however, pasted my brown paper into some rude likeness of the picture,—and packed up colours and note-books finally for a rapid run home; when, as so often happens in the first cessation of an overstrain, the day after leaving Venice I was stopped at Padua by a sharp fit of nervous fever.

145. I call it 'nervous,' not knowing what else to call it,—for there was no malarian taint or other malignity in it, but only quick pulse, and depressed spirit, and the nameless ailing of overwearied flesh. Couttet put me to bed instantly, and went out to buy some herb medicines,—which Paduan physicians are wise enough yet to keep,—and made me some tisane,* and bade me be patient, and all would be well. And, indeed next day I was up, in armchair; but not allowed to stir out of the extremely small back room of the old inn, which commanded view only of a few deep furrowed tiles and a little sky. I sent out George to see if he could find some scrap of picture to hang on the blank wall; and he brought me a seven-inch-square bit of fifteenth century tempera, a nameless saint with a scarlet cloak and an embossed nimbus, who much comforted me.

I was able to travel in a day or two; but the mental depression, with some weakness of limb, remained, all across Lombardy, as far as Vogogna, where a frosty morning glittered on the distant Simplon; and though I could not walk up the pass of Gondo, there was no more sadness in me, afterwards, than I suffered always in leaving either Italy or the Alps.

146. Which, however, in its own kind, became acute again a day or two afterwards, when I stopped on a cloudless afternoon at Nyon, where the road branches away for Paris. I had to say good-bye to Mont

Blanc—there visible in his full cone, through the last gap given by the Chablais mountains as they rise eastward along the lake-shore.

Six months before, I had rhymed to his snows in such hope and delight, and assurance of doing everything I wanted, this year at last; and now, I had only discovered wants that any number of years could not satisfy; and weaknesses, which no ardour of effort or patience of practice could overcome.

Thus, for the first time, measuring some of the outer bastions of the unconquerable world, I opened my English letters; which told me that my eldest Croydon cousin, John, in whose prosperity and upward rounding of fortune's wheel all of us had been confident, was dead in Australia.*

So much stronger than I, and so much more dutiful, working for his people in the little valley of Wandel, out in the great opposite desolate country; and now the dust of it laid on him, as on his brother the beach-sand on this side the sea.* There was no grief, for me, in his loss, so little had I known, and less remembered, him; but much awe, and wonder, when all the best and kindest of us were thus struck down, what my own selfish life was to come to, or end in.

147. With these thoughts and fears fastening on me, as I lost sight first of Mont Blanc, and then of the lines of Jura, and saw the level road with its aisle of poplars in perspective vista of the five days between Dijon and Calais, the fever returned slightly, with a curious tingling, and yet partly, it seemed to me, deadness of sensation, in the throat, which would not move, for better nor worse, through the long days, and mostly wakeful nights. I do not know if diphtheria had been, in those epochs, known or talked of; but I extremely disliked this feeling in the throat, and passed from dislike into sorrowful alarm, (having no Couttet now to give me tisane,) and wonder if I should ever get home to Denmark Hill again.

Although the poetical states of religious feeling taught me by George Herbert's rhymes, and the reading of formal petition, whether in psalter or litany, at morning and evening and on Sunday forenoon, were sincere enough in their fanciful or formal ways, no occasion of life had yet put me to any serious trial of direct prayer. I never knew of Jessie's or my aunt's sicknesses,* or now of my cousin John's, until too late for prayer; in our own household there had been no instantly dangerous illness since my own in 1835; and during the long threatening of 1841 I was throughout more sullen and rebellious than frightened. But now, between the Campo Santo and Santa Maria Novella, I had been brought into some knowledge of the relations that might truly exist between God and His creatures; and thinking what my father and mother would feel if I did not get home to them through those poplar avenues, I fell gradually into the temper, and more or less tacit offering, of very real prayer.

Which lasted patiently through two long days, and what I knew of the nights, on the road home. On the third day, as I was about coming in sight of Paris, what people who are in the habit of praying know as the consciousness of answer, came to me; and a certainty that the illness, which had all this while increased, if anything, would be taken away.

Certainty in mind, which remained unshaken, through unabated discomfort of body, for another night and day, and then the evil symptoms vanished in an hour or two, on the road beyond Paris; and I found myself in the inn at Beauvais entirely well, with a thrill of conscious happiness altogether new to me.

148. Which, if I had been able to keep!—— Another 'had been' this, the gravest of all I lost; the last with which I shall trouble the reader.

That happy sense of direct relation with Heaven is known evidently to multitudes of human souls of all faiths, and in all lands; evidently often a dream,—demonstrably, as I conceive, often a reality; in all cases, dependent on resolution, patience, self-denial, prudence, obedience; of which some pure hearts are capable without effort, and some by constancy. Whether I was capable of holding it or not, I cannot tell; but little by little, and for little, yet it seemed invincible, causes, it passed away from me. I had scarcely reached home in safety before I had sunk back into the faintness and darkness of the Under-World.

CHAPTER VIII

THE STATE OF DENMARK*

149. THE house on Denmark Hill, where my father and mother, in the shortening days of 1845, thankfully received back their truant, has been associated, by dated notepaper, with a quarter of a century of my English life; and was indeed to my parents a peaceful, yet cheerful, and pleasantly, in its suburban manner, dignified, abode of their declining years. For my father had no possibilities of real retirement in him; his business was the necessary pride and fixed habit of his soul: his ambition, and what instinct of accumulative gain the mercantile life

inevitably begets, were for me only; but involved the fixed desire to see me moving in the western light of London, among its acknowledged literary orders of merit; and were totally inconsistent with the thought, faintly and intermittingly haunting my mother and me, that a rose-covered cottage in the dells of Matlock or the vale of Keswick, might be nearer the heavenly world, for *us*, than all the majesty of Denmark Hill, connected though it was, by the Vauxhall Road and convenient omnibuses, with St James's Street and Cavendish Square.

But the house itself had every good in it, except nearness to a stream, that could with any reason be coveted by modest mortals. It stood in command of seven acres of healthy ground (a patch of local gravel there overlying the London clay); half of it in meadow sloping to the sunrise, the rest prudently and pleasantly divided into an upper and lower kitchen garden; a fruitful bit of orchard, and chance inlets and outlets of woodwalk, opening to the sunny path by the field, which was gladdened on its other side in springtime by flushes of almond and double peach blossom. Scarce all the hyacinths and heath of Brantwood redeem the loss of these to me, and when the summer winds have wrecked the wreaths of our wild roses, I am apt to think sorrowfully of the trailings and climbings of deep purple convolvulus which bloomed full every autumn morning round the trunks of the apple trees in the kitchen garden.

150. The house itself had no specialty, either of comfort or inconvenience, to endear it; the breakfast-room, opening on the lawn and farther field, was extremely pretty when its walls were mostly covered with lakes by Turner[1] and doves by Hunt;* the dining and drawing-rooms were spacious enough for our grandest receptions,—never more than twelve at dinner, with perhaps Henry Watson and his sisters in the evening,—and had decoration enough in our Northcote portraits,* Turner's Slave-ship, and, in later years, his Rialto, with our John Lewis, two Copley Fieldings, and every now and then a new Turner drawing. My own work-room, above the breakfast-room, was only distinct, as being such, in its large oblong table, occupying so much of the—say fifteen by five and twenty—feet of available space within book-cases, that the rest of the floor virtually was only a passage round it. I always wrote on the flat of the table,—a bad habit, enforced partly by

---

[1] Namely, Derwentwater; Lake Lucerne, with the Righi, at sunset; the Bay of Uri, with the Rothstock, from above Brunnen; Lucerne itself, seen from the lake; the upper reach of the lake, seen from Lucerne; and the opening of the Lake of Constance, from Constance. Goldau, St Gothard, Schaffhausen, Coblentz, and Llanthony, raised the total of matchless Turner drawings in this room to eleven.

the frequent need of laying drawings or books for reference beside me. Two windows, forming the sides of a bow blank in the middle, gave me, though rather awkwardly crossed, all the light I needed: partly through laziness and make-shiftiness, partly in respect for external symmetry,—for the house had really something of an architectural air at the back,—I never opened the midmost blank wall, though it considerably fretted me: the single window of my bed-room above, looking straight south-east, gave, through the first ten or twelve winters at Denmark Hill, command of the morning clouds, inestimable for its aid in all healthy thought. Papa and mamma took possession of the quiet western rooms, which looked merely into the branches of the cedar on the front lawn.

151. In such stateliness of civic domicile, the industry of midlife now began for me, little disturbed by the murmur of London beyond the bridges, and in no wise by any enlargement of neighbourly circle on the Hill itself; one family alone excepted,* whose affection has not failed me from then till now,—having begun in earlier times, out of which I must yet gather a gleam or two of the tremulous memory.

In speaking of Mr Dale's school, I named only my younger companions there; of whom Willoughby had gone to Cambridge, and was by this time beyond my ken; but Edward Matson sometimes came yet to dine with us at Denmark Hill, and sometimes carried me down to Woolwich, to spend a day amidst its military displays and arts, with his father, and mother, and two sweet younger sisters. Where I saw, in Major Matson, such calm type of truth, gentleness, and simplicity, as I have myself found in soldiers or sailors only; and so admirable to me that I have never been able, since those Woolwich times, to gather myself up against the national guilt of war, seeing that such men were made by the discipline of it.

But at Mr Dale's were also two senior pupils, little known to me except, Henry Dart by his large hazel eyes, and Edmund Oldfield by his already almost middle-aged aspect of serene sagacity. When I went to Oxford, I found Dart at Exeter College, where we established poetical friendship, and contended in all honour for the Newdigate, reading our best passages to each other, for improving censure. Dart, very deservedly, won it that year, and gave promise of generous distinction afterwards; but the hazel eyes were too bright, and closed, in a year or two, to this world's ambition.

152. I do not know how it chanced that the art impulse which animated Edmund Oldfield's grave sagacity did not manifest itself to me till much later. He was the elder brother of a large group of clever

lads and lasses, amiable in the extreme, yet in a slightly severe and evangelical manner; whose father was in some tangible relation to mine as one of the leading men of business on the Hill; their mother known to us by sight only, as a refined and still beautiful woman,—evangelical *without* severity; both of them occupying, with such of their children as were that way minded, the pew before us in Mr Burnet's chapel, whereat sometimes in my younger days we went to hear a gloomier divinity than that of my beloved and Anacreontic Doctor Andrews.

153. We might never have known more of them, unless, among the sacred enthusiasms of Camberwell parish, the fancy had arisen to put a painted window into the east end of the pretty church,* just built for it by Mr Gilbert Scott. Edmund Oldfield, already advanced far beyond me in Gothic art scholarship, was prime mover in the matter, but such rumour as existed in the village of my interest in architecture justified him in expecting some help from me. I had already quite fixed notions of what the colour of glass should be, and in these Edmund concurred. The tracery of the east window seemed to us convertible into no dishonouring likeness of something at Rheims or Chartres. Hitherto unconscious of my inability to compose in colour, I offered to design the entire window head; and did, after some headstrong toil, actually fill the required spaces with a mosaic presenting an orthodox cycle of subjects in purple and scarlet, round a more luminous centre of figures adapted from Michael Angelo. Partly in politeness, partly in curiosity, the committee on the window did verily authorize Edmund Oldfield and me to execute this design; and I having fortunately the sense to admit Edmund's representations that the style of Michael Angelo was not exactly adapted to thirteenth century practice, in construction of a vitrail,* the central light was arranged by him on more modest lines; and the result proved on the whole satisfactory to the congregation, who thereupon desired that the five vertical lights might be filled in the same manner. I had felt, however, through the changes made on my Michael Angelesque cinquefoil,* that Mr Oldfield's knowledge of Gothic style, and gift in placing colour, were altogether beyond mine; and prayed him to carry out the rest of the window by himself. Which he did with perfect success, attaining a delicate brilliancy purer than anything I had before seen in modern glass.

154. I should have been more crushed by this result, had I not been already in the habit of feeling worsted in everything I tried of original work; while since 1842, I was more and more sure of my faculty of seeing the beauty and meaning of the work of other minds. At this time, I might assuredly have been led by Edmund Oldfield into a study of all

the painted glass in England, if only Edmund had been a little more happy in his own power: but I suppose his immediate success was too easy to divert him from the courses of study which afterwards gave him his high position in the British Museum, not enough recognized by the public, and, I believe, farther obscured by the ill humour or temper of Mr Panizzi. If only—I may still sometimes indulge in a 'might have been,' for my friends—he had kept to Gothic foils and their glass, my belief is that Edmund Oldfield could have done for England great part of what Viollet le Duc* did for France, with the same earnestness, and with thrice the sensibility. But the sensibility taking in him the form of reserve, and the restless French energy being absent, he diffused himself in serene scholarship till too late, and retired from the collisions and intrigues of the Museum too early.

Our temporary alliance among the traceries of Camberwell had for immediate consequence to me, an introduction to his family, which broke the monastic laws of Denmark Hill to the extent of tempting me to a Christmas revel or two with his pretty sisters; whereat I failed in my part in every game, and whence I retired in a sackcloth of humiliation, of which the tissue had at once the weight of a wet blanket, and the sting of horsehair.

155. I have only once named, among my Christ Church companions, Charles Newton. He was considerably my senior, besides being a rightly bred scholar, who knew his grammar and his quantities;* and, while yet an undergraduate, was doing accurately useful work in the Architectural Society. Without rudely depreciating my Proutesque manner of drawing, he represented to me that it did not meet all the antiquarian purposes of that body; and, always under protest, I drew a Norman door for Newton, (as the granite veins of Trewavas Head for Dr Buckland,) with distinct endeavour to give the substantial facts in each, apparent to the vulgar mind. And if only—once more pardon, good reader, but this is really an 'if' that I cannot resist—if only Newton had learnt Irish instead of Greek, Scotch instead of Egyptian, and preferred, for light reading, the study of the Venerable Bede to that of Victor Hugo,——well, the British Museum might have been still habitable; the effigy, as the bones, of Mausolus would have rested in peace;* and the British public known more than any Idylls of kings* have yet told them, of personages such as Arthur, Alfred, and Charlemagne.

156. There remained yet some possibilities, even after Charles Newton became Attic and diplomatic, of some heroic attachment between us, in the manner of Theseus and Pirithous.* In fact, for some

years after my Camberwell window and Campo Santo entanglements, Theseus retained, I believe, some hope of delivering me from those Lethean chains;* nor until so late as the year 1850,* when, as we crossed the Great St Bernard together, Charles spoke heresies against the Valley of Chamouni, remarking, with respect to its glacial moraines, that 'he thought more housemaids were wanted in that establishment,' and on the other hand, I expressed myself respecting the virtues of diplomatists, and the value of the opinions of the British Peerage on Art and Science, in a manner which caused Newton to observe (not without foundation) that 'there was the making of Robespierre in me,'—not till then, I repeat, did it become clear to either of us that the decisions of Minos were irrevocable.

We yet examined the castle of Verrex together, as once the aisles of Dorchester; and compared in peace, at Milan, the Corinthian graces of St Lorenzo with the Lombardic monsters of St Ambrogio. Early the next morning Newton left me, in the Albergo Reale, not without inner tears on both sides, and went eastward I know not where. Ever since, we have been to each other, he as the Heathen, and I as the Publican, both of us finding it alike impossible to hear the Church.

157. The transition to Denmark Hill had, however, in the first pride of it, an advantage also in giving our family Puritanism, promotion to a distinguished pew in Camden Chapel, quite near the pulpit. Henry Melvill, afterwards Principal of Haileybury, was the only preacher I ever knew whose sermons were at once sincere, orthodox, and oratorical on Ciceronian principles. He wrote them from end to end with polished art, and read them admirably, in his own manner; by which, though the congregation affectionately expected it, they were always deeply impressed. He arranged his sermons under four or five heads, and brought each in its turn to a vigorously pointed climax, delivering the last words of each paragraph with two or three energetic nods of his head, as if he were hammering that much of the subject into the pulpit cushion with a round-headed mallet.[1]

---

[1] The hackneyed couplet of Hudibras respecting clerical use of the on the pulpit cushion is scarcely understood by modern readers because of the burlesqued rhythm leaning falsely on the vowel:—

> 'The pulpit, drum ecclesiastic,
> Is beat with fist instead of *a* stick.'

The couplet, like most of the poem, has been kept in memory more by the humour of its manner than the truth of its wit. I should like myself to expand it into—

> The pulpit, drum ecclesiastic,
> Keeps time to truth politely plastic,

Then all the congregation wiped their eyes, blew their noses, coughed the coughs they had choked over for the last quarter of an hour, and settled themselves to the more devoted acceptance of the next section.

158. It is the habit of many good men—as it was confessedly, for instance, that of the infant, Samuel—Wilberforce, Bishop of Oxford—not to allow themselves to doubt or question any part of Bible teaching. Henry Melvill, being of the same Episcopal school, and dutifully forbidding himself any dangerous fields of enquiry, explained with accuracy all that was explicable in his text, and argued the inexplicable into the plausible with great zeal and feeling;—always thoroughly convincing himself before he attempted to convince his congregation.

(It may be noted in passing that Dean Stanley, on the other hand, used his plausibility to convince his congregation without convincing himself, or committing himself to anything in particular; while Frederic Maurice secured his audiences' religious comfort, by turning their too thorny convictions the other side up, like railroad cushions.)

For the rest, Mr Melvill was entirely amiable in the Church visitant, though not formidable in the Church militant. There were not many poor in the district to be visited; but he became at once a kindly and esteemed friend to us, as, for the present, serenely feeding lambs of his flock; and I shall always remember gratefully the unoffended smile with which one day, when he had called late, and I became restless during his conversation because my dinner was ready, he broke off his talk, and said, 'Go to your dinner.'

I was greatly ashamed of myself for having been so rude; but went to my dinner,—attended better to Mr Melvill's preaching ever afterwards,—and owe to him all sorts of good help in close analysis, but

> And wakes the Dead, and lulls the Quick,
> As with a death's-head on a stick.

Or, in the longer rhythm of my old diary—

> Who, despots of the ecclesiastic drum,
> Roll the rogues' muffled march, to the rogues' 'kingdom come.'—

For indeed, since I wrote the paragraph about the pulpit of Torcello, in 'The Stones of Venice,' Vol. II, Chap. II, it has become hourly more manifest to me how far the false eloquence of the pulpit—whether Kettledrummle's at Drumclog, with whom it is, in Gibbon's scornful terms, 'the safe and sacred organ of sedition,' or the apology of hired preachers for the abuses of their day—has excited the most dangerous passions of the sects, while it quenched the refiner's fire and betrayed the reproving power of the gospel.*

especially, my habit of always looking, in every quotation from the Bible, what goes before it and after.[1]

159. But to these particulars I must return by-and-bye;* for my business in this chapter is only to give account of the materials and mental resources with which, in my new study at Denmark Hill, looking out on the meadow and the two cows, I settled myself, in the winter of 1845, to write, as my father now justly expected me to do without farther excuse, the second volume of 'Modern Painters.'*

It is extremely difficult to define, much more to explain, the religious temper in which I designed that second volume. Whatever I know or feel, now, of the justice of God, the nobleness of man, and the beauty of nature, I knew and felt then, nor less strongly; but these firm faiths were confused by the continual discovery, day by day, of error or limitation in the doctrines I had been taught, and follies or inconsistencies in their teachers: while for myself, it seemed to me quite sure, since my downfall of heart on last leaving France, that I had no part nor lot in the service or privileges of the saints; but, on the contrary, had such share only in the things of God, as well-conducted beasts and serenely-minded birds had: while, even among the beasts, I had no claim to represent myself figuratively as a lion couchant, or eagle volant,* but was, at my best and proudest, only of a doggish and piggish temper, content in my dog's chain, and with my pig's-wash, in spite of Carlyle;* and having no mind whatever to win Heaven at the price of conversion like St Ranier's, or mortification like St Bruno's.

160. And that my father much concurred with me in these, partly stubborn, partly modest, sentiments, appeared curiously on the occasion of registering his arms at the Heralds' College for painting, as those of the Bardi, and no more under the Long Acre limitation, 'vix ea nostra,' on the panel of his own brougham.* It appeared, on enquiry at the Heralds' Office, that there was indeed a shield appertaining to a family, of whom nothing particular was known, by the name of Rusken: Sable, a chevron, argent,* between six lance-heads, argent. This, without any evidence of our relation to the family, we could not, of course, be permitted to use without modification: but the King-at-Arms registered it as ours, with the addition of three crosses crosslets on the chevron, gules, (in case of my still becoming a clergyman!); and we carried home, on loan from the college, a book of crests and

---

[1] I have never forgotten his noble sermon, one day, on the folly of reading 'Eye hath not seen the things God has prepared for them that love Him,' without going on to the end of the verse, 'but He hath revealed them unto us by His Spirit.'*

mottoes; crests being open to choice in modern heraldry, (if one does not by chance win them,) as laconic expressions of personal character, or achievement.

Over which book, I remember, though too vaguely, my father's reasoning within himself, that a merchant could not with any propriety typify himself by Lord Marmion's falcon,* or Lord Dudley's bear;* that, though we were all extremely fond of dogs, any doggish crest would be taken for an extremely minor dog, or even puppy, by the public; while vulpine types, whether of heads or brushes, were wholly out of our way; and at last, faute de mieux, and with some idea, I fancy, of the beast's resolution in taking and making its own way through difficulties, my father, with the assent, if not support, of my mother and Mary, fixed, forsooth, upon a boar's head, as reasonably proud, without claim to be patrician; underwritten by the motto 'Age quod agis.'* Some ten or twelve years, I suppose, after this, beginning to study heraldry with attention, I apprehended, that, whether a knight's war-cry, or a peaceful yeoman's saying, the words on the scroll of a crest could not be a piece of advice to other people, but must be always a declaration of the bearer's own mind. Whereupon I changed, on my own seal, the 'Age quod agis' into 'To-day,' tacitly underlined to myself with the warning, 'The night cometh, when no man can work.'*

161. But as years went on, and the belief in fortune, and fortune-telling, which is finally confessed in Fors Clavigera, asserted itself more distinctly in my private philosophy,* I began to be much exercised in mind as to the fortunate, or otherwise, meaning of my father's choosing a pig for my crest; and that the more, because I could not decide whether it was lawful for me to adopt the Greek mode of interpretation, according to which I might consider myself an assistant of Hercules in the conquest of the Erymanthian boar,* or was restricted to the Gothic reading which would compel me to consider myself a pig in personâ,—(as the aforesaid Marmion a falcon, or Albert of Geierstein* vulture,—) and only take pride in the strength of bristle, and curl of tusk, which occasioned, in my days of serious critical influence, the lament of the Academician in Punch:

> 'I paints and paints,
> Hears no complaints,
> And sells before I'm dry,
> Till savage Ruskin
> Sticks his tusk in,
> And nobody will buy.'*

Inclining, as time went on, more and more to this view of the matter, I rested at last in the conviction that my prototype and patron saint was indeed, not Hercules, but St Anthony of Padua,* and that it might in a measure be recorded also of little me, that 'il se retira d'abord dans une solitude peu éloignée du bourg de Côme, puis dans un sépulcre fort éloigné de ce bourg, enfin dans les masures d'un vieux château au-dessus d'Héraclée, où il vécut pendant vingt ans. Il n'est pas possible de raconter tout ce qu'il eut à souffrir dans ces trois retraites, tant par les rigueurs qu'il exerça sur lui-même que par la malice du démon, qui mit tout en oeuvre pour le tromper par ses artifices, ou pour l'abattre par ses menaces et ses mauvais traitements, qui allèrent quelquefois jusqu'à le laisser pour mort des coups qu'il lui donna. Antoine triompha de tout; et ce fut pour le récompenser de tant de combats et de tant de victoires que Dieu le rendit puissant en oeuvres et en paroles pour guérir toutes sortes de maladies spirituelles et corporelles, chasser les démons aussi bien des corps que des âmes, se faire obéir par les bêtes les plus cruelles, par les éléments et les autres créatures les moins soumises à la volonté de l'homme.'[1]*

162. I must not, however, anticipate course of this eventful history* so far as to discuss at present any manner of the resemblance in my fate, or work, or home companionships, to those of St Anthony of Padua; but may record, as immediately significant, the delight which both my mother and I took in the possession of a really practical pig-stye in our Danish farmyard, (the coach-house and stables being to us of no importance in comparison); the success with which my mother directed the nurture, and fattening, of the piglings; the civil and jovial character of the piglings so nurtured, indicated especially by their habit of standing in a row on their hind-legs to look over the fence, whenever my mother came into the yard: and conclusively by the satisfaction with which even our most refined friends would accept a present of pork—or it might be, alas! sometimes of sucking pig—from Denmark Hill.

163. The following example of such acknowledgments, addressed to my father, is farther interesting in its post (or side) script, referring to the civil war in Switzerland, and fixing, therefore, the letter, otherwise without date of year, to 1845, when I was beginning to prepare for my first adventurous journey.

---

[1] 'Dictionnaire des Sciences Ecclésiastiques.' I assumed, of course, in adopting this patron saint, that he would have the same domestic pets as St Anthony of the Desert.

47, QUEEN ANN (no street!) WEST,
Thursday, 27 Fe^y.

'My dear Sir,

'Have the goodness to offer my respectful thanks to Mrs Ruskin for the kind present of a part of the little fat friends, & its—————[1] Portugal onions for stuffing them included, &c., &c. Hoping you are all well,

'Believe me,

'Most truly obliged,

'J. M. W. TURNER.'

J. RUSKIN, ESQ.

In the *Times*, sad news from Switzerland.*

Neither do I think it irrelevant, in this place, to foretell that, after twenty years' various study of the piglet character, (see, for instance, the account of the comfort given me by the monastic piglet at Assisi,[2]) I became so resigned to the adoption of my paternally chosen crest as to write my rhymed travelling letters to Joan,[3] most frequently in my heraldic character of 'Little Pig'; or, royally plural, 'Little Pigs,' especially when these letters took the tone of confessions, as for instance, from Keswick, in 1867:

> When little pigs have muffins hot,
> And take three quarters for their lot,
> Then, little pigs—had better not.

---

[1] Turner always indicates by these long lines the places in his letters where his feelings become inexpressible.

[2] 'In one of my saddest moods, I got some wholesome peace and refreshment by mere sympathy with a Bewickian little pig, in the roundest and conceitedest burst of pig-blossom.'*—'Fors,' Letter XLVIII.

[3] Now Mrs Arthur Severn.

And again, on the occasion of over-lunching myself before ascending Red Pike, in the same year:

> As readers, for their minds' relief,
> Will sometimes double down a leaf,
> Or rather, as good sailors reef
> Their sails, or jugglers, past belief
> Will con-involve a handkerchief—
> If little pigs, when time is brief
> *Will*, that way, double up their beef,
> Then—little pigs will come to grief.

And here is what may, it seems to me, gracefully conclude this present chapter, as a pretty and pathetic Pigwiggian chaunt,* from Abbeville, in 1858.

> If little pigs,—when evening dapples,
> With fading clouds, her autumn sky,—
> Set out in search of Norman Chapels,
> And find, instead, where cliffs are high,
> Half way from Amiens to Etaples,
> A castle, full of pears and apples,
> On donjon floors laid out to dry;
> —Green jargonelles, and apples tenny,*—
> And find their price is five a penny,
> If little pigs, then, buy too many,
> Spare to those little pigs a sigh.

CHAPTER IX

THE FEASTS OF THE VANDALS*

164. THE reader of 'to-day' who has been accustomed to hear me spoken of by the artists of to-day as a super-annuated enthusiast, and by the philosophers of to-day as a delirious visionary, will scarcely believe with what serious interest the appearance of the second volume of 'Modern Painters' was looked for, by more people than my father and mother,—by people even belonging to the shrewdest literary circles, and highest artistic schools, of the time.

165. In the literary world, attention was first directed to the book by Sydney Smith, in the hearing of my severest and chiefly antagonist master, the Rev. Thomas Dale, who with candid kindness sent the following note of the matter to my father:—

'You will not be uninterested to hear that Mr Sydney Smith (no mean authority in such cases) spoke in the highest terms of your son's work, on a public occasion, and in presence of several distinguished literary characters. He said it was a work of transcendent talent, presented the most original views, and the most elegant and powerful language, and would work a complete revolution in the world of taste. He did not know, when he said this, how much I was interested in the author.'

166. My father was greatly set up by this note, though the form of British prudence which never specifies occasion or person, for fear of getting itself into a scrape, is provokingly illustrated by its imperfect testimony. But, it mattered little who the other 'literary characters' might have been, for Sydney's verdict was at this time, justly, final, both in general society and among the reviewers; and it was especially fortunate for me that he had been trained in his own youth, first by Dugald Stewart, and then by the same Dr Thomas Brown who had formed my father's mind and directed his subsequent reading. And, indeed, all the main principles of metaphysics asserted in the opening of 'Modern Painters' had been, with conclusive decision and simplicity, laid down by Sydney himself in the lectures he gave on Moral Philosophy at the Royal Institution in the years 1804–5–6, of which he had never enough himself recognized the importance. He amplified and embodied some portions of them afterwards in the Edinburgh Review; but 'considering that what remained could be of no farther use, he destroyed several, and was proceeding to destroy the whole, when, entreaty being made by friends that the portions not yet torn up might be spared, their request was granted;'[1] and these despised fragments, published in 1850 under the title of Elementary Sketches of Moral Philosophy, contain, in the simplest and securest terms, every final truth which any rational mortal needs to learn on that subject.

Had those lectures been printed five years sooner, and then fallen in my way, the second volume of 'Modern Painters' would either never have been written at all, or written with thankful deference to the exulting wit and gracious eloquence with which Sydney had discerned and adorned all that I wished to establish, twenty years before.

167. To the modern student, who has heard of Sydney Smith only as a jester, I commend the two following passages, as examples of the most wise, because most noble, thought, and most impressive, because

---

[1] See note to Introduction, in the edition of 1850.

steel-true, language, to be found in English literature of the living, as distinguished from the classic, schools:—

'But while I am descanting so minutely upon the conduct of the understanding, and the best modes of acquiring knowledge, some men may be disposed to ask, "Why conduct my understanding with such endless care? and what is the use of so much knowledge?" What is the use of so much knowledge?—what is the use of so much life! What are we to do with the seventy years of existence allotted to us? and how are we to live them out to the last? I solemnly declare that, but for the love of knowledge, I should consider the life of the meanest hedger and ditcher as preferable to that of the greatest and richest man here present: for the fire of our minds is like the fire which the Persians burn in the mountains,—it flames night and day, and is immortal, and not to be quenched! Upon something it *must* act and feed,—upon the pure spirit of knowledge, or upon the foul dregs of polluting passions. Therefore, when I say, in conducting your understanding, love knowledge with a great love, with a vehement love, with a love coeval with life, what do I say, but love innocence, love virtue, love purity of conduct, love that which, if you are rich and great, will sanctify the blind fortune which has made you so, and make men call it justice; love that which, if you are poor, will render your poverty respectable, and make the proudest feel it unjust to laugh at the meanness of your fortunes; love that which will comfort you, adorn you, and never quit you,—which will open to you the kingdom of thought, and all the boundless regions of conception, as an asylum against the cruelty, the injustice, and the pain that may be your lot in the outer world,—that which will make your motives habitually great and honourable, and light up in an instant a thousand noble disdains at the very thought of meanness and of fraud! Therefore, if any young man here have embarked his life in pursuit of knowledge, let him go on without doubting or fearing the event; let him not be intimidated by the cheerless beginnings of knowledge, by the darkness from which she springs, by the difficulties which hover around her, by the wretched habitations in which she dwells, by the want and sorrow which sometimes journey in her train; but let him ever follow her as the Angel that guards him, and as the Genius of his life. She will bring him out at last into the light of day, and exhibit him to the world comprehensive in acquirements, fertile in resources, rich in imagination, strong in reasoning, prudent and powerful above his fellows in all the relations and in all the offices of life.'*

168. 'The history of the world shows us that men are not to be counted by their numbers, but by the fire and vigour of their passions;

by their deep sense of injury; by their memory of past glory; by their eagerness for fresh fame; by their clear and steady resolution of ceasing to live, or of achieving a particular object, which, when it is *once* formed, strikes off a load of manacles and chains, and gives free space to all heavenly and heroic feelings. All great and extraordinary actions come from the heart. There are seasons in human affairs when qualities, fit enough to conduct the common business of life, are feeble and useless, and when men must trust to emotion for that safety which reason at such times can never give. These are the feelings which led the Ten Thousand over the Carduchian mountains; these are the feelings by which a handful of Greeks broke in pieces the power of Persia: they have, by turns, humbled Austria, reduced Spain; and in the fens of the Dutch, and in the mountains of the Swiss, defended the happiness, and revenged the oppressions of man! God calls all the passions out in their keenness and vigour, for the present safety of mankind. Anger, and revenge, and the heroic mind, and a readiness to suffer;—all the secret strength, all the invisible array of the feelings;—all that nature has reserved for the great scenes of the world. For the usual hopes, and the common aids of man, are all gone! Kings have perished, armies are subdued, nations mouldered away! Nothing remains, under God, but those passions which have often proved the best ministers of His vengeance, and the surest protectors of the world.'"

169. These two passages of Sydney's express, more than any others I could have chosen out of what I know of modern literature, the roots of everything I had to learn and teach during my own life; the earnestness with which I followed what was possible to me in science, and the passion with which I was beginning to recognize the nobleness of the arts and range of the powers of men.

It was a natural consequence of this passion that the sympathy of the art-circles, in praise of whose leading members the first volume of 'Modern Painters' had been expressly written, was withheld from me much longer than that of the general reader; while, on the other hand, the old Roman feuds with George Richmond were revived by it to the uttermost; and although, with amused interest in my youthful enthusiasm, and real affection for my father, he painted a charming water-colour* of me sitting at a picturesque desk in the open air, in a crimson waistcoat and white trousers, with a magnificent port-crayon in my hand, and Mont Blanc, conventionalized to Raphaelesque grace, in the distance, the utmost of serious opinion on my essay which my father could get from him was 'that I should know better in time.'

170. But the following letter from Samuel Prout, written just at the

moment when my father's pride in the success of the book was fast beguiling him into admission of its authorship, at least in our own friendly circle, expresses with old-fashioned courtesy, but with admirable simplicity and firmness, the first impression made by my impetuous outburst on the most sensible and sincere members of the true fellowship of English artists, who at that time were doing each the best he could in his own quiet way, without thought either of contention with living rivals, or of comparing their modest work to the masterpieces of former time.

'HASTINGS, *July 2nd*, 1843.

'DEAR SIR,

'I beg to apologize for not sooner acknowledging, with my best thanks, your kindness in adding another to many obligations.

'Please to believe that I am ambitious of meriting your many acts of kind consideration, but I am ashamed and vexed to feel a consciousness of apparent rudeness, and a trial of patience which nothing can extenuate. I must fear that my besetting sin of idleness in letter-writing has been displeasing to you, although your note is politely silent on the subject.

'I am sorry to say that for months together my spirits have sunk so low, that every duty and every kindness have been sadly neglected.

'In consequence of this nervous inactivity, the Water Colour Exhibition contains almost all I have been able to accomplish since last year. The drawing of Petrarch's House, which you wished me to make, was finished some time since, but is so unlike what I am sure you expected, that I deferred saying anything about it till another was made. Alas! the things I ought to have done have not been done.* I intended bringing it to town with me, and asking the Favour that it might remain in your possession till I had made something more worthy. My trip to town has been put off month after month, and I expect the resolution will not awake till the last day of seeing sights. Should you not be in town, both drawings shall be left at Foord's.[1]

'Permit me to say that I have been indulged with a hasty perusal of a work on art and artists by "A Graduate of Oxford."* I read the volume with intense interest, the sentiments and language riveting my

---

[1] The letters quoted in the text of 'Praeterita' will always be given without omissions even of trivial passages. Of those arranged in 'Dilecta,' I give only the portions which seem to me likely to interest the reader; and even take leave to drop superfluous sentences without stars or other note of the omission, but so that the absolute meaning of the writer shall be always kept.

attention to every page. But I mourn lest such splendid means of doing eminent service to art should be lost. Had the work been written with the *courteousness* of Sir Joshua Reynolds' lectures, it would have been "a standard work," the author held in high estimation for his learning, and the volume recommended for instruction and usefulness. Perhaps nothing helps more certainly to an accession of influence, and an accumulating power of doing good, than the *language* in which we dictate. We approach an unassuming courteous manner with respect, confidence, and satisfaction, but most persons shrink back from sarcasm. Certainly every author who writes to do good will write with firmness and candour, *cleaving to what is right, but cautious of giving pain or offence.*

'I hope some day to give the book a more careful perusal; *it made me think*, and when I lay hold of it again, I will endeavour to test it by my experience and the judgment of others; and as I have a little *cooled* from the *rage* I felt at first to find my "darlings" set at nought, I trust in spite of its biting bitterness I shall feel more ashamed of myself, and more respect for the opinions of the author.

'Pardon, dear sir, this presuming to tire your patience with my humble opinions; and should it be true what I have just heard, that you know the author, I will rely on your goodness to forgive my objection to opinions in which you are so much interested.

'If it is so, you are indeed honoured, and I trust the powerful "angel-bright talent"* will be directed to do much good for art and artists. Pray give me credit for sincerity in acknowledging that it is art generally I feel for, and as far as I am individually mentioned, I am pleased to find that I have come off beautifully.

'I did not intend to write so much. Kindly pardon quantity and quality.

'And believe me to remain, dear Sir,
'With the greatest respect,
'Yours truly and obliged,
'S. PROUT.

'J. J. Ruskin, Esq.
&c. &c. &c.'

171. I must guard myself, however, very distinctly in giving this letter as an example of the general feeling about the book among the living painters whom it praised, against attributing to them any such admiration of my 'angel-bright talent' as that here expressed by my father's affectionate, and now intimate, friend. The group of

landscapists, headed by Copley Fielding, David Cox, and P. de Wint in the old Water Colour Society, and by David Roberts and Clarkson Stanfield in the Academy (Turner being wholly exceptional, and a wild meteoric phenomenon in the midst of them, lawless alike and scholarless)—this group of very characteristically English landscape painters had been well grounded, every one of them, more or less, in the orthodox old English faith in Dutch painting; had studied it so as to know the difficulty of doing anything as good in its way; and, whether in painting or literature, had studied very little else. Of any qualities or talents 'angel bright,' past or present, except in the rather alarming than dignified explosions round the stable lantern which sometimes take place in a Rembrandt Nativity, Vision to the Shepherds, or the like, none of them had ever felt the influence, or attempted the conception: the religious Italian schools were as little known at that time, to either artist or connoisseur, as the Japanese, and the highest scholarly criticism, with which I had first come to hand-grips in Blackwood,* reached no higher than a sketching amateur's acquaintance with the manner of Salvator and Gaspar Poussin. Taken as a body, the total group of Modern Painters were, therefore, more startled than flattered by my schismatic praise; the modest ones, such as Fielding, Prout, and Stansfield, felt that it was more than they deserved,—and, moreover, a little beside the mark and out of their way; the conceited ones, such as Harding and De Wint, were angry at the position given to Turner; and I am not sure that any of them were ready even to endorse George Richmond's consoling assurance to my father, that I should know better in time.

172. But, with all the kindness of heart, and appreciation of domestic character, partly humorous, partly pathetic, which gave its prevailing tone to the British school of the day, led by Wilkie, Leslie, and Mulready, the entire fellowship of artists with whom we were acquainted sympathized with the partly quaint, altogether pure, strong, and always genial, home-life of my father and mother; nor less with their anxious devotion to their son, and the hopes they entertained for him. Nor, I suppose, was my own status at Denmark Hill without something honourably notable to men of the world, in that, refusing to enter my father's business, I yet stayed serenely under his authority, and, in what seemed to me my own proper line of work, did my utmost to please him. And when (I anticipate now the progress of the next four or five years)—when on any, to us, peculiarly festive occasion,—the return from a journey, publication of a new volume, anniversary of a birthday, or the like,—we ventured to ask our artist friends to rejoice

with us, most of them came, I believe with real pleasure. The early six o'clock dinner allowed them usually a pleasant glance over the meadow and the Norwood Hills in the evening light; the table was just short enough to let the talk flow round without wandering into eddies, or lingering into confidences; there was no guest whom the others did not honour; there was neither effort, affectation, nor restraint in the talk. If the painters cared to say anything of pictures, they knew they would be understood; if they chose rather to talk of sherry, my father could, and would with delight, tell them more about it than any other person knew in either England or Spain; and when the candles came, and the good jests, over the nuts and olives, there was 'frolic wine'* in the flask at every right hand, such as that never Prince Hal nor Jack Falstaff* tasted cup of brighter or mightier.

173. I somewhat admire in myself, at this time, though I perceive it to have been greatly owing to want of imagination, the simplicity of affection with which I kept hold on my Cumberland moors, Calais sands, and French costumes and streets,—as contrasted with the peaks of the Sierra Nevada, the surges of Trafalgar, and the towers of Seville and Granada; of all which I continually heard as the most beautiful and wonderful scenery and architecture of the European world; and in the very midst of which—in the heart of Andalusia, and on the very battle-field of Xeres de la Frontera which gave the Arab his dominion in Spain—I might have been adopted by my father's partner to reign over his golden vineyards, and write the histories of the first Caliphs of Arabia and the Catholic Kings of Spain.

It chanced, however,—or mischanced,—for better or worse, that in the meantime I knew no more the histories of either Arabia or Spain than Robinson Crusoe or his boy Xury;* that the absolutely careful and faithful work of David Roberts showed me the inconstructive and merely luxurious character of Spanish and Arab buildings; and that the painter of greatest power, next to Turner, in the English school, J. F. Lewis, rendered the facts of existing Andalusian life so vividly, as to leave me no hope of delighting or distinguishing myself in any constant relations either with its gaiety or its pride.

174. Looking back to my notices of these and other contemporary artists in the paragraphs added to the first volume of 'Modern Painters,' when I corrected its sheets at Sestri di Levante, in 1846,* I find the display of my new Italian information, and assertion of critical acumen, prevail sorrowfully over the expressions of gratitude with which I ought to have described the help and delight they had given me. Now, too late, I can only record with more than sorrow the passing away

from the entire body of men occupied in the arts, of the temper in which these men worked. It is—I cannot count how many years, since, on all our walls of recklessly ambitious display, I have seen one drawing of any place loved for its own sake, or understood with unselfish intelligence. Whether men themselves, or their buildings, or the scenery in which they live, the only object of the draughtsman, be he great or small, is to overpower the public mind with his greatness, or catch it with his smallness. *My* notions of Rome, says Mr Alma Tadema; *Mine* of Venice, says Miss Clara Montalba; *Ours* of Belgravia and Brighton, say the public and its Graphics,* with unanimous egotism;—and what sensational effects can be wrung out of China or New Zealand, or the miseries and follies of mankind anywhere. Exact knowledge enough—yes, let us have it to fill our pockets or swell our pride; but the beauty of wild nature or modest life, except for the sake of our own picnics or perquisites, none care to know, or to save.

And it is wholly vain, in this state of the popular mind, to try to explain the phase of art in which I was brought up, and of which—little thinking how soon it was to pass away—I wrote so ungratefully.

175. Absolutely careful and faithful, I said, David Roberts was, though in his own restricted terms; fastening on the constant aspect of any place, and drawing that in grey shade, and so much of what might pass for light as enough showed magnitude, distance, and grace of detail. He was like a kind of grey mirror; he gave the greatness and richness of things, and such height and space, and standing of wall and rock, as one saw to be true; and with unwearied industry, both in Egypt and Spain, brought home records of which the value is now forgotten in the perfect detail of photography, and sensational realism of the effects of light which Holman Hunt first showed to be possible. The minute knowledge and acute sensation throw us back into ourselves; haunting us to the examination of points and enjoyment of moments; but one imagined serenely and joyfully, from the old drawings, the splendour of the aisles of Seville or the strength of the towers of Granada, and forgot oneself, for a time.

176. The work of John Lewis was a mirror of men only—of building and scenery as backgrounds for them; all alike rendered with an intensity of truth to the external life, which nothing has resembled before or since. But it was the external and animal life only. Lewis saw in men and women only the most beautiful of living creatures, and painted them as he did dogs and deer, but with a perception of their nature and race which laughs to scorn all the generic study of the scientific schools. Neither Andalusian nor Arab, Turk nor Circassian,

had been painted before his time, any more than described before Byron's; and the endeavours at representation of Oriental character or costume which accompany the travels of even the best-educated English travellers either during or immediately after the Peninsular war,* are without exception the clumsiest, most vulgar, and most ludicrous pieces of work that ever disgraced draughtsmen, savage or civil.

No artist that ever I read of was treated with such injustice by the people of his time as John Lewis. There was something un-English about him, which separated him from the good-humoured groups of established fame whose members abetted or jested with each other; feeling that every one of them had something to be forgiven, and that each knew the other's trick of trade. His resolute industry was inimitable; his colour—founded either on the frankness of southern sunlight, or on its subtle reflections and diffusions through latticed tracery and silken tent—resembled nothing that could be composed in a London studio; while the absence of bravado, sentiment, or philosophy in his subjects—the total subjection alike of the moral and immoral, the heroic and the sensual, to the mere facts of animal beauty, and grace of decoration, left him without any power of appeal either to the domestic simplicity or personal pride of the ordinary English mind. In artistic power and feeling he had much in common with Paul Veronese: but Paolo had the existing pomp and the fading religion of Venice to give his work hold on the national heart, and epic unity in its design; while poor Lewis did but render more vividly, with all his industry, the toy contrabandista or matador of my mother's chimneypiece.

He never dined with us as our other painter friends did; but his pictures, as long as he worked in Spain, were an extremely important element in both my father's life and mine.

177. I have not yet enough explained the real importance of my father's house, in its command of that Andalusian wine district. Modern maps of Spain, covered with tracks of railroad, show no more the courses either of Guadalquiver or Guadiana; the names of railway stations overwhelm those of the old cities; and every atlas differs from every other in its placing of the masses of the Sierras,—if even the existence of the mountain ranges be acknowledged at all.

But if the reader will take ten minutes of pains, and another ten of time, to extricate, with even the rudest sketch, the facts of value from the chaos of things inscrutably useless, in any fairly trustworthy map of Spain, he will perceive that between the Sierra Morena on the north, and Sierra Nevada on the south, the Guadalquiver flows for two hundred miles through a valley fifty miles wide, in the exact midst of which sits Cordova, and half way between Cordova and the sea, Seville; and on the Royal Harbour, Puerto Real, at the sea shore,— Cadiz; ten miles above which, towards Seville, he will find the 'Xeres de la Frontera,' to which, as a golden centre of Bacchic commerce, all the vineyards of that great valley of Andalusia, Vandalusia, or, as Mr Ford puts it, I believe more probably, land of the west,* send down their sun-browned juice; the ground of Macharnudo on Mr Domecq's estate at Xeres itself furnishing the white wine of strongest body in Europe.

178. The power which Mr Domecq had acknowledged in my father, by making him head partner in his firm, instead of merely his English agent, ruled absolutely at Xeres over the preparation of the wines; and, by insisting always on the maintenance of their purity and quality at the highest attainable standard, gave the house a position which was only in part expressed by its standing, until Mr Domecq's death, always at the head in the list of importers. That list gave only the number of butts of wine imported by each firm, but did not specify their price; still less could it specify the relation of price to value. Mr Domecq's two or three thousand butts were, for the most part, old wine, of which the supply had been secured for half a century by the consistent prudence of putting the new vintages in at one end of cellars some quarter of a mile long, and taking the old vintages out at the other. I do not, of course, mean that such transaction was literally observed; but that the vulgar impatience to 'turn over' capital was absolutely forsworn, in the steady purpose of producing the best wine that could be given for the highest price to which the British public would go. As a rule, sherry drinkers are soundly-minded persons, who do not choose to spend a guinea a glass on anything; and the highest normal price for Mr Domecq's 'double-cross' sherry was eighty pounds a butt; rising to two hundred for the older wines, which were only occasionally imported. The highest price ever given was six hundred; but this was at a loss to the house, which only allowed wine to attain the age which such a price represented in order to be able to supply, by the mixture of it with younger vintage, whatever quality the English consumer, in any fit of fashion, might desire.

On the whole, the sales varied little from year to year, virtually representing the quantity of wine annually produced by the estate, and a certain quantity of the drier Amontillado,* from the hill districts of Montilla, and some lighter and cheaper sherries,—though always pure,—which were purchased by the house for the supply of the wider London market. No effort was ever made to extend that market by lowering quality; no competition was possible with the wines grown by Mr Domecq, and little with those purchased on his judgment. My father used to fret, as I have told, if the orders he expected were not forthcoming, or if there seemed the slightest risk of any other house contesting his position at the head of the list. But he never attempted, or even permitted, the enlargement of the firm's operations beyond the scale at which he was sure that his partner's personal and equal care, or, at least, that of his head cellarman, could be given to the execution of every order.

Mr Domecq's own habits of life were luxurious, but never extravagant. He had a house in Paris, chiefly for the sake of his daughters' education and establishment; the profits of the estate, though not to be named in any comparison with those of modern mercantile dynasty, were enough to secure annual income to each of his five girls large enough to secure their marriages in the best French circles: they became, each in her turn, baronne or comtesse; their father choosing their baron or count for them with as much discretion as he had shown in the choice of his own partner; and all the marriages turned out well. Elise, Comtesse des Roys, and Caroline, Princess Bethune, once or twice came with their husbands to stay with us; partly to see London, partly to discuss with my father his management of the English market: and the way in which these lords, virtually, of lands both in France and Spain, though men of sense and honour; and their wives, though women of gentle and amiable disposition, (Elise, indeed, one of the kindest I ever have known,) spoke of their Spanish labourers and French tenantry, with no idea whatever respecting them but that, except as producers by their labour of money to be spent in Paris, they were cumberers of the ground, gave me the first clue to the real sources of wrong in the social laws of modern Europe; and led me necessarily into the political work which has been the most earnest of my life. But these visits and warnings were not till seven or eight years after the time at present rendered account of, in which, nevertheless, it was already beginning to be, if not a question, at least a marvel with me, that these graceful and gay Andalusians, who played guitars, danced boleros, and fought bulls, should virtually get no good of their own beautiful country but the bunch of grapes or stalk of garlic they frugally dined on; that its precious wine was not for them, still less the money it was sold for; but the one came to crown our Vandalic feasts, and the other furnished our Danish walls with pictures, our Danish gardens with milk and honey,* and five noble houses in Paris with the means of beautiful dominance in its Elysian fields.*

179. Still more seriously, I was now beginning to contrast the luxury and continual opportunity of my own exulting days, with the poverty, and captivity, or, as it seemed to chance always, fatal issue of any efforts to escape from these, in which my cousins, the only creatures whom I had to care for, beyond my home, were each and all spending, or ending, their laborious youth.

I must briefly resume their histories, though much apart from mine; but if my heart was cold to them, my mind was often sad for them.

By grotesque freak of Fors, both my aunts married a Mr Richardson—and each left six children, four boys and two girls.

The Perth children were Mary and Jessie, James, John, William, and Andrew; the Croydon children, Margaret and Bridget, John, William, George, and Charles. None left now but William of Croydon.*

180. The Perth boys were all partly weak in constitution, and curiously inconsistent in elements of character, having much of their mother's subtlety and sweetness mixed with a rather larger measure of their father's tannin. The eldest, James, was unlike the other three,—more delicate in feature, and more tractable in temper. My father brought him up to London when he was one- or two-and-twenty, and put him into the counting-house to see what could be made of him: but, though perfectly well-behaved, he was undiligent and effectless—chiefly solicitous about his trousers and gloves. I remember him in his little room, the smaller of the two looking west at top of Herne Hill house, a pleasant, gentle, tall figure of a youth. He fell into rapid decline and died.

Nor long after him, the youngest brother, Andrew, who with fewer palpable follies, had less real faculty than the rest. He learnt farming under a good master in Scotland, and went out to Australia to prove his science; but after a short struggle with the earth of the other side of the world, rested beneath it.

181. The second brother, John, thus left the head of the family, was a stumpily made, snub- or rather knob-nosed, red-faced, bright-eyed, good-natured simpleton; with the most curiously subtle shrewdnesses, and obstinate faculties, excrescent through his simplicity. I believe he first tried to carry on his father's business; not prospering in that, after some pause and little-pleased scrutiny of him, he was established by my father as a wine-agent in Glasgow, in which business and town he remained, in a shambling, hand-to-mouth manner, some thirty years, a torment to my father, of an extremely vexatious kind—all the more that he was something of a possession and vestige of his mother all the same. He was a quite first-rate chess-player and whist-player: in

business, he had a sort of chess and whist instinct for getting the better of people, as if every dozen of sherry were a hand of cards; and would often, for the mere pleasure of playing a trick, lose a customer without really making a penny by him. Good-natured, as I said, with a rude foundation of honesty at the bottom which made my father put up with him, (indeed, so far as I can find out, no one of all my relations was ever dishonest at heart, and most of them have been only too simple,) he never lied about his sherry or adulterated it, but tried to get little advantages in bargains, and make the customer himself to choose the worst wine at the money, and so on—trying always to get the most he could out of my father in the same way, yet affectionate in a dumb-doggish sort, and not ungrateful, he went scamble-shambling on, a plague to the end, yet through all, a nephew.

182. William, the third of the Perth boys, had all John's faults of disposition, but greater powers, and, above all, resolution and perseverance, with a rightly foresighted pride, not satisfied in trivial or momentary successes, but knitting itself into steady ambition, with some deep-set notions of duty and principles of conscience farther strengthening it. His character, however, developed slowly, nor ever freed itself from the flaws which ran like a geological cleavage through the whole brotherhood: while his simplicities in youth were even more manifest than theirs, and as a schoolboy, he was certainly the awkwardest, and was thought the foolishest, of the four.

He became, however, a laborious and sagacious medical student, came up to London to walk the hospitals; and on passing his examination for medical practitioner, was established by my father in a small shop in the Bayswater Road, when he began—without purchase of any former favour, but camped there like a gipsy by the roadside,—general practice, chiefly among the poor, and not enough to live upon for a year or two (without supplemental pork and applesauce from Denmark Hill), but conscientious and earnest, paying largely in gathered knowledge and insight. I shall often have occasion to speak of him hereafter;* it is enough to say in advance that after a few years of this discipline he took his diploma of MD with credit, and became an excellent physician—and the best chess-player I have ever known.*

CHAPTER X

CROSSMOUNT

183. My best readers cannot but be alike astonished and disappointed that I have nothing set down of the conversation, cordial always, and if George Richmond were there, better than brilliant, which flowed at these above described Vandalic feasts. But it seemed to me that all the sap and bloom of it were lost in deliberate narrative, and its power shorn away if one could not record also the expression of the speaker; while of absolutely useful and tenable resulting sense, there was, to my unsympathetic mind, little to be got hold of. Turner resolutely refused to speak on the subject of art at all, and every one of us felt that we must ask him no questions in that direction; while of what any other painter said, I was careless, regarding them all as limited to their own fields, and unable to help me in mine.

I had two distinct instincts to be satisfied, rather than ends in view, as I wrote day by day with higher-kindled feeling the second volume of 'Modern Painters.' The first, to explain to myself, and then demonstrate to others, the nature of that quality of beauty which I now saw to exist through all the happy conditions of living organism; and down to the minutest detail and finished material structure naturally produced. The second, to explain and illustrate the power of two schools of art unknown to the British public, that of Angelico in Florence, and Tintoret in Venice.

184. I have no knowledge, and can form no conjecture, of the extent to which the book in either direction accomplished its purpose. It is usually read only for its pretty passages; its theory of beauty is scarcely ever noticed,—its praise of Tintoret has never obtained the purchase of any good example of him for the National Gallery. But I permit myself—perhaps with vain complacency—the thought that I have had considerable share in the movement which led to the useful work of the Arundel Society* in Italy, and to the enlargement of the National collection by its now valuable series of fourteenth-century religious paintings.

The style of the book was formed on a new model, given me by Osborne Gordon. I was old enough now to feel that neither Johnsonian balance nor Byronic alliteration were ultimate virtues in English prose; and I had been reading with care on Gordon's counsel, both for its arguments and its English, Richard Hooker's 'Ecclesiastical Polity.' I had always a trick of imitating, more or less, the last book I had read with admiration; and it farther seemed to me that for the purposes of argument, (and my own theme was, according to my notion, to be argued out invincibly,) Hooker's English was the perfectest existing model. At all events, I did the best I then knew how, leaving no passage till I had put as much thought into it as it could be made to carry, and chosen the words with the utmost precision and tune I could give them.

For the first time in my life, when I had finished the last sentence, I was really tired. In too long readings at Oxford I got stupid and sleepy, but not fatigued: now, however, I felt distinctly that my head could do no more; and with much satisfied thankfulness, after the revise of the last sheet was sent to printer, found myself on the bows of the little steamer, watching their magical division of the green waves between Dover and Calais.

185. Little steamers they all were, then; nor in the least well appointed, nor aspiring to any pride of shape or press of speed; their bits of sails worn and patched like those of an old fishing-boat. Here, for modest specimen of my then proper art style, I give my careful drawing of the loose lashed jib of one of them, as late as 1854.[1] The immeasurable delight to me of being able to loiter and swing about just over the bowsprit and watch the plunge of the bows, if there was the least swell or broken sea to lift them, with the hope of Calais at breakfast, and the horses' heads set straight for Mont Blanc to-morrow, is one of the few pleasures I look back to as quite unmixed. In getting a Turner drawing I always wanted another; but I didn't want to be in more boats than one at once.

As I had done my second volume greatly to my father's and mother's delight, (they used both to cry a little, at least my father generally did, over the pretty passages, when I read them after breakfast,) it had been agreed that they should both go with me that summer to see all the things and pictures spoken of,—Ilaria, and the Campo Santo, and St Mary's of the Thorn, and the School of St Roch.

Though tired, I was in excellent health, and proud hope; they also at their best and gladdest. And we had a happy walk up and down the quiet streets of Calais that day, before four o'clock dinner.

[1] In which year we must have started impatiently, without our rubrical gooseberry pie,* for I find the drawing is dated '10th May, my father's birthday,' and thus elucidated, 'Opposite,' (*i.e.* on leaf of diary), 'the jib of steamer seen from inside it on the deck. The double curve at the base of it is curious; in reality the curves were a good deal broken, the sail being warped like a piece of wetted paper. The rings by which it holds, being *alternately* round and edge to the eye, are curious. The *lines* are of course seams, which go to the bottom of the sail; the brown marks, running short the same way, are stains.'

186. I have dwelt with insistence in last chapter on my preference of the Hotel de Ville at Calais to the Alcazar of Seville. Not that I was without love of grandeur in buildings, but in that kind, Rouen front and Beauvais apse were literally the only pieces that came up to my mark; ordinary minsters and palaces, however they might set themselves up for sublime, usually hurt me by some manner of disproportion or pretence; and my best joys were in small pieces of provincial building, full of character, and naturally graceful and right in their given manner. In this kind the little wooden belfry of Evreux, of which Prout's drawing is photographed at page 42 of my 'Memoir,'[1]* is consummate; but the Calais one, though of far later and commoner style, is also matchless, far or near, in that rude way, and has been a perpetual delight and lesson to me. Prout has a little idealized it in the distance of the drawing of Calais Harbour, page 40 in the same book; I never tried to draw it myself, the good of it being not in any sculpturesque detail, but in the complex placing of its plain, square-cut props and ties, taking some pretence of pinnacle on them, and being really as structurally useful, though by their linked circletting instead of their weight. There was never time in the happy afternoon to do this carefully enough, though I got a colour-note once of the church-spire, loved in a deeper way, ('Modern Painters,' Vol. IV, Chap. I,) but the belfry beat me. After all, the chief charm of it was in being seen from my bedroom at Desseins, and putting me to sleep and waking me with its chimes.

187. Calais is properly a Flemish, not French town (of course the present town is all, except belfry and church, built in the seventeenth century, no vestige remaining of Plantagenet Calais); it has no wooden houses, which mark the essential French civic style, but only brick or chalk ones, with, originally, most of them, good indented Flemish stone gables and tiled roofs. True French roofs are never tiled, but slated, and have no indented gables, but bold dormer windows rising over the front, never, in any pretty street groups of them, without very definite expression of pride. Poor little Calais had indeed nothing to be proud of, but it had a quaint look of contentment with itself on those easy terms; some dignity in its strong ramparts and drawbridge gates; and, better than dignity, real power and service in the half-mile of pier, reaching to the low-tide breakers across its field of sand.

Sunset, then, seen from the pier-head across those whispering fringes; belfry chime at evening and morning; and the new life of that year, 1846, was begun.

[1] Printed by the Fine Art Society, 1880.

188. After our usual rest at Champagnole, we went on over the Cenis to Turin, Verona, and Venice; whereat I began showing my father all my new discoveries in architecture and painting. But there began now to assert itself a difference between us I had not calculated on. For the first time I verily perceived that my father was older than I, and not immediately nor easily to be put out of his way of thinking in anything. We had been entirely of one mind about the carved porches of Abbeville, and living pictures of Vandyck; but when my father now found himself required to admire also flat walls, striped like the striped calico of an American flag, and oval-eyed saints like the figures on a Chinese teacup, he grew restive. Farther, all the fine writing and polite *éclat* of 'Modern Painters' had never reconciled him to my total resignation of the art of poetry; and beyond this, he entirely, and with acute sense of loss to himself, doubted and deplored my now constant habit of making little patches and scratches of the sections and fractions of things in a notebook which used to live in my waistcoat pocket, instead of the former Proutesque or Robertsian outline of grand buildings and sublime scenes. And I was the more viciously stubborn in taking my own way, just because everybody was with him in these opinions; and I was more and more persuaded every day, that everybody was always wrong.

Often in my other books, and now, once for all, and finally here,—I have to pray my readers to note that this continually increasing arrogance was not founded on vanity in me, but on sorrow. There is a vast difference—there is all the difference—between the vanity of displaying one's own faculties, and the grief that other people do not use their own. Vanity would have led me to continue writing and drawing what every one praised; and disciplining my own already practised hand into finer dexterities. But I had no thought but of learning more, and teaching what truth I knew,—assuredly then, and ever since, for the student's sake, not my own fame's; however sensitive I may be to the fame, also, afterwards.

189. Meantime, my father and I did not get on well in Italy at all, and one of the worst, wasp-barbed, most tingling pangs of my memory is yet of a sunny afternoon at Pisa, when, just as we were driving past my pet La Spina chapel, my father, waking out of a reverie, asked me suddenly, 'John, what shall I give the coachman?' Whereupon, I, instead of telling him what he asked me, as I ought to have done with much complacency at being referred to on the matter, took upon me with impatience to reprove, and lament over, my father's hardness of heart, in thinking at that moment of sublunary affairs. And the spectral Spina of the chapel has stayed in my own heart ever since.

Nor did things come right that year till we got to Chamouni, where, having seen enough by this time of the upper snow, I was content to enjoy my morning walks in the valley with papa and mamma; after which, I had more than enough to do among the lower rocks and woods till dinner time, and in watching phases of sunset afterwards from beneath the slopes of the Breven.

190. The last Chamouni entry, with its sequel, is perhaps worth keeping.

'Aug. 23rd.—Rained nearly all day; but I walked to the source of the Arveron—now a mighty fall down the rocks of the Montanvert;[1] note the intense scarletty purple of the shattered larch stems, wet, opposed with yellow from decomposing turpentine; the alder stems looking much like birch, covered with the white branchy moss that looks like a coral. Went out again in the afternoon towards the Cascade des Peleims; surprised to see the real rain-clouds assume on the Breven, about one-third of its height, the form of cirri,—long, continuous, and delicate; the same tendency showing in the clouds all along the valley, some inclining to the fish-shape, and others to the cobweb-like wavy film.'

'Lucerne, Aug. 31st.—The result of the above phenomena was a little lift of the clouds next morning, which gave me some of the finest passages about Mont Blanc I ever beheld; and then, weather continually worse till now. We have had two days' ceaseless rain, this, the third, hardly interrupted, and the lake right into the town.'

191. There was great joy in helping my mother from the door of the Cygne along a quarter of a mile of extempore plank bridge in the streets, and in writing a rhymed letter in description of the lifted lake and swirling Reuss, to little Louise Ellis (Mr Telford's niece, at this time one of the happy presences in Widmore), of which a line or two yet remain in my ears, about a market boat moored above the submerged quay—

'Full of mealy potatoes and marrowfat pease,
And honey, and butter, and Simmenthal cheese,
And a poor little calf, not at all at its ease,
Tied by the neck to a box at its knees.
Don't you agree with me, dear Louise,
It was unjustifiably cruel in
Them to have brought it in, all that squeeze
Over the lake from Fluelen?'

And so home, that year by Troyes, with my own calf's mind also little at its ease, under confused squeeze of Alps, clouds, and

---

[1] The rocks over which the Glacier des Bois descends, I meant.

architecture; yet finding room still in the waistcoat pocket for notes on the external tracery of St Urbain, which fixed that church for me as the highest type of Gothic construction, and took me off all Italian models for the next four years. The abstraction, however, though St Urbain began it, was not altogether that Saint's fault.

192. The press notices of my second volume had been either cautious or complimentary,—none, to the best of my memory, contemptuous. My friends took much pleasure in it, and the estimate formed of it in the old Scott and John Murray circle was shown by Lockhart's asking me that winter to review Lord Lindsay in the 'Quarterly.'* I was shy of doing this, being well aware that Lord Lindsay knew much more about Italian painting than I did; but I thought no one else likely to do it better, and had another motive to the business,—of an irresistible nature.

The little high-foreheaded Charlotte had by this time become a Scottish fairy, White Lady, and witch of the fatallest sort, looking as if she had just risen out of the stream in Rhymer's Glen, and could only be seen by favouring glance of moonlight over the Eildons. I used to see her, however, sometimes, by the dim lamplight of this world, at Lady Davy's,—Sir Humphrey's widow,—whose receptions in Park Street gathered usually, with others, the literary and scientific men who had once known Abbotsford. But I never could contrive to come to any serious speech with her; and at last, with my usual wisdom in such matters, went away into Cumberland to recommend myself to her by writing a Quarterly Review.

193. I went in the early spring[1] to the Salutation at Ambleside, then yet a country village, and its inn a country inn. But there, whether it was the grilled salmon for breakfast, or too prolonged reflections on the Celestial Hierarchies,* I fell into a state of despondency till then unknown to me, and of which I knew not the like again till fourteen years afterwards. The whole morning was painfully spent in balancing phrases; and from my boat, in the afternoons on Windermere, it appeared to me that the water was leaden, and the hills were low. Lockhart, on the first reception of the laboured MS, asked me to cut out all my best bits, (just as Keble had done before with my prize poem). In both cases I submitted patiently to the loss of my feathers; but was seriously angry and disgusted when Lockhart also intimated to me that a sentence in which I had with perfect justice condemned Mr Gally Knight's representation 'out of his own head' of San Michele

---

[1] 1847.

at Lucca, could not—Mr Gally Knight being a *protégé* of Albemarle Street—appear in the 'Quarterly.' This first clear insight into the arts of bookselling and reviewing made me permanently distrustful of both trades; and hearing no word, neither, of Charlotte's taking the smallest interest in the celestial hierarchies, I returned to town in a temper and state of health in which my father and mother thought that once more the best place for me would be Leamington.

I thought so myself, too; and went penitently again to Jephson, who at once stopped the grilled salmon, and ordered salts and promenade, as before.

194. It chanced that at this time there was staying at Leamington, also under Jephson's care, the son of an old friend, perhaps flame, of my father's, Mrs Farquharson,—a youth now of some two or three-and-twenty, but who seemed to me older than myself, being already a man of some position and influence in Perthshire. A few years before he had come into possession, under trustees, of a large Highland estate, on the condition that he should change his name for that of Macdonald, (properly reduplicate,—Macdonald Macdonald,) considerable sums being reserved in the trustees' hands by the terms of the will, for the purchase of more land. At that time his properties were St Martin's near Perth, where his mother lived; Rossie Castle, above Montrose; another castle, with much rock and moor round it, name forgotten, just south of Schehallien; and a shooting-lodge, Crossmount, at the foot of Schehallien, between Lochs Rannoch and Tummel. The young Macdonald had come to see us once or twice with his mother, at Denmark Hill, and, partly I suppose at his mother's instigation, partly, the stars know how, took a true liking to me; which I could not but answer with surprised thankfulness. He was a thin, dark Highlander, with some expression of gloom on his features when at rest, but with quite the sweetest smile for his friends that I have ever seen, except in one friend of later years, of whom in his place.

He was zealous in the Scottish Evangelical Faith, and wholly true and upright in it, so far as any man can be true in any faith, who is bound by the laws, modes, and landed estates of this civilized world.

195. The thoughtful reader must have noted with some displeasure that I have scarcely, whether at college or at home, used the word 'friendship' with respect to any of my companions. The fact is, I am a little puzzled by the specialty and singularity of poetical and classic friendship. I get, distinctively, attached to places, to pictures, to dogs, cats, and girls: but I have had, Heaven be thanked, many and true friends, young and old, who have been of boundless help and good to

me,—nor I quite helpless to them; yet for none of whom have I ever obeyed George Herbert's mandate, 'Thy friend put in thy bosom; wear his eyes, still in thy heart, that he may see what's there; if cause require, thou art his sacrifice,'* etc. Without thinking myself particularly wicked, I found nothing in my heart that seemed to me worth anybody's seeing; nor had I any curiosity for insight into those of others; nor had I any notion of being a sacrifice for them, or the least wish that they should exercise for my good any but their most pleasurable accomplishments,—Dawtrey Drewitt, for instance, being farther endeared because he could stand on his head, and catch vipers by the tail; Gershom Collingwood because he could sing French songs about the Earthly Paradise; and Alic Wedderburn, because he could swim into tarns and fetch out water-lilies for me, like a water-spaniel.* And I never expected that they should care much for *me*, but only that they should read my books; and looking back, I believe they liked and like me, nearly as well as if I hadn't written any.

196. First then, of this Love's Meinie of my own age, or under it, William Macdonald took to me; and got me to promise, that autumn, to come to him at Crossmount, where it was his evangelical duty to do some shooting in due season.*

I went into Scotland by Dunbar; saw again Loch Leven, Glen Farg, Rose Terrace, and the Inch of Perth; and went on, pensive enough, by Killiecrankie, to the clump of pines which sheltered my friend's lodge from the four winds of the wilderness.

After once walking up Schehallien with him and his keepers, with such entertainment as I could find in the mewing and shrieking of some seventy or eighty grey hares, who were brought down in bags and given to the poorer tenantry; and forming final opinion that the poorer tenantry might better have been permitted to find the stock of their hare-soup for themselves, I forswore further fashionable amusement, and set myself, when the days were fine, to the laborious eradication of a crop of thistles, which had been too successfully grown by northern agriculture in one of the best bits of unboggy ground by the Tummel.

197. I have carelessly omitted noticing till now, that the ambitions in practical gardening, of which the germs, as aforesaid, had been blighted at Herne Hill, nevertheless still prevailed over the contemplative philosophy in me so far as to rekindle the original instinct of liking to dig a hole, whenever I got leave. Sometimes, in the kitchen garden of Denmark Hill, the hole became a useful furrow; but when once the potatoes and beans were set, I got no outlet nor inlet for my excavatory fancy or skill during the rest of the year. The thistle-field at Crossmount

was an inheritance of amethystine treasure to me; and the working
hours in it are among the few in my life which I remember with entire
serenity—as being certain I could have spent them no better. For I had
wise—though I say it—thoughts in them, too many to set down here
(they are scattered afterwards up and down in 'Fors' and 'Munera
Pulveris'*), and wholesome sleep after them, in spite of the owls, who
were many, in the clumps of pine by Tummel shore.

Mostly a quiet stream there, through the bogs, with only a bit of step
or tumble a foot or two high on occasion; above which I was able practically to ascertain for myself the exact power of level water in a current
at the top of a fall. I need not say that on the Cumberland and Swiss
lakes, and within and without the Lido, I had learned by this time how
to manage a boat—an extremely different thing, be it observed, from
steering one in a race; and the little two-foot steps of Tummel were,
for scientific purposes, as good as falls twenty or two hundred feet
high. I found that I could put the stern of my boat full six inches into
the air over the top of one of these little falls, and hold it there, with
very short sculls, against the *level*[1] stream, with perfect ease for any
time I liked; and any child of ten years old may do the same. The nonsense written about the terror of feeling streams quicken as they
approach a mill weir is in a high degree dangerous, in making giddy
water parties lose their presence of mind if any such chance take them
unawares. And (to get this needful bit of brag, and others connected
with it, out of the way at once), I have to say that half my power of
ascertaining facts of any kind connected with the arts, is in my stern
habit of doing the thing with my own hands till I know its difficulty;
and though I have no time nor wish to acquire showy skill in anything,
I make myself clear as to what the skill means, and is. Thus, when I had
to direct road-making at Oxford,* I sate, myself, with an iron-masked
stone-breaker, on his heap, to break stones beside the London road,
just under Iffley Hill, till I knew how to advise my too impetuous pupils
to effect their purposes in that matter, instead of breaking the heads of
their hammers off, (a serious item in our daily expenses). I learned
from an Irish street crossings-sweeper what he could teach me of sweeping; but found myself in that matter nearly his match, from my boy-
gardening; and again and again I swept bits of St Giles' foot-pavements,*
showing my corps of subordinates how to finish into depths of gutter.
I worked with a carpenter until I could take an even shaving six feet
long off a board; and painted enough with properly and delightfully

---

[1] Distinguish carefully between this and a sloping rapid.

soppy green paint to feel the master's superiority in the use of a blunt brush. But among all these and other such studentships, the reader will be surprised, I think, to hear, seriously, that the instrument I finally decided to be the most difficult of management was the trowel. For accumulated months of my boy's life I watched bricklaying and paving;[1] but when I took the trowel into my own hand, abandoned at once all hope of attaining the least real skill with it, unless I gave up all thoughts of any future literary or political career. But the quite happiest bit of manual work I ever did was for my mother in the old inn at Sixt,* where she alleged the stone staircase to have become unpleasantly dirty, since last year. Nobody in the inn appearing to think it possible to wash it, I brought the necessary buckets of water from the yard myself, poured them into beautiful image of Versailles waterworks down the fifteen or twenty steps of the great staircase, and with the strongest broom I could find, cleaned every step into its corners. It was quite lovely work to dash the water and drive the mud, from each, with accumulating splash down to the next one.

198. I must return for a moment to the clumps of pine at Crossmount, and their company of owls, because—whatever wise people may say of them—I at least myself have found the owl's cry always prophetic of mischief to me; and though I got wiser, as aforesaid, in my field of thistles, yet the Scottish Athena put on against me at that time her closed visor (not that Greek helmets ever have a visor, but when Athena* hides her face, she throws her casque forward and down, and only looks through the oval apertures of it). Her adversity to me at this time was shown by my loss of Miss Lockhart, whom I saw for the last time at one of Lady Davy's dinners, where Mr Hope Scott took the foot of the table. Lady Davy had given me Miss Lockhart to take down, but I found she didn't care for a word I said; and Mr Gladstone was on the other side of her—and the precious moments were all thrown away in quarrelling across her, with him, about Neapolitan prisons.[2] He couldn't see, as I did, that the real prisoners were the people outside.

199. Meantime, restraining the ideals and assuaging the disappointments of my outer-world life, the homework went on with entirely useful steadiness. The admiration of tree-branches taught me

---

[1] Of our paviour friends, Mr and Mrs Duprez (*we* always spelt and pronounced Depree), of Langley, near Slough, and Gray's Inn (pronounced Grazen) Lane, in London (see the seventh number of 'Dilecta').* The laying of the proper quantity of sand under the pavement stones being a piece of trowel-handling as subtle as spreading the mortar under a brick.

[2] See above p. 184.

at Fontainebleau, led me now into careful discernment of their species; and while my father, as was his custom, read to my mother and me for half-an-hour after breakfast, I always had a fresh-gathered outer spray of a tree before me, of which the mode of growth, with a single leaf full size, had to be done at that sitting in fine pen outline, filled with the simple colour of the leaf at one wash. On fine days, when the grass was dry, I used to lie down on it and draw the blades as they grew, with the ground herbage of buttercup or hawkweed mixed among them, until every square foot of meadow, or mossy bank, became an infinite picture and possession to me, and the grace and adjustment to each other of growing leaves, a subject of more curious interest to me than the composition of any painter's master-piece. The love of complexity and quantity before noticed as influencing my preference of flamboyant to purer architecture, was here satisfied, without qualifying sense of wasted labour, by what I felt to be the constant working of Omnipotent kindness in the fabric of the food-giving tissues of the earth; nor less, morning after morning, did I rejoice in the traceries and the painted glass of the sky at sunrise.

This physical study had, I find, since 1842, when it began, advanced in skill until now in 1847, at Leamington, it had proceeded into botanical detail; and the collection of material for 'Proserpina' began then, singularly, with the analysis of a thistle-top, as the foundation of all my political economy was dug down to, through the thistle-field of Crossmount.

200. 'Analysis' of thistle-top, I say; not 'dissection,' nor microscopic poring into.

Flowers, like everything else that is lovely in the visible world, are only to be seen rightly with the eyes which the God who made them gave us; and neither with microscopes nor spectacles. These have their uses for the curious and the aged; as stilts and crutches have for people who want to walk in mud, or cannot safely walk but on three legs anywhere. But in health of mind and body, men should see with their own eyes, hear and speak without trumpets, walk on their feet, not on wheels, and work and war with their arms, not with engine-beams, nor rifles warranted to kill twenty men at a shot before you can see them. The use of the great mechanical powers may indeed sometimes be compatible with the due exercise of our own; but the use of instruments for exaggerating the powers of sight necessarily deprives us of the best pleasures of sight. A flower is to be watched as it grows, in its association with the earth, the air, and the dew; its leaves are to be seen as they expand in sunshine; its colours, as they embroider the field, or illumine the forest. Dissect or magnify them, and all you discover or learn at last will be that oaks, roses, and daisies, are all made of fibres and bubbles; and these again, of charcoal and water; but, for all their peeping and probing, nobody knows how.

201. And far more difficult work than this was on foot in other directions. Too sorrowfully it had now become plain to me that neither George Herbert, nor Richard Hooker, nor Henry Melvill, nor Thomas Dale, nor the Dean of Christ Church, nor the Bishop of Oxford, could in anywise explain to me what Turner meant by the contest of Apollo with the Python, or by the repose of the great dragon above the Garden of the Hesperides.*

For such nearer Python, as might wreathe itself against my own now gathering strength,—for such serpent of Eternity as might reveal its awe to me amidst the sands even of Forest Hill or Addington Heath, I was yet wholly unprepared.

All that I had been taught had to be questioned; all that I had trusted, proved. I cannot enter yet into any account of this trial; but the following fragment* of 1847 diary will inform the reader enough of the courses of thought which I was being led into beside the lilies of Avon, and under the mounds, that were once the walls, of Kenilworth.

202. 'It was cold and dark and gusty and raining by fits, at two o'clock to-day, and until four; but I went out, determined to have my walk, get wet or no.

'I took the road to the village where I had been the first day with Macdonald, and about a mile and a half out, I was driven by the rain into a little cottage, remarkable outside for two of the most noble groups of hollyhocks I ever saw—one rose-colour passing into purple, and the other rich purple and opposed by a beautiful sulphur yellow one. It was about a quarter to five, and they (the woman and her mother) were taking their tea (pretty strong, and without milk) and white bread. Round the room were hung several prints of the Crucifixion, and some Old Testament subjects, and two bits of tolerable miniature; one in what I thought at first was an uniform, but it was the footman's dress of the woman's second son, who is with a master in Leamington; the other a portrait of a more distingué-looking personage, who, I found on inquiry, was the eldest son, cook in the Bush inn at Carlisle. Inquiring about the clergyman of the village, the woman—whose name, I found, was Sabina—said they had lost their best earthly friend, the late clergyman, a Mr Waller, I think, who had been with them upwards of eleven years, and had got them into that cottage; her husband having been in his service, and he fretted himself, she said, too much, about getting them into it, and never lived to see them in it after all, dying of decline in London. She spoke of him with tears in her eyes. I looked at the books lying on the table, well used all of them, and found three Bibles, three Prayer Books, a treatise on practical Christianity, another on seriousness in religion, and Baxter's "Saint's Rest."* I asked her if they read no books but religious ones. "No, sir; I should be very sorry if there were any others in my house," said she. As I took up the largest Bible, she said "it was a nice print, but sadly tattered; she wished she could get it bound." This I promised to get done for her, and left her much pleased.

'It had rained hard while I stayed in the cottage, but had ceased when I went on, and presently appeared such a bright bar of streaky sky in the west, seen over the glittering hedges, as made my heart leap again, it put so much of old feelings into me of far-away hills and fountains of morning light; and the sun came out presently, and every shake of the trees shook down more light upon the grass. And so I came to the village and stood leaning on the churchyard gate, looking at the sheep nibbling and resting among the graves (newly watered they lay, and fresh, like a field of precious seed). One narrow stream of light ran in ups and downs across them, but the shadow of the church fell over most—the pretty little grey church, now one dark mass against the intense golden glittering sky; and to make it sweeter still, the church-yard itself rose steeply, so that its own grand line came against this same light at last.'

CHAPTER XI

L'HOTEL DU MONT BLANC

203. THE little inn at Samoens, where I washed the stairs down for my mother,[1] was just behind the group of houses of which I gave a carefully coloured sketch to Mrs John Simon, who, in my mother's old age, was her most deeply trusted friend. She, with her husband, love Savoy even more than I; were kinder to Joseph Couttet to the last, and are so still to his daughter Judith.

The Samoens inn was, however, a too unfavourable type of the things which—in *my* good old times—one had sometimes to put up

---

[1] 'I have myself washed a flight of stone stairs all down, with bucket and broom, in a Savoy Inn, where they hadn't washed their stairs since they first went up them; and I never made a better sketch than that afternoon.' (Ses. and Lil., § 138.)

with, and rather liked having to put up with, in Savoy. The central example of the sort of house one went there to live in, was the Hotel du Mont Blanc at St Martin's; to me, certainly, of all my inn homes, the most eventful, pathetic, and sacred. How to begin speaking of it, I do not know; still less how to end; but here are three entries, consecutive, in my diary of 1849, which may lead me a little on my way.

204. 'St Martin's, evening, July 11th. What a strange contrast there is between these lower valleys, with their over-wrought richness mixed with signs of waste and disease, their wild noon-winds shaking their leaves into palsy, and the dark storms folding themselves about their steep mural precipices,—between these and the pastoral green, pure aiguilles, and fleecy rain-clouds of Chamouni; yet nothing could be more divine than (to-day) the great valley of level cornfield; half, smooth close to the ground, yet yellow and warm with stubble; half, laden with sheaves; the vines in massy green above, with Indian corn, and the rich brown and white cottages (in midst of them).

'July 13th. I walked with my father last night up to the vine-covered cottages under the Aiguille de Varens.

'July 15th, Samoens. We had a stony road to traverse in chars from St Martin's yesterday, and a hot walk this morning over the ground between this (Samoens) and Sixt.* As I passed through the corn-fields, I found they gave me a pleasant feeling by reminding me of Leamington.'

'We' in this entry means only my father and mother and I; poor Mary was with us no more. She had got married, as girls always will,—the foolish creatures!—however happy they might be at home, or abroad, with their own people.

Mary heartily loved her aunt and uncle, by this time, and was sorry to leave them: yet she must needs marry her brother-in-law,* a good, quiet London solicitor, and was now deep in household cares in a dull street, Pimlico way, when she might have been gaily helping me to sweep the stairs at Samoens, and gather bluets[1] in those Leamington-like cornfields.

205. The sentence about 'noon-wind' refers to a character of the great valleys on the north of the main Alpine chain, which curiously separates them from those of the Italian side. These great northern valleys are, in the main, four,—those of the Rhine (the Grisons), of the Reuss (Canton Uri), of the Rhone (Canton Valais), and the Arve

---

[1] The blue centaury-like five gentians in a level cluster. Among the corn, it teaches, like the poppy, that everything isn't meant to be eaten.

(Faucigny),—all of them in ordinarily fine summer weather oppressed by quiet heat in the early part of the day, then burst in upon, by wild wind blowing up the valley about noon, or later; a diurnal storm which raises the dust in whirlwinds, and wholly prevents the growth of trees in any beautiful forms, their branches being daily tormented into every irregular and fretful curve they can be strained to, and their leaves wrung round on the stalks, so that half their vitality is torn out of them.

Strangely, and, so far as I know, without notice by scientific men of the difference, the Italian valleys are, in the greater number of them, redeemed from this calamitous law. I have not lately been in either Val d'Aosta, or the Valtelline, nor ever stayed in the upper valley of the Adige; but neither in the Val Anzasca, the Val Formazza, the Val d'Isella, or the southern St Gothard, is there any trace of the action of malignant wind like this northern one, which I suppose to be, in the essence of it, the summer form of the bise. It arises, too fatally, punctual to the noon, in the brightest days of spring all over western Savoy.

Be that as it may, in the fields neighbouring the two villages which mark the eastern and western extremities of the chain of Mont Blanc,—Sallenches, namely, and Martigny, where I have passed many of the most serviceable days of my life,—this noon wind, associated with inundation, is one of the chief agents in producing the character of the whole scene, and in forming the tempers of the inhabitants. Very early my mind became fixed on this their physical distress, issuing finally not in the distortion of growing trees only, but in abortion of human form and mind, while yet the roots of beauty and virtue remained always of the same strength in the race; so that, however decimated by cretinism,* the Savoyard and Valaisan retain to this day their vigorous personal character, wherever the conditions of ordinary health are observed for them.

206. So earnestly was my heart set on discovering and contending with the neglect and error which were the causes of so great evil to so noble a people, that—I must here anticipate the progress of many years—I was in treaty again and again for pieces of land near the chain of Mont Blanc on which I thought to establish my life, and round which to direct its best energies. I first actually bought the piece of meadow in Chamouni above the chalets of Blaitiere; but sold it on perceiving what ruin was inevitable in the valley after it became a tourist rendezvous. Next, I entered into treaty with the Commune of Bonneville for the purchase of the whole top of the Brezon; but this negotiation came to nothing, because the Commune, unable to see why

anybody should want to buy a waste of barren rock, with pasturage only for a few goats in the summer, concluded that I had found a gold mine or a coal-bed in it, and raised their price on me till I left the Brezon on their hands: (Osborne Gordon having also walked up with me to my proposed hermitage, and, with his usual sagacity, calculated the daily expense of getting anything to eat, up those 4,000 feet from the plain).

207. Next, I was tempted by a grand, fourteenth century, square-set castle, with walls six feet thick, and four round towers, cone-roofed, at the angles, on the west bank of the Arve, below La Roche: but this baronial residence having been for many years used by the farmer to whom it belonged for his fruit store, and the three floors of it only accessible by ladders through trap doors in them, and soaked through with the juice of rotten apples and plums;—so that the most feasible way of making the place habitable would have been to set fire to the whole, and refit the old masonry with an inner lodging of new wood,—(which might as well have been built inside a mountain cave at once as within those six-feet thick of cemented rock,)—I abandoned also the idea of this gloomy magnificence, and remained fancy-free till 1870, when I again was about to enter into treaty for a farm two thousand feet above Martigny, on the ridge separating the Forclaz from the glen of the Trient, and commanding view of the whole valley of the Rhone, westward to Sierre, and northward to Bex. Design ended by my illness at Matlock,* and following sorrow; of which in their due time.

Up to the year with which I am now concerned, however, 1849, when I was just thirty, no plans of this sort had dawned on me: but the journeying of the year, mostly alone, by the Allée Blanche and Col de Ferret round Mont Blanc and then to Zermatt, for the work chiefly necessary to the fourth volume of 'Modern Painters,' gave me the melancholy knowledge of the agricultural condition of the great Alpine chain which was the origin of the design of St George's Guild; and that walk with my father* at St Martin's' virtually closed the days of youthful happiness, and began my true work in the world—for what it is worth.

208. An entry or two from the beginning of the year may be permitted, connecting old times with new.

'April 15th, Wednesday.* Left home, stayed at Folkestone, happy, but with bad cough, and slight feverish feeling, till Monday. Crossed to Boulogne, with desperate cold coming on. Wrote half letter to Miss Wedderburn,' (afterwards Mrs Blackburn,) 'in carriage, going over:' the carriages, of course, in old times being lashed on the deck, one sat inside, either for dignity or shelter.

'April 24th, Tuesday. To Paris on rail. Next morning, very thankfully changing horses, by as lovely sunshine as ever I saw, at Charenton. Slept at Sens. Thursday, Mont-bard; Friday, Dijon. All these evenings I was working hard at my last plate of Giotto.' (G.'s tower, I meant; frontispiece to 'Seven Lamps,' first edition.)

'Stopped behind in the lovely morning at Sens, and went after my father and mother an hour later.[1] It was very cold, and I was driven out by the fires going out, it being in the large room at the back of the yard, with oil pictures only to be got at through my father's bedroom.[2]

'April 29th, Sunday, was a threatening day at Champagnole. We just walked to the entrance of the wood and back,—I colded and coughing, and generally headachy. In the evening the landlady, who noticed my illness, made me some syrup of violets. Whether by fancy, or chance, or by virtue of violet tea, I got better thenceforward, and have, thank God, had no cold since!' (Diary very slovenly hereabouts; I am obliged to mend a phrase or two.)

209. 'Monday, 30th April. To Geneva, through a good deal of snow, by St Cergues; which frightened my mother, they having a restive horse in their carriage. She got out on a bank near where I saw the first gentians, and got into mine, as far as St Cergues.' (It is deserving of record that at this time just on the point of coming in sight of the Alps—and that for the first time for three years, a moment which I had looked forward to thinking I should be almost fainting with joy, and want to lie down on the earth and take it in my arms;—at this time, I say, I was irrecoverably sulky because George had not got me butter to my bread at Les Rousses.)

'Tuesday, 1st May. Walked about Geneva, went to Bauttes', and drew wood anemones.

'Thursday, 3rd May, Chambery. Up the hill that looks towards Aix, with my father and mother; had a chat with an old man, a proprietor of some land on the hillside, who complained bitterly that the priests and the revenue officers seized everything, and that nothing but black bread was left for the peasant.[3]

'Friday, 4th May. Half breakfasted at Chambery; started about seven

---

[1] They had given me a little brougham to myself, like the hunting doctor's in 'Punch,'* so that I could stop behind, and catch them up when I chose.

[2] The inn is fully and exquisitely described by Dickens in 'Mrs Lirriper's Lodgings.'*

[3] Complaints of this kind always mean that you are near a luxurious capital or town. In this case, Aix les Bains.

for St Laurent du Pont, thence up to the Chartreuse, and walked down (all of us); which, however, being done in a hurry, I little enjoyed. But a walk after dinner up to a small chapel, placed on a waving group of mounds, covered with the most smooth and soft sward, over whose sunny gold came the dark piny precipices of the Chartreuse hills, gave me infinite pleasure. I had seen also for the third time, by the Chartreuse torrent, the most wonderful of all Alpine birds—a grey, fluttering stealthy creature, about the size of a sparrow, but of colder grey, and more graceful, which haunts the sides of the fiercest torrents. There is something more strange in it than in the seagull—*that* seems a powerful creature; and the power of the sea, not of a kind so adverse, so hopelessly destructive; but this small creature, silent, tender and light, almost like a moth in its low and irregular flight,—almost touching with its wings the crests of waves that would overthrow a granite wall, and haunting the hollows of the black, cold, herbless rocks that are continually shaken by their spray, has perhaps the nearest approach to the look of a spiritual existence I know in animal life.*

'210. Saturday, May 5th. Back to Chambery, and up by Rousseau's house to the point where the thunder-shower came down on us three years ago.'

I think it was extremely pretty and free-hearted of my mother to make these reverent pilgrimages to Rousseau's house.[1]

With whom I must here thankfully name, among my own masters, also St Pierre. I having shamefully forgotten hitherto the immense influence of 'Paul and Virginia'* amidst my early readings. Rousseau's effective political power I did not know till much later.

211. Richard Fall arrived that Saturday at Chambery; and by way of amends for our lost Welsh tour, (above, p. 190,) I took him to Vevay and Chamouni, where, on May 14th, the snow was still down to the valley; crisp frost everywhere; the Montanvert path entirely hidden, and clear slopes down all the couloirs* perfectly even and smooth—ten to twenty feet deep of good, compact snow; no treacherous surface beds that could slip one over the other.

Couttet and I took Richard up to the cabane* of the Montanvert, memory of the long snow walks at Herne Hill now mingling tenderly

---

[1] 'Les Charmettes.' So also 'un détachement de la troupe' (of his schoolboys) 'sous la conduite de Mr Topffer, qui ne sait pas le chemin, entreprend de gravir le coteau des Charmettes, pour atteindre à l'habitation de Jean-Jacques Rousseau'*—in the year 1833; and an admirably faithful and vivid drawing of the place, as it then stood (unchanged till 1849, when papa and mamma and their little St Preux* saw it), is given by Mr Topffer's own hand on p. 17 of his work here quoted, 'Voyage à la Grande Chartreuse' (1833).

with the cloudless brightness of the Mer de Glace, in its robe of winter ermine. No venturing on that, however, of course, with every crevasse hidden; and nobody at the cabane yet, so we took Richard back to the first couloir, showed him how to use foot and pole, to check himself if he went too fast, or got head-foremost; and we slid down the two thousand feet to the source of the Arveron, in some seven or eight minutes;[1] Richard vouchsafing his entire approval of that manner of progression by the single significant epithet, 'Pernicious!'

It was the last of our winter walks together. Richard did not die, like Charles,* but he went on the Stock Exchange; married a wife, very nice and pretty; then grew rich; held a rich man's faiths in political economy; and bought bad prints of clipper packets in green sea; and so we gradually gave each other up—with all good wishes on both sides. But Richard, having no more winter walks, became too fat and well liking when he was past fifty—and *did* die, then; to his sister's great surprise and mine. The loss of him broke her heart, and she soon followed him.

212. During her forty-five or fifty years of life,* Eliza Fall (had she but been named Elizabeth instead, I should have liked her ever so much better,) remained an entirely worthy and unworldly girl and woman, of true service and counsel always to her brother and me; caring for us both much more than she was cared for;—to my mother an affectionate and always acceptable, calling and chatting, friend: capable and intelligent from her earliest youth, nor without graceful fancy and rational poetic power. She wrote far better verses than ever I did, and might have drawn well, but had always what my mother called 'perjinketty'* ways, which made her typically an old maid in later years. I imagine that, without the least unkind severity, she was yet much of a Puritan at heart, and one rarely heard if ever, of her going to a theatre, or a rout, or a cricket-match; yet she was brilliant at a Christmas party, acted any part—that depended on whalebone—admirably, and was extremely witty in a charade. She felt herself sorrowfully turned out of her own house and place when her brother married, and spent most of her summers in travel with another wise old maid for companion. Then Richard and his wife went to live in Clapham Park; and Eliza stayed, wistfully alone, in her child's home, for a while. The lease expired, I suppose, and she did not care to renew it. The last time I saw her, she was enjoying some sort of town life in New Bond Street.

---

[1] Including ecstatic or contemplative rests: of course one goes much faster than 200 feet a minute, on good snow, at an angle of 30°.

Little I thought, in clasping Richard's hand on the ridge of the Jaman that spring,—he going down into the Simmenthal, I back to Vevay,—that our companying together was ended: but I never have known anything of what was most seriously happening to me till afterwards; this—unastrological readers will please to note—being one of the leaden influences on me of the planet Saturn.*

213. My father and mother were waiting for me at Geneva, and we set out, with short delay, for St Martin's.

The road from Geneva to Chamouni, passing the extremity of the Salève about five miles south of the city, reaches at that point the sandy plateau of Annemasse, where forms of passport had (anciently) to be transacted, which gave a quarter of an hour for contemplation of what the day had to do.

From the street of the straggling village one saw over the undulations of the nearer, and blue level of the distant, plain, a mass of rocky mountains, presenting for the most part their cliffs to the approaching traveller, and tossing their crests back in careless pride, above the district of well inhabited, but seldom traversed, ravines which wind between the lake of Annecy and vale of Sallenches.

Of these the nearest—yet about twelve miles distant—is the before-named Brezon, a majestic, but unterrific, fortalice* of cliff, forest, and meadow, with unseen nests of village, and unexpected balm and honey of garden and orchard nursed in its recesses. The horses have to rest at Bonneville before we reach the foot of it; and the line, of its foundation first, and then of the loftier Mont Vergy, must be followed for seven or eight miles, without hope apparently of gaining access to the inner mountain world, except by footpath.

214. A way is opened at last by the Arve, which, rushing furiously through a cleft affording room only for road and river, grants entrance, when the strait is passed, to a valley without the like of it among the Alps. In all other avenues of approach to their central crests the torrents fall steeply, and in places appear to be still cutting their channels deeper, while their lateral cliffs have evidently been in earlier time, at intervals, connected, and rent or worn asunder by traceable violence or decay. But the valley of Cluse is in reality a narrow plain between two chains of mountains which have never been united, but each independently[1] raised, shattered, and softened into their present forms; while the river, instead of deepening the ravine it descends, has filled it to an

[1] In the same epoch of time, however. See Mr Collingwood's 'Limestone Alps of Savoy.'

unknown depth with beds of glacial sand, increased annually, though insensibly, by its wandering floods; but now practically level, and for the most part tenable, with a little logwork to fence off the stream at its angles, in large spaces of cultivable land.

In several turns of the valley the lateral cliffs go plumb down into these fields as if into a green lake; but usually, slopes of shale, now forest-hidden, ascend to heights of six or seven hundred feet before the cliffs begin; then the mountain above becomes partly a fortress wall, partly banks of turf ascending around its bastions or between but always guarded from avalanche by higher woods or rocks; the snows melting in early spring, and falling in countless cascades, mostly, over the cliffs, and then in broken threads down the banks. Beautiful always, and innocent, the higher summits by midsummer are snowless, and no glacial moraine or torrent defaces or disturbs the solitude of their pastoral kingdom.

Leaving the carriage at Cluse, I always used to walk, through this valley, the ten miles to St Martin's, resting awhile at the springs of Maglan, where, close under the cliff, the water thrills imperceptibly through the crannies of its fallen stones, deeper and deeper every instant; till, within three fathoms of its first trickling thread, it is a deep stream of dazzling brightness, dividing into swift branches eager for their work at the mill, or their ministry to the meadows.

Contrary again to the customs of less enchanted vales, this one opens gradually as it nears the greater mountain, its own lateral cliffs rising also in proportion to its width—those on the left, as one approaches St Martin's, into the vast towers and promontories of the Aiguille de Varens; those on the right into a mountain scarcely marked in any Alpine chart, yet from which, if one could climb its dangerous turf and mural diadem, there must be commanded precisely the most noble view of Mont Blanc granted by any summit of his sentinel chains.

215. In the only map of Switzerland which has ever been executed with common sense and intelligence ('Original von Keller's Zweiter Reisekarte der Schweitz,' 1844), this peak is, nevertheless, left without distinction from that called the 'Croix de Fer,' of which it is only a satellite. But there are any quantity of iron crosses on the Western Alps, and the proper name of this dominant peak is that given in M. Dajoz's lithographed 'Carte des rives du Lac de Genève,'[1]—'Mont Fleury';

---

[1] Chez Briquet et Fils, éditeurs, au bas de la Cité à Genève, 1860; extremely careful in its delineation of the lower mountain masses, and on the whole the best existing map for the ordinary traveller. The Alpine Club maps give nothing clearly but the taverns and footpaths.

though the more usual one with the old Chamouni guides was 'Montagne des Fours'; but I never heard any name given to its castellated outwork. In Studer's geological map* it is well drawn, but nameless; in the Alpine Club's map of South-Western Alps, it is only a long ridge descending from the Mont Fleury, which, there called 'Pointe Percée,' bears a star, indicating a view of Mont Blanc, as probably of Geneva also, from that summit. But the vision from the lower promontory, which commands the Chamouni aiguilles with less foreshortening, and looks steep down into the valley of Cluse from end to end, must be infinitely more beautiful.

216. Its highest ridge is just opposite the Nant d'Arpenaz, and might in future descriptions of the Sallenche mountains be conveniently called the 'Tower of Arpenaz.' After passing the curved rock from which the waterfall leaps into its calm festoons, the cliffs become changed in material, first into thin-bedded blue limestone and then into dark slates and shales, which partly sadden, partly enrich, with their cultivable ruin, all the lower hill-sides henceforward to the very gate of Chamouni. A mile or two beyond the Nant d'Arpenaz, the road ascends over a bank of their crumbling flakes, which the little stream, pendent like a white thread over the mid-cliff of the Aiguille de Varens, drifts down before it in summer rain, lightly as dead leaves. The old people's carriage dips into the trough of the dry bed, descends the gentle embankment on the other side, and turns into the courtyard of the inn under one of the thin arches, raised a foot or two above the gap in the wall, which give honourable distinction either to the greater vineyards or open courts, like this one, of hospitable houses. Stableyard, I should have said, not courtyard; no palatial pride of seclusion, like M. Dessein's, but a mere square of irregular stable,—not even coach-house, though with room for a carriage or two: but built only for shelter of the now unknown char-à-banc,* seat for three between two pairs of wheels, with a plank for footing, at a convenient step from the ground. The fourth side of the yard was formed by the front of the inn, which stood with its side to the road, its back to the neglected garden and incorrigible streamlet: a two-storied building of solid grey stone, with gabled roof and garrets; a central passage on the second floor giving access to the three or four bedrooms looking to back and front, and at the end to an open gallery over the road. The last room on the left, larger than the rest, and with a window opening on the gallery, used to be my father's and mother's; that next it, with one square window in the solid wall, looking into the yard, mine. Floors and partitions all of rough-sawn larch; the planks of the passage floor uncomfortably thin

and bending, as if one might easily fall through; some pretence of papering, I think, in the old people's state room. A public room, about the size of my present study, say twelve paces by six within its cupboards, and usually full of flies, gave us the end of its table for meals, and was undisturbed through the day, except during the hour when the diligence dined.

217. I should have said that my square window looked *over*, rather than *into* the yard, for one could scarcely see anything going on there, but by putting one's head out: the real and prevalent prospect was first into the leaves of the walnut tree in the corner; then of the mossy stable roofs behind them; then of the delicately tin-mailed and glittering spire of the village church; and beyond these, the creamy, curdling, overflowing seas of snow on the Mont Blanc de St Gervais. The Aiguille de Bionnassay, the most graceful buttress ridge in all the Alps, and Mont Blanc himself, above the full fronts of the Aiguille and Dome du Gouté, followed further to the left. So much came into the field of that little four-feet-square casement.

If one had a mind for a stroll, in half a minute's turn to the left from the yard gate, one came to the aforesaid village church, the size of a couple of cottages, and one could lean, stooping, to look at it, on the deeply lichened stones of its low churchyard wall, which enclosed the cluster of iron crosses,—floretted with everlastings, or garlands of fresh flowers if it was just after Sunday,—on two sides; the cart-path to the upper village branching off round it from the road to Chamouni. Fifty yards further, one came to the single-arched bridge by which the road to Sallenche, again dividing from that of Chamouni, crosses the Arve, clearing some sixty feet of strongly-rushing water with a leap of lovely elliptic curve; lovely, because here traced with the lightest possible substance of masonry, rising to its ridge without a pebble's weight to spare,[1] and then signed for sacred pontifical work by a cross high above the parapet, seen from as far as one can see the bridge itself.

218. Neither line, nor word, nor colour, has ever yet given rendering of the rich confusions of garden and cottage through which the winding paths ascend above the church; walled, not with any notion of guarding the ground, except from passing herds of cattle and goats, but chiefly to get the stones off the surface into narrowest compass, and, with the easy principle of horticulture,—plant everything, and let what can, grow;—the under-crops of unkempt pease, potatoes, cabbage,

---

[1] Of course, in modern levelled bridges, with any quantity of overcharged masonry, the opening for the stream is not essentially an arch, but a tunnel, and might for that matter be blown through the solid wall, instead of built to bear it.

hemp, and maize, content with what sun can get down to them through luxuriantly-branched apple and plum trees, and towering shade of walnuts, with trunks eight or ten feet in girth; a little space left to light the fronts of the cottages themselves, whose roof and balconies, the vines seem to think, have been constructed for their pleasure only, and climb, wreathe, and swing themselves about accordingly wherever they choose, tossing their young tendrils far up into the blue sky of spring, and festooning the balconies in autumn with Correggian* fresco of purple, relieved against the pendent gold of the harvested maize.

The absolute seclusion and independence of this manner of rural life, totally without thought or forethought of any foreign help or parsimonious store, drinking its wine out of the cluster, and saving of the last year's harvest only seed for the next,—the serene laissez faire* given to God and nature, with thanks for the good, and submission to the temporary evil of blight or flood, as due to sinful mortality; and the persistence, through better or worse, in their fathers' ways, and use of their fathers' tools, and holding to their fathers' names and fields, faithfully as the trees to their roots, or the rocks to their wild flowers—all this beside us for our Sunday walk, with the grey, inaccessible walls of the Tower of Arpenaz above, dim in their distant height, and all the morning air twice brighter for the glow of the cloudless glaciers, gave me deeper and more wonderful joy than all the careful beauty and disciplined Tightness of the Bernese Oberland, or even the stately streets of my dearest cities of Italy.

219. Here is a little bit of diary, five years later, giving a detail or two of the opposite hillside above Sallenche.

'St Martin's, 26th July, 1854.'* I was up by the millstream this evening, and climbed to the right of it, up among the sloping waves of grass. I never was so struck by their intense beauty,—the masses of walnut shading them with their broad, cool, clearly-formed leafage; the glossy grey stems of the cherry trees, as if bound round tight with satin, twining and writhing against the shadows; the tall pollards of oak set here and there in the soft banks, as if to show their smoothness by contrast, yet themselves beautiful, rugged, and covered with deep brown and bright silver moss. Here and there a chestnut—sharp, and soft, and starry;[1] and always the steep banks, one above another, melting[2] into terraces of pure velvet, gilded with corn; here and there a black jet-black—crag of slate breaking into a frown above them, and

---

[1] I meant—the leaves themselves, sharp, the clustered nuts, soft, the arrangement of leaves, starry.

[2] 'Melting'—seeming to flow into the levels like lava; not cut sharp down to them.

mouldering away down into the gloomy torrent bed, fringed on its opposite edge, a grisly cliff, with delicate birch and pine, rising against the snow light of Mont Blanc. And opposite always the mighty Varens lost in the cloud its ineffable walls of crag.'

220. The next following entry is worth keeping, as a sketch of the undisturbed Catholicism among these hills since the days of St Bernard of Annecy, and Mont Velan.

'Sallenches, Sunday, 10th June (1849). The waitress here, a daughter of the landlord, asked me to-day whether Protestants all said grace before meat, observing me to do so. On this we got into conversation, out of which I have elicited some points worth remembering; to wit, that some of the men only go to confession once a year, and that some of them, to spare their memories, write their sins,—which, however, they cannot deliver on paper to the confessor, but must read them aloud. Louise appeared much horror-struck at the idea which such a procedure admits, of "losing one's sins;" and of their being found by some one who was not a confessor. She spoke with great pleasure of the Capucins,* who come sometimes; said they were such delightful confessors, and made "des morales superbes,"* and that they preached so well that everybody listened with all their might, so that you might tap them on the back and they would never turn round. Of the Jesuits she spoke with less affection, saying that in their great general confessions, which took several days, two or three commandments at a time, they would not allow a *single* sin to be committed by the persons coming to them in the meantime, or else they refused them absolution—refusal which takes place sometimes for less cause. They had a poor old servant, who could only speak patois; the priest couldn't understand her, nor she him, so that he could not find out whether she knew her catechism. He refused absolution, and the poor old creature wept and raved about it, and was in a passion with all the world. She was afterwards burnt in the great fire here! I went to mass, to hear how they preached: the people orderly, and church perfectly full. The sermon by a fat stuttering curé, was from the "Receive not the grace of God in vain," on the Sacraments. "Two of these called Sacramens des Morts, because they are received by persons in a state of spiritual death; the five others called Sacramens des Vivants, because they presume, in those who receive them, a state of spiritual life. The three sacraments of Baptism, Confirmation, and Orders, can only be received once; because they impress an indelible seal, and make men what they were not; and what, after they are once, they cannot unmake themselves. Baptism makes people children or subjects of God; Confirmation makes them soldiers of God, or soldiers of His Kingdom; and Orders make them magistrates of the Kingdom. If you have received baptism, you are therefore an 'enfan de Dieu.'"* What being an "enfan de Dieu" meant was not very clear; for the ineffaceability of baptism was illustrated by the instance of Julian the Apostate, who did all he could to efface it—"Mais la mort," said the preacher, growing eloquent, "le poursuivit jusqu'à"—(he stopped, for he did not know exactly where *to*)—"la tombe; et il est descendu aux enfers, portant cette marque, qui fera éternellement sa honte et sa confusion.""*

221. I wonder at the lightness of these entries, now; but I was too actively, happily, and selfishly busy, to be thoughtful, except only in scholarly way; but I got one of the sharpest warnings of my life only a day after leaving papa and mamma at St Martin's,—(cruel animal that I was!—to do geology in the Allée Blanche, and at Zermatt.) I got a chill by stopping, when I was hot, in the breeze of one of the ice streams, in ascending to the Col de Bon Homme; woke next morning in the châlet of Chapiù with acute sore throat; crossed the Col de la Seigne scarcely able to sit my mule, and was put to bed by Couttet in a little room under the tiles at Courmayeur, where he nursed me as he did at Padua; gave me hot herb-tea, and got me on muleback again, and over the Col de Ferret, in a day or two; but there were some hours of those feverish nights which ought to have made my diaries more earnest afterwards. They go off, however, into mere geology and school divinity* for a while, of which this bit, written the evening after crossing the Col de Ferret, is important as evidence of my beginning to recognise what James Forbes had proved of glacier flow:—

'The most magnificent piece of ruin I have yet seen in the Alps is that opposite the embouchure of the lower glacier of the Val de Ferret, near Courmayeur; the pines are small indeed, but they are hurled hither and thither, twisted and mingled in all conditions of form, and all phases of expiring life, with the chaos of massy rocks, which the glacier has gnashed down, or the opposite mountain hurled. And yet, farther on, at the head of the valley, there is another, in its way as wonderful; less picturesque, but wilder still,—the remains of the eboulement* of the Glacier de Triolet caused by the fall of an aiguille near the Petits Jorasses—the most phrenzied accumulation of moraines I have ever seen; not dropped one by one into a heap, and pushed forward by the ice ploughshare, but evidently borne down by some mingled torrent of ice and rock and flood, with the swiftness of water and the weight of stone, and thrown along the mountain-side like pebbles from a stormy sea;—but the ruins of an Alp instead of the powder of a flint bed.

The glacier torrent of Triolet is almost lost among them, but that below, coming just from the base of the Jorasses, is exquisite beyond description in the play of its currents, narrow eddies of white nevè round islands of rock—falling in upon each other in deep and eddying pools; flowing forth again in massy sheets of ice, feeding, not one glacier stream, but cascade above cascade, far into the mountain gulph.'*

And so on, of divers matters, through four hundred and fifty pages; not all as good as that, but the core of what I had to learn and teach about gneiss and ice and clouds;—George indefatigably carrying his little daguerreotype box up everywhere, and taking the first image of the Matterhorn, as also of the aiguilles of Chamouni, ever drawn by the sun. A thing to be proud of still, though he is now a justice of peace, somewhere in Australia.

222. The following entries, in June, of which the two last come in the midst of busy and otherwise happy days, are all with which I permit myself to trouble the reader for this time.

'Chamouni, Sunday, June 17th. Quiet south rain till twelve o'clock. I have been abstracting the book of Revelation, (they say the French are beaten again at Rome, and another revolution in Paris*); many signs seem to multiply around us, and yet my unbelief yields no more than when all the horizon was clear. I was especially struck with the general appellation of the system of the world. As the "Mystery of God," Chap. x 7, compared with Hebrews xi 6, which I read this morning in our usual course.[1] Theme enough for the day's thought.

'Halfpast five. Pouring still, but I got out before dinner during a fine blink, which lasted just long enough to let me, by almost running, and leaping all the streams, reach the end of the pine wood next the source of the Arveron. There I had to turn to the left to the wooden bridge, when behold a sight new to me; an avalanche had evidently taken place from the (upper) glacier into the very bed of the great cataract, and the stream was as nearly choked as could be with balls and ellipsoids of ice, from the size of its common stones to that of a portmanteau, which were rolling down with it wildly, generally swinging out and in of the water as it waved; but when they came to the shallow parts, tumbled

---

[1] Read the 5th, 6th, and 7th verses in succession:—'AND THE ANGEL WHICH I SAW STAND UPON THE SEA AND UPON THE EARTH LIFTED UP HIS HAND TO HEAVEN, AND SWARE BY HIM THAT LIVETH FOR EVER AND EVER, WHO CREATED HEAVEN, AND THE THINGS THAT THEREIN ARE, AND THE EARTH, AND THE THINGS THAT THEREIN ARE, AND THE SEA, AND THE THINGS WHICH ARE THEREIN, THAT THERE SHOULD BE TIME NO LONGER: BUT IN THE DAYS OF THE VOICE OF THE SEVENTH ANGEL, WHEN HE SHALL BEGIN TO SOUND, THE MYSTERY OF GOD SHOULD BE FINISHED, AS HE HATH DECLARED TO HIS SERVANTS THE PROPHETS.'

and tossed over one another, and then plunging back into the deep water like so many stranded porpoises, spinning as they went down, and showing their dark backs with wilder swings after their plunge,—white, as they emerged, black, owing to their clearness as seen in the water; the stream itself of a pale clay-colour, opaque, larger by one half than ever I saw it, and running, as I suppose, not less than ten miles an hour; the whole mass, water and ice, looking like some thick paste full of plums, or ill-made pine-apple ice, with quantities of fruit in it, and the whole looking like a solid body; for the nodules of ice hardly changed their relative position during the quarter of a minute they were severally in sight, going down in a mass, thundering and rumbling against the piles of the bridge. It made me giddy to look at it; and the more, because, on raising the eye, there was always the great cataract itself startling one, as if it had just begun and seeming to increase every instant, bounding and hurling itself hither and thither, as if it was striving to dash itself to pieces, not falling because it could not help it; and behind there was a fearful storm coming up by the Breven, its grisly clouds warping up, as it seemed, against the river and cataract, with pillars of hail behind. I stayed till it began, and then crept back through the wood, running from one tree to another—there is really now a bit of blue sky over the Pavillon.[1]

223. 'June 18th. Evening, nine o'clock. I must not write much, it is past bed-time; went to source of Arveron with my father and mother and Miss Dowie;[2] never saw it so lovely; drew afterwards near the source, piny sketch, well begun. After tea walked up nearly to my beloved old place on the Breven, and saw a solemn sunset, yet not very bright; the granulated rosy crags of La Cote especially. Thank God for permitting me to sit on that slope once more thus strong in health and limb.

'Chamouni, day 13th, Monday, June 25th. Up rather late this morning, and lost time before breakfast over camera-lucida;* drove to Argentière with my mother, who enjoyed her drive exceedingly; back at one o'clock to my usual place (Les Tines, till four); out after dinner, rambling about Breven with sketch-book in search of a view of Aiguille du Plan; didn't find one, but found some wild strawberries, which were a consolation. The day has been fine, with scattered clouds; in the evening a most curious case of floating cap cloud, *hooding* the Mont Blanc summit without touching it, like gossamer blown upwards from

[1] The green mountain at the base of the Aiguille du Gouté.
[2] Sybilla. See 'Fors,' Letter 90th, 'Lost Jewels,' p. 165.

a field; an awning of slender threads waving like weeds in the blue sky,'
(as weeds in a brook current, I meant), 'and drawn out like floss silk as
fine as snow. This cloud, that does not *touch* the snow, but hovers over
it at a certain height following the convexity of the mountain, has
always seemed most unaccountable to me.

'224. Chamouni, day 14th, Tuesday, June 26th. Heavy, rounded,
somewhat dirty clouds on the Pavillon (halfpast six); but summit bright
and clear, and all very promising.

'Get following books if possible—"Mémoires de la Société de
Physique et d'Histoire Naturelle de Genève" (t. iv, p. 209), on the val-
ley of Val Orsine, by M. Necker; "Actes de la Société Helvétique des
Sc. Nat.," 1837, p. 28, 1839, p. 47, on Nagelflue pebbles.

'Evening. After one of the most heavenly walks I ever took in
Chamouni among the woods of the Pèlerins, I come in to hear of my
poor cousin Mary's death.'* How well I recollect sitting with her on the
slopes of the Breven, and reasoning about the height of La Cote: she
knows it now, better than I, and thinks it less.

'Chamouni, day 15th, Wednesday, June 27th. One of the heavenly
Alpine mornings, all alight: I have been trying to get some of the effect
of sunrise on the Montanvert, and aerial quality of aiguilles,—in vain.
Slanting rays now touch the turf by the châlet of Blaitière,* as perhaps
they touch poor Mary's grave.'

CHAPTER XII

OTTERBURN

225. IN blaming myself, as often I have done, and may have occasion
to do again, for my want of affection to other people, I must also express
continually, as I think back about it, more and more wonder that ever
anybody had any affection for *me*. I thought they might as well have got
fond of a camera lucida, or an ivory foot-rule: all my faculty was merely
in showing that such and such things were so; I was no orator, no actor,
no painter but in a minute and generally invisible manner; and I couldn't
bear being interrupted in anything I was about.

Nevertheless, some sensible grown up people *did* get to like me!—the
best of them with a protective feeling that I wanted guidance no less
than sympathy; and the higher religious souls, hoping to lead me to the
golden gates.

226. I have no memory, and no notion, when I first *saw* Pauline,

Lady Trevelyan; but she became at once a monitress-friend in whom I wholly trusted,—(not that I ever took her advice!)—and the happiness of her own life was certainly increased by my books and me. Sir Walter, being a thorough botanist, and interested in pure science generally, did not hunt, but was benevolently useful, as a landlord should be, in his county. I had no interests in county business at that time; but used to have happy agricultural or floral chats with Sir Walter, and entirely admired his unambitious, yet dignified stability of rural, and celestial, life, there amidst the Northumbrian winds.

Wallington is in the old Percy country, the broad descent of main valley leading down by Otterburn from the Cheviots. An ugly house enough it was; square set, and somewhat bare walled, looking down a slope of rough wide field to a burn, the Wansbeck, neither bright nor rapid, but with a ledge or two of sandstone to drip over, or lean against in pools; bits of crag in the distance, worth driving to, for sight of the sweeps of moor round them, and breaths of breeze from Carter Fell.

There were no children of its own in Wallington, but Lady Trevelyan's little niece, Constance Hilliard, nine years old when I first saw her there, glittered about the place in an extremely quaint and witty way; and took to me a little, like her aunt. Afterwards her mother and she, in their little rectory home at Cowley (near Hillingdon), became important among my feminine friendships, and gave me, of such petting and teasing as women are good for, sometimes more than enough.

227. But the dearness of Wallington was founded, as years went on, more deeply in its having made known to me the best and truest friend of all my life; *best* for me, because he was of my father's race, and native town; *truest*, because he knew always how to help us both, and never made any mistakes in doing so—Dr John Brown. He was staying at Wallington when I stopped there on my way to give my Edinburgh lectures;* and we walked together, with little Connie, on the moors: it dawned on me, so, gradually, what manner of man he was.

This, the reader capable of learning at all—(there are few now who can understand a good Scotchman of the old classic breed)—had better learn, straightway, from the record he gave of his own father's life,[1] of which I must give here this one passage of his childhood. His father was a young pastor, crowned in perfectness of faithful service, together with his 'modest, calm, thrifty, reasonable, happy-hearted' wife, his student-love; this their son, five years old,—just at the age

---

[1] Letter to Rev. John Cairns. Edmonston & Douglas, 1861.

when I looked back to the creation of the world, for *me*, in Friar's Crag, of Derwentwater; *my* mother, thrifty and reasonable also, meantime taking care that not more than two plums should be in my pie for dinner; my father, also thrifty and reasonable, triumphing in his travel at Whitehaven, a 'wanderer,' like the pedlar in the 'Excursion,' selling sherry instead of bobbins;*—all of us as happy as cicadas* (and a little more). Now hear Dr John Brown:—

228. 'On the morning of the 28th May, 1816, my eldest sister Janet and I were sleeping in the kitchen-bed with Tibbie Meek, our only servant. We were all three awakened by a cry of pain—sharp, insufferable, as if one were stung. Years after we two confided to each other, sitting by the burnside, that we thought that "great cry" which arose at midnight in Egypt must have been like it. We all knew whose voice it was, and, in our nightclothes, we ran into the passage, and into the little parlour to the left hand, in which was a closet-bed. We found my father standing before us, erect, his hands clenched in his black hair, his eyes full of misery and amazement, his face white as that of the dead. He frightened us. He saw this, or else his intense will had mastered his agony, for, taking his hands from his head, he said, slowly and gently, "Let us give thanks," and turned to a little sofa[1] in the room; there lay our mother, dead. She had long been ailing. I remember her sitting in a shawl,—an Indian one with little dark green spots on a light ground,—and watching her growing pale with what I afterwards knew must have been strong pain. She had, being feverish, slipped out of bed, and "grandmother," her mother, seeing her "change come," had called my father, and they two saw her open her blue, kind, and true eyes, "comfortable" to us all "as the day"—I remember them better than those of any one I saw yesterday—and, with one faint look of recognition to him, close them till the time of the restitution of all things.'

He had a precious sister left to him; but his life, as the noblest Scottish lives are always, was thenceforward generously sad,—and endlessly pitiful.

229. No one has yet separated, in analyzing the mind of Scott, the pity from the pride; no one, in the mind of Carlyle, the pity from the anger.

Lest I should not be spared to write another 'Praeterita,'* I will give, in this place, a few words of Carlyle's, which throw more lovely light

---

[1] 'This sofa, which was henceforward sacred in the house, he had always beside him. He used to tell us he set her down upon it when he brought her home to the manse.'

on his character than any he has written,—as, indeed, his instantly vivid words always did; and it is a bitter blame and shame to me that I have not recorded those spoken to myself, often with trust and affection, always with kindness. But I find this piece, nearly word for word, in my diary of 25th October, 1874. He had been quoting the last words of Goethe, 'Open the window, let us have more light'* (this about an hour before painless death, his eyes failing him).

I referred to the 'It grows dark, boys, you may go,' of the great master of the High School of Edinburgh.[1] On which Carlyle instantly opened into beautiful account of Adam's early life, his intense zeal and industry as a poor boy in a Highland cottage, lying flat on the hearth to learn his Latin grammar by the light of a peat fire. Carlyle's own memory is only of Adam's funeral, when he, Carlyle, was a boy of fourteen, making one of a crowd waiting near the gate of the High School, of which part of the old black building of the time of James I was still standing—its motto, 'Nisi Dominus, frustra,'* everywhere. A half-holiday had been given, that the boys might see the coffin carried by,—only about five-and-twenty people in all, Carlyle thought 'pig-bellied persons, sympathetic bailies, relieving each other in carrying the pall.' The boys collected in a group, as it passed within the railings, uttered a low 'Ah me! Ah dear!' or the like, half sigh or wail—'and he is gone from us then!'

'The sound of the boys' wail is in my ears yet,' said Carlyle.

230. His own first teacher in Latin, an old clergyman. He had indeed been sent first to a schoolmaster in his own village, 'the joyfullest little mortal, he believed, on earth,' learning his declensions out of an eighteen-penny book! giving his whole might and heart to understand. And the master could teach him nothing, merely involved him day by day in misery of non-understanding, the boy getting crushed and sick, till (his mother?) saw it, and then he was sent to this clergyman, 'a perfect sage, on the humblest scale.' Seventy pounds a year, his income at first entering into life; never more than a hundred. Six daughters and two sons; the eldest sister, Margaret, 'a little bit lassie,'—then in a lower voice, 'the flower of all the flock to *me*.' Returning from her little visitations to the poor, dressed in her sober prettiest, 'the most amiable of possible objects.' Not beautiful in any notable way afterwards, but 'comely in the highest degree.' With dutiful sweetness, 'the right hand of her father.' Lived to be seven-and-twenty. 'The last time that I wept aloud in the world, I think was at her death.'

---

[1] It was *his* Latin grammar, the best ever composed, which my Camberwell tutor threw aside, as above told, for a 'Scotch thing.'*

Riding down from Craigenputtock to Dumfries,—'a monstrous precipice of rocks on one hand of you, a merry brook on the other side.... In the night just before sunrise.'

He was riding down, he and his brother, to fetch away her body,—they having just heard of her death.

A surveyor (?), or some scientific and evidently superior kind of person, had been doing work which involved staying near, or in, her father's house, and they got engaged, and then he broke it off. 'They said that was the beginning of it.' The death had been so sudden, and so unexpected, that Mary's mother, then a girl of twelve or thirteen, rushed out of the house and up to the cart,[1] shrieking, rather than crying, 'Where's Peggy?'

I could not make out, quite, how the two parts of the family were separated, so that his sister expected them to bring her back living, (or even well?). Carlyle was so much affected, and spoke so low, that I could not venture to press him on detail.

This master of his then, the father of Margaret, was entirely kind and wise in teaching him—a Scotch gentleman of old race and feeling, an Andrea Ferrara* and some silver-mounted canes hanging in his study, last remnants of the old times.

231. We fell away upon Mill's essay* on the substitution of patriotism for religion.

'Actually the most paltry rag of'—a chain of vituperative contempt too fast to note—'it has fallen to my lot to come in with. Among my acquaintance I have not seen a person talking of a thing he so little understood.' The point of his indignation was Mill's supposing that, if God did not make everybody 'happy,' it was because He had no sufficient power, 'was not enough supplied with the article.' Nothing makes Carlyle more contemptuous than this coveting of 'happiness.'

Perhaps we had better hear what Polissena and the nun of Florence ('Christ's Folk,' IV) have to say about happiness, of *their* sort;* and consider what every strong heart feels in the doing of any noble thing, and every good craftsman in making any beautiful one, before we despise any innocent person who looks for happiness in this world, as well as hereafter. But assuredly the strength of Scottish character has always been perfected by suffering; and the types of it given by Scott in Flora MacIvor, Edith Bellenden, Mary of Avenel, and Jeanie Deans,*—to name only those which the reader will remember without

---

[1] 'Rushed at the cart,' his words. Ending with his deep 'Heigh dear,' sigh. 'Sunt lachrymae rerum.'*

effort,—are chiefly notable in the way they bear sorrow; as the whole tone of Scottish temper, ballad poetry, and music, which no other school has ever been able to imitate, has arisen out of the sad associations which, one by one, have gathered round every loveliest scene in the border land. Nor is there anything among other beautiful nations to approach the dignity of a true Scotswoman's face, in the tried perfectness of her old age.

232. I have seen them beautiful in the same way earlier, when they had passed through trial; my own Joanie's face owes the calm of its radiance to days of no ordinary sorrow—even before she came, when my father had been laid to his rest under Croydon hills, to keep her faithful watch by my mother's side, while I was seeking selfish happiness far away in work which to-day has come to nought. What I have myself since owed to her,—life certainly, and more than life, for many and many a year,—was meant to have been told long since, had I been able to finish this book in the time I designed it. What Dr John Brown became to me, is partly shown in the continual references to his sympathy in the letters of 'Hortus Inclusus';* but nothing could tell the loss to me in his death, nor the grief to how many greater souls than mine, that had been possessed in patience through his love.

I must give one piece more of his own letter, with the following fragment, written in the earlier part of this year, and meant to have been carried on into some detail of the impressions received in my father's native Edinburgh, and on the northern coast, from Queen's Ferry round by Prestonpans to Dunbar and Berwick.

Dr Brown goes on:—'A year ago, I found an elderly country-woman, a widow, waiting for me. Rising up, she said, "D' ye mind me?" I looked at her, but could get nothing from her face; but the voice remained in my ear, as if coming from the "fields of sleep," and I said by a sort of instinct, "Tibbie Meek!" I had not seen her or heard her voice for more than forty years.'*

233. The reader will please note the pure Scotch phrase 'D' ye mind me?' and compare Meg Merrilies' use of it. 'At length she guided them through the mazes of the wood to a little open glade of about a quarter of an acre, surrounded by trees and bushes, which made a wild and irregular[1] boundary. Even in winter, it was a sheltered and snugly sequestered spot; but when arrayed in the verdure of spring, the earth

---

[1] It might have been 'irregular,' in ground just cut up for building leases, in South Lambeth; wild, yet as regular as a disciplined army, had it been the pines of Uri. It *was* a 'waste of blossom,' a shade of weeping birches.

sending forth all its wild flowers; the shrubs spreading their waste of blossom around it, and the weeping birches, which towered over the underwood, drooping their long and leafy fibres to intercept the sun, it must have seemed a place for a youthful poet to study his earliest sonnet, or a pair of lovers to exchange their first mutual avowal of affection. Apparently it now awakened very different recollections. Bertram's brow, when he had looked round the spot, became gloomy and embarrassed. Meg, after muttering to herself, "This is the very spot," looked at him with a ghastly side glance,—"D'ye mind it?"

'"Yes," answered Bertram, "imperfectly I do."

'"Ay," pursued his guide, "on this very spot the man fell from his horse—I was behind that bourtree[1] bush at the very moment. Now will I show you the further track—*the last time ye travelled it, was in these arms.*"'*

That was twenty years before, for Bertram's nurse; (compare Waverley's and Morton's;) Dr Brown's Tibbie; my own father's* Mause; my Anne; all women of the same stamp; my Saxon mother not altogether comprehending them; but when Dr John Brown first saw my account of my mother and Anne in 'Fors,' *he* understood both of them, and wrote back to me of 'those two blessed women,' as he would have spoken of their angels, had he then been beside them, looking on another Face.*

234. But my reason for quoting this piece of 'Guy Mannering' here is to explain to the reader who cares to know it, the difference between the Scotch 'mind' for 'remember,' and any other phrase of any other tongue, applied to the act of memory.

In order that you may, in the Scottish sense, 'mind' anything, first there must be something to 'mind'—and then, the 'mind' to mind it. In a thousand miles of iron railway, or railway train, there is nothing in one rod or bar to distinguish it from another. You can't 'mind' which sleeper is which. Nor, on the other hand, if you drive from Chillon to Vevay, asleep, can you 'mind' the characteristics of the lake of Geneva. Meg could not have expected Bertram to 'mind' at what corner of a street in Manchester—or in what ditch of the Isle of Dogs—anything had past directly bearing on his own fate. She expected him to 'mind' only a beautiful scene, of perfect individual character, and she would not have expected him to 'mind' even that, had she not known he had persevering sense and memorial powers of very high order.

---

[1] Elder, in modern Scotch; but in the Douglas glossary, *Bower* bush.

Now it is the peculiar character of Scottish as distinct from all other scenery on a small scale in north Europe, to have these distinctively 'mindable' features. One range of coteau by a French river is exactly like another; one turn of glen in the Black Forest is only the last turn re-turned; one sweep of Jura pasture and crag, the mere echo of the fields and crags of ten miles away. But in the whole course of Tweed, Teviot, Gala, Tay, Forth, and Clyde, there is perhaps scarcely a bend of ravine, or nook of valley, which would not be recognisable by its inhabitants from every other. And there is no other country in which the roots of memory are so entwined with the beauty of nature, instead of the pride of men; no other in which the song of 'Auld lang syne'* could have been written,—or Lady Nairn's ballad of 'The Auld House.'*

* * * * *

235. I did not in last 'Praeterita'* enough explain the reason for my seeking homes on the crests of Alps, in my own special study of cloud and sky; but I have only known too late, within this last month, the absolutely literal truth of Turner's saying that the most beautiful skies in the world known to him were those of the Isle of Thanet.

In a former number of 'Praeterita'* I have told how my mother kept me quiet in a boy's illness by telling me to think of Dash, and Dover; and among the early drawings left for gift to Joanie are all those made—the first ever made from nature—at Sevenoaks,* Tunbridge, Canterbury, and Dover. One of the poorest-nothings of these, a mere scrawl in pen and ink, of cumulus cloud crossed by delicate horizontal bars on the horizon, is the first attempt I ever made to draw a sky,— fifty-five years ago. That same sky I saw again over the same sea horizon at sunset only five weeks ago. And three or four days of sunshine following, I saw, to my amazement, that the skies of Turner were still bright above the foulness of smoke-cloud or the flight of plague-cloud;* and that the forms which, in the pure air of Kent and Picardy, the upper cirri were capable of assuming, undisturbed by tornado, unmingled with volcanic exhalation, and lifted out of the white crests of ever-renewed tidal waves, were infinite, lovely and marvellous beyond any that I had ever seen from moor or alp; while yet on the horizon, if left for as much as an hour undefiled by fuel of fire, there was the azure air I had known of old, alike in the lowland distance and on the Highland hills. What might the coasts of France and England have been now, if from the days of Bertha in Canterbury, and of Godefroy in Boulogne, the Christian faith had been held by both nations in peace, in this pure air of heaven? What might the hills of Cheviot and the vale of Tweed have been now, if from the days of Cuthbert in Holy Isle, and of Edwin in Edinburgh, the Crosses of St George and St Andrew had been borne by brethren; and the fiery Percy and true Douglas laid down their lives only for their people?

FOLKESTONE, 11*th October*, 1887.

END OF VOL. II

VOLUME III

CHAPTER I

THE GRANDE CHARTREUSE

MONT BLANC REVISITED
(Written at Nyon in 1845.)

O Mount beloved, mine eyes again
Behold the twilight's sanguine stain
　　Along thy peaks expire.
O Mount beloved, thy frontier waste
I seek with a religious haste
　　And reverent desire.

They meet me, 'midst thy shadows cold,—
Such thoughts as holy men of old
　　Amid the desert found;—
Such gladness, as in Him they felt
Who with them through the darkness dwelt,
　　And compassed all around.

Ah, happy, if His will were so,
To give me manna here for snow,
　　And by the torrent side
To lead me as He leads His flocks
Of wild deer through the lonely rocks
　　In peace, unterrified;

Since, from the things that trustful rest,
The partridge on her purple nest,
　　The marmot in his den,
God wins a worship more resigned,
A purer praise than He can find
　　Upon the lips of men.

Alas for man! who hath no sense
Of gratefulness nor confidence,
　　But still regrets and raves,
Till all God's love can scarcely win
One soul from taking pride in sin,
　　And pleasure over graves.

> Yet teach me, God, a milder thought,
> Lest I, of all Thy blood has bought,
> Least honourable be;
> And this, that leads me to condemn,
> Be rather want of love for them
> Than jealousy for Thee.

1. THESE verses, above noticed (p. 218), with one following sonnet,* as the last rhymes I attempted in any seriousness, were nevertheless themselves extremely earnest, and express, with more boldness and simplicity than I feel able to use now with my readers, the real temper in which I began the best work of my life. My mother at once found fault with the words 'sanguine stain,' as painful, and untrue of the rose-colour on snow at sunset; but they had their meaning to myself,— the too common Evangelical phrase, 'washed in the blood of Christ,'* being, it seemed to me, if true at all, true of the earth and her purest snow, as well as of her purest creatures; and the claim of being able to find among the rock-shadows thoughts such as hermits of old found in the desert, whether it seem immodest or not, was wholly true. Whatever might be my common faults or weaknesses, they were rebuked among the hills; and the only days I can look back to as, according to the powers given me, rightly or wisely in entireness spent, have been in sight of Mont Blanc, Monte Rosa, or the Jungfrau.

When I was most strongly under this influence, I tried to trace,—and I think have traced rightly, so far as I was then able,—in the last chapter of 'Modern Painters,' the power of mountains* in solemnizing the thoughts and purifying the hearts of the greatest nations of antiquity and the greatest teachers of Christian faith. But I did not then dwell on what I had only felt, but not ascertained,—the destruction of all sensibility of this high order in the populations of modern Europe, first by the fine luxury of the fifteenth century, and then by the coarse lusts of the eighteenth and early nineteenth: destruction so total that religious men themselves became incapable of education by any natural beauty or nobleness; and though still useful to others by their ministrations and charities, in the corruption of cities, were themselves lost,—or even degraded, if they ever went up into the mountain to preach, or into the wilderness to pray.*

2. There is no word, in the fragment of diary recording, in last 'Praeterita,'* our brief visit to the Grande Chartreuse, of anything we saw or heard there that made impression upon any of us. Yet a word was said, of significance enough to alter the courses of religious thought in me, afterwards for ever.

I had been totally disappointed with the Monastery itself, with the pass of approach to it, with the mountains round it, and with the monk who showed us through it. The building was meanly designed and confusedly grouped; the road up to it nothing like so terrific as most roads in the Alps up to anywhere; the mountains round were simplest commonplace of Savoy cliff, with no peaks, no glaciers, no cascades, nor even any slopes of pine in extent of majesty. And the monk who showed us through the corridors had no cowl worth the wearing, no beard worth the wagging, no expression but of superciliousness without sagacity, and an ungraciously dull manner, showing that he was much tired of the place, more of himself, and altogether of my father and me.

Having followed him for a time about the passages of the scattered building, in which there was nothing to show,—not a picture, not a statue, not a bit of old glass, or well-wrought vestment or jewellery; nor any architectural feature in the least ingenious or lovely, we came to a pause at last in what I suppose was a type of a modern Carthusian's cell, wherein, leaning on the window sill, I said something in the style of 'Modern Painters,' about the effect of the scene outside upon religious minds. Whereupon, with a curl of his lip, 'We do not come here,' said the monk, 'to look at the mountains.'* Under which rebuke I bent my head silently, thinking however all the same, 'What then, by all that's stupid, do you come here for at all?'

3. Which, from that hour to this, I have not conceived; nor, after giving my best attention to the last elaborate account of Carthusian faith, 'La Grande Chartreuse, par un Chartreux, Grenoble, 5, Rue Brocherie, 1884,' am I the least wiser. I am informed by that author that his fraternity are *Eremite** beyond all other manner of men,—that they delight in solitude, and in that amiable disposition pass lives of an angelic tenor, meditating on the charms of the next world, and the vanities of this one.

I sympathize with them in their love of quiet—to the uttermost; but do not hold that liking to be the least pious or amiable in myself, nor understand why it seems so to them; or why their founder, St Bruno,— a man of the brightest faculties in teaching, and exhorting, and directing; also, by favour of fortune, made a teacher and governor in the exact centre of European thought and order, the royal city of Rheims,—should think it right to leave all that charge, throw down his rod of rule, his crozier of protection, and come away to enjoy meditation on the next world by himself.

And why meditation among the Alps? He and his disciples might as easily have avoided the rest of mankind by shutting themselves into a penitentiary on a plain, or in whatever kind country they chanced to be born in, without danger to themselves of being buried by avalanches, or trouble to their venerating visitors in coming so far up hill.

Least of all I understand how they could pass their days of meditation without getting interested in plants and, stones, whether they would or no; nor how they could go on writing books in scarlet and gold,—(for they were great scribes, and had a beautiful library,)—persisting for centuries in the same patterns, and never trying to draw a bird or a leaf rightly—until the days when books were illuminated no more for religion, but for luxury, and the amusement of sickly fancy.

4. Without endeavouring to explain any of these matters, I will try to set down in this chapter, merely what I have found monks or nuns like, when by chance I was thrown into their company, and of what use they have been to me.

And first let me thank my dear Miss Edgeworth for the ideal character of Sister Frances, in her story of Madame de Fleury,* which, read over and over again through all my childhood, fixed in me the knowledge of what a good sister of charity can be, and for the most part is, in France; and, of late, I suppose in Germany and England.

But the first impression from the life of the secluded Sisterhoods[1] was given me at the Convent of St Michael, on the summit of the isolated peak of lava at Le Puy, in Auvergne, in 1840. The hostess-sister who showed my father and me what it was permitted to see of chapel or interior buildings, was a cheerful, simple creature, pleased with us at once for our courtesy to her, and admiration of her mountain home, and belief in her sacred life. Protestant visitors being then rare in Auvergne, and still more, reverent and gentle ones, she gave her pretty curiosity free sway; and enquired earnestly of us, what sort of creatures we were,—how far we believed in God, or tried to be good, or hoped to go to heaven? And our responses under this catechism being in their sum more pleasing to her than she had expected, and manifesting, to her extreme joy and wonder, a Christian spirit, so far as she could judge, in harmony with all she had been herself taught, she proceeded to cross-examine us on closer points of Divinity, to find out, if she could, why we were, or unnecessarily called ourselves, anything else

---

[1] Of the Brotherhoods, of course the first I knew* were those of St Bernard; but these were not secluded for their own spiritual welfare, any more than our coastguardsmen by the Goodwin sands; and are to be spoken of elsewhere, and in quite other relations to the modern world.

than Catholic? The one flaw in our faith which at last her charity fastened on, was that we were not *sure* of our salvation in Christ, but only hoped to get into heaven,—and were not at all, by that dim hope, relieved from terror of death, when at any time it should come. Whereupon she launched involuntarily into an eager and beautiful little sermon, to every word of which her own perfectly happy and innocent face gave vivid power, and assurance of sincerity,—how 'we needed to be *sure* of our safety in Christ, and that every one might be so who came to Him and prayed to Him; and that all good Catholics were as sure of heaven as if they were already there;' and so dismissed us at the gate with true pity, and beseeching that we would prove the goodness of God, and be in peace. Which exhortation of hers I have never forgotten; only it has always seemed to me that there was no entering into that rest of hers but by living on the top of some St Michael's rock too, which it did not seem to me I was meant to do, by any means.

But in here recording the impression made on my father and me, I must refer to what I said above of our common feeling of being, both of us, as compared with my mother, reprobate and worldly characters, despising our birthright like Esau,* or cast out, for our mocking ways, like Ishmael.* For my father never ventured to give me a religious lesson; and though he went to church with a resigned countenance, I knew very well that he liked going just as little as I did.

5. The second and fourth summers after that, 1842 and 1844, were spent happily and quietly in the Prieuré[1] of Chamouni, and there of course we all of us became acquainted with the curé, and saw the entire manner of life in a purely Catholic village and valley,—recognising it, I hope, all of us, in our hearts, to be quite as Christian as anything we knew of, and much pleasanter and prettier than the Sunday services, in England, which exhaust the little faith we have left.

Wordsworth, in his continental notices of peasant Catholicism, recognises, also at Chamouni, very gracefully this external prettiness—

> 'They too, who send so far a holy gleam,
>   As they the Church engird with motion slow,
> A product of that awful mountain seem
>   Poured from its vaults of everlasting snow.
> Not virgin lilies marshalled in bright row,
>   Not swans descending with the stealthy tide,

---

[1] Not in the Priory itself, but the Hotel de l'Union. The whole village is called 'The Priory.'

> A livelier sisterly resemblance show
> Than the fair forms that in long order glide
> Bear to the glacier band, those shapes aloft descried.'*

But on me, the deeper impression was of a continuous and serene hold of their happy faith on the life alike of Sunday and Monday, and through every hour and circumstance of youth and age; which yet abides in all the mountain Catholic districts of Savoy, the Waldstetten, and the Tyrol, to their perpetual honour and peace; and this without controversy, or malice towards the holders of other beliefs.

6. Next, in 1845, I saw in Florence, as above told, the interior economy of the monasteries at Santa Maria Novella,—in the Franciscan cloisters of Fésole, and in Fra Angelico's, both at San Domenico and San Marco. Which, in whatever they retained of their old thoughts and ways, were wholly beautiful; and the monks with whom I had any casual intercourse, always kind, innocently eager in sympathy with my own work, and totally above men of the 'world' in general understanding, courtesy, and moral sense.

Men of the *outer* world, I mean, of course,—official and commercial. Afterwards at Venice I had a very dear and not at all monastic, friend, Rawdon Brown; but *his* society were the Venetians of the fifteenth century. The Counts Minischalchi at Verona, and Borromeo at Milan, would have been endlessly kind and helpful to me; but I never could learn Italian enough to speak to them. Whereas, with my monkish friends, at the Armenian isle of Venice, and in any churches or cloisters through North Italy, where I wanted a niche to be quiet in, and chiefly at last in Assisi, I got on with any broken French or Italian I could stutter, without minding; and was always happy.

7. But the more I loved or envied the monks, and the more I despised the modern commercial and fashionable barbaric tribes, the more acutely also I felt that the Catholic political hierarchies, and isolated remnants of celestial enthusiasm, were hopelessly at fault in their dealing with these adversaries; having also elements of corruption in themselves, which justly brought on them the fierce hostility of men like Garibaldi in Italy, and of the honest and open-hearted liberal leaders in other countries. Thus, irrespectively of all immediate contest or progress, I saw in the steady course of the historical reading by which I prepared myself to write the Stones of Venice, that, alike in the world and the Church, the hearts of men were led astray by the same dreams and desires; and whether in seeking for Divine perfection, or earthly pleasure, were alike disobeying the laws of God when they withdrew from their direct and familiar duties, and ceased, whether in

ascetic or self-indulgent lives, to honour and love their neighbour as themselves.*

While these convictions prevented me from being ever led into acceptance of Catholic teaching by my reverence for the Catholic art of the great ages,—and the less, because the Catholic art of these small ages can say but little for itself,—I grew also daily more sure that the peace of God rested on all the dutiful and kindly hearts of the laborious poor; and that the only constant form of pure religion was in useful work, faithful love, and stintless charity.

8. In which pure religion neither St Bruno himself nor any of his true disciples failed: and I perceive it finally notable of them, that, poor by resolute choice of a life of hardship, without any sentimental or fallacious glorifying of 'Holy poverty' as if God had never promised full garners for a blessing; and always choosing men of high intellectual power for the heads of their community, they have had more directly wholesome influence on the outer world than any other order of monks so narrow in number, and restricted in habitation. For while the Franciscan and Cistercian monks became everywhere a constant element in European society, the Carthusians, in their active sincerity, remained, in groups of not more than from twelve to twenty monks in any single monastery, the tenants of a few wild valleys of the north-western Alps; the subsequent overflowing of their brotherhood into the Certosas of the Lombard plains being mere waste and wreck of them; and the great Certosa of Pavia one of the worst shames of Italy, associated with the accursed reign of Galeazzo Visconti. But in their strength, from the foundation of the order, at the close of the eleventh century, to the beginning of the fourteenth, they reared in their mountain fastnesses, and sent out to minister to the world, a succession of men of immense mental grasp, and serenely authoritative innocence; among whom our own Hugo of Lincoln, in his relations with Henry II and Coeur de Lion, is to my mind the most beautiful sacerdotal figure known to me in history. The great Pontiffs have a power which in its strength can scarcely be used without cruelty, nor in its scope without error; the great Saints are always in some degree incredible or unintelligible; but Hugo's power is in his own personal courage and justice only; and his sanctity as clear, frank, and playful as the waves of his own Chartreuse well.[1]

9. I must not let myself be led aside from my own memories

---

[1] The original building was grouped round a spring in the rock, from which a runlet was directed through every cell.

into any attempt to trace the effect on Turner's mind of his visit to the Chartreuse, rendered as it is in the three subjects of the Liber Studiorum,—from the Chartreuse itself, from Holy Island, and Dumblane Abbey. The strength of it was checked by his love and awe of the sea, and sailor heroism, and confused by his classical thought and passion; but in my own life, the fading away of the nobler feelings in which I had worked in the Campo Santo of Pisa, however much my own fault, was yet complicated with the inevitable discovery of the falseness of the religious doctrines in which I had been educated.

10. The events of the ten years 1850–1860, for the most part wasted in useless work, must be arranged first in their main order, before I can give clear account of any thing that happened in them. But this breaking down of my Puritan faith, being the matter probably most important to many readers of my later books, shall be traced in this chapter to the sorrowful end. Note first the main facts of the successive years of the decade.

1851. Turner dies, while I am at first main work in Venice, for 'The Stones of Venice.'

1852. Final work in Venice for 'Stones of Venice.' Book finished that winter. Six hundred quarto pages of notes for it, fairly and closely written, now useless. Drawings as many—of a sort; useless too.

1853. Henry Acland in Glenfinlas with me. Drawing of gneiss rock made; now in the school at Oxford. Two months' work in what fair weather could be gleaned out of that time.

1854. With my father and mother at Vevay and Thun. I take up the history of Switzerland, and propose to engrave a series of drawings of the following Swiss towns: Geneva, Fribourg, Basle, Thun, Baden, and Schaffhausen. I proceed to make drawings for this work, of which the first attempted (of Thun) takes up the whole of the summer, and is only half done then. Definition of Poetry, for 'Modern Painters,' written at Vevay, looking across lake to Chillon. It leaves out rhythm, which I now consider a defect in said definition; otherwise good,—'The arrangement, by imagination, of noble motive for noble emotion.' I forget the exact words,* but these others will do as well, perhaps better.

11. 1855. Notes on Royal Academy begun. The spring is so cold that the hawthorns are only in bud on the 5th of June. I get cough, which lasts for two months, till I go down to Tunbridge Wells to my doctor cousin, William Richardson, who puts me to bed, gives me some syrup, cures me in three days, and calls me a fool for not coming to him before, with some rather angry warnings that I had better not keep a cough for two months again. Third volume of 'Modern Painters' got

done with, somehow, but didn't know what to call it, so called it 'Of Many Things.' But none of *these* were 'done with,' as I found afterwards, to my cost.

1856. With my father and mother to Geneva and Fribourg. Two drawings at Fribourg took up the working summer. My father begins to tire of the proposed work on Swiss towns, and to inquire whether the rest of 'Modern Painters' will ever be done.

1857. My mother wants me to see the Bay of Cromarty and the Falls of Kilmorock. I consent sulkily to be taken to Scotland with that object. Papa and mamma, wistfully watching the effect on my mind, show their Scotland to me. I see, on my own quest, Craig-Ellachie, and the Lachin-y-Gair forests, and finally reach the Bay of Cromarty and Falls of Kilmorock, doubtless now the extreme point of my northern discoveries on the round earth. I admit, generously, the Bay of Cromarty and the Falls to be worth coming all that way to see; but beg papa and mamma to observe that it is twenty miles' walk, in bogs, to the top of Ben Wyvis, that the town of Dingwall is not like Milan or Venice,—and that I think we have seen enough of Scotland.

12. 1858. Accordingly, after arranging, mounting, framing, and cabinetting, with good help from Richard Williams of Messrs Foord's,* the Turner drawings now in the catacombs of the National Gallery, I determine to add two more Swiss towns to my list, namely, Rheinfelden and Bellinzona, in illustration of Turner's sketches at those places; and get reluctant leave from my father to take Couttet again, and have all my own way. I spend the spring at Rheinfelden, and the summer at Bellinzona. But Couttet being of opinion that these town views will come to no good, and that the time I spend on the roof of 'cette baraque'* at Bellinzona is wholly wasted, I give the town views all up, and take to Vandyke and Paul Veronese again in the gallery of Turin. But, on returning home, my father is not satisfied with my studies from those masters, and piteously asks for the end of 'Modern Painters,' saying 'he will be dead before it is done,' Much ashamed of myself, I promise him to do my best on it without farther subterfuge.

1859. Hard writing and drawing to that end. Fourth volume got done.* My father thinks, himself, I ought to see Berlin, Dresden, Munich, and Nuremberg, before the book is finished. He and my mother take their last continental journey with me to those places. I have my last happy walk with my father at Konigstein.

1860. I work hard all the winter and early spring—finish the book,* in a sort; my father well pleased with the last chapter, and the engraved drawings from Nuremberg and Rheinfelden. On the strength of this piece of filial duty, I am cruel enough to go away to St Martin's again, by myself, to meditate on what is to be done next. Thence I go up to Chamouni,—where a new epoch of life and death begins.*

13. And here I must trace, as simply and rapidly as may be, the story of my relations with the Working Men's College.

I knew of its masters only the Principal, F. D. Maurice, and my own friend Rossetti. It is to be remembered of Rossetti with loving honour, that he was the only one of our modern painters who taught disciples for love of them. He was really not an Englishman, but a great Italian tormented in the Inferno of London; doing the best he could, and teaching the best he could; but the 'could' shortened by the strength of his animal passions, without any trained control, or guiding faith. Of him, more hereafter.*

I loved Frederick Maurice, as every one did who came near him; and have no doubt he did all that was in him to do of good in his day. Which could by no means be said either of Rossetti or of me: but Maurice was by nature puzzle-headed, and, though in a beautiful manner, *wrong*-headed; while his clear conscience and keen affections made him egotistic, and in his Bible-reading, as insolent as any infidel of them all. I only went once to a Bible-lesson of his; and the meeting was significant, and conclusive.

14. The subject of lesson, Jael's slaying of Sisera. Concerning which, Maurice taking an enlightened modern view of what was fit and not, discoursed in passionate indignation; and warned his class, in the most positive and solemn manner, that such dreadful deeds could only have been done in cold blood in the Dark Biblical ages; and that no religious and patriotic Englishwoman ought ever to think of imitating Jael by nailing a Russian's or Prussian's skull to the ground,—especially after giving him butter in a lordly dish. At the close of the instruction, through which I sate silent, I ventured to enquire, why then had Deborah the prophetess declared of Jael, 'Blessed above women shall the wife of Heber the Kenite be'? On which Maurice, with startled and flashing eyes, burst into partly scornful, partly alarmed, denunciation of Deborah the prophetess, as a mere blazing Amazon; and of her Song as a merely rhythmic storm of battle-rage, no more to be listened to with edification or faith than the Norman's sword-song at the battle of Hastings.

Whereupon there remained nothing for *me*,—to whom the Song of Deborah was as sacred as the Magnificat,*—but total collapse in sorrow and astonishment; the eyes of all the class being also bent on me in amazed reprobation of my benighted views, and unchristian sentiments. And I got away how I could, and never went back.

That being the first time in my life that I had fairly met the lifted head of Earnest and Religious Infidelity—in a man neither vain nor ambitious, but instinctively and innocently trusting his own amiable feelings as the final interpreters of all the possible feelings of men and angels, all the songs of the prophets, and all the ways of God.

15. It followed, of course, logically and necessarily, that every one of Maurice's disciples also took what views *he* chose of the songs of the prophets,—or wrote songs of his own, more adapted to the principles of the College, and the ethics of London. Maurice, in all his addresses to us, dwelt mainly on the simple function of a college as a collection or collation of friendly persons,—not in the least as a place in which such and such things were to be taught, and others denied; such and such conduct vowed, and other such and such abjured. So the College went on,—collecting, carpentering, sketching, Bible criticising, etc., virtually with no head; but only a clasp to the strap of its waist, and as many heads as it had students. The leaven of its affectionate temper has gone far; but how far also the leaven of its pride, and defiance of everything above it, nobody quite knows. I took two special pupils out of its ranks to carry them forward all I could. One I chose; the other chose me—or rather, chose my mother's maid Hannah; for love of whom he came to the College, learned drawing there under Rossetti and me,—and became eventually, Mr George Allen of Sunnyside; who, I hope, still looks back to his having been an entirely honest and perfect working joiner as the foundation of his prosperity in life. The other student I chose myself, a carpenter* of equal skill and great fineness of faculty; but his pride, wilfulness, and certain angular narrownesses of nature, kept him down,—together with the deadly influence of London itself, and of working men's clubs, as well as colleges. And finally, in this case, and many more, I have very clearly ascertained that the only proper school for workmen is of the work their fathers bred them to, under masters able to do better than any of their men, and with common principles of honesty and the fear of God, to guide the firm.

16. Somewhat before the date of my farewell to Maurician free-thinking, I had come into still more definite collision with the Puritan dogmata which forbid thinking at all, in a séance* to which I was invited, shyly, by my friend Macdonald,—fashionable séance of Evangelical doctrine, at the Earl of Ducie's; presided over by Mr Molyneux, then a divine of celebrity in that sect; who sate with one leg over his other knee in the attitude always given to Herod at the massacre of the Innocents in mediaeval sculpture; and discoursed in tones of consummate assurance and satisfaction, and to the entire comfort and consent of his

Belgravian audience, on the beautiful parable of the Prodigal Son.* Which, or how many, of his hearers he meant to describe as having personally lived on husks, and devoured their fathers' property, did not of course appear; but that something of the sort was necessary to the completeness of the joy in heaven over them, now in Belgrave Square, at the feet—or one foot—of Mr Molyneux, could not be questioned.

Waiting my time, till the raptures of the converted company had begun to flag a little, I ventured, from a back seat to enquire of Mr Molyneux what we were to learn from the example of the *other* son, not prodigal, who was, his father said of him, 'ever with me, and all that I have, thine'?* A sudden horror, and unanimous feeling of the serpent having, somehow, got over the wall into their Garden of Eden, fell on the whole company; and some of them, I thought, looked at the candles, as if they expected them to burn blue.* After a pause of a minute, gathering himself into an expression of pity and indulgence, withholding latent thunder, Mr Molyneux explained to me that the home-staying son was merely a picturesque figure introduced to fill the background of the parable agreeably, and contained no instruction or example for the well-disposed scriptural student, but, on the contrary, rather a snare for the unwary, and a temptation to self-righteousness,—which was, of all sins, the most offensive to God.

Under the fulmination of which answer I retired, as from Maurice's, from the séance in silence; nor ever attended another of the kind from that day to this.

17. But neither the Puritanism of Belgravia, nor Liberalism of Red Lion Square, interested, or offended, me, otherwise than as the grotesque conditions of variously typhoid or smoke-dried London life. To my old Scotch shepherd Puritanism, and the correspondent forms of noble French Protestantism, I never for an instant failed in dutiful affection and honour. From John Bunyan and Isaac Ambrose, I had received the religion by which I still myself lived, as far as I had spiritual life at all; and I had again and again proof enough of its truth, within limits, to have served me for all my own need, either in this world or the next. But my ordained business, and mental gifts, were outside of those limits. I saw, as clearly as I saw the sky and its stars, that music in Scotland was not to be studied under a Free Church precentor, nor indeed under any disciples of John Knox, but of Signior David; that, similarly, painting in England was not to be admired in the illuminations of Watts' hymns; nor architecture in the design of Mr Irons' chapel in the Grove. And here I must take up a thread of my mental history, as yet unfastened.

18. I have spoken several times* of the effect given cheaply to my drawings of architecture by dexterous dots and flourishes, doing duty for ornament. Already, in 1845, I had begun to distinguish Corinthian from Norman capitals, and in 1848, drew the niches and sculpture of French Gothic with precision and patience. But I had never cared for ornamental design until in 1850 or '51 I chanced, at a bookseller's in a back alley, on a little fourteenth century Hours of the Virgin,* not of refined work, but extremely rich, grotesque, and full of pure colour.

The new worlds which every leaf of this book opened to me, and the joy I had, counting their letters and unravelling their arabesques as if they had all been of beaten gold,—as many of them indeed were,—cannot be told, any more than—everything else, of good, that I wanted to tell. Not that the worlds thus opening were themselves new, but only the possession of any part in them; for long and long ago I had gazed at the illuminated missals* in noblemen's houses (see above, p. 9), with a wonder and sympathy deeper than I can give now; my love of toil, and of treasure, alike getting their thirst gratified in them. For again and again I must repeat it, my nature is a worker's and a miser's; and I rejoiced, and rejoice still, in the mere quantity of chiselling in marble, and stitches in embroidery; and was never tired of numbering sacks of gold and caskets of jewels in the Arabian Nights: and though I am generous too, and love giving, yet my notion of charity is not at all dividing my last crust with a beggar, but riding through a town like a Commander of the Faithful,* having any quantity of sequins and ducats in saddle-bags (where cavalry officers have holsters for their pistols), and throwing them round in radiant showers and hailing handfuls; with more bags to brace on when those were empty.

19. But now that I had a missal of my own, and could touch its leaves and turn, and even here and there understand the Latin of it, no girl of seven years old with a new doll is prouder or happier: but the feeling was something between the girl's with her doll, and Aladdin's in a new Spirit-slave to build palaces for him with jewel windows. For truly a well-illuminated missal is a fairy cathedral full of painted windows, bound together to carry in one's pocket, with the music and the blessing of all its prayers besides.

And then followed, of course, the discovery that all beautiful prayers were Catholic,—all wise interpretations of the Bible Catholic;—and every manner of Protestant written services whatsoever either insolently altered corruptions, or washed-out and ground-down rags and débris of the great Catholic collects, litanies, and songs of praise.

'But why did not you become a Catholic at once, then?'

It might as well be asked, Why did not I become a fire-worshipper? I *could* become nothing but what I was or was growing into. I no more believed in the living Pope than I did in the living Khan of Tartary. I saw indeed that twelfth century psalters were lovely and right, and that presbyterian prayers against time, by people who never expected to be any the better for them, were unlovely and wrong. But I had never read the Koran, nor Confucius, nor Plato, nor Hesiod, and was only just beginning to understand my Virgil and Horace. How I ever came to understand *them* is a new story, which must be for next chapter:* meantime let me finish the confessions of this one in the tale of my final apostacy from Puritan doctrine.

20. The most stern practical precept of that doctrine still holding me,—it is curiously inbound with all the rest,—was the Sabbath keeping; the idea that one was not to seek one's own pleasure on Sunday, nor to do anything useful. Gradually, in honest Bible reading, I saw that Christ's first article of teaching was to unbind the yoke of the Sabbath, while, *as* a Jew, He yet obeyed the Mosaic law* concerning it; but that St Paul had carefully abolished it altogether, and that the rejoicing, in memory of the Resurrection, on the Day of the Sun, the first of the week, was only by misunderstanding, and much wilful obstinacy, confused with the Sabbath of the Jew.

Nevertheless, the great passages in the Old Testament regarding its observance held their power over me, nor have ceased to do so; but the inveterate habit of being unhappy all Sunday did not in any way fulfil the order to call the Sabbath a delight.*

I have registered the year 1858 as the next, after 1845, in which I had complete guidance of myself. Couttet met me at Basle, and I went on to Rheinfelden with great joy, and stayed to draw town and bridges completely (two of the studies are engraved in 'Modern Painters').

21. I think it was the second Sunday there, and no English church. I had read the service with George, and gone out afterwards alone for a walk up a lovely dingle on the Black Forest side of the Rhine, where every pretty cottage was inscribed, in fair old German characters, with the date of its building, the names of the married pair who had built it, and a prayer that, with God's blessing, their habitation of it, and its possession by their children, might be in righteousness and peace. Not in these set terms, of course, oh every house, but in variously quaint verses or mottoes, meaning always as much as this.

Very happy in my Sunday walk,* I gathered what wild flowers were in their first springing, and came home with a many-coloured cluster, in which the dark-purple orchis was chief. I had never examined its structure before, and by this afternoon sunlight did so with care; also it seemed to me wholly right to describe it as I examined; and to draw the outlines as I described, though with a dimly alarmed consciousness of its being a new fact in existence for me, that I should draw on Sunday.

22. Which thenceforward I continued to do, if it seemed to me there was due occasion. Nevertheless, come to pass how it might, the real new fact in existence for me was that my drawings did not prosper that year, and, in deepest sense, never prospered again. They might not have prospered in the course of things,—and indeed, could not without better guidance than my own; nevertheless, the crisis of change is marked at Rheinfelden by my having made there two really pretty colour-vignettes which, had I only gone on doing the like of, the journey would have been visibly successful in everybody's sight. Whereas, what actually followed those vignettes at Rheinfelden was a too ambitious attempt at the cliffs of the Bay of Uri, which crushed the strength down in me; and next, a persistently furious one to draw the entire town, three fortresses, and surrounding mountains of Bellinzona, gradually taming and contracting itself into a meekly obstinate resolve that at least I would draw every stone of the roof right in *one* tower of the vineyards,—'cette baraque,' as Couttet called it.

I *did* draw every stone, nearly right, at last in that single roof; and meantime read the Plutus of Aristophanes, three or four times over in two months, with long walks every afternoon, besides. Total result on 1st of August—general desolation, and disgust with Bellinzona,—cette baraque,—and most of all with myself, for not yet knowing Greek enough to translate the Plutus. In this state of mind, a fit took me of hunger for city life again, military bands, nicely-dressed people, and shops with something inside. And I emphasized Couttet's disapproval of the whole tour, by announcing to him suddenly that I was going, of all places in the world, to Turin!

23. I had still some purpose, even in this libertinage, namely, to outline the Alpine chain from Monte Viso to Monte Rosa. Its base was within a drive; and there were Veroneses in the Royal gallery, for wet days. The luxury of the Hôtel de l'Europe was extremely pleasant after brick floors and bad dinners at Bellinzona;—there was a quiet little opera house, where it was always a kindness to the singers to attend to the stage business; finally, any quantity of marching and manoeuvring by the best troops in Italy, with perfect military bands, beautifully tossing plumes, and pretty ladies looking on. So I settled at Turin for the autumn.

There, one Sunday morning, I made my way in the south suburb to a little chapel which, by a dusty roadside, gathered to its unobserved door the few sheep of the old Waldensian faith who had wandered from their own pastures under Monte Viso into the worldly capital of Piedmont.

The assembled congregation numbered in all some three or four and twenty, of whom fifteen or sixteen were grey-haired women. Their solitary and clerkless preacher, a somewhat stunted figure in a plain black coat, with a cracked voice, after leading them through the languid forms of prayer which are all that in truth are possible to people whose present life is dull and its terrestrial future unchangeable, put his utmost zeal into a consolatory discourse on the wickedness of the wide world, more especially of the plain of Piedmont and city of Turin, and on the exclusive favour with God, enjoyed by the between nineteen and twenty-four elect members of his congregation, in the streets of Admah and Zeboim.*

Myself neither cheered nor greatly alarmed by this doctrine, I walked back into the condemned city, and up into the gallery where Paul Veronese's Solomon and the Queen of Sheba* glowed in full afternoon light. The gallery windows being open, there came in with the warm air, floating swells and falls of military music, from the courtyard before the palace, which seemed to me more devotional, in their perfect art, tune, and discipline, than anything I remembered of evangelical hymns. And as the perfect colour and sound gradually asserted their power on me, they seemed finally to fasten me in the old article of Jewish faith, that things done delightfully and rightly, were always done by the help and in the Spirit of God.*

Of course that hour's meditation in the gallery of Turin only concluded the courses of thought which had been leading me to such end through many years. There was no sudden conversion possible to me, either by preacher, picture, or dulcimer. But that day, my evangelical beliefs were put away, to be debated of no more.

CHAPTER II

MONT VELAN

24. I WAS crowded for room at the end of last chapter, and could not give account of one or two bits of investigation of the Vaudois character, which preceded the Queen of Sheba crash. It wasn't the Queen herself,—by the way,—but only one of her maids of honour, on whose

gold brocaded dress, (relieved by a black's head, who carried two red and green parrots on a salver,) I worked till I could do no more;—to my father's extreme amazement and disgust, when I brought the petticoat, parrots, and blackamoor, home, as the best fruit of my summer at the Court of Sardinia; together with one lurid thunderstorm on the Rosa Alps, another on the Cenis, and a dream or two of mist on the Viso. But I never could make out the set of the rocks on the peak of Viso; and after I had spent about a hundred pounds at Turin in grapes, partridges, and the opera, my mother sent me five, to make my peace with Heaven in a gift to the Vaudois churches. So I went and passed a Sunday beneath Viso; found he had neither rocks nor glaciers worth mentioning, and that I couldn't get into any pleasant confidences with the shepherds, because their dogs barked and snarled irreconcileably, and seemed to have nothing taught them by their masters but to regard all the rest of mankind as thieves.

I had some pious talk of a mild kind with the person I gave my mother's five pounds to: but an infinitely pleasanter feeling from the gratitude of the overworn ballerina at Turin, for the gift of as many of my own. She was not the least pretty; and depended precariously on keeping able for her work on small pittance; but did that work well always; and looked nice,—near the footlights.

I noticed also curiously at this time, that while the drawings I did to please myself seemed to please nobody else, the little pen-and-ink sketches made for my father, merely to explain where I was, came always well;—one, of the sunset shining down a long street through a grove of bayonets, which he was to imagine moving to military music, is pleasant to me yet. But, on the whole, Turin began at last to bore me as much as Bellinzona; so I thought it might be as well to get home. I drove to Susa on the last day of August, walked quietly with Couttet over the Cenis to Lans-le-bourg next day; and on 2nd September sent my mother my love, by telegram, for breakfast-time, on her birthday, getting answer of thanks back before twelve o'clock; and began to think there might be something in telegraphs, after all.

25. A number of unpleasant convictions were thus driven into my head, in that 1858 journey, like Jael's nail through Sisera's temples; or Tintoret's arrow between St Sebastian's eyes*—I must return a moment to Mr Maurice and Deborah before going on to pleasanter matters. Maurice was not, I suppose, in the habit of keeping a skull on his chimney-piece, and looking at it before he went to sleep, as I had been, for a long while before that talk; or he would have felt that whether it was by nail, bullet, or little pin, mattered little when it was

ordained that the crowned forehead should sink in slumber. And he would have known that Jael was only one of the forms of 'Dira Necessitas'—she, Delilah, and Judith, all the three of them; only we haven't any record of Delilah's hymn when she first fastened Samson's hair to the beam: and of Judith nobody says any harm;—I suppose because she gave Holofernes wine, instead of milk and butter.* It was Byron, however, not Deborah, who made *me* understand the thing; the passage he paraphrased from her, in the Giaour, having rung in my ears ever since I wrote the Scythian banquet-song*—

> 'The browsing camels' bells are tinkling,
> His mother looked from her lattice high,' etc.

And I felt now that I had myself driven nails enough into my mother's heart, if not into my father's coffin; and would thankfully have taken her home a shawl of divers colours on both sides, and a pretty damsel or two, in imitation of Sisera:* but she always liked to choose her damsels for herself.

It was lucky, in her last choosing, she chanced on Joan Agnew; but we are a far way yet from Joanie's time, I don't quite know how far. Turner died, as I said, in 1851: Prout had left us still earlier;* there could be no more sharing of festivities on my birthday with *him*. He went home to De-Crespigny Terrace from Denmark Hill one evening, seeming perfectly well and happy;—and we saw him no more.

26. And my dog Wisie,* was he dead too? It seems wholly wonderful to me at this moment that he should ever have died. He was a white Spitz, exactly like Carpaccio's dog in the picture of St Jerome;* and he came to me from a young Austrian officer, who had got tired of him,—the Count Thun, who fell afterwards at Solferino. Before the dog was used enough to us, George and I took him to Lido to give him a little sea bath. George was holding him by his forepaws upright among the little crisp breakers. Wisie snatched them out of his hands, and ran at full speed—into Fairyland, like Frederick the Great at Mollwitz.* He was lost on Lido for three days and nights, living by petty larceny, the fishermen and cottagers doing all they could to catch him; but they told me he 'ran like a hare and leaped like a horse.'

At last, either overcome by hunger, or having made up his mind that even *my* service was preferable to liberty on Lido, he took the deep water in broad daylight, and swam straight for Venice. A fisherman saw him from a distance, rowed after him, took him, tired among the weeds, and brought him to me—the Madonna della Salute having been propitious to his repentant striving with the sea.

From that time he became an obedient and affectionate dog, though of extremely self-willed and self-possessed character. I was then living on the north side of St Mark's Place, and he used to sit outside the window on the ledge at the base of its pillars greater part of the day, observant of the manners and customs of Venice. Returning to England, I took him over the St Gothard, but found him entirely unappalled by any of the work of Devils on it—big or little. He saw nothing to trouble himself about in precipices, if they were wide enough to put his paws on; and the dog who had fled madly from a crisp sea wave, trotted beside the fall of the Reuss just as if it had been another White Dog, a little bigger, created out of foam.

27. Reaching Paris, he considered it incumbent upon him to appear unconscious of the existence of that city, or of the Tuileries gardens and Rue Rivoli, since they were not St Mark's Place; but, half asleep one evening, on a sofa in the entresol at Meurice's, and hearing a bark in the street which sounded Venetian,—sprang through the window in expectation of finding himself on the usual ledge—and fell fifteen feet[1] to the pavement. As I ran down, I met him rushing up the hotel stairs, (he had gathered himself from the stones in an instant), bleeding and giddy; he staggered round and round two or three times, and fell helpless on the floor. I don't know if young ladies' dogs faint, really, when they are hurt. He, Wisie, did not faint, nor even moan, but he could not stir, except in cramped starts and shivers. I sent for what veterinary help was within reach, and heard that the dog might recover, if he could be kept quiet for a day or two in a dog-hospital. But my omnibus was at the door—for the London train. In the very turn and niche of time I heard that Macdonald of St Martin's* was in the hotel, and would take charge of Wisie for the time necessary. The poor little speechless, luckless, wistfully gazing doggie was tenderly put in a pretty basket, (going to be taken where? thinks the beating heart,) looks at his master to read what he can in the sad face—can make out nothing; is hurried out of the inexorable door, downstairs; finds himself more nearly dead next day, and among strangers. (*Two miles* away from Meurice's, along the Boulevard, it was.)

He takes and keeps counsel with himself on that matter. Drinks and eats what he is given, gratefully; swallows his medicine obediently; stretches his limbs from time to time. There was only a wicket gate, he saw, between the Boulevard and him. Silently, in the early dawn of the

---

[1] Thirteen feet nine, I find, on exact measurement—coming back to Meurice's to make sure. It is the height of the capitals of the piers in the Rue Rivoli.

fourth or fifth day—I think—he leaped it, and along two miles of Parisian Boulevard came back to Meurice's.

I do not believe there was ever a more wonderful piece of instinct certified. For Macdonald received him, in astonishment,—and Wisie trusted Macdonald to bring him to his lost master again. The Schehallien chief brought him to Denmark Hill; where of course Wisie did not know whether something still worse might not befall him, or whether he would be allowed to stay. But he was allowed, and became a bright part of my mother's day, as well as of mine, from 1852 to 1858, or perhaps longer. But I must go back now to 1854–6.

28. 1854. The success of the first volume of 'Modern Painters' of course gave me entrance to the polite circles of London; but at that time, even more than now, it was a mere torment and horror to me to have to talk to big people whom I didn't care about. Sometimes, indeed, an incident happened that was amusing or useful to me;—I heard Macaulay spout the first chapter of Isaiah, without understanding a syllable of it;—saw the Bishop of Oxford taught by Sir Robert Inglis to drink sherry-cobbler through a straw;*—and formed one of the worshipful concourse invited by the Bunsen family, to hear them 'talk Bunsenese' (Lady Trevelyan), and *see* them making presents to—each other—from their family Christmas tree, and private manger of German Magi. But, as a rule, the hours given to the polite circles were an angering penance to me,—until, after I don't know how many, a good chance came, worth all the penitentiary time endured before.

I had been introduced one evening, with a little more circumstance than usual, to a seated lady, beside whom it was evidently supposed I should hold it a privilege to stand for a minute or two, with leave to speak to her. I entirely concurred in that view of the matter; but, having ascertained in a moment that she was too pretty to be looked at, and yet keep one's wits about one, I followed, in what talk she led me to, with my eyes on the ground. Presently, in some reference to Raphael or Michael Angelo, or the musical glasses,* the word 'Rome' occurred; and a minute afterwards, something about 'Christmas in 1840.' I looked up with a start; and saw that the face was oval,—fair,—the hair, light-brown. After a pause, I was rude enough to repeat her words, 'Christmas in 1840!—were you in Rome *then?*' 'Yes,' she said, a little surprised, and now meeting my eyes with hers, inquiringly.

Another tenth of a minute passed before I spoke again.

'Why, I lost all that winter in Rome in hunting *you!*'

It was Egeria herself! then Mrs Cowper-Temple. She was not angry; and became from that time forward a tutelary power,—of the brightest and happiest; differing from Lady Trevelyan's, in that Lady Trevelyan hadn't all her own way at home; and taught me, therefore, to look upon life as a 'Spiritual combat;' but Egeria always had her own way every-where,—thought that I also should have mine,—and generally got it for me.

29. She was able to get a good deal of it for me, almost immedi-ately, at Broadlands, because Mr Cowper-Temple was at that time Lord Palmerston's private secretary: and it had chanced that in 1845 I had some correspondence with the government about Tintaret's Crucifixion;—not the great Crucifixion in the Scuola di San Rocco, but the bright one with the grove of lances in the Church of St Cassan, which I wanted to get for the National Gallery.* I wrote to Lord Palmerston about it, and believe we should have got it, but for Mr Edward Cheney's putting a spoke in the wheel for pure spite. However, Lord Palmerston was, I believe, satisfied with what I had done; and, now perhaps thinking there might be some trustworthy offi-cial qualities in me, allowed Mr Cowper-Temple to bring me, one Saturday evening, to go down with him to Broadlands. It was dark when we reached the South-Western station. Lord Palmerston received me much as Lord Oldborough receives Mr Temple in 'Patronage;'—gave me the seat opposite his own, he with his back to the engine, Mr Cowper-Temple beside me;—Lord Palmerston's box of business papers on the seat beside *him*. He unlocked it, and looked over a few,—said some hospitable words, enough to put me at ease, and went to sleep, or at least remained quiet, till we got to Romsey. I forget the dinner, that Saturday; but I certainly had to take in Lady Palmerston; and must have pleased her more or less, for on the Sunday morning, Lord Palmerston took me himself to the service in Romsey Abbey: drawing me out a little in the drive through the village; and *that* day at dinner he put me on his right hand, and led the conversation dis-tinctly to the wildest political theories I was credited with,[1] cross-examining me playfully, but attending quite seriously to my points; and kindly and clearly showing me where I should fail, in practice. He disputed no principle with me, (being, I fancied, partly of the same mind with me about principles,) but only feasibilities; whereas in every talk permitted me more recently by Mr Gladstone, *he* disputes *all* the

---

[1] The reader-will please remember that the 'Life of the Workman'* in the 'Stones of Venice,' the long note on Education at the end of first volume of 'Modern Painters,'* and the fierce vituperation of the Renaissance schools in all my historical teaching, were at this time attracting far more attention, because part of my architectural and pictorial work, than ever afterwards the commercial and social analyses of 'Unto This Last.'

principles before their application; and the application of all that get past the dispute. D'Israeli* differed from both in making a jest alike of principle and practice; but I never came into full collision with him but once. It is a long story, about little matters; but they had more influence in the end than many greater ones,—so I will write them.

30. I never went to official dinners in Oxford if I could help it; not that I was ever really wanted at them, but sometimes it became my duty to go, as an Art Professor; and when the Princess of Wales came, one winter,* to look over the Art Galleries, I had of course to attend, and be of what use I could: and then came commands to the dinner at the Deanery,—where I knew no more how to behave than a marmot pup! However, my place was next but one to D'Israeli's, whose head, seen close, interested me; the Princess, in the centre of the opposite side of the table, might be glanced at now and then,—to the forgetfulness of the evils of life. Nobody wanted *me* to talk about anything; and I recovered peace of mind enough, in a little while, to hear D'Israeli talk, which was nice; I think we even said something to each other, once, about the salmon. Well—then, presently I was aware of a little ripple of brighter converse going round the table, and saw it had got at the Princess, and a glance of D'Israeli's made me think it must have something to do with *me*. And so it had, thus:—It had chanced either the day before, or the day before that, that the Planet Saturn had treated me with his usual adversity in the carrying out of a plot with Alice in Wonderland.* For, that evening, the Dean and Mrs Liddell dined by command at Blenheim: but the girls were not commanded; and as I had been complaining of never getting a sight of them lately, after knowing them from the nursery, Alice said that she thought, perhaps, if I would come round after papa and mamma were safe off to Blenheim, Edith and she might give me a cup of tea and a little singing, and Rhoda show me how she was getting on with her drawing and geometry, or the like. And so it was arranged. The night was wild with snow, and no one likely to come round to the Deanery after dark. I think Alice must have sent me a little note, when the eastern coast of Tom Quad was clear. I slipped round from Corpus through Peckwater, shook the snow off my gown, and found an armchair ready for me, and a bright fireside, and a laugh or two, and some pretty music looked out, and tea coming up.

31. Well, I think Edith had got the tea made, and Alice was just bringing the muffins to perfection—I don't recollect that Rhoda was there; (I never did, that anybody else was there, if Edith was; but it is

all so like a dream now, I'm not sure)—when there was a sudden sense of some stars having been blown out by the wind, round the corner; and then a crushing of the snow outside the house, and a drifting of it inside; and the children all scampered out to see what was wrong, and I followed slowly;—and there were the Dean and Mrs Liddell standing just in the middle of the hall, and the footmen in consternation, and a silence,—and—

'How sorry you must be to see us, Mr Ruskin!' began at last Mrs Liddell.

'I never was more so,' I replied. 'But what's the matter?'

'Well,' said the Dean, 'we couldn't even get past the parks; the snow's a fathom deep in the Woodstock Road. But never mind; we'll be very good and quiet, and keep out of the way. Go back to your tea, and we'll have our dinner downstairs.'

And so we did; but we couldn't keep papa and mamma out of the drawing-room when they had done dinner, and I went back to Corpus, disconsolate.

Now, whether the Dean told the Princess himself, or whether Mrs Liddell told, or the girls themselves, *somehow* this story got all round the dinner-table, and D'Israeli was perfect in every detail, in ten minutes, nobody knew how. When the Princess rose, there was clearly a feeling on her part of some kindness to me; and she came very soon, in the drawing-room, to receive the report of the Slade Professor.

32. Now, in the Deanery drawing-room, everybody in Oxford who hadn't been at the dinner was waiting to have their slice of Princess—due officially—and to be certified in the papers next day. The Princess,—knowing whom she had to speak to,—*might* speak to, or mightn't, without setting the whole of Oxford by the ears next day, simply walked to the people she chose to honour with audience, and stopped, to hear if they had anything to say. I saw my turn had come, and the revolving zodiac brought its fairest sign to me: she paused, and the attendant stars and terrestrial beings round, listened, to hear what the marmot-pup had to say for itself.

In the space of, say, a minute and a half, I told the Princess that Landscape-painting had been little cultivated by the Heads of Colleges,—that it had been still less cultivated by the Undergraduates, and that my young-lady pupils always expected me to teach them how to paint like Turner, in six lessons. Finding myself getting into difficulties, I stopped: the Princess, I suppose, felt I was getting *her* into difficulties too; so she bowed courteously, and went on—to the next Professor, in silence.

33. The crowd, which had expected a compliment to Her Royal Highness of best Modern Painter quality, was extremely disappointed: and a blank space seemed at once to form itself round me, when the door from the nurseries opened; and—enter Rhoda—in full dress!

Very beautiful! But just a snip too short in the petticoats,—a trip too dainty in the ankles, a dip too deep of sweetbriar-red in the ribands. Not the damsel who came to hearken, named Rhoda,—by any means;— but as exquisite a little spray of rhododendron ferrugineum* as ever sparkled in Alpine dew.

D'Israeli saw his opening in an instant. Drawing himself to his full height, he advanced to meet Rhoda. The whole room became all eyes and ears. Bowing with kindly reverence, he waved his hand, and introduced her to—the world. '*This* is, I understand, the young lady in whose art-education Professor Ruskin is so deeply interested!'

And there was nothing for *me* but simple extinction; for I had never given Rhoda a lesson in my life, (no such luck!); yet I could not disclaim the interest,—nor disown Mr Macdonald's geometry! I *could* only bow as well as a marmot might, in imitation of the Minister; and get at once away to Corpus, out of human ken.

34. This gossip has beguiled me till I have no time left to tell what in proper sequence should have been chiefly dwelt on in this number,—the effect on my mind of the Hospice of St Bernard, as opposed to the Hermitage of St Bruno. I must pass at once to the outline of some scenes in early Swiss history, of which the reader must be reminded before he can understand why I had set my heart so earnestly upon drawing the ruined towers of Fribourg, Thun, and Rheinfelden.

In the mountain kingdom of which I claimed possession by the law of love, in first seeing it from the Col de la Faucille, the ranges of entirely celestial mountain, the 'everlasting clouds'* whose glory does not fade, are arranged in clusters of summits definitely distinct in form, and always recognizable, each in its own beauty, by any careful observer who has once seen them on the south and north. Of these, the most beautiful in Switzerland, and as far as I can read, or learn, the most beautiful mountain in the world, is the Jungfrau of Lauterbrunnen. Next to her, the double peaks of the Wetterhorn and Wellhorn, with their glacier of Rosenlaui; next to these, the Aiguille de Bionnassay, the buttress of Mont Blanc on the south-west; and after these loveliest, the various summits of the Bernese, Chamouni, and Zermatt Alps, according to their relative power, and the advantage of their place for the general observer. Thus the Blumlis Alp, though only ten thousand feet high, has far greater general influence than the Mont Combin, which is nearly as high as Mont Blanc, but can only be seen with difficulty, and in no association with the lowlands.

35. Among subordinate peaks, five,—the Tournette of Annecy, the Dent du Midi of Bex, the Stockhorn, south of Thun, Mont Pilate at Lucerne, and the High Sentis of Appenzell,—are notable as outlying masses, of extreme importance in their effect on the approaches to the greater chain. But in that chain itself, no mountain of subordinate magnitude can assert any rivalship with Mont Velan, the ruling alp of the Great St Bernard.

For Mont Velan signals down the valley of the Rhone, past St Maurice, to Vevay, the line of the true natural pass of the Great St Bernard, from France into Italy by the valley of Martigny, and Val d'Aosta; a perfectly easy and accessible pass for horse and foot, through all the summer; not dangerous even in winter, except in storm; and from the earliest ages, down to Napoleon's, the pass chosen by the greatest kings, and wisest missionaries. The defiles of the Simplon were still impassable in the twelfth century, and the Episcopate of the Valais was therefore an isolated territory branching up from Martigny; unassailable from above, but in connection with the Monastery of St Bernard and Abbey of St Maurice, holding alike Burgundian, Swiss, and Saracen powers at bay, beyond the Castle of Chillon.

And I must remind the reader that at the time when Swiss history opens, there was no such country as France, in her existing strength. There was a sacred 'Isle of France,' and a group of cities,—Amiens, Paris, Soissons, Rheims, Chartres, Sens, and Troyes,—essentially French, in arts, and faith. But round this Frank central province lay Picardy, Normandy, Brittany, Anjou, Aquitaine, Languedoc, and Provence, all of them independent national powers: and on the east of the Côte d'Or,[1] the strong and true *kingdom* of Burgundy, which for centuries contended with Germany for the dominion of Switzerland, and, from *her* Alpine throne, of Europe.

36. This was, I have said, at the time 'when Swiss history opens'—*as such*. It opens a century earlier, in 773, as a part of all Christian history, when Charlemagne convoked his Franks at Geneva to invade Italy, and dividing them there into two bodies, placed Swiss mountaineers at the head of each, and sending one division by the Great St Bernard, under his own uncle, Bernard,[2] the son of

---

[1] The eastern boundary of France proper is formed by the masses of the Vosges, Côte d'Or, and Monts de la Madeleine.

[2] Don't confuse *him* with St Bernard of Annecy, from whom the pass is named; nor St Bernard of Annecy with St Bernard of Dijon, the Madonna's chosen servant.

Charles Martel, led the other himself over the Cenis. It was for this march over the Great St Bernard that Charlemagne is said to have given the foresters of the central Alps their three trumpets—the Bull of Uri, the Cow of Unterwald, and the Horn of Lucerne; and, without question, after his Italian victories, Switzerland became the organic centre of civilization to his whole empire.* 'It is thus,' says M. Gaullieur, 'that the heroic history of old Zurich, and the annals of Thurgovie and Rhétie, are full of the memorable acts of the Emperor of the West, and among other traditions the foundation of the Water-church, (Wasserkirche,) at Zurich, attaches itself to the sight of a marvellous serpent who came to ask justice of the Emperor, in a place where he gave it to all his subjects, by the Limmat shore.'

37. I pause here a moment to note that there used to be indeed harmless water serpents in the Swiss waters, when perfectly pure. I myself saw those of the Lac de Chêde, in the year 1833, and had one of them drawn out of the water by the char-a-banc driver with his whip, that I might see the yellow ring round its neck. The colour of the body was dark green. If the reader will compare the account given in 'Eagle's Nest'* of one of the serpents of the Giesbach, he will understand at once how easily the myths of antiquity would attach themselves among the Alps, as much to the living serpent as to the living eagle.

Also, let the reader note that the *beryl*-coloured water of the Lake of Zurich and the Limmat gave, in old days, the perfectest type of purity, of all the Alpine streams. The deeper blue of the Reuss and Rhone grew dark at less depth, and always gave some idea of the presence of a mineral element, causing the colour,* while the Aar had soiled itself with clay even before reaching Berne. But the pale aquamarine crystal of the Lake of Zurich, with the fish set in it, some score of them— small and great—to a cube fathom, and the rapid fall and stainless ripple of the Limmat, through the whole of its course under the rocks of Baden to the Reuss, remained, summer and winter, of a constant, sacred, inviolable, supernatural loveliness.

By the shore of the Limmat then, sate Charlemagne to do justice, as Canute by the sea:—the first 'Water church' of the beginning river is his building; and never was St Jerome's rendering of the twenty-third Psalm sung in any church more truly: 'In loco, pascue, ibi collocavit me, *super aquam refectionis educavit.*'* But the Cathedral Minister of Zurich dates from days no longer questionable or fabulous.

38. During the first years of the tenth century, Switzerland was disputed between Rodolph II, King of Burgundy, and Bourcard, Duke of Swabia. The German duke at last defeated Rodolph, near Winterthur;

but with so much difficulty, that he chose rather thenceforward to have him for ally rather than enemy; and gave him, for pledge of peace, his daughter BERTHA, to be Burgundian queen.

Bertha, the daughter of the Duke Bourcard and Regilinda, was at this time only thirteen or fourteen. The marriage was not celebrated till 921—and let the reader remember that marriage,—though there was no Wedding March played at it, but many a wedding prayer said,—for the beginning of all happiness to *Burgundy*, *Switzerland*, and *Germany*. Her husband, in the first ten years after their marriage, in alliance with Henry the Fowler of Germany, drove the Saracen and Hungarian nomad armies out of the Alps: and then Bertha set herself to efface the traces of their ravages; building, everywhere through her territories, castles, monasteries, walled towns, and towers of refuge; restoring the town and church of Soleure in 930, of Moutiers in the Jura, in 932; in the same year endowing the canons of Amsoldingen at Thun, and then the church of Neuchâtel; finally, towards 935, the church and convent of Zurich, of which her mother Regilinda became abbess in 949, and remained abbess till her death;—the Queen Bertha herself residing chiefly near her, in a tower on Mont Albis.

39. In 950 Bertha had to mourn the death of her son-in-law Lothaire, and the imprisonment of her daughter Adelaide on the Lake of Garda. But Otho the Great, of Germany, avenged Lothaire, drove Berenger out of Italy, and himself married Adelaide, reinstating Conrad of Burgundy on the throne of Burgundy and Switzerland: and then Bertha, strong at once under the protection of the king her son, and the emperor her son-in-law, and with her mother beside her, Abbess of the Convent des Dames Nobles of Zurich, began her work of perfect beneficence to the whole of Switzerland.

In the summer times, spinning from her distaff as she rode, she traversed—the legends say, with only a country guide to lead her horse, (when such a queen's horse would need leading!)—all the now peaceful fields of her wide dominion, from Jura to the Alps. My own notion is that an Anne-of-Geierstein-like maid of honour* or two must have gleamed here and there up and down the hills beside her; and a couple of old knights, perhaps, followed at their own pace. Howsoever, the queen verily *did* know her peasants, and their cottages and fields, from Zurich to Geneva, and ministered to them for full twelve years.

40. In 962, her son Conrad gave authority almost monarchic, to her Abbey of Payerne, which could strike a coinage of its own. Not much after that time, her cousin Ulrich, Bishop of Strasbourg, came to visit her; and with him and the king her son, she revisited all the religious

institutions she had founded, and finally, with them both, consecrated the Church of Neuchâtel to the Virgin. The Monastery of the Great St Bernard was founded at the same time.

I cannot find the year of her death, but her son Conrad died in 993, and was buried beside his mother at Payerne.

And during the whole of the 11th century, and more than half of the 12th, the power of Bertha's institutions, and of the Church generally, increased in Switzerland; but gradually corrupted by its wealth of territory into a feudal hierarchy, against which, together with that of the nobles who were always at war with each other, Duke Berthold IV, of Zaehringen, undertook in 1178, the founding of FRIBOURG in Uchtland.

The culminating point of the new city above the scarped rocks which border the Sarine (on the eastern bank?) was occupied by the Château de Tyre (Tyrensis), ancient home of the Counts of that country, and cradle, it is believed, of the house of Thierstein. Berthold called his new town Freyburg, as well as that which existed already in his states of Breisgau, because he granted it in effect the same liberties, the same franchises, and the same communal charter (Handfeste) which had been given to the other Fribourg. A territory of nine leagues in circumference was given to Fribourg in Uchtland, a piece which they still call 'the old lands.' Part of the new colonists came from Breisgau, Black Forest people; part from the Roman Pays de Vaud. The Germans lived in the valley, the others on the heights. Built on the confines of France and Germany, Fribourg served for the point of contact to two nations until then hostile; and the Handfeste of Fribourg served for a model to all the municipal constitutions of Switzerland. Still, at this day, the town is divided into two parts, and into two languages.

41. This was in 1178. Twelve years later, Berthold V, the greatest and the best of the Dukes of Zaehringen, made, of the village of Burgdorf in the Emmenthal, the town of Berthoud, the name given probably from his own; and then, in the year 1191, laid the foundations of the town of BERNE.

He chose for its site a spot in the royal domain, for he intended the new city to be called the Imperial city; and the place he chose was near a manor which had served in the preceding century for occasional residence to the Rodolphian kings. It was a long high promontory, nearly an island, whose cliff sides were washed by the Aar. The Duke of Zaehringen's Marshal, Cuno of Babenberg, received orders to surround with walls the little island on which stood the simple hamlet of Berne, now become the powerful city of Berne, praiseworthy at first in the democratic spirit of its bourgeois, and afterwards in its aristocracy, whose policy, at once elevated, firm, consistent, and ambitious, mingled itself in all the great affairs of the neighbouring countries, and became a true power, upon which the sovereigns of the first order had sometimes to count.

Lastly, Berthold built the Castle of Thun, where the Aar issues out of its lake; castle which, as may be seen at the present day, commanded the whole level plain, opening to Berne, and the pass into the Oberland.

42. Thus the three towns Fribourg, Berne, and Thun, form, at the close of the twelfth century, the triple fortress of the Dukes of Zaehringen, strengthened by a body of burghers to whom the Dukes have granted privileges till then unknown; this Ducal and Civic allied power asserting itself in entire command of Switzerland proper, against the Counts of Savoy in the south, the Burgundian princes in the east, and the ecclesiastical power of Italy, vested in the Bishops of Sion, in the Valais,—thence extending from the mouth of the Rhone into the Pays de Vaud, and enthroned there at Payerne by the bequests of Queen Bertha. The monks of her royal abbey at Payerne, seeing that all the rights they possessed over the Pays de Vaud were endangered by the existence of Fribourg, opposed the building of the Church of St Nicholas there, asserting that the ground assigned to it and its monastery belonged to the Abbey of Payerne. Berthold IV was on the point of attacking the monks on their own rock when the nobles of the Vaud interfered, as mediators.

Four of them—Amé, Count of Geneva, Vauthier of Blonay, Conrad of Estaveyer, and Rodolph of Montagny—compelled Berthold to ratify the privileges, and resign the lands, of the monks of Payerne, by a deed signed in 1178; the church and monastery of St Nicholas being founded at Fribourg under their rule. And this constitution of Fribourg, whether the Dukes of Zaehringen foresaw it or not, became the fecund germ of a new social order. The 'Commune' was the origin of the 'Canton,' 'and the beneficent aera of communal liberty served for *acheminement** to the constitutional liberties and legislative codes of modern society.'

43. Thus far M. Gaullieur, from whose widow I leased my own chalet at Mornex, and whose son I instructed, to the best of my power, in clearing land of useless stones on the slope of the Salève,—under the ruins of the old Château de Savoie, the central castle, once, of all Savoy; on the site of which, and summit of its conical hill-throne, seated himself, in his pleasure villa, all the summer long, my very dear friend and physician, old Dr Gosse of Geneva; whose mountain garden,

about three hundred feet above mine, was indeed enclosed by the remaining walls and angle towers of the Castle of Savoy, of which the Doctor had repaired the lowest tower so as to serve for a reservoir to the rain rushing down the steep garden slopes in storm,—and to let none of it be wasted afterwards in the golden Salève sunshine.

'C'était une tour de guerre,' said the Doctor to me triumphantly, as he first led me round the confines of his estate. 'Voyez. C'était une tour de guerre. J'en ai fait une bouteille!'*

44. But that walk by the castle wall was long after the Mont Velan times of which I am now telling;—in returning to which, will the reader please note the homes of the four Vaudois knights who stood for Queen Bertha's monastery: Amé of Geneva, Vauthier of Blonay, Conrad of Estaveyer, and Rodolph of Montagny?

Amé's castle of Geneva stood on the island, where the clock tower is now; and has long been destroyed: of Estaveyer and Montagny I know nothing; but the Castle of Blonay still stands above Vevay, as Chillon still at the head of her lake; but the château of Blonay has been modified gradually into comfort of sweet habitation, the war towers of it sustaining timber-latticed walls, and crowned by pretty turrets and pinnacles in cheerful nobleness—trellised all with fruitage or climbing flowers; its moats now all garden; its surrounding fields all lily and meadowsweet, with blue gleamings, it may be of violet, it may be of gentian; its heritage of human life guarded still in the peacefully scattered village, or farmhouse, here and there half hidden in apple-blossom, or white with fallen cherry-blossom, as if with snow.

45. I have already told how fond my father was of staying at the Trois Couronnes of Vevay, when I was up among the aiguilles of Chamouni. In later years, I acknowledged his better taste, and would contentedly stay with him at Vevay, as long as he liked,—myself always perfectly happy in the fields and on the hillsides round the Château Blonay. Also, my father and mother were quite able at any time to get up as far as Blonay themselves; and usually walked so far with me when I was intent on the higher hills,—waiting, they, and our old servant, Lucy Tovey, (whom we took abroad with us sometimes that she might see the places we were always talking of), until I had done my bit of drawing or hammering, and we all went down together, through the vineyards, to four o'clock dinner; then the evening was left free for me to study the Dent d'Oche and chains of crag declining southwards to Geneva, by sunset.

Thus Vevay, year after year, became the most domestic of all our foreign homes. At Venice, my mother always thought the gondola would upset; at Chamouni, my father, that I should fall into the Mer de Glace; at Pisa, he would ask me, 'What shall I give the coachman?' and at Florence, dispute the delightfulness of Cimabue. But at Vevay, we were all of a mind. My father was professionally at home in the vineyards,—sentimentally in the Bosquet de Julie; my mother liked apple orchards and narcissus meads as much as I did; and for me, there was the Dent du Midi, for eternal snow, in the distance; the Rochers de Naye, for climbing, accessibly near; Chillon for history and poetry; and the lake, in the whole breadth of it from Lausanne to Meillerie, for Turnerian mist effects of morning, and Turnerian sunsets at evening; and moonlights,—as if the moon were one radiant glacier of frozen gold. Then if one wanted to go to Geneva for anything, there were little steamers,—no mortal would believe, now, how little; one used to be afraid an extra basket of apples would be too much for them, when the pier was full of market people. They called at all the places along the north shore, mostly for country folks; and often their little cabins were quite empty. English people thought the lake of Geneva too dull, if they had ever more than an hour of it.

46. It chanced so, one day, when we were going from Vevay to Geneva. It was hot on the deck, and we all went down into the little cabin, which the waves from the paddle wheels rushed past the windows of, in lovely wild masses of green and silver. There was no one in the cabin but ourselves (that is to say, papa, mamma, old Anne, and me), and a family whom we supposed, rightly, to be American, of the best sort. A mother with three daughters, and her son,—he in charge of them all, perhaps of five or six and twenty; his sisters younger; the mother just old enough to *be* their mother; all of them quietly and gracefully cheerful. There was the cabin table between us, covered with the usual Swiss news about nothing, and an old caricature book or two. The waves went on rushing by; neither of the groups talked, but I noticed that from time to time the young American cast somewhat keen, though entirely courteous, looks of scrutiny at my father and mother.

In a few minutes after I had begun to notice these looks, he rose, with the sweetest quiet smile I ever saw on any face (unless, perhaps, a nun's, when she has some grave kindness to do), crossed to our side of the cabin, and addressing himself to my father, said, with a true expression of great gladness, and of frank trust that his joy would be understood, that he knew who we were, was most thankful to have met us, and that he prayed permission to introduce his mother and sisters to us.

The bright eyes, the melodious voice, the perfect manner, the simple, but acutely flattering, words, won my father in an instant. The New Englander sat down beside us, his mother and sisters seeming at once also to change the steamer's cabin into a reception room in their own home. The rest of the time till we reached Geneva passed too quickly; we arranged to meet in a day or two again, at St Martin's.

And thus I became possessed of my second friend, after Dr John Brown; and of my first real tutor, Charles Eliot Norton.

CHAPTER III

L'ESTERELLE

SALLENCHES SAVOY, 9*th September*, 1888.

47. THE meeting at St Martin's with Norton and his family was a very happy one. Entirely sensible and amiable, all of them; with the farther elasticity and acuteness of the American intellect, and no taint of American ways. Charles himself, a man of the highest natural gifts, in their kind; observant and critical rather than imaginative, but with an all-pervading sympathy and sensibility, absolutely free from envy, ambition, or covetousness:[1] a scholar from his cradle, nor only now a *man* of the world, but a *gentleman* of the world, whom the highest born and best bred of every nation, from the Red Indian to the White Austrian, would recognize in a moment, as of their caste.

In every branch of classical literature he was my superior; knew old English writers better than I,—much more, old French; and had active fellowship and close friendship with the then really progressive leaders of thought in his own country, Longfellow, Lowell, and Emerson.

All the sympathy, and all the critical subtlety, of his mind had been given, not only to the reading, but to the trial and following out of the whole theory of 'Modern Painters;' so that, as I said, it was a real joy for him to meet me, and a very bright and singular one for both of us, when I knocked at his door in the Hôtel du Mont Blanc at five in the morning; and led him, as the roselight flushed the highest snow, up the winding path among the mountain meadows of Sallenches.

---

[1] I mean, covetousness of beautiful things, the only sort that is possible to people like Charles Norton or me. He gave me his best Greek 'Fortune,' a precious little piece of flying marble, with her feet on the world, engraved with hexagonal tracery like a honeycomb. We both love its honey—but best, given by each other.

I can see them at this moment, those mountain meadows, if I rise from my writing-table, and open the old barred valves of the corner window of the Hotel Bellevue;—yes, and there is the very path we climbed that day together, apparently unchanged. But on what seemed then the everlasting hills, beyond which the dawn rose cloudless, and on the heaven in which it rose, and on all that we that day knew, of human mind and virtue,—how great the change, and sorrowful, I cannot measure, and, in this place, I will not speak.

48. That morning gave to me, I said my first tutor;[1] for Dr John Brown, however, far above me in general power, and in the knowledge proper to his own profession, yet in the simplicity of his affection liked everything I wrote, for what was true in it, however imperfectly or faultfully expressed: but Norton saw all my weaknesses, measured all my narrownesses, and, from the first, took serenely, and as it seemed of necessity, a kind of paternal authority over me, and a right of guidance;—though the younger of the two,—and always admitting my full power in its own kind; nor only admitting, but in the prettiest way praising and stimulating. It was almost impossible for him to speak to any one he cared for, without some side-flash of witty compliment; and to me, his infinitely varied and loving praise became a constant motive to exertion, and aid in effort: yet he never allowed me in the slightest violation of the laws, either of good writing, or social prudence, without instant blame, or warning.

I was entirely conscious of his rectorial power, and affectionately submissive to it; so that he might have done anything with me, but for the unhappy difference in our innate, and unchangeable, political faiths.

49. Since that day at Sallenches it has become a matter of the most curious speculation to me, what sort of soul Charles Norton would have become, if he had had the blessing to be born an English Tory, or a Scotch Jacobite, or a French Gentilhomme, or a Savoyard Count. I think I should have liked him best to have been a Savoyard Count; say, Lord of the very Tower of Sallenches, a quarter of a mile above me at the opening of the glen,—habitable yet and inhabited; it is half hidden by its climbing grapes. Then, to have read the 'Fioretti di San Francesco,'* (which *he* found out, New Englander though he was, before I did,) in earliest boyhood; then to have been brought into instructively grievous collision with Commerce, Liberty, and

---

[1] Gordon was only my master in Greek, and in common sense; he never criticized my books, and, I suppose, rarely read them.

Evangelicalism at Geneva; then to have learned Political Economy from Carlyle and me; and finally devoted himself to write the History of the Bishops of Sion! What a grand happy, consistent creature he would have been,—while now he is as hopelessly out of gear and place, over in the States there, as a runaway star dropped into Purgatory; and twenty times more a slave than the blackest nigger he ever set his white scholars to fight the South for; because all the faculties a black has may be fully developed by a good master (see Miss Edgeworth's story of the grateful Negro),[1]*—while only about the thirtieth or fortieth part of Charles Norton's effective contents and capacity are beneficially spent in the dilution of the hot lava, and fructification of the hot ashes, of American character;—which are overwhelming, borne now on volcanic air,—the life of Scotland, England, France, and Italy.* I name Scotland first, for reasons which will be told in next 'Praeterita,'—'Joanna's Care.' Meantime, here is the last letter I have from Norton, showing how we have held hands since that first day on Geneva lake.

'SHADY HILL, *April 9th*, 1887.

50. 'It is very good of you, my dearest Ruskin, to send me such a long, pleasant letter not punishing me for my silence, but trusting to—

> "My thought, whose love for you,
> Though words come hindmost, holds his rank before."*

You are doing too much, and your letter gives me a fear lest, out of care for me, you added a half-hour of effort to the work of a too busy day. How long it is since I first began to preach prudence to you! and my preaching has availed about as much as the sermons in stones* avail to convert the hard-hearted. Well, we are glad to take each other as we are, you ever imprudent, I ever——(I leave the word to your mercy).

'The last number* of "Praeterita" pleased me greatly. There was a sweet tone in it, such as becomes the retrospect of a wise man as he summons the scenes of past life before his eyes; the clearness, the sharp-cut outline of your memories is a wonder, and their fulness of

---

[1] I showed the valley of Chamouni, and the 'Pierre-a-Bot' above Neuchâtel, to Mrs Beecher Stowe and her pretty little daughter Georgie—when Georgie was about sixteen, and wouldn't let me say a word against Uncle Tom: howbeit, that story of the Grateful Negro, Robinson Crusoe, and Othello, contain, any of the three, more alike worldly and heavenly, wisdom than would furnish three 'Uncle Tom's Cabins.'

light and colour. My own are very different. I find the outlines of many of them blurred, and their colours faint. The loss* that came to me fifteen years ago included the loss of vividness of memory of much of my youth.

'The winter has been long and hard with us. Even yet there are snowbanks in shady places, and not yet is there a sign of a leaf. Even the snowdrops are hardly venturing out of the earth. But the birds have come back, and to-day I hear the woodpeckers knocking at the doors of the old trees to find a shelter and home for the summer. We have had the usual winter pleasures, and all my children have been well, though Lily is always too delicate, and ten days hence I part with her that she may go to England and try there to escape her summer cold. She goes out under Lowell's charge, and will be with her mother's sister and cousins in England. My three girls have just come to beg me to go out with them for a walk. So, good-bye. I will write soon again. Don't you write to me when you are tired. I let my eyes rest for an instant on Turner's sunset, and your sunrise from Herne Hill, which hang before me; and with a heart full of loving thanks to you,—I am ever your affectionate

'C. E. N.

'My best love to Joan,—to whom I mean to write.'

Somewhat more of Joan (and Charles also) I have to tell, as I said, in next 'Praeterita.'

51. I cannot go on, here, to tell the further tale of our peace and war; for the Fates wove for me, but a little while after they brought me that friend to Sallenches glen, another net of Love,* in which alike the warp and woof were of deeper colours.

Soon after I returned home, in the eventful year 1858, a lady wrote to me from—somewhere near Green Street, W.,*—saying, as people sometimes did, in those days, that she saw I was the only sound teacher in Art; but this farther, very seriously, that she wanted her children—two girls and a boy—taught the beginnings of Art rightly; especially the younger girl, in whom she thought I might find some power worth developing:—would I come and see her? I thought I should rather like to; so I went, to near Green Street; and found the mother—the sort of person I expected, but a good deal more than I expected, and in all sorts of ways. Extremely pretty still, herself, nor at all too old to learn many things; but mainly anxious for her children.

Emily, the elder daughter, wasn't in; but Rosie was,—should she be sent for to the nursery? Yes, I said, if it wouldn't tease the child, she might be sent for. So presently the drawing-room door opened, and Rosie came in, quietly taking stock of me with her blue eyes as she walked across the room; gave me her hand, as a good dog gives its paw, and then stood a little back. Nine years old,* on 3rd January, 1858, thus now rising towards ten; neither tall nor short for her age; a little stiff in her way of standing. The eyes rather deep blue at that time, and fuller and softer than afterwards. Lips perfectly lovely in profile;—a little too wide, and hard in edge, seen in front; the rest of the features what a fair, well-bred Irish girl's usually are; the hair, perhaps, more graceful in short curl round the forehead, and softer than one sees often, in the close-bound tresses above the neck.

52. I thought it likely she *might* be taught to draw a little, if she would take time; I did not expect her to take *pains*, and told her mother so, at once. Rosie says never a word, but we continue to take stock of each other. 'I thought you *so* ugly,' she told me, afterwards. She didn't quite mean that; but only, her mother having talked much of my 'greatness' to her, she had expected me to be something like Garibaldi, or the Elgin Theseus;* and was extremely disappointed.

I expressed myself as ready to try what I could make of Rosie; only I couldn't come every other day all the way in to Green Street. Mamma asked what sort of a road there was to Denmark Hill? I explained the simplicity and beauty of its ramifications round the Elephant and Castle, and how one was quite in the country as soon as one got past the triangular field at Champion Hill. And the wildernesses of the Obelisk having been mapped out, and determined to be passable, the day was really appointed for first lesson at Denmark Hill—and Emily came with her sister.

53. Emily was a perfectly sweet, serene, delicately-chiselled marble nymph of fourteen, softly dark-eyed, rightly tender and graceful in all she did and said. I never saw such a faculty for the arrangement of things beautifully, in any other human being. If she took up a handful of flowers, they fell out of her hand in wreathed jewellery of colour and form, as if they had been sown, and had blossomed, to live together so, and no otherwise. Her mother had the same gift, but in its more witty, thoughtful, and scientific range; in Emily it was pure wild instinct. For an Irish girl, she was not witty, for she could not make a mistake; one never laughed at what she said, but the room was brighter for it. To Rose and me she soon became no more Emily, but 'Wisie,' named after my dead Wisie. All the children, and their father, loved animals;—my

first sight of papa was as he caressed a green popinjay which was almost hiding itself in his waistcoat. Emily's pony, Swallow, and Rosie's dog, Bruno, will have their day in these memoirs;* but Emily's 'Bully' was the perfectest pet of all;—he used to pass half his day in the air, above her head, or behind her shoulders, holding a little tress of her long hair as far out as he could, on the wing.

54. That first day, when they came to Denmark Hill, there was much for them to see;—my mother, to begin with, and she also had to see them; on both sides the sight was thought good. Then there were thirty Turners, including the great Rialto; half-a-dozen Hunts; a beautiful Tintoret; my minerals in the study; the loaded apple trees in the orchard; the glowing peaches on the old red garden wall. The lesson lost itself that day in pomiferous talk, with rustic interludes in the stables and pigsty. The pigs especially, it was observed, were highly educated, and spoke excellent Irish.

When next they came, lessons began duly, with perspective, and the analysis of the essential qualities of triangles! I must state here, generally, that ever since the year I lost in efforts to trisect an angle myself, education, both in drawing and ethics, has been founded by me on the *pleasant* and pretty mysteries of trigonometry! the more resolutely, because I always found ignorance of magnitudes at the root of modern bad taste and frivolity; and farther, because all the grace, and much of the sentiment, both of plant and mountain form, depends on the angle of the cone they fill with their branches, or rise into with their cliffs.

These geometrical lessons are always accompanied, when I have girls to teach, by the most careful pencil study of the forms of leaves as they grow, whether on ground or branch.

55. In botanical knowledge, and perception of plant-character, my eldest Irish pupil, mamma, was miles and miles my superior;* and in powers of design, both the children were so; but the fine methods of measurement and delineation were new to all of them; nor less the charm of faithfully represented colour, in full daylight, and in the open air. Having Turner's mountain drawings of his best time beside us, and any quantity of convolvuluses, hollyhocks, plums, peaches, and apples, to bring in from the garden, the afternoon hours went fast: but so much more in talk than work, that I soon found, if either triangles or bindweeds were to come to anything, it must be under the governess's superintendence, not mamma's: and that I should have to make my way to Green Street, and up to the schoolroom, after all, on at least two out of three of the lesson days. Both the children, to my extreme

satisfaction, approved of this arrangement, and the final order was that whenever I happened to go through Green Street, I should pay them a visit in the nursery. Somehow, from that time, most of my London avocations led me through Green Street.*

It chanced above all things well for me that their governess was a woman of great sense and power, whom the children entirely loved, and under whom mamma put herself, in the schoolroom, no less meekly than they; partly in play, but really also a little subdued by the clear insight of the fearlessly frank preceptress into her own faults. I cannot call them 'foibles,' for her native wit and strength of character admitted none.

56. Rosie had shortly expressed her sense of her governess's niceness by calling her 'Bun;' and I had not been long free of the schoolroom before she wanted a name for me also, significant of like approval. After some deliberation, she christened me 'Crumpet'; then, impressed by seeing my gentleness to beggars, canonized me as 'Saint Crumpet,' or, shortly and practically, 'St C.,'—which I remained ever afterwards; only Emily said one day to her sister that the C. did in truth stand for 'Chrysostom.'*

The drawing, and very soon painting, lessons went on meantime quite effectively, both the girls working with quick intelligence and perfect feeling; so that I was soon able, with their mother's strong help, to make them understand the essential qualities both of good painting and sculpture. Rose went on into geology; but only far enough to find another play-name for me—'Archegosaurus.' This was meant partly to indicate my scientific knowledge of Depths and Ages; partly to admit me more into family relations, her mother having been named, by her cleverest and fondest friend, 'Lacerta,'*—to signify that she had the grace and wisdom of the serpent, without its poison.

And things went on,—as good girls will know how, through all that winter;—in the spring, the Fates brought the first whirlpool into the current of them, in that (I forget exactly why) it was resolved that they should live by the Cascine of Florence in the spring, and on the Lung' Arno, instead of in the park by the Serpentine. But there was the comfort for me that Rosie was really a little sorry to go away; and that she understood in the most curious way how sorry *I* was.

Some wise, and prettily mannered, people have told me I shouldn't say anything about Rosie at all.* But I am too old now to take advice, and I won't have this following letter—the first she ever wrote me—moulder away, when I can read it no more, lost to all loving hearts.

57. DEAREST S^T CRUMPET—I am so sorry—I <u>couldn't</u> write before, there wasn't one bit of time—I am so sorry you were di_ssap̂pointed—I only got yr letter yesterday (Sunday), & we only got to Nice late on Saturday afternoon—So I have got up so early this morning to try & get a clear hour before breakfast to write to you, which you see I'm doing—So you thought of us, dear St Crumpet, & we too thought so much of you—Thank you very much for the Diary letter; it was so nice of you to write so long a one—I have so much to tell you too Arichigosaurus so I will begin from Dover, & tell what befel us up to Nice—Emily asks me to say that she did a picture at Dover of Dover Castle in a fog—I think it was to please you—Well we had a roughish passage, but we[1]

sat on deck & didn't mind—We thought & talked about you— Every great wave that came we called a ninth wave and we thought how pleasant it w^d be to sit in a storm and draw them, but I think if you had wanted it done I'd have tryed to do it St Crumpet—There was what do you think at the prow of our steamer—yr brother Archigosaurus, an alligator, and we said it was you—Well so we got to Calais, breakfasted at the Table d'Hôte there, and then began that weary railroad journey from Calais to Paris—The scenery was just the same all the way— I suppose you know it—Those long straight rows of poplars cut even at the tops & flat uninteresting country. I drew the pôplars in perspective for you St Crumpet—We got to Paris on

Friday evening & stayed till Wednesday—No, I couldn't I tell you, there wasn't one bit of time or do you think I would not have seized it directly for I know yr thinking why didn't she write—Its too long to say all we did & didn't do in Paris, so I'll only tell about the Louvre and Notre Dame. We went to the Louvre. Oh St Crumpet how we thought of you there—How we looked and talked about the Titians you told us to look at particularly the glass ball one & the white Rabbit*—Yes we looked so much at them and we did, all of us, think them so very beautiful—I liked two portraits of Titian's of two dark gentlemen with earnest eyes better than any I think. We thought his skins (I mean the skins he made his picture-people have) so very beautifully done & we looked at the pinks at the corners of the eyes & thought of the Portrait of Lord Bute's* & you again St Crumpet.

---

[1] I leave pauses where the old pages end.

58. We liked the picture of Paul Veronese of the children playing with the dog very much I think one of them the most prominent with dark eyes & not looking at the dog is very beautiful. Why does Paul Veronese put his own family in the pictures of sacred subjects, I wonder? I liked the little puppy in the boys arms trying to get away—The statues in the Louvre I think most beautiful. Is it wrong St Crumpet to like that noble Venus Victrix* as well as Titian. If it is, am I a hardened little tinner? Oh but they are so beautiful those statues there's one of a Venus* leaning against a tree with a Lacerta running up it—Notre Dame they are spoiling as quick as they can by colouring those grand old pillars with ugly daubs of green and yellow etc. Is not that 'light' in the French?[1] It's a bore saying all we thought of Paris, I must get on to the mountains not to say Alps—Don't be Kinfishery[2] dear St Crumpet; how good it was of you to give yr Turners that you love so much to the Oxford Museum* From Paris we started early on Wednesday morning & travelled all day & all the night in the train—Yes you would have said 'Poor Posie' I <u>was</u> bored But we got over it very well—It was so pleasant to be running after the sun to the south (Dont be Kingfishery) & awaking at about 5 in the morning to see long plains of greyheaded silvery olives and here and there pink perky peach trees dancing among them—And there were groups of dark cool cypress trees pointing upwards, & hills & grey rocks sloping to the sea—the Mediterranean So we shook off our sleepiness, at least Papa Mama and I did for Emily & Adèle still slept; & saw behind those peaks of craggy hills a pink smile coming in the sky telling us that the morning had come really at last So we watched & suddenly there rose (popped w^d be a better word for it really rose in one instant)

such a sun—'nor dim, nor red'* (you know the verse) & then dipped back again below the hills It was so beautiful—But I shocked Mama by saying 'Jack in the box' which awoke Emily who declared of course she had been wide awake and had seen it all. Why do people always do that, St Crumpet? This was just before we came to Marseilles. It had been snowing the day before & it was nice to go to sleep & wake up in the summer—We got to Toulon and there we spent the day & oh Archigosaurus we saw so many Lacertas there; again we thought of you—How can you wish to be a parrot[3]—are you not our saint—You wouldn't look a bit nice in a gold laced cap; don't you know blue is the

---

[1] Referring to a debate over Mrs Browning's poem in defence of them; the one in which she says, rightly, that they are no more 'light' than a rifle-ball is.*

[2] *King*fishery. Sitting sulkily on a branch.

[3] I suppose I had not expressed this farther condition, of being her father's parrot.

colour you should wear. At Toulon it was like July—I don't like such heat—Transplantation & scorching is too much for an Irish rose—But I sat with

Mama and Emily on a rock & sketched Toulon Harbour, (or rather tried to) for you St Crumpet. Then the next we posted, the country was so beautiful some of it & towards evening we saw snowy peaks, they were the mountains of Savoy. I was pretty tired that night & we had to sleep at Frejus such a disagreeable place. The next day we had six horses to our carriage for it was a hilly road. We walked about two hours of the way over the hills[1] You know what sort of a view there was at the top, St Crumpet & how one stands & stares & says nothing because the words of Grand, Glorious, Beautiful etc cannot in one quarter express what one thinks. You the author of M-Ps c^d describe it Irish roses can't. But I can tell you how my cousins the moorland roses nodded at me as I passed and how they couldn't understand why Irish hedge roses bloomed in July instead of March

59. I can tell you how the fields were white with Narcissi, how the roads were edged with mauve-coloured anemones & how the scarlet anemones stood up in the meadows tantalizing me in the carriage so much because I wanted to feel them And there were myrtles (wild) growing close to the blue Mediterranean & Mama lay down on them by the seaside at Cannes while Papa and I were talking to a perfectly deaf old French fisherman who gave his[2] to me as he caught them putting them half alive into my hands, oh, you w^d have been alive there Archigosaurus. How I wish you had been there. Well we got here (Nice) on Saturday evening & we climbed up an old Roman Ampitheatre and saw of all sunsets the most glorious. We said it was like Light in the West, Beauvais,* and again we thought of you Oh St Crumpet I think of you so much & of all your dearnesses to me

I wish so very much that you were happy—God can make you so—We will try not to forget all you taught us—It was so nice of you. Thank you so much from both of us.—Mama is very glad you went to Dr Ferguson She says you must not give him up. How very kind of you to see & talk to our old man Certainly the name is not beautiful We have all read your letter* & we all care for it That was indeed a 'dear Irish labourer.'

---

[1] The Pass of the Esterelle, between Frejus and Nice; more beautiful, always, to me, than all the groves and cliffs of the Riviera.—1889.

[2] 'Fish' to be understood; also that the fisherman was not 'perfectly' deaf, for papa could not have talked with his eyes only, as Rose could.

I like him so much; such a nice letter. I hope M^r & Mrs Ruskin are well now. Will you give them our love please & take for yourself as much as ever you please. It will be a great deal if you deign to take all we send you. I like Nice but I don't much like being transplanted except going home. I am ever your rose.

Postscript

Yes, write packets—trunks, & we shall like them so much. Indeed I couldn't write before, I'll try to write again. You must see how we think of you & talk of you—rose posie.

CHAPTER IV

JOANNA'S CARE*

60. THE mischances* which have delayed the sequence of 'Praeterita' must modify somewhat also its intended order. I leave Rosie's letter to tell what it can of the beginning of happiest days; but omit, for a little while, the further record of them,—of the shadows which gathered around them, and increased, in my father's illness; and of the lightning which struck him down in death—so sudden, that I find it extremely difficult, in looking back, to realize the state of mind in which it left either my mother or me. My own principal feeling was certainly anxiety for her, who had been for so many years in every thought dependent on my father's wishes, and withdrawn from all other social pleasure as long as she could be *his* companion. I scarcely felt the power I had over her, myself; and was at first amazed to find my own life suddenly becoming to her another ideal; and that new hope and pride were possible to her, in seeing me take command of my father's fortune,* permitted by him, from his grave, to carry out the theories I had formed for my political work, with unrestricted and deliberate energy.

My mother's perfect health of mind, and vital religious faith, enabled her to take all the good that was left to her, in the world, while she looked in secure patience for the heavenly future: but there was immediate need for some companionship which might lighten the burden of the days to her.

61. I have never yet spoken of the members of my grandmother's family, who either remained in Galloway,[1] or were associated with my early days in London. Quite one of the dearest of them at this time, was

---

[1] See above, pp. 41–4.

Mrs Agnew, born Catherine Tweddale, and named Catherine after her aunt, my father's mother. She had now for some years been living in widowhood; her little daughter, Joan, only five years old when her father died, having grown up in their pretty old house at Wigtown,[1] in the simplicity of entirely natural and contented life; and, though again and again under the stress of domestic sorrow, untellable in the depth of the cup which the death-angels filled for the child, yet in such daily happiness as her own bright and loving nature secured in her relations with all those around her; and in the habits of childish play, or education then common in the rural towns of South Scotland: of which, let me say at once that there was greater refinement in them, and more honourable pride, than probably, at that time, in any other district of Europe;[2] a certain pathetic melody and power of tradition consecrating nearly every scene with some past light, either of heroism or religion.

62. And so it chanced, providentially, that at this moment, when my mother's thoughts dwelt constantly on the past there should be this

---

[1] Now pulled down and the site taken for the new county buildings. The house as it once stood is seen in the centre of the wood-cut at page 6 of Gordon Fraser's Guide,* with the Stewartry hills in the distance. I have seldom seen a truer rendering of the look of an old Scottish town.

[2] The following couple of pages, from 'Redgauntlet,' put in very few words the points of difference between them and the fatally progressive follies and vanities of Edinburgh:—

"'Come away, Mr Fairford; the Edinburgh time is later than ours,' said the Provost.

"'And come away, young gentleman,' said the Laird; "I remember your father weel, at the Cross, thirty years ago. I reckon you are as late in Edinburgh as at London; *four* o'clock hours, eh?"

"'Not quite so degenerate,' replied Fairford; "but certainly many Edinburgh people are so ill-advised as to *postpone their dinner* till three, that they may have full time to answer their London correspondents."

"'London correspondents!' said Mr Maxwell; "and pray, what the devil have the people of Auld Reekie to do with London correspondents?"

"'The tradesmen must have their goods,' said Fairford.

"'I Can they not buy our own Scottish manufactures, and pick their customers' pockets in a more patriotic manner?"

"'Then the ladies must have fashions,' said Fairford.

"'Can they not busk the plaid over their heads, as their mothers did? A tartan screen, and once a year a new cockernony from Paris, should serve a countess; but ye have not many of *them* left, I think. Mareschal, Airley, Winton, Wemyss, Balmerino—ay, ay, the countesses and ladies of quality will scarce take up too much of your ballroom floor with their quality hoops nowadays."

"'There is no want of crowding, however, sir,' said Fairford; "they begin to talk of a new Assembly Room."

"'A new Assembly Room!' said the old Jacobite Laird. "Umph—I mind quartering three hundred men in the Assembly Room you *have*. But, come, come: I'll ask no more questions—the answers all smell of new lords, new lands."'*

child near us,—still truly a child, in her powers of innocent pleasure, but already so accustomed to sorrow, that there was nothing that could farther depress her in my mother's solitude. I have not time to tell of the pretty little ways in which it came about, but they all ended in my driving to No. 1, Cambridge Street, on the 19th April, 1864: where her uncle (my cousin, John Tweddale) brought her up to the drawing-room to me, saying, 'This is Joan.'*

I had seen her three years before, but not long enough to remember her distinctly: only I had a notion that she would be 'nice,'[1] and saw at once that she *was* entirely nice, both in my mother's way and mine; being now seventeen years and some—well, for example of accuracy and conscience—forty-five days, old. And I very thankfully took her hand out of her uncle's, and received her in trust, saying—I do not remember just what,—but certainly *feeling* much more strongly than either her uncle or she did, that the gift, both to my mother and me, was one which we should not easily bear to be again withdrawn. I put her into my father's carriage at the door, and drove her out to Denmark Hill. Here is her own account of what followed between my mother and her:—

63. 'I was received with great kindness by the dear old lady, who did not inspire *me*, as she did so many other people, with a feeling of awe! We were the best of friends, from the first. She, ever most considerate of what would please *me*, and make me happy; and I, (ever a lover of old ladies!) delighted to find it so easily possible to please *her*.

'Next morning she said, "Now tell me frankly, child, what you like best to eat, and you shall have it. Don't hesitate; say what you'd really like,—for luncheon to-day, for instance." I said, truthfully, "Cold mutton, and oysters"; and this became a sort of standing order (in months with the letter *r!**)—greatly to the cook's amusement.

'Of course I respectfully called the old lady "*Mrs Ruskin*"; but in a day or two, she told me she didn't like it, and would I call her "Aunt" or "Auntie"? I readily did so.

'The days flew in that lovely garden, and as I had only been invited to stay a week, until Mr Ruskin should return home,[2] I felt miser-able when he did come, thinking I must go back to London streets, and noise; (though I was always very happy with my good uncle and aunts).

---

[1] And the word means more, with me, than with Sydney Smith (see his Memoirs); but it means *all* that *he* does, to begin with.*

[2] I must have been going away somewhere* the day after I brought her to Denmark Hill.

'So, when the last evening came, of my week, I said, with some hesitation, "Auntie, I had better go back to my uncle's to-morrow?"

'She flung down her netting, and turned sharply round, saying, "Are you unhappy, child?" "Oh no!" said I, "only my week is up, and I thought it was time——"

'I was not allowed to finish my sentence. She said, "Never let me hear you say anything again about going; as long as you are happy here, stay, and we'll send for your clothes, and make arrangements about lessons, and everything else here."

'And thus it came about that I stayed *seven years!*—till I married; going home now and then to Scotland, but always getting pathetic little letters there, telling me to "come back as soon as my mother could spare me, that I was much missed, and nobody could ever fill my place." And Auntie was very old then (not that she ever could bear being called *old*, at ninety!), and I could not ever bear the thought of leaving her!'

64. Thus far Joanie; nor virtually have she and I ever parted since.* I do not care to count how long it is since her marriage to Arthur Severn; only I think her a great deal prettier now than I did then: but other people thought her extremely pretty then, and I am certain that everybody *felt* the guileless and melodious sweetness of the face. Her first conquest was almost on our threshold; for half an hour or so after we had reached Denmark Hill, Carlyle rode up the front garden, joyfully and reverently received as always; and stayed the whole afternoon; even, (Joan says) sitting with us during our early dinner at five. Many a day after that, he used to come; and one evening, 'in describing with some rapture how he had once as a young man had a delightful trip into Galloway, "where he was most hospitably entertained in the town of Wigtown by a Mr Tweddale," I (Joan) said quietly, "I *am* so glad! That was my grandfather, and Wigtown is my native place!" He turned in a startled, sudden way, saying, "Bless the child, is that so?" adding some very pretty compliments to my place and its people, which filled my heart with great pride. And, on another occasion, after he had been to meet the Queen at Dean Stanley's,* in describing to us some of the conversation, he made us laugh by telling how, in describing to Her Majesty the beauty of Galloway, that "he believed there was no finer or more beautiful drive in her kingdom than the one round the shore of the Stewartry, by Gatehouse of Fleet," he got so absorbed in his subject that, in drawing his chair closer to the Queen, he at last became aware he had fixed it on her dress, and that she could not move till he withdrew it! Do you think I may say farther' (Of course, Joanie), 'that

Carlyle as a young man often went to my great aunt's (Mrs Church) in Dumfriesshire; and he has several times told me that he considered *her* one of the most remarkable and kindest women he had ever known. On one occasion while there, he went to the little Cummertrees Church, where the then minister (as a joke sometimes called "Daft Davie Gillespie") used to speak his mind very plainly from the pulpit, and while preaching a sermon on "Youth and Beauty being laid in the grave," something tickled Carlyle, and he was seen to smile; upon which Mr Gillespie stopped suddenly, looked with a frown at Carlyle (who was sitting in my aunt's pew), and said, "Mistake me not, young man; it is *youth alone* that *you* possess." This was told to me, (Joan,) by an old cousin of mine who heard it, and was sitting next Carlyle at the time.'

65. I am so glad to be led back by Joanie to the thoughts of Carlyle, as he showed himself to her, and to me, in those spring days, when he used to take pleasure in the quiet of the Denmark Hill garden, and to use all his influence with me to make me contented in my duty to my mother; which he, as, with even greater insistence, Turner, always told me was my first;—both of them seeing, with equal clearness, the happiness of the life that was possible to me in merely meeting my father's affection and hers, with the tranquil exertion of my own natural powers, in the place where God had set me.

Both at the time, and ever since, I have felt bitter remorse that I did not make Carlyle free of the garden,* and his horse of the stables, whether we were at home or not; for the fresh air, and bright view of the Norwood hills, were entirely grateful and healing to him, when the little back garden at Cheyne Row was too hot, or the neighbourhood of it too noisy, for his comfort.

66. And at this time, nearly every opportunity of good, and peace, was granted in Joan's coming to help me to take care of my mother. She was perfectly happy herself, in the seclusion of Denmark Hill; while yet the occasional evenings spent at George Richmond's, or with others of her London friends, (whose circle rapidly widened,) enabled her to bring back to my mother little bits of gossip which were entirely refreshing to both of us; for I used to leave my study whenever Joanie came back from these expeditions, to watch my mother's face in its glittering sympathy. I think I have said of her before, that although not witty herself, her strong sense gave her the keenest enjoyment of kindly humour, whether in saying or incident; and I have seen her laughing, partly *at* Joanie and partly *with* her, till the tears ran down her still brightly flushing cheeks. Joan was never tired of telling her whatever

gave her pleasure, nor of reading to her, in quieter time, the books she delighted in, against which, girls less serenely—nay, less religiously, bred, would assuredly have rebelled,—any quantity, for instance, of Miss Edgeworth and Richardson.

(I interrupt myself for a moment to express, at this latter time of life, the deep admiration I still feel for Richardson. The follies of modern novel writing render it impossible for young people to understand the perfection of the human nature in his conception, and delicacy of finish in his dialogue, rendering all his greater scenes unsurpassable in their own manner of art. They belong to a time of the English language in which it could express with precision the most delicate phases of sentiment, necessarily now lost under American, Cockney, or scholastic slang.)

67. Joanie herself had real faculty and genius in all rightly girlish directions. She had an extremely sweet voice, whether in reading or singing; inventive wit, which was softly satirical, but never malicious; and quite a peculiar, and perfect, sense of clownish humour, which never for an instant diminished her refinement, but enabled her to sing either humorous Scotch, or the brightest Christy Minstrel* carols, with a grace and animation which, within their gentle limits, could not be surpassed. She had a good natural faculty for drawing also, not inventive, but realistic; so that she answered my *first* lessons with serviceable care and patience; and was soon able to draw and paint flowers which were a great deal liker the flowers themselves than my own elaborate studies;—no one said of them, 'What wonderful drawing!' but everybody said, 'How like a violet, or a buttercup!' At that point, however, she stayed, and yet stays, to my sorrow, never having advanced into landscape drawing.

But very soon, also, she was able to help me in arranging my crystals; and the day divided itself between my mother's room, the mineral room, the garden, and the drawing-room, with busy pleasures for every hour.

68. Then, in my favourite readings, the deep interest which, in his period of entirely central power, Scott had taken in the scenery of the Solway, rendered everything that Joanie could tell me of her native bay and its hills, of the most living interest to me; and although, from my father's unerring tutorship, I had learned Scott's own Edinburgh accent with a precision which made the turn of every sentence precious to me, (and, I believe, my own rendering of it thoroughly interesting, even to a Scottish listener,)—yet every now and then Joanie could tell me something of old, classic, Galloway Scotch, which was no less

valuable to me than a sudden light thrown on a chorus in Aeschylus would be to a Greek scholar;—nay, only the other day I was entirely crushed by her interpreting to me, for the first time, the meaning of the name of the village of Captain Clutterbuck's residence,— Kennaquhair.[1]

69. And it has chiefly been owing to Joan's help,—and even so, only within the last five or six years,—that I have fully understood the power, not on Sir Walter's mind merely, but on the character of all good Scotchmen, (much more, good Scotchwomen,) of the two lines of coast from Holy Island to Edinburgh, and from Annan to the Mull of Galloway. Between them, if the reader will glance at any old map which gives rivers and mountains, instead of railroads and factories, he will find that all the highest intellectual and moral powers of Scotland were developed, from the days of the Douglases at Lochmaben, to those of Scott in Edinburgh,—Burns in Ayr,—and Carlyle at Ecclefechan, by the *pastoral* country, everywhere habitable, but only by hardihood under suffering, and patience in poverty; defending themselves always against the northern Pictish war of the Highlands, and the southern, of the English Edwards and Percys, in the days when whatever was loveliest and best of the Catholic religion haunted still the—then *not* ruins,—of Melrose, Jedburgh, Dryburgh, Kelso, Dunblane, Dundrennan, New Abbey of Dumfries, and, above all, the most ancient Cave of Whithorn,—the Candida Casa of St Ninian; while perfectly sincere and passionate forms of Evangelicalism purified and brightened the later characters of shepherd Cameronian life, being won, like all the great victories of Christianity, by martyrdoms, of which the memory remains most vivid by those very shores where Christianity was first planted in Scotland,—Whithorn is I think, only ten miles south of Wigtown Bay; and in the churchyard of Wigtown, close to the old Agnew burying-ground, (where most of Joanie's family are laid,)

---

[1] 'Ken na' where'! Note the cunning with which Scott himself throws his reader off the scent, in the first sentence of 'The Monastery,' by quoting the learned Chalmers 'for the derivation of the word "*Quhair*," from the winding course of the stream; a definition which coincides in a remarkable degree with the serpentine turns of the Tweed'! ('It's a *serpentine turn* of his own, I think!' says Joanie, as I show her the sentence,) while in the next paragraph he gives an apparently historical existence to 'the village of which we speak,' by associating it with Melrose, Jedburgh, and Kelso, in the 'splendour of foundation by David I.,' and concludes, respecting the lands with which the king endowed these wealthy fraternities, with a grave sentence, perhaps the most candid ever written by a Scotsman, of the centuries preceding the Reformation: 'In fact, for several ages the possessions of these Abbies were each sort of Goshen, enjoying the calm light of peace and immunity, while the rest of the country, occupied by wild clans and marauding barons, was one dark scene of confusion, blood, and unremitted outrage.'

are the graves of Margaret MacLachlan, and Margaret Wilson,* over which in rhythm is recorded on little square tombstones the story of their martyrdom.

70. It was only, I repeat, since what became practically my farewell journey in Italy in 1882, that I recovered the train of old associations by re-visiting Tweedside, from Coldstream up to Ashestiel; and the Solway shores from Dumfries to Whithorn; and while what knowledge I had of southern and foreign history then arranged itself for final review, it seemed to me that this space of low mountain ground, with the eternal sublimity of its rocky seashores, of its stormy seas and dangerous sands; its strange and mighty crags, Ailsa and the Bass, and its pathless moorlands, haunted by the driving cloud, had been of more import in the true world's history than all the lovely countries of the South, except only Palestine. In my quite last journey to Venice* I was, I think, justly and finally impressed with the sadness and even *weakness* of the Mediterranean coasts; and the temptation to human nature, there, to solace itself with debasing pleasures; while the very impossibility of either accumulating the treasures, or multiplying the dreams, of art, among those northern waves and rocks, left the spirit of man strong to bear the hardships of the world, and faithful to obey the precepts of Heaven.

71. It is farther strange to me, even now, on reflection—to find how great the influence of this double ocean coast and Cheviot mountain border was upon Scott's imagination; and how salutary they were in withdrawing him from the morbid German fancies which proved so fatal to Carlyle:* but there was this grand original difference between the two, that, with Scott, his story-telling and singing were all in the joyful admiration of that past with which he could re-people the scenery he gave the working part of his day to traverse, and all the sensibility of his soul to love;[1] while Carlyle's mind, fixed anxiously on the future, and besides embarrassed by the practical pinching, as well as the unconfessed shame, of poverty, saw and felt from his earliest childhood nothing but the faultfulness and gloom of the Present.

---

[1] Yet, remember, so just and intense is his perception, and so stern his condemnation, of whatever is *corrupt* in the Scottish character, that while of distinctly evil natures—Varney, Rashleigh, or Lord Dalgarno*—he takes world-wide examples,—the unpardonable baseness of so-called respectable or religious persons, and the cruelties of entirely selfish soldiers, are always Scotch. Take for the highest type the Lord Lindsay of 'The Abbot,' and for the worst, Morton in 'The Monastery,' then the terrible, *because* at first sincere, Balfour of Burleigh in 'Old Mortality'; and in lower kind, the Andrew Fairservice and MacVittie of 'Rob Roy,' the Peter Peebles of 'Redgauntlet,' the Glossin of 'Guy Mannering,' and the Saddletree of the 'Heart of Midlothian.'

It has been impossible, hitherto, to make the modern reader understand the vastness of Scott's true historical knowledge, underneath its romantic colouring, nor the concentration of it in the production of his eternally great poems and romances. English ignorance of the Scottish dialect is at present nearly total; nor can it be without very earnest effort, that the melody of Scott's verse, or the meaning of his dialogue, can ever again be estimated. He must now be read with the care which we give to Chaucer; but with the greater reward, that what is only a dream in Chaucer, becomes to us, understood from Scott, a consummate historical morality and truth.

72. The first two of his great poems, 'The Lay of the Last Minstrel' and 'Marmion,' are the re-animation of Border legends, closing with the truest and grandest battle-piece that, so far as I know, exists in the whole compass of literature[1];—the absolutely fairest in justice to both contending nations, the absolutely most beautiful in its conceptions of both. And that the palm in that conception remains with the Scotch, through the sorrow of their defeat, is no more than accurate justice to the national character, which rose from the fraternal branches of the Douglas of Tantallon and the Douglas of Dunkeld. But,—between Tantallon and Dunkeld,—what moor or mountain is there over which the purple cloud of Scott's imagination has not wrapt its light, in those two great poems?—followed by the entirely heroic enchantment of 'The Lady of the Lake,' dwelling on the Highland virtue which gives the strength of clanship, and the Lowland honour of knighthood, founded on the Catholic religion. Then came the series of novels, in which, as I have stated elsewhere,* those which dealt with the history of other nations, such as 'Ivanhoe,' 'Kenilworth,' 'Woodstock,' 'Quentin Durward,' 'Peveril of the Peak,' 'The Betrothed,' and 'The Crusaders,' however attractive to the general world, were continually weak in fancy, and false in prejudice; but the literally *Scotch* novels, 'Waverley,' 'Guy Mannering,' 'The Antiquary,' 'Old Mortality,' 'The Heart of Midlothian,' 'The Abbott,' 'Redgauntlet,' and 'The Fortunes of Nigel,' *are*, whatever the modern world may think of them, as faultless, throughout, as human work can be: and eternal examples of the ineffable art which is taught by the loveliest nature to her truest children.

Now of these, observe, 'Guy Mannering,' 'Redgauntlet,' a great part of 'Waverley,' and the beautiful close of 'The Abbot,' pass on the two coasts of Solway. The entire power of 'Old Mortality' rises out of them,

---

[1] I include the literature of all foreign languages, so far as known to me: there is nothing to approach the finished delineation and flawless majesty of conduct in Scott's Flodden.*

and their influence on Scott is curiously shown by his adoption of the name 'Ochiltree' for his bedesman of Montrose, coming, not from the near hills, as one at first fancies, but from the Ochiltree Castle, which in Mercator's old map of 1637 I find in the centre of the archbishopric, then extending from Glasgow to Wigtown, and correspondent to that of St Andrew's on the east,—the subordinate bishopric of Candida Casa, answering to that of Dunkeld, with the bishoprics of the isles Sura, Mura, and Isla. It is also, Mercator adds in his note, called the 'bishopric of Galloway.'

73. 'Even I,' says Joanie, again, 'remember old people who knew the real "Old Mortality."'* He used to come through all the Galloway district to clean and re-cut the old worn gravestones of the martyrs; sometimes, I have been told, to the long since disused kirkyard of Kirkchrist, the place where my great aunt, Mrs Church (Carlyle's friend, of whom I have spoken) began her married life. Kirkchrist is just on the opposite side from Kirkcudbright, overlooking the River Dee.'

I must go back to a middle-aged map of 1773, to find the noble river rightly traced from its source above Kenmure Castle to the winding bay which opens into Solway, by St Mary's Isle; where Kirkchrist is marked as Christ K, with a cross, indicating the church then existing.

I was staying with Arthur and Joan, at Kenmure Castle itself in the year 1876, and remember much of its dear people: and, among the prettiest scenes of Scottish gardens, the beautiful trees on the north of that lawn on which the last muster met for King James; 'and you know,' says Joanie, 'the famous song that used to inspire them all, of "Kenmure's on and awa, Willie!"'[1] The thoughts come too fast upon me, for before Joanie said this, I was trying to recollect on what height above Solway, Darsie Latimer pauses with Wandering Willie, in whom Scott records for ever the glory,—not of Scottish music only, but of all *Music*, rightly so called,—which is a part of God's own creation, becoming an expression of the purest hearts.

74. I cannot pause now to find the spot,[2] and still less the churchyard in which, at the end of Wandering Willie's tale, his grandsire wakes: but, to the living reader, I have this to say very earnestly, that

---

[1] 'Lady Huntley plays Scotch tunes like a Highland angel. She ran a set of variations on "Kenmure's on and awa'," which I told her were enough to raise a whole countryside. I never in my life heard such fire thrown into that sort of music.'—*Sir Walter writing to his daughter Sophia. Lockhart's 'Life,'* vol. iv, page 371.

[2] It is on the highest bit of moor between Dumfries and Annan. Wandering Willie's 'parishine' is only thus defined in 'Redgauntlet'—'They ca' the place Primrose Knowe.'

the whole glory and blessing of these sacred coasts depended on the rise and fall of their eternal sea, over sands which the sunset gilded with its withdrawing glow, from the measureless distances of the west, on the ocean horizon, or veiled in silvery mists, or shadowed with fast-flying storm, of which nevertheless every cloud was pure, and the winter snows blanched in the starlight. For myself, the impressions of the Solway sands are a part of the greatest teaching that ever I received during the joy of youth:—for Turner, they became the most pathetic that formed his character in the prime of life, and the five Liber Studiorum subjects, 'Solway Moss,' 'Peat Bog, Scotland,' 'The Falls of Clyde,' 'Ben Arthur,' and 'Dumblane Abbey,' remain more complete expressions of his intellect, and more noble monuments of his art, than all his mightiest after work, until the days of sunset in the west came for *it* also.

75. As 'Redgauntlet' is, in its easily readable form, inaccessible, now-adays, I quote at once the two passages which prove Scott's knowledge of music, and the strong impression made on him by the scenery between Dumfries and Annan. Hear, first, of Darsie Latimer's escape from the simplicity of his Quaker friends to the open downs of the coast which had formerly seemed so waste and dreary. 'The air I breathed felt purer and more bracing; the clouds, riding high upon a summer breeze, drove in gay succession over my head, now obscuring the sun, now letting its rays stream in transient flashes upon various parts of the landscape, and especially upon the broad mirror of the distant Firth of Solway.'

A moment afterwards he catches the tune of 'Old Sir Thom a Lyne,' sung by three musicians cosily niched into what you might call a *bunker*,[1] a little sandpit, dry and snug, surrounded by its banks, and a screen of furze in full bloom. Of whom the youngest, Benjie, 'at first somewhat dismayed at my appearance, but calculating on my placability, almost in one breath assured the itinerants that I was a grand gentleman, and had plenty of money, and was very kind to poor folk, and informed *me* that this was Willie Steenson, "Wandering Willie, the best fiddler that ever kittled thairm (cat-gut) with horsehair." I asked him if he was of this country. "*This* country!" replied the blind man, "I am of every country in broad Scotland, and a wee bit of England to the boot. But yet I am in some sense of this country, *for I was born within hearing of the roar of Solway.*"'

76. I must pause again to tell the modern reader that no word is ever used by Scott in a hackneyed sense. For three hundred years of

[1] This is a modern word, meaning, first, a large chest; then, a recess scooped in soft rock.

English commonplace, *roar* has rhymed to *shore*, as *breeze* to *trees*; yet in this sentence the word is as powerful as if it had never been written till now! for no other sound of the sea is for an instant comparable to the breaking of deep ocean, as it rises over great spaces of sand. In its rise and fall on a rocky coast, it is either perfectly silent, or, if it strike, it is with a crash, or a blow like that of a heavy gun. Therefore, under ordinary conditions, there may be either *splash*, or *crash*, or *sigh*, or *boom*; but not *roar*. But the hollow sound of the countless ranks of surfy breakers, rolling mile after mile in ceaseless following, every one of them with the apparent anger and threatening of a fate which is assured death unless fled from,—the sound of this approach, over quicksands, and into inextricable gulfs of mountain bay, this, heard far out at sea, or heard far inland, through the peace of secure night—or stormless day, is still an eternal voice, with the harmony in it of a mighty law, and the gloom of a mortal warning.

77. 'The old man preluded as he spoke, and then taking the old tune of "Galashiels" for his theme, he graced it with a wildness of complicated and beautiful variations; during which it was wonderful to observe how his sightless face was lighted up under the conscious pride and heartfelt delight in the exercise of his own very considerable powers.

'"What think you of that now, for threescore and twa?"'

I pause again to distinguish this noble pride of a man of unerring genius, in the power which all his life has been too short to attain, up to the point he conceives of,—from the base complacency of the narrow brain and dull heart, in their own chosen ways of indolence or error.

The feeling comes out more distinctly still, three pages forward, when his wife tells him, 'The gentleman is a gentleman, Willie; ye maunna speak that gate to him, hinnie.' 'The deevil I maunna!' said Willie,[1] 'and what for maunna I? If he was ten gentles, he *canna draw a bow like me, can he?*'

78. I need to insist upon this distinction, at this time in England

---

[1] Joanie tells me she has often heard the fame of the *real* Wandering Willie spoken of: he was well known in travel from the Border right into Galloway, stopping to play in villages and at all sorts of out-of-the-way houses, and, strangely, succeeded by a *blind woman* fiddler, who used to come led by a sister; and the chief singing lessons in Joanie's young days were given through Galloway by a *blind man*, who played the fiddle to perfection; and his ear was so correct that if in a class of fifty voices one note was discordant, he would stop instantly, tap loudly on the fiddle with the back of his bow, fly to the spot where the wrong note came from, pounce on the person, and say, 'It was *you*, and it's no use denying it; if I can't *see*, I can *hear!*' and he'd make the culprit go over and over the phrase till it was conquered. He always opened the class with a sweeping scale, dividing off so many voices to each note, to follow in succession.

especially, when the names of artists, whose birth was an epoch in the world's history, are dragged through the gutters of Paris, Manchester, and New York, to decorate the last puffs written for a morning concert, or a monthly exhibition. I have just turned out of the house a book in which I am told by the modern picture dealer that Mr A., B., C., D., or F. is 'the Mozart of the nineteenth century'; the fact being that Mozart's birth wrote the laws of melody for all the world as irrevocably as if they had been set down by the waves of Solway; and as widely as the birth of St Gregory in the sixth century fixed to *its* date for ever the establishment of the laws of musical expression.* Men of perfect genius are known in all centuries by their perfect respect to all law, and love of past tradition; their work in the world is never innovation, but new creation; without disturbing for an instant the foundations which were laid of old time. One would have imagined—at least, any one but Scott would have imagined—that a Scottish blind fiddler would have been only the exponent of Scottish feeling and Scottish art; it was even with astonishment that I myself read the conclusion of his dialogue with Darsie Latimer: '"Are ye in the wont of drawing up wi' all the gangrel bodies that ye meet on the high road, or find cowering in a sand-bunker upon the links?" demanded Willie.

'"Oh, no! only with honest folks like yourself, Willie," was my reply.

'"Honest folks like me! How do ye ken whether I am honest, or what I am? I may be the deevil himsell for what ye ken; for he has power to come disguised like an angel of light; and besides, he is a prime fiddler. He played a sonata to *Corelli*, ye ken."'

79. This reference to the simplest and purest writer of Italian melody being not for the sake of the story, but because Willie's own art had been truly founded upon him, so that he had been really an angel of music, as well as light to him. See the beginning of the dialogue in the previous page. '"Do you ken the Laird?" said Willie, interrupting an overture of Corelli, of which he had whistled several bars with great precision.'

I must pause again, to crowd together one or two explanations of the references to music in my own writings hitherto, which I can here sum by asking the reader to compare the use of the voice in war, beginning with the cry of Achilles on the Greek wall, down to what may be named as the two great instances of modern choral war-song: the singing of the known Church-hymn[1] at the Battle of Leuthen ('Friedrich,'

---

[1] *Psalm*, I believe, rather; but see my separate notes on St Louis' Psalter (now in preparation).

vol. ii, p. 259), in which 'five-and-twenty thousand victor voices joined':

> 'Now thank God one and all,
> With heart, with voice, with hands,
> Who wonders great hath done
> To us and to all lands;'

and, on the counter side, the song of the Marseillaise on the march to Paris, which began the conquests of the French Revolution, in turning the tide of its enemies. Compare these, I say, with the debased use of modern military bands at dinners and dances, which inaugurate such victory as *we* had at the Battle of Balaclava,* and the modern no–Battle of the Baltic, when our entire war fleet, a vast job of ironmongers, retreated, under Sir C. Napier, from before the Russian fortress of Cronstadt.*

80. I preface with this question the repetition of what I have always taught, that the Voice is the eternal musical instrument of heaven and earth, from angels down to birds. Half way between them, my little Joanie sang me yesterday, 13th May, 1889, 'Farewell, Manchester,' and 'Golden Slumbers,' two pieces of consummate melody, which can only be expressed by the voice, and belonging to the group of like melodies which have been, not invented, but inspired, to all nations in the days of their loyalty to God, to their prince, and to themselves. That Manchester has since become the funnel of a volcano, which, not content with vomiting pestilence, gorges the whole rain of heaven, that falls over a district as distant as the ancient Scottish border,—is not indeed wholly Manchester's fault, nor altogether Charles Stuart's fault; the beginning of both faults is in the substitution of mercenary armies for the troops of nations *led* by their *kings*. Had Queen Mary led, like Zenobia, at Langside; had Charles I charged instead of Prince Rupert at Naseby; and Prince Edward bade Lochiel follow *him* at Culloden, we should not to-day have been debating who was to be our king at Birmingham or Glasgow. For the rest I take the bye-help that Fors gives me in this record of the power of a bird's voice only.[1]

---

[1] 'An extraordinary scene is to be witnessed every evening at Leicester in the freemen's allotment gardens, where a nightingale has established itself. The midnight songster was first heard a week ago, and every evening hundreds of people line the roads near the trees where the bird has his haunt. The crowds patiently wait till the music begins, and the bulk of the listeners remain till midnight, while a number of enthusiasts linger till one and two o'clock in the morning. Strange to say, the bird usually sings in a large thorn bush just over the mouth of the tunnel of the Midland main line, but the songster is heedless of noise, and smoke, and steam, his stream of song being uninterrupted for

81. But the distinction of the music of Scotland from every other is in its association with sweeter natural sounds, and filling a deeper silence. As Fors also ordered it, yesterday afternoon, before Joanie sang these songs to me, I had been, for the first time since my return from Venice, down to the shore of my own lake, with her and her two youngest children, at the little promontory of shingle thrown out into it by the only mountain brook on this eastern side, (Beck Leven,) which commands the windings of its wooded shore under Furness Fells, and the calm of its fairest expanse of mirror wave,—a scene which is in general almost melancholy in its perfect solitude; but, when the woods are in their gladness, and the green—how much purer, how much softer than ever emerald!—of their unsullied spring, and the light of dawning summer, possessing alike the clouds and mountains of the west,—it is, literally, one of the most beautiful and strange remnants of all that was once most sacred in this British land,—all to which we owe, whether the heart, or the voice, of the Douglas 'tender and true,' or the minstrel of the Eildons, or the bard of Plynlimmon, or the Ellen of the lonely Isle,—to whose lips Scott has entrusted the most beautiful Ave Maria that was ever sung, and which can never be sung rightly again until it is remembered that the harp is the true ancient instrument of Scotland, as well as of Ireland.[1]

I am afraid of being diverted too far from Solway Moss, and must ask the reader to look back to my description of the Spirit of music in

four or five hours every night. So large has been the throng of listeners that the chief constable has drafted a number of policemen to maintain order and prevent damage.'—*Pall Mall Gazette*, May 11th, 1889.

[1] Although the violin was known as early as 1270, and occurs again and again in French and Italian sculpture and illumination, its introduction, in superseding both the voice, the golden bell, and the silver trumpet, was entirely owing to the demoralization of the Spanish kingdom in Naples, of which Evelyn writes in 1644, 'The building of the city is, for the size, the most magnificent in Europe. To it belongeth three thousand churches and monasteries, and those best built and adorned of any in Italy. They greatly affect the Spanish gravity in their habit, delight in good horses, the streets are full of gallants on horseback, and in coaches and sedans, from hence first brought into England by Sir Sanders Duncomb; the country people so jovial, and addicted to music, that the very husbandmen almost universally play on the guitar, singing and composing songs in praise of their sweethearts, and will commonly go to the field with their fiddle,—they are merry, witty, and genial, all which I attribute to the excellent quality of the air.'

What Evelyn means by the *fiddle* is not quite certain, since he himself, going to study 'in Padua, far beyond the sea,' there learned to play on 'ye theorba, taught by Signior Dominico Bassano, who had a daughter married to a doctor of laws, that played and sung *to nine* several instruments, with that skill and addresse as few masters in Italy exceeded her; she likewise composed divers excellent pieces. I had never seen any play on the *Naples viol* before.'

the Spanish chapel at Florence ('The Strait Gate,'* pages 134 and 135), remembering only this passage at the beginning of it, 'After learning to reason, you will learn to sing: for you will want to. There is much reason for singing in the sweet world, when one thinks rightly of it. None for grumbling, provided always you *have* entered in at the strait gate. You will sing all along the road, then, in a little while, in a manner pleasant for other people to hear.'

82. I will only return to Scott for one half page more, in which he has contrasted with his utmost masterhood the impressions of English and Scottish landscape. Few scenes of the world have been oftener described, with the utmost skill and sincerity of authors, than the view from Richmond Hill sixty years since; but none can be compared with the ten lines in 'The Heart of Midlothian,' edition of 1830, page 374. 'A huge sea of verdure, with crossing and intersecting promontories of massive and tufted groves, was tenanted by numberless flocks and herds, which seemed to wander unrestrained, and unbounded, through the rich pastures. The Thames, here turreted with villas, and there garlanded with forests, moved on slowly and placidly, like the mighty monarch of the scene, to whom all its other beauties were but accessories, and bore on his bosom a hundred barks and skiffs, whose white sails and gaily fluttering pennons gave life to the whole.

'As the Duke of Argyle looked on this inimitable landscape, his thoughts naturally reverted to his own more grand and scarce less beautiful domains of Inverary. "This is a fine scene," he said to his companion, curious perhaps to draw out her sentiments; "we have nothing like it in Scotland." "It's braw rich feeding for the cows, and they have a fine breed o' cattle here," replied Jeanie; "but I like just as weel to look at the craigs of Arthur's Seat, and the sea coming in ayont them, as at a' thae muckle trees."'

83. I do not know how often I have already vainly dwelt on the vulgarity and vainness of the pride in mere magnitude of timber which began in Evelyn's 'Sylva,' and now is endlessly measuring, whether Californian pines or Parisian towers,—of which, though they could darken continents, and hide the stars, the entire substance, cost, and pleasure are not worth one gleam of leafage in Kelvin Grove, or glow of rowan tree by the banks of Earn, or branch of wild rose of Hazeldean;—but I may forget, unless I speak of it here, a walk in Scott's own haunt of Rhymer's Glen,[1] where the brook is narrowest in

---

[1] 'Captain Adam Ferguson, who had written, from the lines of Torres Vedras, his hopes of finding, when the war should be over, some sheltering cottage upon the Tweed,

its sandstone bed, and Mary Ker stopped to gather a wild rose for me. Her brother, then the youngest captain in the English navy, afterwards gave his pure soul up to his Captain, Christ,—not like banished Norfolk, but becoming a monk in the Jesuits' College, Hampton.

84. And still I have not room enough to say what I should like of Joanie's rarest, if not chiefest merit, her beautiful dancing. *Real* dancing, not jumping, or whirling, or trotting, or jigging, but dancing,—like Green Mantle's in 'Redgauntlet,' winning applause from men and gods, whether the fishermen and ocean Gods of Solway, or the marchmen and mountain Gods of Cheviot.[1] Rarest, nowadays, of all the gifts

within a walk of Abbotsford, was delighted to see his dreams realized; and the family took up their residence next spring at the new house of Toftfield, on which Scott then bestowed, at the ladies' request, the name of *Huntley Burn*;—this more harmonious designation being taken from the mountain brook which passes through its grounds and garden,—the same famous in tradition as the scene of Thomas the Rhymer's interviews with the Queen of Fairy.

'On completing this purchase, Scott writes to John Ballantyne:—"Dear John,— I have closed with Usher for his beautiful patrimony, which makes me a great laird. I am afraid the people will take me up for coining. Indeed these novels, while their attractions last, are something like it. I am very glad of *your* good prospects. Still I cry, *Prudence! Prudence!* Yours truly, W. S."'—*Lockhart's 'Life,'* vol. iv, page 82.

[1] I must here once for all explain distinctly to the most matter-of-fact reader, the sense in which throughout all my earnest writing of the last twenty years I use the plural word 'gods.' I mean by it, the totality of spiritual powers, delegated by the Lord of the universe to do, in their several heights, or offices, parts of His will respecting men, or the world that man is imprisoned in;—not as myself knowing, or in security believing, that there are such, but in meekness accepting the testimony and belief of all ages, to the presence, in heaven and earth, of angels, principalities, powers, thrones, and the like,—with genii, fairies, or spirits ministering and guardian, or destroying or tempting; or aiding good work and inspiring the mightiest. For all these, I take the general word 'gods,' as the best understood in all languages, and the truest and widest in meaning, including the minor ones of seraph, cherub, ghost, wraith, and the like; and myself knowing for an indisputable fact, that no true happiness exists, nor is any good work ever done by human creatures, but in the sense or imagination of such presences. The following passage from the first volume of 'Fors Clavigera' gives example of the sense in which I most literally and earnestly refer to them:—

'You think it a great triumph to make the sun draw brown landscapes for you! That was also a discovery and some day may be useful. But the sun had drawn landscapes before for you, not in brown, but in green, and blue, and all imaginable colours, here in England. Not one of you ever looked at them, then; not one of you cares for the loss of them, now, when you have shut the sun out with smoke, so that he can draw nothing more, except brown blots through a hole in a box. There was a rocky valley between Buxton and Bakewell, once upon a time, divine as the vale of Tempe; you might have seen the gods there morning and evening,—Apollo and all the sweet Muses of the Light, walking in fair procession on the lawns of it, and to and fro among the pinnacles of its crags. You cared neither for gods nor grass, but for cash (which you did not know the way to get). You thought you could get it by what the *Times* calls "Railroad Enterprise." You enterprised a railroad through the valley, you blasted its rocks away, of cultivated womankind. It *used* to be said of a Swiss girl, in terms of commendation, she 'prays well and dances well;' but now, no human creature can pray at the pace of our common prayers, or dance at the pace of popular gavottes,—more especially the last; for however fast the clergyman may gabble, or the choir-boys yowl, their psalms, an earnest reader can always *think* his prayer, to the end of the verse; but no mortal footing can give either the right accent, or the due pause, in any beautiful step, at the pace of modern waltz or polka music. Nay, even the last quadrille I ever saw well danced, (and would have given half my wits to have joined hands in,) by Jessie and Vicky Vokes, with Fred and Rosina, was in truth *not* a quadrille, or four-square dance, but a beautifully flying romp. But Joanie could always dance everything *rightly*,[1] having not only the brightest light and warmth of heart, but a faultless foot; faultless in freedom—never narrowed, or lifted into point or arch by its boot or heel, but level, and at ease; small, *almost* to a fault, and in its swiftest steps rising and falling with the gentleness which only Byron has found words for—

> 'Naked foot,
> That shines like snow—and falls on earth as mute.'*

The modern artificial ideal being, on the contrary, expressed by the manner of stamp or tap, as in the Laureate's line—

> 'She tapped her tiny silken-sandalled foot.'*

heaped thousands of tons of shale into its lovely stream. The valley is gone, and the gods with it; and now, every fool in Buxton can be at Bakewell in half-an-hour, and every fool in Bakewell at Buxton; which you think a lucrative process of exchange, you Fools everywhere!'

[1] Of *right* dancing, in its use on the stage, see the repeated notices in 'Time and Tide.' Here is the most careful one:—'She did it beautifully and simply, as a child ought to dance. She was not an infant prodigy; there was no evidence, in the finish or strength of her motion, that she had been put to continual torture through half her eight or nine years. She did nothing more than any child, well taught, but painlessly, might do. She caricatured no older person,—attempted no curious or fantastic skill. She was dressed decently,—she moved decently,—she looked and behaved innocently,—and she danced her joyful dance with perfect grace, spirit, sweetness, and self-forgetfulness. And through all the vast theatre, full of English fathers and mothers and children, there was not one hand lifted to give her sign of praise but mine.

'Presently after this came on the forty thieves, who, as I told you, were girls; and there being no thieving to be presently done, and time hanging heavy on their hands, arms, and legs, the forty thief-girls proceeded to light forty cigars. Whereupon the British public gave them a round of applause.

'Whereupon I fell a-thinking; and saw little more of the piece, except as an ugly and disturbing dream.'

From which type the way is short, and has since been traversed quickly, to the conditions of patten, clog, golosh, and high-heeled bottines, with the real back of the foot thrown behind the ankle like a negress's, which have distressed alike, and disgraced, all feminine motion for the last quarter of a century,—the slight harebell having little chance enough of raising its head, once well under the hoofs of our proud maiden-hood, decorate with dead robins, transfixed humming birds, and hot-house flowers,—for its 'Wedding March by Mendelssohn.' To think that there is not enough love or praise in all Europe and America to invent one other tune for the poor things to strut to!

85. I draw back to my own home, twenty years ago, permitted to thank Heaven once more for the peace, and hope, and loveliness of it, and the Elysian walks with Joanie, and Paradisiacal with Rosie, under the peach-blossom branches by the little glittering stream which I had paved with crystal for them. I had built behind the highest cluster of laurels a reservoir, from which, on sunny afternoons, I could let a quite rippling film of water run for a couple of hours down behind the hay-field, where the grass in spring still grew fresh and deep. There used to be always a corncrake or two in it. Twilight after twilight I have hunted that bird, and never once got glimpse of it: the voice was always at the other side of the field, or in the inscrutable air or earth. And the little stream had its falls, and pools, and imaginary lakes. Here and there it laid for itself lines of graceful sand; there and here it lost itself under beads of chalcedony. It wasn't the Liffey, nor the Nith, nor the Wandel; but the two girls were surely a little cruel to call it 'The Gutter'! Happiest times, for all of us, that ever were to be; not but that Joanie and her Arthur are giddy enough, both of them yet, with their five little ones, but they have been sorely anxious about me, and I have been sor-rowful enough for myself, since ever I lost sight of that peach-blossom avenue, 'Eden-land' Rosie calls it sometimes in her letters. Whether its tiny river were of the waters of Abana, or Euphrates, or Thamesis, I know not, but they were sweeter to my thirst than the fountains of Trevi or Branda.*

86. How things bind and blend themselves together! The last time I saw the Fountain of Trevi, it was from Arthur's father's room— Joseph Severn's, where we both took Joanie to see him in 1872, and the old man made a sweet drawing of his pretty daughter-in-law, now in her schoolroom; he himself then eager in finishing his last picture of the Marriage in Cana,* which he had caused to take place under a vine trellis, and delighted himself by painting the crystal and ruby glitter-ing of the changing rivulet of water out of the Greek vase, glowing

into wine. Fonte Branda I last saw with Charles Norton,[1] under the same arches where Dante saw it. We drank of it together, and walked together that evening on the hills above, where the fireflies among the scented thickets shone fitfully in the still undarkened air. *How* they shone! moving like fine-broken starlight through the purple leaves. How they shone! through the sunset that faded into thunderous night as I entered Siena three days before, the white edges of the mountainous clouds still lighted from the west, and the openly golden sky calm behind the Gate of Siena's heart, with its still golden words, 'Cor magis tibi Sena pandit,'* and the fireflies everywhere in sky and cloud rising and falling, mixed with the lightning, and more intense than the stars.

BRANTWOOD,
June 19th 1889.

[1] I must here say of Joanna and Charles Norton this much farther, that they were mostly of a mind in the advice they gave me about my books; and though Joan was, as it must have been already enough seen, a true-bred Jacobite, she curiously objected to my early Catholic opinions as roundly as either Norton or John P. Robinson. The three of them—not counting Lady Trevelyan or little Connie, (all together *five* opponent powers)—may be held practically answerable for my having never followed up the historic study begun in Val d'Arno, for it chanced that, alike in Florence, Siena, and Rome, all these friends, tutors, or enchantresses were at different times amusing themselves when I was at my hardest work; and many happy days were spent by all of us in somewhat luxurious hotel life, when by rights I should have been still under Padre Tino in the sacristy of Assisi, or Cardinal Agostini at Venice, or the Pope himself at Rome, with my much older friend than any of these, Mr Rawdon Brown's perfectly faithful and loving servant Antonio. Of Joanna's and Connie's care of *me* some further history will certainly, if I live, be given in No. VII, 'The Rainbows of Giesbach'; of Charles Norton's visit to me there also.

APPENDIX

[THIS passage was omitted, probably at the instruction of Joan Severn, from the end of 'L'Esterelle' in the original publication of *Praeterita*, where it followed directly from the chapter as reproduced above.]

CHAMOUNI, 18th September, 1888.—I was repeating over this letter to myself last night, the nearly full moon keeping me awake, not unwillingly, with unclouded light, as she rose above the Dôme, and set over the Breven, while the higher two stars of Orion's belt seemed to pause above the peak of the Aiguille Blaitiere, a film of white cloud filling the valley to the south, stretching upwards to Mont Blanc—the aiguilles all silver-grey in moonlight.

Repeating it—and thinking over its character as distinguished from that of other children's letters. There is no precocity in it. Any girl of real power, well taught, would feel and write, in all sincerity, just as this Rose does, of pictures, statues, flowers, and hills. But the quite singular character of the letter is its sympathy. There is not a sentence in which the child is thinking of herself. She knows exactly what *I* am feeling, and thinking only of that, without a shadow of vanity, or of impulsive egoism. Her one thought always is, 'Can I help him, or give him any joy?' the consciousness of her own power being so habitual and frank that it is used as simply, as (?when) she first gave me her hand, her subsequent knowledge of me being deeper than a child's only in its religious anxiety that I should believe as she believed. And in the year 1860 the 'new epoch of life,' above spoken of, began for me in this wise, that my father and mother could travel with me no more, but Rose, in heart, was with me always, and all I did was for her sake.

BRIEG, SIMPLON, 20th September.—As much for her sake, that is to say, as of old, for theirs, and more distinctly also in the choice and tenour of it, beginning with *Unto This Last*, composed at Chamouni in walks to and fro under the wood of the Arveron. I recollect an American—not friend, but the intimate companion—asking me who Rosie-Posie was,—the words sometimes being said aloud unconsciously.

Then in 1860, I could not bear being so far away from her, when she was at her home in Ireland, so, having it also in my mind to write some day the analysis of sea-waves which had baffled me in *Modern Painters*, I stayed at Boulogne instead of going on to the Alps, taking a little bedroom and parlour under the sandhills north of the pier, and set myself to watch sea and sky, Rose writing to me every week punctually, and Emily sometimes interlining a word or two, leaning over her shoulder. I taught myself to write what writing is possible to me in answer to these letters, but learned much more than that in the days when there were no waves to be looked at, except the little ones on the sands, which were if anything more puzzling than the great ones.

I had given up learning Greek by Gordon's, I finally think, quite wise advice, and Latin, because I hated Lucretius, and was teased by Tacitus. But now, when Rose began to ask me questions about her Greek Testament, and the thoughts I had first expressed in *Unto This Last* could receive support from Homer and Xenophon and Horace, it was needful for such purpose at least to make what verbal knowledge I had, sound.

I took the bit in my teeth, sent for my Plato to Boulogne, with Xenophon's *Economist*, and Horace, and read sometimes not more than a line a day of each, but that as perfectly as grammar and dictionary would do it. Gradually I gained real scholarship in pure plain Greek and in lyric Latin. I cannot translate a Greek chorus, nor do I know the force of the words used by Plato and Horace in every other writer; but I know what Plato and Horace mean themselves by them, and *feel* in meaning, better than most other scholars. But Gordon's warning came fatally true. I lost at least half of the precious years between 1860 and 1870 in gaining this scholarship, wholly useless in argument with modern writers formed in the French and American schools, and taking the place in my own life and time which ought to have been given to finish my well begun work in geology, or begin earlier that which I must leave merely hinted in *Love's Meinie*.

If only I were back once again in the bright little room at Boulogne—with a Rosie letter on the table—and for all other companionship, a shrimp or a limpet in a bucket—she herself taught me to catch crawfish in the Liffey— what a history of streams and woods we could have written together!

I *did* learn more at Boulogne, however, of shrimps and limpets than one can find in books; and of waves, at least the look of them from the deck of a Boulogne lugger. For one day, as I was watching the mackerel boats come in, the captain of one which had moored alongside the pier came up the wooden ladder steps close beside me. I liked the intelligent and kindly face, and after watching the play of it a while, in his talk with the people he met, asked him if he would take me out with him to see some mackerel fishing. After a little debate, he consented and from that time forward, took me out with him in the bright mornings, and brought me in with the next tide, sometimes in open sea leaving me at the tiller even in a brisk breeze; but he would never let me bring the boat into harbour. The prettiest piece of sailing I saw was one intensively warm night with high wind, the whole sea phosphorescent in its foam, the boat running gunwale under, the currents of blue fire floating continually over the lower side of the deck. For the rest, in sunny mornings, I saw beautiful things in the colours of the fresh caught fish, but could not reconcile it with my Utopian principles of Creation that any should have poisonous spines in their fins, and still less with my Utopian principles of society that my good and thoughtful sailing master should only be a Boulogne pilot.

EXPLANATORY NOTES

ALL references to Shakespeare are to *The Oxford Shakespeare: The Complete Works*, ed. Stanley Wells and Gary Taylor (2nd edn., OUP, 2005); those to the Bible are to the King James Version (KJV): JR's allusions to the Bible in *Praeterita* are always to KJV.

ABBREVIATIONS

CJRCEN	*The Correspondence of John Ruskin and Charles Eliot Norton*, ed. John Lewis Bradley and Ian Ousby (Cambridge: Cambridge UP, 1987)
Diary	*The Diaries of John Ruskin*, ed. Joan Evans and J. H. Whitehouse, 3 vols. (Oxford: Clarendon, 1956–9), continual pagination; all references simply to 'diary' are to these volumes
JJR	John James Ruskin, JR's father
JR	John Ruskin
JMO'G	Joyce O'Gorman
JRCJS	*John Ruskin's Correspondence with Joan Severn: Sense and Nonsense Letters*, ed. Rachel Dickinson (Oxford: Legenda, 2009)
LE	*Library Edition*
MR	Margaret Ruskin, JR's mother
MS Diary	the manuscript diaries of John Ruskin preserved in the Ruskin Library of the University of Lancaster, MS1–26.
OED	*Oxford English Dictionary*, 2nd (electronic) edn.

AUTHOR'S PREFACE

5 *passing . . . account of*: JR's omissions are discussed in the Introduction, pp. x, xx–xxi.

father: JJR.

old house: 28 Herne Hill, where the Ruskins moved in March 1823 (it was demolished *c*.1912). Herne Hill was, then, an affluent area of south London.

visionary flowers: Shelley, 'The Question' (1820), l. 33.

hope . . . them: JR's faith in immortal life by this point was probably far more troubled than this line suggests.

VOLUME I

7 *The Springs of Wandel*: the Wandle is a river in south-west London with its principal source ('springs') in Croydon, south London.

somewhat violently: see Introduction, p. xvi.

violent: extreme.

7 *Pope's translation*: completed in 1720 and influential throughout the nineteenth century.

8 *Hooker and George Herbert*: JR drew on the style of the Anglican divine Richard Hooker (1654–1700) especially in *Modern Painters*, II (1846). He said in 1840 that he admired the poet George Herbert (1593–1633) 'above everything' (*LE* i. 409) and always associated him with the best he had learned in his life.

kings: JR's shorthand for those with a recognized right and ability to rule.

Tydides or Idomeneus: warriors in Homer's *Iliad*. Tydides is the patronymic of Diomedes.

Redgauntlet: the eponymous hero of Scott's novel (1824), set in eighteenth-century Scotland.

father's sister: Jessie Richardson.

my grandfather: John Thomas Ruskin.

grave: in the churchyard of St John the Evangelist, Shirley, Croydon (recently restored).

No. 54: the house was demolished in 1969. There are now apartments on the site.

9 *Long Acre*: this area, close to Covent Garden, had many coach-and-harness establishments.

Abbot at Kinross, and the Monastery in Glen Farg: Scott's novels *The Abbot* and *The Monastery* were both published in 1820. The first is set partly in Loch Leven Castle, near Kinross; the second involves a place named 'Glendearg'.

White Lady . . . Loch Leven: the 'White Lady' is in *The Monastery* while Mary Queen of Scots is imprisoned on Loch Leven in *The Abbot*.

FitzJames of the Lady of the Lake: Fitz-James is King James V in disguise in Scott's poem *The Lady of the Lake* (1810).

Marmion: Douglas is the hero of Scott's poem *Marmion* (1808), on the battle of Flodden.

Tantallon . . . Archibald . . . Snowdoun: Tantallon is a castle in East Lothian; Archibald is from *Marmion*; the Knight of Snowdoun is Fitz-James in *The Lady of the Lake*.

'Restoration' . . . 29th of May: the day of Charles II's restoration to the English throne. The oak apple commemorated the future Charles II's escape from the Roundhead army by hiding in an oak tree after the battle of Worcester (1651).

10 *grandmother*: Margaret Ruskin (Senior).

Simone Memmi's King's Head: Memmi's painting of the ruler's head is in the Spanish Chapel at Santa Maria Novella, Florence (it is admired in chapter 5 of *Mornings of Florence* (1877)).

My maternal grandfather . . . as I have said: William Cock. JR had not referred to him before in the *Praeterita* version of this section (see Note on the Text, p. xxiv).

not clear on that point: indeed not: Cock was landlord of the King's Head (see previous paragraph).

St George's Company: the first name of JR's Guild of St George: see Introduction, pp. xvi.

11 *my aunt*: Bridget Richardson.

13 *face of a child . . . painting in a classical subject*: Northcote's *The Sylvan Doctor* is currently lost though a photograph of it remains (*LE* xxxv, facing p. 22).

St George's schools: the Guild was to have its own schools. JR wrote some textbooks (including the science studies of the 1870s and 1880s) in part for use in them.

circulating library: multi-volume novels and other books could be borrowed a volume at a time from these subscription institutions (it was the books that circulated, not the libraries).

Seven Champions of Christendom: Richard Johnson's *Renowned History of the Seven Champions of Christendom* (1596–7), a romance version of the lives of the patron saints of England, Scotland, Wales, Ireland, as well as France, Italy, and Spain.

14 *Fors*: see Introduction, p. xvi n.

Hannah: 1 Samuel 1: 11.

sons of Zebedee . . . His to give!: Mark 10: 35–41.

15 *admired Raphael*: JR gradually changed his mind about what he had once thought Raphael's 'divine art' (*LE* i. 77). By the time of 'Pre-Raphaelitism' (1853), Raphael emblematizes the 'degradation' of the 'intellect and the art of Italy' when he paints, in the Vatican, Theology led by Christ and Poetry led by the pagan Apollo (*LE* xii. 148).

'he would have been a Bishop': the Ruskins, like others, moved between private non-established chapels and the Church of England (that is, a Church with bishops). They were worshipping at St Bride's Fleet Street before 1841, moving on to Camden Chapel. JR was involved in the 1844 rebuilding of St Giles's church, Camberwell: his 'unconversion' in 1858 (see p. 318) followed after attendance at the French service in the Waldensian (Protestant) chapel of Turin.

I have said somewhere before: in *Fors* for December 1872 (*LE* xxvii. 421).

16 *The quality of the Macharnudo vintage . . . never impair*: these are likely to be JJR's often repeated salesman's words (with some remembrance of Falstaff on sack, *2 Henry IV*, iv. iii.).

17 *Rogers' Italy . . . carefully at Turner's work*: the long poem *Italy* by Samuel Rogers (1763–1855) was illustrated in 1830 by artists including Turner, whose watercolours (reproduced in steel engraving) are less illustrations

to Rogers's text than his own depictions of Italy. Literally the first Turner JR *may* have seen was *The Wreck of the Minotaur* in 1828 on the Isle of Wight.

18 *'dickey'* . . . *derivation*: *OED* is uncertain of the etymology of 'dickey'. JR prints a letter about it in *Dilecta* (*LE* xxxv. 585) claiming it is ultimately from the Latin *tego*: 'to cover'.

Bob Sawyer's arrangements with Sam: in Dickens's *Pickwick Papers* (1836–7), ch. 50, Bob Sawyer and Sam Weller share the dickey seat in Mr Pickwick's coach.

Anne: Anne Strachan.

19 *posting*: exchanging horses on a long journey.

caparisoned: harnessed.

oriel: properly, an upper-storey bay window.

20 *Midsummer holiday*: JR means this only colloquially: the accepted 'Midsummer holiday' since medieval times has usually been 23–8 June.

first gooseberry pie of the year: young gooseberries can be picked in mid-May to encourage growth of larger fruit, ripening properly in July. It is possible to eat the May crop, but 10 May is early indeed.

21 *'Standard in Cornhill'*: the 'Standard' was a disused water pump at Cornhill in the City of London, which served as a measurement of distance to and from the capital.

viator: traveller.

Cold Harbour: 'place of shelter from the weather for wayfarers, constructed by the wayside. Hence, a frequent name of a locality', *OED*.

bricked over for the convenience of Mr Biffin: the Effra flowed above ground from Norwood and Dulwich into the Thames until it was channelled underground. The Victorian sewage systems incorporated the river and now only the outfall is visible (at Vauxhall Bridge). 'Mr Biffin' is unknown.

22 *forget the name of a man to whom I owe so much!*: JJR bought the lease of Herne Hill from a Mr T. J. Moores in 1829.

all the fruit was forbidden: in Genesis, only one fruit—of the 'knowledge of good and evil' (Genesis 2: 17)—is forbidden.

there were no companionable beasts: while Adam names the animals in Eden, they are not, in fact, his companions.

Cock-Robinson-Crusoe: compounded of the traditional rhyme 'Who Killed Cock Robin?' and the eponymous hero of Daniel Defoe's 1719 novel. JR means 'perky', like a 'Cock Robin', but alone like 'Robinson Crusoe'.

23 *High School of Edinburgh*: the Royal High School, Edinburgh, with twelfth-century origins, where both JJR and Walter Scott had been educated.

Brantwood: the painting remains in the Brantwood collection. Brantwood, JR's home 1872–1900, is on the eastern shore of Coniston Water in the English Lake District.

tragedy of Douglas: a blank verse tragedy by the Scottish dramatist John Home, first performed in 1756, which concerns an abandoned illegitimate child and the fatal disorder that ensues from his recognition.

Castle Spectre: 'Monk' Lewis's popular play of 1797: a drama of the Gothic supernatural, it was set in medieval Conw[a]y.

24 *Count Robert of Paris*: Scott's penultimate novel, published in 1831 (Scott died the following year): it is set in Constantinople during the First Crusade.

wretches who were tormenting and selling the wrecked intellect: in 1826, the financially over-extended printing business (James Ballantyne & Co), of which Scott was a partner, collapsed during economic downturn, leaving debts over £126,000. In a commercial environment without limited liability, Scott was personally liable to substantial loss. His future earnings were sequestered to pay it off, and he undertook major writing projects to raise money, including fiction, *The Life of Napoleon Buonaparte* (1827), and a complete edition of his novels. By his death in 1832, he had repaid over £51,000.

My father . . . concealment of the Ballantyne partnership: JJR severely apportions blame to an individual, but the partnership's business model was not exceptional, and the external financial environment was hostile. Scott did not, anyway, 'conceal' the partnership.

Compare the 52nd paragraph . . . The Bible of Amiens: 'the duty enforced upon me in early youth of reading every word of the gospels and prophecies as if written by the hand of God, gave me the habit of awed attention which afterwards made many passages of the profane writers, frivolous to an irreligious reader, deeply grave to me' (*LE* xxxiii. 119).

25 *Scottish paraphrases*: the principal hymnal of the Church of Scotland.

love for the Law of God: Psalm 119, the longest of the psalms, is a celebration of divine law.

eighth of 1st Kings being one: 1 Kings 8 is sixty-six verses long, and describes King Solomon's worship at the Ark.

'Shall any . . . ashes of the urn?': unknown.

28 *Wombwell's menagerie*: George Wombwell (1777–1850) founded his Travelling Menagerie in 1810: it was the most famous animal show of the time.

30 *Crystal Palace*: this glass and iron edifice was designed by Joseph Paxton for the 1851 Great Exhibition then moved from Hyde Park to Sydenham Hill, south London, in 1854. It was destroyed by fire in 1936.

coup-de-soleil: sunstroke.

31 *Magna Charta*: Magna Carta, the 'Great Charter', signed on 15 June 1215 by King John (1199–1216), defined the powers of the monarch in relation to the barons. It is often seen as the starting point of the English constitution.

31 *law of England might preserve Banstead . . . otherwise unremunerative duty*: 'In December 1876 the lord of the manor of Banstead (Sir John Hartopp, Bart.) was proposing to build on, and enclose parts of, Banstead Downs and Heath. The freeholders and copyholders of the manor formed a Preservation Committee, a member of which, Mr W. Hale White . . . wrote to Ruskin, who guaranteed £100 towards the expenses of the committee. An action (Robertson v. Hartopp) was commenced, and after long, costly, and complicated litigation, the committee gained its object' (*LE* xxxv. 49).

32 *the principle . . . in 'Proserpina' . . . seeds and fruits . . . flowers for the fruit*: 'The flower exists for its own sake,—not for the fruit's sake' (*LE* xxv. 249). JR's point is that the beauty of flowers is God's gift to human beings, not merely instrumental to attract pollinating insects. *Proserpina* (1875–86), on botany, mostly considered flowers and plants in relation to the myths with which they were historically associated.

Dame Wiggins . . . Peacock at Home . . . Frank . . . Harry and Lucy . . . Joyce's Scientific Dialogues: *Dame Wiggins of Lee, and her Seven Wonderful Cats* is a comic poem published in 1823 and reissued by JR, illustrated by Kate Greenaway, in 1885—the same year in which this chapter appeared. *Peacock at Home* is a poem by Catherine Ann Turner Dorset (1750?–1817?), published in 1807. 'Frank' and 'Harry and Lucy' are from Maria Edgeworth's children's tales, *Early Lessons* (1801); *Scientific Dialogues . . . an Easy Introduction to Natural and Experimental Philosophy* by Jeremiah Joyce (1763–1816) began in 1800 and was often reissued.

33 *in my seventh year*: JR was not unique in producing imitation publications in early youth: it was not uncommon among educated, literary children (the Brontës are obvious comparisons).

34 *according to my practice to this day*: a wry comment on the number of incomplete multi-part books JR had in hand in later years.

36 *Manfred*: the hero of Byron's Faustian dramatic poem *Manfred* (1816–17) is tortured by his own guilt to suicide.

37 *Adam's Latin Grammar*: Alexander Adam's widely used *The Principles of Latin and English Grammar*. see Introduction, pp. xii–xiii.

38 *Scott's Tales of a Grandfather*: Scott's history of Scotland (and later France), published from 1828.

lignum vitae: ('wood of life', Latin), a hard commercial wood.

voussoir: wedge-shaped stone used in arch building.

Waterloo Bridge: the neoclassical granite bridge across the Thames at London with nine arches. It was opened in 1817, and commemorated the Battle of Waterloo (1815).

so fond of its toy bricks, except Miss Edgeworth's Frank: Frank receives a 'box full of little bricks' from Henry in Part IV of Edgeworth's tale.

paviours: those who lay paving.

39 *Eudosia . . . 'On the Universe'*: 'Eudosia' refers to the 'good gifts' of Creation: for the poem itself, see *LE* ii. 269–71.

Deucalion: JR's book on geology (1875–83): it included extensive accounts of mountain formation.

40 *Don Quixote . . . most offensive of books to me*: JR changed his mind about Cervantes's *Don Quixote* (1605–15), disliking the satirical presentation of knighthood as a poor model of manliness.

41 *Burd Helen, the Twa Corbies*: traditional Scottish ballads. The first is about longing to be dead in the grave with Helen; the latter about two crows eating a dead knight.

a year afterwards: actually three years afterwards, in 1783.

somewhat rough tanner: Patrick (Peter) Richardson (born in 1774 and died, 20 July 1824, in Bridgend, Perth) was a man of some social standing (e.g., a member of the Perth tanner's guild court in 1821). He married Jessie (20 November 1783–18 May 1828) on 1 November 1801 in St Cuthbert's, Edinburgh.

42 *Peter—not Simon—the tanner*: cf. Acts 9: 43: 'And it came to pass, that he tarried many days in Joppa with one Simon a tanner' (with a play on St Peter the Apostle's original name of Simon).

my little cousin Jessie: Janet/'Jessie' Richardson (1819/20–7).

'Dux': leader, 'Duke'.

'Mause' . . . 'Old Mortality': Mause Headrigg is a stern, but comic, Presbyterian retainer in Scott's *Old Mortality* (1816).

43 *wild Amorite*: in Deuteronomy 1: 7, the Amorites are a mountain-dwelling people.

slight bias against Evangelical religion . . . my later works: JR's writing in the 1870s and 1880s was critical of the narrow-mindedness of Evangelicalism in general (see e.g. *St Mark's Rest*) and of the narrowness of 'my own pert little Protestant mind' (*LE* xxiv. 277) in youth in particular.

a pure dove-preistess . . . Highland Dodona: Dodona was the ancient oracle at Epirus where the prophetesses were known, according to Herodotus, as 'doves'.

Little Peter: Patrick (1810–18).

She had been much saddened . . . my mother's words accurately: Jessie's children included the younger Jessie; Catherine (1810–17); Mary (1815–49), and two other infant girls: both Margaret (1816–17), who died at 6 months, and Helen (died at 3 weeks in 1817), passed away in the same year as Catherine.

jargonel pears: jargonelle pears were particularly associated with Perth in the nineteenth century.

44 *for molinary purposes*: that is, a mill-stream.

tansy: widespread plant of aster family, with bright yellow flowers.

Medusa: a Gorgon in Greek myth whose look could turn human beings to stone.

45 *gleaning*: retrieving loose corn from the ground after harvesting.

46 *It came on after a long walk . . . water on the brain*: the connection is that water on the brain, *hydrocephalus*, was treated in the nineteenth century by digitalis, extracted from foxgloves.

happy, happy: a conjunction particularly associated with Keats, e.g. 'Ode on a Grecian Urn' (1817), ll. 21 and 25.

47 *Beresford Chapel, Walworth*: Walworth, south London: Beresford Chapel (now on John Ruskin Street, Camberwell) was demolished after 1989 and the site is now occupied by apartments.

48 *a sermon of Blair's . . . Bingley's Natural History*: all appropriately Protestant reading. Hugh Blair (1718–1800) was a leading Scottish preacher whose 5-volume *Sermons* (1777–1801) went into many editions. The references thereafter are to John Bunyan's *The Pilgrim's Progress* (1678) and *The Holy War* (1682); Francis Quarles' *Emblems* (1635), a set of biblical paraphrases and reflective passages; and John Foxe's *The Book of Martyrs* (1563), a study of Christian martyrs widely admired by Puritans and influential on Protestant perceptions of Catholics. *The Lady of the Manor* (1823–9) and *Henry Milner* (1822–37) are children's stories by the Evangelical Mary Martha Sherwood (1775–1851); the *Youth's Magazine* is an Evangelical magazine with children's stories; *Alfred Campbell the Young Pilgrim* (1825) is by Barbara Hofland (1770–1844), a poet and writer of moral tales; 'Bingley's Natural History' is, probably, William Bingley's *Animated Nature; or, Elements of the Natural History of Animals* (1814).

Miss Andrews . . . 'Angel in the House': Andrews's daughter, Emily, married Coventry Patmore (1823–96), author of the influential poem *The Angel in the House* (1854–61), in 1847.

'Tambourgi, Tambourgi': from Byron's *Childe Harold*, canto ii.

49 *Anacreontic metre*: the metre of a seven-syllable line used by the Greek lyric poet Anacreon (582–485 BCE) in poems on wine and love.

Cruikshank's illustrations to Grimm: the British illustrator George Cruickshank (1792–1878) illustrated the Grimm brothers' fairy tales in *German Popular Stories* (1823–6). JR thought them the 'finest [etchings] next to Rembrandt's' (*LE* xv. 222).

Caxton's New Bath Hotel: Matlock's New Bath Hotel was opened in 1802 (it is still a hotel). By 'Caxton' JR refers to the Saxton family, who were owners and proprietors of the hotel.

galena: lead ore mineral.

50 *'Iteriad'*: the word alludes to *Iliad*, meaning 'epic of a journey'.

52 *Herne Hill Station*: opened in 1862.

big geography book: *Geography, Illustrated on a Popular Plan; for the Use of Schools and Young Persons* (1806–10) by 'the Rev. J. Goldsmith' (actually, the publisher and bookseller Sir Richard Phillips, 1767–1840).

53 *Joanie*: Joan Severn.

I leave the unfinished folly . . . may see it: published in *Poems* (2 vols., 1891), *LE* ii. 340–87.

54 *'Scotch thing'*: see Introduction, p. xxii.

55 *Salvador*: JJR's courier about whom little is known.

Rembrandt's Supper at Emmaus: the painting (1648) remains in the Louvre. JR recalls Rose looking at Veronese's version in 'L'Esterelle', p. 342.

fatal dinner at Mr Domecq's: JR thought this dinner was fatal to his chances of marrying Adèle Clotilde Domecq, daughter of Pedro Domecq, with whom he fell in love as a teenager. There is an account on p. 116.

56 *trying to trisect an angle*: trisecting an angle with a compass and straight edge is a celebrated impossibility.

Parnassus and Plynlimmon: the first is a mountain near Delphi, Greece, sacred to Apollo and the Muses; Plynlimon is the highest point of the Welsh Cambrian Mountains.

57 *John . . . Bridget*: the children were: John (1803–?); William (1806–?); George (1808–?); Charles (1811–34); Margaret (1804–?); Bridget (1814–?51). Bridget married Isaac Fox and, like John, emigrated to Australia. On Charles, see note to p. 91.

I never liked invalids: wry comment on JR's increasing frailty.

ruddy as the boy David: 1 Samuel 17: 42.

58 *tadpole-haunted ditch in Croxted Lane*: the destruction of the rural Croxted Lane in Dulwich, south London, and its transformation into a rubbish-strewn urban cart-road is mourned in JR's *Fiction, Fair and Foul* (*LE* xxxiv. 265–7). It is now Croxted Road, the A2199.

Messrs Smith, Elder, & Co.: a major nineteenth-century publishing house, which issued many of Ruskin's works as well as those by, among others, Charlotte Brontë, Robert Browning, and George Gissing.

59 *Forget-me-not*: the first literary annual, running from 1822 to 1847.

Thomas Pringle . . . Lockhart's Life of Scott: Thomas Pringle (1789–1834), Scottish editor, poet, and writer on South Africa, is mentioned by Lockhart's *Life of Sir Walter Scott* (1837–9), though not with a 'sprinkling of honour'.

Parks and Livingstones: Mungo Park (1771–1806) and David Livingstone (1813–73), Scottish explorers of Africa.

60 *Ettrick Shepherd*: the nickname of James Hogg (1770–1835), Scottish poet and novelist.

Elusinian initiation and Delphic pilgrimage: Elusinian refers to the initiation ceremonies at Eleusis, Greece, in honour of Demeter and Persephone; 'Delphic' refers to the great ancient Greek Oracle of Apollo at Delphi.

polished minstrel of St James's Place: Rogers's house was at 22 St James's Place, Westminster, overlooking Green Park and he designed the interior decoration himself.

61 *conversation*: JR's relationship with Rogers later improved, and they corresponded.

61 *I have elsewhere related*: it is not clear to what JR is referring. There are two letters to Hogg (one from JJR and the other from JR) reproduced in Mary Gray Garden's *Memorials of James Hogg* (1895), which may have been provided by JR. JJR's refers to a brief visit from the poet. But JR does not 'relate' the event anywhere.

Miss Edgeworth's story of Lazy Lawrence . . . Harry and Lucy: the first is a story in Edgeworth's *The Parent's Assistant* (1796), set near Clifton: the journey to Matlock occurs in *Harry and Lucy Concluded* (1825).

I have said somewhere . . . first memory . . . Derwentwater: JR remembered in *Modern Painters*, III (1856), ch. 17: 'The first thing which I remember, as an event in life, was being taken by my nurse to the brow of Friar's Crag on Derwent Water; the intense joy, mingled with awe, that I had in looking through the hollows in the mossy roots, over the crag, into the dark lake, has associated itself more or less with all twining roots of trees ever since' (*LE* v. 365).

62 *I have written . . . wise to print*: the writing referred to is now lost.

The Menai Bridge . . . tube . . . tower to tower: Telford's initial bridge across the Menai Straits from the north Wales mainland to the island of Anglesey had a wooden deck. By 'tube' JR refers to Robert Stephenson's Britannia Bridge, built as a tubular railway bridge in 1850.

64 *chiasoi*: JR means 'crossed' or 'diagonally intersected'.

'Chiasognathos Grantii': properly, *Chiasognathus granti* ('Grant's Stag-beetle'). A paper on this creature, described as a new genus, *Chiasognathus*, was sent to the Cambridge Philosophical Society by a Dr Grant from the *Forte* and read on 16 May 1831.

65 *'Star and Garter'*: a renowned hotel in Richmond, London, overlooking the Thames, whose guests included foreign monarchs and celebrities: it was demolished in 1919.

coruscant: glittering, sparkling.

'faggot against anthracite': JR is remembering a description of the battle of Dettingen (1743) quoted in Carlyle's *History of Friedrich II* (1858–65), Bk. 14, ch. 5, which actually reads, 'fire of anthracite-coal *versus* flame of dry wood'. The battle saw British, Austrian, and Hanoverian forces defeat the French.

Spain: the marriage was in Lisbon, Portugal.

66 *'long-drawn aisle'*: from Gray's 'Elegy Written in a Country Churchyard' (1751), l. 39.

the first chapter of the Antiquary . . . Spanish: in fact, in chapter 2 of Scott's novel *The Antiquary* (1816), the landlord rejects port and brings claret. Robert Cockburn and George Wauchope established their port business in 1815.

67 *I read all Captain Marryat's . . . Walton . . . by heart*: Frederick Marryat (1792–1848) was an English author of popular sea-stories; Izaac Walton's *The Compleat Angler* (1653) is the most celebrated British book

on river fishing. *The Deerslayer* (1841) and *The Pathfinder* (1840) are two adventure novels by the American author James Fenimore Cooper (1789–1851).

little black silkworm . . . mulberry leaf: the domesticated silkworm, *Bombyx mori*, eats mulberry leaves almost exclusively.

68 *rez-de-chaussée*: ground floor.

windmills on Mont Martre: until the middle of the nineteenth century, Montmartre, a hill in north central Paris, had many windmills.

69 *Earth shaker*: ancient Greek epithet for Poseidon, god of the sea, storms, and earthquakes.

early and late: *Praeterita* never returned to discuss Chelsea in any detail. Nanny Clowsley remains unknown.

70 *like Aladdin's trap-door*: in 'Aladdin and the Wonderful Lamp', Aladdin passes through a trapdoor and finds the lamp.

'Vix ea nostra voco': 'I scarcely call these things our own' (Ovid, *Metamorphoses*, 13.141). JR sees the appropriateness of this motto for a *hired* carriage (he may have known it from Scott's *Waverley*, ch. 10).

71 *Murray*: John Murray (1808–92), third-generation publisher, launched *Murray's Guides* with *A Handbook for Travellers on the Continent* (1836). The guides became staples for English travellers.

valet-de-place: guide to travellers.

73 *Three Kings*: the *3 Könige am Rhein* or *Des Trois Rois* is an ancient inn (begun *c.*1681) in Basel. It opened as a 'luxury' grand hotel in 1844 and has recently been restored to its nineteenth-century condition.

74 *Clapham Junction*: this busy train station opened in 1863.

destruction of the myth of William Tell: this demythologization bothered JR elsewhere though there seems no obvious source for it. He may refer to the general nineteenth-century concern with the relationship between 'historical' narratives and myth including the work of the German 'Higher Critics' on the Bible.

tunnelled Gothard: the Gothard Rail Tunnel, joining Göschenen with Airolo, was constructed between 1871 and 1881.

grapes dropped blood . . . Morgarten Glen: the battle of St Jakob an der Birs in August 1444 saw the Swiss defeated by a French force, though Swiss bravery was long remembered. The Swiss employed pikes instead of the previously preferred halberds.

were there paddle-packets across Atlantic?: commercial transatlantic steam service began in 1838.

75 *'all sorts and conditions of men'*: a phrase from the Book of Common Prayer.

St Bernard of La Fontaine . . . St Bernard of Talloires . . . Aosta: JR describes the vision of St Bernard (1090–1153), Abbot of Clairvaux (born in Fontaine-lès-Dijon). St Bernard of Talloires is St Bernard of Menthon, born near Annecy, who established the hospices at the Great and Little St Bernard Passes in the Alps.

76 *Renaissance evil*: this is JR's great contention. The fault-line of western culture, as he saw it from *The Stones of Venice* (1851–3) onwards, was the division between the faithful God-centred Gothic age, and the corruption of the human-centred Renaissance.

Portia's villa,—Juliet's palace: in *The Merchant of Venice* and *Romeo and Juliet* respectively.

'mount of marble, a hundred spires': Tennyson, 'The Daisy' (1855), l. 60.

Burford's panorama in Leicester Square: panoramas (long painted displays of landscapes or historical events) were popular at the beginning of the nineteenth century. Barker/Burford's, in Leicester Square, London, ran between 1792 and 1865.

78 *amourette*: flirtation/affair.

79 *Saussure's 'Voyages dans les Alpes'*: Horace-Bénédict de Saussure (1740–99), Swiss Alpinist, published his geological study between 1779 and 1796.

Mineralogy: the *Manual of Mineralogy* by the Edinburgh academic Robert Jameson (1774–1854).

Agora: assembly place (Greek).

80 *Martha*: see Luke 10: 41.

'though still the house affairs would draw her thence': *Othello*, I. iii. 146.

82 *science of Political Economy*: the precursor of what is now economics. Political economy grew from moral philosophy and was concerned with matters of commerce and the relations of consumption and production, usually from philosophical, societal, and legal perspectives. The new economics would prefer mathematical, statistical, and theoretical procedures. JR mocked the assumption that political economy was a science in the first essay of *Unto This Last* (1860).

Adam Smith's 'Wealth of Nations': JR owned the 1811 Edinburgh edition of this 1776 work on the free market.

honourable and distinguished merchant: an important theme of *Unto This Last* where JR argued that moral behaviour from employers as well as merchants would transform capitalism.

Dr Thompson's or Mr Murray's new system of chemistry: Thompson is unknown; 'Murray's' is probably John Murray, *Elements of Chemistry* (Edinburgh, 1801).

Gregory's 'Economy of Nature': George Gregory's *The Economy of Nature Explained and Illustrated: on the Principles of Modern Philosophy*, 3 vols. (1796).

83 *Agnes . . . life*: Dickens, *David Copperfield*, ch. 62. Agnes remains silently loyal to David throughout his unwise marriage to Dora.

Grace Nugent and Lord Colambre: not entirely a happy allusion. In Edgeworth's *The Absentee* (1812), Lord Colambre falls in love with Grace

Nugent whom he presently learns is illegitimate. He despairs, for he feels he can never marry such a woman. But subsequently he discovers that Grace is not only legitimate, but an heiress.

84 *the now not very young people were married*: John James and Margaret were married on 27 February 1818: she was 37, he 33.

85 *common ways . . . perfect peace*: Proverbs 3: 17.

His capital was either . . . St Catherine's Docks: St Katharine Docks (opened in 1828) were near JJR's offices at 7 Billiter Street: his cellars were at Tower Wharf, near the Tower of London.

86 *savoir faire*: 'know how'.

injured lip: see p. 45.

87 *barouche*: a four-wheeled hooded carriage, associated with the leisured classes.

Londonian chapel . . . Roman basilica: Beresford Chapel had a stern, simplified Romanesque facade, with a plain galleried interior.

88 *some years since effaced from sight and memory of men*: by 1875, Henry Ritchie wrote to JR saying that 'not one brick is left standing upon another that composed the walls of No. 7 Billiter Street' (Lancaster University, Ruskin Foundation, L85, 27 August 1875). Towering over the Street is now the skyscraper of 30 St Mary Axe (the Gherkin).

Wardell . . . believe: John and William Wardell, 7 Billiter Street, were wine merchants.

89 *brick wall of the brewery*: unknown: 8 Billiter St (presumably opposite 7) was a cider merchant's in 1823, and housed a 'General Porter' in 1851. 11 Billiter Street was a pub, the Crown and Thistle, in the late 1830s, but the brewery may have been on an adjacent street.

90 *sparkle of Jin Vin . . . steadiness of Tunstall*: the 'sharp-witted, active, able-bodied, and well-voiced apprentices, namely, Jenkin Vincent and Frank Tunstall' in Scott's *The Fortunes of Nigel* (1822), set in London. JR owned the manuscript, bought by JJR.

Margaret: the heroine of *The Fortunes of Nigel*, who lives on Fleet Street.

91 *couldn't save him*: see the *Bristol Mercury*, 2285 (8 Feb. 1834): 'Drowned by the upsetting of a boat off Portsmouth, on the 27th ult. Charles Thomas Richardson, in the 27th year of his age, son of Mr George Richardson, of Croydon'. Charles is buried in Wootton parish church, Isle of Wight.

92 *Vester, Camenae*: ['yours, O muses']: Horace, *Odes*, 3.4.21.

I think it must have been as early as 1832: Richard was not at Shrewsbury at this point.

93 *Rev. George Croly . . . Henry Neele, Esq.*: see Glossary of Persons Mentioned. *The Chronicles of London Bridge* (1827), a history, was written by Richard Thompson (1794–1865).

94 *Continental Annual and Friendship's Offering*: the first is probably *The Continental Annual and Romantic Cabinet*, edited by William Kennedy and

illustrated by Prout (Smith, Elder, 1832); *Friendship's Offering* was another Smith, Elder periodical, from 1824 to 1844.

94 *Noctes Ambrosianae*: seventy-one imaginary conversations in *Blackwood's Magazine* (1822–35), usually set in an Edinburgh tavern: they include relatively racy descriptions of women.

shipwreck in Don Juan: the shipwreck in Byron's satiric *Don Juan* (1819–24) is in canto ii, followed by a scene of dog and man-eating.

'*Juan and Haidée*': the romance in *Don Juan*, canto ii.

Cain, Werner, the Deformed Transformed, and Vision of Judgment: Byron's *Cain* (1821); *Werner* (1822); *The Deformed Transformed* (1824); *The Vision of Judgment* (1822) is a parody of Southey's *A Vision of Judgment* (1821).

95 *Corsair ... Giaour ... Richard III ... Solomon*: the *Corsair* is the protagonist of Byron's semi-autobiographical *The Corsair* (1814); the Giaour ('unbeliever', 'infidel') is from Byron's *The Giaour: A Fragment of a Turkish Tale* (1813); 'Richard III' is the malevolent eponymous protagonist of Shakespeare's play. The Old Testament monarch Solomon was the first king of Israel: JR is thinking of his reputation for wisdom.

Victor Hugo down to Doctor Watts: JR claimed to dislike the novels of the French writer Victor Hugo (1802–85). But Hugo's conception of the Renaissance as inferior to the medieval world in his most famous novel *Notre-Dame de Paris* (1831, *The Hunch-back of Notre Dame*) was quietly influential on *The Stones of Venice*. Isaac Watts (1674–1748) was an English hymn writer.

Alice Bridgenorth: the daughter of the Puritan Major Bridgenorth in Scott's *Peveril of the Peak* (1823).

Madge Wildfire: a madwoman in Scott's *The Heart of Midlothian* (1818).

Margherita Cogni ... wife of Faliero: the first was Byron's real-life Venetian mistress; the second is Angiolina, in Byron's play of ducal treachery, *Marino Faliero*.

Esther's religious aunt in Bleak House: Miss Barbary in Dickens's *Bleak House* (1852–3), perhaps merged with the severe Mrs Clennam in *Little Dorrit* (1855–7).

Humphrey Clinker: *The Expedition of Humphry Clinker* is Tobias Smollett's epistolary novel of 1771. The Ruskins were committed readers of eighteenth-century fiction. JR and JJR had a shared fondness in particular for Matthew Bramble, the characterful, angry, but morally centred squire in *Humphry Clinker*. Bramble's voice, perhaps, echoes in the voice of *Fors Clavigera*. Even JR's last dog at Brantwood was called Bramble.

97 '*The Whigs abuse him ... unshadows the Rialto*': *The Works of Lord Byron: Letters and Journals*, ed. R. E. Prothero (1904), iv. 239–40 (with minor transcription changes).

Murray: John Murray (1778–1843), Byron's publisher.

98 *I have no patience ... Dunciad*: Pope's *The Rape of the Lock* (1712–17); 'Essay on Man' (1732–4), *Dunciad* (1728–43). JR came to admire Pope,

and was considering writing a biography of him in the summer of 1873 (*LE* xxvii. 586 n.).

Ayrshire ploughman: Robert Burns (1759–96), Scottish national poet.

Beatrice's 'ottave' . . . Songs of Tuscany: Beatrice of Piano degli Ontani, poet and mother of eight children, silences a crowd with her singing and receives tribute as the 'greatest poet of our mountain' (*LE* xxxii. 209) in *Roadside Songs of Tuscany*, translated and illustrated by Francesca Alexander, and edited by JR in 1885.

99 *Homer to tell me . . . top of Ossa*: in the Odyssey, book 11, Ossa is thrown onto nearby Mount Olympus.

Of no use for Pope . . . nothing of the sort: 'Trees, where you sit, shall crowd into a shade', Alexander Pope, *Pastorals*, ii. 74. JR was dissatisfied with any conception of nature animated by human emotion (the 'pathetic fallacy'), in *Modern Painters*, III (1856), ch. 12.

I rejoiced in all the stories . . . St John: Pallas is Pallas Athena, Greek goddess of Wisdom; Venus, Roman goddess of love; Achilles the Greek warrior hero of Homer's *Iliad*; Eneas is Aeneas, the Trojan hero of Virgil's *Aeneid* who founds Rome; Elijah is the Old Testament prophet of the ninth century BCE; and St John was still widely believed at this point to be the author of both the Fourth Gospel and the Book of Revelation.

'as idle tales; and they believed them not': they were not the words of Peter but of Mary Magdalene and other women concerning the risen Jesus that the Apostles regarded as idle tales (Luke 24: 11).

Shakespeare said the Alps voided their rheum on the valleys: Henry V, III. v. 52.

'the glacier's cold . . . day by day': Manfred, I. i. 68–9 (slight misquotation).

100 *The witch of the Staubbach . . . in her cutty sark*: the 'witch of the Staubbach' is Byron's 'Witch of the Alps' in *Manfred* whom Manfred refuses to serve; the rat is from Shakespeare's *Macbeth*, I. iii. 8; Nannie is one of the beguiling witches in a cutty sark ('short skirt') that Tam watches in Burns's poem 'Tam o'Shanter' (1791), and who pulls off his horse's tail.

sea-king Conrad: the protagonist of Byron's *The Corsair*.

Coleridge's long, lank, brown, and ancient, mariner: Coleridge's 'The Rime of the Ancient Mariner' (1798–1834), l. 226.

Windsor woods: Pope describes these woods in his political poem, *Windsor Forest* (1713).

tinkling cymbal: 1 Corinthians 13: 1.

Lachin-y-Gair: where Mary Duff came from, it is also commemorated in Bryon's poem of this name (1807).

Chillon and of Meillerie: Byron's *The Prisoner of Chillon* (1816) recorded the heroic solitude of François Bonivard as a prisoner in the Swiss Château de Chillon. Meillerie, in the Haute-Savoie, was visited by Byron and Shelley as they were investigating places mentioned in Rousseau's *Julie, ou la nouvelle Héloïse* (1761).

100 *Foscari and Falier*: two doges of Venice, the former the subject of Byron's
     drama *The Two Foscari* (1821) and the latter, the only doge to be executed
     for treachery, of his *Marino Faliero* (1821).

     White Maid of Avenel: the ghostly White Lady in Scott's *The Monastery*.

     Rogers . . . 'St Preux has stood': 'where Tell leaped ashore' is a quotation
     from the 'Meillerie' section of Rogers's *Italy*; 'Here St Preux has stood' is
     from earlier in the same section.

     Portia . . . Miranda: Portia from *The Merchant of Venice*; Miranda from
     The Tempest.

     trenches: cuts into (*OED*, 1.1).

101 *'Poor Louise'*: the doleful 'Lay of Poor Louise' is in chapter 10 of Scott's
     The Fair Maid of Perth (1828).

     'Coast Scenery': Stanfield's *Coast Scenery: A Series of Views in the British
     Channel* (1836). The plate referred to is no. 3.

     Turner's . . . Bible series: JR refers to engravings in *Landscape Illustrations
     of the Bible: . . . from Original Sketches . . . Engraved by W. and E. Finden*
     (1836).

     'cyanometer': an instrument for measuring 'blueness' of sky.

102 *Croyland*: Crowland, Lincolnshire town with a partially ruined medieval
     abbey.

     Dict^re des Sciences Eccles^ques: Richard and Giraud's *Bibliothèque sacrée, ou,
     dictionaire universel* (1822–7 edn.).

     in present political junctures: this chapter was issued in February 1886: by
     April, W. E. Gladstone (1809–98), four times British prime minister, had
     introduced the Government of Ireland ('First Home Rule') Bill which
     would have created a devolved assembly for portions of Ireland.

     'Rue St Jacques . . . Pelican': 'St James' Street, at the sign of the Pelican'.

     'qui si . . . Benoist': 'who also became a nun with the Benedictine Order'.

103 *de grande probité . . . sans reproche*: 'of great integrity, authority, and with-
     out reproach'.

     eschevins: aldermen.

     Marguilliers: church wardens/parish officers.

104 *I might haunt them . . . Rob Roy*: in Scott's *Rob Roy* (1817), vol. ii, ch. 3,
     Rob Roy hides in the crypt of Glasgow Cathedral and passes on a secret
     message.

     coteaux: slopes.

     American tin: 1812 saw the first American canning factory, and, after the
     Civil War (1861–5), canning became a major industry.

     modistes: milliners/those who are 'modish'.

105 *'Our Fathers have told us'*: JR's planned ten-part series on Christian
     history, particularly in the thirteenth century, had the general title of

Our Fathers Have Told Us. It reached only its first part (*The Bible of Amiens*, 1880–5); the eighth was to be on Rouen.

108 *'pertes'*: losses.

'*Taillés à pic, et entrecoupées'*: 'cut straight down, and interspersed'.

109 *derniers rochers, and calotte*: the 'last rocks' and a rounded cavity ('calotte' is an architectural term).

110 *see the passage . . . through sympathy*: there is no exact parallel in *Seven Lamps of Architecture* (1849). How human presence makes a landscape valuable, though, is the main theme of *The Poetry of Architecture* (1837–8).

'*Not till we can . . . peopled garden'*: see *The Correspondence of Thomas Carlyle and Ralph Waldo Emerson 1834–1872*, ed. C. E. Norton, 2 vols. (Boston: Osgood, 1883), i. 18. Carlyle is himself quoting an unnamed source, in fact, and it is part of his elaborate compliment to Emerson for sending him a gift across the ocean. JR slightly misrepresents what Carlyle is doing.

more than Carlyle's wife to him: Carlyle's unhappy marriage to Jane Welsh Carlyle had been revealed by Froude's publication of *Reminiscences* (1881), a volume of great interest to JR.

112 *as will be seen*: there is no further reference to the Rigi in *Praeterita*.

Quem tu, Melpomene: from Horace's *Odes*, 4. 3, meaning: 'He whom thou, Melpomene'. But the sense comes from the rest of the passage: 'Hast welcomed with thy smile, in life arriving, | Ne'er by boxer's skill shall be | Renown'd abroad, for Isthmian mastery striving; | Him shall never fiery steed | Draw in Achaean car a conqueror seated; | Him shall never martial deed | Show, crown'd with bay, after proud kings defeated, | Climbing Capitolian steep: | But the cool streams that make green Tibur flourish, | And the tangled forest deep, | On soft Aeolian airs his fame shall nourish' (Conington's translation).

pantiles: the Pantiles is now the name for the old commercial centre of Tunbridge Wells, which, from the early eighteenth century, had been distinguished by its many terracotta pantiles. Most had gone by the time the Ruskins visited.

113 *laced and buttoned surtout*: a (cavalry) frock coat.

114 *another place*: JR does so only briefly, p. 150.

drop their h's: the standard nineteenth-century indicator of uneducated speech.

West-end wine merchant: could this be a slip for West *Country*? Certainly, there was a William Watson, wine merchant, in Bristol in 1820.

Clos-Vougeot . . . Champagne: Clos-Vougeot is a Burgundy *grand cru*; Hochheimer, more usually known in English as 'Hock', is a popular German wine from the Rheingau; 'still Champagne' refers not to actual champagne without bubbles, but to the still wines that were, at this point, available from the champagne area.

116 *'la toilette de Madame'*: 'My Lady's Wardrobe' is an old French game where the players sit in a circle, except the leader. Each seated player has taken the name of some item of the lady's wardrobe. The leader says: 'My lady wants her gown', and the 'gown' must rise at once and the leader takes the vacated place, and so on. If a player does not rise immediately, he or she owes a forfeit.

for whom it was written: Vincenzo Bellini (1801–35) wrote the opera *I Puritani* (1835), based loosely on Scott's *Old Mortality*, for the singers Giulia Grisi, Luigi Lablache, Giovanni Battista Rubini, and Antonio Tamburini.

117 *Taglioni*: Marie Taglioni (1804–84) was an Italian-Swedish ballerina of international fame. In 1845, JR mourned the demolitions at the Ca' d'Oro on Venice's Grand Canal. Shortly afterwards, more destruction followed, ordered by Taglioni, who had been given the Ca' d'Oro as a Venetian home. It seems JR did not know this connection.

Grisi and Malibran . . . Patti . . . as soon as possible: Maria Malibran (1808–36) and Adelina Patti (1843–1919) were among the best-known of nineteenth-century sopranos; 'Là ci darem la mano' is Don Giovanni and Zerlina's duet in Mozart's *Don Giovanni* (1787).

'Come mai . . .' . . . 'A te o cara': 'Come mai posso vivere' may be an earlier version of the 'Canzonetta Fiorentina' by M. R. Lacy in his *Alcuni canti popolari* (London: Lonsdale, 1846?). If so, JR had, probably, a high baritone voice, and some vocal dexterity. 'A te o cara' is Talbot's love aria to Elvira from *I Puritani*. JR, with 'true lover's sentiment', had Adèle in mind. For Mr Marshall, see note to p. 157.

118 *to enforce with benefit . . . autobiography*: this was not done.

White of Selborne, or Vicar of Wakefield . . . Whistonian: the first is the naturalist the Revd Gilbert White (1720–93); the Vicar of Wakefield is the eponymous hero of Oliver Goldsmith's 1766 novel; Whistonian refers to William Whiston (1667–1752), scientist and Arian.

cometic: Whiston thought Noah's flood had been caused by a comet, and argued for the periodicity of comets in general.

square caps on: that is, undergraduates with mortar boards.

'Knut the king came sailing by': almost certainly the four-line passage of verse in Middle English, preserved in the twelfth-century *Liber Eliensis*: 'Merie sungen ðe muneches binnen Ely, | ða Cnut ching reu ðerby. | "Roweth, cnites, noer the land | And here we ther muneches saeng"' ('Merrily sang the monks in Ely as king Cnut rowed past. [He said]: "Row, lads, closer to land, and let us hear the song of those monks"').

119 *southern cross*: the Crux, small constellations with a cross-like appearance, visible best from the southern hemisphere.

George the Third . . . French Catholics: King George III was opposed to Catholic Emancipation, believing it to be contrary to his coronation oath.

Mercredi des cendres: 'Ash Wednesday' (French), the beginning of the penitential season of Lent in the western Christian calendar.

Mr Traddles, Mr Toots, and Mr Winkle: Traddles is an impoverished, luckless, but kind-hearted young man in Dickens's *David Copperfield* (1849–50); Toots is the ardent young lover in *Dombey and Son* (1846–7); and Winkle a young man with pretentions to sport in *Pickwick Papers*.

Norwood dinner: in *David Copperfield*, ch. 26, David dines with his employer, Mr Spenlow, and becomes 'a captive and a slave' to his childlike daughter, Dora.

120 *Spanish-born . . . Transubstantiation*: JR refers to the English defeat of the Spanish Armada (1588), a Protestant victory over a Catholic power; the battle of Waterloo (1815), a British alliance defeating the French forces of Napoleon Bonaparte; and the theological concept of transubstantiation, the Catholic belief that Christ is literally present in the consecrated bread and wine of the Mass, which remains alien to Protestant conceptions of the Eucharist.

Our connection . . . 'Friendship's Offering': the story was 'Leoni: A Legend of Italy', published in 1837 and reproduced in *LE* i. 288–304.

Hours of Idleness: Byron's juvenilia, published in 1807: it contained 'Lachin y Gair'.

121 *I remember nothing more of that year, 1836*: JR's diaries are blank from 1836 to 1838.

Herodotus: JR's degree was the standard mixture of classics and mathematics.

122 *Bride of Abydos*: Byron's poem published in 1813.

Sensitive Plant and Epipsychidion: two Shelley poems, published in 1820 and 1821 respectively. JR's initial enthusiasm for Shelley faded: 'cast aside Shelley as shallow and verbose', he said in 1857 (*LE* xv. 227).

'prickly . . . blue': 'The Sensitive Plant', *LE* iii. 60 (JR omits the punctuation).

'it was a little . . . mosaic paven': Shelley, 'The Isle', ll. 1–2 (slight misquotation).

the Revolt of Islam: (1818), Shelley's poem about freedom from religion.

Prometheus . . . something of Aeschylus: Shelley's *Prometheus Unbound* (1820) drew on *Prometheus Bound*, still regarded in the early nineteenth century as written by Aeschylus.

matriculate: to be registered as a student.

Christ Church: Oxford's cathedral college, founded in 1524, and favoured by aristocrats. Entry at the two ancient Universities of Oxford and Cambridge, as evident here, was partly related to an ability to pay.

123 *Gentlemen-Commoners . . . Servitors . . . our Reformed University*: gentlemen-commoners were undergraduates paying higher fees, who acquired thereby a higher social rank; servitors acted as servants to college Fellows

in return for reduced charges. Oxford was significantly reformed and remodelled by the time JR wrote *Praeterita*: science was well established and the concept of research was more widely accepted, the professoriate was rethought, governance structures changed, and social distinctions of the sort described largely removed.

123 *good as Bossuet's . . . Primate of England*: Jacques-Bénigne Bossuet (1627–1704) was a celebrated French preacher at Louis XIV's court. By 'Primate of England', JR means Archbishop of Canterbury (though the Archbishop of York is properly 'Primate of England', Canterbury of '*all* England').

124 *choice of Hercules*: between Virtue and Pleasure.

125 *Davie Gellatly*: Davie Gellatley, from Scott's *Waverley*, is a retainer who keeps on the 'windy side of insanity' (ch. 12).

all very well for Abraham to do what angels bid him: Genesis 22: 11–19. The angel first bids Abraham slay his son.

gone with Him up to the mountain . . . Lake of Galilee: JR is probably thinking of Matthew 17: 1–2, the scene of the Transfiguration, and of John 6: 1, where Jesus crosses Galilee.

126 *City of Destruction*: Christian's journey in Bunyan's *The Pilgrim's Progress* is from the City of Destruction to Mount Zion.

Gothic chapel: Peckwater is built in eighteenth-century neoclassical style.

college chapel: also, distinctively, Oxford's cathedral. This looked considerably different to the present appearance of the cathedral, which was, apart from anything else, given a neo-Norman east window by Scott in 1853.

choir: the part of the cathedral with canons' and college members' stalls. The Jacobean choir of the cathedral that JR knew was removed after his time and is now in St Peter's, Cassington.

127 *first shrine of St Frideswide*: Frithuswith (*c*.650–727), patron saint of Oxford: Christ Church is on the site of her priory. Her shrine (in the north-east chapel of the cathedral) has been variously desecrated.

fifteenth century: it is actually *c*.1640.

The west window . . . Adoration of the Shepherds: a puzzling reference. Ackermann's *History of the University of Oxford* (1814) shows the old *east* window of the Cathedral as a nativity scene with angels and shepherds. Or is JR confusing Christ Church with New College, with Joshua Reynolds's painted west window, which depicts the nativity? The first mistake seems more likely.

greatest divine . . . greatest scholar: JR may (ironically) mean by 'greatest divine' the holder of the Regius professorship of divinity, who was a canon of Christ Church (at this point, Renn Dickson Hampden, 1793–1868); by the greatest scholar, he may simply mean the Regius Professor of Greek (Thomas Gaisford, dean).

128 *Dean Abbot*: JR is comparing Christ Church to a monastery.

Gorgonian cold: Gorgons in Greek myth turned human beings to stone by looking at them. See also note to p. 44.

great council hall of Venice: the Sala del Maggior Consiglio in the Palazzo Ducale.

first from a second future: two forms of Latin future tense (indicative and imperative).

where the Pelasgi lived, or where the Heraclidae returned from: it is not clear where Pelasgians, allies of Troy, come from in Homer's *Iliad*; the 'Return of the Heraclidae' is the name for the conquest of Peloponnesus by the Dorians.

130 *lèse-majesté*: offence against a sovereign.

Hospice of the Grimsel: the portion of JR's 'Letter' in verse to Richard Fall written during this storm is given in *LE* ii. 431–4.

131 *north side of Canterbury*: Canterbury is the Christ Church quadrangle leading to Merton street. It is one of the curious features of this chapter that JR does not mention the Christ Church picture collection here, begun in 1765, and containing Oxford's largest collegiate collection of Old Masters.

plains of Troy: Acland published *The Plains of Troy: Illustrated by a Panoramic Drawing Taken on the Spot* in 1839.

excellent college tutor: W. L. Brown.

'Duckling Astray': JR refers to Harrison Weir's illustration in the *Children's Prize*, 12 (Dec. 1873), which he also mentioned, in a discussion of children's reading, in *Fors*, February 1875 (*LE* xxviii. 257).

132 *I can't make out . . . unflinchingly given*: an omitted passage here ends: 'I learned four dialogues of Plato—of Theology, the Thirty-nine Articles;—of myself—[of] the world I was to live in—nothing' (*LE* xxxv. 610).

133 *'little go'*: slang term for the first of three examinations for an Oxford degree.

οραʹ . . . *Iphigenia in Tauris*: 'the vacant space | Between the triglyphs *(mark it well)* enough | Is open to admit us', from Euripides' *Iphigenia in Tauris* (*c*.414–412 BCE), trans. R. Potter (1781).

triglyph: a tablet of a Doric frieze with vertical channels: an obscure piece of knowledge.

Erinnys: better known as the Eumenides, the Greek personifications of just punishments/curses.

Holbein . . . Durer . . . Titian . . . Bonifazio's Bishops: JR refers to Hans Holbein's portrait of *Erasmus* (1523), now in the National Gallery, London, and Albrecht Dürer's *Philipp Melanchthon* (1526), now in the Museum of Fine Arts, Boston. Titian was a prolific portraitist of noblemen and grandees; it is not clear to which painting of a bishop by the Veronese painter Bonifazio (1487–1553) JR refers.

Tom: Tom Quad, the main quadrangle of Christ Church.

134 *ghostly*: spiritual.

Anathema: in the sense of 'set apart' or 'sacred', rather than 'accursed'.

134 *the present Dean*: Henry George Liddell. 'Anagke' is Greek for 'constraint'/'necessity'. Liddell wrote to JR to say that he was grateful for the 'kindly expressions' in *Praeterita*: 'Kindly I call them, though I am sensible that, under the kindliness, lies severe censure' (*LE* xxxv. 203 n.).

Cardinal's Square: that is, Tom Quad (Christ Church was founded in 1525 as Cardinal College, by Cardinal Wolsey).

135 *Frank*: Francis Buckland.

Herschel: Sir John Herschel (1792–1871), English mathematician and astrologer.

Carolina lizards: see Buckland in Glossary of Persons Mentioned.

136 *thirty years afterwards*: twenty years afterwards (1857).

137 *Circassian*: JR perhaps means Caucasian, but neither term is very meaningful.

138 *head of my college*: William Gaisford.

without any bush: that is, without advertisement or display.

140 *modestest of presidents*: from 1831, Fielding was president of the Old Water-Colour Society.

Newman Street: 26 Newman Street, London, Fielding's long-term home.

Volume of Conversations: the critic William Hazlitt (1778–1830) published some of Northcote's 'conversations' in the *New Monthly Magazine* (1826), then as a book, *Conversations of James Northcote Esq., R.A.* (1830).

141 *I hope to reprint . . . preserved*: this was not done.

142 *Queen Anne Street*: 47 Queen Ann Street West, Turner's house from 1810 and, later, gallery.

Quilleboeuf, or the 'Keelmen heaving in coals': Turner's *Quillebeuf, at the Mouth of Seine* (1833) is now in Lisbon (it was in the Royal Academy in 1833) and his *Keelmen Heaving in Coals by Moonlight* (1835) is in the National Gallery of Art, Washington.

Fountain of Indolence, or Golden Bough: Turner's *The Fountain of Indolence* (1834) is part of the Beaverbrook Collection, New Brunswick; *The Golden Bough* (1834) is in the Tate collection.

Juliet and her Nurse, Rome from Mount Aventine, and Mercury and Argus: Turner's *Juliet and her Nurse* (1836) is in a private collection; *Rome from Mount Aventine* (1836) is in the National Gallery of Scotland; and *Mercury and Argus* (before 1836) in the National Gallery of Canada.

an article in Blackwood's Magazine: the 'article' was 'Exhibitions' (actually a brief review) in October 1836.

fragment: this fragment, with its claim that Turner's imagination is 'Shakespearian in its mightiness', is reproduced in *LE* iii. 635–40 (iii. 638).

143 *immortality*: the claim of Wordsworth's 'Ode: Intimations of Immortality' (1807).

144 *'haunted me like a passion'*: Wordsworth, 'Tintern Abbey' (1798), l. 78.

I took stones for bread . . . Devil's bidding: Jesus is tempted by the devil to turn stones into bread in the first temptation in the wilderness (Matthew 4: 3–4).

Sermon on the mount: pun on Jesus' 'Sermon on the Mount', the most substantial collection of Jesus' teaching (Matthew 5–7).

sonnets to the celandine . . . poor little Psychidion: Wordsworth wrote three poems on the celandine, 'To the Small Celandine', 'To the Same Flower', and 'The Small Celandine', in 1802–3. Shelley's autobiographical 'Epipsychidion' (1821) records his passion for the young Teresa ('Emilia') Viviani. 'Epipsychidion' means 'the story of a soul'.

promising literary work: *The Poetry of Architecture*, JR's collection of essays on the eighteenth-century theme of the role of architecture in landscape.

145 *umquwhile*: 'former' (archaic).

an essay nine foolscap pages long: JR's 'Essay on the Relative Dignity of the Studies of Painting and Music and the Advantages to be Derived from their Pursuit' survives and is reproduced in *LE* i. 267–85.

146 *'Onward . . . still and deep'*: *The Lady of the Lake*, I. xiii. 1–2.

steamer: the first steamer on the Loch commenced service in 1843.

147 *Kataphusin*: 'according to nature' (Greek).

concealment of name: the title page of the first edition of *Modern Painters* I gave the authorship as only 'A Graduate of Oxford', though JR did not continue with the *nom de plume*. Debates about anonymous publication in the Victorian period, particularly in journalism, focused on the (unwarranted claim to) authority that anonymity was sometimes thought to imply.

four little volumes of Johnson—the Idler and the Rambler: *The Idler* (1758–60) and *The Rambler* (1750–2) are two collections of essays, almost all by Dr Johnson.

148 *cobwebs of German metaphysics*: JR was no friend of German thought. Here, he may have Samuel Taylor Coleridge, Thomas Carlyle, George Eliot, and G. H. Lewes in mind as interpreters of German philosophy for British readers, which JR thought obfuscatory.

149 *Why, I know not . . . close abruptly*: the magazine itself ceased.

'it will be seen . . . eternal battlements': this is from chapter 4, 'The Mountain Cottage: Westmoreland' (*LE* i. 52).

'Guarda e Passa': 'non ragionam di lor, ma guarda e passa': 'Do not speak of them, but look and pass on' (Dante, *Inferno*, iii. 51).

150 *Irvingite persuasion*: follower of Scottish preacher and spiritual revivalist Edward Irving (1792–1834).

portion for foxes: Psalm 63: 10.

151 *Newdigate*: the annual prize for the best undergraduate poem at the University of Oxford: JR won it with 'Salsette and Elephanta' in 1839.

152 *High German . . . Newton's Principia*: JR means Old High German, an early stage of German before the eleventh century. Together with formal French, Immanuel Kant's *The Metaphysics of Morals* (1797), and Isaac Newton's *Philosophiae Naturalis Principia Mathematica* (1687), this obviously comprises an absurdly advanced curriculum.

153 *told in Fors*: this story is given in *Fors* for May 1883 (*LE* xxix. 426–8).

clouds that gather round the setting sun: Wordsworth, 'Immortality Ode', l. 201.

Miserere: ('have mercy [on me]') in the Agnus Dei of the Latin Mass and Psalm 51.

'blazed every rose-carved buttress fair': Scott, *Lay of the Last Minstrel*, VI. xxiii. 42.

VOLUME II

155 *confragose*: 'rough with breaks, or shattered parts; broken': this is the only example *OED* gives.

'horrid': bristling, rough, shaggy (*horridus*).

156 *another place*: cf. pp. 210–13.

Peepy choked himself with his teetotum: Peepy Jellyby is a neglected small child in Dickens's *Bleak House* (1852–3); a 'teetotum' is a form of spinning top.

Arabia Felix: 'Happy Arabia', a term, formally, for southern Arabia including, now, the Yemen.

'On the Old Road': JR's account of his 'first editor', W. H. Harrison, written in 1878, was included in his collection, *On the Old Road* (1885). It compared modern journalism with that of JR's youth. Pringle had died in 1834.

157 *Cartoons*: Raphael's seven designs for tapestries intended for the Sistine Chapel hung in the Cartoon Gallery of Hampton Court till 1865: they are now in London's V&A.

maze: Hampton Court's celebrated hedge maze, planted at some point between 1689 and 1695.

coins of Cnossus . . . Minotaur: Knossos (or Labyrinth) is the centre of Minoan civilization at Crete; Daedalus is the legendary architect of the Cretan labyrinth, in which the Minotaur, half bull and half man, was imprisoned, until slain by Theseus.

I have much unprinted MSS . . . as it can: JR considered the coins of Knossos in appendix 21 of *The Stones of Venice*, I. The lecture on 'The School of Athens' in 1870 (from *Aratra Pentelici*) discussed Greek coinage, and JR reflected on the moral significance of the Minotaur as a figure of modern lust in Lecture 6 of *Ariadne Florentina* (1872).

mamma Monro: Mrs Gray's mother.

Mr Marshall on the trumpet stop: William Marshall (1806–75), organist of Christ Church cathedral (1825–46) and a respected teacher, was playing the old 'Father' Smith organ at Christ Church, built *c.*1680. It was rebuilt in 1848 (and had two trumpet stops).

158 *daughter*: Charlotte Harriet Jane Lockhart (1828–58) was the daughter of John Gibson Lockhart (1794–1854), author of *The Life of Sir Walter Scott*.

160 *'piped into a new creed by the whine of an organ pipe'*: JR is half-remembering himself on the subject of converts in appendix 12 of *The Stones of Venice*, I: 'to be blown into a change of religion by the whine of an organ pipe' (*LE* ix. 437). The (conventional) point is the contrast between the beguiling aesthetic quality of Catholic worship and an austere Protestantism.

Protestant Cavalier, not Protestant Roundhead: that is, JR wished to preserve the best of the past rather than, like the Cromwellian Roundheads in the English Civil War, as he sees them, upturn it.

161 *Finden's Bible*: see note to p. 101 above.

Mr Windus's Llanberis or Melrose: Turner's *Llanberis Lake and Snowdon—Caernarvon, Wales* (*c.*1830–5) is now in the National Gallery, London; the location of *Melrose Abbey: Moonlight*, commissioned by Walter Fawkes (*c.*1822), is unknown.

'Richmond Bridge, Surrey': JR acquired this in 1839 for 55 guineas: it is now in the British Museum.

162 *the Gosport*: JR also bought this in 1839 (for 60 guineas): it is now in Portsmouth Art Gallery.

who St Aldate was: St Aldate appears to have been a bishop of Gloucester who died in 577, but there is much uncertainty.

drawing of Winchelsea: this was bought in January 1840 for 55 guineas: it is now in the British Museum.

163 *Topffer's rivalless caricatures*: Rodolphe Töpffer's *Histoire de M. Jabot* (1833), a prototype of the comic, is a satirical account of a social upstart.

the Harlech: JR bought this for £63 in 1840. It is now in a private collection in the USA.

166 *I think she might also have told . . . amuse the midges*: this is more criticism of evolutionary biology, including of Darwin's *The Various Contrivances by which Orchids are Fertilized by Insects* (1862).

squash before 'tis a peascod: *Twelfth Night*, i. v. 152.

David Roberts . . . Holy Land: JR refers to *The Holy Land, Syria, Idumea, Arabia, Egypt, & Nubia, from drawings made on the spot by D. Roberts . . . With historical descriptions by the Revd George Croly* (1842–9).

167 *bise*: a north, or north-north-west wind in Switzerland/France.

Grimaldi: Joseph Grimaldi (1778–1837) was a famous English clown, thought to be the first white face clown.

167 *the last time I was at Sestri*: this was in 1872, when JR was with Joan and Arthur Severn, Mrs Hilliard and Miss Constance Hilliard.

168 *Pieta by Michael Angelo*: this pietà is no longer thought to be by Michelangelo.

At Genoa, I did not even hunt down the Vandykes: Van Dyck was based in Genoa during a six-year visit to Italy from 1621, painting portraits of aristocratic families.

carrioles: 'small open carriage[s] with a seat for a single person', *OED*.

slackening wheels of Pharaoh: Exodus 14: 24–5.

'Woe is me, Alhama': Byron's 'A Very Mournful Ballad of the Siege and Conquest of Alhama' concerns the Christian conquest of Alhama, Granada.

'the Moorish King rode up and down': a slight misquotation of Byron's first line.

sirocco: a hot blighting wind in Mediterranean countries.

169 *Cerito*: Francesca Cerrito (1817–1909), Italian ballerina.

bajocco: an Italian copper coin of little value.

'a trifle from Matlock': this was a popular phrase used on trinket boxes from this Derbyshire town in the nineteenth century. Its origin is unknown.

'Bacchus and Ariadne' . . . (we supposed classic) original: perhaps a copy of the painting of that name by Carle van Loo (1705–65), now in a private collection.

smoked: none of the Ruskins smoked (JR disapproved of tobacco throughout his active life), but candle and lamp oil will have done the damage.

170 *1845*: see pp. 220–3.

Pisa . . . Byron and Shelley: both poets lived in Pisa in 1821.

Misericordia: a volunteer Christian care association.

Spina Chapel: the small Gothic church of Santa Maria della Spina in Pisa was built in 1230: it was dismantled and reassembled, somewhat altered, higher above the River Arno in 1871.

171 *Newgate-like palaces*: JR compares the many fortress-like rusticated stone palazzi of central Florence with London's Newgate Prison.

Rogers in the Lorenzo Chapel: JR refers to Michelangelo's tombs in the Medici chapel of the church of San Lorenzo, Florence (in the 'Florence' section of Rogers's *Italy*, the poet thinks the statues so lifelike that they breathe).

Bacchus . . . Raphael's St John: Michelangelo's marble sculpture of *Bacchus* (1497) is now in Florence's Bargello; the 'knife grinder' is JR's term for the *Arrotino* ('blade sharpener'), a sculpture from the first century BCE, which is still in the Uffizi's Tribuna (it is now thought to be a portion of a larger *Flaying of Marsyas*). The statue of the *Venus de' Medici*, from the same period, remains in the Uffizi, and JR *did* change his mind about this, coming to see it as a beautiful representation of female form. Raphael's painting *St John the Baptist* (1518) is now in the Galleria dell'Accademia, Florence.

Angelico . . . Madonna . . . Venus Marina: Fra Angelico's *Madonna di Pontassieve* (1435–50?) and Botticelli's painting *The Birth of Venus* (*c*.1486), are still in the Uffizi. JR's term ('Venus of the Sea') is his own.

172 *Is the ruin of it yet spared?*: an error. The 'ruins' are actually the remains of the unfinished massive addition to the original cathedral (completed 1263) that were halted by the plague in 1348 and not resumed. They are still there.

Aeolian: as in an Aeolian (wind) harp.

good Roman emperor . . . Trajan: Trajan was Roman emperor between 98 and 117 CE. JR is alluding to Machiavelli's concept of 'Five Good Emperors', later developed by Edward Gibbon.

Marcus Antoninus . . . Socrates: Marcus Antoninus, usually known as Marcus Aurelius, was a Roman philosopher-emperor between CE 161 and 180, and last of the 'Five Good Emperors'. He was not a contemporary with the ancient Greek philosopher Socrates (*c*.469–399 BCE).

Nanny Clowsley's: see p. 69.

'I am in Rome' . . . Rogers': the first words of the 'Rome' section from Rogers's *Italy*.

173 *I had no distinct idea what the Forum was*: JR is perhaps still thinking of Rogers who describes visitors 'often saying to themselves | "This was the Roman Forum"'. The Forum was the centre of Rome's legal, ceremonial, and economic activity.

Arch of Severus: a triumphal arch (203 CE) commemorating the Parthian victories of Emperor Septimius Severus, 194–9 CE.

tufo and pozzolana: both forms of volcanic ash, the latter often used as a kind of cement.

all the great religious paintings . . . lower story of the Sistine: Pietro Perugino (*c*.1445–1523) was one of the painters who decorated the walls of the Sistine Chapel, 1477–80; the Chapel of Pope Nicholas V was decorated by Fra Angelico; the Sistine Chapel itself, the best known of the chapels in the Apostolic Palace, the Pope's residence in the Vatican, was built by Pope Sixtus IV (1471–84).

Raphael's Transfiguration, and Domenichino's St Jerome: the *Last Communion of St Jerome* (1614) by Domenico Zampieri ('Domenichino') is often compared to Raphael's *Transfiguration* (1516–20), usually thought his last painting: both are in the Pinacoteca Vaticana.

Sir Joshua's verdict on the Stanze: the four 'Stanze di Raffaello' ('Raphael's rooms') in the Vatican Palace contain Raphael's frescoes on biblical, religious, historical, and mythical themes. Reynolds, in *Discourse* 5, said that they were among paintings 'justly considered as the greatest efforts of our art which the world can boast'.

173 *decisively ascertaining that they could not give me the least pleasure*: JR, in his lecture 'Pre-Raphaelitism', made more of this. He said: 'On one wall of that chamber [Raphael] placed a picture of the World or Kingdom of Theology, presided over by Christ. And on the side wall of that same chamber he placed the World or Kingdom of *Poetry*, presided over by *Apollo*. And from that spot, and from that hour, the intellect and the art of Italy date their degradation' (*LE* xii. 148).

Domenichino . . . deference to Sir Joshua: in the *Discourses*, Domenichino is among those painters who, admirably, 'had opinions of their own'.

174 *Parnassus to the Disputa*: the *Parnassus* is the third part of the Stanze, after *The Disputation of the Sacrament* and *The School of Athens* (see note to p. 173).

'Stones of Venice': an error: it was 'Pre-Raphaelitism'. See note to p. 173.

where Mr Severn lived at that time: 18 via di San Isodoro, Rome.

175 *Prodigal Son*: Luke 15: 11–32.

Apollo Belvidere: *Apollo Belvedere*, a classical sculpture, in the Vatican museums, sculpted *c*.350–325 BCE, has been long celebrated as the epitome of classical aesthetics.

176 *fair English girl*: Georgina Tollemache.

177 *the Pope*: Gregory XVI (1831–46).

'Gente, e qui l'uccellatore': 'People, here is the bird catcher', from Mozart's *The Magic Flute* (1791), Act 1 ('Der Vogelfänger bin ich ja').

Cumae: ancient Greek settlement near Naples in Italy and location of the home of the Cumean Sybil and entrance to the underworld used by Aeneas in the *Aeneid*.

'Time and Tide': *Time and Tide* (1867) comprised twenty-five letters to a working man of Sunderland on the laws of work.

178 *'Unto This Last'*: JR's collection of four essays on political economy.

helping princesses . . . bottom: an allusion to the Grimm brothers' story 'The Frog-Prince'.

George the Fourth . . . Amurath the Fifth: JR *did* bear some resemblance to the profile of George III on his copper coinage; by George IV, JR probably does not mean a physical link so much as a remembrance of the King's gluttonous lifestyle (JR often accused himself of over-indulgence). 'Amurath the Fifth' seems an imprecise and mildly racist assumption that an Ottoman or 'Eastern' ruler would naturally be a man of pride. The name may be taken from *2 Henry IV*, v. ii. 48.

180 *Advent Sunday*: beginning of the Christian penitential season before Christmas.

over the rich evergreen oaks of the Borghese gardens: the gardens of the Villa

Borghese. The evergreen oak (*Quercus ilex*) is characteristic of Mediterranean landscapes.

'Qu'elle . . . pas un mot': 'that she did not understand a word'.

dum pituita molestat: 'cum pituita molesta est', Horace, *Epistles*, i. i. 108: 'when his phlegm is troublesome'.

181 *finished by Moscheles*: Ignaz Moscheles (1794–1870) was a Bohemian pianist and resident before the mid-1840s in London.

'Coeli Enarrant': 'the heavens declare': JR's *Coeli Enarrant* (1885) was, as its subtitle made clear, a set of *Studies of Cloud Form and its Visible Causes Collected and Completed out of 'Modern Painters'*.

182 *Dogana*: (lit. 'customs' in Italian): JR means a customs officer.

183 *Leoni*: see note to p. 120.

'It now is evening . . . Brundusium's wall': from Dante, *Purgatorio*, canto iii in Cary's translation (Virgil is explaining why he does not have a shadow). Virgil died in modern Brindisi (Brundusium).

birdless lake: 'Avernus' is from the Greek, 'without birds'.

'Nec te . . . Avernis': 'Nor did Hecate set you over the groves of Avernus in vain', *Aeneid*, 6. 118 (Aeneas is speaking to the Cumean Sybil). JR saw something of himself in the Sybil-prophet, and also considered the prophetic power of other modern 'sybils' later in his life (the weather being one in the 1870s and 1880s). He thought of Venice as a source of prophetic teaching, calling the city the Avernus of the Adriatic and a 'Sea Sibyl' (*LE* vii. 440) in 1860.

184 *till forty years afterwards*: see Lecture 6 of *Ariadne Florentina* for JR's discussion of *Sybils*.

Falernian: the celebrated wine from ancient Italy.

scoria: a form of dried sponge-like volcanic rock.

Mr Gladstone . . . in the Neapolitan prisons: Gladstone had been troubled by the state of Neapolitan justice, writing *Two Letters to the Earl of Aberdeen, on the State Prosecutions of the Neapolitan Government* in 1851.

except Byron: cf. 'Italia! oh Italia! thou who hast | The fatal gift of beauty, which became | A funeral dower of present woes and past— | On thy sweet brow is sorrow ploughed by shame', *Childe Harold*, canto iv.

contadina: peasant girl.

185 *grave*: JR's diary for 20 March 1841 records that he was more cheerful: 'More blood again to day [. . .] I don't think it matters much'.

nothing new to be done, nor said: JR's slightly fatalistic tone is different from his diary for 22 March, which records: 'doctor says it is nothing'.

Benediction: the Easter blessing, at this point one of the Pope's various formal benedictions across the Christian year.

'Natural History of Enthusiasm': Isaac Taylor, the author of this influential 1829 study, encouraged a steady Protestantism, pointing out the distortions produced by excessive enthusiasm in religion.

186 *'Farquharson'*: or 'Fergusson' in the diary: still unknown.

187 *'Fate cannot harm me; I have dined, to-day'*: the last line of Smith's 'Recipe for a Salad' (1839?).

not even beginning of railway bridge: this transport link to Venice was completed in 1846.

Sir Philip . . . sea at all: Sidney was in Venice 1573–4.

'expected to see . . . rather than pleasure': the quotation is from Lady Craven's *A Journey Through the Crimea to Constantinople* (London, 1789), 93. The visit was actually in 1785 and she was more pleased with Venice than JR allows.

Evelyn: the English writer and diarist Sir John Evelyn (1620–1706) visited Venice between 1645 and 1646 (see the *Diary* for June and July 1645).

188 *centres of my life work*: see p. 103.

bournes: 'bournes' is correct though some transcribers give it as 'homes'. The diary continues: 'there might have been another [home with Adèle], but that has become all pain' (6 May, in the 1841 MS *Diary*).

'There is moon . . . on the grey water': JR is slightly misleading again. The diary goes on: '& I am happier than I have been—these 5 years—so happy—happier than in all probably I shall ever be again in my life' (1841 MS *Diary*).

What good of religion, love, admiration or hope: an allusion to Wordsworth's 'We live by Admiration, Hope, and Love', Book 4, *The Excursion* (1814). This was one of JR's favourite lines.

189 *"Mais, Monsieur . . . suffira"*: 'But, Sir, a pound will be a little—large! I will give you half that; you will see if that will be sufficient'.

"si tu . . . savoir": very informal French meaning something like 'if you aren't careful, you'll know it'.

Turner's work: this is an addition, written on the otherwise blank verso page opposite the entry for 6 June 1841 (1841 MS *Diary*). JR may mean 'Turner Work', that is, *Modern Painters*.

191 *Agassiz' 'Poissons Fossiles'!*: the Swiss glacial scientist and palaeontologist Jean Agassiz (1807–73) published his *Recherches sur les poissons fossiles* ('Studies of Fish Fossils'), establishing a classification system, in five well-illustrated volumes, 1833–43.

lithographer's: lithography, invented in 1796, is a process for transferring images to paper using a greased stone.

192 *'Broken Chain'*: this gloomy Gothic poem is reproduced in *LE* ii. 124–80.

'King of the Golden River': written in 1841 and published 1851, this was JR's only piece of fiction, a fairy tale about generosity rewarded over greed.

Alison's 'Europe' and Turner's 'Chemistry': Archibald Alison's *Modern History of Europe from the French Revolution to the Fall of Napoleon*

(1833–42) was regarded even in its own day as a wordy history of the Revolutionary period. 'Chemistry' is probably Edward Turner's *Elements of Chemistry* (1827).

sunrise of Dickens on us . . . 'Sketches' . . . Pickwick . . . Nickleby: Dickens published his collection of writing for newspapers and periodicals as *Sketches by Boz* in 1836; his popular comic tales, *The Pickwick Papers*, appeared serially between April 1836 and November 1837, and the novel of growing up, *Nicholas Nickleby*, between April 1838 and October 1839.

written to amuse a little girl: JR wrote this story for Euphemia (Effie) Gray, whom he later married (in 1848).

193 *vivants instead of fossiles*: living instead of fossilized.

'on a glacier . . . final rest': adapted from the 'Jorasse' section of Rogers's *Italy*.

Kenilworth Castle: Turner's painting of this name (1830) is now in the Fine Arts Museum, San Francisco. A version was included in Turner's *Picturesque Views in England and Wales* (1825–38). JR's diary for 2 September 1841 indicates he had been reading Scott's novel, *Kenilworth* (1821), while at Leamington (Kenilworth Castle being close by).

The diary says '. . . word or a look': this reference is puzzling. JR's diary records this meeting at a dinner on 22 June 1840 (entry for 23 June), but does not give this passage. In the manuscript, the entry simply stops after the statement that the dinner occurred, and JR has drawn a line. Later, some unrelated material has been added below the line in the remaining space, written with the diary turned the other way up. Although many pages of the diary have been torn out *after* this point, it seems that the entry for 23 June had been completed and the portion quoted in *Praeterita* was never there.

194 *Michael Angelo . . . of the Last Judgment*: Michelangelo's huge fresco, on the east wall of the Sistine Chapel, was completed in 1541.

195 *ice-study of '79*: JR refers to his chapter on ice crystal structure, 'Bruma Artifex', vol. ii, ch. 3, of *Deucalion*.

'Read the Clementina part of "Sir Charles Grandison"': Samuel Richardson's *Sir Charles Grandison* (1753) was widely admired in the nineteenth century. JR reads the section concerning the love of Grandison for the Italian noblewoman, Clementina della Porretta, whose Catholicism is an obstacle to their union.

I find my first lessons from Harding were also at this time: JR is reminded of Harding while writing *Praeterita* because his diary for 20 November 1841, open in front of him, records a lesson.

196 *Mr Munro of Novar*: Hugh Andrew Johnstone Munro (1797–1864), art collector and patron of Turner.

Carthages and Romes: JR refers to Turner's *Dido Building Carthage* (1815), now in the National Gallery, London; and Roman paintings including

Ancient Rome: Agrippina Landing with the Ashes of Germanicus (exhibited 1839), now in the Tate collection.

197 *one day on the road to Norwood*: this 'conversion' narrative has a faint echo of St Paul's on the road to Damascus (Acts 22): JR's diaries give no comparable account of this event.

find no entry of it: JR's diary for 1842 begins only on 26 May.

complimentary double-fourth: JR, after his absence, was eligible only for a Pass degree, but his work was sufficiently good to be given honorary inclusion in the Honours list. At this point, it was by no means unusual to leave university without a degree, and intentionally sitting only for the Pass school was common.

198 *Peru for fear of earthquakes*: JR is perhaps thinking of the earthquake in Lima in October 1746 when at least 5,000 people were killed: it was the most deadly in the country's recorded history until 1970 and is still commemorated.

tree of Jesse on a painted window: from a reference in Isaiah 11: 1, this is the family tree of the Messiah's descent from Jesse through David. There are fine early examples in Chartres Cathedral and Dorchester Abbey.

199 *getting to the top of them*: an allusion to Alpine climbing, which JR tended to think was childish and ignorant, and said as much in the first lecture of *Sesame and Lilies* (1865). The Alpine Club (for mountaineers) had been founded in 1857.

Languidly, but not idly . . . nowhere: JR, again, does not record in any detail this event in his diary for June 1842: 'As unprofitable a week as I ever spent in my life', he noted for 7 June, though adding, 'But I got some new ideas in my evening walk at Fontainebleau'.

200 *'He hath . . . time'*: Ecclesiastes 3: 11.

I had wanted . . . 'Harry and Lucy': in *Harry and Lucy Concluded* (1825), vol. iii.

201 *too late for her*: MR was 61 in 1842.

La Cloche, at Dijon . . . La Cygne, at Lucerne: two hotels.

Siberian crabs: a popular name for a species of (crab)apple, *Malus baccata*, with edible fruit.

202 *formal term-keeping at Oxford*: there were (and are) residence requirements for Oxford degrees.

Camberwell church window: see pp. 244–5.

"Slaver": Turner's *The Slave Ship* or *Slavers Throwing Overboard the Dead and Dying—Typhoon Coming on* was first exhibited in 1840: it is now in the Museum of Fine Arts, Boston.

second volume: *Modern Painters*, II (1846) is the most theoretical of the five volumes.

More and more deeply every hour . . . road over it: the question of the influence of mountains, or lack of it, had troubled JR in 'The Mountain Gloom' in *Modern Painters*, IV (1856). Napoleon and his army crossed the Great St Bernard Pass in May 1800.

203 *reach it easily*: the Ruskins left Dover on 14 May and arrived at Geneva on 30 May 1844.

battles at Chalons and Leipsic: the battle of Châlons (274) marked the end of the short-lived Gallic Empire; the battle of Leipzig (1813) was a major defeat of Napoleon.

Aire: Industrial Revolution cotton mills used the current of the river Aire, running through Yorkshire, for power.

sand of Berlin: the national Prussian Military Academy, established in 1810, was eventually located on Unter den Linden, Berlin.

contrat sociale: JR means 'civil society under law', but the term also alludes to Jean-Jacques Rousseau's *Du contrat social* (1762) with its argument against the divine right of kings.

Exchange . . . builder's commission on the cost: JR's readers might have remembered his criticism of the Bradford Exchange in 'Traffic' (1864) where he said the Bradfordians were only pretending to care about their new building. He saw large commission fees as improper: particularly those, as he said in the *Fors* letter for May 1875, for work 'taken out of the hands of the old village carpenter' (*LE* xxviii. 304).

204 *no foxes to hunt, no birds to shoot*: two activities associated for JR with an idle upper class.

feluccas: a term used loosely to mean traditional wooden sailing boats.

205 *Shakespeare's Cliffs*: 'Shakespeare Cliff', on the Dover cliffs, was named after the Dover cliff scene in Shakespeare's *King Lear*, Folio, IV. v. There was to be a chapter of *Praeterita* with this name.

206 *Mr Bautte's*: the business established by Jean-François Bautte (1772–1837), Swiss watchmaker, jeweller, and inventor. MR owned a watch from this company, which is now at Brantwood.

207 *as if Perdita were looking on to learn*: in *The Winter's Tale*, IV. iv. 140–1, Florizel says to Perdita: 'When you do dance, I wish you | A wave o'th'sea'.

little streams . . . leaped like chamois: cf. Psalm 114: 6: '[. . .] Ye mountains, that ye skipped like rams; and ye little hills, like lambs?'

208 *1st June, 1844*: actually 30 May.

209 *give an account further on*: see 'L'Hotel du Mont Blanc'.

210 *the uselessness of San Carlo's memory*: St Charles Borromeo (1538–84) was an Italian reforming educationalist.

solfataras: Solfatara is a volcanic crater near Naples, but JR means 'volcanoes' in general.

15th June: the following extract is adapted from the diary entry for 15 *July* 1844.

Linaria Alpina: purple-flowered Alpine toadflax.

210 *Cassiopeia*: W-shaped constellation in the night sky of the northern
hemisphere.

211 *That evening James Forbes and his wife were with us*: in *Deucalion*, JR
describes this meeting as one that connected him in a direct line of descent
with the wisdom of Forbes. When shown JR's drawing, Forbes' 'eye grew
keen,' he wrote, 'and his face attentive, as he examined the drawings; and
he turned instantly to me as to a recognized fellow-workman,—though yet
young, no less faithful than himself (*LE* xxvi. 220). JR's diary entry for
16 July 1844, however, records that the meeting was, instead, a 'most
uncomfortable chat'.

a field of cirri . . . cirrostrati . . . actynolite: 'cirri' is the plural of cirrus: thin
strips of feathery cloud. When they are numerous, they form a cloud pattern called cirrostratus. Green actinolite is a green, splintery mineral, with
iron content.

212 *since Christ broke bread for His multitude*: the miracle of the loaves and
fishes, Matthew 15: 29–39.

213 *'La sobriété . . . jusqu'aux larmes'*: 'Frugality, the normal companion of love
of one's work, is still a noticeable quality of these valley-dwellers. This
rye-bread, which I told you they only eat when it's six months old, is softened in whey or buttermilk, and this kind of soup becomes their main
nourishment; cheese or a bit of salted-down old cow or goat are kept for
feast-days or days when the work is heavy; as for fresh meat, that is never
eaten, it's too costly a dish. The rich people of the region live with the
same attitude to food; I used to see our host in Macugnaga, who was nothing other than poor, each evening fetch from a locked place a few cloves
from a bunch of garlic, one of which he solemnly distributed to his wife
and the same quantity to each of his children, and this clove of garlic was
the only seasoning for a piece of dry bread, which they crushed between
two stones and ate for their supper. Those amongst them who work away
come at least every two years to spend several months in their home village, and, although, when they are away from home, they usually eat better, they easily return to the local food and when they depart, it is with
deep regret; I have witnessed one or two of these leave-takings and they
have moved me to tears.' [JMO'G]

Walkley Museum: Walkley is an area north-west of Sheffield that JR visited
in 1875 to see a former pupil, Henry Swan. He established a small museum
there to present high quality replicas and representatives of major features
of European art to Sheffield's industrial workers. The collection is now in
the Millennium Gallery, Sheffield.

more than thirty chamois: curiously, the diary (27 July 1844) actually says
'more than twenty'.

'Pour les voir . . . ils sont': 'In order to see them, one must go where
they are'.

says the diary: for 27 July 1844.

214 *myrtilles and mica-slate*: *myrtilles* are bilberries; mica-slate is highly strati-
fied rock composed of mica and quartz.

wild Rubens sketch . . . Veronese beneath it: Rubens's study for *The Terrors of
War* (1837–8) was discussed in Anna Jameson's account of Rogers's collection in her *Companion to the Private Galleries of London* (1844), 407.
Jameson lists Veronese's study *for Mary Magdalene Anointing the Feet of
the Saviour* in the collection too (p. 398).

215 *'The Entombment'*: Titian's *Entombment of Christ* (*c*.1523–6).

John and Gentile Bellini, by John Bellini: the identity of the painter of this
picture, now called *Portrait de deux jeunes hommes*, is disputed: perhaps
Gentile Bellini or Giovanni Cariani.

Campo Santo: the large cloister near the Duomo in Pisa: its frescos (largely
destroyed in the Second World War) are now usually ascribed to Buonamico
Buffalmacco (the Triumph of Death, the Last Judgement); Benozzo
Gozzoli (the story of the Patriarchs); Andrea Bonaiuti, Antonio Veneziano,
and Spinello Aretino (the stories of Pisan saints); and Taddeo Gaddi (the
story of Job). Stories from Genesis were contributed by Piero di Puccio
(JR's titles).

216 *no diaries*: JR went abroad during 1845 (without his parents): there were
regular letters home but no diary.

Turner's 'Liber Studiorum': inspired by the *Liber Veritatis* ('book of truth')
of Claude Lorrain (*c*.1604/5–82), Turner began sketching for the *Liber
Studiorum* ('book of studies') in 1806. Plates were published between 1807
and 1819. Its overall subject was landscape art, divided into six types:
Pastoral, Marine, Mountainous, Historical, Architectural, and 'Elevated
or Epic Pastoral'.

Rio's 'Poésie Chrétienne,' . . . Lord Lindsay's . . . 'Christian Art': two influential books for JR. Alexis-Francois Rio's *De la poésie Chrétienne* (1836,
English translation in 1854) drew attention to overlooked European medieval art. There is some confusion about Alexander Lindsay, 8th Earl of
Balcarres. He did not publish his *Sketches of the History of Christian Art*
until 1847. Lindsay was assured of the moral purpose of art and agreed
with Rio in celebrating early Italian artists including Giotto and Fra
Angelico. JR reviewed Lindsay's book when it appeared in the *Quarterly
Review*, June 1847.

Tribune: of the Uffizi (see p. 171).

'la vieille . . . Martigny': 'old Switzerland took up its weapons, fought off
the Bas Valaisans, who were defeated and massacred at the Trient Bridge,
near to Martigny'.

'pour expulser . . . gouvernement': 'to expel the Jesuits, and overthrow the
government'.

'renversée': 'overthrown'. There were attempts in 1844 and 1845 to bring
down the conservative government of the Canton.

217 *no more pains with me*: the exact reasons for JR's final rupture with Turner remain a mystery. It seems that Turner in some way impugned JR's integrity.

'*une issue encore plus tragique que la première*': 'a result more tragic than the first' (some thirty-five rebels were killed and many more imprisoned).

soldanelle: *Soldanella alpina*, violet-purple Alpine flower.

218 *scout*: Oxford term for college servant.

A rhyme . . . and another . . . last serious exertions of my poetical powers: these are reproduced in *LE* ii. 223 and 238. The first also appears on pp. 303–4. The latter—vituperative indeed—begins: 'Have you in heaven no hope—on earth no care— | No foe in hell—ye things of stye and stall, | That congregate like flies, and make the air | Rank with your fevered sloth[?]'.

220 *Litany and all*: the 1662 Prayer Book notes that the Litany, or General Supplication, could be 'sung or said after Morning Prayer, upon Sundays, Wednesdays, and Fridays'. It is a long responsorial prayer for deliverance and safety, which aptly includes the petition: 'That it may please thee to preserve all who travel by land, by water'.

thirteen years later before I made a sketch on Sunday: JR drew flower heads in his diary for 23 May 1858, adding below them on 24 February 1868: 'This drawing of Orchises was the first I ever made on Sunday: and marks, henceforward, the beginning of total change in habits of mind.'

loveliest Christian tomb in Italy: JR refers to the early Renaissance tomb (1406–13) of Ilaria del Caretto by Jacopo della Quercia (*c*.1374–1438) in Lucca Cathedral, which was, in its serenity and fidelity, the epitome of Christian sculpture to JR; its grace suggested an ideal form of womanhood too. See p. 222.

221 *Don Whiskerandos*: the Spanish lover in Sheridan's burlesque on theatrical production, *The Critic* (1779).

Tanagra: a town in ancient Greece known for terracotta figures of men, women, and children made in moulds for mass sale, from the fourth century BCE onwards.

Chantrey in Lichfield, Roubilliac in Westminster: in 1820, Ellen Jane Robinson asked the English sculptor Francis Chantrey (1781–1841) for a monument to her dead daughters, Ellen-Jane and Marianne. Known as 'The Sleeping Children', it is at the end of the south choir aisle in Lichfield Cathedral. Westminster Abbey contains a number of sculptures by the French sculptor Louis-François Roubiliac (Roubillac) (1705?–1762), including his bust of Handel and of the Duke of Argyll.

dying gladiator: presumably a reference to the late third century BCE marble statue (a Roman copy of a Greek original) known as *Galata Morente* ('The Dying Gaul') in the Capitoline Museums, Rome.

222 *the beauty of Clotilde and Cécile*: see p. 118.

the living Egeria of Araceli: Georgina Tollemache (Egeria was a water nymph in the legendary history of Rome). 'Araceli' is the ancient Basilica di Santa Maria in Aracoeli, on the Capitoline Hill, Rome.

Fra Bartolomeo . . . the Magdalene, with St Catherine of Siena: the Italian Renaissance painter Fra Bartolom(m)eo (1472–1517) painted *God the Father with Sts Catherine of Siena and Mary Magdalen* in 1509: it is now in Museo e Pinacoteca Nazionale, Lucca.

223 *Cary's Dante, and Sismondi's 'Italian Republics,' and Lord Lindsay*: JR, a lifelong reader of Dante, remained loyal to the blank verse translation (1814) of the *Divine Comedy* by Henry Francis Cary (1772–1844); the *Histoire des républiques italiennes du Moyen Âge* (1809–18) by the Swiss writer Jean Charles Léonard de Sismondi (1773–1842) was an important work in outlining the achievement of medieval Italy (and was later a force in the Risorgimento's developing conception of a unified Italy). JR is mis-remembering when he read Lord Lindsay, whose book was not published for another two years.

render to every man according to his work: Psalm 42: 12.

224 *Hast thou . . . here, below*: the second and third stanzas of Herbert's 'The Bag'.

memory: JR's remembered version only slightly alters punctuation and exchanges 'heavens' for Herbert's 'sky'.

No matter for their names: see note to p. 215.

'Yet in my flesh I shall see God': Job 19: 26.

225 *patriarchal life*: that is, strictly, the period of Abraham, Isaac, and Jacob, in the Old Testament.

'Dies Irae,' instead of 'Dies Amoris': 'Dies Irae' ('Day of Wrath') is a phrase from the Latin Requiem: 'Dies Amoris' ('Day of Love') is JR's alternative vision of the Last Day.

226 *a flask of Aleatico*: it is an indication of the change in tastes from the nineteenth century to the present that JR drinks at 4 p.m. wine from Aleatico grapes that are now primarily the basis of dessert wines.

228 *what no one who sees her now could conceive*: the medieval centre of Florence was significantly remodelled throughout the nineteenth century.

229 *I wrote a complete critical and historical account*: this has not been located.

Araby the blest: Milton, *Paradise Lost*, iv. 63.

230 *'Ça vaut . . . peine'*: 'it's worth the trouble'.

Ambassador: the secretary to the British Embassy at Florence at this point was Henry Edward Fox, 4th Baron Holland (1802–59), a Christ Church man.

P. P. C. card: 'pour prendre congé' (in effect, 'I am leaving'). JR follows standard Victorian diplomatic etiquette.

231 *'pietra serena'*: Italian grey sandstone.

'the most beautiful valley in the Alps': exact quotation unknown: Murray's *Handbook for Travellers in Switzerland* (1838) recorded that the journey to

Vogogna was the 'most wild, interesting, and beautiful that I have yet made; and the Val Anzasca I have distinguished in my mind as the happy valley'.

233 *Dr Zimmermann*: J. G. Zimmerman (1728–95), author of *Solitude* (first translated into English, 1798).

234 *kind of pain of which Carlyle so wildly complains*: Carlyle continually described authorship as a torment. 'Friedrich' is his *History of Friedrich II of Prussia, Called Frederick the Great*.

235 *mossy cell*: Milton's 'Il Penseroso' (pub. 1645), l. 169.

cruelty of Leontes . . . Helena's lord: Leontes is the jealous king from *The Winter's Tale*; the Dane is Hamlet; Iago is the villain of *Othello*; Iachimo from *Cymbeline* claims to have slept adulterously with Innogen; Tybalt is the violent antagonist in *Romeo and Juliet*; Edmund is the treacherous son in *King Lear*; 'Isabel's brother' is Claudio in *Measure for Measure* who sleeps with his betrothed before marriage and thus commences the events of the play; Helena's lord is the prejudiced and heartless Bertram of *All's Well that Ends Well*.

236 *'Pour que George . . . la fois'*: 'In order for George to be [*lit.* go] well, it is necessary to give him food to eat a lot and often.'

237 *Laws of Fésole*: this was published in parts between 1877 and 1878 with the subtitle *A Familiar Treatise on the Elementary Principles and Practice of Drawing and Painting as Determined by the Tuscan Masters*.

'mare maggiore': JR believed the aged Tintoretto had declared of his life's work: 'È faticoso lo studio della pittura, e sempre si fa il mare maggiore' ('The study of painting is endless, and always [takes one into] a greater sea').

Daguerre: Louis-Jacques-Mandé Daguerre (1787–1851) was a French artist and scientist, credited with the invention of the daguerreotype, an early form of nineteenth-century photography.

238 *Mr Boxall . . . Milan . . . engraved*: Sir William Boxall (1800–79) was an English painter who, from 1866, was director of the National Gallery. His picture after Leonardo was engraved by Frederick Christian Lewis (1779–1856) and published in 1850. Lewis had provided etchings for Turner's *Liber Studiorum*.

'So be it when I shall grow old': from Wordsworth's short poem on the rainbow, 'My heart leaps up when I behold' (1807).

239 *Adoration of the Magi*: this picture is in the lower hall of the Scuola di San Rocco.

'Ç'a ne va . . . après': 'It is not going well.' 'You are not aware of it at present, but you will be later.'

tisane: any kind of herbal tea.

240 *my eldest Croydon cousin, John . . . dead in Australia*: see p. 57.

as on his brother the beach-sand on this side the sea: see pp. 90–1.

Jessie's or my aunt's sicknesses: see p. 57.

241 *The State of Denmark*: JR's joke about Denmark Hill: an allusion to Marcellus's words in *Hamlet*: 'Something is rotten in the state of Denmark' (I. iv. 67).

242 *doves by Hunt*: William Henry Hunt's picture of a dead dove was bought by JJR in 1852.

Northcote portraits: see p. 13.

243 *one family alone excepted*: the Oldfields.

244 *pretty church*: the medieval church of St Giles, Camberwell, burned down the day before JR's twenty-second birthday (7 February 1841). The new church was designed by George Gilbert Scott and opened in 1844 (JJR had given £100. 10s. to the fund). Edmund Oldfield and JR designed a portion of the east window (though JR's involvement was minimal). The window was badly damaged in the Second World War, though is now repaired.

vitrail: 'stain-glassed window' (French).

cinquefoil: architectural term for a five-division or five-'leaved' ring or arch top.

245 *Viollet le Duc*: Eugène Emmanuel Viollet-le-Duc (1814–79) was a French architect and major exponent of the French Gothic revival: his approach to restoration, including at Notre-Dame de Paris, never suited JR's understanding of the need to preserve rather than replace the fabric of the past.

quantities: that is, the system of Latin verse scansion. Charles Newton was previously mentioned on p. 131.

if only Newton had learnt Irish instead of Greek . . . rested in peace: JR wrote on 23 April 1881: 'Newton's pride in discovering Mausolus, and their engineers' whistling over his Asiatic mummy, have entirely corrupted and thwarted the uses of the British Museum Art Galleries [. . . If] I showed you a photograph of the head of Mausolus without telling you what it was, I will undertake that you saw with candid eyes in it nothing more than the shaggy poll of a common gladiator' (*LE* xxxvii. 352–4).

Idylls of kings: JR is thinking of Tennyson's *The Idylls of the King* (1856–85), a long Arthuriad.

Theseus and Pirithous: two heroes of ancient Greece who take an oath of friendship, impressed by each other's strength and courage.

246 *Lethean chains*: Lethe is the river of forgetfulness in ancient Greek religion.

1850: actually 1851

247 *The hackneyed couplet . . . power of the gospel*: The first couplet is from Samuel Butler's *Hudibras* (1663–78), I. i. 11–12 ('And pulpit, drum ecclesiastick, | Was beat with fist, instead of a stick'). In *The Stones of Venice*, II, JR remarks that 'When the sermon is good we need not much concern ourselves about the form of the pulpit. But sermons cannot always be good; and I believe that the temper in which the congregation set themselves to

listen may be in some degree modified by their perception of fitness or
unfitness, impressiveness or vulgarity, in the disposition of the place
appointed for the speaker' (*LE* x. 30). Kettledrummle's sermon (after
Drumclog) is from Scott's *Old Mortality* (bk. 1, ch. 18, is headed with the
same quotation from *Hudibras* used by JR here). The quotation from
Edward Gibbon, which describes 'The pulpit', is from chapter 37 of the
one-volume version (1837) of *The Decline and Fall*. The 'refiner's fire' is a
reference to Malachi 3: 2.

248 *'Eye hath not seen . . . us by His Spirit'*: 1 Corinthians 2: 9–10.

But to these particulars I must return by-and-bye: JR returns neither to Bible
reading nor to Melvill.

second volume of 'Modern Painters': volume II was published on 24 April
1846 (JR had reached home on 4 November 1845).

lion couchant, or eagle volant: terms from heraldry: a lion lying down with
head raised; an eagle with its wings extended as if flying.

in spite of Carlyle: an allusion to the eighth of Carlyle's *Latter-Day
Pamphlets* (1850), which offers a philosophical system from a pig's point of
view, beginning: 'The Universe, so far as sane conjecture can go, is an
immeasurable swine's-trough, consisting of solid and liquid, and of other
contrasts and kinds;—especially consisting of attainable and unattainable,
the latter in immensely greater quantities for most pigs. 2. Moral evil is
unattainability of Pig's-wash; moral good, attainability of ditto'.

his own brougham: JR is recalling an anecdote of Giotto's life: ' "Paint me my
arms,—" said Giotto, as the youth threw him his white shield with that
order—"he speaks as if he were one of the Bardi!" Our English panel-painter
had lost the consciousness that there yet remained above him, so much as
one, of the Bardi' (*LE* xxii. 267). The Bardi were a distinguished Florentine
family. Giotto painted his frescoes *The Life of St Francis* in the Bardi Chapel
of Florence's Santa Croce. On Long Acre and the motto, see p. 70.

Sable, a chevron, argent: in heraldry, sable is the term for black tincture;
a chevron is a V-shape form; argent is the term for silver tincture; gules
for red.

249 *Lord Marmion's falcon*: Marmion, in Scott's poem, is distinguished by
a falcon on his shield.

Lord Dudley's bear: the bear that 'brooks no one to cross his awful path' is
the emblem of the Earl of Leicester in Scott's *Kenilworth* (ch. 7).

'Age quod agis': 'Do what you are doing'/'Concentrate on your business'.

'The night cometh, when no man can work': John 9: 4.

fortune, and fortune-telling . . . private philosophy: the notion of a ruling *fors*
(fate/fortune) was developed throughout *Fors Clavigera*.

Erymanthian boar: one of the Twelve Labours of Hercules was capturing
the monstrous boar of Mount Erymanthos.

Albert of Geierstein: aristocrat with a vulture as his crest in Scott's novel
Anne of Geierstein (1829).

'*I paints and paints . . . nobody will buy*': JR slightly misquotes the 'Poem by a Perfectly Furious Academician', which first appeared in *Punch*, 24 May 1856, p. 209.

250 *St Anthony of Padua*: JR means St Anthony of Egypt (*c*.251–356), who is the patron saint of pigs and pig farmers, and is often represented with a pig. See JR's footnote on this page.

'*il se retira d'abord . . . de l'homme*': 'he retreated first of all into an isolated place not far from the little town of Cooma, then into a sepulchre a long way from this town, finally into the tumbledown buildings of an old castle above Herakleopolis, where he lived for twenty years. It's impossible to recount all that he had to suffer in these three periods of retreat, as much from the rigours he put himself through as from the malice of the demon, who did everything to deceive him by his tricks or to weaken him by his threats and his evil assaults, whose blows sometimes went so far as to leave him for dead. Anthony overcame everything; and it was to reward him for so many struggles and so many victories that God made him powerful in word and deed to cure all sorts of spiritual and physical illnesses, to cast out demons both from bodies as well as from souls, to make the most cruel beasts, the elements and the other creatures, who are most rebellious to the will of man, obey him.' [JMO'G]

eventful history: *As You Like It*, II. vii. 164.

251 *In the Times, sad news from . . . Switzerland*: The *Times* for 21 February 1845 (p. 6, cols. 4–5) included a long report on 'Troubles in Switzerland', particularly in relation to Lausanne and the expulsion of the Jesuits (which finally occurred in 1848).

'*In one of my saddest moods . . . pig-blossom*': *Fors* for December 1874: the quotation is from *LE* xxviii. 208. 'Bewickian' refers to Thomas Bewick (1753–1828), the English wood engraver, who illustrated *A General History of Quadrupeds* (1790), which includes a section on 'The Hog Kind'.

252 *Pigwiggian chaunt*: JR wrote a number of these fanciful 'Pigwiggian Chaunts'.

tenny: orange-brown tincture in heraldry (tawny).

The Feasts of the Vandals: JR first called this chapter 'Symposia Andalusica'. The new title plays on the assumption that the name of Andalusia in Spain comes from the Vandals ('Vandalusia'), who invaded in the fifth century CE (a doubtful etymology). The chapter is about Spain, the sherry trade, and family entertainments around JJR's business.

254 '*But while I am descanting . . . offices of life*': from *Elementary Sketches of Moral Philosophy* (1850), 111–13 (with only minor changes to the original punctuation).

255 '*The history of the world . . . protectors of the world*': *Elementary Sketches*, 423–4. Smith refers to the retreat of the 'Ten Thousand' Greek mercenaries during the attempt of Cyrus to seize the Persian throne in 401 BCE. The Greeks defeated the armies of the Persian king, though Cyrus was killed. By the 'handful of Greeks' defeating Persia, Smith means the battle

of Marathon in 490 BCE, where Athenian forces defeated a larger army in the first Persian invasion of Greece.

255 *a charming watercolour*: George Richmond's portrait is reproduced as the frontispiece for *LE* iii. The original was lost to fire in 1941.

256 *Alas! the things I ought to have done have not been done*: cf. the General Confession in the Book of Common Prayer. 'We have offended against thy holy laws, We have left undone those things which we ought to have done, And we have done those things which we ought not to have done'.

'A Graduate of Oxford': JR's pseudonym for the first edition of *Modern Painters*, I.

257 *'angel-bright talent'*: cf. 'Talents angel-bright' in Edward Young's *The Complaint, or, Night Thoughts* (1742–5), Night Sixth, l. 273.

258 *first come to hand-grips in Blackwood*: see p. 142 for the initial article against Turner that prompted JR's defence of Turner.

259 *'frolic wine'*: from Robert Herrick's 'Ode to Ben Jonson' (l. 10), about meeting at feasts.

Prince Hal nor Jack Falstaff: Prince Hal, later Henry V, and Sir John Falstaff are tavern companions in Shakespeare's *1 Henry IV*.

than Robinson Crusoe or his boy Xury: Crusoe escapes from slavery with the boy Xury at the beginning of Defoe's novel. As it happens, Crusoe displays vague conceptions of Spanish history in chapter 12.

paragraphs added . . . in 1846: JR added material for the third edition of *Modern Painters*, I, partly in response to criticism. He included new discussion of Samuel Prout.

260 *Graphics*: JR is thinking of illustrated newspapers in general, and *The Graphic* in particular, founded in 1869 as a competitor to the *London Illustrated News*.

261 *Peninsular war*: the prolonged campaigns from 1807 to 1814 as British, Portuguese, and Spanish forces tried to stop Napoleon's army invading the Iberian Peninsula. The war's conclusion opened up the peninsula to travel again (and made possible JJR's sherry business).

262 *Vandalusia, or, as Mr Ford puts it, . . . land of the west*: Richard Ford's celebrated *A Handbook for Travellers in Spain* (1845), i. 144, names the area 'Vandalucia'.

Amontillado: a type of sherry that is a little darker than *fino*: it is named after the Montilla region of Spain.

263 *Danish gardens with milk and honey*: Danish, of course, because of 'Denmark Hill'; 'milk and honey' is a conventional biblical phrase (e.g. Deuteronomy 11: 9) referring to the Promised Land.

Elysian fields: Paris's Avenue des Champs-Élysées.

264 *None left now but William of Croydon*: William Richardson died shortly after these words were written.

265 *I shall often have occasion hereafter*: only once, in fact: on p. 310.

best chess-player I have ever known: JR shared this family enthusiasm for, and ability at, chess. It was a significant occupation of his later years, often by correspondence.

266 *Arundel Society*: this society (1849–97) endeavoured to develop British understanding of early Italian art. It published scholarship, and engravings of pictures, architecture, and sculpture. JR was a Council member and his contributions included his *Giotto and His Works at Padua* (1853–60).

267 *without our rubrical gooseberry pie*: see p. 20.

268 *'Memoir'*: the Fine Art Society's reprint of JR's *Notes by Mr Ruskin on Samuel Prout and William Hunt* (1880).

271 *to review Lord Lindsay in the 'Quarterly'*: JR reviewed Lord Lindsay's *Sketches of the History of Christian Art* in the *Quarterly Review* (June 1847).

Celestial Hierarchies: Lindsay briefly catalogues the 'heavenly hierarchies' in chapter 3 of *Sketches*.

273 *'Thy friend . . . thou art his sacrifice'*: from Herbert's "The Church-Porch: Perirrhanterium'.

Dawtrey Drewitt . . . Gershom Collingwood . . . Alic Wedderburn . . . like a water-spaniel: Dr Drewitt remembered this referred 'to some games with Mrs Severn's children at Brantwood, and to some snakes in his rooms at Oxford' (*LE* xxxv. 424 n.). Wedderburn recorded that 'Collingwood and I were at Brantwood one summer, not long after a visit to Oxford of Princess Alice of Hesse, for whom Ruskin had promised to paint a water-lily. One Sunday afternoon we drove Ruskin up to a tarn, where water-lilies grew. But those within reach were poor flowers, while those out in the middle looked (and were) fine. Collingwood and I tossed which of us should strip and swim out to them. I won, jumped in, and brought back—I think, with their stalks in my mouth—some of the lilies' (*LE* xxxv. 425 n.).

evangelical duty . . . season: the idea of shooting as a 'duty' depended in part on the fact that the sport employed many estate staff: shooting kept them in work.

274 *'Munera Pulveris'*: subtitled *Six Essays on the Elements of Political Economy*, *Munera Pulveris* was issued 1862–3.

when I had to direct road-making at Oxford: JR had engaged a party of undergraduates at Oxford in 1874 to improve a road west of the city.

I swept bits of St Giles' foot-pavements: in 1872, under the remit of what would become the Guild of St George, JR hired street-cleaners for Church Lane, St Giles, London.

275 *in the old inn at Sixt*: in the next chapter (see p. 278), JR places this incident at Samoens.

Athena: Greek goddess of wisdom and war, had an owl as a symbol, and was associated with a classical helmet or *casque*.

see the seventh number of 'Dilecta': *Dilecta* never reached this far.

277 *what Turner meant . . . contest of Apollo with the Python . . . Garden of the Hesperides*: two great topics of *Modern Painters*, V. In chapter 10, JR considers the *Garden of Hesperides* as Turner's representation of the wayward spiritual state of England; in chapter 11, *Apollo and the Python* represents the 'strife of purity with pollution; of life with forgetfulness; of love, with the grave' (*LE* vii. 420). See Introduction, p. xx.

following fragment: this is from the entry for 7 August 1847 (with the usual minor changes and transcription errors).

278 *Baxter's "Saint's Rest"*: Richard Baxter, *The Saints Everlasting Rest: or, a Treatise of the Blessed State of the Saints in their Enjoyment of God in Glory* (1650, and many times reissued in the nineteenth century).

279 *Sixt*: JR omits the end of this sentence from the diary (entry for 15 July 1849): 'which I passed so sorrowfully five years ago'.

brother-in-law: her *brother's* brother-in-law. Dr William Richardson's second wife was Miss Bolding: her brother, John Parker Bolding, married Mary Richardson, who died in 1849: they had one child, John James (22 May 1848–19??). John Parker Bolding of Bromfield Gardens, Richmond Hill, Surrey, died in 1888.

280 *cretinism*: the sicknesses of Alpine dwellers long puzzled JR: it was his subject in 'The Mountain Gloom' in *Modern Painters*, IV. 'Cretinism' was an accepted nineteenth-century term for stunted mental and physical development as a consequence of iodine deficiency that led also to the enlargement of the thyroid gland (goitre).

281 *illness at Matlock*: JR did not reach this far in *Praeterita*. The illness was in 1871.

walk with my father: JR refers to his walk 'under the aig[uille] de Varens' with JJR on 13 July 1849 (diary).

April 15th, Wednesday: 18 April (1849) according to the diary.

282 *like the hunting doctor's in 'Punch'*: unidentified.

'Mrs Lirriper's Lodgings': in Dickens's *Mrs Lirriper's Legacy* (1864), chapter 1, Mrs Lirriper says she stayed in the 'pleasantest-situated inn my dear! Right under the two towers, with their shadows a changing upon it all day like a kind of a sundial, and country people driving in and out of the courtyard in carts and hooded cabriolets and such like, and a market outside in front of the cathedral, and all so quaint and like a picter'.

283 *I had seen . . . the most wonderful of all Alpine birds . . . animal life*: entry untraced. Most likely, JR is describing an Alpine Accentor (*Prunella collaris*).

'un détachement . . . Rousseau': 'a group [of schoolboys], led by Mr Topffer, who did not know the way, began to climb the hill at Charmettes, to reach the house of Jean-Jacques Rousseau'.

St. Preux: see note to p. 100.

'Paul and Virginia': JR refers to Jacques-Henri Bernardin de Saint-Pierre's novel *Paul et Virginie* (1787).

couloirs: narrow, steep, and vertical crevasses, fissures, gullies, or scars on a mountain side.

cabane: hut, cabin.

284 *Richard did not die, like Charles*: see p. 91.

forty-five or fifty years of life: actually sixty.

'perjinketty': from the Scottish dialectal word *perjink*: prim or finicky.

285 *planet Saturn*: JR (who was, incidentally, an Aquarius) merely alludes to the association of Saturn with lead as, supposedly, the oldest metal.

fortalice: an archaic term for a fortress.

287 *Studer's geological map*: *Carte geologique de la Suisse* by Bernhard Studer and Arnold Escher von der Linth (1853).

char-à-banc: more accurately a larger vehicle than JR suggests, with wooden benches (which is what the name literally means) arranged looking to the sides not straight ahead.

289 *Correggian*: referring to the sensuous Italian painter Antonio da Correggio (1489–1534).

laissez faire: 'leave/allow to do'—a theory of economics involving the absence of state intervention, though JR uses it here to mean something like 'permission to continue freely'.

26th July, 1854: this is eleven days after the annulment of JR's marriage to Effie Gray.

290 *Capucins*: the Capuchins, established at the beginning of the sixteenth century, are an order of friars, derived from the Franciscans.

"des morales superbes": '[such] excellent moral tales/fables'.

291 *'enfan de Dieu'*: child of God.

"Mais la mort . . . confusion": 'But death pursued him there to—the tomb; and he descended into hell, bearing this mark, which was to be his shame and confusion for ever.'

school divinity: that is, the sort of discussion associated with medieval theology. JR may have glanced at the 'Autumnal Journey 1849' section of his diary (beginning October 1849), which commenced with detailed biblical discussion.

eboulement: JR uses this to mean a 'collapse' or 'remains of landslide'.

292 *'The most magnificent . . . mountain gulph'*: from the diary entry of 2 August 1849.

they say the French are beaten again at Rome, and another revolution in Paris: JR's news of events surrounding the Siege of Rome—an early stage of Italian unification—was arriving late. The Italian patriot commander Giuseppe Garibaldi (1807–82) had driven French forces, arriving to aid the Pope, from Rome at the end of April 1849, but the French had then laid siege. The Romans capitulated at the end of June and the victorious

French entered Rome on 3 July. There was no additional revolution in France.

293 *camera-lucida*: an optical sketching aid that allowed artists to trace features of a scene in front of them from an image projected onto paper.

294 *Mary's death*: Mary Richardson, who had long lived with the Ruskins.

châlet of Blaitière: JR briefly owned land above this in 1863.

295 *Edinburgh lectures*: JR's *Lectures on Architecture and Painting* (1854) were delivered in Edinburgh in November 1853: they began with medieval Italy and ended with a buoyant affirmation of Pre-Raphaelitism.

296 *selling sherry instead of bobbins*: the 'Wanderer' in the first book of Wordsworth's *The Excursion* (1814) is for a time a Pedlar (though is not described selling bobbins).

cicadas: tree crickets, associated with warm parts of Europe.

Lest I should not be spared . . . 'Praeterita': JR wrote this chapter in Folkestone in October 1887 when ill: see Introduction, pp. xviii–xix. He means another *instalment* of *Praeterita*.

297 *more light*: G. H. Lewes's *Life of Goethe* (1875) reports that Goethe's last audible words were *'More light!'*, p. 566.

'Scotch thing': see Introduction, p. xxii.

'Nisi Dominus, frustra': the motto of the city of Edinburgh: 'without the Lord, [all is] in vain'.

298 *'Sunt lachrymae rerum'*: (sunt lacrimae rerum): 'there are tears over things' *Aeneid*, 1.462. These words are sometimes thought the pessimistic heart of Virgil's outlook.

Andrea Ferrara: the name traditionally inscribed on all the Scottish broadswords of exceptional quality.

Mill's essay: J. S. Mill's *Three Essays on Religion* had been published, post-humously, in the year of this conversation (1874).

their sort: JR refers to part 4 ('The Nun's School in Florence') of *Christ's Folk in the Apennines* by Francesca Alexander and edited by JR (1887), which was going through the press as he was writing this chapter. There, a nun declares a 'confirmed belief that her life of teaching, cooking, and sewing is the most delightful and exhilarating possible' (*LE* xxxii. 287–8). This is followed by a story from Polissena involving a blind girl giving a necklace to the Madonna in exchange for sight: her eyes recover, but then she says she misses the necklace. At that, her sight is taken away permanently.

types of it given by Scott . . . Deans: Flora MacIvor is a Jacobite preparing for the 1745 uprising in *Waverley*; Edith Bellenden is loved by Henry Morton, the hero of *Old Mortality*, though her family opposes him; Mary of Avenel is caught in a troubled romance in *The Monastery*; and Jeanie Deans is the heroine of *The Heart of Midlothian*, who bravely walks from Scotland to London.

299 *'Hortus Inclusus'*: JR's collection of letters to the Beever sisters of the Thwaite, Coniston (1887).

forty years: from Brown's *Supplementary Chapter* (see Glossary of Persons Mentioned), 414 n.

300 *was in these arms*: from Scott's *Guy Mannering*, ch. 53.

my own father's: JR means his aunt's.

looking on another Face: cf. Matthew 18: 10.

301 *'Auld lang syne'*: a farewell song by Robert Burns (1788).

'The Auld House': Baroness Nairne's nostalgic song (not a ballad) about 'mony cherish'd memories' appears in the *Life and Songs of the Baroness Nairne* (1869).

I did not in last 'Praeterita': see pp. 280–1.

In a former number of 'Praeterita: the passage referred to was omitted in revision.

Sevenoaks: the picture of Sevenoaks, from 1831, was exhibited at Coniston in 1900; on the back is written: 'I believe my very first study from nature'.

plague-cloud: the term that JR used to describe weather diseased by human pollution and God's judgement that culminated in *The Storm-Cloud of the Nineteenth Century*.

VOLUME III

304 *These verses ... with one following sonnet*: JR omits the penultimate stanza of the first poem, dated 9 June 1845 and first published in 1850 (*LE* ii. 235). The sonnet is 'The Glacier' (*LE* ii.240), first published in 1846.

'washed in the blood of Christ': cf. 'These are they which came out of great tribulation, and have washed their robes, and made them white in the blood of the Lamb', Revelation 7: 14.

the power of mountains: in the last chapter of *Modern Painters*, IV, 'The Mountain Glory'.

went up into the mountain to preach, or into the wilderness to pray: in Matthew 5: 1, Jesus goes up a mountain to preach the 'Sermon on the Mount', and withdraws to the wilderness to pray in Luke 5: 16.

in last 'Praeterita': this should be 'last but one'.

305 *I had been totally disappointed ... mountains*: this story had also been told in *The Stones of Venice*, III and in *Modern Painters*, V.

Eremite: hermits.

306 *Madame de Fleury*: the 'good Sister Frances' appears in 'Madame de Fleury' from Edgeworth's *Tales of Fashionable Life* (1809).

Of the Brotherhoods, of course the first I knew: see *LE* i. 505, for JR's visits to the Hospice on the Great St Bernard in 1835. JR did not speak of the

Brotherhoods in any detail elsewhere after this: perhaps he was to discuss them in the ninth part of *Our Fathers Have Told Us*, on 'Pastoral forms of Catholicism, reaching to our own times' (*LE* xxxiii. 187).

307 *Esau*: Genesis 25: 29–34.

Ishmael: Genesis 21: 9.

308 *'They too . . . aloft descried'*: from Wordsworth's 'Processions: Suggested on a Sabbath Morning in the Vale of Chamouny' in the *Memorials of a Tour of the Continent, 1820* (1822), with minor alterations.

309 *to honour and love their neighbour as themselves*: Leviticus 19: 18.

310 *'The arrangement . . . emotion' . . . I forget the exact words*: 'the suggestion, by the imagination, of noble grounds for the noble emotions' (*Modern Painters*, III, 5.28).

311 *Messrs Foord's*: Foord's of Windsor were for many years JR's framers.

'cette baraque': 'this shed'/'hut'.

Fourth volume got done: an odd error: *Modern Painters*, IV was issued with *Modern Painters*, III in 1856.

finish the book: *Modern Painters*, V was issued on 14 June 1860. The last chapter, 'Peace', quietly answered his father's impatience with the slow progress of the book: 'Looking back over what I have written', JR said, 'I find that I have only now the power of ending this work,—it being time that it should end, but not of concluding it; for it has led me into fields of infinite inquiry where it is only possible to break off with such imperfect result as may, at any given moment, have been attained' (*LE* vii. 444).

312 *a new epoch of life and death begins*: this was, for JR, a real turning point, as from now (1860) his concentration was more on social and economic criticism than art. He said in a lecture in November 1877, 'I got this volume [*Modern Painters*, V] bound in the Valley of St Martin's in that summer [1860], and in the Valley of Chamouni I gave up my art-work, and wrote this little book [*Unto this Last*], the beginning of the days of reprobation' (*LE* xxii. 512).

Of him, more hereafter: *Praeterita* did not return to Rossetti.

Jael's slaying of Sisera . . . Magnificat: Maurice's text is Judges 5. Israel seeks to be freed from the army of King Jabin, which is led by Sisera. Jael, the wife of Heber the Kenite, kills Sisera after offering him hospitality (including 'butter in a lordly dish' (v. 25)), and God, in turn, gives victory to Israel. Deborah, a prophetess, salutes Jael (Yael) in her song, which includes the verse: 'Blessed above women shall Jael the wife of Heber the Kenite be, blessed shall she be above women in the tent' (v. 24). J. R. Green described the beginning of the battle of Hastings (1066) in 1874 as follows: 'A general charge of the Norman foot opened the battle; in front rode the minstrel Taillefer, tossing his sword in the air and catching it again while he chaunted the song of Roland' (*History of the English People* (1880), vol. i, ch. 2). The Magnificat is Mary's song in the New Testament at the

Annunciation, beginning 'My soul doth magnify the Lord, And my spirit hath rejoiced in God my Saviour' (Luke 1: 46–7).

313 *The other student . . . a carpenter*: JR refers to a carpenter known now only as 'Mr Butterworth'.

séance: *OED*'s first sense: 'A sitting of [. . .] a number of persons assembled for discussion, or instruction by a lecturer, or the like'.

314 *Prodigal Son*: Luke 15.

'ever with me, and all that I have, thine': Luke 15: 31. The son who has remained at home rebukes his father for not celebrating his loyalty (Luke 15: 29–30).

burn blue: a candle burning blue is a traditional sign of a ghost's or devil's presence.

315 *I have spoken several times*: the passages referred to were omitted in JR's revisions.

Hours of the Virgin: that is, an illuminated manuscript of a liturgy for the Virgin Mary.

illuminated missals: full texts and instructions for the celebration of mass.

Commander of the Faithful: a term to describe a caliph, ruler of a Muslim state (JR was careful in later life to present an eclectic faith position).

316 *next chapter*: JR did not return to this topic in the next chapter, but see p. 365.

Mosaic law: the Ten Commandments, received by Moses (including 'Remember the sabbath day, to keep it holy', Exodus 20: 8).

Sabbath a delight: Isaiah 58: 13.

Very happy in my Sunday walk: see the story told on p. 220.

318 *Admah and Zeboim*: 'And that the whole land thereof is brimstone, and salt, and burning, that it is not sown, nor beareth, nor any grass groweth therein, like the overthrow of Sodom, and Gomorrah, Admah, and Zeboim, which the Lord overthrew in his anger, and in his wrath', Deuteronomy 29: 23.

Paul Veronese's Solomon and the Queen of Sheba: in the Galleria Sabauda, Turin, this painting is sometimes attributed to Benedetto Caliari (1538–98), Veronese's brother.

Spirit of God: there is no exact biblical source for this idea.

319 *Tintoret's arrow between St Sebastian's eyes*: in the Scuola di San Rocco. The arrow is actually in the saint's forehead.

320 *'Dira Necessitas' . . . milk and butter*: 'Dira Necessitas' ('grim necessity') is probably meant to be 'saeva necessitas' ('savage necessity') of Horace, *Odes*, 1.25.17. Delilah betrays Samson to the Philistines in Judges 16. She cuts off his hair, the source of his strength, having made a number of attempts to weaken him, one of which involves weaving strands of his hair in a loom (a 'beam'); Judith saves Israel from the Assyrians by decapitating their leader Holofernes in the Book of Judith when he is drunk (a story

excluded from the Protestant Bible). In fact, Holofernes orders his own wine: it is not given to him by Judith.

320 *Scythian banquet-song*: written in 1838, this is reproduced on *LE* ii. 57–69. The song refers to a skull being used as a drinking cup.

in imitation of Sisera: Judges 5: 30.

Prout had left us still earlier: see Prout in Glossary of Persons Mentioned. He had died a year after Turner, not 'earlier'.

Wisie: also the nickname for Rose La Touche's sister, Emily.

Carpaccio's dog in the picture of St Jerome: the dog attends in fact on St *Augustine* receiving a vision of St Jerome's death in Carpaccio's sequence in the Scuola di San Giorgio degli Schiavoni in Venice.

ran . . . Mollwitz: 'The King vanishes from Mollwitz Field [. . .] for sixteen hours, into the regions of Myth, "into Fairyland," as would once have been said', Carlyle wrote in book 12 of *Frederick the Great*, referring to the battle of Mollwitz (1741) in the War of Austrian Succession.

321 *Macdonald of St Martin's*: see William Farquharson in Glossary of Persons Mentioned.

322 *to drink sherry-cobbler through a straw*: the bishop was Samuel Wilberforce. JR claims this tale for 1854, but he told a very similar story to W. H. Harrison in 1847.

musical glasses: a cryptic allusion to Oliver Goldsmith's *The Vicar of Wakefield*: 'The two ladies threw my girls quite into the shade; for they would talk of nothing but high life, and high lived company; with other fashionable topics, such as pictures, taste, Shakespear, and the musical glasses' (ch. 9).

323 *it had chanced that in 1845 . . . St Cassan . . . National Gallery*: the attempt was actually made in 1851. The picture is still in San Cassiano.

'Life of the Workman': ch. 6 of *The Stones of Venice*, II, 'The Nature of Gothic', was reissued as a separate pamphlet in 1854 with the subtitle 'And Herein of the True Functions of the Workman in Art'.

long note on Education . . . 'Modern Painters': 'Logical Education' is a note at the end of volume IV (not I) of *Modern Painters* (*LE* vi. 482–5).

324 *D'Israeli*: an earlier family spelling of the surname of Benjamin Disraeli (1804–81), twice British Prime Minister.

one winter: the only known visit of the Prince of Wales to Oxford during JR's time was in the summer: June 1875.

Planet Saturn . . . Alice in Wonderland: JR had said that Saturn had a leaden influence on him on p. 285; Lewis Carroll's Alice in Wonderland was modelled on Alice Liddell, daughter of Christ Church's Dean.

326 *rhododendron ferrugineum*: the *Alpenrose* or snow-rose, of the Alps.

'everlasting clouds': from Rogers's *Italy* ('The Alps').

328 *This was, as I have said . . . empire*: this section and much afterwards closely

follows, in JR's translation or paraphrase, Eusèbe-Henri-Alban Gaullieur's *La Suisse: historique et pittoresque* (1855). See Introduction, p. xx.

account given in 'Eagle's Nest': JR mentions his encounter with a 'small steel-grey serpent' (*LE* xxii. 196) in Lecture 6 (1872) of *The Eagle's Nest*. He wrote on the mythic and moral meaning of snakes in the 'Living Waves' chapter (1880) of *Deucalion*.

causing the colour: this is a quiet allusion to the topic of one of JR's earliest publications: his essay, 'Enquiries on the Causes of the Colour of the Water of the Rhine' (Loudon's *Magazine of Natural History*, 1834).

By the shore of the Limmat . . . refectionis educavit: JR is confusing Zurich's Grossmünster, commenced at the beginning of the twelfth century, and which stands on the site of a church legendarily founded by Charlemagne, with the tenth-century Wasserkirche. His quotation from St Jerome's translation of the Bible into Latin, the Vulgate, is from Psalm 23 (22 in the Vulgate): 'He maketh me to lie down in green pastures: he leadeth me beside the still waters'. The point is that both churches are next to the water.

329 *maid of honour*: JR means a maid of honour as benign as the heroine of Scott's *Anne of Geierstein*.

331 *acheminement*: 'route', 'transmission'.

332 *'C'était une tour de guerre' . . . 'Voyez . . . une bouteille!'*: 'It was a tower of war:' . . . 'Look. It was a tower of war. I have made it a bottle!'

335 *'Fioretti di San Francesco'*: *The Little Flowers of St Francis* is an anonymous late fourteenth-century Italian text based on the life of St Francis.

336 *Miss Edgeworth's story of the grateful Negro*: Edgeworth's story, written in 1802, was collected in the *Tales and Miscellaneous Pieces* (1825).

lava . . . Italy: JR's volcanic metaphor may be an allusion to the devastating explosion of Krakatoa in May 1883, which coloured the world's sky for several years afterwards.

"My thought . . . rank before": adapted from Shakespeare's *Sonnet* 85, ll. 11–12.

sermons in stones: *As You Like It*, II. i. 17.

The last number: vol. II, ch. X.

337 *The loss*: Susan Sedgwick Norton, Norton's wife, had died on 17 February 1872 after the birth of their son Richard.

net of Love: JR met Rose La Touche, as he goes on to explain, in 1858.

Green Street, W.: actually, 10 Great Cumberland Place, then Norfolk Street, London (this confusion *might* result from JR's periodical association of Rose with the colour green).

338 *Nine years old*: an odd error: Rose La Touche was 10 on 3 January 1858.

Elgin Theseus: JR means one of the warriors in the Elgin Marbles in the British Museum.

339 _will have their day in these memoirs_: these points were not reached.

my superior: JR reprints a letter on botany from Mrs La Touche in _Proserpina_, reinforcing this point (_LE_ xxv. 523–5).

340 _I should pay them a visit . . . Green Street_: it is impossible now to recover the details of JR's visits to the La Touches in his early part of his relationship with them. But surviving evidence suggests it was slower to develop than narrated here.

'_Chrystostom_': that is, from St John Chrysostom (_c._347–407), whose added Greek surname _chrysostomos_ means the 'golden-mouthed'.

'_Lacerta_': 'lizard' (Latin).

I shouldn't say anything about Rosie at all: Joan Severn was particularly anxious about what JR might say of Rose (see Introduction, pp. xvii–xviii). Norton had written more generally to JR on 4 June 1888 saying that if he could write a portion of _Praeterita_, 'I should omit some things which you will tell' (_CJRCEN_, 500).

341 _Titians you told us to look at . . . white Rabbit_: Rose looks at Titian's _Allegory of Alfonso d'Avalos_ (JR thought it was a portrait of Titian and his mistress (_LE_ xii. 458)) and _The Virgin and Child with Saint Catherine and a Shepherd_, known as _The Madonna of the Rabbit_. Both are still in the Louvre.

Portrait of Lord Bute's: unknown reference.

342 _Paul Veronese . . . Venus Victrix_: Rose refers to the foreground of Veronese's _Supper at Emmaus_ (_c._1559), still in the Louvre: two children play with a dog, one looking away; another boy holds a puppy. By _Venus Victrix_, she may mean the Louvre's _Venus de Milo_ or even the _Winged Victory of Samothrace_.

a Venus: not a Venus but an Apollo: _Apollo Sauroctonos_ (Apollo the Lizard-killer). It is still in the Louvre.

Referring to a debate . . . rifle–ball is: JR is glossing Rose's allusion to the opening of Book 6 of Elizabeth Barrett Browning's _Aurora Leigh_ (1856): 'The English have a scornful insular way | Of calling the French light. The levity | Is in the judgment only'. Browning goes on to ask about the 'lightness' of a bullet. Rose is referring to Viollet-le-Duc's restoration of Notre-Dame de Paris from 1845 onwards.

Oxford Museum: JR had presented some Turner watercolours to the University of Oxford, including those of French rivers.

'_nor dim, nor red_': from l. 97 of Coleridge's _The Rime of the Ancient Mariner_ (1798–1834).

343 _Light in the West, Beauvais_: Rose is thinking of JR's spectacular cloud drawing entitled 'Light in the West, Beauvais', engraved for _Modern Painters_, V.

your letter: JR's letter to Rose is lost.

344 _Joanna's Care_: see Introduction, pp. xvii–xviii.

mischances: there were nine months between Chapters II and III of Volume III, and four months between Chapters I and II.

father's fortune: JR inherited an estate of £120,000 together with property worth another £3000 on the (sudden) death of his father on 3 March 1864.

345 *Gordon Fraser's Guide*: Gordon Fraser, *Wigtown and Whithorn: Historical and Descriptive Sketches, Stories and Anecdotes* (1877). The picture referred to here is the frontispiece.

'*Come away, Mr Fairford . . .' . . . 'new lords, new lands*': from the beginning of chapter 11 of *Redgauntlet*.

346 '*This is Joan*': Joan provided these details (see Introduction, pp. xvii–xviii). On 9 May 1886, JR had written to her to say: 'I can't make out about the times I used to be alone in the D. Hill drawing room with mama in the evening. Were you much away from us, after you came?—What year did you come first in to stay?' (*JRCJS*, 224–5).

And the word . . . begin with: JR is thinking of 'Definition of a Nice Person' in *A Memoir of Sydney Smith, by his Daughter, Lady Holland*, i (1855 edn.), 246: 'A nice person is neither too tall nor too short, looks clean and cheerful, has no prominent feature, makes no difficulties, is never misplaced, sits bodkin, is never foolishly affected, and is void of affectations. A nice person helps you well at dinner, understands you, is always gratefully received by young and old, Whig and Tory, grave and gay [etc.]'.

in months with the letter r l: oysters, it was long thought in Great Britain, could only be eaten in months with an 'r' in them (colder months where there was less chance of them being off).

going away somewhere: if Joan arrived, as she says, on 19 April 1864, JR was in Bradford on 21–2 April, then at Winnington School, Cheshire, until after 29 April. He was back in Denmark Hill by 6 May.

347 *nor virtually have she and I ever parted since*: see Introduction, pp. xviii–xix.

meet the Queen at Dean Stanley's: Carlyle met the Queen as described in 1869.

348 *make Carlyle free of the garden*: 'allow Carlyle free access to the garden'.

349 *Christy Minstrel*: Edwin Pearce Christy (1815–62) founded the Christy's Minstrels in 1843 (a black-face minstrel group) and it was re-formed in Great Britain as Raynor & Pierce's Christy Minstrels in 1857. JR's fondness for pantomime and popular entertainment is well attested.

351 *Margaret MacLachlan, and Margaret Wilson*: two Presbyterian martyrs, drowned in 1685 in the Solway Firth for refusing allegiance to the King.

last journey to Venice: in October 1888. JR left few records of his feelings and thoughts during this trip, which ended in a breakdown in Paris. He had been often silent in Venice, unable to tell his companion, the architect Detmar Blow (1867–1939), about the city, or introduce him to friends.

351 *morbid German fancies . . . fatal to Carlyle*: JR thought that Carlyle's immersion in German thought and writing, to which JR was never sympathetic, had weakened his ideas and influence.

   Varney, Rashleigh, or Lord Dalgarno: Varney from *Kenilworth*; Rashleigh from *Rob Roy*; Dalgarno from *The Fortunes of Nigel*.

352 *Flodden*: the battle fought between Scotland and England on 9 September 1513 in Northumberland, in which the English were victors. It is the subject of *Marmion*.

   as I have stated elsewhere: see *Fiction, Fair and Foul* (1880/1881).

353 *real 'Old Mortality'*: the stonemason Robert Paterson (1715–1801) spent forty years carving and erecting gravestones for the Covenanters, and provided Scott with his model for Old Mortality.

356 *laws of musical expression*: Pope Gregory the Great (540–604) has often been credited with the invention of the Gregorian plainchant that bears his name.

357 *Battle of Balaclava*: fought in 1854 in the Crimean War, this was an indecisive engagement involving the disastrous Charge of the Light Brigade.

   no-Battle of the Baltic . . . Cronstadt: Admiral Sir Charles Napier (1786–1860) was rebuked by British newspapers for deciding not to attack Kronstadt in the Baltic campaign of the Crimean.

359 *'The Strait Gate'*: JR refers to the fifth chapter of *Mornings in Florence* (1875–7).

361 *'Naked foot . . . as mute'*: Byron's *The Corsair*, ii. 1010–11.

   'She tapped her tiny silken-sandalled foot': 'Prologue' to Tennyson's *The Princess*, l. 149.

362 *Trevi or Branda*: the first in Rome, the second in Siena.

   Marriage in Cana: this was left unfinished at Severn's death.

363 *Cor magis tibi Sena pandit*: 'More than her gates, Siena opens her heart to you.'

GLOSSARY OF PERSONS MENTIONED

THIS glossary gives details of many of those either in JR's circle, or who were important to him and/or his family. The information given does not constitute a comprehensive biography for each person listed, but only salient details that relate to, or help explain, JR's references. JR's spelling of names is not reliable (though the nineteenth century had a slightly different attitude to consistency in the spelling of names from our own time): his variants have mostly been silently corrected or normalized in this list.

HENRY ACLAND (1815–1900), fellow student with JR at Christ Church and lifelong friend, he was a distinguished physician: Lee's Reader in Anatomy at Oxford from 1845 and Regius Professor of Medicine from 1857. Acland was an important influence on the development of science as a university discipline at Oxford. JR fell out with him over vivisection.

SIR PEREGRINE ACLAND (1789–1871), of 'Fairfield', Stogursey near Bridgwater, Somerset, inherited Turner drawings purchased by his uncle, the eccentric philanthropist, drunk, and pro-slavery MP John Fuller (1757–1834).

ALEXANDER ADAM (1741–1809), appointed Rector of the High School, Edinburgh, in 1768, he was the author of the widely used *The Principles of Latin and English Grammar* (1772), which Dale wanted to stop JR reading (see Introduction, p. xxii). Always a respected figure in JR's mind.

JOAN AGNEW, *see* Joan Severn

FRANCESCA ALEXANDER (1837–1917), American illustrator and translator. JR 'edited' (primarily a matter of selection and preface/postscript) some of her work, including *Roadside Songs of Tuscany* (1885) and *Christ's Folk in the Apennines* (1887).

GEORGE ALLEN (1832–1907), initially a craft carpenter, he was taught drawing by JR at the Working Men's College and later married Hannah Hobbes, MR's maid. Allen was subsequently established by JR as his publisher and he published, among many other works, *Praeterita* itself. Allen was frustrated, it seems, by the errors and misrepresentations in the autobiography. George Allen became George Allen & Unwin in 1914 with still-standing offices opposite the British Museum.

DR EDWARD ANDREWS (1787–1841), preacher at Beresford Chapel, Walworth, whose school JR was attending by 1829. His daughter Emily Augusta (1824–62) married the poet Coventry Patmore (1823–96), author of *The Angel in the House* (1854–63). Her face was the subject of Browning's 'A Face' in *Dramatis Personae* (1864).

GEORGE BEAUMONT (1753–1827), art patron and painter, and early major donor to the National Gallery: he aggressively disapproved of Turner's work.

DR JOHN BROWN (1810–82), Edinburgh physician and writer who wrote an early appreciation of *Modern Painters*; he was a friend of JR. JR quotes his *Supplementary Chapter to the Life of Rev. John Brown, D.D. A Letter to Rev. John Cairns, D.D.* (1860) in *Praeterita*.

RAWDON BROWN (1806–83), English historian of Venice who was an unofficial host to many English visitors to the city. He worked extensively on the *Calendar of State Papers and Manuscripts Relating to English Affairs* (1864–81) in the Venetian state archives, and assisted JR in his work on *The Stones of Venice*. Their views on politics were dissimilar.

DR THOMAS BROWN (1778–1820), a refined, French-inspired philosopher and poet who succeeded to the chair in moral philosophy at Edinburgh in 1810–11. A friend of MR's mother.

REVD WALTER LUCAS BROWN (1805–62), graduate of, and subsequently tutor at, Christ Church, where he taught JR Greek: he was later vicar of Wendlebury, Oxfordshire.

FRANCIS BUCKLAND (1826–80), son of William Buckland, zoologist and surgeon.

DR WILLIAM BUCKLAND (1784–1856), eccentric English geologist and canon of Christ Church, whose house was full of animals, many of which he ate. Buckland moved away from Old Testament accounts of the Deluge and, it is now recognized, his timescales of geology helped modestly to prepare the ground for Darwin.

ARTHUR BURGESS (d. 1887?), JR's assistant, engraver, and photographer who worked in Verona with JR and at Oxford, assisting in the preparation of teaching materials. Burgess was initially a wood engraver, and met JR first in 1860.

THOMAS CAMPBELL (1777–1844), Scottish poet who was instrumental in the foundation of the University of London.

FRANCIS RICHARD CHARTERIS (1818–1914), Lord Elcho, British soldier and politician, who was at Christ Church with JR.

EDWARD CHENEY (1803–84), art collector and watercolourist, he was a collector of Italian painting and unofficial adviser to the National Gallery on its Italian collections. He lived for a time in Venice and was a friend of Rawdon Brown. JR visited Cheney in his Shropshire home, Badger Hall. His publications included *Despatches of Venetian Ambassadors* (1864).

SIR JAMES CLARK (1788–1870), First Physician to Queen Victoria and a specialist in consumption: called on to advise on JR's sickness while at Oxford.

WILLIAM COCK (1754–87), JR's maternal grandfather, landlord of the King's Head, Market Street, Croydon. He apparently died after a riding accident and was buried in Croydon parish churchyard.

W(ILLIAM) G(ERSHOM) COLLINGWOOD (1854–1932), biographer, novelist, and artist, who met JR while a student at Oxford and helped on the Hinksey Road project. He became JR's friend and assistant at Brantwood, and eventually his biographer. Collingwood was Professor of Fine Art at the University of Reading.

WILLIAM CRAWSHAY (1788–1867), the 'Iron King', who built the family home, Cyfarthfa Castle, at Merthyr Tydfil, Wales.

GEORGE CROLY (1780–1860), writer, Tory, and clergyman, he became Rector of St Stephen, Walbrook, in 1835. JJR thought him a good model for his son.

REVD THOMAS DALE (1797–1870), clergyman who taught JR at Grove Lane, Camberwell. He was professor of English language and literature at University College London (1828–30) and of English literature and history at King's College London (1835–40) where he also taught JR. Dale was, from 1835, vicar of St Bride's, Fleet Street. Although JR maintained a friendship and correspondence, he never forgot Dale's 'blasphemous' treatment of Adam's *Principles of Latin and English Grammar* (see Introduction, p. xxii).

HENRY DART (1817–87), attended Dale's school and later won the Newdigate Prize at Oxford in 1838 with 'The Exile of St Helena', beating JR, his friend, who won it the following year. Dart was called to the Bar in 1841. He translated the *Iliad* into English hexameters (1862–5).

EARL OF DESART, John Cuffe 3rd Earl of Desart (1818–65), Irish politician.

DOMECQ FAMILY, JR fell in love as a teenager with the daughter of JJR's business partner, Pedro Domecq. He usually gave her name as Adèle Clotilde (Spanish: Adela Clotilde), and she was born in 1821. She married the French baron Melchor José Miguel Julian de Du-Quesne in 1840, and died sometime after 23 February 1886 (when JR told a friend that he knew she was still living). The other younger daughters were Cecilia Eulalia (1822–86), later Countess de Chabrillan; Elisa (Elise) (1823–68), later Countess Des-Roys; and Carolina (1824–?), later Countess de Bethune.

FREDERICK GEORGE DAWTREY DREWITT (1848–1942), pathologist and watercolourist who had graduated from Christ Church in natural science in 1871. Drewitt had attended JR's Oxford lectures and became a friend.

MARY DUFF OF LACHIN-Y-GAIR (1788–1858), married the port merchant Robert Cockburn in 1805. Aged 9, she had been the object of Byron's adoration (he was also 9). The Irish poet and balladeer Thomas Moore (1779–1852) in his *Life of Byron*, vol. i (1854), records Byron's account of himself as '"utterly, devotedly fond of that girl, at an age when I could neither feel passion, nor know the meaning of the word"'.

JOHANN-LUDWIG RUDOLF DURHEIM (1811–95), Swiss artist whom JR met in Florence in 1845 and corresponded with until 1856. At one point JR asked William Holman Hunt to support him.

SIR HERBERT EDWARDES (1819–68), army officer and politician in India, known for defeating the revolt at Multan in 1848 in the Second Anglo-Sikh War, and for his able administration. He was a devout Christian, about whom JR wrote in *A Knight's Faith* (1885). He married the step-daughter of Dr Grant.

RICHARD WHITEMAN FALL (1820–78), an early friend of JR who accompanied him on his 1849 tour. Fall was at Shrewsbury School, 1834–7. He became a partner in the Palmer, Mackillop, Dent, & Co, a company that traded in the capital markets including, in 1854, arranging for the first European capital loan to Turkish state finances. His sister, Eliza Fall (1821–81), published *Poems* (1851) under the name Mary Maynard.

WILLIAM MACDONALD COLQUHOUN FARQUHARSON (1822–93), he took the name Macdonald on succeeding to the ownership of St Martin's Abbey, Perth; Glen Shee, Blairgowrie; and The Craig, Montrose in 1841.

WALTER FAWKES MP (1769–1825), friend and patron of Turner, who lived at Farnley Hall, Wharfedale.

COPLEY FIELDING (1787–1855), English landscape painter who taught JR, and who is much discussed in *Modern Painters*.

JAMES FORBES (1809–68), Scottish physicist and glacial scientist whose integrity JR sought to defend against others, including the physicist John Tyndall (1820–93).

J(AMES) A(NTHONY) FROUDE (1818–94), historian and biographer of Carlyle, who issued Carlyle's *Reminiscences* in 1881. A furore followed (*Reminiscences* exposed many of Carlyle's faults and the unhappiness of his marriage), but JR felt the candour of Carlyle's writing admirable.

THOMAS GAISFORD (1779–1855), Regius Professor of Greek and Dean of Christ Church, University of Oxford, from 1831.

WILLIAM GAISFORD (1822–43), Thomas Gaisford's son, whom JR carried back to his room at Christ Church when William was drunk: he drowned, aged 21.

MISS GALE, apparently related by marriage to Arthur Severn. She lived with her sister at Burgate House in the precincts of Canterbury Cathedral (now St Augustine's Library).

DR GLOAG, (Scottish) doctor in Rome who attended on JR and who seems to have worked with Thomas Carlyle's brother, Dr John Carlyle.

OSBORNE GORDON (1813–83), JR's tutor at Christ Church and friend, later vicar of Easthampstead, Berkshire. He was also the son of a wine merchant.

DR GEORGE GRANT (1792?–1857), a friend and neighbour of JJR, and probably sometime surgeon on board HMS *Forte*. He took his MD from Edinburgh in 1824 and lived in later life on Richmond Hill, Surrey, where he married the widow Mrs Sidney (whose daughter married Sir Herbert Edwardes).

EUPHEMIA (EFFIE) CHALMERS GRAY (1828–97), the sharp, active, and independently minded woman whose family knew the Ruskins, and who married JR in 1848. Effie was gifted and regarded social success highly. Her marriage began with a relatively happy period in Venice, but then deteriorated. Parental interference did not help, and JR remained largely detached from Effie, with whom, in truth, he had little in common. The marriage was annulled, it is generally believed, on the grounds of non-consummation and 'incurable impotence' in July 1854, though JR denied the latter charge. Effie later married the Pre-Raphaelite John Everett Millais (1829–96). JR almost never referred to her in writing again, though she intervened with damaging revelations in his relationship with Rose in 1870.

MR AND MRS RICHARD GRAY, almost all details are lost of the Grays (sometimes Greys) of Camberwell, JJR's friends. In 1813, Richard Gray was married in Lisbon to Miss Mary Monro, daughter of the late Edinburgh merchant John Monro. Richard Gray was then described as a 'merchant' by the *Scots Magazine* (1813). They later lived in Camberwell Grove, near the Ruskins, with Mary's mother and her poodle.

THOMAS GRIFFITH (n.d.), art dealer, at whose house JR met Turner on 22 June 1840.

ROBERT GRIMSTON (1816–84), sportsman and supporter of telegraphy.

SIR WILLIAM GULL (1816–90), eminent physician of the royal household, he was known for work on the disease he first named as *anorexia nervosa*. He cared for JR during his 1882 illness.

JAMES DUFFIELD HARDING (1798–1863), English landscape painter and one of JR's tutors.

CONSTANCE (CONNIE) HILLIARD (later Mrs W. H. Churchill), Lady Trevelyan's niece, whom JR met first when she was 11. She was the daughter of the Revd J. C. Hilliard of Cowley, Uxbridge, with whom JR often stayed in the 1870s.

JOHN ('GEORGE') HOBBS (*c*.1825–1892), JR's valet who left the Ruskins to travel to Australia where he became a magistrate in New South Wales, dying in 1892.

'THE REV. MR HOWELL', William Howels (1778–1832), Welsh Evangelical preacher, he was from 1817 minister at the Chapel-of-Ease, Long Acre. His sermons were published in 2 volumes, 1834–6.

WILLIAM HENRY HUNT (1790–1864), English watercolourist, known for his detailed studies from life.

WILLIAM HOLMAN HUNT (1827–1910), English painter and founder-member of the Pre-Raphaelite Brotherhood. JR devoted much attention to the interpretation of his painting, and thought that his 'sensational realism' eclipsed the achievement of David Roberts.

ROBERT HUSSEY (1801–56), a graduate, and from 1835 Censor, of Christ Church, Oxford. From 1842, he was the first Regius Professor of Ecclesiastical History.

THOMAS HENRY HUXLEY (1825–95), evolutionary biologist, champion of Darwin, and Professor of Natural History at the Royal School of Mines. T. H. Huxley was associated in JR's mind with the apparent triumph of the new 'materialist' science over natural theology. JR met Huxley in the meetings of the Metaphysical Society in the 1870s and, in *Praeterita*, envisaged his mind as crudely literal, with no space for either imagination or faith.

SIR ROBERT INGLIS (1786–1855), English conservative politician.

JOSEPH IRONS (1785–1852), Evangelical preacher who was minister at the Grove Chapel, Camberwell, between 1818 and his death.

ANNA JAMESON (1794–1860), Irish-born writer whose work on Shakespeare's heroines (*Characteristics of Women: Moral, Poetical and Historical* (1832)) JR valued. She wrote widely on art, including the five volumes of *Sacred and Legendary Art* (1848–64). *Praeterita* was notoriously dismissive of her artistic knowledge and judgement.

DR HENRY JEPHSON (1798–1878), successful physician and philanthropist at Royal Leamington Spa, who treated patients, including JR, with the spa spring waters and dietary regimes.

SIR WILLOUGHBY JONES (1820–84), MP for Cheltenham, Conservative politician, and Norfolk landowner, he attended Thomas Dale's school with JR.

JOHN KEBLE (1792–1866), poet, clergyman, and Oxford Movement leader. He pruned JR's Newdigate prize poem for reading aloud in his capacity as Professor of Poetry at Oxford, 1831–41.

LORD KILDARE, Charles William FitzGerald (1819–87), 4th Duke of Leinster, was Kildare's MP (1847–52).

(HENRY) GALLY KNIGHT (1786–1846), country squire, fiction writer, and author of *Ecclesiastical Architecture of Italy* (1842–4). A passage criticizing him was kept out of JR's review of Lord Lindsay's *Christian Art*, and included in *The Stones of Venice*: '[Readers] will find a drawing of the entire front [of San Michele, Lucca] in Gally Knight's *Architecture of Italy*. It may serve to give them an idea of its general disposition, and it looks very careful and accurate; but every bit of the ornament on it *is drawn out of the artist's head*. There is not *one line* of it that exists on the building' (*LE* ix. 431).

HERBERT KYNASTON (1809–78), tutor in Greek at Christ Church, and later High (Head) Master of St Paul's School, London.

EDWIN LANDSEER (1802–73), English painter, particularly of animals, and one of the most celebrated of the age. His later career was overshadowed by mental breakdown.

JOHN FREDERICK LEWIS (1804–76), English orientalist painter, and son of the engraver Frederick Christian Lewis. JR thought him the 'painter of greatest power . . . in the English school' next to Turner and was particularly enthusiastic about *A Frank Encampment in the Desert of Mount Sinai* in *Academy Notes* (1856), saying it was akin to Titian and Veronese. JR thought there was something 'un-English about him': he lived away from Great Britain between 1837 and 1851, working in Egypt from 1841 to 51.

HENRY GEORGE LIDDELL (1811–98), educated at Christ Church, he served as Dean, 1855–91. He was a classical scholar and one of the editors of the celebrated Liddell and Scott *Greek-English Lexicon* (1843–). JR knew, in particular, three of his daughters: Alice (1852–1934), who was Lewis Carroll's model for Alice in Wonderland; Edith (1854–76); and Rhoda (1859–1949).

JOHN CLAUDIUS LOUDON (1783–1843), Scottish proprietor of the *Architectural Magazine*.

THOMAS BABINGTON MACAULAY (1800–59), historian and Whig politician. His progressive theory of history, most evident in *The History of England* (1848–55), was antagonistic to JR's conviction that modern Europe's future lay in turning back to the values of the (medieval) past.

GEORGE MACDONALD (1824–1905), Scottish Christian fantasy writer and minister, he assisted in communications between JR and Rose La Touche.

F(REDERICK) D(ENISON) MAURICE (1805–72), Christian Socialist minister who was one of the founders, in 1854, of the Working Men's College, at which JR taught.

'MAISIE' (n.d.), the woman in charge of domestic arrangements at 7 Billiter Street, JJR's offices, discussed on p. 88. In real life she may have been the person noted in the 1851 Census as 'M[illegible, but not Maisie or Marion] Elizabeth Skane'. She was listed as 'House Keeper', aged 43, and born in 'Horseleydown', Surrey.

GIUSEPPE MAZZINI (1805–72), Italian pro-unification political thinker.

HENRY MELVILL (1798–1871), graduated from Peterhouse, Cambridge, in 1821, and was Principal of the East India College, Haileybury, 1843–57. He was a residentiary canon of St Paul's, 1856–71, and one of the most popular preachers in London.

JAMES MILLINGEN (1774–1845), Dutch-English archaeologist and writer on coins who died in Florence on 1 October 1845, just after JR's disappointing visit to him (p. 230).

DR THOMAS MUNRO (1759–1833), a noted physician of the mentally ill (his patients included King George III), as well as a painter and art collector. He held informal art evenings that Turner attended in London.

ALEXANDER NASMYTH (1758–1840), Scottish portrait and landscape painter. He taught JJR painting at Edinburgh High School.

HENRY NEELE (1798–1828), English poet, editor of Shakespeare's *The Tempest*, and suicide.

CHARLES NEWTON (1816–94), educated at Christ Church, he was an assistant at the British Museum in 1840 and British Consulate in the east (1852–60) when he discovered the mausoleum of Halicarnassus. He was later keeper of Greek and Roman antiquities at the British Museum until 1885. He married Mary, Arthur Severn's sister.

JAMES NORTHCOTE (1746–1831), English historical and portrait painter, whose portrait of JR still hangs in the dining room, Brantwood. He was also the author of a *Life of Titian* (1830), written with William Hazlitt.

CHARLES ELIOT NORTON (1827–1908), American art critic, Dante scholar, and friend of English men and women of letters including JR and Carlyle: he was professor of the History of Art at Harvard from 1875 to 1898: JR called him 'my first real tutor', though it is fair to say that Norton never really understood JR's politics or affections. There were criticisms of Norton in *Dilecta* but Joan ensured they were not published. Norton, who was one of JR's executors, supervised the burning of letters at Brantwood after JR's death.

EDMUND OLDFIELD (1817–1902), attended Thomas Dale's school with JR and worked with him on the east window of St Giles, Camberwell. Oldfield went on to the British Museum as a curator and became an adviser on ecclesiastical restoration. His publications included *Catalogue of Select Examples of Ivory Carvings from the 2nd to the 16th Century* (1855). Oldfield served on the committee (1902) for JR's memorial in Westminster Abbey.

CONSTANCE (CONNIE) OLDHAM (1852–1924), JR's god-daughter and niece of Edmund Oldfield, she attended Winnington School (and is 'May', *The Ethics of the Dust* (1866)).

JOHN HENRY PARKER (1806–84), bookseller, architectural historian, and author of the influential *Glossary of Terms used in Grecian, Roman, Italian, and Gothic Architecture* (1838).

THOMAS PRINGLE (1789–34), Scottish editor, poet, and writer on South Africa.

SAMUEL PROUT (1783–1852), English watercolourist, particularly of continental street scenes, whom JR much admired. He had an eye for picturesque detail and elegant decay. Prout, who lived on Denmark Hill, died on 10 February 1852 after attending JR's thirty-third birthday party at the Ruskins' house also on Denmark Hill.

EDWARD BOUVERIE PUSEY (1800–82), Regius Professor of Hebrew and Oxford Movement leader.

BRIDGET RICHARDSON (née Cock, 1783–1830), MR's sister, and JR's aunt, who lived in Croydon and married George Richardson (1782–1861), baker.

JANET (JESSIE) RICHARDSON (née Ruskin, 1783–1828), JJR's sister who married Patrick Richardson, merchant, in 1804, and lived in Perth. JR remembered her and the loss of her children.

GEORGE RICHMOND (1809–96), English painter and portraitist. He had been in the circle of 'The Ancients', inspired by the poet-engraver William Blake (1757–1827) and the painter Samuel Palmer (1805–81). He moved towards more widely appreciated portraiture in his later years.

DAVID ROBERTS (1796–1864), Scottish painter, who was particularly known for his orientalist work including in the Holy Land. He was initially encouraged by Turner.

ABBÉ ROSINI, Giovanni Rosini (1776–1855), Professor of Rhetoric at the University of Pisa, and later *conservatore* of the Campo Santo. JR mistakenly called him the 'Professor of the Belli Arti in Pisa' in the 1883 'Epilogue' to *Modern Painters*, II (*LE* iv. 351).

JOHN ROWBOTHAM (1798?–1846), author of works on geography, and French, German, and Latin grammars: one of JR's home tutors.

CHARLES RUNCIMAN (1794–1878), artist and an early drawing teacher of JR.

JOHN JAMES RUSKIN (1785–1864), JR's father. Educated at Edinburgh High School, JJR was sent to London at the age of 16 to enter commerce: in 1814, he helped establish the sherry importing company of Ruskin, Telford, and Domecq, for which he became the leading salesman. JJR's father committed suicide in 1817, and JJR married his cousin Margaret in February 1818. Prudent financially and the key figure in JR's sense of critical authority, he was powerfully difficult, supportive, critical, and unswervingly interested in his son's life and career.

JOHN THOMAS RUSKIN (1761–1817), JJR's father and JR's grandfather, John Thomas was born in London on 22 October 1761 and married Catherine Tweddale in 1781 in Aberdeenshire. He was a grocer and merchant. Debt apparently drove him to kill himself on 30 October 1817, it was thought by cutting his throat, in the house where JR would later marry.

MARGARET RUSKIN (1756?–1817), JR's maternal grandmother, who married William Cock, of the King's Head, Croydon.

MARGARET RUSKIN (1781–1871), JR's mother: devoutly Evangelical, she was an ever-present figure in JR's life, and he never disobeyed her. JR thought that she obtained many of her Evangelical principles from Mrs Rice's day school in Croydon. Much caricatured by subsequent writers, MR taught JR ethical principles, and the Bible, which he thought permanently shaped his mind.

CHARLES ROBERT SCOTT-MURRAY (1818–82), of Danesfield House, Marlow; High Sheriff of Buckinghamshire.

ARTHUR SEVERN (1842–1931), the son of the English painter Joseph Severn, Arthur was educated at Westminster School. He met Joan Agnew in 1867/8, and subsequently married her. Severn came to know JR closely, and left a biographical sketch of him edited in 1967 as *The Professor*.

JOAN SEVERN (née Agnew, 1846–1924), JR's relative who originally looked after MR and increasingly took responsibility for JR's household: she was his principal (and sometimes controversial) carer after his mental illness of 1878 to his death. JR wrote prolifically to her, and she played a significant role both in the final shape of *Praeterita* and the future of his estate. See also Introduction, pp. xvii–xix.

JOSEPH SEVERN (1793–1879), English painter and friend of the poet John Keats, who was with him while he was dying. Father of Arthur Severn.

EMMA SIDNEY (?–1904), daughter of James Sidney of Richmond, Surrey, and later under the guardianship of Dr Grant. She married Sir Herbert Edwardes in 1850.

DR JOHN AND MRS JANE SIMON (later Sir John and Lady Jane), JR's friends. Sir John (1816–1904) was President of the Royal College of Surgeons and a leading authority on sanitation.

SYDNEY SMITH (1771–1845), Edinburgh clergyman, wit, and founder of the *Edinburgh Review*. His *Elementary Sketches of Moral Philosophy, Delivered at the Royal Institution in the Years 1804, 1805, and 1806* were published posthumously in 1849. JR, on pp. 252–5, associated himself with Smith's circle, and thought *Modern Painters*, II affirmed Smith's ideas. JR was able to study the *Sketches* during his mental illness of the summer, 1886: 'the only moral philosophy worth reading', he said (*CJRCEN*, 495).

CLARKSON FREDERICK STANFIELD (1793–1867), English painter of marine subjects.

ARTHUR PENRHYN STANLEY (1815–81), educated at Rugby and author of *The Life and Correspondence of Thomas Arnold* (1844) concerning his former headmaster. Stanley was Dean of Westminster from 1863.

ANNE STRACHAN (c.1794–1871), JR's nurse and then MR's maid, she lived her whole adult life in the Ruskins' service.

MRS FANNY TALBOT (1824–1916), generous supporter of the Guild of St George and the National Trust, and an important correspondent with JR.

GEORGINA TOLLEMACHE (1821?–1901), later Lady Mount-Temple. JR met her properly in 1853 having glimpsed her in Rome in 1840. She supported JR during the distress of his relationship with Rose La Touche, and she organized séances at Broadlands, her home, after Rose's death. JR thought for a time that the spirit of Rose had contacted him during these.

ROSE LA TOUCHE (1848–75), young Irish girl whom JR met first when she was 10 (though he oddly said in *Praeterita* that she was 9). JR hoped to marry her, but religious differences kept her apart as well, later, as an intervention from Effie Millais and Rose's growing illness (which may have been a form of *anorexia nervosa*). Rose's death in 1875 devastated JR, and she remained a presence in his life thereafter. Joan and others were worried about what JR might say of her in *Praeterita*.

PAULINE, LADY TREVELYAN (1816–66), English artist who gathered a circle of Pre-Raphaelites and poets around her at Wallington Hall, Northumberland, with her husband Sir Walter Trevelyan. She was a close friend of JR, and died while on a European tour with him. A projected chapter of *Praeterita* was to deal with this event. She was the aunt of JR's secretary at Brantwood (for the period 1876–82), the artist

Laurence Hilliard (1855?–87). His early death in 1887 brought back memories of Lady Trevelyan's loss.

CATHERINE TWEDDALE, later Ruskin (1763–1817), JR's paternal grandmother and wife of John Thomas Ruskin.

ALEXANDER WEDDERBURN (1854–1931), JR's follower and editor, he met JR while studying at Balliol College, Oxford, and knew him at Brantwood. One of JR's executors, he was a co-editor of *The Library Edition of the Works of John Ruskin*, 39 volumes (Allen, 1903–12) though the bulk of the work was undertaken by his co-editor, Sir Edward Tyas Cook (1857–1919).

SAMUEL WILBERFORCE (1805–73), Bishop of Oxford: his argument with T. H. Huxley over evolution in the Oxford Museum in 1860 became mythologized as a conflict between 'materialist science' and natural theology.

DAVID WILKIE (1785–1841), Scottish painter, who died on his return from a painting tour to the Holy Land. Turner's *Peace: Burial at Sea* commemorates his funeral off the coast of Malta.

GODFREY WINDUS (1790–1867), retired coach-maker and collector of Turner and other English painters. JR had freedom to visit Windus's fifty or so Turners at his house in Tottenham Green whenever he wished.

INDEX

American Literature

British and Irish Literature

Children's Literature

Classics and Ancient Literature

Colonial Literature

Eastern Literature

European Literature

Gothic Literature

History

Medieval Literature

Oxford English Drama

Poetry

Philosophy

Politics

Religion

The Oxford Shakespeare

A complete list of Oxford World's Classics, including Authors in Context, Oxford English Drama, and the Oxford Shakespeare, is available in the UK from the Marketing Services Department, Oxford University Press, Great Clarendon Street, Oxford OX2 6DP, or visit the website at www.oup.com/uk/worldsclassics.

In the USA, visit www.oup.com/us/owc for a complete title list.

Oxford World's Classics are available from all good bookshops. In case of difficulty, customers in the UK should contact Oxford University Press Bookshop, 116 High Street, Oxford OX1 4BR.

	Late Victorian Gothic Tales
JANE AUSTEN	Emma
	Mansfield Park
	Persuasion
	Pride and Prejudice
	Selected Letters
	Sense and Sensibility
MRS BEETON	Book of Household Management
MARY ELIZABETH BRADDON	Lady Audley's Secret
ANNE BRONTË	The Tenant of Wildfell Hall
CHARLOTTE BRONTË	Jane Eyre
	Shirley
	Villette
EMILY BRONTË	Wuthering Heights
ROBERT BROWNING	The Major Works
JOHN CLARE	The Major Works
SAMUEL TAYLOR COLERIDGE	The Major Works
WILKIE COLLINS	The Moonstone
	No Name
	The Woman in White
CHARLES DARWIN	The Origin of Species
THOMAS DE QUINCEY	The Confessions of an English Opium-Eater
	On Murder
CHARLES DICKENS	The Adventures of Oliver Twist
	Barnaby Rudge
	Bleak House
	David Copperfield
	Great Expectations
	Nicholas Nickleby
	The Old Curiosity Shop
	Our Mutual Friend
	The Pickwick Papers